P9-DXL-432

Pacific Press

PACIFIC

>>THE UNAUTHORIZED STORY OF VANCOUVER'S NEWSPAPER MONOPOLY

PRESS

MARC EDGE

NEW STAR BOOKS
VANCOUVER
2001

New Star Books Ltd.
107 - 3477 Commercial Street
Vancouver, BC V5N 4E8
www.NewStarBooks.com

Cover by Rayola Graphic Design
Typeset by New Star Books
Printed & bound in Canada by Transcontinental Printing
1 2 3 4 5 05 04 03 02 01

Publication of this work is made possible by grants from the Canada Council, the British Columbia Arts Council, and the Department of Canadian Heritage Book Publishing Industry Development Program.

NATIONAL LIBRARY OF CANADA CATALOGUING IN PUBLICATION DATA

Edge, Marc, 1954-
Pacific Press

ISBN 0-921586-88-4

1. Pacific Press — History. 2. Newspaper publishing — British Columbia — Vancouver — History — 20th century. 3. Canadian newspapers (English) — British Columbia — Vancouver — History — 20th century. I. Title.
PN4919.V362E33 2001 070.5'722'0971133 C2001-911329-3

This book is dedicated to the memory of

John Allan "Jack" Edge (1919-1985),

who was there in Victory Square.

Each paper has assured its readers that it will retain its former character. Since the chief characteristic of each paper was its bitter competitive spirit toward the other, this character-retention will be quite a trick, something like watching a wrestling match between Siamese twins.

SCOTT YOUNG, *Globe and Mail,* 1957

CONTENTS

FOREWORD

by Pierre Berton

Marc Edge's fascinating study of the rise (and fall) of Pacific Press is invaluable for several reasons.

First, it is a welcome and much-needed chapter in the ongoing history of journalism in Canada. Edge has filled in the blanks and provided the details for future historians who chronicle the newspaper world of the twentieth century.

Second, it is also an important chapter in the continuing history of British Columbia — a magnificent source for those who will focus on the story of this province during the period under review.

Most important, however, Edge's carefully researched investigation provides a case study of that flawed concept the business world calls "synergy."

Vancouver, when I knew it, was perhaps the liveliest newspaper town in Canada, if not in North America, reflecting the ebullient nature of the West Coast. The city rejoiced in three lively, indeed vivacious daily newspapers, all competing with one another to be first with the news.

In my day — *circa* 1946 — the *Vancouver Daily Province* set the standard for responsible, informed journalism. Look at it now, a sleazy tabloid, with few redeeming qualities. The *Vancouver Sun* was its feisty and aggressive rival, proudly boasting of its local ownership and fitting neatly into the ebullient city that it served. The smaller *News-Herald*, on which I cut my teeth, was formed by the staff of the failed *Vancouver Star* and managed, through sheer persistence and a few bright ideas, to hold its own against the competition.

We were not ruled by the bottom line in those days. After all, the publishers themselves were journalists (like Robert Elson, who went on to become managing editor of *Life* magazine) or were the intimates of journalists. The Cromie brothers, who ran the *Sun*, hobnobbed with their reporters and editors; the *Province* hierarchy drank with their underlings in the beer parlour of the Commercial Hotel.

No man better epitomized that bubbling era than Hal Straight, the hard-drinking, hard-driving *Sun* managing editor. His whole purpose was to beat the *Province* in the circulation war that marked those days. We used to gather in his kitchen of a Saturday night and plot the defeat of our enemy. "Don't worry," Straight used to say, "one day there'll be an act of God, and we'll be ready."

And when that time came — in the form of a printer's strike — Straight *was* ready. With Don Cromie's help he kept the *Sun* publishing, while the *Province* closed down.

Straight believed in competition. It kept us on our toes and he rewarded us for it. One day an irate citizen marched into the *Sun* office demanding that a reporter be fired for filching a photograph from his bureau drawer during a police investigation.

"Fire him?" cried Straight. "I'm going to give him a raise."

Television helped to change all this. When the screen carried instant news, the newspaper scoop was dead. But the real enemies of aggressive (and sometimes costly) Vancouver-style journalism have been the large, semi-anonymous corporations that swallow newspapers whole, merge them, water them down, and in the interests of greater and greater profit, all but destroy them. That is what happened in Vancouver, as Marc Edge's book shows.

It began after Don Cromie sold the *Sun* following his brother's death. But the real death knell was administered by the news conglomerate, Pacific Press. At that point, the two surviving Vancouver dailies were no longer at arm's length.

How ironic that the very daily newspapers which, in their editorials, praised free and unfettered competition in the market place, should themselves be the victims of the opposite concept. *Free enterprise?* Marc Edge's remarkable study quotes chapter and verse to make it crystal clear that, in Vancouver, that vaunted ideal is as tattered as yesterday's front page.

PREFACE

Two events that occurred during the fall of 2000 while I was researching the history of Pacific Press pointed me toward an increasingly inescapable conclusion. The more I delved into the past, the more clearly recent events surrounding the partnership of the *Vancouver Sun* and *Province* came into context. As the most egregious example of the trend toward concentration of ownership that characterized the Canadian newspaper industry during the latter decades of the twentieth century, the amalgamated Vancouver dailies suddenly stood as a harbinger of what could be expected in the future. As objects of commodification, the news media have increasingly become the possessions of business people with overt political loyalties. It was perhaps inevitable that media outlets under such ownership would become instruments of political persuasion in what seems to be a return to the days of the "party press" from which newspapers evolved a century ago in their quest for a mass audience. Some scholars have noted that in the 1990s the press became transformed by a renewed political purpose. Paul Mongerson has dubbed the latest version the "power press," because it acts not as a neutral conveyor of objective information but as an advocate of political propaganda; not as a watchdog on powerful institutions in society, but as a "vigilante" and arguably the most powerful institution of all.[1]

The first event was an opportunity to question Neil Reynolds, the new editor of the *Vancouver Sun,* about his Libertarian beliefs and how they would affect news coverage by Vancouver's leading daily. A journalist of enormous reputation, Reynolds made no secret of his political leanings or the fact he was once national leader of and a federal candidate for the Libertarian Party of Canada, a right-wing fringe group devoted to the elimination of government regulation. According to author Doug Fetherling, Reynolds, the son of a Methodist minister, "is fond of saying, with just a pinch of hyperbole, that like all sons of Methodist ministers, he was a communist at 16. . . . He came to libertarianism from the left, rather than from the right, as is usual."[2] Fetherling, whom Reynolds had installed as "writer-in-residence" at the *Kingston Whig-Standard* back in the 1970s, recalled that his boss once announced he was "proud to be Canada's most conservative newspaper editor at the head of Canada's most left-wing daily newspaper."[3] Fetherling, now writing for Reynolds at the *Sun* under the name George, described the political position of libertarians in his 1993 history of the *Whig-Standard*, which was a respected and vigorous if somewhat quirky independent Ontario daily until its 1990 purchase by Southam.

> They are not just tax rebels. Like the anarchists of old, they maintain that both socialists and conservatives form governments in order to impose their will on the population, the one believing in individual freedom before equality, the other in equality before freedom. Why can't society have both, the anarchists ask.[4]

Presenting himself to local scrutiny on the academic circuit in November 2000, Reynolds outlined the new political activism he brought to Vancouver's largest newspaper. "The *Vancouver Sun* believes in limited government and in the innate moral right to global trade," he told a lunch-hour gathering at the School of Journalism at the University of B.C. "Making the world become one through commerce."[5] Asked whether the *Sun*'s front-page crusade for drug legalization that fall indicated readers could expect to read more of the Libertarian Party position in his paper's news columns, Reynolds allowed that this was a reasonable assumption.

A second occurrence that November cast grave aspersions on the credibility of the *Province* and raised even more serious questions about political manipulation of the news. I received a telephone call one evening during the federal election campaign from a former colleague at the tabloid who complained that the paper's new editor was rearranging coverage of Stockwell Day between editions to cast the Alliance Party leader in a better light. Vivienne Sosnowski, who had been appointed along with Reynolds that summer to replace Pacific Press editors who had been shuffled off to corporate owner Hollinger's *Chicago Sun-Times*, was coming into the *Province* newsroom between editions to go through the newspaper's election coverage, my outraged source charged, and had been replacing stories that made Day look bad with more favorable coverage. The blatant favoritism reached a climax on the evening of November 15, I was told, when Sosnowski ordered dropped from *Province* pages an article on a poll that showed support for the Alliance leveling off. That same evening she was said to have scrapped a story in the paper's first edition about the CBC television comedy show *This Hour Has 22 Minutes* starting a petition to have Day change his first name to Doris. Yet a third story in that day's first edition unfavorable to Day, this one detailing his fundamentalist religious views, including his belief that dinosaurs roamed the earth with humans only 6,000 years ago, was replaced by one outlining his views on law and order. Wasn't this awful, my source asked, and could I do anything to help expose such blatant bias? Well, I responded, "Yes, and no." Stuck in the 1970s in my research on Pacific Press, I was also up to my ears in teaching a Simon Fraser University course on the newspaper industry. I promised to do what I could and phoned a reporter at the alternative weekly *Georgia Straight*, who said he would look into it but never followed up. I assumed the story had died a natural death until just before Christmas, when a radio item announced that a complaint had been lodged with the B.C. Press Council by the advocacy group Campaign for Press and Broadcasting Freedom "on behalf of un-named *Province* journalists." For the next week I watched the pages of the *Province*, expecting to see the obligatory news item on the complaint against it.

Perusing the pages of tabloid triviality was personally painful. Since leaving the *Province* in exasperation almost eight years earlier, I had been unable to take the newspaper seriously and hardly able to even pick up what some of my erstwhile colleagues derisively referred to as "The Comic." Having started on the *Province* in the 1970s when it was a serious newspaper, respected in at least some quarters, my journalistic self-esteem had suffered like that of many others at the daily after its 1983 conversion to tabloid format and its ensuing preoccupation with triviality. I had been fortunate to be assigned to the courthouse beat about that time and thus had missed much of the subsequent silliness rampant in the newsroom, but by 1993 I eagerly accepted a Southam buyout offer. On leaving, I sympathized with some former colleagues who felt trapped there by circumstance and/or obligation, knowing that if they left they would likely never work again at a major daily in an industry dominated by one giant corporation, and certainly not in Vancouver, where both dailies are owned by the same company. From tales I heard afterward, conditions in the *Province* newsroom seemed to do nothing but worsen due to understaffing and an increasingly confrontational management style. Holding two business degrees, I was always amazed at how inept some of my journalistic superiors had proven as managers, but under the ownership of Conrad Black's worldwide Hollinger empire, the executives imported to Pacific Press seemed to bring a new nastiness. Management prerogative being one of the privileges of ownership, I could only shake my head at the tales I heard at the Press Club, until even it died a slow death after the *Sun* and *Province* newsrooms moved downtown to Granville Square.

Another privilege of owning the Pacific Press dailies, which Hollinger acquired from the imploded Southam chain, seemed to be increased promotion of the right-wing agenda favored by Black and his business partners, David Radler and Peter White.[6] I had learned, while doing research in the doctoral program in the E.W. Scripps School of Journalism at Ohio University, that when Radler became publisher of such Hollinger newspapers as the *Sun-Times* in Chicago and the *Jerusalem Post* in Israel, he had imposed a new conservatism on them.[7] Black, of course, was renowned as the reactionary publisher of Hollinger's *Daily Telegraph* in London, while White is an overt political operative, having been active in both the Progressive Conservative Party and the Alliance. With their cleverly leveraged buyout of the Southam dailies, the Hollinger principals seemed to be following a formula of gaining "value added" from their acquisitions by installing editors who would promote their political agenda, most notably Reynolds, who had first been hired to remake the *Ottawa Citizen* into Hollinger's flagship in the nation's capital.

After a week, when no mention of the complaint made against it by its own journalists had appeared in the *Province*, I telephoned my old city editor, Don MacLachlan, who had moved "upstairs" to head corporate communications at Pacific Press, and asked why. "We were never officially informed of a complaint against us," insisted MacLachlan, suggesting a call to Bill Bachop at the Press Council office in Victoria.

"It's not the Press Council's function to dictate the editorial content of the papers," said Bachop, explaining why the complaint never got past his desk.

It was then that the significance of the new reality at the Pacific Press dailies under Hollinger hit me. The *Province* had always been conservative politically and, according to Allan Fotheringham, under the direction of editor and publisher Paddy Sherman it had loyally favored the provincial Social Credit Party of W.A.C. Bennett. But the *Sun* had been founded as a Liberal Party newspaper in the early twentieth century, although as a commercial enterprise it had evolved into a less blatantly partisan publication, a small "l" liberal daily under Cromie family ownership and then under Max Bell's FP Publications. Since then the *Sun* had swung to the right — a Conservative Party supporter in the 1980s under publisher Clark Davey, and now with Reynolds it was apparently an instrument of far-right advocacy. From a politically balanced pair, Vancouver's newspapers had moved to stake out positions on the far right and farther right of the political spectrum, with a resulting imbalance.

Perhaps, I thought, there *was* something I could do to help make this known. From discussions with Reynolds, who was kind enough that November to come up Burnaby Mountain and speak to my class at SFU, I got the impression that his admission of political advocacy was coupled with an earnest belief that readers are fully aware of this bias. From my research into the history of the Pacific Press dailies, I knew that even while I worked there I had not been aware of the veiled political agendas to which the dailies kept. This suggested to me that most outsiders could be similarly ignorant of these leanings, and my journalistic instincts told me the entire issue made for an interesting feature article. I queried *Media* magazine, the quarterly publication of the Canadian Association of Journalists, and received an assignment to write a cover story for their Spring 2001 issue on the *Province* newsroom controversy. By then the underground group Guerrilla Media had posted on its web site the *Province* pages containing the controversial election coverage changes in what seemed to me an interesting example of the "New Media" outlets on the Internet countering the information control hitherto enjoyed by the "Old Media."[8] By February, the *Province* newsroom's hostilities boiled over in a week-long "byline strike" by journalists to protest the suspension of a shop steward, which was followed by editors removing bylines for an additional two weeks in retaliation under what I called a "byline lockout." That gave me the "news hook" I needed to hang the story on, after which I could get into what was by then old news about the Press Council complaint, with the requisite denials and recriminations all around.

When I interviewed them, some of my former *Province* colleagues painted a ghastly picture of the management practices instituted by Radler as publisher of both the Pacific Press dailies before he bowed out when Hollinger sold the former Southam dailies to television network CanWest Global Communications. "I've never encountered such hostility in any newsroom where I've worked," said Janet Ingram-Johnson, a veteran of twenty-five years on the *Province* news desk. Senior editors parachuted in from other corporate titles often didn't even bother to learn the names of *Province* copy editors during their time in Vancouver, she said, simply referring to them as "you" in stating their commands. "There isn't a meaningful level of courtesy between the managers and staff in the newsroom. It's a very miserable place to work. It's atrocious."[9] But more worrisome were accusations that under Radler the newspaper had become a mouthpiece for the Alliance Party. "From the stories I was directed to run, I certainly had the impression that the managers in the newsroom were under orders to reflect the Alliance Party point of view and certainly to promote Stockwell Day," said Ingram-Johnson. "It appeared our managers in our newsroom were on a mission to promote the right-wing point of view, and that was reflected in the coverage." My old roommate from Calgary, *Province* copy editor Shane McCune, was at first as reluctant to stick his neck out as most of his colleagues. He had already felt the effects of the climate of managerial vindictiveness when his raucous and opinionated, but perhaps too progressive, "Citizen Shane" column had been canceled. "I was not privy to any of these decisions, although I was on the election team," he finally observed on the record under prodding. "I've never seen anything like it."[10]

If the Pacific Press dailies are to henceforth be organs of political advocacy, what we are witnessing out here on the West Coast cutting edge of the limits of newspaper ownership and management certainly seems to represent a swing back to the days of the blatantly partisan party press. If so, readers should be fully informed of the leanings of the dailies and the fact their news coverage choices will reflect the political positions of their editors and owners. But making political advocacy the new mission of the *Vancouver Sun* and *Province*, similar to that of Black's start-up *National Post*, could prove an expensive effort if those on the other end of the ideological spectrum become alienated instead of persuaded and desert the dailies in disgust. Abandoning the pretence of objectivity, as discredited as the concept has become, will add a lack of credibility to the Pacific

Press dailies' already diminished relevance, and will do nothing to reverse their decades-long decline in circulation.

This book comprises the research into Pacific Press conducted for my doctoral dissertation. It examines a time period bounded by the 1957 formation of the company, with some necessary background, and the 1991 *Sun* switch to morning publication, with a smattering of update. As stated in the subtitle, it is an "unauthorized" history in that Pacific Press in no way contributed to it. Not that they refused, but I didn't really ask. When I did seek to reproduce photographs from their archives to illustrate the book after it was completed, however, permission was refused by *Sun* executive editor Shelley Fralic and *Province* managing editor Malcolm Kirk. Thus readers unfamiliar with the Pacific Press premises and the participants in its history will have to use their imaginations.

Following is the preface to the dissertation, slightly revised for book publication.

Pacific Press was an arrangement which both fascinated and frustrated many who worked there and no doubt completely mystified many observers who tried to make sense from the outside of what on earth was going on at 6th Avenue and Granville Street in Vancouver. But with the passing of the millennium just ended, Pacific Press ceased to exist, at least in name. When television network CanWest Global Communications acquired the *Vancouver Sun* and *Province,* along with most of the other Southam newspapers, late in 2000, it changed the name of the holding company that publishes both Vancouver dailies to Pacific Newspaper Group. Now that the newspapers are linked with BCTV, the largest television operation in the province, the news media in Greater Vancouver have entered the new Age of Convergence, with multimedia co-ownership and cooperation leading to "synergies" that supposedly make the whole greater than the sum of its parts, at least in business terms.

The Age of Convergence follows the Age of Concentration, which during the latter decades of the twentieth century saw most of Canada's newspapers come under the control of a few giant chains. The steady march toward chain ownership of newspapers that had formerly been family-owned or otherwise independent began to concern many in the 1960s and led to the formation in 1969 of the Special Senate Committee on Mass Media, chaired by Senator Keith Davey, to examine the issue. The Davey Committee forced media corporations to open their books for the first time and found their profits "astonishing."[11] The irony, according to the Committee's 1970 report, was delicious in its hypocrisy. "An industry that is supposed to abhor secrets is sitting on one of the best-kept, least-discussed secrets, one of the hottest *scoops*, in the entire field of Canadian business — their own balance sheets."[12] By 1970 "genuine" newspaper competition existed in only five Canadian cities, the Senate report noted, with the Southam, Thomson, and FP Publications chains controlling 44.7 percent of the country's daily newspaper circulation, compared with 25 percent in 1958.

> This tendency could . . . lead to a situation whereby the news (which we must start thinking of as a public resource, like electricity) is controlled and manipulated by a small group of individuals and corporations whose view of What's Fit to Print may closely coincide with . . . What's Good For Business . . . There is some evidence, in fact, which suggests we are in that boat already.[13]

Stating that its intention was not to determine whether the tendency toward press monopoly was a good thing or a bad thing — "*of course* it's a bad thing" — the committee reasoned that the real-world problem was to strike a balance. "How do you reconcile the media's tendency toward monopoly with society's need for diversity?"[14] Included in the measures it recommended to deal with the problem was a Press Ownership Review Board to approve — or, more likely, disapprove — newspaper sales or mergers. The Board's basic guideline would be that "*all* transactions that increase concentration of ownership in the mass media are undesirable and contrary to the public interest — unless shown to be otherwise."[15] While the Davey Committee's findings and recommendations were bruited about thoroughly across Canada for years, its key recommendation for stemming the tide of press ownership concentration was never enacted. "We had to conclude that we have in this country not the press we need, but rather the press we deserve," recalled Davey. "The sad fact is that the media must self-regulate because most Canadians are not prepared to demand the press they need."[16]

Implementation of a Press Ownership Review Board, similar to what exists in Great Britain, would likely have prevented the events of August 27, 1980, the date which lives in Canadian newspaper infamy as "Black

Wednesday." Closure on that day of the *Ottawa Journal* by Thomson and the *Winnipeg Tribune* by Southam resulted in national outrage on a scale which suggested to most observers that the time had arrived for restrictions on the growth of newspaper chains. Even the owners admitted such a need. A Royal Commission on Newspapers, called almost immediately by Prime Minister Pierre Trudeau to investigate the situation, pointed out less than a year later what was obvious to everyone. "Newspaper competition, of the kind that used to be, is virtually dead in Canada," reported the commission chaired by Tom Kent. "This ought not to have been allowed to happen."[17]

Southam and Thomson by then controlled 59 percent of the nation's daily newspaper circulation between them, the Kent Commission observed, warning that without a brake being applied to the inexorable economic forces which contributed to concentration of ownership, the situation would only grow worse. But a proposed Canada Newspaper Act to control ownership concentration was never enacted, as the federal government changed from Liberal to Conservative. Reaction of newspaper publishers who stood on their right to "freedom of the press" was swift and furious. The *Globe and Mail* lambasted the report as a "veritable idiot's delight of interference in the ownership and operation of the nation's press."[18] Kent, a former editor of the *Winnipeg Free Press*, reiterated the fundamental conundrum first enunciated by Davey: that press regulation was unlikely if left to politicians beholden for their re-election to public opinion molded to a great extent by news coverage. The vituperative nature of the publishers' campaign against controls on press ownership, Kent observed, "fully confirms the analysis of the state of the problems of the newspaper industry."[19]

The resulting inaction led to Canada having in the 1980s the most highly concentrated newspaper ownership in the world.[20] "At the national level, no developed country has so concentrated a newspaper industry," concluded Peter Dunnett in his 1988 book, *The World Newspaper Industry*. "In Canada the newspaper market is unusual in that it is still growing and could accommodate new entrants."[21] The closures by Southam and Thomson of long-publishing dailies in Winnipeg and Ottawa, each of which left the other with a local monopoly, overshadowed events in Vancouver, where Thomson sold the *Sun* to Southam, which already owned the *Province*. That made Pacific Press the worst example of daily newspaper monopoly in Canada, because as a joint monopoly it has served ever since to keep competition out of the market, unlike in Ottawa and Winnipeg, where other dailies eventually appeared.

The story of Pacific Press is one which has long needed telling. Over the years there has been no shortage of local rumination on the subject, most of it lost into the ether as radio airwaves and thus out of our collective consciousness. At least one previous attempt has been made to publish a history of Pacific Press, but to date the literature on newspaper journalism in Canada has lacked such a work. I hope the following effort provides a comprehensive examination of the subject. Like all journalists, I fear most of all some major omission of the record. In unearthing some very interesting material I have become resigned to the fact that inevitably after its publication additional information will come to light which allows a more informed perspective. Given that this is a first effort at a long-overdue task, I can only beg in advance the reader's indulgence of its inevitable oversights.

My first glimpse of Pacific Press came as a grade school student on a class tour of the newly opened building at 6th and Granville in 1966. A year later I began an intermittent association with the enterprise as a dependent contractor. As a carrier for the *Sun* in South Burnaby during the late 1960s, I became enamored of journalism as a profession by reading the columns of Allan Fotheringham, Jim Taylor, Denny Boyd, and Jack Wasserman. Much reading time was spent in the paper "shack" awaiting arrival of the delivery trucks, which often came late, if at all, during the production disruptions of late 1969 and early 1970. The three-month shutdown of Pacific Press in 1970 marked the end of my career as a "paper boy," as I became increasingly preoccupied with greater pursuits. My university years drew me to student journalism, and in 1974 I was fortunate enough to begin writing as a sports reporter for the *Province*. After graduating from Simon Fraser University with a degree in commerce, I moved on to a job in the business section of the *Calgary Herald* in the late 1970s. While there I watched with interest from a safe distance the escalating labor tensions at Pacific Press, which led to its eight-month shutdown beginning on Halloween 1978.

It was a vacancy caused by that strike which provided me the opportunity to return to Vancouver as a business reporter for the *Province* following the resumption of publication in 1979. It was a fascination with the complex labor relations at Pacific Press which led me to pursue a Master's degree in the subject at Michigan State University while on a leave of absence from the *Province* in 1982. That led me to a position on the Newspaper Guild executive committee in 1984, which proved interesting during the seven-week strike at Pacific Press that spring. My involvement as a member of the Guild's bargaining committee that year was an eye-opening experience, but not one I wished to continue, union politics being like politics of any kind. After a career move into news, I was fortunate to be assigned to the courthouse beat just as the *Province* switched to tabloid format in 1983. A decade later, as Southam desperately downsized its workforce in an ultimately unsuccessful attempt to stave off corporate takeover, I accepted a buyout offer and left to pursue other interests. Those included sailing the Pacific aboard my forty-foot ketch *Markenurh* for two years starting in 1995, and returning to school in 1997 for a doctorate in Mass Communication in the E.W. Scripps School of Journalism at Ohio University.[22]

When it came time to choose a subject for the major research effort that would be my dissertation, I decided it should be on the newspaper arrangement with which my fortunes had been intertwined for much of the previous three decades. It was not an easy choice, however, and I do not mind admitting I was daunted by taking on such a challenge. But I consider myself fortunate to have studied historical research under Professor Patrick Washburn, who is one of the foremost journalism historians in the United States. It is to him I owe the greatest debt of gratitude for enabling me to undertake this research. I also wish to thank everyone who assisted my research and who read draft versions of various portions of the manuscript. I especially would like to acknowledge St. Clair Balfour, whose first-hand recollections of the circumstances surrounding the formation of Pacific Press were invaluable, and Allan Fotheringham, whose accounts of the pivotal events at the *Vancouver Sun* in the mid-1970s were important. Paddy Sherman's contributions, while not in time for my dissertation, cleared up some lingering questions and provided some needed balance to the book. I am grateful to Pierre Berton not only for his reminiscences of the prehistory of Pacific Press, but also for his kind words of encouragement on reading the draft manuscript. I would like to thank Professor Bob Hackett of the School of Communication at Simon Fraser University and Professor Mary Lynn Young of the School of Journalism at the University of British Columbia for their comments and encouragement on reading portions of the draft manuscript. Other readers whose comments are appreciated include Mike Tytherleigh, Patrick Nagle, Phil Needham, Rolf Maurer, Robert Dykstra, John Jensen, Doug Harrison, James Compton, Donald Gutstein, Terry Glavin, Albert Rose, Wendy Fitzgibbons, and Mark Leier. Clive Cocking and Sean Rossiter were of assistance in providing access to published but unindexed or unavailable material. Larry "DaVinci" Campbell helped me obtain the 1957 autopsy report into the death of Sam Cromie. Denny Boyd and Douglas Sagi were of great assistance in providing correspondence related to the 1987 "Cheesecake rebellion" at the *Vancouver Sun*. Gerry Haslam was generous not only with his recollections but also in providing documents relating to the conversion of the *Province* to tabloid format. I am grateful to George Brandak of the Special Collections and University Archives division of the University of British Columbia Library for alerting me to the existence of the Stuart Keate papers, without which this history would be nowhere near as complete as it is. I had incorrectly assumed that Mr. Keate's 1980 memoirs, which have to date provided the best available perspective on the inner workings of Pacific Press, would be the extent of his contribution to this project since his passing. On examining his personal papers, however, I was excited to find much relevant material which he chose not to include in his book *Paper Boy*. Of course, all errors and omissions are my responsibility as researcher.

I would lastly, but hardly leastly, like to thank my editor, Audrey McClellan, who was of enormous assistance in organizing, smoothing, and even correcting the manuscript, despite my sometimes determined resistance.

The history of Pacific Press is a case study of the adverse effects of removing competition from the marketplace for ideas. I hope its telling will provide some insights into how better to facilitate healthy journalism by showing how unchecked corporate control over the news has proven a disservice to the community and, ultimately, to the owners of the press. The Pacific Press paradox was one of a monopoly that worked, in large part, to the disadvantage of those entangled in it, as I hope the following exposition of the facts demonstrates.

Pacific Press

INTRODUCTION

Moving to Mornings

On the morning of September 16, 1991, residents of Vancouver awoke to the sight of newspaper carriers wearing baggy caps, vests, and knickerbockers, handing out free copies to startled commuters on city streets. Topping off the period costumes, designed to recall the garb of street urchin "newsies" of a bygone era, were newspaper bags emblazoned with the name of the city's leading daily newspaper, the *Vancouver Sun*. The publicity stunt was intended to draw attention to a long-planned move by the *Sun*, which that day switched from afternoon publication, where it had languished with declining circulation for years, to the more prosperous morning field.

The change in publication time had proven problematic, however, as the militant Vancouver press unions balked at the move. New printing presses purchased for the project had also proven unreliable. And bad publicity, which had been plaguing the *Sun*'s journalistic efforts for years and had helped turn many Vancouverites off the newspaper-reading habit, suddenly reached a pinnacle in 1991. Internal problems had led to the acrimonious departure of the paper's editor-in-chief that spring. As a result, the *Sun*'s switch to morning publication had twice been postponed. It had first been planned for January as an "all-day" newspaper with both morning and afternoon editions. A second target date of May had also been scrubbed when management could not reach an agreement with the newspaper's unions and instead decided to convert the *Sun* to a morning-only newspaper.

Such a switch in publication time was not uncommon and had been made by more than 150 newspapers in North America since 1976, including sixteen in 1990 alone.[1] Afternoon newspapers had become a dying breed since nightly television news had siphoned off much of their readership over the previous two decades in a syndrome known across the continent as "Death in the Afternoon," and Vancouver had the highest rate of evening television news viewing in Canada.[2]

But in Vancouver the switch of the *Sun* to the morning field was unusual because its owner already published a morning newspaper there, one which had proven popular since its conversion to tabloid format in 1983. Both the *Sun* and tabloid *Province* were published by Pacific Press, a holding company owned by the largest newspaper chain in Canada, Toronto-based Southam Inc.

The absentee ownership had also contributed to the estrangement of Vancouverites from their daily newspapers. The phenomenon of "western alienation" was well-known in British Columbia, which was isolated from the rest of Canada and particularly from the centre of economic, political, and media power in central Canada.[3] Rafe Mair, the latest radio star in a long tradition of Vancouver "hotliners," referred to the Pacific Press dailies derisively on his popular talk show as the "*Don Mills Sun* and the *Don Mills Province*," after the Toronto suburb where Southam was headquartered. Their coverage, Mair noted, often offered little relevance to the grassroots issues of the day. "Both papers were totally out of touch with the community they were supposed to serve and represent, and it showed."[4]

To many in Vancouver the switch in *Sun* publication time was symptomatic of the malaise the city's daily newspaper monopoly had fallen into over decades without competition, noted the *Financial Times*.

> Some media observers say the real story lies in a lack of competition. They point out that the broadsheet *Sun* will be pitted in mock combat against its corporate stablemate, the tabloid *Province*. . . . Indeed, in the weeks leading up to the *Sun*'s Sept. 16 switch to morning publication, there seemed to be far more co-operation than competition between the two papers. . . . Some say that in a truly competitive market, the papers would be forced to provide a fresher product.[5]

To promote the change in *Sun* publication time, management of the newspaper embarked on the most expensive advertising campaign ever undertaken by the daily, with television and radio ads saturating the market. The gaily costumed street vendors were the final phase of a $700,000 multi-media onslaught described by former *Sun* journalist Ian Gill in the *Georgia Straight* alternative weekly newspaper as "one of the most bizarre advertising and promotional campaigns this city has ever seen."[6] Ironically, full-page advertisements in the *Sun* had focused on some of the reasons readers said they did *not* want their leading daily newspaper delivered in the morning. "If I Wanted Yesterday's News, I'd Just Buy a Fish," read the headline on one.

The campaign of reverse psychology had been orchestrated by the New York-based public relations firm Burson-Marsteller, which was best-known for undertaking damage control of such disasters as the Tylenol poisoning scare and Exxon's despoiling of Prince William Sound in Alaska with a massive oil tanker spill. The *Sun*'s switch to morning publication was shaping up as a journalistic disaster of similar proportions, and the participation of Burson-Marsteller was providing even more bad publicity. The controversial spin doctors had only weeks earlier been blasted by one of the *Sun*'s own columnists for their work with the giant forest companies that reap the bounty of B.C.'s greatest natural resource. Burson-Marsteller's creation of an industry advocacy group called the Forest Alliance to create a positive image for harvesting of the province's old-growth timber stands, noted Stephen Hume, should be considered in light of the firm's earlier work on such white-washing projects as a military junta's "dirty war" in South America. "In Argentina, Burson-Marsteller was hired to make the world think better of a government widely known to be butchering its own citizens," wrote Hume.[7] The *Sun*'s choice of a crisis communication expert was appropriate, quipped the *Prince Rupert Daily News* in an editorial. "After all, the paper has been butchering its readers for years."[8]

It seemed that Pacific Press could not make both of its daily newspapers successful at the same time. While the *Province* had pushed its circulation up by 50,000 since its conversion to tabloid format and threatened to soon break the 200,000 barrier, the *Sun* had suffered a corresponding decline. Its circulation had fallen from 250,000 in 1985 to 210,000 and threatened to pass the *Province* going the other way, falling below the psychological barrier of 200,000 it had passed in 1957 shortly after gaining the then-preferred afternoon market to itself. Even as Southam prepared to reposition its flagship *Sun* as a morning newspaper, the move threatened to steal circulation from the *Province*.

A newspaper consultant brought in by Southam to oversee the *Sun*'s conversion had seen several similar projects succeed, but University of Arizona professor Michael Burgoon admitted that the situation at Pacific Press was unique in that it was the first time newspapers owned by the same company had been moved into direct competition in the same time period.[9] *Chicago Tribune* media writer James Warren found that local management was not optimistic about the *Sun*'s move succeeding. "Privately, some Pacific Press executives and editors are queasy," reported Warren while visiting Vancouver that May for the annual American Newspaper Publishers Association convention. "They worry that some people won't want longer, more thoughtful *Sun* articles in the morning; that the *Province*, with cheaper ad rates, will be a short-shrifted stepchild; and that one paper may benefit from later printing deadlines for news and sports."[10] To produce two newspapers at once, noted the *Globe and Mail* national newspaper, Pacific Press resources would be stretched to their limits, which risked producing products with compromised content.

> To get both papers on subscribers' doorsteps by 6 a.m., copy deadlines for both papers have shifted to as early as 3 o'clock the previous afternoon. Some subscribers who will receive early editions will get no evening news, sports scores or theatre and concert reviews. Anticipating *Province* readers' concerns, editor-in-chief Brian Butters wrote in a column, "if a particular story or sports result is not in the edition you get . . . it will be published in the following day's paper." Critics are calling that delivering "yesterday's news tomorrow."[11]

The *Sun* had always been the moneymaker at Pacific Press, and its profits had for years more than offset *Province* losses, at least when the newspapers published without interruption. But since the mid-1980s, growth of the *Province* coupled with advertising inroads made by community newspapers had cut sharply into the *Sun*'s bottom line. Despite the popularity of the *Province* with readers and advertisers, an extended recession in the resource-based economy of British Columbia in the mid-

1980s had prevented it from turning a profit and the best it had been able to do was reduce its losses. The result of diminishing the *Sun* flagship at Pacific Press had thus turned the corporate bottom line from black ink to red, as the Vancouver newspaper partnership became a curious economic contradiction: a money-losing monopoly.

The newspaper crisis in Vancouver had evolved over more than three decades since the *Sun* had entered into a partnership with the competing *Province* newspaper in 1957. Before the dailies set up shop together in a government-sanctioned monopoly, the city had enjoyed vigorous newspaper competition between not just two, but three dailies. Both the *Sun* and *Province* published in the afternoon back then as, before the rise of television, mornings were not yet the preferred publication time for newspapers. The morning *Herald*, owned by press baron Roy Thomson, was barely surviving against the afternoon giants, which battled it out in a decade-long newspaper war. Competition had kept prices down for both readers and advertisers, as the *Sun* and *Province* promoted their products fiercely in a race for first place. Competition for news was also strong, with "scoops" jealously guarded and a sensational brand of journalism practised, especially on the lively pages of the *Sun*.

The locally controlled firm promoted itself as "Vancouver's Only Home-Owned Newspaper" against the corporate *Province*, which since the 1920s had been part of the Southam chain based in Toronto. Distaste for Eastern absentee ownership on Canada's West Coast had played a role in the *Sun*'s surge into first place in the Vancouver circulation war after a violent strike at the *Province* in 1946 had seen Southam publish using non-union "scab" printers. The use of strikebreakers in the strong union town had proven disastrous for the *Province*, which had been the leading daily in Vancouver until then. A labor boycott immediately dropped its circulation, and the young Cromie brothers, who had inherited the *Sun* from their father, took full advantage of the boycott to pull ahead of their corporate competition in circulation and advertising sales.

After a decade the newspaper war became one of attrition, and Southam feared the inevitable result would be one daily dying, most likely its *Province*. The newspaper chain, which published some of the largest dailies across the county, had poured millions of dollars into its Vancouver operation in a decade-long attempt to regain the circulation lead it had lost to the *Sun*, but by 1956 it became obvious to Southam executives they would have to settle for second place behind the *Sun* in Vancouver, and second-place newspapers were a disappearing species across North America as advertisers followed readers to the leading daily in each town, followed by even more readers who were as interested in advertising as in news. The resulting death spiral had already seen dozens of newspapers die for lack of advertising revenue, and after its *Province* lost the account of the largest department store in town, Southam saw the same scenario eventually playing out in Vancouver.

In an attempt to stave off extinction for its *Province* and to stem the millions of dollars in losses it had suffered in competition with the *Sun*, Southam convinced *Sun* publisher Don Cromie to enter into an equal partnership such as had proliferated in the U.S. since the 1930s. A "joint operating agreement," as it was known south of the border, saw two newspapers amalgamate production in one printing plant, with morning and afternoon dailies saving capital costs by sharing presses and splitting profits equally. The controversial arrangements had drawn criticism for raising prices and quashing competition, and were widely thought to violate U.S. anti-trust laws against businesses collaborating to create a lucrative monopoly. By 1957, no legal challenge had been made to the cozy arrangements, however, and Southam was confident it could defend a partnership with the *Sun* in Vancouver against federal "anti-combines" regulations designed to prevent competitors from going into business together by claiming "economic necessity" to preserve the *Province* from the always-fatal "circulation spiral." The chain bought up Thomson's *Herald* and folded it, moved the *Province* to morning publication, and paid the Cromies a multi-million-dollar dowry as an "equalization" payment for entering into an equal partnership with a less-profitable competitor.

The new Pacific Press indeed drew the attention of federal regulators, who ruled it was an illegal combination. Lengthy hearings were held under the Restrictive Trade Practices Act, and after evidence was presented to support Southam's argument that the arrangement was essential to save the *Province* and thus preserve competing editorial voices in Vancouver, the Pacific Press merger was allowed to stand. A stipulated court order to prevent changes to the ownership arrangement was never entered, however, and over the years incremental changes to the partnership had increased the concentration of its ownership.

The government-sanctioned monopoly should have insured a profitable future for Pacific Press, as despite the *Province* losing even more money than before with its move to morning publication, increased profits of the *Sun* from soaring circulation in the absence of afternoon competition more than offset the losses. It was a "bizarre arrangement," according to long-time *Sun* publisher Stuart Keate, who retired in 1978, which one year "left the *Sun* with a bottom line of $2.25 million on its gross profit of $12 million and the *Province* with exactly the same reward on a loss of $1 million."[12] But economic, social, labor, and technological forces converged to nullify most of the financial benefits of monopoly for Pacific Press. The lack of local daily newspaper competition over the decades resulted in a bland product which no longer excited Vancouverites, many of whom got out of the reading habit during regular and prolonged shutdowns of both newspapers by a multitude of unions, some of which were the most militant in the country.

Labor problems at Pacific Press became so serious during the 1970s that in frustration with the unworkable partnership Southam bought the other half of Pacific Press from the Thomson worldwide conglomerate that had acquired the *Sun*, which went through a series of corporate owners after passing from Cromie family hands in 1963. Sole ownership of Pacific Press consolidated a situation that had already been ruled unlawful twenty years earlier, as former *Province* editor Bob McConnell, then publisher of Southam's *Montreal Gazette*, admitted in 1980. "Canadian combines legislation, weak though it may be, makes it quite clear that such a two-paper combination is illegal," McConnell told a meeting of the Canadian Association of Advertisers in Montreal. "It was found to be illegal, incidentally, in the case of Pacific Press, which exists only under special and very specific dispensation from the combines branch."[13]

Population growth in the Vancouver suburbs starting in the 1960s had also eaten into the advertising and circulation revenue of the Pacific Press dailies, as weeklies sprang up in the outlying areas to provide better service for neighborhood merchants than the metropolitan dailies could. Some of the community newspapers in Greater Vancouver had expanded to twice- or even thrice-weekly publication as advertisers and readers increasingly scorned the expensive dailies for their local paper. The suburban press became profitable by capturing community advertising with free distribution to every home in its market area. When the Pacific Press unions shut down the dailies regularly every few years, the independent entrepreneurs pounced on the extra advertising revenue to reap an extraordinary bonanza. Competition from community newspapers had become such a serious problem for Pacific Press that between 1989 and 1991 Southam bought up the biggest moneymakers in a series of acquisitions that precipitated yet a third federal inquiry into the ever-increasing concentration of newspaper ownership in Vancouver.

The federal Competition Tribunal hearings provided a scathing indictment of the dailies. Ten days before the *Sun*'s long-delayed morning debut, expert testimony on what so ailed Pacific Press that its parent corporation had been forced to buy up most of its competition brought bad publicity of a kind which could not be countered by any paid advertising campaign. Newspaper consultant Ted Bolwell, a former managing editor of Canada's largest daily, the *Toronto Star*, testified on September 6 that his analysis of the Pacific Press dailies showed they produced a poor but pricey product. "Some of the worst printing quality is in *The Sun* and *The Province*," said Bolwell, adding that his survey of the newspapers conducted during the previous spring had shown that thin news coverage by the Pacific Press papers gave "short shrift" to local events. "*The Sun* consistently carried only two or three Vancouver stories in its first news section, plus a couple to a few more in its second section," testified Bolwell, who had turned down the job of *Sun* publisher in 1978. "The tabloid *Province* sometimes carried less local news."[14] The Vancouver dailies were regularly scooped on news by their suburban competition, Bolwell added, and some of these stories never appeared in the *Sun* or *Province*.

Market penetration of the Pacific Press papers was declining even more rapidly than the worrisome downward trend being experienced by the industry as a whole, the consultant continued, dropping vital retail advertising linage and further diminishing the company's bottom line. The poor financial performance by Pacific Press was in spite of its charging advertising rates out of all proportion to the quality of the product offered, Bolwell noted. "The rates are probably the highest in Canada, which is unusual for a paper whose circulation is plummeting."[15] He concluded that Southam's monopoly in Vancouver was unusual for failing to capitalize on its lack of daily competition. "Despite owning the only two daily newspapers in Canada's third-largest metropolitan area — in the only major city, in fact, without daily competition — Pacific Press was floundering."[16]

In an attempt to head off a Bureau of Competition Policy order that it sell several of the community newspapers it had acquired because the resulting market control would allow Southam to raise advertising rates as high as it wanted, the newspaper chain provided its own expert witness to contradict the claim. But the report by management consultant Angus Reid, better known as a political pollster, used poor methodology in concluding that the market for daily newspaper retail advertising was different from that exploited by community papers, Bolwell argued. More significantly, the study produced in an attempt by Southam to counter the divestiture order suffered from a clear conflict of interest, as Bruce Constantineau reported in a story buried on the *Sun*'s inside business pages.

> "His definition of retail advertisers is far broader than what is germane to the case," Bolwell said. "In short, it's worthless." Justice Max Titelbaum appeared surprised when Bolwell mentioned that Southam owns the Angus Reid polling organization. "What did you say?" he asked Bolwell. When Bolwell repeated himself, Titelbaum grinned.[17]

This study examines the genesis of the Pacific Press problem that led to a situation unique in Canadian newspapers, where a government-sanctioned monopoly proved such a financial disaster that it contributed to the demise of one newspaper chain and by 1991 was threatening the ownership of another. Beginning with the antecedent conditions that led to formation of the mechanical amalgamation between the *Vancouver Sun* and *Province* in 1957, it examines the economic, political, social, technological, and labor forces which led to not only a disappearance of daily newspaper competition in Canada's third-largest city, but to an almost total absence of newspaper competition of any kind in Greater Vancouver. It is much more an "economic" history than a "journalistic" history and aims to chronicle the editorial natures of the respective newspapers only to the extent they affected them as business enterprises.[18]

The literature of journalism is replete with the reminiscences of reporters, editors, publishers, and columnists which often make for fascinating reading. Several former Pacific Press journalists (all notably from the *Sun* side) have had their memoirs published, and these are referred to liberally. But this history of Pacific Press aims to examine an under-researched area of Canadian newspaper organizations as businesses, albeit businesses unlike others in that they greatly affect social and political aspects of our communities. Pacific Press has played no small part in the unique nature of Vancouver since its 1957 inception, and its history is one which has long needed telling.

1 The Deal

St. Clair Balfour watched from the western shore of Bowen Island as the big motor yacht eased into the bay. His anticipation rose as he heard the anchor chain rattle out along the boat's bow roller and down into the water. Then, hearing the roar of the twin diesel engines reversing thrust as the helmsman guided the *Tempest IV* astern to set the anchor's flukes in the mud of Howe Sound, he could hold himself back no longer.[1] Tearing off his shirt and casting it aside on the beach, Balfour plunged into the water and began to swim toward the yacht, now lying perhaps 50 yards offshore. The frigid water made him stroke faster, as he had forgotten how cold the water was on Canada's West Coast. The sweltering day that summer of 1956 had made a swim seem an attractive idea, but as he approached the waiting craft he could think of little else than climbing up as quickly as possible out of the icy bay and into the sun's warming rays again.

The helmsman was there as he approached, attaching the boarding ladder and offering Balfour a hand up onto the boat's deck as the gasping swimmer shivered involuntarily against his chill. The two men shook hands warmly, as they had become good friends in the short time they had known each other. Balfour respected Larry Dampier's keen business intellect and admired the young executive's rise to head a major food company headquartered just outside nearby Vancouver. For his part, Dampier found Balfour, scion of the country's largest newspaper publishing empire, an amiable acquaintance on his frequent trips west from Southam's offices in Toronto to Vancouver, where one of the company's newspapers, the *Daily Province*, was published.[2] Now general manager of

Southam Press Ltd., the 46-year-old Balfour had become increasingly preoccupied with the situation in Vancouver, where a bitter war between the *Province* and its rival, the *Vancouver Sun*, threatened to leave only one survivor. This trip for Balfour, while nominally to enjoy some of the West Coast's famous salmon fishing, was a fishing trip in more ways than one. He wanted to negotiate a truce with the *Sun*'s owners and arrange a partnership under which the newspapers could coexist, perhaps even flourish.

Balfour felt at ease on the water, having been a U-boat hunter as a corvette captain in the Royal Canadian Navy during the Second World War, in which he had earned the Distinguished Service Cross. He had worked his way up in the ranks of the family firm, starting in the early 1930s as a police reporter on Southam's original *Hamilton Spectator* where, according to a 1952 feature in *Saturday Night* magazine, "he became known as an aggressive news gatherer."[3] He learned the business side of newspapering on the staff of Southam's *Winnipeg Tribune*, where he worked in the circulation and advertising departments before returning to Hamilton and eventually being promoted to publisher. His no-nonsense demeanor and jutting jaw impressed many, according to the *Saturday Night* profile.

> It would be ridiculous to say that he might have attained his rapid rise in the company without his family connection but it is also certain that his training and aggressiveness would have taken him far on any newspaper. Balfour has worked hard for the job he now holds. Anything but a glad-hander (his reticence is often mistaken for aloofness), he is respected by the men who work for him. They know him for a good newspaperman — firm and uncompromising in his principles.[4]

From the boat's deck, Balfour could see north up Howe Sound, which was rimmed by the towering peaks of the Coast Mountain range, even now, at the height of summer, still covered in snow. Looking toward shore, he saw the Bowen Island property where he had been staying as a guest of the Cromie family, owners of the *Sun*. At adjacent Camp Gates, the *Sun* held a summer camp for the newspaper's carriers and orchestrated a raucous salmon derby. Bowen Island served as a getaway for the wealthy family, only a dozen miles from downtown Vancouver yet a world of wilderness away.

A friend of the Cromie brothers, Don and Sam, whose father had rescued — some said stolen — the *Sun* from the brink of bankruptcy in 1917, Dampier was along for the ride, literally. He liked nothing better than to pilot the sixty-three-foot Cromie family yacht from its berth in downtown Vancouver's Coal Harbor to the retreat on Bowen Island. If he was able to help work out a deal between the publishers of the two newspapers, so much the better. But as a businessman, he knew Vancouver readers and advertisers had benefited from the all-out war between the newspapers. The *Sun* and *Province* were each so intent on taking advertising away from the other that they often offered deep discounts to gain business. Similarly with subscriptions, the two newspapers were so desperate to sign up new readers and thus influence the balance of power between publications that they had engaged in some generous giveaways and contests with expensive prizes.

From Balfour's point of view, the Cromies had fired the first shot in the newspaper war almost a decade earlier. Southam thought it had an agreement with the *Sun*'s owners that neither newspaper would take advantage of a strike at the other to gain circulation. But in 1946 the militant printers of the International Typographical Union (ITU) had gone to war with Southam, striking five of the chain's dailies in retaliation for the company's strikebreaking tactics at the *Winnipeg Tribune*. Southam kept printing its newspapers from behind picket lines, using non-union printers and management personnel to continue publishing, but Balfour realized now that had been a terrible mistake in a strong union town like Vancouver, where the epithet "scab" was truly a four-letter word. The resource-based economy of British Columbia, which relied heavily on the forest industry, resulted in a highly unionized labor force led by the powerful International Woodworkers of America. A labor boycott against the *Province* remained in place for years after the ITU strike ended, dropping its circulation to second place behind the *Sun*. The dispute even became immortalized in song:

> *Lay that* Province *down, babe,*
> *Lay that* Province *down;*
> *That scab-run rag is blackballed*
> *In this union town.*[5]

The irony was that the *Province* had been the first Southam paper to agree in 1945 to the ITU's demand that the international union's bylaws, one of which made the five-day week mandatory, not be subject to arbitration. Three of the chain's other papers in Ottawa, Edmonton, and Hamilton, where Balfour was then assistant publisher, also went along with the change. The Cromies, who a few years earlier had been the first Canadian newspaper owners to certify the American Newspaper Guild to represent its editorial employees, also agreed to the provision. But in Winnipeg, where memories of the violent general strike of 1919 still caused lingering resentment toward organized labor, both dailies refused. The ITU appealed to Southam to intervene in Winnipeg, where its *Tribune* had begun printing a joint edition with the rival *Free Press* from behind the ITU picket line, but the company insisted it was a local issue and held to its policy of allowing its publishers decision-making autonomy.[6] In Hamilton, Balfour continued publishing his *Spectator* using non-union printers, while the striking compositors published their own thrice-weekly union tabloid, the *Hamilton News*.[7] In Edmonton, Southam's *Journal* joined forces with the rival *Bulletin* to publish a joint edition as the Winnipeg papers had done. In Ottawa, Southam's *Citizen* resumed publishing after an interruption of several days, during which the competing *Journal* refused to take advantage of the strike, even running an editorial urging *Citizen* readers to return to that newspaper when it reappeared. The *Journal* also refused to accept advertising from businesses that had been exclusive customers of the *Citizen* before the strike.[8]

Southam was not worried about Vancouver because in late 1945 *Province* publisher Leigh Spencer had negotiated a "united front" of publishers, gaining the agreement of Don Cromie and the morning *News-Herald*'s Clayton "Slim" Delbridge that their papers would set type for the *Province* if the ITU walked out there. That would have resulted in a shutdown of their papers as well after printers there refused to handle "struck work." The committee of publishers, Spencer reported to head office, was even considering a jointly published newspaper such as was being put out in Winnipeg and Edmonton, but the deal fell apart when Cromie backed out several days later, fearing the effect on his paper's other unions, especially the Newspaper Guild.[9]

When the *Province* was struck by ITU pickets on June 5, 1946, the Cromies first froze *Sun* circulation at its April level of 105,000 and began to ration advertising. But that changed by the end of the month "due to public pressure," according to the Sun Publishing Company annual report of 1946. The company had arranged for delivery of enough logs to run a Sunday shift at the Powell River Company's pulp mill to provide extra newsprint for expansion of the *Sun*.

> The company removed most restrictions on classified advertising, accepted about half of the display advertising offered, and increased the daily gross press run by degrees until by the end of August it was frozen at an average daily net sale of 125,000. The present concrete demand for unsolicited *Sun* subscriptions is estimated at 10,000. Had it not been for the Sunday run at the mill it is estimated that little or no circulation increase would have been possible.[10]

Soon the *Sun* was taking full advantage of its hobbled rival, selling all the new subscriptions, and especially classified advertising, it could find newsprint to print. Don Cromie learned from his father the importance of advertising in attracting readers and called the classified ads "white gold."[11] The Cromies had long taken pride in the fact their newspaper was locally owned and operated, unlike the *Province*, and under Robert Cromie in the 1920s and 1930s had trumpeted that fact daily across the front page of the *Sun*, declaring it "The Only Vancouver Newspaper Owned by Vancouver Men." When the senior Cromie died suddenly at age 48 in 1936, his sons were too young to take active control of the *Sun*, so his widow, Bernadette, headed the paper's board of directors.[12] The front-page banner thus had to be changed to the gender-neutral "Vancouver's Only Home-Owned Newspaper."

It was Mrs. Cromie's labor sympathies that allowed the Guild to get its first contract at the *Sun* in 1941, and the regard for unions rubbed off on her son Don.[13] "They'll be the real power in the capitalist system before another 50 years and maybe sooner," he declared while publisher.[14] Just weeks before the ITU struck the *Province*, Cromie had fanned the flames of labor unrest in a speech to the Pacific Northwest Circulation Managers Association. "Labor is too powerful to be ignored and capitalists must recognize labor-management teams," Cromie told the meeting at the Hotel Vancouver. "If we continue to fight labor we will have government more and more in control, which is a greater danger."[15] Pierre Berton, who had been a reporter for Cromie's *Sun* after the war, quoted his former boss in a 1948 feature in *Maclean's* magazine as saying, "The Guild is my conscience." Berton added ominously, "There has never been a strike at the *Sun*."[16] Now corporate rival Southam, which was run from its boardroom in Toronto, expected cooperation in its vulnerable hour even as it published using scab printers. Cromie would have none of it, and soon the banks of telephone solicitors he hired swelled the *Sun*'s subscription list, and the extra ads almost doubled the size of the paper's editions. Within two years the *Sun* would boast more classified advertising linage than any other newspaper in Canada, and more than all but three newspapers in the U.S.[17]

The *Province* was hindered by a lack of leadership as the strike began, with publisher Spencer laid up in the hospital.[18] The paper did not publish for six weeks, during which it lost $300,000 in revenue.[19] When Southam brought in four replacement printers on July 12 from its paper in Calgary, which was organized by a different union, they were followed into the *Province* building in Victory Square by picketers, who attacked and evicted them. Hours later, classified advertising manager W.B. Mackie was grabbed in the building's lobby, pulled outside, and beaten up. The next day, eight printers from Winnipeg got into the *Province* building, but one had to be rescued by his colleagues from the clutches of picketers, who were roughing him up.[20]

That summer had been a long, hot one for labor unrest across the province, including a shutdown of the forest industry, and a union coordinating committee had been set up to force a complete stoppage in all strikebound industry in British Columbia.[21] Soon the ranks of picketers outside the downtown *Province* offices were swelled by striking mineworkers and members of other unions. Southam responded by bringing in executives from the company's head office to run the presses, including Peter Southam, who had worked for fifteen years at the *Province* and had recently helped get the *Ottawa Citizen* back on the street. Gordon Southam, promotions manager for the *Province*, trained as a stereotyper in the art of engraving photographs for inclusion on printing plates. While training replacements, the company went to court on July 15 with affidavits detailing the picket-line violence and obtained an injunction against the ITU pickets. But as Charles Bruce noted in his 1968 official Southam history, that only made the situation outside the *Province* building worse, as "plenty of militant union men had time to spare. That night 200 boilermakers marched singing around the *Province*. The next morning, 'protest' picket lines included fishermen, steelworkers, boilermakers, metal and chemical workers, and woods workers."[22]

The international headquarters of the pressmen's union ordered its members to honor their contract with the company and report for work, and preparations were made inside the *Province* building to publish an edition the next day. That plan fell apart at the last minute when a thousand angry unionists massed outside in Victory Square. Bruce gave *Province* publisher Leigh Spencer's version of events.

> Four of their men had gone to lunch and after contact with the pickets had come back in a state of nerves bordering on collapse. Spencer went down to the pressroom. His informants had not exaggerated. "One of the men was so over-wrought that he was in tears and so nervous he could not talk and the others were in not much better condition. The upshot of it was the entire press crew walked off the plant and I could not stop them."[23]

It took until July 22 before a press run of 10,000 copies could be printed without aid of union pressmen, stereotypers, or printers. The pressmen then returned again, and that led union truckers to report to deliver the next day's edition. The result, according to Bruce, was nothing less than a "rousing riot."[24] Three trucks made it through the growing picket line, but "each truck's passage heightened the truculent excitement of the gathering crowd."[25] The next truck away from the loading dock was set upon by picketers, as described in the next day's editions of the *Sun*.

> The van drove across Pender [Street] with angry sympathizers scrambling aboard. There were insufficient police to cope with the trouble. Bundles of papers were thrown out of the van and scattered across the street. The van was brought to a stop and overturned. As a streetcar crossed the scattered papers, a spark set fire to them, and firemen had to be called.[26]

Of the seventeen rioters arrested, none were printers, instead numbering seamen, machinists, and foundry workers.[27] Following the riot, a police convoy allowed trucks manned by *Province* office workers to deliver 75,000 copies of the next day's edition. Union truckers returned, despite ITU picketing under restrictions imposed by the court injunction. Heavy union pressure discouraged both subscribers and advertisers, and it wasn't until the September 11 edition that department store advertising was again placed in the paper. That day's papers never got on the press, however, as the pressmen's union was threatened with expulsion from the local labor council if it handled the work. Management went back to running the presses, but when the paper was finally printed, union truckers refused to deliver it. The office workers had to resume their delivery rounds, but by then three days of editions had been missed. As legal action continued, eventually the pressmen and truckers returned to work. Three picketers who attacked Mackie were fined, and nine of the seventeen charged in the July 22 riot were convicted and given jail terms or fined.[28]

A lawsuit brought by Southam against six local ITU officers went to court in late 1947, and early the next year a judge ruled the strike illegal and ordered the defendants to pay the company a nominal $10,000 in damages.[29] The amount was never paid as the claim was waived when the strike was finally settled in late 1949.[30] But irreparable harm had been done to the reputation, and readership, of the *Province*. While post-war circulation had stood at about 125,000 for the *Province* to 100,000 for the *Sun*, soon these positions were reversed as a result of the strike. Many unionists would never buy the *Province* again.

Southam would not easily relinquish market leadership to the *Sun*. Before long it began offering inducements to subscribers in a desperate attempt to win back top spot in circulation. The *Province* owners realized that newspaper economics dictated they were in a struggle for survival since advertisers naturally patronize the largest-circulation newspaper in a city because it reaches more of their potential customers. Readers in turn find the larger paper more useful because they are as interested in ads as they are in news. The result is a vicious cycle of attrition for the second paper. The "circulation spiral," as it was known, had resulted in the consolidation and closure of hundreds of newspapers across North America since their heyday early in the twentieth century. Many economists had come to believe that due to the cost-saving advantages of large size, known as "economies of scale," the newspaper business was a natural monopoly like railroads or telephones. A 1945 study of newspaper mortality had pointed to "seemingly 'inexorable' economic trends . . . such factors as the loss of advertising revenue to radio, the preference of advertisers of fewer media with larger circulations and the increased cost of machinery, newsprint, labor, taxes and nearly every other item of the newspaper's expenses."[31] Major cities in North America that had boasted several daily newspapers at the turn of the century saw the number dwindle over the years to one or two through mergers, closures, and the increasing cost of starting up new publications, as Oscar Garrison Villard chronicled in his 1944 book, *The Disappearing Daily*. "There is no promise today of the sudden rise of new dailies, only the certainty that we shall see a still greater decrease in the number now extant, which is already quite too small."[32]

Vancouver, which once had four newspapers publishing daily, by 1956 had only three, and the third was barely hanging on. The morning *Herald*, which had been founded in the 1930s as the *News-Herald*, had been passed from hand to hand recently. Its latest owner, Roy Thomson, lived in Great Britain, where he owned the daily *Scotsman* in Edinburgh and was building an international newspaper empire. The Toronto-born press baron, who would be honored by Queen Elizabeth in 1964 as Lord Thomson of Fleet, had tried unsuccessfully several times to unload his money-losing *Herald* on Southam or the Cromies. The morning paper's biggest drawback was its publication time, as before television news became widely available the most popular newspaper publishing time was in the afternoon. The *Sun* and *Province* vied for supremacy in the p.m. market, however, leaving the mornings to the third-place *Herald*, which sold barely 30,000 copies a day. Southam spared no expense in its bid to reclaim its lost lead over the *Sun*, and the Cromies responded in a bid to maintain market supremacy. Soon the newspapers were spending wildly to attract subscribers. Stuart Keate, publisher of the nearby *Victoria Times*, watched the newspaper war with a keen eye and recalled it as "a decade of frantic competition which did little credit to either paper" in his home town.

> Instead of returning to its role as a low-keyed, responsible journal, the *Province* sought to match the *Sun* with sensational headlines and a "scoop" for each edition. All this was accompanied by a promotion assault in which each newspaper spent $500,000 a year to seduce the populace with a bewildering array of give-aways — sets of steak knives, Panda dolls, TV lamps and cheap insurance policies.[33]

In 1953, Southam had doubled the promotion budget for the *Province* to a half-million dollars but was only able to increase its share of the Vancouver newspaper market marginally, as the *Sun* clung stubbornly to its lead with 50 percent more circulation than its rival.[34] Balfour, now second in command to his cousin Philip Fisher, who was president of the Southam newspaper empire their grandfather had founded, knew the bleeding had to stop for the sake of business. He knew Don Cromie was not averse to cooperation, having read a letter the *Sun* publisher had written in 1950 to Fisher in which he made an overt overture. "Perhaps you'll find it worth considering whether the Vancouver public would get its best newspaper service and value from a co-operating morning-evening operation," wrote Cromie.[35] The problem was that Cromie wanted to be the majority partner in any arrangement with Southam. He had proposed an arrangement in which the *Province* would move to morning publication, leaving the afternoon field to the *Sun*, but Cromie was asking for 60 percent ownership of such a joint venture, meaning Southam would have to give up control of the *Province*. Balfour offered instead to buy the *Sun*, but Cromie would not sell. The two had gone back and forth for months on the question of ownership split until Balfour finally sensed he was close to getting the *Sun* publisher to agree to an equal partnership. He had worked carefully to bait his line, and now on this four-day fishing trip to Howe Sound, he hoped to land his catch.

The equal partnership Balfour proposed, with mechanical and distribution facilities shared, was a common arrangement in the United States, having by 1956 been agreed to in more than a dozen cities. Called joint operating agreements, the first had been made in 1933 in Tucson, Arizona, and the partnerships proved popular, spreading across the nation. But not everybody was happy with the cozy arrangements, pointing out that eliminating competition between newspapers inevitably resulted in higher advertising and subscription prices. Some questioned whether they violated U.S. anti-trust laws designed to prevent companies working together to their mutual advantage and the consumer's detriment.

In Canada, newspapers owned by the same company had shared production facilities before, but not in a market the size of Vancouver, Canada's third-largest city. In the early 1950s, the *Victoria Times* and the *Colonist* in B.C.'s nearby capital on Vancouver Island had amalgamated production facilities, forming a jointly owned company, Victoria Press Limited.[36] But Balfour knew that any partnership between Southam and the *Sun*, now fierce competitors in Vancouver, would be a hard sell with the federal government's competition watchdog. In Canada, laws against monopoly practices were known as "anti-combines" legislation and were administered by the Restrictive Trade Practices Commission in Ottawa. The intent was the same as in the U.S. — to protect the consumer from companies conspiring together to extract monopoly profits — but that was not often the result north of the border. Balfour figured he could make such a partnership fly with the federal regulators, but he decided to cross that hurdle only after he had a deal with Cromie.

Of more pressing concern this summer day was persuading Cromie to call a truce in their newspaper war and agree to an equal partnership. Cromie could be convinced to make a deal, Balfour believed, because he knew Southam's nationwide resources far outstripped his own and he was therefore bound to be the loser in a long-term battle, as Southam could simply afford to endure the losses longer. While Balfour knew Southam could win in the long run, he also knew the cost would be enormous, draining the newspaper chain's resources and diverting its attention and capital investment from the competitive markets where its seven other dailies were published. In Vancouver, its plant needed upgrading desperately. A 1956 study of *Province* facilities found them cramped and antiquated, with printers "continually stepping over one another."[37] Its presses were old, and for every color printed, an entire "set" of eight pages had to be dropped from the press run, often requiring an extra section to be printed, with higher labor costs resulting, as the study noted. "Nowadays, with more colour being used by advertisers, this results in a third section having to be printed on [an] extra shift."[38] Both publishers needed to upgrade to faster, higher-capacity presses capable of using the new color printing technology, but neither could afford to make such a major investment while pouring all their resources into a circulation war. The best compromise for both sides was the peace of a partnership, but Southam would only settle for an equal share. The *Province* was willing to move to morning publication and the *Herald* could be cheaply bought up from Thomson and killed off for its network of carriers and list of subscribers, but Cromie was unwilling to enter into an equal partnership with what would be a weaker twin publishing in the smaller morning market and thus contributing less to the common enterprise. He wanted to be compensated with cash up front, and Southam was willing to pay for the partnership. The only question was how much.

Balfour had come to the West Coast not to make Cromie a cash offer, but to convince him that an equal partnership was the best alternative for both sides because it was the only option, other than a fight to the death. The amount of an equalization payment could be negotiated later, but Balfour wanted to come away from his fishing trip with Cromie's agreement in principle to an equal partnership. Balfour pondered his strategy as the fishing party was ferried aboard by the yacht's tender. A brace of brothers completed the crew, Don and Sam Cromie, fresh from getting out that day's edition in Vancouver, and the Foley brothers, down from the pulp and paper capital of Powell River, fifty miles up the coast. The Foley family ran the Powell River Company, one of the province's largest newsprint plants, and as the *Sun*'s arrangements during the ITU strike showed, newspapers like to stay in close contact with their biggest suppliers.

In attempting to convince Cromie to divide up the market, Balfour was simply continuing the company strategy of his grandfather. William Southam had worked his way up from delivering the *London Free Press* in Ontario to superintendent of the newspaper's plant at 33 in 1877, when he bought a half-interest in the *Hamilton Spectator* for $4,000.[39] Twenty years later, as *Spectator* publisher, he began the family's newspaper empire by sending his sons Wilson and Harry to Ottawa to purchase the *Citizen*. Collusion between publishers in the nation's capital was already well organized by that time, with heads of the three dailies meeting regularly to set advertising rates. The cooperation had begun in 1895 in response to double-dealing by the McKim advertising agency, which had worked each publisher against the others to obtain lower ad rates.[40] By 1920, after the *Ottawa Journal* bought the rival *Free Press*, collusion between it and Southam's *Citizen* reached a maximum, according to historian Minko Sotiron, when a deal was reached under which the papers would jointly promote one daily if its circulation fell more than 5 percent below the other's.

> A formula was introduced by which one paper would receive financial compensation if the other exceeded it in advertising, circulation, or profit. The *Citizen*'s Harry Southam considered the agreement eliminated "waste in the production and distribution of our newspapers" brought about "by the years of futile and useless competition."[41]

When the Southam company expanded to Western Canada, it campaigned for similar cooperation between publishers, first in Calgary where its *Herald*, purchased in 1907, dominated the competition and forced closure of the rival *News-Telegram* in 1920; then in Winnipeg, where it purchased the *Tribune* in 1920. When it moved to Canada's West Coast in 1923 by buying the *Province*, Southam took over Vancouver's leading daily. The second-place *Sun* lambasted the Eastern control publicly, but privately publisher Robert Cromie was willing to cooperate with his new corporate rival, due perhaps to the fact that in a moment of financial desperation he had gone to the Southams for a loan, and for a time the parent company of the rival *Province* held the third mortgage on his printing plant.[42] Cromie had advocated dividing up the Vancouver afternoon market between the two papers, and according to the official Southam history, eventually an agreement was reached after the third paper in the market, the *Star*, folded.

> Early in 1933 the *Province* and *Sun* did in fact agree to stabilize the circulation position in various classifications (city carrier, city total, and so on) with the *Sun* at 86 per cent of the *Province* overall, the agreement providing that either paper making gains in any classification would cease efforts to get new subscribers while the other took steps to catch up. They couldn't get together on advertising.[43]

The Depression of the 1930s continued the newspaper shakeout that the Great War years had begun. The number of Canadian dailies fell from 138 in 1913 to 109 by the Crash of 1929, only to dip to 90 by 1938.[44] The Second World War brought a shortage of newsprint, which had to be rationed like many wartime commodities. After the war, newsprint was no more plentiful when price controls were lifted, and under the law of supply and demand the price of a ton more than doubled in a dozen years, from $54 to $130, forcing more dailies out of business.[45] By 1956 there was an acute shortage of newsprint, and earlier in the same summer that Balfour visited Bowen Island, the crisis had led to action by publishers, with the Canadian Daily Newspaper Publishers Association confronting the Newsprint Association on July 11 to demand stepped-up production.[46]

The rising costs and circulation war in Vancouver had caused both the *Sun* and the *Province* to forego needed capital improvements to their printing plants, as neither Southam nor the Cromies were prepared to make such a major investment under uncertain conditions. The *Province* was in a cost squeeze not only due to rising newsprint prices but also because of higher labor rates, as Cromie's penchant to give the unions what they wanted meant Southam had to match the wage increases.[47] In addition to generous wages, the *Sun* provided its employees with a 37½-hour workweek, a pension plan, life insurance, hospital and surgery insurance, a $3,000 banquet every year, subsidized cafeteria meals, walls covered in art, soft music, and a lucrative profit-sharing plan, splitting anything the paper made over $150,000 with its workers. Cromie, who once said he'd "rather turn out a good newspaper than make money, has fixed it so he won't make too much," Pierre Berton noted in a 1948 *Maclean's* feature.

> Last year, strangled by newsprint shortages, the paper made only $90,000. Cromie, anticipating bigger profits, gave his staff some in advance anyway — about two days pay each. He didn't ask for it back. Now, paradoxically, staff members view with alarm the present *Sun* spending spree. . . . The profit-sharers are inclined to wonder suspiciously if the music and other frills are worth the money.[48]

The conditions were ripe for cooperation, and the next day Balfour and Don Cromie went off to fish the waters near Keats Island, just the two of them in a small, outboard-powered skiff. There, in the middle of Howe Sound, the two shook hands on the deal that would create Pacific Press. Agreeing finally to the principle of equal partnership, the pair left the amount of equalization Southam would pay the Cromies until later, after accountants had valued the operations of each.

Soon back in Toronto from his successful West Coast fishing trip, Balfour made a meeting with Southam's lawyer, Alec MacIntosh, one of his first priorities. They had to prepare their strategy for dealing with government regulators, who theoretically had the power to scotch the deal Balfour had just made. Together the pair traveled to Ottawa to inform the head of the Restrictive Trade Practices Commission of the agreement. Many years later, long after his retirement from the newspaper business, Balfour would recall the meeting in the mandarin's office. "I remember him at that time saying, 'Mr. MacIntosh, I'm going to have to make inquiries and I suppose the longer we take, the better you'd like it.' . . . I just remember him smiling and saying 'I suspect that the longer we take . . .' or words to that effect."[49]

2 The Tower

Don Cromie, back from Bowen Island, waited for the elevator in the lobby of the old Sun Tower in downtown Vancouver. And waited. And waited some more. The aging lift was legendary for slow motion. But the pause perhaps gave the publisher — once described by *Sun* columnist Jack Scott as "a restless man, all bone, sinew and nerve ends" — a moment to reflect on events of that summer of 1956.[1] Even as his newspaper's still-secret marriage with Southam's *Province* was being consummated, a bitter provincial election campaign was under way across British Columbia, and the government wanted Cromie in jail for the *Sun*'s coverage of it. The fact that a minister of the Crown was facing allegations of bribery had not stopped Premier W.A.C. Bennett from calling an election at summer's end. And though the scandal had caused forest minister Robert Sommers to resign his portfolio while an investigation was held, it had not prevented him from standing for re-election. Even before criminal charges could be laid, however, Sommers launched a preemptive strike, filing a libel lawsuit against lawyer David Sturdy, who had brought to light allegations the minister had accepted cash and gifts from applicants for timber-cutting rights.

When the matter became an issue in the election campaign, Cromie and Vancouver's other newspaper publishers were put in an awkward position. Reporting the brouhaha would risk a contempt charge, since the matter was now before the courts. But when Conservative leader Deane Finlayson raised the allegations in a campaign speech, reading portions of Sturdy's statement of defence aloud, the *Sun* ran the story, as had the *Herald*. Now Sommers had gone to court seeking an order to put Finlayson, Cromie, and *Herald* publisher Gerry Brown in Burnaby's nearby Oakalla prison farm for contempt of court.[2] (The charges were thrown out after a Conservative Party lawyer from Saskatchewan, John Diefenbaker, who would be elected prime minister the next year, flew out to the coast to defend Finlayson.) The Sommers drama would last for more than two years, and the contempt charge against Cromie's newspaper would not be the last.[3]

A growing crowd was now waiting in the Sun Tower lobby for the snail-like elevator to arrive. The publisher greeted each employee personally, as he was on a first-name basis with most of his staff. "Cromie loves informality the way some men love order," a *Time* magazine profile a few years earlier had noted.[4] Pierre Berton described Cromie in *Maclean's* as "tall, willow-thin, probe-nosed, sandy-haired, nervous" and noted he had been voted the best-dressed man in the building. "He wears saddle-stitched, light-colored fedoras, tan corduroy suits, brilliant green-and-scarlet-flowered ties, loud sweaters and socks."[5] In *Saturday Night* magazine, Jack Scott called Cromie "fastidious . . . a stickler for punctuality," but observed that he "confronts the world with what is, for an intense man, a deceptively bland appearance and laconic style of speaking."[6] Despite being publisher of the city's leading daily, Cromie was, according to Scott, "a little known figure" in Vancouver, unlike his "ebullient" younger brother Sam, who served as the paper's representative at its free swimming and skiing lessons and annual salmon derby. "Something of an eccentric," wrote Scott, "[Don] Cromie is most often and accurately compared with his father. . . . Of four sons, Don alone seems to have been destined to voluntarily fill the publisher's chair."[7]

Don seemed to have inherited his father's business sense while the elder Cromie's charm and charisma went mostly to Sam. Together they made a good team, but Don had an unpredictability that was sometimes unnerving. "*Sun* men know that they can see him any time, [but] are not sure what will happen once they get inside his office," noted *Time* magazine in 1949.[8] In his 1948 *Maclean's* article, Berton told the story of how Cromie "once banged a hatchet down on the desk of O. Leigh Spencer, former *Province* publisher, during a get-together on ad rates, after he'd been told that Spencer carried a gun in his vest pocket."[9] His management skills often rubbed others the wrong way, but by the time his victory in Vancouver's newspaper war was about to be acknowledged with a million-dollar dowry from Southam, Cromie was considerably more easygoing. "*Sun* department heads who have learned to live with his bluntness and sometimes caustic wit agree he is mellowing," noted Scott in his 1957 profile of Cromie in *Saturday Night*. "'Don has finally heard about the soft sell,' one observes."[10]

The copper-domed tower, where the growing contingent of *Sun* staff waited for the eventual elevator, had been built in 1911 in a warehouse district on the outskirts of what was then Vancouver's central business district, near the deepwater docks of Burrard Inlet, to house the city's leading newspaper of the day, which back then was not the *Sun* but the *Vancouver World*. The seventeen-storey World Tower, as it was then known, briefly held the distinction of being the tallest building in the British Empire, no small point of pride for a remote outpost on the edge of the Canadian frontier, before being surpassed by Toronto's twenty-storey Royal Bank building.[11] After Cromie's father bought the *World* in 1924 and folded it into his *Sun*, the World Tower was taken over by the Bekins moving company and used for storage while the *Sun* published from its old offices on the opposite side of Beatty Street. But after a 1937 fire razed the wooden *Sun* building, a move across the street again made the Tower a newspaper building, with neon piping added to the copper dome and a brilliant beacon installed on its roof to symbolize the shining *Sun*.

Robert Cromie was a legendary figure in Vancouver newspapering. A world traveler, promoting Vancouver wherever he went, he wrote pamphlets on the faraway places he visited, such as Russia and China. He was always bringing home interesting dinner guests, many of them visitors to Vancouver like the muckraking journalist Lincoln Steffens, whom Don Cromie would remember later as "a tiny little fellow with a pointy beard and a black, sloping hat that gave him quite a dramatic appearance."[12] The senior Cromie also told his son of his long friendship with U.S. president Franklin D. Roosevelt, whom he helped, during a visit to Washington, enunciate a rationale for his "New Deal" economic policy prescribed at the depths of the Depression of the 1930s. As Don recalled many years later in an oral history of Vancouver newspapers:

> It got great publicity across the country and was very heavily played in the *Sun* because my father asked the question at a news conference ... [Roosevelt] proceeded to enunciate slowly ten points that set the objectives and goals of the New Deal, all of which had been written out by himself and my father the day before over tea. Nobody ever knew that.[13]

Despite having no formal education, the elder Cromie was a brilliant businessman. The story of how he came to the coast had long since passed into Vancouver newspaper folklore. Born in Quebec of Irish and Australian parents in 1887, he was working as a teenaged bellhop at Winnipeg's famous Mariaggi hotel about 1905 when he was summoned to bring ice and soda to the room of Colonel Jack Stewart, a visiting construction magnate from Vancouver. Given a sizeable tip, the young Cromie returned half of it, saying it was too much. Impressed with this integrity, Stewart hired Cromie as his personal assistant in Vancouver.

Stewart had emigrated from Scotland to Canada at 20 in 1882, working his way west to Vancouver, where he found employment as an axeman clearing the city site. He was working on June 13, 1886, when fire destroyed the fledgling town and he had survived the flames only by seeking refuge in the waters of False Creek.[14] The lucrative Pacific Great Eastern railway contract, which Stewart had obtained in 1909 along with his American partners, Timothy Foley and Pat Welch, would become one of the longest-running fiascos in B.C. history. Begun in 1912, construction of the line had stalled by 1916 two-thirds of the way from Vancouver to Fort George (soon to become Prince George), 400 miles away in the province's northern interior. The firm of Foley, Welch and Stewart, then the leading railway and heavy construction contractors on the continent, was unable to complete the project because of cost overruns and soon needed the provincial government's help to pay the interest on millions of dollars in loans. While the Colonel beat a hasty retreat to build rail lines across the battlefields of Europe during the First World War, his partners and assistant Cromie were left to explain what had become of the $25 million paid out for construction of the PGE. A select committee of the provincial legislature formed to investigate the scandal heard testimony that a half million dollars had gone to pay off a vice-president of the PGE to ensure the contract, issued without going to public tender, went to

Foley, Welch and Stewart. Skipping the country before his testimony was complete, the recipient confessed he used much of the money to pay off members of the Conservative provincial government and the press. A $1,000 payment went to editorial writer George Morden of the *North Shore Press* in return for his "ardent support" of the project, while $250 went to W.A. Harkin of the *Province*.[15]

Buying off the *Vancouver Sun* was quite unnecessary, Cromie testified in June 1917, as Stewart had used part of the $763,000 he distributed to members of the opposition Liberal Party to buy outright the evening newspaper, which was then a Liberal Party organ.[16] The PGE contract was canceled by motion of the provincial legislature, and a lawsuit was launched against Foley, Welch and Stewart, claiming $6.9 million in excess profits, which later was settled for $1.1 million.[17] A 1924 Royal Commission report eventually absolved the government of blame.[18]

As Don Cromie stood waiting for the elevator in the lobby of the Sun Tower in that summer of 1956, Bennett's Social Credit administration had just weeks earlier finally finished the PGE rail line to Prince George, forty-four years after it was started. The first train pulled into Prince George on August 29, which "Wacky" Bennett trumpeted to great effect in his campaign for re-election. Somehow in the confusion of the 1917 scandal around the PGE, which came to stand in the minds of many British Columbians for "Prince George Eventually," Robert Cromie came into ownership of the *Sun*. It was an acquisition that went unexplained for almost seventy years. "How the newspaper passed permanently into the possession of Mr. Cromie is another of the mysteries of Vancouver newspaperdom," declared a 1946 history of Vancouver newspapers by longtime *Province* editorial writer Dan McGregor.[19]

Regardless of how he acquired the *Sun*, Robert Cromie soon proved deft at advancing it. Borrowing money from Colonel C.B. Blethen, publisher of the nearby *Seattle Times*, he first bought the competing *News-Advertiser* in September 1917, paying only a reported $100,000 for it in a brilliant move, according to McGregor. "At one stroke, Mr. Cromie did two good pieces of business. He eliminated a rival . . . and he added that rival's circulation to his own."[20] To the *Sun*'s 10,000 readers were added the *News-Advertiser*'s 8,000, leaving it as the only morning newspaper, with the *Province* and the *World* publishing in the afternoon. In 1924, a year after Southam bought the *Province* from founder Walter Nichol, Cromie bought the faltering *World* for $475,000 from owner Charles Campbell and began publishing it as the *Evening Sun* while continuing to publish a *Morning Sun*.

The only problem was that Cromie had neglected to extract a promise from Campbell to stay out of the Vancouver newspaper game, in which he emerged again as a player two months later, starting a new afternoon paper dubbed the *Evening Star*. More worrisome to Cromie in the renewed competition was the *Star*'s penny pricing, with six-day home delivery offered at thirty cents a month, compared with fifty cents for the *Evening Sun* and 75 cents for the *Province*. Cromie dropped his subscription price to 25 cents to undercut the *Star*, and Campbell quickly sold out to General Victor Odlum, a First World War hero who had been editor of the *World* in 1905 at age 25. Cromie made a series of deals with Odlum starting in 1926. First they agreed to stabilize monthly subscription rates at forty cents. Then Cromie made a bold move, persuading Odlum to swap the *Star* for his old *Morning Sun*. Thus, the *Star* was folded into the *Evening Sun*, and the *Morning Sun* became the *Morning Star*. Eyebrows were raised at the time, but the move proved a master stroke, as *Maclean's* magazine observed in 1928.

> What the public did not realize, and what Cromie apparently understood, was that ... his evening paper, getting into the homes, had a far more promising future, from a revenue point of view, than the morning paper, which went to the offices and was consequently held in light regard by the advertisers bidding for the attention of women, who do the family buying.[21]

As proof of Cromie's foresight, the magazine cited the fact that *Sun* circulation had grown in four years from 17,000 to more than 70,000, noting "it is no secret that the big afternoon daily, evolved from the little sheet of dubious origin . . . is a highly prosperous concern."[22] The Cromie formula for editorial success was to make his locally owned newspaper a champion for Vancouver and Western Canada, while scorning his Southam competition and its absentee Eastern ownership. Stuart Keate, who as publisher of the *Sun* would take Cromie's paper to its greatest heights, remembered it from growing up in Vancouver during the 1930s as "the working-man's paper — at once raucous, rambunctious and dedicated to the proposition that the simple business of a newspaper was to raise hell. . . . It also espoused with the utmost vigour the curious enthusiasms of its publisher." By comparison, according to Keate, the market-leading *Province* was "staid, stodgy and eminently respectable. . . . It viewed events with quiet objectivity, rarely raised its voice, and generally reflected the conservative stance of the Establishment."[23]

The *Star* folded in 1932 after its staff refused Odlum's demand to take a pay cut. *Time* magazine observed a few years later that "with two well-entrenched evening dailies in the field [population 246,593], a morning paper in Vancouver seemed an economic impossibility."[24] That did not stop a group of *Star* staffers from starting their own morning daily, the *News-Herald*. A public sympathetic to such a cooperative effort during the depths of the Depression helped the new paper grow within five years to a circulation of 20,000, making it the largest morning paper in the country west of Toronto.[25]

The elder Cromie's business acumen was doubtless due to his foresight, which also gained him a reputation for eccentricity. He was a fitness buff well before the jogging craze and a health-food devotee and vegetarian long before such a lifestyle was common. "He is a physical culturist of the first water," observed *Maclean's* in a 1928 profile. "An ordinary café, or club plate dinner, eaten by a friend, causes 'Bob' Cromie acute mental agony, for he can visualize in awful detail the calamitous chemical reactions of wrong food combinations. His friends describe his own meals as 'weird.'"[26]

The most-repeated Robert Cromie story is that of the editor who, on accepting his publisher's invitation to lunch, soon found himself embarked on a brisk ten-mile walk to Cromie's Point Grey home for a plate of raw vegetables. The irony was that Cromie, about whom *Maclean's* predicted "Canada is to hear a great deal," died at 48 of heart failure on May 11, 1936, while on a visit to Victoria for a speaking engagement before the Chamber of Commerce, where he was to recount his most recent trip to the Orient.[27] His funeral was the largest Vancouver had ever seen, and his will bequeathed half ownership of the *Sun* to his widow, Bernadette, born of a founding Vancouver family — the tinsmithing shop of her father, Edward McFeely, was one of the few buildings to survive the Great Fire of 1886 — and 10 percent to each of their five children. Mrs. Cromie took over as publisher in name only, with operations of the *Sun* directed by the paper's business manager, P.J. Salter. Eldest son Robert Cromie Jr. was named vice-president despite being just 24, but the combination was not successful, and the *Sun* went into a period of decline. Bob Jr., as a staff member later recalled, "didn't like to make waves — he was just a nice guy."[28] The effect was that the editorial direction of the paper was set by accountant Salter, whose instinct was to emulate the successful *Province*, which made the *Sun* increasingly redundant to readers, and circulation fell.

Don Cromie, who was just twenty when his father died, had already dropped out of journalism school at the nearby University of Washington in Seattle. "I found myself messing around in type boxes — old fashioned type boxes — and doing things like that for which I had no aptitude," he remembered.[29] He switched his major to English but never finished his degree. Scott's 1957 profile in *Saturday Night* magazine summarized his life experience.

> He served an apprenticeship as a cub reporter on the *Sun*, rode the rods through the United States in one depression year on his father's advice that it would give him a liberal education, enrolled briefly in the London University's School of Economics, took a Cook's tour through Russia in 1936 and returned to complete his basic training on the news desk of the *Toronto Star*.[30]

Cromie had received his job offer directly from *Star* publisher Joseph Atkinson while taking a tour of the paper's building with circulation manager Ralph Cowan in 1940.[31] He was working in Toronto when his younger brother Sam, who objected to the way the *Sun* was being run into the ground, convinced Don to return home to help steer the family ship. With the war on, the physically robust Sam Cromie was about to be called up to serve in the RCAF, and from what he saw going on at the Sun Tower, he got the feeling the *Sun* would no longer be a Cromie family newspaper when he got out of the service. Don agreed to take over as managing editor, but with the strong-willed Sam away the *Sun* was almost sold out from under him. If it hadn't been for the intervention of sports editor Hal Straight, it would have been. Straight was a legend in Vancouver newspapering before leaving to take a job as publisher of the *Edmonton Bulletin*. "A reincarnation of Walter Burns, the hard-driving editor in . . . *The Front Page*," was the way Straight was described by Pierre Berton, whom he hired away from the *News-Herald* after being promoted to managing editor of the *Sun*. "He claimed he had spilled more hooch than most people consume in a lifetime."[32] A giant of a man who had been a notable amateur athlete in his youth, Straight was, according to Berton, "the perfect managing editor for what was then one of the most colorful daily newspapers in Canada."[33] He was not above such stunts as putting apple-blossom perfume into the printer's ink for a feature on tree flowers, or convincing an itinerant evangelist to "walk through the composing room during a typographers' slowdown carrying a placard reading: 'It's Later Than You Think.'"[34] Straight secured his place in *Sun* legend when he abruptly settled a dispute with his city editor, who balked at following orders from a former sportswriter. The incident, according to Berton, set the town buzzing. "Straight simply picked him up and stuffed him into one of the big wire baskets behind the city desk."[35]

During the Second World War, Straight was still sports editor when Bob Cromie Jr. agreed, since the *Sun* had been losing money during the years since his father's death, with Salter's decision to sell the paper to Victor Sifton, owner of the *Winnipeg Free Press,* for $750,000. But Straight had made friends with an industry expert who had been brought in from Chicago to value the *Sun* for the buyers and who frequented the newspaper's sports department to get the baseball scores. The American confided to Straight that the *Sun* was actually worth more like a million dollars, and the sports editor passed the information on to Don Cromie, urging him to use the valuation to get the sale voted down at the shareholders meeting called to approve it. It did not happen that way, however, and the sale was approved. Straight recalled what happened next for a 1982 oral history of Vancouver newspapers.

> After the meeting, he [Don Cromie] came up to the sports department and I got mad at Don for not exposing the report. Finally, I arranged for him to phone his brother, Sam, who was in Edmonton in the air force, and have Sam phone his mother — she had the stock — that night, and Don would be there, and they'd ask her not to sell. So they did that.[36]

With the check already in the mail from Winnipeg, the sale was nixed.[37] Bob Cromie Jr. got out of the newspaper business and went into cattle ranching up-country. Salter quit, leaving Don to take over as publisher. Cromie offered Straight a promotion to city editor the next day at his home in West Vancouver, but Straight protested that his background was in sports and that he was inexperienced in the news business. Straight instead boldly asked for the managing editor's job Cromie had vacated, but the *Sun*'s new publisher balked. "How can you be managing editor when you can't be a city editor?" he asked.[38] Straight had a quick answer, as recalled by Berton. "'Easy,' said Straight. 'I'll hire a good city editor.' He did — by luring Himie Koshevoy away from the *Province*."[39] A veteran journalist who began his career in 1932 on the old *Vancouver News* before it became hyphenated with the *Star* survivors as the *News-Herald*, Koshevoy was a brilliant acquisition for the Cromies because in addition to being a solid newsman, he possessed a flair for the offbeat that soon characterized the *Sun*. A persistent prankster, he once ran the same story on the front page three straight days, just to see if anyone would notice. Nobody did.[40] Stuart Keate, who worked on the *News-Herald* in the 1930s, described Koshevoy as "a gentle, gnome-like character who would have looked perfectly at home in a rock-garden, with water streaming from his mouth. He was also celebrated as the town's most avid punster. Why had he been kicked out of his campus fraternity? 'Because,' said Himie, deadpan, 'I refused to pay my Jews.'"[41] Together the enormous Straight and diminutive Koshevoy formed a Mutt-and-Jeff management team that would soon treat Vancouverites to some of the liveliest newspapering ever seen in Canada.

Things began looking up even more when Sam returned home after the war to run the production side of *Sun* operations as mechanical vice-president. The brothers became known as the "boy publishers," as Berton observed in his 1948 *Maclean's* article. "The name didn't stick. In . . . six years the *Sun*'s circulation has rocketed from 75,000 to 150,000. The Cromie boys have long since proved that they are dry behind the ears."[42] Don Cromie's first order of business after taking over as publisher was to remake the *Sun* into the type of feisty newspaper his father had produced. Under the guidance of Straight and Koshevoy, the editorial direction that had emulated the conservative coverage of the *Province* returned to the philosophy of Robert Cromie or, as Berton called it, "the *Sun* brand of raucous, racy, hard-hitting, ruggedly independent and highly irreverent journalism."[43] *Time* magazine listed in 1949 some of the changes by the *Sun*'s new publisher, who "hired some of the best reporters in town, remade the *Sun*'s hodge-podge front page, using clearer type and more pictures. . . . filled the first section of the paper with stories for men (including sports and finance), put women's pages, comics and classified ads into sections two and three."[44]

The ITU strike at the *Province* gave the Cromies the chance to take the lead on their competition, and they never looked back. The *Sun* emphasized local coverage, with the paper's sole correspondent outside B.C. being posted in the nation's capital of Ottawa. Its political stance was Liberal, laced with broadsides against absentee Eastern ownership and relentless criticism of federal monopolies in broadcasting (the Canadian Broadcasting Corporation) and the airline industry (Trans-Canada Airlines, later renamed Air Canada). Like his father, who was known to slip his lead columnist a five-dollar bill to disagree with that day's editorial, Cromie encouraged his columnists to freely differ from the policies prescribed on the paper's editorial page. Two of the *Sun*'s most high-profile columnists were vigorously left-wing. Elmore Philpott even ran for parliament with Cromie's blessing.[45] Jack Scott's column often ran with a disclaimer or even a rebuttal from Cromie. A writer for *Saturday Night* magazine noted in 1953 the proliferation of columnists in the city, counting eighteen among the three dailies. Of the eight *Sun* columnists, it deemed Scott "an opinionated veteran . . . and a smooth writer," while Philpott was "probably the best-liked and respected of all the denizens of this bizarre journalistic jungle."[46] Berton observed the editorial battles at his alma mater with keen interest from his new posting in Toronto at *Maclean's*.

> Philpott and the editorial writers often snipe at each other from journalistic foxholes on opposite sides of the page. *Sun* readers have become used to picking up the paper to find an editorial attacking Scott, a feature story refuting Philpott, a Philpott column refuting a previous editorial attack and half a dozen letters to the editor violently denouncing or praising one and all.[47]

Scott observed in his 1957 profile of his publisher that Cromie was a "strong believer in retailing many shades of opinion," and noted he had even annoyed his reporting staff by slashing the news hole by an entire page to create space opposite the editorials to print opposing opinions.[48] According to Keate, Cromie became concerned in the mid-1950s about the length of *Sun* editorials and news stories and imported a New York word-count specialist to do a study. "The visiting semanticist recommended that no editorial should exceed 300 words, and no sentence nineteen words," Keate recalled.[49]

Cromie's formula was wildly successful, as *Sun* circulation soared from 160,000 in 1949, when it ranked as the country's fifth-largest daily, to more than 190,000 by 1954. The *Province*, after dropping below 100,000 in circulation for the five years after its disastrous strike, was by then back up over 120,000 as a result of its increasingly vigorous promotional efforts.[50] Competition between the two evening papers had turned into an all-out war and created a climate for newspapering that reminded many, including Berton, of "the rough-and-ready, buccaneering brand of journalism that made Chicago famous in the '20's."[51] *Maclean's* columnist George Bain recalled the formula as "Bright writing, big headlines and outrageous stunts. . . . at *The Sun*, when the story was big, they played it big. With big headlines, bylines and plenty of space."[52] The secret to the *Sun*'s success, Scott noted in 1957, was that "the front-running position in circulation made little change in the *Sun*'s long-time 'second-newspaper look' of aggressive news coverage with an emphasis on local stories, a stable of controversy-hungry columnists and globe-trotting feature writers."[53]

But Cromie had one problem that prevented him from running away from his evening rival. Berton's many talents included cartooning, which he had done at the *News-Herald* before the war, and song-writing.[54] He immortalized Cromie's quest for the scarce newsprint on which to print more and thicker copies of the *Sun* after the ITU strike, in a composition for quartet performed at an annual soiree known as the "Fourth Estate Frolic," which was held at the Hotel Vancouver.

> *Cromie wanted paper like Dracula wanted blood*
> *He really had to have the stuff to stem the* Province *flood*
> *He used up every ounce he had to stretch each daily issue*
> *And that is why our men's room has clear run out of tissue.*[55]

By 1951, with newsprint still in short supply, Cromie was about to go into the black market and pay exorbitant prices to a commodities broker in New York when he lunched with his old friend Slim Delbridge, a stock promoter who had taken over the morning *News-Herald* a few years earlier with a group of investors. The ever-interested Keate, then publisher of the nearby *Victoria Times*, recounted in his memoirs the deal they made.

> The *News-Herald* quota, while not large, was significant when valued at the price Cromie intended to pay for paper in New York. Before the luncheon was ended, Delbridge had agreed to sell the *News-Herald* to the *Sun*. . . . Cromie got the morning newspaper and its quota for no more than he would have been compelled to pay for newsprint in New York.[56]

Over Delbridge's protests, Cromie proceeded to starve the morning paper for its precious newsprint, which he used to pad his lead over the *Province*. The *News-Herald* was down to a thin ten-page edition, of which only 30,000 copies were being printed daily, when Cromie flipped the ailing title to Roy Thomson in 1952.[57] Thomson's expanding international media empire had started with a chain of smaller newspapers across Canada, but most were moneymakers due to the fact they enjoyed local monopolies. Thomson soon found the fierce competition in Vancouver not to his liking and tried repeatedly to unload his renamed *Herald* on both Southam and the *Sun*.

For Cromie, making peace with Southam made a lot of sense. Newspapers had become big business, and independent, family-owned dailies like his were becoming an endangered species. Chains like Southam and Thomson were expanding and reaping the advantages of scale economies, which allowed them to reduce costs through centralized management. The chains were also better-equipped through diversification to weather the bad times that could put individual newspapers out of business. It was a conundrum that while daily newspaper circulation soared to record levels in the mid-1950s, the cost squeeze was killing long-established titles at a rapid rate. In a three-year period in the 1950s, no fewer than four Montreal dailies suspended publication, including the 146-year-old *Herald*, which had been acquired by the rival *Star* in 1938 and converted to the country's lone English-language tabloid, modeled after the successful *New York Daily News*.[58]

As he finally boarded the arriving elevator, Cromie was also no doubt mindful of the fact that in Edmonton, where Straight had gone for a job as publisher of the venerable *Bulletin*, that paper's death in 1951 was the result of its being *too* successful, as the Canadian Press wire service had reported.

> The newspaper had increased its circulation 66 per cent in three years and its advertising linage 88 per cent. He [Straight] said it was now confronted with the problem of building a new plant and buying a new press at an outlay of $1,000,000. In addition, the paper was unable to obtain adequate newsprint supplies.[59]

The *Bulletin* was the second-oldest newspaper in Western Canada, after the *Battleford Herald* in neighboring Saskatchewan. It would have beaten the Battleford paper to publication, but its first printing press, transported by founder Frank Oliver from Winnipeg in an ox cart, ended up at the bottom of the Saskatchewan River when the raft Oliver built to cross the river tipped. Oliver had to return to Winnipeg and order a new press from Philadelphia.[60] But the press was designed for a sixteen-page paper, and the *Bulletin* had increased in size to an average of twenty-seven pages per edition and 30,000 circulation under the aggressive ownership of *Calgary Albertan* publisher and oil magnate Max Bell, who had bought the newspaper in 1948. Its competition, Southam's *Edmonton Journal*, sold almost twice as many copies in the provincial capital of 150,000. In announcing its demise, the *Bulletin* noted the growing problem on its front page. "Many newspapers have been forced out of business in centres of population much larger than Edmonton and the trend is that the number of cities able to support more than one newspaper is steadily decreasing."[61] Straight told his old colleagues at the Sun Tower "we forced ourselves out of business," but denied he was heading to Victoria to take over as publisher of the *Victoria Times*, which Bell had just bought in the British Columbia capital.[62]

Finally back in his fourth-floor office, Cromie took a long-distance telephone call from Toronto. It was St. Clair Balfour calling from Southam headquarters with an interesting proposition to settle the question of how much compensation Cromie and his *Sun* would receive for agreeing to an equal partnership with the smaller *Province*. Cromie had been holding out for $4 million up front, with Southam stuck on its offer of $3.5 million. Balfour was obviously a gambling man, because he offered to flip a coin to decide the amount, and was even willing to let Cromie perform the toss right there in his Vancouver office. The Southam man had a sense of daring, having previously won a similar flip with Jack Kent Cooke over a $50,000 difference in the sale price of a printing company in Toronto.[63] Cromie, however, was unwilling to risk such a large sum on mere chance. "I was a gambling man, but half-a-million was a bit too rich for my blood, and I balked," he told Ben Metcalfe in a 1986 interview. "I think even Nick the Greek would have balked at a phone toss for half-a-million."[64]

3 The Balance Wheel

Sam Cromie was everything his older brother Don was not. Robust, outgoing, and charismatic, he was the most popular executive at the *Vancouver Sun*, doubtless due in part to his Friday afternoon habit of taking the composing room staff across the street for beer at the Lotus Hotel. He had a way with people that put them at ease and made it difficult for them to dislike him. His infectious laugh resonated throughout the halls of the Sun Tower. Allan Fotheringham, who began his writing career in the sports section of the *Sun* in the mid-1950s, described Cromie as "an impossibly handsome charmer."[1] He remembers him as a well-dressed, larger-than-life figure who drove a fancy car and parted his thick, dark hair down the middle in the style of a 1930s movie star.[2]

Shortly after returning home from a Second World War stint in England as a flight lieutenant in the Royal Canadian Air Force, Cromie decided to throw his hat into the civic politics ring — despite being only 28 years old — running for city council as a Non-Partisan Association candidate. When the votes in the 1946 election were counted, he had not only topped the polls, but he had also made history as Vancouver's youngest-ever elected alderman. He even served as acting mayor after the sudden death of Gerry McGeer in 1947 and donned the ceremonial robes and chain of office to preside over his final council meeting, making him the youngest to fill that position, too.[3]

Cromie had been urged by the NPA to run for a second term in office and had even been approached by the Liberal Party to run for parliament, but in 1948 he decided instead to devote his full attention to the family business. The *Sun* was busy padding its lead over the strike-hobbled *Province*, and he was his publisher brother's close partner in that project. The pair made a good team for several reasons. As mechanically minded as Don Cromie was not, Sam had a fascination for anything with moving parts, so he concentrated his efforts on the production side of the newspaper business. He had started in the circulation department of the *Sun* and worked as a district manager, supervising carriers on news routes in the west-side Point Grey and Dunbar districts. Sam even tried his hand in the *Sun*'s newsroom, working in the sports department covering boxing.[4] Sam was soon appointed the paper's production manager, studying complicated typesetting machines during a stint at the Intertype company's factory in New York and one at the firm's San Francisco office. He paid his dues in the *Sun*'s deafening pressroom, wearing ink-stained coveralls. He became the paper's first vice-president in 1951 and by 1955 was Don's right-hand man as assistant publisher. More important for the Cromie family business than Sam's mechanical aptitude and popularity with the staff, however, was the fact that he was as level-headed as his older brother was eccentric. Sam was roundly seen as Don Cromie's "balance wheel."

Sam Cromie was also a bit of a speed demon. He loved sports cars and liked to drive them fast. He had an MG before the war, then graduated to a Jaguar and later a Mercedes-Benz.[5] He was so enamored of the German import that he opened Vancouver's first Mercedes-Benz dealership. "He is mad about cars and a little reckless," noted Berton in his 1948 *Maclean's* feature. "He is the only alderman in the city's history to be penalized with a blue driver's licence, awarded to B.C. drivers who have been tagged for speeding."[6] Like the rest of the Cromies, Sam had grown up on the waters around Vancouver. He owned a cottage at Halfmoon Bay, forty miles up the coast, next door to one owned by childhood friend Bill Dix. The pair would head up to this Sunshine Coast hideaway at any time of the year for a fishing trip — even in the middle of a frosty February. The official reason for their weekend excursion begun February 15, 1957, was an annual visit to inspect the bungalows for winter damage, but despite the time of year the pair and three friends were looking forward to getting out on the water the next day for some fishing.

By midnight the others had gone to bed, but Cromie was anxious to test his new fifteen-horsepower outboard to make sure it was ready for the morning's fishing excursion. Despite the late hour and their intoxicated condition — or perhaps because of it — he and Dix decided to head out on the strait for a midnight test ride. The night was clear, the moon was up, and the waters were calm, but soon something went wrong and suddenly Cromie and Dix were in the water. A police investigation would speculate the boat "may have hit something in the water and overturned, or made too tight a turn and turned over, or the engine could have worked loose and upset them."[7] Sam Cromie reacted calmly, remembering the lessons he had learned in lifesaving class. He first freed his legs, somehow pulling his pants off over his rubber-soled shoes. He set out swimming for shore, but the frigid water soon brought on disabling hypothermia. Back at the cabins, the three guests had no inkling of the mishap which had befallen their hosts. They were not even aware the pair had ventured out on the water. The next morning they awoke to find Dix and Cromie missing and mounted a frantic search. The lighthouse keeper at nearby Merry Island spotted an overturned vessel, and soon Sam's body was found floating face down, 200 yards from his engineless boat. Abrasions on his face suggested he may have reached shore but, exhausted and hypothermic, lost consciousness and been swept back out to sea by the tide.

An autopsy was performed in nearby Sechelt the next day. The *Sun*, as part of its three full pages of coverage, quoted Dr. H.F. Inglis on its front page. "I found no trace of alcohol," said Inglis, which was consistent with the doctor's written report of his examination of Cromie's corpse, which noted "no unusual or alcoholic odor" in his stomach contents.[8] It did not, however, reflect the truth. Cromie had been drinking heavily the night he died. A blood sample sent for analysis showed his alcohol level was .14, almost twice the legal limit for driving of .08, and the equivalent of almost five beer or hard-liquor drinks. "This is very close to what they would diagnose as a critical concentration," noted coroner William McKee at an inquest more than a month later.[9] Results of the inquest were not reported on the pages of the *Vancouver Sun*. Sam Cromie's death by misadventure, Fotheringham noted, marked the moment when "the balance wheel evaporated from the balance act."[10]

Death had claimed both his father and brother at a young age, and Don Cromie was wobbling now without his brotherly balance wheel. But the deal with Southam had been made, although it had not yet been announced. Cromie and Balfour had agreed in a telephone conversation in January to form a separate entity—tentatively called "Company X"—as a holding company to own the assets of both the *Sun* and *Province*, which would in turn be owned equally by Southam and the Sun Publishing Company.[11] But details of the amalgamation were still to be worked out, and the *Sun*'s publisher was now without his trusted right-hand man. He needed a new foil to run the production side of the newspaper, with which he was unfamiliar. The best person he could think of was his friend Larry Dampier, the capable executive at Lever Brothers. Dampier did not know the newspaper business from the ground up as Sam had, but Cromie felt comfortable with him and offered him the job of assistant publisher. Dampier accepted, feeling his Cromie friends needed his help.[12]

The deal with Southam was settled when a compensation payment of $3.85 million was negotiated. But before the amalgamation could be announced, word of the impending marriage leaked out, with speculation rampant on radio and appearing in print on February 26 in the *Victoria Colonist*.[13] Southam president Philip Fisher tried to play down the rumors. "We haven't made any sort of deal so far," he told a national magazine in March. "We may make a deal or we may not. . . . We have been talking to the *Sun* for some time in an attempt to get some sense into the Vancouver newspaper situation, which is too expensive and too highly competitive."[14] On March 25, 1957, the Combines Investigation Act's director of investigation and research, T.D. MacDonald, wrote to Fisher.

> I have been reading in the press about a rumored merger of the *Vancouver Sun* with the *Vancouver Province*. . . . I believe such a merger would put me upon enquiry. . . . It simply means that I would consider it a case in which I should gather all the facts with a view to determining whether they should be placed before the Restrictive Trades Practices Commission.[15]

Two months later, Cromie and Balfour signed the formal agreement to form Pacific Press on May 24. Southam retained the perpetual right to appoint the *Province* publisher, while the Cromies through their Sun Publishing Company would appoint the publisher of the *Sun*. Each publisher, under the agreement, would have "full responsibility and authority" to run their own newspaper, including the "news and editorial content of the said newspapers respectively as well as for the solicitation of advertising and subscriptions."[16] A general manager would be appointed to manage all other departments.[17] A board of directors would consist of four nominees of each owner. Southam, which would move its *Province* to morning publication, negotiated for the assets of Thomson's *Herald*, which held the morning Canadian Press franchise. In exchange for that, its list of subscribers and network of carriers, as well as some pre-paid syndicated features, such as the popular comic strip "Blondie," Southam paid Thomson $260,000 on the understanding it would be reimbursed by Pacific Press after the amalgamation was completed.[18]

On May 30, the deal was officially announced in both newspapers. In a front-page statement in the *Sun*, Don Cromie claimed the amalgamation was necessary for "long-term continuance of local and alert control of the *Sun*." He cited the pressures on continued family ownership of the newspaper. "New generations dilute the centralized ownership which is usually characteristic of vigorous and independent newspapers. Heavy inheritance taxes speed this dilution." He noted that five branches of the Cromie family then owned about 60 percent of the *Sun*, which had about 500 shareholders. To slow the spread of voting control, the Sun Publishing Company had divided its shares between voting and non-voting. "Over a long period, much of our share-holding becomes purchased by Vancouver's public," Cromie explained. "We have guided such sales toward wide distribution in small lots." The Pacific Press rationalization, Cromie told readers, was forced by the need of both companies to invest in new facilities. The *Sun* had planned a new office building, but the competition between dailies had made the necessary enormous construction investment perilous. "The prospect of proceeding while the large Southam Company operated *The Province* seemed unwise," wrote Cromie. "This step should assume either that the *Sun* by then has, or intends to shortly, force *The Province* from the Vancouver newspaper fields." Cromie declared that his newspaper's victory over its competition seemed likely, either by "prudent withdrawal of the Southams or in active struggle for Vancouver readership favour." But the result, he argued, would be unacceptable to local newspaper consumers. "Either type of victory presented the near certainty of a one-ownership, single company, single management newspaper domination of Vancouver," Cromie continued. "Neither the public nor the owners, in a city this size, should be happy with such a single newspaper responsibility if an alternative is available." But while conceding the new business arrangement was "unusual, almost unique,"

Cromie promised readers his newspaper would retain its editorial vigor and compete with its new business partner as strongly as before.

> The new arrangement brings us greater than ever assurance and freedom to work in our own style. . . . Our "style" and our policies have been described in various tempers from excellent to outrageous. . . . We will continue to scoop them with the best columnists, editors and news breaks (except, perhaps, for isolated incidents we'd rather forget). We shall continue our superior condescension towards the conservative policy vision of The Southam Company.[19]

The autonomy clauses in the Pacific Press agreement providing for independent operation of each newspaper, which Cromie pointed out had been placed there at his insistence, were so strong that, in the absence of reasonable conduct, he claimed "either company could wipe out all Vancouver profits and create large over-all losses by extravagances in its respective newspaper." Instead, Cromie said, "we believe that in creating a unique, standoffish operation we have made a real effort at intelligent solution to a strange, modern economic paradox." He concluded his rambling front-page justification of the amalgamation by philosophizing. "Men can't foretell the future. They may and should, however, strive to create atmospheres and conditions in which good policies and ideals are most likely to continue to work and flourish."[20]

For his newspaper, publisher Arthur Moscarella promised on the *Province*'s front page that the new morning paper would compete just as hard as before with its new business partner. "We will retain our character and personality, our 'aliveness.' And we will go after news scoops just as hard as we have been doing with such spectacular success." But he stressed the *Province* would remain as conservative as ever as a morning newspaper. "We will retain the dependability that has been our mark in this city and this province throughout our history. As in the past, we shall not yield to temptations of shallow journalism. We shall fully and vigorously maintain the integrity which has seen this newspaper through some dark days."[21]

The two Vancouver dailies provided most of the coverage Vancouverites would get of the Pacific Press amalgamation. The morning *Herald* had announced its demise two days earlier, blaming rising costs for its inability to carry on and announcing that its readers would soon begin receiving the *Province* instead. But in the *Toronto Globe and Mail*, columnist Scott Young declared it a dark day for journalism in Vancouver, which he said would become, in effect,

> a one-newspaper town, even though two continue to be published.... Each paper has assured its readers that it will retain its former character. Since the chief characteristic of each paper was its bitter competitive spirit toward the other, this character-retention will be quite a trick, something like watching a wrestling match between Siamese twins.[22]

Young's argument was that removing the profit motive would kill honest competition between the papers, to the detriment of the public, which "should get free and untrammelled competition of ideas." Even if the men who were running the newspapers at the time of the amalgamation continued the editorial vigor that Vancouverites were accustomed to, he worried about their successors and "what unanimous torrent of bigotry they might shower on their readers." The outcome, predicted Young, would be irreversible. "It seems to me inevitable that men who sit down with one another every so often to share profits will begin to share ideas and outlooks too. And then who'll oppose the *Sunny Province*, or the *Provincial Sun*? In two papers brought up to use sharp knives and live ammunition, the natural progression now will be to rubber daggers and water pistols.[23]

Both Cromie and Balfour took umbrage at the assault. Cromie wrote a letter to the columnist, complimenting him on how neatly his "Siamese twins" crack summed up the dilemma. "But a chap wearies of the prospect of putting out a leading newspaper with an old pile of bricks and baling wire, with the prospect that someone will need a monopoly to justify a modern plant," Cromie complained. "This way we avoid a monopoly ... and get modern plant and equipment."[24] But the swipe Cromie seemed to find most insulting was that his newspaper would some day come to resemble its competition. "I can't envision the *Vancouver Sun* ever looking, thinking or acting like the Southams' *Province*."[25] For his part, Balfour pointed out the precedents of Scott's privileged position as pundit. "I wonder if he stopped for even a second to think that his column only appeared because four Toronto newspapers [*Mail*, *Empire*, *World*, and *Globe*] had been swallowed or married so that the *Globe and Mail* would be strong enough to survive, pay him a comfortable salary, [and] allow him to write as he pleases."[26]

On June 18, the day after the *Sun* and *Province* began joint publication, federal regulators moved into action, with MacDonald issuing an order under the Combines Investigation Act demanding information from the companies.[27] The companies complied within weeks, but it took almost a year for hearings into the amalgamation to commence. Meanwhile, operations of the two dailies were gradually consolidated, with production of both papers performed at the Sun Tower's composing room and printing done on the *Sun*'s presses beginning in early 1958.[28] *Province* editorial, advertising, executive, and circulation departments continued to operate out of its building at Victory Square, where the executive offices of the new Pacific Press Ltd. also were set up. The mechanical facilities of the *Province* were used to house the engraving departments of both newspapers, and its presses to print the comic sections of both the *Sun* and *Province*.[29]

The switch of its competition to morning publication finally put the *Sun* over the top of its longtime circulation goal of 200,000 by the end of September 1957, and the resulting celebration was remembered by Fotheringham. "When the *Sun* hit the magic circulation figure of 200,000, the annual Christmas blowout at the Commodore Ballroom was capped with a monstrous neon sign onstage blinking out '200,000' while Cromie wheeled out, for circulation manager Herb Gates, a new white Cadillac."[30] *Sun* circulation actually rose to 220,000 by the end of 1957 before falling back under 200,000 briefly after the newspaper raised its subscription price with the New Year. Denny Boyd, who had joined the *Sun* earlier that year as a sportswriter, recalled his first company Christmas party.

> Imperial Rome never did it with more opulence and conspicuous decadence. Liquor flowed like the spring runoff. Aged deskmen and ad salesmen, crazed with Scotch, chased copygirls and switchboard operators all over the Commodore Ballroom. Dancers crunched discarded lobster shells under their feet. Executive secretaries, dressed in hired gowns, performed credible can-can dances. Old resentments bubbled over into brief, clumsy fistfights.[31]

The Restrictive Trade Practices Commission heard evidence in Vancouver starting on June 2, 1958. Among the witnesses called was frustrated advertiser Brendan Kennelly, of Princeton, who testified he had been allocated a small sum by that town's Centennial Committee to advertise its upcoming anniversary celebrations. Told he could not advertise in the *Vancouver Sun* without also placing and paying for an ad in the *Province*, Kennelly testified his group was unable to afford the combination rate. Johnny Toogood, advertising manager of Pacific Press, testified that any advertising other than classified that originated outside the Greater Vancouver retail area was now required to be carried in both papers. "It was mulled over for some considerable time, and from the beginning the Southam Company felt that this was what should be done," Toogood told C. Rhodes Smith, the commission chairman, in Vancouver. "On the other hand the publisher of *The Vancouver Sun* was very much against it because he did not feel it was what he wanted."[32] The combination ad rate of $1 per line was arrived at by adding the previous *Sun* rate of 55 cents and the *Province* rate of 40 cents, plus a nickel for good measure, Toogood testified.

> When we had agreed upon the principle it was decided that each publisher had to have the same revenue from general advertising that he had previously, and the only way to do it was to take the two rates, put them together and then the technical work of putting the rate cards together. I just got the rate card of the Victoria papers and changed it around to our own location, had it printed and sent it out and it was done in a hurry.[33]

Although exceptions to the rule were sometimes made, Toogood testified, enforcement of the combination rate was essential to the financial viability of the *Province*, which derived half its advertising revenue from the general classification. Other morning newspapers in Canada, such as the *Gazette* in Montreal and the *Globe and Mail* in Toronto, had trouble attracting national advertising, he added. "Every other newspaper in Canada in a similar [joint operating] situation had done the same, so one presumed that was the accepted standard."[34] Indeed, research by the commission showed the same requirement existed in the seven other

Canadian cities where two newspapers published jointly: Victoria, London, Quebec, Moncton, St. John, Halifax, and Charlottetown.[35] *Province* publisher Moscarella testified he had discussed with Don Cromie as early as 1953 the possibility of negotiating a truce to their costly newspaper war.

> At that time we were both engaged in a very, very expensive promotional activity, and each of us was canceling out what the other fellow was trying to do. . . . We were at each other's throats all day long. . . . We were doing all kinds of promotion, putting on contests, giving away premiums, spending $50,000 on reader contests, and things of that kind which we would initiate, and the other fellow would sit back and come back with something a little better and bigger than we were doing. It was just one vicious circle.[36]

Moscarella said the initial overture on amalgamation was made by Cromie, who noted that neither newspaper was making much money and if that situation continued, one of them would eventually have to fold. "He made the suggestion at the time that we should consider the question of going into the morning field and he going into the evening field," testified the *Province* publisher. "I said that sounds all right, providing we reverse the situation, that we go into the evening field and he go into the morning field. Of course, he laughed that off, nothing doing, his was the largest paper and he should have the choice of which field in which he should publish."[37]

Cromie testified that despite the fact his newspaper was winning the war, he was also anxious to negotiate a settlement that would see both the *Sun* and *Province* survive. "We did not like to take the gamble that we would be the ones forced out by some circumstances. We were not overly anxious to go through a long process of having them subsidize their paper with eastern money in the hopes of swinging the tables on us, or even if they stayed on indefinitely of forcing the field to support two newspapers at a precarious level."[38] While Southam and the *Sun* claimed that the decision to close the morning *Herald* had been made independently by owner Roy Thomson, Cromie testified that the price for its assets went up after the new Pacific Press partners insisted the *Herald* continue publishing — and thus continue losing money — until the *Province* was ready to move to morning publication. "He complained bitterly that the offer was beginning to cost him money, and I know in fact the price was raised."[39]

Financial figures provided by the companies tended to contradict Southam's argument that the amalgamation should be allowed on the basis of "economic" necessity. They showed that Southam profits had nearly doubled over the previous four years, standing at almost $3.2 million in 1956, while net profit per share increased steadily from $1.44 in 1947 to $4.26 in 1956. Even at the company's Vancouver operations, earnings had recently turned upward after years of losses following the 1946 ITU strike. By 1956, the *Province* was actually making money, turning a profit of $191,460 after taxes, although its earnings were modest when compared to those of the *Sun*, which saw its after-tax earnings in its fiscal year ended August 31, 1956, jump by more than half from the previous twelve months to $950,407.[40]

But by May 1956, Southam faced a setback in its program of nursing the *Province* back to financial health. The newspaper's largest advertiser, the Eaton's department store chain, announced it would no longer place advertising in the second-place *Province* and instead would confine its business to the leading *Sun*. The precipitous move appeared to *Province* management as the precipice of a slippery slope down which it could slide to insolvency. Moscarella proposed a drastic discount for largc advertisers to stem the tide, from a rate of twenty cents a line to only eight cents after a certain amount of linage had been placed, which paid little more than the cost of the extra newsprint involved. But the move failed to hold Eaton's on *Province* pages, and as a result, when the following year's projections were drawn up, which included the generous Cromie wage increases the *Province* had to match, the paper's profit level, which had been slowly rising from a sea of red ink, began to start sinking again. "When we made up our budget [for 1957] the operating profit was substantially less than half of what we showed the previous year, due to the very heavy wage increase cost," Moscarella testified.[41]

Balfour also blamed high labor costs for forcing the Pacific Press amalgamation when hearings resumed in Toronto before commission member A.S. Whiteley on June 17, 1958. "It costs twice as much to produce a page in Vancouver . . . as it does in Ottawa," said Balfour. "In Ottawa and Winnipeg the relative positions of the two newspapers have been practically unchanged for as long as I can remember, and there is not the same, what I might call nervousness as there was in Vancouver, where there had been a complete reversal of the field."[42] He also explained the significance of the Eaton's development.

> Department store advertising is important as a circulation holder and. . . . the other advertisers tend to watch what the department stores are doing and to follow their example. If more advertising is being placed in the *Sun* than the *Province* the tendency of other retail advertisers who may have been up to that time placing equal copy in the two newspapers would be to reduce or cancel their advertising in the *Province* and concentrate on the *Sun.*[43]

The inevitable result of the loss of such a major advertiser would be the death spiral that so many second newspapers had gone into, losing readers as a result, then more advertisers and more readers. The time to act had come, before Southam lost what little bargaining power it had with Cromie, and the deal to amalgamate the *Sun* and *Province* and kill off the *Herald* was only instituting the inevitable, according to the parties. But they held off on plans for construction of a new plant while the federal investigators held their hearings. Under the law, after all, the Restrictive Trade Practices Commission had the power to break up the newly formed Pacific Press as an illegal monopoly.

•

Jack Scott was only one of a succession of talented columnists to grace the pages of the *Vancouver Sun* following its amalgamation with the *Province*, an advantage that played no small part in the evening newspaper's growing dominance of its new bedfellow. Don Cromie's newspaper had a bold slogan, but one that stood scrutiny: "The *Sun* has the writers." Of all the columnists to grace the paper's pages, Scott stood apart from the rest in popularity, earnestness, output, and grace. His position atop the list is the opinion of no less than the others on it. Fotheringham has variously declared Scott "the finest essayist in Canada" (1986)[44], "the most graceful writer of prose in Canadian column-writing" (1993)[45] and "the most beautiful writer in Canadian journalism, his words skipping across the page like a flat pebble across a lake" (1999).[46]

According to Fotheringham in his 1989 book *Birds of a Feather*, "it is hard to imagine a better craftsman" than Scott, who was "worshipped by his readers in the forties and fifties."[47] Denny Boyd, a Scott protege in the 1950s who went on to become the *Sun*'s featured columnist after Fotheringham, remembered Scott as "the most popular columnist the *Sun* ever had." His drawing power, according to Boyd, was enormous. "He once wrote a column saying he was going up to Mountain Highway to pick blueberries; the next day the RCMP had to come in to sort out the traffic chaos created by hundreds of people who just wanted to meet Scott."[48] No less an authority than Pierre Berton, who graduated from featured columnist of the *Toronto Star* to one of Canada's foremost non-fiction writers with dozens of best-selling books, declared Scott the best. "No one has ever touched Jack Scott as a columnist," according to Berton. "He had the common touch. He could make a column out of almost anything — the killing of a mouse; the felling of a Christmas tree. He could make you laugh, he could make you cry, and he could bring a lump to your throat."[49] Berton credits Scott with teaching him the writing craft while the two were young colleagues, first at the briefly tabloid *News-Herald*, then at the *Sun*.

> He was . . . a slender and attractive man with a great wit, a talent for an apt phrase, and a good deal of experience in spite of his youth. He did more than edit my copy; he taught me how to write it. The best advice he ever gave me — so simple, so pertinent — consisted of two sentences. "Always describe the places. Always describe the people." I've never forgotten that.[50]

Scott was born into the newspaper business. His father, an editor at the *Province*, would sit with his young son in the lobby of the old Hotel Vancouver on Saturday afternoons in the 1920s. It was from his father's words of wisdom that the boy learned the secret of his future writing success. "Look at everybody who crosses this lobby," the elder Scott would tell his son. "In every one of them is a story."[51] Scott began his newspaper career at 15 as a copy boy at the *News-Herald* in 1931. By 1940 he was not only the morning newspaper's city editor, but also a columnist, beginning his long-running "Our Town." Soon both Berton and Scott were called up to military service. Following the war they returned to Vancouver and found the *News-Herald*, which they knew as a lively tabloid, had reverted to a boring broadsheet dominated by older men. Before long they were working for the *Sun*, where Scott transferred his column. "Scott was freed of all editorial duties and wrote a column a day for twenty years or so," recalled Berton. "People grabbed the *Sun*, ignored the front page and reached for the section page to read Our Town."[52]

One feature of Scott's writing that endeared him to Vancouverites in the post-war years was his socialist perspective, which was very much in line with the working-class sentiments of *Sun* readers at the time. "They called him a Red, a radical, a troublemaker," said Berton. "He fought for what he believed in. He held no brief for phoneys or fat cats. He was anti-establishment and anti-hero. He was left of centre and so was his pen."[53] According to Boyd, Scott's heart "bled through his shirts," and the condition led to his ascendancy atop the *Sun*'s editorial operations, but it also proved his downfall. When Scott "complained once too often that the paper lacked a social conscience, Cromie said, 'Okay, you run the paper,'" recalled Boyd.[54] Scott's reign as editorial director lasted only five months until he "begged to go back to his column," according to Ben Metcalfe.[55] In that time, some of the most innovative assignments ever were given to the most unlikely of *Sun* reporters — not to mention some of the most generous pay raises. "Glamorous Marie Moreau, the fashion editor who had an office larger than the entire sports department, was sent to Cuba, where she sashayed herself into getting the first interview Fidel Castro had granted," Fotheringham wrote years later. "Football columnist Annis Stukus, a legend himself, was sent to Formosa to interview Chiang Kai-shek."[56] But by the late 1950s the Cold War had put a damper on socialist enthusiasms, even on Canada's notoriously Left Coast. Boyd attributed Scott's downfall as managing editor to office politics in the *Sun* newsroom during an era of rampant McCarthyism.

> He had made the mistake of being drawn into the office. . . . By agreeing to work office hours, Scott made himself vulnerable to office politics. They got him, the Brutus faction in middle management claimed Scott was a pinko and had hired an avowed Communist, the gentle Ray Gardner, as city editor. Scott was brought down and the relationship collapsed in mutual bitterness.[57]

Meanwhile at the *Province*, in contrast to the *Sun*'s rousing success, circulation declined as the Old Lady of Victory Square got even greyer. From 131,811 copies sold on September 30, 1957, according to the semi-annual counting by the Audit Bureau of Circulations, sales dropped to barely 106,000 by the end of 1958.[58] Southam seemingly did little to pick its paper up, in contrast to the vigorous competition it offered the *Sun* during the newspaper war following the ITU strike of 1946. The company cut newsroom staff, claiming fewer journalists were needed on a morning newspaper. In November 1958, Moscarella retired and was replaced as *Province* publisher by Fred Auger, who had been publisher of Southam's *Winnipeg Tribune*. The line of succession at Vancouver's new morning newspaper bucked the trend at Canadian dailies, most of which were headed by experienced journalists.[59] Both Moscarella and Auger came from the advertising side of the newspaper business, with Auger having managed the Vancouver branch of the McKim advertising agency before the war.[60]

Ross Munro, a veteran journalist and former war correspondent for the Canadian Press, who was then editor-in-chief and assistant publisher of the *Province*, was shuffled off to Winnipeg as Auger's replacement at the *Tribune*. Scott Young, who had assessed the Vancouver newspaper amalgamation so harshly the previous year for the *Globe and Mail*, had found slim solace in Munro's editorial leadership of the *Province*. "If you had to pick one man in Canada who is unquestionably honest, you'd never lose by picking Ross Munro," wrote the columnist. "Yet Cromie won't always run the *Sun*, or Munro the *Province*, and who knows what the views of their successors will be."[61]

After the Restrictive Trade Practices Commission gathered financial data and heard testimony in the summer of 1958, it was another year before a "Statement of Evidence" was prepared by the Director of Investigation and Research under the Combines Investigation Act and submitted to the parties on July 17, 1959. The document charged that the agreement between Southam and the *Sun* was more than a mere amalgamation of production facilities by the two companies. As Scott had pointed out in his 1957 feature in *Saturday Night* magazine on the newly formed Pacific Press, "the word 'merger' was studiously avoided on both sides."[62] The word had a legal meaning under the Combines Investigation Act and such combinations between competing businesses were illegal. But the combines investigators did not hesitate to declare a merger. "Pacific Press Limited is a combine in that it is a merger, trust or monopoly because it . . . controls the business of publishing daily newspapers having general circulation in Vancouver, British Columbia, and because such merger, trust or monopoly has operated and is likely to operate to the detriment of the public," declared the Statement of Evidence.[63]

Public detriment resulted from the provision that general advertising had to be carried in both newspapers, it claimed. "It is obvious that a prospective advertiser who is required to pay for two advertisements at a larger cost when he desires only one . . . is prejudiced by such use of a combined rate for general advertisers."[64] The provision had created considerable outrage in Vancouver, despite the fact that such an arrangement was by then also operating in seven other Canadian cities. The purchase of the *Herald* by Southam was, according to the Combines branch, "part of a plan to give Pacific Press Limited ownership of all daily newspapers in Vancouver and to enable it to occupy both the morning and evening fields. . . . The purchase of the right to publish *The Herald* virtually assures Pacific Press Limited that no other publisher can enter the daily newspaper field in that city."[65] The economic justification pleaded by Southam was dismissed by the federal investigators in light of the financial figures.

> Profits from the operation of *The Province* have fallen off and in some years a loss was shown. However, in recent years the operation has shown profits. . . . The Southam Company Limited. . . . simply chose not to compete with Sun Publishing Company Limited. . . . This was undoubtably the most attractive method of ensuring future profit, but it cannot be said that it was the only course, or the only profitable course, open to The Southam Company Limited.[66]

The other illegal action found by the combines investigators was profit pooling. "The earnings of the *Vancouver Sun* are, in effect, subsidizing the operation of *The Province* and . . . advertising rates and selling prices of the *Vancouver Sun* have been raised to accomplish this result."[67] Profit pooling, while illegal under U.S. law, had been going on by then at more than a dozen newspapers operating jointly in that country, but the practice had not yet been challenged by the U.S. Justice Department under federal anti-trust laws. The case against Pacific Press brought under the Combines Investigation Act would be the first case of profit pooling by newspapers tested under Canadian law, and thus the first on the continent. Advertising rates at the *Province* had been unchanged since the amalgamation, the Statement of Evidence noted, but had been increased at the *Sun*. While the increase was claimed by the companies to be required to cover costs, "it appears doubtful that the additional revenue was required by *The Vancouver Sun* as such. Rather it would seem that the additional revenue was required by Pacific Press Limited because of the heavy losses being sustained on publication of *The Province*."[68] The arrangement for independent appointment of publishers by the owning companies was found by the investigators to be "insufficient to prevent detriment from resulting because . . . they are contingent and liable to be changed, with the result that complete control will pass to Pacific Press Limited; and . . . because of the mutual financial interests of the parties, they are unlikely to result in any substantial degree of competition."[69]

The companies were presented with the Statement of Evidence and used it to formulate their arguments why Pacific Press, while found to be an illegal monopoly to the public detriment, should nevertheless be allowed to continue operating. On January 11, 1960, four days of hearings commenced in Vancouver. It was almost exactly three years sincc Pacific Press had first taken form as "Company X." Southam's lawyer, Alec MacIntosh, presented a brief that took issue with the facts as they were found by the Combines branch. The decision to increase *Sun* advertising rates, Southam insisted, was made by the *Sun* without consulting *Province* management. "Neither the management of *The Province* nor any official of The Southam Company Limited had any part in this decision or influenced it in any way."[70] The *Herald*, it claimed, "was shut down by its owners and not by the parties to this hearing."[71] Southam even took issue with the *Globe and Mail* assessment by Scott Young. "Objection is taken to the inclusion in the Statement of Evidence of the published comments of a newspaper columnist who is not available for cross-examination."[72]

The *Sun*'s brief disagreed that the public had been deprived of a choice among independent competing newspapers. "To the extent that the public's choice has been limited, this is a result of economic conditions and not a result of the agreement of May 1957. The agreement is a result and not a cause."[73] The *Sun*'s position was that the commission should restrict itself to ruling on the present Pacific Press agreement and not on some hypothetical alteration agreed to in the future. "The allegations of the Director that the arrangements are contingent and subject to alteration with the inevitable result that complete control of the daily newspaper field will pass to Pacific Press Limited are not correct. Even if they were correct they are irrelevant."[74] With testimony and arguments completed early in 1960, Commissioners Smith and Whiteley adjourned to consider the evidence and arguments, write their report and make recommendations.

4 The Sell-out

Max Bell was nothing if not persistent. The former McGill University football star had taken over the *Calgary Albertan* from his father, George Bell, who had bought it in 1926. But Max Bell did not inherit the newspaper when his father died in 1936 — he had to borrow enough money from friends to convince the Royal Bank to allow him to take over the debt-ridden *Albertan,* of which he became publisher in 1943.[1] The loans were repaid after Bell made a fortune while still in his mid-thirties with an investment in Alberta's Leduc oil fields, which paid off in a major strike in 1947. The youthful millionaire struck many as perpetually preppy. Bruce Hutchison, one of Canada's most respected journalists, first met Bell in 1950 and remembered him as looking "like a college undergraduate . . . this breezy, tanned, athletic fellow with his crew cut and gaudy sports clothes."[2] Stuart Keate, a journalist whom Bell would hire as publisher of two of his newspapers, remembered first meeting his future boss when Bell arrived unannounced in 1949 at the *Time* magazine offices in Montreal, where Keate was Canadian bureau chief, to offer him the job of publisher of his newly acquired *Victoria Times.* "In appearance, Bell was a locker-room guy — athletic, muscular, snub-nosed, blue-eyed, with close-cropped curly grey hair and pink cheeks," recalled Keate. "His dress that first day personified the man: the camel-hair coat reflecting his affluence, the casual golf shirt his indifference to it."[3]

A jet-setting sportsman who was especially fond of horse racing, Bell set his sights on building the newspaper empire his father had started in Western Canada, only to see it fall apart with losses in mining and promotional ventures. By the time Bell the younger was done, he would fashion the country's largest chain of dailies, ahead of even Southam and Thomson. His strategy for convincing newspaper owners to sell was persistence — pursue relentlessly those who had inherited publications but had little interest in carrying on the family tradition. "In each instance, the second-generation owners lacked the will or the spark to carry on the endeavours their pioneer fathers had so laboriously fashioned," observed Keate. "Apparently convinced that they could not compete with the developing chains, they were content to 'take the money and run.'"[4]

Bell first went after the *Edmonton Bulletin*, buying it in 1948 for $650,000 from Charles Campbell, who had purchased it in 1930 after selling the *Vancouver World* to Robert Cromie in 1924. Then Bell bought the *Lethbridge Herald* from playboy Hugh Buchanan, who had inherited the paper from his printer father. Next he set his sights on the *Victoria Times* on the West Coast, picking it up for $750,000 from the Spencer family, which owned a regional chain of department-stores bearing their name.[5] His plan in the capital city of British Columbia, according to Keate, was to buy the competing *Victoria Colonist* and combine production operations of the two newspapers in a common facility. "The [gross] market potential, Bell suggested, was probably in the neighborhood of $5 million a year. With the economies inherent in joint equipment and a combination advertising and circulation rate, such a venture would probably net about $700,000 a year."[6] But Tim Matson, who had inherited the morning paper from his entrepreneur father Sam, proved to be a harder sell than Bell expected. Matson had earlier agreed to sell to Thomson but got cold feet and begged out of the deal. He readily sold Bell a minority interest and agreed to combine production facilities, but Matson balked at surrendering control of the *Colonist*. Within a year of moving into the shared plant of Victoria Press Limited with his aggressive new partner, however, Matson gave in to Bell's repeated offers to name a price for the paper. He named a figure he considered exorbitant, $1 million, to which Bell readily agreed.

Bell merged his four dailies with Victor Sifton's *Winnipeg Free Press* in 1958 to form Federated Papers (FP) Publications Ltd. Sifton also was born into a newspaper family, as he and his brother had inherited the venerable *Free Press* and dailies in Regina and Saskatoon from their father, Clifford Sifton, who in addition to being a newspaper proprietor also had served at the turn of the century in the cabinet of Prime Minister Wilfrid

Laurier. Sifton family acquisition of the *Free Press* from the Canadian Pacific Railroad in 1899 was said to be a sweetheart deal in exchange for political cooperation. The Bell-Sifton alliance was an unlikely one given Prairie newspaper history. Bell's father had been partners with the Meilicke brothers, Hugo and Ted, in the *Regina Leader-Post* and *Saskatoon Star-Phoenix*, but the enterprise fell apart in acrimony when George Bell was ousted in a power play and the papers were sold to the Siftons. Bell launched a long and bitter lawsuit, which was eventually dropped, and for many years Max Bell believed his father was the victim of double-dealing. Keate, who married into the Meilicke family, in his memoirs recalled how Bell and Sifton reconciled the longstanding feud at a Canadian Press meeting in the 1950s.[7]

After their father's death, the Sifton brothers had a falling out and parted company in 1953, with Clifford Sifton Jr. taking the Saskatchewan newspapers while Victor got the Manitoba daily, which ranked among the world's, finest.[8] Joining forces five years later, Sifton and Bell quickly expanded their Western Canadian newspaper empire eastward, buying the *Ottawa Journal* in May 1959 to make FP a national chain. Now picking up major dailies, Bell soon set his sights on the *Vancouver Sun*, seeing it as vulnerable to takeover due to its fractured, second-generation family ownership. Sifton was not convinced the paper could be pried from Don Cromie's grasp, remembering his experience almost twenty years earlier when he had made a deal to buy the *Sun* at a bargain price, only to have the purchase scotched at the last minute by the upstart heir. Bell coveted the *Sun*, which was then the largest daily in Canada west of Toronto and was perfectly positioned in a booming city on the emerging Pacific Rim. No longer engaged in a war of attrition with Southam, the *Sun* was looking forward to a profitable future in a modern new facility with a joint monopoly. To Bell, the *Sun* "continued to loom as a glittering prize," according to Keate. "So Bell began his quiet Chinese water-torture treatment on Don Cromie, calling him whenever he was in Vancouver and letting him know that he was ready to deal at any time."[9]

But Bell was not the only one bidding for the *Sun*. Swedish industrialist Axel Wenner-Gren, who had bought up a large portion of the B.C. interior in the 1950s with plans for a massive development, and the growing U.S. chain headed by Sam Newhouse both made offers which were rebuffed by Cromie.[10] Even the *Sun*'s new business partner was quietly bidding for an ownership interest in the afternoon daily as a strategic move. As early as 1955, even before the deal to form Pacific Press was made, Southam had been a covert purchaser of the publicly traded shares in the Sun Publishing Company, according to the firm's official history.

> As the result of a casual remark by Max Bell to [St. Clair] Balfour, Southams had begun to "hold a basket" under the market for *Sun* stock, buying for investment through an agent without the company's name appearing. When Pacific Press was formed, the Southam company held about 12 per cent of the *Sun*'s voting stock and 8 per cent of the non-voting.[11]

When the Pacific Press deal was made in 1957, Balfour disclosed Southam's ownership interest in the *Sun* to Cromie and promised not to buy any more shares in his newspaper without first letting him know about it. But after the *Sun* became the target of active takeover interest in the early 1960s, the pair agreed Southam should go back into the market for Sun Publishing Company shares in an effort to keep the newspaper from falling into foreign ownership. By 1963 the company held just over 18 percent of the *Sun*'s voting stock.[12]

In September 1960 the Restrictive Trade Practices Commission released a 210-page report on the Pacific Press amalgamation. While stating that "ideally, there should be several newspapers competing for attention in every large centre of population," and emphasizing "the importance of maintaining as much independence as possible in the publication of existing dailies," they decided to allow the Pacific Press merger on the basis of the "economic necessity" argument. "The Commission must accept the evidence . . . that as a business enterprise *The Province* did not have prospects of earnings which would lead its owners to continue its operations indefinitely," the report concluded.[13] Despite the objections of the *Sun*, however, the commissioners insisted on looking to the future of Pacific Press and providing for safeguards against further erosion of the editorial independence of the two newspapers.

> The continued publication of separate newspapers . . . does not immediately represent as serious a danger to the public interest

> . . . as a newspaper monopoly in the hands of a single owner. Nevertheless . . . the further danger of a more complete monopoly exists. . . . The end result might be an appearance of rivalry without serious conviction, such as the rivalry of two articles under different brands produced by the same manufacturer.[14]

As long as the arrangements for the continued existence of the *Sun* and *Province* were "matters of private arrangement," the commissioners concluded, "there is no safeguard that the public interest in a variety of independent newspapers may not be further affected to its disadvantage."[15] Therefore they recommended that "steps should be taken to ensure that no changes are made in the existing agreements which would reduce the degree of independence which now exists."[16] As recent amendments to the Combines Investigation Act appeared to them to have been designed to permit the use of a restraining order in such cases, the commissioners recommended that such a court order be issued.

> In our opinion what is required is a judicial order which would restrain the parties from making any alteration in the agreements without the approval of a court. In the proceedings for such an order a review could be made of the . . . requirement that general advertising must be placed in both papers, which . . . operates to the detriment of anyone who desires to place an advertisement in only one paper.[17]

E. Davie Fulton, a Vancouver lawyer who was Justice Minister in the Conservative government of Prime Minister John Diefenbaker, released the report. When asked if the Justice Department would bring in the recommended restraining order limiting future changes in Pacific Press ownership without court approval, Fulton announced "The usual consideration will be given to what steps ought to be taken."[18] However, the 1968 history of Southam noted that a judicial order was never issued. Pacific Press responded to the recommendation with "written assurance that it [the Justice Department] would be told of any proposed changes, and that the combination requirement for national advertising had been washed out."[19] No further actions were ever taken. Given that more than three years had passed since the Pacific Press amalgamation, the companies knew the chance that the federal government could force them to break up their new creation was slim. "Our conception was that, here we'd made this omelette and no matter what they did, how were they going to unscramble it?" recalled St. Clair Balfour in 1999.[20]

Max Bell had by the early 1960s acquired 10 percent of Sun Publishing Co. from members of the extended Cromie family, which by now numbered about twenty. Youngest brother Pete was the first to sell his shares in 1961, shortly after the *Sun* sold off its independent printing arm, which he managed.[21] Other arms of the diverse Sun Publishing Co. were pieced off to appease family members and their quest for liquidity. One of the first assets to go was the firm's profitable *B.C. Directories*, which was sold to a Chicago company. Next went the company's radio station in Nanaimo on Vancouver Island, CHUB. Then the *Sun* sold a suburban Los Angeles daily it had purchased, the *Garden Grove News*, which had flourished under its recent Canadian ownership and imported talent from north of the border, including popular *Sun* cartoonist Len Norris.[22] Finally, the *Sun* was all that remained of the family empire, and Don Cromie was determined to hold onto the newspaper his father had turned into a going concern and which he had transformed into Western Canada's leading daily.

But the 1960s were a time of rapid newspaper chain expansion in both Canada and the United States. In the U.S., the twin pressures of inheritance tax laws, which encouraged families to sell, and corporate tax laws, which allowed chains to avoid income tax by investing their profits in new acquisitions, pushed chain ownership of dailies from 46.1 percent in 1960 to 61.8 percent in 1967.[23] The post-war boom had fueled expansion of the chains which, according to American scholar Bryce W. Rucker, "greatly intensify their buying during periods of prosperity."[24] The upward pressure on prices caused by U.S. tax laws sent sale prices soaring, such as the record $42 million paid by the Newhouse chain in 1962 for the jointly operating *Times-Picayune* and *States-Item* in New Orleans.[25] In Canada, inheritance tax laws and second-generation family ownership, which created pressure to sell out, combined to contribute to the demise of the independent newspaper. The major chains — Southam, Thomson, and Sifton — controlled about 25 percent of newspaper circulation in 1958, but by the time the 1960s were over, that figure would be almost doubled, to 47.2 percent, with a fourth chain, FP, accounting for most of the expansion.[26]

The trend toward consolidation was evident by the early 1960s, and *Maclean's* writer Douglas Fisher noted in 1962 that the Combines Investigation Act had been "useless in stopping the spread of chain ownership." If the tendency continued, "most of the country's press may someday be owned by a few men in a few big cities," argued Fisher. "But the growth of any newspaper chain means that the opportunities for new newspapers and for the widening of the range of opinion expressed in the country are limited, if not eliminated entirely. When a monopoly newspaper is established in a city it cannot be challenged with any expectation of success."[27]

Don Cromie was increasingly squeezed by the external pressure to sell and internal pressure from his own family. By 1963, almost half of the issued Sun Publishing Company shares were held outside the Cromie family, with 45 percent controlled by would-be acquisitors.[28] Vancouver native Stuart Keate watched the developments closely from his post as FP's closest publisher in Victoria. "Cromie was running a profitable newspaper," noted Keate. "But he wondered if he, as an independent, could withstand the long-term challenge of the Southam group." There were personal reasons for selling the *Sun* in addition to business motives, recalled Keate, who described the publisher as being "shattered" by the drowning death of his younger brother. "There was a history of early deaths in the Cromie family and there were times when Don didn't feel he would make it to age 60."[29]

Bruce Hutchison, who was then Keate's editor at the *Victoria Times*, recalled the breakfast he enjoyed aboard Bell's 137-foot yacht *Campana* in Vancouver harbor during the summer of 1963 with Bell and FP's chain manager, Dick Malone, who had taken over as publisher of the *Winnipeg Free Press* after Victor Sifton died in 1961. Bell was confident he could pry the *Sun* from Cromie's grasp, Hutchison recalled, but his breakfast guests were skeptical, especially given the late Sifton's disappointment more than two decades earlier.

> Assuring us that the *Sun* could be bought at the right price, he left Dick and me on the yacht while he met Don to talk business in millions of dollars. We awaited his return, quite certain that, like

> Victor, he would fail. Within the hour he was back, the necessary stock transfer had been arranged, his big dream, and Dick's, vastly expanded.[30]

According to Keate, Bell "caught Cromie in a receptive mood and offered him $10 a share over the current market value of $20." Cromie sold, Keate claimed, "because he felt a responsibility for the financial security of numerous children and in-laws."[31] Besides, noted Keate, Bell promised Cromie he could stay on as *Sun* publisher "indefinitely."[32] In announcing the sale on the front page of his family's former newspaper, Cromie said "sales by individual family members had made control vulnerable to any interested party with the resources." The passing of Vancouver's largest daily newspaper from a family business to corporate ownership was done partly on the basis of compatibility with the *Sun*'s longtime political position, according to Cromie. "When Mr. Bell made an offer on behalf of his progressive, small 'l' liberal newspaper organization, I was sort of regretfully relieved to settle the question of future control."[33]

Cromie soon realized he had made a mistake. St. Clair Balfour, who had worked closely with the Vancouver publisher to keep the *Sun* from falling into foreign hands, recalled how Cromie agonized over the decision. Telephoning him in Toronto, Cromie told Balfour of FP's offer and asked for his business partner's advice. Balfour urged him not to sell and considered flying out to the West Coast to try to stop the deal. "The first time I saw Cromie after he'd done the deal with FP, he said, 'Why did you let me do it?'" recalled Balfour. "I should have flown to Vancouver and I didn't."[34] Cromie soon tried to buy the *Sun* back but, as Keate put it, "Max Bell was not inclined to sell."[35] Cromie would lament the decision in later years, Ben Metcalfe reported in 1986. "As he stresses now in retrospect, he still cannot understand why he sold his controlling family interest in the *Sun*."[36]

While Cromie had long enjoyed the freedom of being his own boss, flying off to Palm Springs or heading out on his yacht whenever the mood struck him, he was now working for a profit-driven corporation that wanted, according to Keate, "a publisher who was on the job every day."[37] The $85,000 annual salary he paid himself as owner was reduced as an employee to $45,000.[38] But the worst part was working for someone else and having to take orders. The new management wanted to make some modifications to *Sun* operations, which did not go over well with its erstwhile owner, Keate observed.

> For some reason, Cromie laboured under the delusion that he could sell his newspaper and continue to run it in his own way. Max Bell felt differently. . . . Bell believed that "there was some fat on it," . . . and that the new owners could improve its performance by the simple imposition of some sensible management principles. When these took the form of memos from Winnipeg, Cromie blew up and quit.[39]

Denny Boyd, a *Sun* sportswriter at the time, attributes Cromie's downfall as publisher to an embarrassing byline strike by reporters covering the 1963 Grey Cup game at Vancouver's Empire Stadium, which pitted the hometown B.C. Lions against the Hamilton Tigercats in the Canadian Football League championship game. Cromie, a novice football observer who watched the game from the Royal Box, decided that a late tackle by Hamilton lineman Angelo Mosca on the sidelines, which knocked the Lions' star running back Willie Fleming out of the game, was a flagrant foul that cost the local team victory. He ordered the *Sun*'s coverage to reflect his assessment. The sports staff did not share their publisher's opinion and on the advice of their Newspaper Guild shop steward refused to allow their bylines to appear atop the stories they were ordered to write, according to Boyd. "By the end of the next day, every newsroom across Canada was buzzing with the story of the mutiny in the *Sun* sports department. The mutiny story even buried the controversy about the game."[40] Years after the incident, according to Boyd, he learned the inside story from fellow *Sun* columnist Paul St. Pierre.

> According to Paul, who was editing the editorial pages then, Cromie called in and dictated an inflammatory editorial in Paul's absence. Our venerable columnist, Bruce Hutchison, was outraged. . . . Paul agreed it was insane but Cromie, after all, was the publisher. Paul remembers that Hutch said, "Perhaps he's no longer qualified to be publisher." Pressure began to come from Max Bell in Calgary and Cromie was gone within months, resigning under pressure because he overreacted to one play in a crummy football game.[41]

Cromie's tenure as a corporate publisher lasted barely six months. On taking his leave after twenty-two years as publisher, he announced in the *Sun* that "the relief from daily newspaper pressure is highly welcome."[42]

He stayed on as chairman of the Pacific Press board of directors, but only for a few months. By the time Cromie disassociated himself from the newspaper he, his father, and his brothers had built, the acrimony between himself and the newspaper's new owners was obvious. In a statement, Cromie was pointed about the reasons for his resignation. "I disagree with FP leaders over some policies, procedures and manners," he wrote. "On review the association seems fruitless."[43] But FP had not expected Cromie to remain as *Sun* publisher "indefinitely" as he had been promised. On the same summer day that Max Bell bought control of the newspaper, Hutchison recalled that Bell and Dick Malone asked him if he would take over as publisher "when Cromie, as was foreseen, had retired." Hutchison, who was then 62 and happy to be living on Vancouver Island, declined.[44]

The *Sun* languished leaderless for months. Assistant publisher Larry Dampier, the Cromie family friend who had come aboard to help manage the newspaper after Sam Cromie drowned seven years earlier, took over business operations of the *Sun* and hoped he would get the publisher's job, but he lacked any background as a journalist. Malone assumed editorial direction from his office in Winnipeg and suggested the job Cromie had vacated might go unfilled for up to a year, which set the rumor mill at the old Sun Tower into high gear. One school of thought had the job going to Hal Straight, the former *Sun* managing editor who had started a suburban weekly newspaper in North Vancouver, the *North Shore Citizen*, in 1958 after his return from Edmonton.[45] He enjoyed the additional advantage of being a friend of Max Bell, who had hired him as publisher of the *Edmonton Bulletin* after he bought it in 1948. Another rumor had Slim Delbridge, who had been publisher of the closed *Vancouver Herald*, getting the post. And in Victoria, cabinet minister Waldo Skillings rose from his seat in the provincial legislature to announce the job would go to Keate, who told the Canadian Press (truthfully, he claimed in his memoirs) he knew nothing about the matter.[46]

Control of Canadian media outlets by foreign interests was something Balfour strongly opposed, and he lobbied hard to have it outlawed by Ottawa. He met with Prime Minister Lester Pearson in late 1963 to record Southam's opposition to the foreign control that threatened it and other Canadian media institutions with takeover.[47] The issue of foreign ownership of Canadian media had been raised by the 1961 Royal Commission on Publications that recommended ending tax breaks for U.S. magazines, such as *Time* and *Reader's Digest*, which published Canadian editions. The competition these publications, which were produced in the U.S. and reprinted with minor content and advertising changes for the Canadian market, posed for Canadian-produced magazines such as *Maclean's* and *Saturday Night* was seen as unfair by those who feared for the continued survival of such national publications.

Early in 1964, after his meeting with Balfour, and in response to the foreign ownership question, Pearson raised in parliament the possibility his government might extend the protection against foreign competition it was contemplating for magazines to Canada's newspapers as well. The issue split the industry, with many Canadian dailies opposing what they saw as a threat to press freedom, not to mention stock prices. Newly anointed Lord Thomson of Fleet recorded his opposition to the proposal, and the *Toronto Telegram* excoriated Southam for its advocacy of it, claiming the country's largest chain was simply interested in enhancing its opportunities for expansion by banning foreign competition. "This was the only argument, in the course of months of discussion and dissent on the proposal, that angered Balfour," noted Charles Bruce in his Southam history. "Nothing in the company's record, he held, would support the charge."[48]

Before meeting with Pearson, Balfour had brought the matter before the Southam board of directors at the firm's 1963 annual meeting, proposing that the company take a position on the matter, which it did with a resolution firmly in favor of Canadian-only media ownership. But this put the four Southam publishers on the board of directors, including Fred Auger of the *Province*, in an awkward position should they oppose the company's official position personally, professionally, or editorially. In keeping with Southam's long-standing policy of not interfering with the autonomy of its publishers, however, Balfour issued a memo. "If after reading the case which I have made, or after the proposed legislation is introduced, you, or any of our publishers, wishes to disagree editorially, then he should feel free to do so."[49] While most advocated for the measures against foreign media ownership on their newspaper's editorial page,

Edmonton Journal publisher Basil Dean actively opposed it. Dean, who doubled as vice-president of the Canadian Daily Newspaper Publishers Association, voted for a CDNPA resolution of protest against the proposed controls on foreign ownership and was part of a publishers' delegation that presented its opposition to Pearson.[50] In the end, the government decided in 1965 to include newspapers in a budget measure restricting tax deduction of advertising expenses to those placed in Canadian-owned media, which had the same effect as banning foreign ownership.

Acquisition of the *Sun* made FP the largest chain in Western Canada, with a circulation of 463,710 between its six titles, putting Southam suddenly in second place with 379,200 in five dailies.[51] Southam still stood as the largest chain nationally in 1963 on the strength of its Eastern newspapers, but that would soon change. After FP merged with the *Toronto Globe and Mail* in 1965, its quarter-million circulation pushed Max Bell's newspaper empire narrowly ahead of Southam's to rate as Canada's largest chain, with 855,170 in circulation across eight dailies.[52] But in Vancouver, even with Cromie out of the way, Max Bell and FP had problems. A new plant was in the planning stages, and a square block uptown had already been bought to build it on when FP bought the *Sun*.[53] The property on Granville Street, between 6th and 7th Avenues, was just across the Granville Street Bridge from the downtown peninsula, where both the *Sun* and *Province* had always operated. The move from the city's core made sense for several reasons. Property values there had soared, and increased traffic congestion made it difficult for both newspapers' delivery trucks to get in and out of the Sun Tower plant.

The new site sloped gently toward False Creek and provided a spectacular view of the North Shore mountains. On its Granville Street side, several stores and two apartment buildings stood, while a moving and storage company operated on the 6th Avenue side, with several houses on 7th Avenue. Development of the property had been delayed, according to the *Journal of Commerce* in April 1962, with a "shift in plans" calling for a September 1963 deadline for commencing construction.[54] Sale of the *Sun* that summer delayed things even more, and the September deadline came and went without tenders for construction being called. Finally, four firms were selected as candidates to build the new facility, and a November 7 date was set for submitting bids on the estimated $5-million project.[55] But costs soon began soaring, and the original estimate proved wildly optimistic. Excavation of the site, which began in March 1964, was unusually deep, going down 30 feet to house the plant's subterranean presses. The digging proved problematic, as did the use of lightweight concrete, which turned out to be more sensitive to fluctuations in moisture content than normal concrete. Labor shortages also plagued the project, with skilled trades in short supply. Longer hours and additional shifts at overtime rates sent costs spiraling upward. By the time the new Pacific Press Building was opened more than two years after bids were tendered, its price tag had almost tripled from the original estimate to $14 million.[56]

Meanwhile at the Sun Tower, the newspaper's staff and Pacific Press craftsmen were in a restive state. Consolidation of the *Sun* and *Province* production facilities, which had employed about 1,500 workers combined when the amalgamation was announced in 1957, had meant that almost one-third of staff had already become redundant. Instead of two composing rooms, both newspapers were being made up at the Sun Tower, where both also were printed on the *Sun*'s relatively more modern presses. Almost a third of the ITU printers had already been slashed from the payroll — from 350 in 1957 to only 250 by 1965 — and the planned move to a more modern facility made them fear the loss of another thirty-five to forty-five jobs, according to union head Len Guy.[57]

Despite the protests of publishers at the time of amalgamation that editorial competition would remain as vigorous as before, more than 200 jobs also had been eliminated in the two newsrooms, from 760 to 550 by 1965. The fear of more job losses when the staffs of both papers moved into the new building were fueled by an article on the planned facility in the U.S. trade publication *Editor & Publisher* in 1964, which reported the building was designed to accommodate a staff of 825, which was 200 fewer than were then working for Pacific Press. The concern prompted the Newspaper Guild to sign a three-year contract that guaranteed the jobs of all its members on staff at Pacific Press as of July 1, 1964. Such a long-term contract was usually forbidden under the rules set down by the Guild's international headquarters, but the policy was relaxed when local union representative Bill McLeman made a special appeal to Guild officials in Washington, D.C., on the basis of fears for job security.[58]

At the *Sun*, apprehension over the change in ownership extended to top management. Keate received a telephone call from Pacific Press general manager Ed Benson while he was publisher of the *Victoria Times*. "According to Benson, senior *Sun* executives were 'scared to death' and 'full of apprehensions,'" Keate recalled, adding he wondered why he was hearing about the unrest from a man he described as "a master of intrigue."[59] In response to the situation in his home town, Keate, in his capacity as a director of FP, wrote to Bell. "The staff of the *Sun* was in turmoil, jittery and uncertain about its future," Keate recalled warning Bell.[60] He suggested that it might be better to have venerable Bruce Hutchison, who was Keate's editor in nearby Victoria, take over editorial direction from Malone in Winnipeg. The absentee ownership was under heavy criticism in Vancouver, Keate warned Bell, with radio hotliner Jack Webster, a former *Sun* reporter, particularly critical. Local reaction against now-total Eastern ownership of Vancouver's daily newspapers had led to a movement to start a third daily in the city. The situation at the *Sun*, Keate recalled, was "a dog's breakfast, virtually incomprehensible in the light of the business acumen of the paper's new owners."[61]

Bell responded by telephone from Calgary several days later, Keate recalled, and in a thirty-five-minute conversation "did everything but make me a firm offer for the job as publisher of the *Sun*."[62] Noting the salary he was being offered — $36,000 — was considerably less than Cromie (or even Dampier) had received, Keate protested to Bell that his relations with Malone were "at best, prickly." Within a month, Keate was called to a meeting at the Hotel Vancouver with Bell, Hutchison, and Malone to discuss the job, but "what should have been a festive occasion quickly degenerated into a confrontation with all the elan and *joie de vivre* of the Nuremburg trials."[63] To Keate's astonishment, Malone began reading a four-page, typewritten document setting out his expectations for the new *Sun* publisher. Included in this "solemn ukase," as Keate called it, was an admonishment against being a "'big shot', bon vivant type of publisher." Malone instead wanted one who would keep to a strict nine-to-five routine and even work Saturday mornings to set a good example, taking only three weeks of holidays without extra long weekends, avoiding out-of-town business trips and "the social swing and cocktail circuit, the Press Club," and other social organizations. "It is quite impossible to be one of the boys on the town one night and hold the serious respect of the staff on the following day," Keate recalled Malone reading.

> I sat in the hotel room, listening to Malone reading this sombre catalogue of Thou-Shalt-Nots — actually *reading* it, with an occasional furtive glance to ensure that I was Getting the Message — with mounting dismay. I felt a bit like a juvenile delinquent being lectured by a stern and disapproving father. . . . The person he had described, and the procedures indicated, were the precise antithesis of my own style, personality, and philosophies of leadership.[64]

Malone prefaced his job description for the new *Sun* publisher with an analysis of FP's new acquisition which, he said, "has many good things in its favour." The document outlined the *Sun*'s strengths and weaknesses, to Malone's mind. "It has been a bright, aggressive and successful operation, it does have a flair and liveliness which it is very important to preserve and it also has on its staff many people of considerable competence. As against this, it is often considered irresponsible, a bit junky and bigoted on some issues."[65] The FP chain manager urged a "slow, steady program to achieve the outlook and respect needed," and building a "feeling of security" among employees. "To imagine that we should simply discharge half the executives is utter madness," noted Malone. "It would require several years to rebuild staff morale afterwards and we would lose considerable time in training new executives into their jobs."[66]

Promising to think it over, Keate appealed privately to Bell that he could not possibly accept such "impossible" and "insulting" rules and insisted Bell get Malone to back off. The whole thing turned into a "Mexican stand-off," according to Keate, and he finally accepted the job. "Before we broke up, Bell put his hand on my shoulder and said: 'Stu, I want you to know that you were my first and only choice for this job,'" Keate recalled of the meeting that sealed his appointment.[67] But the *Sun* publisher learned years later from Hutchison and Malone that Bell, about whom Keate was assembling material for a biography, was not being truthful. A typewritten note in Keate's personal papers outlines a meeting he had with Hutchison and Malone at the Hotel Vancouver on December 12, 1974, in which they revealed the Calgary oilman's original choice. "In January 1964 MB told RSM and BH he wanted Hal Straight as publisher of the *Sun*. 'No way,' said Dick. 'He's a thug and a crook. Totally unacceptable.' Max turned red, angry said: 'He's my friend. Don't call him a crook.'

However [Max] yielded and agreed SK should be publisher. Seconded by BH and (according to RSM), RSM."[68]

The only remaining problem pending announcement of Keate's appointment was informing Dampier of the decision after the FP board had approved it, but word leaked out at the annual Canadian Press meeting in Toronto, and the story was expected to be in the next day's editions of the *Toronto Telegram*. "Malone scurried around, found Dampier, and on the mezzanine lobby of the Royal York Hotel advised him that he would not be getting the top job at the *Sun*," recalled Keate. "Although disappointed, he took the news with good grace and promised his loyal support."[69]

Meanwhile, the change in ownership of the *Sun* had prompted calls for a Royal Commission on press ownership. New Democratic Party leader Tommy Douglas raised the issue in parliament, pressing Liberal prime minister Lester Pearson on the question for weeks without response. Douglas Fisher, the former *Maclean's* magazine writer who had been elected member of parliament for Port Arthur in Ontario, asked Justice Minister Guy Chevier, according to a report in *Canadian Printer & Publisher*, "whether a restraining order. . . . against Pacific Press was still in effect. Chevier said he would reply later."[70]

On his arrival as publisher in 1964, Stu Keate aimed at making the *Sun* less parochial, as it seemed preoccupied with local news. "My aim was to reduce the strident tone of its columns; to take the paper out beyond the bounds of British Columbia to concern itself with national and international affairs; and in the process to make it as independent and responsible as humanly possible," he recalled.[71] Together with Bruce Hutchison, his old colleague from Victoria, who served as editorial director by remote from his camp at Shawnigan Lake on Vancouver Island, Keate set about revamping the *Sun*. One of his first tasks in changing the paper's direction was to dethrone Erwin Swangard, who was a hard-driving managing editor but seemed to the new publisher "to belong to the 'Front Page' school of another era. It soon became apparent we could never produce the kind of newspaper we wanted with Swangard in charge of the news columns."[72] In his place the *Sun*'s new publisher wanted to promote the capable Bill Galt, who was Swangard's assistant managing editor. Galt was a graduate of the Columbia School of Journalism, had been the *Sun*'s Washington correspondent, and, according to Keate, "enjoyed the respect of the newsroom because reporters knew he could do any job they undertook, only better."[73] But Swangard did not make the transition easy, as Keate noted in a 1966 letter to Hutchison.

> For some months now, Swangard has been waging a not-too-subtle campaign with me to get Galt away from the post of Assistant Managing Editor. . . . Swangard seems to have some insecurity about a strong man in behind him, and rarely passes up an opportunity to cry Bill down. . . . Swangard is an excellent man in many respects — a tireless worker and strong expediter. But in other ways . . . he embarrasses me and, more importantly, the paper.[74]

Keate told Hutchison that while Galt "may not be as hot an administrator as Swangard, I believe he can be trained and that his other qualities more than make up for any deficiency in this regard."[75] When he moved against Swangard, the managing editor would not go without a fight. "In due course, I advised him that he would be retired at age sixty," recalled Keate. "Swangard balked. There ensued some acrimonious negotiations, at the end of which there were threats of legal action for wrongful dismissal. Before it reached that point, we 'settled out of court' with a graduated series of payments totalling some $85,000."[76] Within a few years of Keate taking over as publisher of the *Sun*, the newspaper had been completely re-made, according to Hutchison. "It was a paper so different from its earlier slam-bang news treatment and feverish headlines as to be almost unrecognizable if you looked over the old files in the library."[77]

Talent seemed to fall into Keate's lap at the *Sun*. Jack Wallace, a "newspaper doctor" with the Hearst newspaper chain in the U.S., showed up one day and refused to leave without a job offer. According to Keate, the typography buff "had made up his mind to leave San Francisco, settle in Vancouver and that was that."[78] With Wallace in charge of the newspaper's redesign, the *Sun* began to win awards for its page layout. Lisa Hobbs of the *San Francisco Chronicle*, author of four books including a best-seller on China, moved with her husband to the rain forest of Vancouver Island so favored by Hutchison. She first worked out a deal with Galt to write features from the Island, then took over the *Sun*'s television column and ultimately became the paper's associate editor and the first woman to sit on its editorial board. Eric Downton, a foreign correspondent for fifteen years with the *Daily Telegraph*, came aboard, and the closure of the *Vancouver Times* made the services of witty sportswriter Jim Taylor available.[79]

While under Keate the *Sun* had remained liberal since its takeover by Max Bell and FP Publications in 1963, down the street at the *Province*, the morning daily had become even more conservative in its editorial stance under publisher Fred Auger. Soon the Southam paper would suffer an embarrassment that pointed up in no uncertain terms the political polarization of the Pacific Press publications. In a 1965 *Saturday Night* column, Doug Collins observed that the *Province* "began to shed its once-respectable clothing" five years earlier with an infamous election-eve hoax spread across its front page.[80] The provincial election of 1960 featured a strong socialist challenge to the Social Credit government of W.A.C. Bennett. The Co-operative Commonwealth Federation, or CCF, as it was known then, looked poised to take power with a minority government because the vote was split four ways between the socialists, Social Credit, Conservatives, and Liberals. But a last-minute "fear" campaign led by the *Province* raised the specter of businesses fleeing B.C. and taking jobs with them if the CCF won office. "Are we going to flirt with a group of wooly idealists who want to invest huge sums of our tax money to experiment with state ownership?" the *Province* asked in a front-page editorial, noting the socialists were "already half-married to the labor bosses and highly vulnerable to communist infiltration."[81]

The editorial was tied to a news story bannered across the top of the page, which quoted Alberta oil magnate Frank McMahon as warning that the election of the CCF would endanger a planned $450-million oil and gas project in northern B.C. which would provide 10,000 permanent jobs. "I feel it is my public duty to make plain to everyone the enormous stakes involved in this election," McMahon told the *Province*.[82] Bennett won re-election two days later with a slim six-seat majority, and opposition leaders blamed McMahon's eleventh-hour warnings on the *Province* front page for galvanizing the anti-socialist vote around the Socred government.[83] There was only one problem, according to Allan Fotheringham. "There were no

10,000 jobs available or under threat," the *Sun* columnist wrote a dozen years later. "There was no $450,000,000 development."[84] The front-page *Province* story, Fotheringham charged, was "concocted . . . out of a phoney threat by McMahon," who was a "good friend" of Bennett.[85]

The scare tactic, charged Fotheringham, was a classic example of the "roorback" technique, named for an 1844 hoax aimed at a U.S. presidential candidate and eventual election victor. James Polk's political opponents floated a phoney story on election eve about a "Baron Roorback," who claimed Polk had branded slaves with an iron. The obscure word "roorback" survives as a term signifying any bogus accusation leveled against a political opponent when there is no time to set the record straight.[86] The *Province*, according to Fotheringham, "sold" its front page to McMahon with the phoney story and alarmist editorial. "Other unbylined, unsourced stories on the page abandoned any pretence at news objectivity and became editorialized election eve warnings."[87] The roorback, noted Collins, marked a sharp rightward turn by the already conservative morning newspaper.

> The paper pleads regularly that the rope and the knout are the answer to crime . . . It loves The Bomb, which it describes as a lifesaver, and sees itself as a leading element in the contest to save Christ's earth from Communism. When Tommy Douglas was elected in Burnaby-Coquitlam, its lead editorial was titled "National Socialist Headquarters. . . .", and State Secretary Maurice Lamontagne, who once asked here for some Western understanding of affairs in Quebec, was branded A Dangerous Canadian.[88]

Soon the morning newspaper's running battles with the federal leader of the socialist party would erupt into a full-scale war of words on the floor of the House of Commons in Ottawa and result in a Royal Commission into *Province* editorial content.

5 The Times

Val Warren was a salesman extraordinaire. Broadcaster Jack Webster, a former *Vancouver Sun* writer, found him "an exceedingly persuasive spokesman."[1] *Maclean's* magazine described him in 1963 as "a hard-driving and humorless adman."[2] Donald Stainsby, a longtime *Vancouver Sun* journalist, referred to him in a 1964 *Saturday Night* magazine article as "a much-scorned, cigar-smoking stocky man of 41."[3] A former National Film Board cameraman, Warren was on his way from Ottawa to a promised studio job in Hollywood after the Second World War when he stopped off in Vancouver to visit relatives, fell in love with the city and decided to stay. Getting into the advertising business, Warren handled "the comparatively small accounts of local merchants that the big-time agencies scorn," convincing one client, a dog-food manufacturer, to declare his product "fit for human consumption," according to Stainsby. "He and the client looked admiringly at a sample can, then the client handed it to Warren, 'Okay, Val,' he said, 'eat it.'"[4] He started a billboard company he confidently called National Outdoor Advertising and took over the unprofitable Time O'Day company, which sold advertising messages that ran between time announcements on a telephone line. By tripling call volume, according to a 1963 profile in *Marketing* magazine, Warren turned the venture into a "booming business."[5] He also started up a weekly newspaper, a free-circulation "shopper" called *Metro Times*.

But Warren had bigger dreams than such middling enterprises. In 1958, shortly after Pacific Press was formed, he was approached by a group of merchants and asked to investigate the possibility of starting up a third daily newspaper in Vancouver to compete with the new monopoly. At first deciding such a venture was impractical due to high start-up costs of $10-$15 million, Warren changed his mind when he spotted a report in a trade magazine of a new printing process being developed. Offset printing, which replaced the cumbersome letterpress printing plates composed out of molten lead on manual typesetting machines, was a process in which thin plastic sheets were engraved photographically, using "cold type" set by stenographers on punched tape. It lowered the capital equipment start-up costs of newspapers and cut the labor costs of composition. Unlike letterpress printing, the process also allowed crisp color reproduction, approaching the photographic quality of glossy magazines.

Offset printing had been used for several years at many weekly and small-circulation daily newspapers in the U.S. on presses built by R. Hoe and Co., but the trade-off for automated higher-quality reproduction was a slower printing speed, and the process was thus unsuitable for large-circulation daily newspaper production. When Warren spotted a report of a breakthrough by the Danish company Aller, which allowed for offset printing at five times previous speeds, he knew the process had become suitable for large-scale daily publication. Instead of $10-$15 million in start-up costs for a conventional printing plant, Warren calculated he could get a third daily off the ground in Vancouver for $4-$5 million using offset printing. "This was the breakthrough that formed the trenches for the invasion of the newspaper world," Warren told *Marketing* in 1963. "Failure is impossible — we haven't even considered it."[6] He negotiated with Hoe, which imported the French-built presses, for the Canadian rights to the process and planned a nationwide chain of dailies to be printed on the Aller-designed presses. Warren turned down an offer of financing from Hoe, deciding instead to raise capital with a public share offering. He signed a lease calling for $20,000 a month to be paid for the $3 million in presses.

Setting up a booth at the annual Pacific National Exhibition agricultural fair in East Vancouver during the summer of 1963, Warren showed a color promotional film to potential investors and distributed survey results that suggested more than 80,000 subscribers would buy a third daily newspaper in Vancouver, which he claimed could expect to earn $6.5 million in annual revenue.[7] Warren raised $1.65 million within a year by selling shares at $10 apiece, mostly to small investors in blocks of $300 to $400.[8] He recruited a solid corps of veteran newsmen, including former *Province* managing editor Bill Forst as editorial director, former *Province* and *News-Herald* managing editor Aubrey Roberts as assistant publisher, and former *Star* publisher General Victor Odlum, who had been out of the newspaper business for more than thirty years and was then 83, as chairman of the board. From the beginning, Warren played on public distaste for the Pacific Press monopoly, which had lost any local ownership since the *Sun* had been bought in 1963 by FP Publications. "For a long time now there has been some mild concern in Vancouver over the city's general newspaper situation," noted *Marketing* magazine in assessing the new daily's chances. "There is a feeling around that both papers are the same."[9] *Maclean's* magazine headlined its 1963 report of Warren's ambitions "Hot, hopeful rumors for Vancouverites who are fed up with their newspaper," and continued, "His confidence is buoyed by his conviction that Vancouver is fed up with Pacific Press, the Southam-Max Bell holding company that owns both the *Sun* and *Province*."[10]

An undated "information package" prepared for the *Times*' board of directors set out the anti-Pacific Press strategy. "Since the merger took place, the public has felt, and witnessed with shock, the difference it made to our city. . . . Sensationalism has run rampant from front page to editorial page. . . . Ad rates have increased dramatically."[11] Noting a development at the *Los Angeles Times* in 1963, which saw typesetters who had been rendered redundant by new technology given lifetime job guarantees and transferred to other duties, the document saw an opportunity to exploit the resulting labor unrest at Pacific Press. "Merging two mechanical staffs into one publishing plant, with various unions involved, we predict that labor will obviously take the same stand and demand that no man lose his job."[12] The document noted that many of the applications for employment received by the *Times* had come from Pacific Press employees wanting out for other reasons than money. "Pacific Press employees are at a low ebb of fear for their jobs which, coupled with the news of a new newspaper entering in this market serves to create more havoc amongst them for jobs, and future security."[13] The information package provided to directors foresaw one possible obstacle the Pacific Press papers could pose to the success of the *Vancouver Times*.

> There is a possibility that pressure will be brought to bear on leading advertisers to stay out of the *Times*, but the only two motives that could be used are loss of preferred ad position in the newspaper, and offering space for less money. . . . however, this approach seems unlikely. The two large publishing groups who now control the Pacific Press have a fifty year history of respect for profits.[14]

To avoid labor troubles of its own, the *Times* signed an unusual "vertical" contract with the ITU, giving the printers jurisdiction over all mechanical departments at the newspaper in contrast to the multiplicity of craft union certifications at Pacific Press. For a plant site, Warren chose a building on the outskirts of town in East Vancouver that formerly housed a Volkswagen dealership. Among the columnists recruited were Jack Webster, a popular radio talk show host on CKNW; Doug Collins, an opinionated veteran writer and broadcaster; and Jim Taylor, an acerbic sportswriter from the *Victoria Colonist*. The paper was planned to be published in two sections and be both a broadsheet and a tabloid. A broadsheet news section would wrap around a tabloid section, which would alternately focus on entertainment, sports, business, women's, and other features. A tabloid classified advertising section would contain free ads, with vendors expected to pay up only on sale of their merchandise. Of the planned forty-eight pages daily, a dozen would be in full color.[15] The first edition was planned for September 5, 1964, and promotion went into high gear at that summer's PNE fair, with a large booth set up to sell subscriptions. By the time the *Times* hit the streets with a thick sixty-six-page inaugural edition, it had signed up 73,000 customers, which proved too many for the fledgling newspaper to deliver, reported *Canadian Printer & Publisher.*

> Routes were based on a predicted 50,000. Consequently, some areas received first-day editions 24 hours late. To compound the problem, only about 80,000 copies were run and none were available in corner stores. Some were filched from doorsteps, and one carrier lost his entire load of papers when he put his bag down at the side of the road to make a delivery. An antiquated make-shift switchboard couldn't cope with the volume of calls for a week.[16]

In addition to its early delivery difficulties, the new *Times* also suffered from production problems. A scanner broke down and color photographs practically disappeared from the paper, disappointing many who had been sold on the idea of a colorful alternative. The offset presses still weren't operating at full capacity, and production difficulties dictated 10 p.m. deadlines, early for an afternoon newspaper. "Gradually deadlines were brought more into line," reported *Canadian Printer & Publisher*, "but two weeks after first edition, the time lag between editorial deadlines and pressrun was still considered too long."[17] The problems caused the promised full-color advertising to be delayed and ads were scarce generally, with some of the initial news sections carrying as little as 12 percent advertising. "We've signed up three or four department stores and the supermarkets, but they appeared reticent [*sic*] to get started," said assistant publisher Aubrey Roberts. "But we're getting there, slowly."[18]

Public reaction to the *Times* was mixed. "The 'entirely different' format promised by the *Times* . . . had the anticipated impact on the public, but for many the new look was too radical," noted *Canadian Printer & Publisher*. "Each potential subscriber had his own concept of what the 'difference' would be."[19] Subsequent editions in the paper's first week of publication averaged sixteen broadsheet news pages, with an eight-page classified advertising section and a sixteen-page tabloid magazine. "They used to say we wouldn't get off the ground," said Warren. "Now they're trying to say we won't last. Well, we've got off the ground and there is no chance of us going broke for the next ten years. Failure is impossible."[20] The publisher's enthusiasm reflected the initial success of the new daily newspaper he had conceived. "Warren admits that it feels good to talk like this after six years of being taunted and mocked as an inexperienced babe in newsprint," wrote Stainsby in *Saturday Night*. "There can be little doubt that he saw a magnificent chance when others didn't, and he grabbed it."[21]

But even before it published its first edition, the seeds of the *Times*' demise had been sown. Of the $1.8 million received from share sales by then, almost $1 million had gone to initial organization, development. and finance costs.[22] By the time the first papers hit the streets, the *Times* was so cash-strapped that it had less than $200,000 on hand to meet working costs and a payroll of more than 300. "This was the pinched shoe from which *The Times*, faced with poor response from advertisers, was never able to escape," according to Webster.[23] Warren, who controlled the *Times* board of directors through his ownership of all 6,000 Class B shares of the company, which gave him the right to appoint three of the seven board members and hold the deciding vote as president, had also received, in addition to his $51,178 salary as publisher starting in 1962, $75,000 for the "goodwill" of his closed weekly shopper, *Metro Times*, along with reimbursement for more than $37,000 in expenses for the "pilot" publication.[24] The cozy financial arrangements the publisher made for himself created tension with other executives as money became increasingly tight at the new daily. Warren's management style didn't help matters, according to Webster.

> It is no secret that Warren's personality created many a clash with fellow directors, executives and staff. . . . An early blow to staff morale came with the abrupt resignation, a few days after the first edition, of the first managing editor, Geoffrey Molyneux, regarded as a brilliant newspaperman. Molyneux decided there was no future for him on the *Times* and he went back east.[25]

Assistant publisher Aubrey Roberts resigned in December after, according to Webster, "a face-to-face disagreement with Warren over financial matters."[26] Next to go was editorial director Bill Forst in January, after another disagreement with Warren. According to *Times* business editor Bruce Young, a "palace revolt" brewed over Christmas while Warren was vacationing in the Caribbean, but it fell apart after he was tipped off by telegram and hopped back home on the next jet to nip the revolution in the bud, emerging stronger than ever. An earlier revolt had resulted in Warren handing over his position as publisher to Odlum, according to Young, but he won the Christmas confrontation. "Warren asserted full control over the company once again," noted Young. "Odlum technically remained as publisher but actually slid out of the picture."[27] After Forst was ousted in his January confrontation with Warren, managing editor Brud Delany transformed the *Times* from a "solid, lacklustre newspaper," according to the *Times* business editor, into a "vigorous and slightly left-of-centre paper aimed at intellectuals. The approach attracted a solid readership of 50,000 a day."[28]

But while the *Times* had a loyal core of readers, the same was not true of advertisers, who were not convinced that by buying space in the new evening daily they could reach customers who did not already read the *Sun* or *Province*. Circulation also declined as the novelty wore off. By spring the *Times* was in desperate financial straits. On March 26 the newspaper could not afford to pay its non-mechanical staff and prepared a front-page editorial that Webster described as "unique in newspaper history."[29] Under the headline "*Times* fights for survival," the editorial issued a plea for support. "Why do we exist? And who are we fighting? Have you forgotten that the daily press of our city was under one-company control? Have you forgotten the brand of journalism that permeated this community?"[30] The *Times* editorial blamed everyone in sight for its plight, except its own management.

> There are those in our community who — from the first week of publication — have judged *The Times* abruptly and harshly: complaints ranging from not getting a newspaper on time to "*The Times* stands for nothing, thereby accomplishes nothing." There are leading advertisers in our community who, to date, have never bought an ad in *The Times*, not even a congratulatory ad in our inaugural issue.[31]

The editorial pointed out succinctly the chicken-or-egg conundrum facing the *Times* and every other trailing newspaper: ads attract readers, without whom advertisers don't buy space. "Lack of advertising content, in the first few months of publication, caused hundreds of people to cancel their subscriptions because ads are news and without them you are half a newspaper."[32] The lack of advertising was the paper's biggest problem, as Young noted that on some days the paper did not contain $400 worth of advertising. "To all intents and purposes, advertising revenue was nonexistent," wrote Young in *Canadian Printer & Publisher*. "Retailers in Greater Vancouver simply didn't use the *Times*."[33] Pacific Press had a stranglehold on retail advertising in Vancouver by dint of its wider coverage of homes, noted the *Times* business editor. "The *Times* had only one half-decent advertising contract in its brief life — one page a week for a small grocery chain that found the cost of advertising with the Pacific Press too rich for its blood."[34] The specter of Pacific Press was raised in the front-page *Times* editorial, which made a veiled reference to interference with its operations by the entrenched *Sun* and *Province*. "Fighting a two-newspaper, one-company-control octopus on all levels of our society has been a 24-hour-a-day job. We have a hundred bonafide reasons to holler 'foul' on the front page of *The Times* — but we have not."[35] When radio hotliner Webster, one of his own columnists, pressed Warren on the issue, however, he offered no examples. "To be frank, I was prepared to believe his allegation if publisher Warren could produce proof," offered Webster. "But when I challenged him publicly he wouldn't, or couldn't amplify his allegations."[36]

The other complaint addressed in the front-page editorial of March 27 was that of editorial content. In defense of its product, the *Times* editorial fairly scolded the readers and advertisers who had scorned it. "What did you expect from a new newspaper — 90 pages daily? Top columnists? Forty pages in ads every day, from the first day of publication? Did you expect an editorial policy that satisfied every member of our community daily? Then you expected too much."[37] While it had launched itself with great promises of editorial vigor, in print the *Times* had lodged itself firmly on the fence. "The news pages did not live up to the advance billing that *The Times* would step on toes and stir things up to get them moving," noted Webster. "The *Vancouver Times* wavered and waffled in its editorial policies. It was neither fish nor fowl nor plain red herring."[38] The *Times* admitted its failings editorially in its front-page plea, in which it asked for more time to find its way.

> No, we have not reached the pinnacle of editorial success we set out to achieve, but we make no further apologies for our product — a daily newspaper. A new newspaper needs time to mold a policy, time to learn how to step hard and decide in which direction; and we are learning every day. In another six months we will be that much better a newspaper from front page to comics.[39]

There was, however, a good reason for the *Times* to be wishy-washy editorially. From its inception, there had been rumors that the new daily was created by supporters of the Social Credit provincial government of Premier W.A.C. Bennett, who were fed up with the slings and arrows of the Liberal *Vancouver Sun* and the Conservative *Province*. Warren denied it, and the paper's editorial policy bent over backwards to reveal no bias on behalf of Social Credit. But when the financial difficulties of the *Times* became public, Warren hinted he had a buyer for the newspaper, which caused speculation that the money would come from Socred sources.[40]

Part of the impetus behind the *Vancouver Times* had in fact been political, and it did have Social Credit sympathies. The undated, unsigned "information package" provided to *Times* directors had listed among the reasons to create a new daily the unfavorable coverage of the provincial government by the Pacific Press dailies. "The *Sun*, carrying the Liberal party banner, accelerated one of the most vicious vengeance campaigns ever waged in the Canadian press. It has set out to undermine, obstruct and destroy the Social Credit party that has been in power in B.C. for twelve years, and today enjoys a whopping majority in the House."[41] The political motivation seemed an open secret from the outset and had been broadly hinted at in the trade magazine *Canadian Printer & Publisher* as early as its January 1963 issue. While recording Warren's insistence the new daily would be "non-partisan and have no political affiliations," the magazine noted: "It has been known for some time that the Social Credit party, if not actually the government, has been interested in establishing a newspaper, because of the faint support for Social Credit shown by most existing B.C. papers."[42]

The non-mechanical payroll that had been missed on Friday, March 26, was postponed until the following Wednesday, and in its front-page editorial the *Times* issued a plea for a further cash infusion. In its first seven months of operation, the new daily had lost $1.3 million, including $235,000 in one month alone.[43] Cost controls were non-existent initially, according to Young. "In the first three months alone the editorial staff went through $200 worth of ballpoint pens, a small item but one of many that added up."[44] Now *Times* management clamped down on costs and asked for $100,000 from the public in the form of debenture sales to help see the newspaper through its money problems. The appeal was successful in raising $90,000 and the missed payday was made up as promised.[45]

In its next edition the *Times* announced it had received an overwhelming response to its call. "We are not going to throw in the sponge," another front-page editorial promised.[46] In that issue it also made a bold gambit which sought to solve its advertising problem, but which ultimately may have worsened it. A full page inside that day's editions of the *Times* was devoted to an attack on its most reluctant customer. Under the headline "This space reserved for Woodward's Stores Ltd.," the *Times* set out its grievances against the province's largest retailer. "For reasons unknown to us *The Times* has been denied any ads from Woodward's since our commencement of publication," the editorial complained. "We do not think this is fair to our subscribers. We are also certain that we now enjoy a wide readership, and that ads run in *The Times* can prove to be productive, if given a chance."[47] *The Times* offered Woodward's two free pages of advertising a week, free of charge, until the department store chain decided the customer response was worth paying for.

Not only was the ploy unsuccessful, it may even have backfired as other retailers wondered why they should pay for ads when the *Times* was offering free space to a major competitor. "The public reaction to this open pressure play was double-edged," noted Webster. "Some people felt the store should have advertised, if only in a token manner, as a gesture of support for a new community venture. Others felt *The Times* was guilty of advertising blackmail in the poorest taste."[48] Radio reporter Mark Raines approached Woodward's executives for their reaction, but was unable to obtain an interview, instead being given a statement from the retailer that said, in effect, "If we decide to advertise, we'll pay for it, but we won't submit to intimidation."[49]

Douglas Fisher, the *Maclean's* writer who had sounded the alarm about chain ownership of Canadian newspapers a few years earlier, now took up the *Times*' cause in the federal parliament. Fisher, who had been elected in Ontario under the NDP banner, pressed Justice Minister Guy Favreau in the House of Commons on the charges of "foul practices it has encountered from its competitors and whether, in the light of those statements and the previous [RTPC] report, the combines branch could take another look at the press situation in Vancouver?"[50] *The Times* made the federal attention its top story under the headline "Pacific Press probe urged in Commons."[51] It followed the story the next day with an exclusive under the front-page headline "MP explains need for Pacific Press probe."

> In an interview with *The Times*, Fisher stressed he is not accusing Pacific Press of being a restrictive monopoly. "But it seems to me that when a newspaper cries 'foul,' as *The Times* has, then there are at least some practices that bear investigation by the commission. . . . A new study is now valid to see whether the *Sun* and *Province* are co-operating to keep advertising revenue away from *The Times*, and to keep distribution points to themselves."[52]

It seemed that in its desperate hour the best hope for the *Times* was that its Pacific Press competition would be shut down by a strike. The ITU had voted overwhelmingly to walk out in support of its demands for job guarantees in the face of automation in the new plant Pacific Press was building. Warren told creditors that in the event of a strike at Pacific Press, the *Times* was preparing to double its edition size and boost its press run to 80,000.[53] At the same time, he boldly announced a second newspaper for his planned nationwide chain, telling a group of Toronto admen in early April that an *Edmonton Times* would be launched in 1966 and that a similar title in Quebec would be announced soon. "In five years he expects all five papers to be rolling," reported *Marketing*. "Each paper will be financed by the community. There will be no financial link between the papers, but as a co-operative they will set up an Ottawa office together to pool features and combine sales efforts, for example."[54]

In April, Warren and his struggling daily received a boost when Vancouver's hottest media commodity suddenly became available, and the *Times* scooped him up. Pat Burns had created a sensation in 1963 with a radio genre he named the "Hot Line" after a news item of the day—the Kennedy-Khrushchev phone link of the Cuban Missile Crisis. During his five hours of daily air time, the gravel-voiced CJOR host not only fielded phone calls from listeners; he also placed them to unsuspecting victims. His tactics would cause federal regulators to rewrite the rules and threaten to take CJOR off the air, but his popularity prompted competing radio stations to quickly assemble their own phone-in shows, pressing their most opinionated commentators into service. Outspoken and persuasive, Burns attracted an enormous following with his blunt criticism and conspiracy theories. Soon a quarter of a million listeners across the Pacific Northwest were tuning him in every night, and a radio phenomenon had been spawned. *Maclean's* magazine reported in 1964 that within six months CJOR's ratings increased by 1,500 percent.

> These days, his mail averages a thousand letters a week from listeners who can't get his line, and every day at least fifty people line up outside his studio hoping to button-hole him for a little personal conversation. Once when there was a power failure at

> CJOR and Burns went off the air, his fans bombarded other Vancouver stations with claims that someone had thrown a bomb into his studio. And when he took off for a holiday early in October, the same fans spread a panicky rumor that he had been assassinated.[55]

Time magazine declared Burns "hypnotic."[56] The mellifluous quality of the hotliner's "greatest natural asset — that deep, resonant voice" — lent an air of credibility to his arguments, according to a 1966 *Maclean's* report on the growing talk radio phenomenon. "Somehow, when Burns opens his mouth (which is often) the most commonplace observation can sound like the pronouncements of a heroic liberator revealing a new bill of rights for a long-oppressed people."[57] His aural persuasiveness, the *Maclean's* writer found, was magnified by his "sometimes monumental" rudeness and his self-styled role of advocate for the common man.[58] Other stations in the highly competitive Lower Mainland radio market quickly pressed into service their own versions of Burns, whom *Vancouver Sun* columnist Jack Wasserman dubbed, "The Mouth That Roars." Radio giant CKNW in nearby New Westminster soon found its boast of being B.C.'s most listened-to station in jeopardy. In self-defense, CKNW management dragged their lead commentator, Jack Webster, as he recalled, "kicking and screaming into the talk show business. . . . They convinced me to give it a try by explaining how much more money I could earn. I was earning good money, and the station provided a car. They doubled it!"[59] Webster would go on to enjoy a longer career and achieve greater fame than Burns, but starting out in the mid-1960s he could barely compete with the antics of CJOR's wild new populist force.

The Canadian radio regulatory body of the day, the Board of Broadcast Governors, put a stop to one of Burns' favorite tactics in 1965, making it illegal to put anyone on the air without their prior agreement. It also took seriously the many complaints it received about the accusatory commentator. With the station's broadcasting licence up for renewal that spring and hearings set to deal with complaints about its programming, CJOR president Marie Chandler weighed the peril of continuing with Burns against the hotliner's demands for more money and exemption from censorship by the station — and handed Burns his walking papers.[60] His fans threatened to boycott sponsors who stayed with the station, which even suffered a bomb scare.[61] "Burns' 25 sponsors withdrew $70,000 worth of business after the firing, and he boasted that he would take his trade — and his people — with him," reported *Time.*[62] As dramatic as the parting was, Burns and his girlfriend/manager played it for all it was worth, according to *Maclean's*.

> Suddenly, Burns was off the air. Vancouver was stunned. Nobody seemed to know where Burns was, and the only source of information was Burns' attractive lady agent, Elaine Alexander, who tersely told the press there would be no statement. A few days later, there was an announcement that a public meeting would be held, at which time Burns would tell all. When the time came, even Burns couldn't believe the turnout.[63]

The downtown rally was scheduled for the evening of March 29 and the result, according to *Time*, was a thirty-block, "monstrous traffic jam, as 10,000 people tried to fight, shove and shoehorn their way into the 2,800-seat Queen Elizabeth Theatre."[64] Caught in the crush of cars was Burns, who told *Maclean's*, "I wondered what the reason was, never for a moment thinking that it had to do with me. Fortunately some of the other drivers recognized me and let me through — otherwise I never would have made it."[65] Reported the *Times*, "All traffic routes to the QET were clogged with cars. By 7:30 there was a line of cars stretching from the Georgia Viaduct up Main to about four blocks past the CNR station. People drove around the area aimlessly looking for parking. Nearby areas were logjammed with cars, back and side lanes looked like long, thin secondhand car lots."[66] According to the *Sun*, by 5 p.m. there were already more people crowded outside the theatre than it could hold, including "men and women of all age groups from students upwards. Mink coats mingled with head scarves."[67] A bomb threat, which proved bogus, brought the riot squad and fire departments rushing to the scene. When the doors opened at 6 p.m., it took only seven minutes to fill every seat. Outside, the overflow crowd milled about in the rain, listening on loudspeakers as Burns held the early arrivals inside rapt for hours with his allegations about the "conspiracy" that took him off the air. "The establishment trembled and you, the great unwashed, had a voice," Burns told the crowd, blaming the extinguishment of his Hot Line on "the empires of patronage and privilege."[68]

Suddenly seeing a way out of his newspaper's financial crisis, Val Warren seized the opportunity to cash in on Burns' popularity and signed him as a *Vancouver Times* columnist in an attempt to boost his flagging daily's circulation. A front-page announcement on April 1 proved to be no April Fool's Day put-on, and the paper's overworked switchboard "lit up like a Christmas tree."[69] The *Times* announced it would devote "a half page presentation of his strongly-opinionated views on a society with which he often finds himself at angry odds."

> This time, though, he is out in the open where the Burns haters, sometimes as dedicated as his devotees, will have the opportunity for rebuttal. For every half page of Burns that *The Times* publishes there will be equal space for those who feel they have cause to hit back. He will be on his own and critics, who charged in the past that those he attacked were not given fair opportunity to reply, can now have their innings.[70]

The result, according to *Marketing* magazine, was a smash hit. "Four days later, when Burns' first full-page 'Court of Public Opinion' appeared, the *Times*' circulation was reported to be 50,000 and screaming to 60,000. Newsstands couldn't supply the demand."[71] More importantly for the *Times*, some of the advertisers that had bought air time on Burns' radio show, such as the Vancouver-based department store Hamilton Harvey, which had rented the Queen Elizabeth Theatre for his public rally, indeed followed Burns onto the pages of the *Times*. Things suddenly began looking up for Warren's ailing daily. "A snap poll of media men, taken after the first two columns were out, yields the opinion that Burns alone cannot save the *Times* — but he'll help to give the paper another three to six months," reported *Marketing* magazine.[72] Amid renewed hope, Warren continued his campaign to convince Woodward's to come on board as a *Times* advertiser. Another full-page editorial devoted to the department store chain's continued absence from the *Times* ran April 13 and addressed the backlash management had felt after the paper's initial attack on the retailer. "Some said it was an unethical effort," the editorial admitted. "We were hurt and bleeding, on the brink of having to still our presses. If we were to go under, we wanted all to know how hard we had tried." But still Woodward's refused to patronize the paper, with which its relations had been "strained from the outset," according to *Times* business editor Bruce Young.[73]

Before April was up, the annual shareholders meeting of the Times

Publishing Company Ltd. was scheduled, and Warren had to report publicly that by the end of December the fledgling enterprise had lost "an awful lot of money — $903,000."[74] But Warren declared that the months since had been a "growth period," with revenues in March up 38 percent over those for January, with costs down by 32 percent.[75] "He admitted the paper has required more money to get off the ground than originally estimated," reported the *Times*. "He said the losses in the shake-down period were twice those anticipated and knocked a big hole in the company's financial reserves. . . . 'I shudder to tell you the risk we ran in those first 90 days.'"[76]

But Warren was putting a brave face on a desperate situation. In May he needed a moratorium from creditors on $200,000 in overdue bills, and he had to ask the Hoe company for more time to pay $100,000 the *Times* owed on the lease of its presses.[77] Before May was out, Warren decided to throw in the sponge after all and announced the *Times* would convert to a weekly publication in June. "The move from a daily to a weekly is being made to prevent further losses of working capital, and arrive into a profit area, by reducing labor and material costs by 50 percent," explained the *Times* on its front page of May 26. The new *Times Weekly*, it announced, would join a "select group" of respected newspapers across the globe that published only once a week, including the *Sunday Times* of London, *Paris Match*, *Der Spiegel*, and *The Economist*. The *Times* predicted its new weekly incarnation would "attract even larger numbers of readers in the weeks ahead. Immediate goal is a weekly circulation of 75,000, rising to 100,000 within the next few months."[78] At a press conference, Warren declared that circulation of the *Times Weekly* could go as high as 150,000 and enable it to re-enter the daily field. The *Vancouver Sun* noted that the largest weekly newspaper in the area was the *North Shore Citizen*, with a circulation of 16,000.[79] Staff of the *Times* was slashed by half in preparation for its conversion, but others in management objected to the capitulation and reasoned that with the prickly Warren out of the way their newspaper might have a fighting chance of remaining a daily, according to Young.

> To the schemers, it seemed that even as a daily the paper could only survive if new advertising were forthcoming as a result of Warren's ouster — Woodward's advertising in particular. Warren

> heard of the plot and called the participants into his board room. For an hour, he scolded, berated and harangued them. "Go back to your jobs — I'll see what can be done to save this paper," he said. Two hours later Warren called a staff meeting and announced he was stepping out of the picture.[80]

At first insisting he be reimbursed the $30,000 he had paid for his controversial 6,000 Class B shares, which gave him control of the *Times'* board of directors, Warren later agreed to turn them over without payment.[81] According to Bill Bell, a former *News-Herald* city editor who was a member of the *Times'* board of directors, Odlum bought the shares for $1 after Warren approached two investment groups that indicated a willingness to refinance the *Times*, but after the paper's progenitor turned over his controlling interest, Odlum double-crossed him. "As soon as Warren left, the general promptly installed himself as the new publisher and made it known he did not favor selling control to any group other than *Times* shareholders," revealed Bell in a 1979 letter to the editor of the *Sun*.[82] Two days after announcing its conversion to a weekly, the *Times* abruptly reversed field and ran, in red ink, a banner front-page headline befitting the outbreak of war: "TIMES TO STAY DAILY, WARREN STEPS DOWN." Reported the *Vancouver Sun*, "Warren told the meeting he reached his decision because of rumors and talk that he was the stumbling block in the newspaper's drive to get more advertising to make ends meet."[83] Of Warren's departure, Webster observed, "It was not before time."[84]

Instead of turning to the financiers Warren had approached, an issue of 200,000 new Class A shares was authorized for sale at $5 apiece to raise capital, but provincial superintendent of brokers Bill Irwin, noting that $3 million had already been invested in the *Times* by the public, restricted sale to current shareholders to prevent spread of what had obviously become a highly speculative venture.[85] A meeting of shareholders was scheduled for June 2 at the Hotel Vancouver in hopes of gaining the needed financial support. Former Warren lieutenants Forst and Roberts, who had earlier jumped ship after clashing with the paper's founder, clambered back aboard. "It must be impressed on everyone concerned, not only with the *Times*, but with the basic concepts of free expression of opinion and independent presentation of news and advertising that this newspaper represents their last hope for a community-owned newspaper within their lifetimes," pleaded Forst in a front-page column on the "day of decision."[86] With that edition the *Times* appropriated the former boast of the *Vancouver Sun* before it came under absentee corporate ownership, emblazoning under its front-page flag "Vancouver's Only Home-Owned Newspaper."

At the shareholders' meeting, Odlum announced that Warren's contentious Class B shares would be nullified. Odlum told the assembly of more than 1,000 that he would personally take over business operations of the *Times* and Bell would become managing director. Managing editor Brud Delany resigned and Mike Tytherleigh, the paper's magazine editor, was named to fill his spot. An immediate $50,000 was required to continue publication, the meeting was told, but when the checks and pledges were collected from the audience, only just over $19,000 was counted. Announcing that an additional $10,000 had been pledged by *Times* employees, Bell said a decision on continuing the *Times* as a daily would be deferred until the 6,000 shareholders who had not attended the meeting were solicited for support. The *Times* headlined developments triumphantly on its front page the next day: "'Owners' rally round paper." But the *Vancouver Sun* saw the result less optimistically, under the headline "*Times* Faces New Financial Crisis." Noting Warren's absence from the meeting, the *Sun* reported that several speakers were "highly critical of his operation of the paper." It quoted Odlum as calling Warren "'a man of many skills — a bit of a dreamer.' He said he and the former president had been 'friendly enemies' and there was a deep difference of opinion."[87] City editor Barney McKinley told the meeting he resigned, according to the *Sun*. "He added the paper's news staff now consists of Forst, managing editor Mike Tytherleigh and two women writers."[88]

Under Tytherleigh, the *Times* again changed its look, according to Young, this time out of necessity. "With a staff so thin that he could only spare one man for straight reporting work, he brought out a North American copy of the popular British newspapers — big headlines, an informal approach and a breezy, if shallow, outlook. He could not pretend to cover the news, especially the local news. Circulation dropped to 40,000."[89] And while relations with Woodward's improved after Warren's ouster and "amicable discussions" were held, according to Young, nothing more resulted and advertising sales by a decimated staff dwindled.

> When Warren left, the so-called "tin cup approach" stayed. The salesmen sold stock instead of advertisements. There was apparently no other way of meeting a monthly deficit that persisted in running well over the $50,000 mark, even after drastic economies. The scramble to raise funds to meet payrolls became part of life at the *Times*. Advertising salesmen were switched onto collecting receivables instead of soliciting new sales. Circulation men had to concentrate on collections rather than subscription drives.[90]

It seemed the *Times* could not shake its association with Warren, who continued with his plans for a nationwide chain of publicly funded offset dailies. In a front-page bid to divorce the *Times* from its founder, publisher Odlum issued a "Categorical Message" on June 15. "Notwithstanding gossip to the contrary, William Val Warren is no longer connected with *The Times* in any capacity," wrote Odlum. "He has no control over, or influence on, the policies which the paper will espouse. . . . It will be completely independent."[91] That brought action by Warren's lawyers, and an apology appeared a few days later. "It was not the intention of the publisher or the members of the Board of Directors to cast any aspersions whatsoever on the integrity and ability of Mr. Warren."[92] The financial shell game continued until finally the plug was pulled abruptly on August 6, with a final-edition headline of "We're Taking a Pause," announcing the paper's demise. Most of the remaining 150 employees had not been paid for the final eight weeks. Much of the July circulation income had gone toward the necessities of ink and newsprint. Suppliers had been refusing for months to deliver without immediate cash payment. Even up until the last day, directors of the newspaper were meeting with an unnamed Vancouver financier who was prepared to invest $500,000 in exchange for control of the *Times*, according to Young. The business editor said the offer was rejected by the directors, who felt the arrangement was "not compatible with the interests" of the other shareholders, "most of them little people who had been induced to invest in Vancouver's 'third daily newspaper.'"[93]

Webster's long analysis of "the somewhat pathetic end of a bold experiment," appeared in the next day's *Vancouver Sun*, having obviously been prepared well in advance. While giving Warren "full credit for achieving the seemingly impossible," he gave the compliment with a back-handed swipe. "Virtually by his own efforts . . . he did produce a newspaper. Little more can be said in his favor."[94] Like almost everyone else, Webster blamed Warren's naïveté, most of all. "There is no doubt in my mind that Warren never took off his rose-tinted glasses when predicting the financial future of his paper." But the broadcaster thought the paper might have succeeded under better management.

> At one time, in my view, *The Times* had a chance, but only under different and more efficient management. It is significant that until the end, *The Times* maintained a circulation of 40,000 copies a day. These were people who liked the paper and wanted to see direct competition for *The Sun* and *The Province*. Other Vancouver people obviously resented the apparent monopoly of Pacific Press. . . . *The Times*' promoters were banking, too, on advertiser resentment against Pacific Press. It failed to materialize.[95]

Webster lamented for the future of newspaper competition in Vancouver. "It will be many years, I fear, before another effort is made to build a third daily newspaper from the ground up."[96] In fact, the effect of competition from a third daily newspaper had only caused Pacific Press to prosper. The leading *Sun* "grew fatter," with its circulation now up to 240,000, observed former *Times* business editor Bruce Young in *Canadian Printer & Publisher*. "The day the *Times* announced it could carry on no longer, a top advertising man at the *Sun* expressed his regret," reported Young. "Not because he felt any remorse over the death of an upstart but because its very presence had spurred his salesmen to greater than usual efforts."[97] Warren blamed the Pacific Press monopoly for preventing his *Times* from taking flight. Fourteen years after his daily dream died, he outlined a fundamental problem posed by the presence of two well-established newspapers occupying the market in a joint monopoly. "Many advertisers, when first approached to buy an ad in the *Times*, gave a donation rather than meet the wrath of Pacific Press," Warren revealed. "Preferred lineage [*sic*] rates, preferred page positions and co-operation tidbits cannot be trifled with."[98]

Vancouver was a booming city with a rapidly growing population, but most of the migrants came from other parts of the country, and they did not always share the underdog sympathies of longtime residents. The popular indignation of native Vancouverites that Warren and his followers had been counting on to support the *Times* in its bid to fill a perceived newspaper vacuum had gone the same way as "the dynastic Cromie boast of a locally owned newspaper blown away by a prevailing easterly wind," according to Ben Metcalfe in a 1986 history of local newspapers for *Vancouver* magazine.

> What they found was that, while they did have a truly local newspaper in embryo, there was no vacuum nor enough popular indignation or money to support them. The truth was that Vancouver newspaper readers, comprising more and more "naturalized" than Old Vancouverites, were caring less and less that their newspapers were owned in the east.[99]

6 Siamese Twins

Ormond Turner was a *Province* columnist who might as well have come right out of the newspaper's comics page. According to former colleague Lyndon Grove, the mustachioed one-time actor was a "pre-Garry Trudeau 'Doonesbury' character, part Zonker, part Duke."[1] *Sun* business writer Alan Daniels thought Turner combined "a columnist's instincts with the ethics of a carny operator and explored the limits of both."[2] Turner once caused a row during a press conference by the visiting pop band Dave Clark Five. "The musicians, dallying with some groupies, were 45 minutes late appearing and said they would permit just one question per reporter," recalled *Sun* columnist Denny Boyd. "The first question came from Ormond Turner and it was: 'Who the hell do you jerks think you are, keeping us waiting?'"[3] Like many journalists of the day, Turner was a heavy drinker who was known for an ingenious method of making "last call" at the closest beer parlor to the *Province*'s Victory Square newsroom despite working a shift that ended at midnight. "At 11:55 p.m. he'd phone the Cecil Hotel and order 18 beers," recalled Boyd. "He and a mate would be there at 12:05, five minutes after closing time, and they'd knock those beers down and be gone by 12:30."[4]

As a columnist, Turner was the antithesis of Jack Scott. While Scott wrote his revered "Our Town" column in the *Vancouver Sun*, Turner's column in the *Province* was titled "Around Town" and was more of a gossip column, with items of interest to denizens of Vancouver's night clubs. And while the socialist Scott was union-friendly in his column, Turner reflected his newspaper's politics with an antagonism toward organized labor. One anti-union campaign Turner began researching at the beer parlor of Burnaby's Admiral Hotel caused such a furor that it prompted a Royal Commission in 1965, the only such investigation in the nation's history of allegations made in the press.[5] In his column on February 19, 1965, Turner began making charges of union vote-fixing in aid of candidates running in the 1963 federal election under the banner of the socialist New Democratic Party. A poll captain surveyed the voters list on the day after the April 8 election, looking for likely candidates for volunteer work during the next vote, Turner reported, adding that the man noticed some names appeared on the voters list in more than one riding.

> He found dozens more names which appeared on more than one list and expanded his search to every federal and provincial constituency in the province. He now has a list of 2,000 names which appeared fraudulently and after 5,000 hours of voluntary work on the lists has damning evidence of what appears to be a conspiracy to fake votes.[6]

One Granville Street address in Vancouver, Turner reported, had eighty-five registered voters supposedly living in a building so small that such a number of residents would have had to sleep seven to a room. Other addresses were found to be simply fictitious when checked. In a riding where the election result was so close it was still in dispute almost two years later, Turner reported his informant's claim of a 3 percent duplication in names. While noting provisions for voters to be enumerated in more than one riding, Turner claimed the irregularities found were simply too enormous to be explained away so easily. "A voter is allowed to register in two different places — at his home and his place of work if it is not the same locality and our man claims enumerators are deliberately being deceived. Someone is using the second registration as a vote for their candidate. There's a lot more to come on this."[7] Indeed there was. Three days later, Turner claimed he had corroboration in the form of a confession.

> A local union official has privately admitted that at least six B.C. unions have conspired to get NDP candidates elected fraudulently by entering fictitious names on the voters lists. He said that

> union members (and others) then went to the polls and used the phoney names to help elect NDP candidates. He didn't seem proud to have been involved in this illegal and shocking subversion of Canada's election laws.[8]

Setting out the alleged scheme in detail, Turner described how union hiring halls, after dispatching members to an out-of-town job during the seven-week registration period preceding an election, would ensure the workers were enumerated to vote at their work site as well as in their home ridings. This might happen more than once as tradesmen moved between jobs during the election campaign, Turner said, adding the duplicate registrations seemed to be done with a purpose. "On election day, SOMEONE casts these votes," charged the columnist. "In every riding where this has been proved to happen, the NDP has benefitted, with or without that party's knowledge."[9] The political fallout from Turner's columns began close to home but soon reached the nation's capital. Both the provincial legislature and federal parliament were in session at the time. In Victoria, NDP member Dave Barrett, a social worker elected in the Fraser Valley riding of Dewdney, rose in the House on February 23 to denounce Turner's reporting as "scurrilous" and a "vicious attack." Demanding that Turner be reprimanded, Barrett promised retribution. "There are laws in this land that protect us from these kinds of statements," warned Barrett. "Certain action that we will be taking will make sure this columnist doesn't forget his statement."[10]

The next day in Ottawa, NDP leader Tommy Douglas, the firebrand former Prairie preacher who had been elected in the suburban Vancouver riding of Burnaby-Coquitlam, was incensed when he received a copy of Turner's February 22 column in the mail. Usually Douglas and his socialist comrades were confined to bantering from the margins in parliament, always finishing a distant third in the polls to the Liberals and Conservatives, who alternated in forming the federal government. But the 1963 election had seen the Liberals gain only a few more seats than the incumbent Conservatives of Prime Minister John Diefenbaker and just fewer than the number required to form a majority government. With nine elected members, the NDP thus held the balance of power in parliament, which gave the party great influence with Liberal leader Lester Pearson, who ascended to prime minister by forming a minority government with NDP support. Douglas used his leverage with the government to push his party's progressive policies, including his own pet project, universal medicare.

Before the first item of business could be raised in the afternoon session of the House of Commons on February 24, Douglas rose on a question of privilege. What should have been a simple matter of ordering an investigation resulted in a bitter debate that saw the government defeated in a vote in which the NDP and Conservatives combined to outnumber the Liberals. If the question had been one of confidence in the government, and not a mere matter of member's privilege, the required result would have been dissolving parliament for an election call. "This copy of the *Vancouver Province* only came to my hand this morning," Douglas told parliament, holding aloft the February 22 edition and reading Turner's allegations. "This article casts a serious reflection upon the trade unions in the province of B.C., and calls into question the legality of the election of certain members of this party."[11] Douglas demanded an investigation into Turner's charges. "This apparently reasonable request could have been satisfied in five minutes," recalled Southam News political columnist Charles Lynch. "As it was, it took an hour and a half of parliamentary infighting in which the government got egg on its face, a speaker's ruling was reversed, and Turner achieved a measure of fame that caused several political columnists in the gallery to turn green with envy."[12]

Unknown to Douglas, Transport Minister Jack Pickersgill somehow had a copy of Turner's next column, which addressed the local howls of outrage following his initial allegations of electoral impropriety. Now it was the turn of a minister of the Crown to quote Turner in the House of Commons. "What's the NDP mad about?" Pickersgill read from Turner's reply. "I never said that their party was involved in a conspiracy to get phoney votes — I said that at least six trade unions were involved in a bid to get phoney votes for the NDP." The transport minister argued that a question of privilege, such as Douglas was raising, had to affect the House or one if its members. "But the author of this article has indicated clearly that he is making no accusation against the house or any member of it."[13] The intervention only served to inflame Douglas further. "This attempt to muddy the waters by bringing in something ... irrelevant has a very strange aroma," he snapped.[14] He moved for an investigation by the country's chief electoral officer, but Speaker Alan Macnaughton ruled his motion out of order. "Macnaughton got carried away by the fine legal points in Douglas' motion and neglected to bring some horse sense to bear on the problem," wrote Lynch. "He seemed to regret it the moment he had uttered it, but the deed was done, and the best he could do was invite Douglas to appeal his ruling."[15]

Douglas, according to the Canadian Press, was "bristling with anger" when he demanded an answer from Macnaughton. "I should like to know whether you are ruling that a statement saying there are members of this House, belonging to this party, who were elected by fraudulent means, is not a question of privilege?"[16] In the background, NDP member Colin Cameron, whose riding on Vancouver Island had been specifically mentioned in Turner's allegations, called the Speaker's ruling "bloody disgraceful" and suggested a more direct way of dealing with the matter. "I am giving notice now, Mr. Speaker," said Cameron, "that I shall make a substantive motion tomorrow to call this individual, Ormond Turner, before the bar of the house."[17] Ruling that motion also out of order, Macnaughton as much as agreed he had ruled too hastily on the motion Douglas had made. "I admit that I could have asked for a general discussion or for some comments before rendering my decision."[18]

Then Harold Winch rose. A founder of the NDP during the depths of the Depression thirty years earlier, when it was known as the Co-operative Commonwealth Federation (CCF), Winch had been elected eleven times since to serve federally or provincially, had never won his riding by less than 3,000 votes, and in the 1963 election had received more than twice as many votes as his nearest rival in working-class Vancouver East. "I have never felt so upset as I am at the present moment," intoned Winch, as some honorable members shouted "shame" in the background.

> Mr. Speaker, as the defender of elected members and the defender of democratic principles, are you saying that . . . we cannot ask for the protection of this house by demanding an investigation into the innuendo and lies directed at those six members in this group who come from British Columbia? I say, sir, that if there ever was a point of privilege, it is this.[19]

Macnaughton admitted having "personal sympathy" with the NDP's indignation over Turner's allegations. "Nevertheless, in effect, what is asked for today is an inquiry into a matter which happened . . . two years ago." When Douglas renewed his call for an investigation into Turner's charges, the Speaker practically pleaded that the NDP leader "obviously sees the difficulty of the Chair; nevertheless, rightly or wrongly a decision has been given. If the honorable member is dissatisfied with that decision I invite him to appeal it, because even the Chair is perhaps in the position of making an error." Douglas replied, "I am most distinctly not satisfied with Your Honour's ruling, and I therefore regretfully appeal that ruling."[20] When the yeas and nays were heard, Macnaughton declared majority support for his ruling, but when some House mathematicians rose to question his hearing, division was called and MPs were polled. "One by one, Liberals stood and were counted on an issue that none of them knew the slightest thing about a few moments earlier," wrote Lynch.[21] The vote count was 114 to 108 against the speaker's ruling, and an investigation into the allegations of the *Province* columnist was ordered. The result was "a blow *The Province* met boldly," according to Doug Collins in a *Saturday Night* magazine column. "Ormond was shown on the front page, looking serious, a putative three pounds of evidence spread before him," noted Collins. "Editorially, the paper crowed and flapped its wings at all the great doings."[22] The next day the *Province*'s front-page recap of events in parliament noted that "none of the members could explain how such a simple issue had sparked so much debate Wednesday and resulted in such heated argument on both sides."[23]

When the office of chief electoral officer turned out to be vacant, B.C. Supreme Court Chief Justice Nathan Nemetz, a longtime labor lawyer and mediator, was appointed a one-man Royal Commission and began investigating Turner's charges, enlisting the aid of the RCMP. Within a month, hearings began at the Hotel Vancouver. Called to testify on the first day, Turner revealed that 90 percent of his published information came from Coquitlam druggist Morland Brown, who on election day had been a Liberal poll captain in the riding where Douglas was elected. Brown had telephoned him with the information about duplicate entries he had counted in thousands of hours spent poring over voters lists, Turner told Nemetz, noting evidence of many incorrect addresses as well. Under cross-examination by lawyer Tom Berger, appearing for the B.C. Federation of Labour, Turner testified the source for his allegation that the duplicate entries had been arranged by unions to benefit the NDP was a union member, whose name he could not recall, whom he had met in 1958 at the Admiral Hotel beer parlor in Burnaby. "I believe I knew his name at the time," Turner testified. "This is called backgrounding a story."[24]

Brown, described in the *Province* as "quiet-spoken. . . . slight, scholarly," testified he first noticed duplicate voters list entries while serving as a polling-station scrutineer for Burnaby-Coquitlam Liberal candidate Tom Kent, erstwhile editor of the *Winnipeg Free Press*. He told Nemetz he had spent as many as eight hours a day going through lists and found that most of the duplications involved workers in logging camps. In one mountainous poll in the Burnaby-Coquitlam riding, he said, he found that 42 percent, or twenty-nine of the poll's sixty-eight registered voters, were also listed in other B.C. ridings. But he admitted he had no evidence of wrongdoing. "I have no proof of any illegal voting and I never claimed I had."[25] Getting to the bottom of Turner's claimed corroboration in the form of a union official's confession required a three-week adjournment of the hearings. RCMP officers searched in the interim for his informants, the names of whom had been kept secret during testimony. When the inquiry resumed, according to the *Province*, "a cloak-and-dagger element descended on the usual calm atmosphere" with the testimony of two "mystery witnesses."[26]

The source for Turner's confession claim turned out to be publicist Lyn Morrow, the Conservative candidate in Burnaby-Coquitlam, who testified she had discussed with Brown his findings about name duplications. Investigating further, she told Nemetz she passed on to Turner details of a conversation she later had over lunch with an official of the B.C. Federation of Labour. "I said, 'Was Tommy [Douglas] responsible for the double listings too?' and he said, 'Oh, no, we did that.'"[27] The first thing the named labor man knew about his involvement in the brouhaha was when he was summonsed by the RCMP while at home the night before his testimony. "I must say I was fantastically angry at the things now laid to my doorstep," John McNevin told Nemetz the next day. "I've been up all night." McNevin, the Fed's secretary-treasurer, testified he could recall no conversation such as Morrow had related to Turner.

With testimony completed, lawyers Berger and John Laxton, representing the NDP, took turns flaying Turner and the *Province* publicly. "He is not only incompetent, but also malicious and irresponsible," Berger told Nemetz, calling "fantasy" the columnist's claims of impropriety.[28] "Turner's story was hatched by a confused Liberal, brought to life by a treacherous Conservative, written by a dishonest columnist and published by an irresponsible newspaper," Laxton added. "No language is too strong when applied to Turner. You should use the knife to cut out the cancer this kind of journalism creates."[29] The best Turner's lawyer could do was point out that some discrepancies had indeed been found on the

1963 election lists. Collins noted that *Province* coverage of the hearings into its columnist's wild allegations became increasingly tentative. "As time went on the paper backed into its leads more and more nervously," recalled Collins. "Towards the end, it was reduced to giving prominence to its lawyer's claim that the columnist was a man who did what he thought proper for his country."[30]

Nemetz released his report in August, reaching "the ineluctable conclusion that nothing of substance emerges that would support any of the serious charges made by Mr. Turner."[31] While finding Brown "an honest and straightforward witness," Nemetz added that the columnist went well beyond the information he had in making his allegations. "It appears to me that in a mood of zealous investigatory journalism Mr. Turner drew inferences from Mr. Brown's statements and material which cannot be supported."[32] Turner's column the next morning was apologetic in a brief lead item. "It was something I thought should be looked into," Turner explained. "It has been, and that's that. No malice was intended anywhere, and where any hurt was felt, I'm sorry."[33] Noting that Turner's column soon disappeared from *Province* pages, Collins called it "The Story That Never Was" and a "real humiliation" for thc morning daily. "It isn't often that a newspaper is forced to put on sackcloth and sit on the stool of repentance."[34] Turner retired from the *Province* shortly thereafter and became editor of the monthly magazine *Phenomena*, published by the Vancouver Flying Saucer Club, of which he was elected president in 1968.[35]

By the end of 1965, the long-awaited Pacific Press Building was finally ready for occupation. The mammoth 350,000-square-foot, four-storey edifice occupied almost the entire square block between the main thoroughfare of Granville Street and adjacent Hemlock Street to the east, and between 6th and 7th Avenues uptown, just south of the Granville Street Bridge, which spanned False Creek and connected the downtown peninsula with the rest of the city. The site had not been the original choice of either Southam, which had purchased property to the west for a possible plant site on False Creek near the south end of the Burrard Bridge, or the *Sun*, which had bought up parcels of land adjacent to its Sun Tower with an eye to adding a new printing plant next door. In their quest for more printing capacity to extend their circulation lead over the

Province during the ITU strike, the Cromies had acquired in 1949 two used presses from the *Indianapolis News*, which had been made redundant by its amalgamation of production facilities with the *Indianapolis Star*. A one-storey "Mechanical Building" was built on Beatty Street, next to the Sun Tower, to house the presses. Completed in 1950, the building was intended to be built higher as necessary, with six or seven additional storeys eventually added. Chicago architect Morton Pereira, a specialist in newspaper plant design, was hired in 1956 to draw plans and commission engineering surveys for the completed building.[36]

Even after the amalgamation that formed Pacific Press the next year, the new partners planned to build on the *Sun* site adjacent to the Georgia Viaduct until further engineering studies raised doubts about whether the *Sun*'s Mechanical Building could be expanded sufficiently to house the presses eventually required to print both newspapers. "These doubts arose because of the limited amount of land held or procurable and because of certain questions relating to air rights," noted the Restrictive Trade Practices Commission in 1960.[37] The Granville Street site was thus acquired in the early 1960s and Pereira was commissioned again to design the Pacific Press Building, which was presented in print as a futuristic design that even incorporated a roof-top helicopter landing pad. But construction was delayed with the 1963 change in ownership of the *Sun*, and when the South Granville soil was finally broken in early March 1964, the original $5 million cost estimate began spiraling out of sight due to construction difficulties and labor shortages. It took until the end of October for the foundation to be excavated and the concrete poured.

The building was designed to be built entirely of concrete rather than structural steel, and use of a new lightweight concrete caused much of the delay. "Application of lightweight concrete is a new trend in high-rise construction but is practically unheard of in anything under 20 stories," reported the *Journal of Commerce*.[38] The biggest drawback of lightweight concrete turned out to be its sensitivity to moisture, which in the rainy Vancouver climate proved problematic. "It is very, very sensitive to fluctuations in moisture content," noted R.G. Saunders of contractor Smith Bros. & Wilson. "This has to be very rigidly controlled."[39] The project was labor-intensive and skilled trades were in short supply, with longer hours and extra shifts needed at overtime rates for such classifications as bricklayers, stonemasons, plasterers, tinsmiths, tile setters, acoustic ceiling and insulation applicators.[40] By the end of 1965, when the project was finally completed, the original cost estimate had almost tripled to $14 million. When finished, the boxish structure was hailed by the *Journal of Commerce* as "evidence that imaginative approaches to design beyond functional practicality are possible by ingenious application of conventional construction methods and materials — concrete." It even found artistic merit in the gleaming new structure.

> The exterior of the building is clad in a skin of white pre-cast quartz aggregate concrete panels, which are articulated to attain a pleasant play of light and shade as the sun shifts from east to west. Also at night when the building is floodlit one gets an equally delightful distribution of shadows. This was achieved by just a simple sloping of the top and bottom of the panels. There is an ever-changing kaleidoscope of shades as one moves about the building. The material is expressive of contemporary technology.[41]

The design was described as "a deliberate break . . . with the steel-and-glass cube concept that has become popular architecture, limiting the scope of expression and creativity of the architect and making cities dull, boring and looking alike."[42] The aim was to create a design with "all the virtues of classicism and yet is a modern expression of today's homes without being just another box," said architect Adrian Lozano. "We tried from the very beginning not to lose the basic expression of the concrete frame."[43] The concrete expressionism even extended from the columns on the outside to those on the inside. "No attempt was made to hide the columns anywhere," noted the *Journal of Commerce*. "In the press room, for example, they have been treated very much like a painting by Piet Mondrian, who was the strictest and most 'architectural' of all abstract painters."[44]

From form to functionality, the building was ultramodern and innovative for the mid-1960s. One feature in use at only one other printing plant in North America was an automated system to deliver each day's required newsprint from a storage area to the presses. "The paper doesn't feel the touch of human hand until it is picked up as bundles of newspapers at the truck bays," reported *Canadian Printer & Publisher*.[45] The Pacific Press Building also was one of the first newspaper plants in the world to be fully air-conditioned, including the pressroom, but it contained neither boilers nor furnaces to heat it, instead recycling the body heat of employees and heat generated by lighting, presses, and the forty tons of molten lead used to compose the letterpress printing plates, which had to be kept at a constant 590 degrees Fahrenheit.[46] The recycling system had its skeptics, according to *Province* reporter Tom Hazlitt, but "to the surprise of traditionalists, the new-fangled heat pump system ... worked well."[47] *Province* employees were especially impressed with the sparkling new premises, said Hazlitt, considering their former quarters at Victory Square. "The tasteful furnishings and polished floors were a little overwhelming to newspaper veterans, most of whom have spent their careers in surroundings that can only be described as grubby."[48]

The move into the new building was set for the publication break over Christmas, which also included a weekend, and required 200 employees and movers working through Christmas Eve and Christmas Day. Two giant cranes moved heavy equipment, and vehicles of all types shuttled back and forth in a procession across False Creek bridges in snowy weather and treacherous road conditions, according to Hazlitt. "At one point, the two giant cranes, four radio-controlled trucks, seven forklift vehicles and 12 moving vans were in simultaneous service."[49]

Printing was performed at both the new location and the Sun Tower's Mechanical Building for almost a year before the new presses were phased in. The entire third floor of the new Pacific Press Building was devoted to editorial and composing operations, with a joint clipping library separating the *Sun* and *Province* newsrooms at the front of the building and providing a meeting point for competing journalists. The cohabitation arrangement reflected the senior status of the *Sun*, which got the 6th Avenue side for its newsroom, overlooking downtown and the spectacular North Shore mountains when they could be seen through the rain clouds. The *Province* newsroom was relegated to the upslope side, which provided no such impressive view, except from the publisher's office on the western Granville Street side, where a glimpse northward could be caught through store fronts. Upon its departure from historic Victory Square, which had been landscaped at Southam's expense to surround the cenotaph laid after the First World War, a statue was erected to mark the *Province*'s presence across the street for sixty-seven years, as its old building became a department store. Unveiled by park board chairman George Puil in 1967, the memorial was described in the *Province* as forming "the letters V and P in a modernistic design of solid cast aluminum."[50]

More modern art was commissioned to adorn the new premises of

Pacific Press, including a reflecting pool outside fed by water from a fountainhead of black Canadian granite carved in the form of a shell by sculptor William Koochin. In the building's lobby was a brass-and-steel sculpture by George Norris "representing the newspaper industry in an abstract form."[51] The 36-year-old Victoria sculptor declined to attend the unveiling of his unusual artwork, which had been almost a year in the making, at the Pacific Press Building's official opening on March 14, 1966, because "he felt the structure might mean different things to different people," according to the *Sun*.[52] Instead the ten-foot-high sculpture of a figure holding aloft a web of printing plates containing headlines from Vancouver's past was unveiled by *Sun* publisher Stu Keate, who described it as "an endeavour to epitomize the spirit of communications."[53] In an essay in that day's editions of the *Sun*, Norris described his sculpture as "kind of a fantasy" that simply came to him as he worked. "It could be thought of as the none-too-gentle transformation of three-dimensional life into two-dimensional print," explained Norris. "Then again, maybe the whole thing suggests a sculpture of Babel . . . so many incomprehensible and misunderstood words!"[54]

But it was the twelve-foot-high bronze sculpture by Jack Harman of a four-member "Newspaper Family," comprising mother, father, son, and infant daughter, at the front of the building that drew the most comment and even embroiled the two newspapers, according to Keate, "in a quarrel which set the whole town laughing."

> With some of the prudery common to medical art-work, Harmon [*sic*] had presented the two males without reproductive equipment. . . . When the finished work was hoisted into place, in a garden in front of Pacific Press, it was discovered that the young boy had suddenly sprouted a penis. The father had not. This was, at the very least, a biological contradiction which puzzled many viewers and enraged Fred Auger, who argued that Harmon [*sic*] had breached his contract with the ad-lib appendage.[55]

This soon became the object of considerable public outcry, exposed as it was to passersby on one of Vancouver's busiest thoroughfares. Religious groups registered their opposition to Vancouver's first nude statue, according to Keate. "An elderly woman telephoned me in near-hysteria to cry: 'I have to avert my eyes when the bus stops in front of your building.

How *dare* you show that little boy's privates in public!'"[56] As Auger tried to pass the embarrassing work on to the Vancouver Art Gallery, only to have the donation vetoed by Keate, the *Sun* publisher recalled that the pranksters came out in full force. "After a series of clandestine raids, the offending organ became a sort of hitching-post for a variety of ornaments: a glazed doughnut, a garland of buttercups, even a condom."[57] In one memorable incident, the infamous University of B.C. engineers, notorious for nocturnally hoisting Volkswagen Beetles into improbable locations, were believed responsible for painting the controversial appendage bright red. *Province* reporter Kathy Tait caught the culprits "red-handed" as she drove past the building early on a Sunday morning in August 1966, calling police from a nearby gas station.[58] The color enhancement soon became compounded, according to Keate, when a maintenance man was dispatched to remove the paint. "The emissary assigned to this task (who said it was embarrassing to perform such an act on busy Granville Street) unfortunately decided to do the job with Brillo. The result was twofold: the red gave way to a gleaming bronze, and the statue was immediately christened by staff members as 'Le coq d'or.'"[59]

Before the first anniversary of the building they shared, relations between the Pacific Press publishers became more seriously strained. A controversy involving the church where Keate was a parishioner saw the *Sun* publisher pictured on the front page of the *Province*, which led to an angry exchange of correspondence between him and Auger. CBC television broadcast part of a "psychedelic service" featuring jazz music, poetry readings, and a "go-go girl" at University Hill United Church near the end of November 1966. The resulting furor led to a vote of confidence in Rev. James McKibbon, minister at Keate's church, St. Anselm's. McKibbon had devised the psychedelic service, which was described by another minister as an "experiment to simulate brain expansion which LSD users claim to experience."[60] The vote was held in the week before Christmas, by secret ballot of parishioners, and *Province* reporter Malcolm Turnbull was turned away at the church door as an interloper. The morning paper's front-page account the next day featured a picture of the *Sun* publisher with a cutline that read "Stuart Keate tried to keep press out." According to the *Province* report, the press was barred from the meeting. "Persons entering the church were screened and questioned to ensure they were active parishioners," reported the *Province*. "*Vancouver Sun* publisher Stuart Keate, a member of the congregation, stood at the door to identify any newsmen so they would not be admitted."[61] Keate, who had long been an outspoken champion of press freedom, was furious and sent a memo to Auger charging him with "dirty pool."

> To send out a photographer to take a "grab shot" of me through a church window, at a private parish meeting — at which I had no formal or official role at all — is hitting below the belt. If the publisher of *The Province* was involved in any news story, it would be referred to me as a matter of policy, so I cannot excuse you. The total effect of your picture, story and cut-lines is to portray me as a suppressor of news, which is a monstrous and vicious distortion of my whole life in the press.[62]

The *Sun* publisher complained to Auger that it was "not the first time you have shafted me," and pointed to the reprinting in the *Province* of "the only hostile editorial in Canada" about Keate's mediation of the CBC dispute over the firing of the hosts of the controversial television news magazine show *This Hour Has Seven Days* as a "similar distortion" of the facts. "I have always regarded you as a friend of mine but it is now quite obvious that you are not," Keate's memo concluded. "In my book, you are not to be trusted."[63] Auger tried three times to call Keate, who admitted to Dick Malone that he refused to speak to him. "I suppose in due course I will but I am going to make perfectly plain to him that my position is unchanged and that, from now on, we will operate at arm's length," Keate wrote in a letter to the Winnipeg-based general manager of the FP Publications chain. "This will strain the atmosphere around Pacific Press, and make life more difficult, but I feel very keenly about this thing. He has deliberately lied."[64] The genesis of the story, Keate told Malone, came when he was in Auger's office on an unrelated matter and mentioned he would be in attendance at the church meeting that evening.

> I told him that I had been asked to "be on the lookout for the press" and laughingly commented: "What a job for a guy in my position!" Fred laughed too, and agreed that it was impossible. When I got to the church I pointed out to the people's warden, a lawyer named Russ Twining, that I couldn't be placed in such a position. He

> agreed and asked me if I would witness signatures of parishioners as they signed the [membership verification] document.[65]

Unable to get Keate to speak to him on the phone for two days, Auger apologized in a memo but denied any responsibility for the fiasco. "Surely you haven't been counting on me to keep you out of the paper," wrote Auger. "I don't expect it either and that's why I stay as far as possible from road blocks and public affairs."[66] Keate was not disposed to forgive his Pacific Press counterpart, replying, "Your apology is of small comfort to me, since I have been demeaned and defamed across Canada by your lousy, untrue page 1 story and sleazy picture."[67] The *Province* picture and story had been sent out on the Canadian Press wire service and appeared in newspapers across the country, but a belated correction had been sent out after a CP editor, according to Keate, "smelled something fishy and began to check around."[68] His investigation found that Keate neither knew nor talked to the *Province* reporter, who was instead turned away by a vestryman, and that the story ran on "orders from higher ups."[69] Keate told Auger that, being a former chairman of the Freedom of the Press Committee of the Canadian Daily Newspaper Publishers Association, he had received "a spate of calls from across Canada" asking why he was keeping the press out of meetings.

> I have for 35 years in the press, fought for press freedoms. . . . As president of CDNPA and CP I have written and spoken on the subject for the past 17 years. So you shafted me. Okay; now we know the ground rules. If we weren't in Pacific Press I'd sue you down to your socks. Under the circumstances, we have to live under the same roof. To me, it is not a very pleasant prospect.[70]

7 The Legend

Bruce Hutchison was a legend in Canadian journalism by the 1960s. Starting his newspaper career as a sportswriter on the *Victoria Times* in 1918 right out of high school at age 16, he also wrote fiction for U.S. magazines such as *Collier's* and *The Saturday Evening Post*, often illustrating the pieces himself. One of his short stories, "Park Avenue Logger," was made into a Hollywood feature film, and he wrote a weekly column on Canadian affairs for the Boston-based *Christian Science Monitor* for more than fifty years. He also wrote more than 100 articles for *Maclean's* magazine. "His life output was something like 20 million words, one or two of which (so the joke went) were poorly chosen," noted *Sun* columnist Vaughn Palmer.[1] Hutchison never attended university but received four honorary degrees, and was Canada's greatest journalist according to many, including *Sun* columnist Denny Boyd. "He turned words into jewellery, his thoughts bursting off the page with the brilliant clarity of diamonds."[2]

Hutchison covered Ottawa and Washington and other world capitals as a correspondent for the *Times*, the *Province*, and the *Vancouver Sun*, winning three National Newspaper Awards. He wrote fifteen books, receiving three Governor General's Awards for works such as *The Incredible Canadian*, a biography of Prime Minister Mackenzie King, and *The Unknown Country*, a best-seller that, according to longtime *Maclean's* editor Peter C. Newman, "came as close as any text in defining Canada's identity." Newman described the tall, bespectacled editorialist as "crusty" and deemed him the "dean and mentor" of English-language print journalism in Canada.

> His talent was to draw large conclusions from small events, and his graceful literary style helped obliterate the distance that usually separates a journalist from his subjects. . . . Perhaps Hutchison's most endearing quality was his almost physical affection for Canada, a passionate love affair that colored everything he said and wrote. . . . He was perpetually angry with any politician bold enough to pretend he could run Canada, yet he also had a deep sympathy for just how tough a country it was to govern.[3]

Growing up in Victoria during the 1930s, Pierre Berton regularly read Hutchison's "Loose Ends" column in the *Times* and considered it "one of the best newspaper columns ever published in Canada."[4] Berton credited Hutchison's books, such as *The Fraser* and *The Struggle for the Border*, with turning him from a journalist into an historian. "I owe him a very great debt, for it was he who first taught me that the Canadian past could be interesting," recalled Berton. "His books of popular history have been my single most important influence."[5] Hutchison's column in the *Times* ran for thirty-five years, even after he went to work covering the legislature for the *Province* in 1929 and then switched to the *Vancouver Sun* in 1938.

When the Second World War began, Hutchison was Ottawa correspondent for the *Sun*, which dispatched him to Washington in 1940 to cover the U.S. presidential election campaign. At the behest of Prime Minister King, Hutchison was recruited for a secret propaganda campaign to help influence American public opinion toward entering the war. On tour with Republican candidate Wendell Willkie, an isolationist who opposed American involvement in another European conflict, Hutchison's clandestine assignment was to meet with local editors along the campaign route and persuade them against a policy of neutrality. "The whole notion of such unofficial diplomacy struck me as ridiculous, and no worse candidate could have been chosen for it — a secret agent out of some farce by Evelyn Waugh, a script written for James Bond," Hutchison recalled. "But as I was doing nothing of use to my country in wartime I agreed to attempt this mad mission."[6] While Hutchison doubted the effectiveness of his secret assignment, Willkie became an interventionist following his narrow defeat at the polls by Franklin D. Roosevelt, and soon the U.S. was supplying war aid to Britain.

Later in the war, Hutchison was assigned by Henry Luce's *Fortune* magazine to profile the great *Winnipeg Free Press* editor John F. Dafoe. In Winnipeg on that assignment he met Victor Sifton, the paper's owner and publisher. When Dafoe died in 1944, Sifton offered to make Hutchison his successor, but the West Coast native refused to move from his home on Vancouver Island to the frigid climes of prairie Manitoba. To describe his rainforest retreat, Hutchison had coined the term "Lotusland," which eventually grew in general usage to refer to the entire province of British Columbia. He likened his rustic estate at Shawnigan Lake, north of Victoria, to the paradise found by the sailors of Ulysses in Tennyson's epic poem *The Lotus Eaters*. "No one who has entered here ever wanted to leave again."[7] As a compromise, Sifton agreed to make Hutchison co-editor of the *Free Press* and a columnist while allowing him to remain on the coast, and the arrangement was agreeable to the westerner. "By this time I had seen that my own departure from the *Sun* would suit its new publisher, Don Cromie, equally well, and I realized, too, that he needed a man who would live in Vancouver, a sacrifice of convenience that I was not prepared to make," Hutchison recalled. "Besides, Cromie's idea of journalism and mine were separated by several light years, at least."[8]

But Sifton's quest for a top-flight editor-in-residence to replace Dafoe soon saw Tom Kent, an editorial writer for *The Economist* in London, hired as Hutchison's *Free Press* co-editor. "Among all the journalists of my acquaintance, this pale and icy young man was the most facile, a wonder of speed and self-confidence," Hutchison recalled. "Where we old-timers might take two hours to write a leader [editorial] he could dash it off in ten minutes, letter-perfect, in the *Economist*'s bravura style of metaphor and sarcasm."[9] Hutchison found that he and Kent differed over what the British Columbian's contribution to the newspaper's editorial page should be.

> Kent understandably did not want me as more than a casual contributor to the *Free Press*. He wanted younger men by his side who could be trained in his luxuriant writing style and the new, foolproof economic theories imported from London to enlighten Canada's darkness. . . . As Kent put it, I could write about the woods, the birds, and the flowers — easy work as he imagined, never having descended to such trivia.[10]

At his camp in the woods around Shawnigan Lake, Hutchison was digging a new hole for his outhouse when Don Cromie wandered by and, in "an absurd scene," offered him the editor's job at the *Vancouver Sun*.

"Hardly pausing in my work, I declined with thanks," recalled Hutchison. "I continued to decline for the next several days as Cromie and his wife stayed at our camp and he continued to press me. In my demented scale of values, a good privy, symbol of the outdoor life, stood far ahead of any office job on the mainland."[11] But being on the outs with Kent in Winnipeg, Hutchison was open to offers — as long as they did not require him to leave his beloved Vancouver Island. When he turned down Max Bell in 1950 for the publisher's job at his original employer, the *Victoria Times*, Hutchison had recommended Stuart Keate, then Canadian bureau chief for *Time* magazine in Montreal. Sending Keate a note of congratulations when he took the publisher's job, Hutchison dropped a broad hint that his services were available. "I remember when the *Times* was a great little paper and I sometimes wish I were back in it."[12] Keate recalled he could barely believe his luck in having "the best newspaper editor in Canada *volunteering* his services to his old alma mater."[13] Keate quickly enlisted Hutchison to write three columns a week, and when *Times* editor Harry Hudges retired a year later, Keate offered Hutchison the job of rebuilding the newspaper from its moribund state into a strong editorial voice. "One rainy night in the summer of 1952, Stu Keate came stumbling down our trail at the lake, that day's edition of the *Times* burning in his hand as a makeshift lantern, and offered me the editorship of his paper on my own outrageous conditions," recalled Hutchison. "I could work, he said, in my house or the office, the hours unspecified, the pay handsome (and quickly doubled by Max)."[14] According to Palmer, who edited a collection of Hutchison's writings, he was one of the most influential editorialists in Canada in the middle decades of the twentieth century.

> His opinions were widely cited, sometimes on the floor of the House of Commons, and once, in 1952, the members of the B.C. Legislature were so outraged by one of his opinions in the *Victoria Times* that they came within a few votes of summoning his publisher before the bar of the House to apologize. Hutchison responded by reprinting the offending editorial on the front page, just in case anyone missed it the first time. (The offending editorial was one of a series that won its author the National Newspaper Award for 1952.)[15]

The arrangement at the *Times* worked well, according to Hutchison, because he and Keate got along famously due to the younger publisher's "instinct for news, his zest for life, and his natural gifts as a leader of men."[16] When FP Publications bought the *Vancouver Sun* in 1963, Dick Malone, general manager of the growing chain, convinced Hutchison to apply his talents to supervising that paper's editorial page as he had that of the *Free Press* and the *Times*, by remote control from Shawnigan Lake. After Keate was appointed nine months later to replace Cromie as publisher of the *Sun*, they joined forces again, determined to remake the newspaper into a more responsible journal. Its apprehensive staff waited, "probably for an attempt to make their gaudy, boisterous paper a dull echo of the sober *Winnipeg Free Press*," according to Hutchison. "This was the last thing that Dick, Stu, or I intended. All we wanted was a *Sun* with more content and less froth, more world news and less local crime, more accuracy and less sensation."[17] According to Allan Fotheringham, *Sun* staffers were immediately buoyed by the simultaneous presence and absence of Hutchison, who brought a touch of class to the newspaper's pages. "Hutchison was an idol to those of us who knew him, not only for the languorous ease of his writing but for the astounding — miraculous — way he conducted his entire career," recalled Fotheringham. "The miracle was never going to the office. A genius! No semi-literate editors to deal with. No fools at the next desk. No niggling accountants badgering over some expense account."[18]

By 1969, five years after Keate and Hutchison assumed editorial control of the *Sun*, its circulation was up to 261,000, placing it second in Canada behind only the *Toronto Star* and marginally ahead of the *Globe and Mail*. The paper was also a rich moneymaker, with the largest classified advertising linage in the country. It helped that the *Sun* had the evening field to itself, as working-class Vancouver had traditionally run counter to the trend toward morning newspapers in other cities and been, according to Keate, a "tough morning-paper town."[19] The result was that as circulation of the *Sun* soared past 260,000, that of the morning *Province* dipped perilously close to 100,000. The *Sun*'s new corporate owner began to find the morning paper's losses a drain on its bottom line, as under the Pacific Press agreement profits and losses of each publication were split equally. FP Publications was also less generous to its workers than the Cromies had been and insisted to new partner Southam that a harder line be taken against the Pacific Press unions. Southam, having been burned by the International Typographical Union (ITU) during the 1946 *Province* strike, was reluctant to attempt publication behind picket lines as all three Toronto papers — the *Star*, *Telegram*, and *Globe and Mail* — had been doing since a strike by printers that began during the summer of 1964. Initially using managers and office staff to operate the equipment abandoned by ITU members, the papers did not miss an edition and later hired replacement printers and defecting strikers to continue publication as the dispute dragged on for seven years.[20] The Toronto papers launched a joint recruitment campaign across the country to hire replacements, but their ads that summer of 1964, which offered "permanent positions with excellent salaries" to experienced printers, were barred from the Pacific Press papers by ITU members, who refused to handle them as boycotted work, or "hot."[21] The ads did appear in other dailies composed by ITU printers, including in the *Columbian* in nearby New Westminster.

The success of the Toronto newspapers in publishing with replacement workers did not escape the notice of Pacific Press management. Even before the move into the automated new plant in 1965, preparations were made for training non-union personnel in the use of composing room equipment prior to bargaining for a new contract. The operation, in a building adjacent to the old Sun Tower, was protested by the ITU's Len Guy as a "strikebreaking school." He told a meeting of the Vancouver and District Labour Council in November 1964 that he confronted Ed Benson, general manager of Pacific Press, about the training facility. "He said the school was in addition to the company's strike insurance of more than $1 million and company representatives also said the company had contacted non-union firms for the purpose of setting advertisements if a strike was engaged in," Guy told his brother unionists.[22]

Relations between Benson and the printers' leader became strained that fall when the Pacific Press GM was quoted as telling hoteliers in a speech that labor negotiators "are not the equal to their counterparts." Benson, a metallurgical engineer by profession who had worked as a mining company executive before heading Pacific Press in 1959, told a *Sun* reporter he had been misquoted. "Trade union leadership is more in need of executive training than is its management counterpart," Benson claimed was his actual wording. "They are not equals in the sense of economic training."[23] He had made similar statements the previous year in an interview with *Province* business columnist Pat Carney. "One thing I've run across — with some union people — and I don't say it looking down my long nose — is that I try to outline our plan, but when I get to cash flow, I lose them."[24] Carney described Benson as looking more like a union official than a management executive. "A big man, Ed Benson prowls his office in his shirt sleeves, chain-smoking cigars — real ones, not the elegant kind."[25] She reported he was frustrated by dealing with unionists who just did not understand his plans, such as those he devised for retraining craftsmen displaced by new technology to do work in other departments. "I have run into more obstacles than an Orangeman would have if he ran in the recent election for Pope," said Benson.[26]

After the papers moved into the new Pacific Press Building at the end of 1965, Benson resumed his preparations for publishing during a strike in case contract negotiations were unsuccessful in 1967. He resurrected his school for training replacement workers and added a new tactic with applications to the federal Department of Transport and city hall for helicopter landing rights on the Pacific Press parking lot. The company claimed the purpose of a heliport was for "relaying photographs, newspaper staff or visitors from the airport or games at Empire Stadium."[27] The unions suspected the move was designed to allow Pacific Press to bring in replacement workers during a strike without having to cross a picket line.

The first union to have its collective agreement expire that year was the Newspaper Guild, on June 30. Local Guild officers had obtained permission from the union's international office for an unusually long three-year deal in 1964 in exchange for job security guarantees going into the new Pacific Press Building, and the company wanted to continue that precedent to lock up its non-mechanical staff contractually until mid-1970. That proposal was a non-starter with the Guild, and talks broke down in May with a conciliator being named. The assisted negotiations broke off on the eve of contract expiration, and the following week the conciliator issued his report, recommending a 10 percent wage increase over a two-year contract. That was readily accepted by the company, but rejected by negotiators for the Guild. With rising inflation, they wanted an increase from $147.50 to $200 weekly for the "key rate" classification for senior reporters and advertising salesmen. That amounted to a 35 percent increase, and to back its demands the Guild took a strike vote in early

October. The result was 81 percent in favor of a walkout, but Guild officer Bill McLeman announced that 48-hour strike notice would not be immediately served in hopes of resuming negotiations.[28]

Carney, who by 1967 was writing her business column for the *Sun*, expressed dismay at the turn of events. "Frankly, I don't have the faintest idea what it is all about," she confessed to readers. "What we want is more money, only that wasn't what we voted on. And, of course, nobody actually wants to go on strike. Only we apparently voted for a strike just to make sure that it wasn't necessary to go on strike. You follow?"[29] From what she was able to discover from buttonholing union and management officials in the halls of the Pacific Press Building, Carney said she discovered the real issue was not money but the Guild's attempt at union solidarity by having ITU observers sit in on its talks with the company. "They won't discuss anything while we have the printers sitting with us in negotiations," Carney quoted one unnamed shop steward as saying. Management was adamant, she reported, quoting an executive anonymously in response. "We might want to tell your union something which we wouldn't want to tell another union," reasoned the manager. Guild members were confused about whether management was bluffing or out to break the union, according to Carney. "The real issue is whether you support your union," she quoted a co-worker as saying. "If you vote no to striking, Management will figure that the union doesn't have the backing of the workers, and you won't get as much money. If you vote yes, Management will take it as a show of strength and will concede more ground."[30]

Meanwhile, Pacific Press management opened up a new front in its battle with the newspaper unions, taking the pressmen to court. When that union asked for a government-supervised strike vote on October 6, along with the printers, mailers, and stereotypers, the company claimed that a clause in the agreement the pressmen had signed separately from the other craft unions in 1965 provided for binding arbitration if a new contract could not be negotiated. Company lawyer George Robson went to B.C. Supreme Court for an injunction against a walkout by pressmen. "Robson said that if the pressmen's union does go on strike, Pacific Press will have great difficulty in producing newspapers, 'if at all,'" reported the *Province*.[31] The bid failed, however, when the judge, according to the *Sun*, ruled that "he could not conclude on the material before him that the union would act illegally and strike prior to the termination of its agreement with the company."[32] Talks with the craft unions resumed following expiration of their contracts on October 31, made more urgent by a government-supervised strike vote that passed by more than 90 percent. By the second week of November, the war of words between Benson and Guy escalated over the company's continuing operation of its mechanical training school. Guy said Benson told him "he is making intensive preparations to produce *The Sun* and *Province* without our help."[33] Benson responded the next day with an offer to shut down the school on one condition. In a letter to the ITU, he noted that the union had taken a strike vote and thus could serve 48-hour strike notice on the company at any time. Benson said he was "unwilling to leave the company completely unprotected" and suggested as a "mutual gesture of good faith" that the sides compromise.

> I will stop the preparations which are now underway, and you will agree that for every day from the date of cessation, you will add one day to the period which you will use to formally advise us of strike action. By way of example: if our bargaining lasts, say, 14 days and there is an impasse and you decide to serve strike notice, you would then give us 14 days' plus 48 hours' notice. I think this is an honorable arrangement to settle our difference of opinion.[34]

The company also announced it would accept an offer of mediation by the provincial labor department.[35] Guild negotiators rejected the company's latest offer of a 14 percent wage increase over two years, with the union's Bill McLeman calling the offer "clearly inadequate and terribly disappointing."[36] Three days later, the Guild and three of the four craft unions, except for the pressmen, served strike notice. Guy said the move was made "because the unions have been unable to get the company to bargain realistically."[37] He vowed the unions would neither bargain nor accept the government's offer of mediation while Benson continued his training school. "We were forced to get a settlement under threat of a strikebreaking school last time," noted Guy. "As a result in the last year of a three-year contract we only got about one-third of what other unions settled for."[38] The B.C. Federation of Labour waded into the fracas the next day, accusing Pacific Press of the "despicable act of recruiting strikebreakers." It issued a statement saying it had "concrete proof" that the company was recruiting replacements from outside the province.

> It is difficult to understand how a company that uses 20th century production techniques reverts to the 18th century in its dealings with its employees. . . . Here we have a monopolistic company which arbitrarily lays down its own terms to advertisers and subscribers and . . . is equally as arbitrary in its dealings with its employees. . . . Our federation has little doubt that should a strike take place the trade unionists in this province will immediately discontinue advertising and subscribing to the *Vancouver Sun* and *Province*. I am firmly convinced that the labor movement of B.C. will not tolerate scab newspapers.[39]

Two days later, the Guild suspended talks with the company after rejecting a new offer of 22.5 percent over three years but offered to accept a contract of twenty-eight months, which would result in simultaneous expiration with the craft union contracts. Guild president Dave Manley accused the company of archaic tactics. "You have stooped to a new low in labor relations that we never expected to see here in Vancouver when you imported into this city and into this plant that most contemptible of all human beings — the professional strikebreaker."[40] Benson denied the charge and rejected the Guild's wage demand. "Pacific Press is not prepared to agree to the $200 pay rate and if you think you are going to get $200 in 28 months, forget it."[41]

The next afternoon's editions of the *Sun* and the following morning's *Province* carried a full-page ad headlined "Pacific Press working conditions, wages and fringe benefits are among the best in Canada."[42] It called the union demands "unrealistic" in the prevailing economic climate. "At a time when every responsible person is urging caution and restraint to combat rampant inflation which is destroying our standard of living [it] does nothing more than encourage inflation and government-imposed monetary controls," it read. "No one wants that."[43] The ad also took a swipe at one of the company's unions, singling its members out as unworthy of the wages they were seeking. "Our mailers, who are semi-skilled workers, earn $3.69 per hour on day work and $3.94 per hour at night. A 35 per cent increase in pay would give them $10,000 a year — pretty fancy wages for someone who bundles and sorts newspapers."[44]

Relations went from bad to worse the next day when Benson gave an interview on radio, saying increased security around the Pacific Press plant had been instituted "because of pilfering over a long period."[45] That drew the ire of printers composing pages for the next morning's *Province,* and they staged a temporary work stoppage that night, telling a *Sun* reporter they "objected mostly to a Benson statement they interpreted as accusing them of being thieves."[46] The job action brought an emergency 10 p.m. meeting between Benson and Guy, which resulted in agreement for work — and talks — to resume. Premier W.A.C. Bennett got involved from Ottawa, where he was attending a federal-provincial finance ministers conference, suggesting in a telephone interview with the *Sun* that both sides accept an interim agreement and resume talks in six months. "A lot of my friends are reporters and press men," said the premier. "They may criticize me once in a while but the newspapers are very important to the economy. . . . I know very well that the press men, the employees, don't want to go on strike and I know very well the company doesn't want to shut down its plant."[47] The Guild rejected the premier's suggestion as unrealistic. "We have been negotiating for six months," said Bill McLeman. "There is no reason to think if we waited another six months and started again we would not be in the same position again."[48]

Then the B.C. Federation of Labour went public with the information it claimed to have about professional strikebreakers being employed by Pacific Press. John McNevin, the Fed's assistant secretary who had been subpoenaed on short notice two years earlier to testify at the inquiry into *Province* columnist Ormond Turner's allegations of union vote-fixing, also told a press conference that helicopter landing rights obtained by the company would be used to drop replacement workers behind picket lines. "He said federation inquiries have indicated that Okanagan Helicopters has refused a company request for service and Northern Helicopters say they have not yet been approached but would have to take 'a good look at the use of their services for this purpose,'" reported the *Province.*[49] McNevin also charged that the company had hired a well-known U.S. "scab-herder," Leroy Norton, and announced that a former journalist and failed politician was considering the matter.

> According to our information this man comes in prior to a strike and endeavors to recruit various strikebreakers across the country and assist the company in putting out newspapers behind a picket line. We feel this type of person is undesirable and have

> asked for his deportation. Deputy Immigration Minister Tom Kent has indicated an investigation will be held if it is proved Norton is doing this type of work.[50]

Benson issued a statement denying Pacific Press had imported strike-breakers. "A strike-breaker is defined in the dictionary as a person hired to take the job of a man who is on strike," quibbled the Pacific Press general manager. "No such activity is involved here."[51] He noted that officials from the national and international offices of some of the unions involved had come to Vancouver to assist in negotiations. "One newspaper expert from the U.S. who visits Vancouver newspapers regularly has been instructing senior management officials and supervisory employees in the operation of certain basic machines."[52] Security measures were instituted at the Pacific Press Building the next day, which brought tensions almost to the boiling point. Extra Pinkerton security guards were brought in and employees were required to show company-issued photo identification at entrances in order to be admitted. A notice posted on bulletin boards throughout the plant warned that further restrictions could be imposed to "limit employees to their places of work, washrooms and the cafeteria and that special passes would be issued for employees moving between departments."[53] Closed-circuit television cameras were installed at the plant's loading bays, and a helicopter landing pad was painted on the executive parking lot adjacent to the building. Windows overlooking the pressroom from a public viewing gallery were boarded up, and the rear entrances of outside businesses leasing office space on the 7th Avenue side of the Pacific Press Building were sealed off.

Matters came to a head when an attempted delivery of cots to the plant was halted after stereotypers walked off the job in protest. Benson claimed no knowledge of the beds, but Guy said unionists were "at a loss to understand how the general manager could be unaware of what is going on in his own plant. . . . We can only consider that we are being provoked into taking strike action."[54] Benson ordered the delivery trucks away and held talks with his union counterparts that were described as "amicable" and resulted in the lifting of security measures. Notices posted on bulletin boards read: "Following today's negotiating sessions, both company and union representatives agreed that there should be no provocative acts by either party."[55] The United Press International wire service saw things shaping up into a "full-scale war of attrition" at Pacific Press. "If a strike is held, and the threat grows more certain daily, indications are it will be a long one," reported UPI.[56] On Vancouver Island, the Victoria Newspaper Guild local protested coverage of the dispute by the newspaper cooperative Canadian Press, pointing out the absence of any reference in CP reports out of the wire service's Vancouver bureau to the slowdown by printers at Pacific Press, the training school, the allegations of an imported American strike-breaker, or the condemnation by Vancouver mayor Tom Campbell of the installation of closed-circuit TV cameras. "This has been noticed by our members, who are able to contrast CP coverage with that of Vancouver radio and television stations," said a statement by the Victoria Newspaper Guild. [57] The dispute was headlined "The ugly face of monopoly" on the front page of the labor newspaper *Pacific Tribune.*

> This attempt at union busting comes natural to monopolies like Pacific Press. The tendency of all monopolies is to use their economic power to dominate and have their way. They are thoroughly undemocratic and a threat to the public's interests. . . . Pacific Press has foisted itself on Vancouver life, and hangs like an albatross around the neck of the city, blocking the door to any competition and making a mockery of the "free press" about which both papers claim to be champions.[58]

Talks continued, and the company made a "final" offer to the craft unions of an increase of 65 cents an hour over two years, leaving the bargaining table when it claimed the unions turned the offer down. Guy accused the company of "neglecting to tell the complete story" and instead insisted the unions had accepted the offer and that talks had only broken down when they "attempted to use part of the money offered to adjust the night employees' differential."[59] The impasse resulted in printers stopping work for a study session, which left the *Sun* having to consolidate its three editions into one on November 29, and empty spaces appearing where news stories should have been on twenty-one of the forty-six pages printed for the next morning's *Province.* A full-page apology appeared on an otherwise blank front page of the morning paper. "The stoppage occurred despite the assurances by representatives of the International Typographical Union that such incidents would not be repeated," it insisted.[60] Large, bold type in the middle of the front page stated the company's position succinctly. "Nobody wants a strike . . . but we've reached our limit."[61]

The job action resulted in more talks that suddenly produced an agreement with the craft unions the next day, leaving only the Newspaper Guild contract unsettled. Given the lower level of militancy in the Guild compared to the craft unions, the company felt the threat of a shutdown by strike was past and made an increase of 16 percent over twenty-eight months its "final" offer. The Guild countered with a demand of 22 percent over the same period, which was rejected by Pacific Press. When the company refused to budge, McLeman telephoned the *Province* newsroom just before 10 p.m. on December 7, announcing that a strike would commence the following morning. "The Guild has no other choice when the company refuses adamantly to budge from its 16 per cent offer and would give no consideration to the last guild proposal, greatly reduced in order to avoid this regrettable situation," said McLeman.[62]

The announcement brought the intervention of Mayor Campbell, who said he feared that if the strike was not settled quickly "that's the end of the *Province*."[63] Before noon the next day, Campbell convinced the union to withdraw its pickets so the *Sun* could be published while talks between the company and Guild continued, declaring, "It's a deal."[64] But Campbell's efforts were soon quashed when the talks broke down just before 1:30 that afternoon and the picket lines went back up. According to the Canadian Press, the talks failed due to a disagreement over the mayor's role. "The company said it had not rejected the mayor as mediator but that the government conciliation officer had done so," reported CP. "The guild said it wanted the mayor as mediator but the company did not."[65]

The development put the Pacific Press craft unions in an awkward position. "The mechanical departments of Pacific Press were at work, but were expected to stop as soon as they realized the building was again being picketed by striking Guild employees," reported the *Columbian*. "Pacific Press said in a statement it intended to continue publication regardless of a strike by the 670 members of the Vancouver Newspaper Guild."[66] But the craft unions did not walk out in response to the Guild strike, as they had been expected to do. Instead, the printers stayed on the job following a hastily called meeting on the composing room floor. Almost as unexpectedly, when a delivery truck carrying cots and mattresses appeared at the Pacific Press loading dock, Guild pickets parted peacefully to let them into the building. They also allowed successive shifts of printers through to replace those on duty, as reported by the Canadian Press.

> The printers, who earlier had said they would respect guild picket lines, reported for work promptly for the evening and morning shifts. Picket lines parted to let them in the building. Paddy Sherman, editor-in-chief of the *Province,* suggested in an interview that the strikers had permitted printers to enter to prevent supervisory personnel from getting out a paper.[67]

On the picket line outside the building, Guild members filled buckets with box lunches for the printers to hoist up to the third-floor composing room so they would not have to leave their posts, thus preventing management replacements from taking over the typesetting machines.[68] "The printers, members of the International Typographical Union, had remained on duty within the building 24 hours a day since the strike began," reported the *Columbian.* The obstructionist tactics succeeded, and soon talks between the company and Newspaper Guild resumed. In a marathon seventeen-hour bargaining session, an agreement was reached at 3 a.m. on December 11, just in time for *Province* staff to produce a sixteen-page edition for delivery that morning.[69] An 8 a.m. meeting attended by 400 Guild members ratified the deal, according to the *Province,* with a "near-unanimous voice vote."[70] Terms of the agreement were little more than the company's last offer, admitted McLeman, who said that for some categories, such as classified advertising salesmen, the increases ranged as high as the originally demanded 35 percent. The deal was made with a last-minute sweetener that bumped the key rate an extra $5.15 a week, to $177.50, in the final month of the contract. The company estimated the total package cost it "between 17 and 18 per cent."[71] McLeman said he regretted having to take strike action. "It was the only weapon we had," he told a *Sun* reporter. "Our needs were great and we had to show the company we were serious."[72]

According to one-time *Sun* religion editor Sean Rossiter in a 1980 article for *Vancouver* magazine, the three-day strike in 1967 made the Guild a power "only because the craft guilds supported it by reporting to work but standing idly by their machines."[73] It also put the Guild firmly in the debt of the printers and left Ed Benson flummoxed by the unionists he claimed did not understand economics but somehow got the better of him anyway.

But it was only Round One.

8 The Showdown

By the end of the 1960s, relations between the corporate partners at Pacific Press grew "increasingly chilly," according to then-*Sun* publisher Stuart Keate, as FP shareholders became exasperated with rising costs of production and the financial underperformance of the *Province*.[1] The mounting losses of its morning bedfellow drained the afternoon giant's profits in the partnership, which Keate characterized as "a bizarre arrangement which [one year] left the *Sun* with a bottom line of $2.25 million on its gross profit of $12 million and the *Province* with exactly the same reward on a *loss* of $1 million."[2] Howard Webster, a major FP shareholder since folding his *Globe and Mail* into the chain in 1965, was one of the loudest critics of the Pacific Press arrangement, according to Keate: "Webster contended that a partnership was just that; that there was no law suggesting that a winner could go on indefinitely subsidizing a loser. At one point he brought along a New York lawyer who argued that the Vancouver omelette could, indeed, be unscrambled."[3] But the contract entered into between the Cromies and Southam in 1957 proved under Canadian law to be perfectly valid, according to Keate.[4]

Next to Webster, the biggest FP advocate of rearranging the Pacific Press partnership was the chain's general manager, Dick Malone, the penny-pinching publisher of the *Winnipeg Free Press*. Starting his newspaper career in the late 1920s as a reporter for the *Toronto Star*, Malone had moved west during the Depression and went to work for the Sifton family, first on their Regina and Saskatoon papers, then in 1936 on their flagship *Free Press*. Called up from the officer reserves during the Second

World War, he served as an aide to Defence Minister James Ralston, establishing the army's public relations division and founding the Canadian military newspaper *The Maple Leaf.* He landed in Sicily on invasion day and was present at both the liberation of Paris and the Japanese surrender aboard the USS *Missouri* in Tokyo Bay. He rose by war's end to the rank of brigadier, a title he would wear for the rest of his life. He directed operations of the growing FP chain from his headquarters in Winnipeg with military efficiency.

Robert Fulford of the independently owned *Toronto Star* profiled the FP braintrust in 1966. "Malone, in conversation, is the sort of man who makes cliches spring instantly to mind — he's a hard-headed, no-nonsense man; he watches, one imagines, with an 'eagle eye,' all the details of the FP papers. It comes as no surprise that he was a success in the Army."[5] Malone's book *Missing From the Record,* about relations between Canadian officers and British General Bernard Montgomery, for whom he was a liaison officer, was a "curious, stiff-necked little book," according to Fulford. "A man who had a dashing, exciting war managed to make his account of it sound like an inter-office memo."[6] Malone's need to be in control extended even to his interview with Fulford, whom he went out of his way to insult, according to the reporter. "For instance, the other day he instructed me: 'Now look, I've given you a straight story. You write it straight or I'll get on to Ralph' — meaning Ralph Allen, the managing editor of *The Star.*"[7]

Keate, who felt the Brigadier's wrath often during his years as publisher of FP papers in Victoria and Vancouver, singled out Malone as "the only person I found difficult to get along with, in more than forty years in the business."[8] Malone's penchant for badgering his publishers at all hours, even at home, led Keate's daughter Kathryn to pen a verse to the tune of "Mary Ann," a calypso hit. "All day, all night Dick Malone/Call me daddy on de tely-phone/Why can't he leave us alone?/Goddam! Sumbitch! Dick Malone!"[9] Keate took his share of shots at Malone in his 1980 autobiography *Paper Boy.* "It is difficult to resist the view that Malone was a bully — a man who had to gratify some inner daemon by pushing other people around."[10] Unlike the Southam chain and even penurious Thomson, which more or less left their publishers alone to run their own operations, FP was micro-managed under the firm hand of the Brigadier who, according to Keate, "felt he had to inject his own views on everything from reportorial assignments to Red Cross contributions."[11] When FP acquired the

Montreal Star in 1973, *Time* magazine profiled Malone, recalled Keate, with a picture of him clutching the "inevitable" cigar.

> The caption under the picture read: "No penchant for interfering." The horse-laughs engendered by this statement were enough to rock the Fordham University seismograph to an 8.2 reading on the Richter scale. A great many FP employees — too many, in fact — felt that they had to wire Malone before going to the bathroom.[12]

The Brigadier's most infuriating character trait was his outright refusal to even consider the views of others, which made him, according to former *Time* journalist Keate, "the most splendid example of the doctrine of uninterruptability since Henry Luce."[13] Malone's dogmatic doggedness helped make relations between Southam and FP in the Pacific Press partnership increasingly problematic. "Dick Malone and I did not get on together on the Pacific Press board as Cromie and I had," recalled St. Clair Balfour. "It was always a case of Malone wanting the *Province* to cut back its expenses. Dick Malone would hear, but he didn't listen."[14] Keate recalled that during quarterly meetings of the Pacific Press board of directors, Malone took to "muttering dark threats from time to time" about the growing *Province* losses, which began closing in on $2 million a year.

> This performance infuriated Dick Malone, who came to each Pacific Press board meeting in Vancouver loaded with tough questions. Why, he demanded to know, did the *Province* need almost as many circulation personnel when it had roughly half the numbers of the *Sun*? . . . In frustration, Malone declared that he would refuse to approve annual financial statements and budgets and "wanted his dissent recorded.". . . To Clair Balfour's credit, he never lost his cool. [15]

The biggest cost of production at Pacific Press was labor, as under Cromie family ownership the *Sun*'s unions had been richly rewarded with generous wages, which Southam's *Province* had to match. Comparative financial figures presented to the Restrictive Trade Practices Commission hearings into the Pacific Press amalgamation showed that by the time of the merger in 1957, labor costs of composing a column of type for the *Province* were more than one quarter higher than at any other Southam paper, and half again more than at most. The high cost of labor was one of the reasons advanced by Southam for the economic necessity of allowing the amalgamation, as the commission's report noted: "The financial position of *The Province* was affected by the fact that labour costs in Vancouver were relatively high. While *The Sun* had to meet the same conditions it was in a much better position to do so because of its much larger revenues."[16] Since the Pacific Press cohabitation at 6th and Granville began, the newspaper unions had bargained hard not only to preserve jobs that might otherwise have been made redundant by automation, but also to keep their wages apace with rising inflation. Now with the Newspaper Guild coming of age during the short strike of 1967, which was not only supported by the printers but made possible by them, the new solidarity between unions was made more significant by the fact that in 1969 all collective agreements would expire simultaneously on Halloween. A "joint council" was formed by the union heads to bargain as one with the company, which similarly strengthened its resolve, at FP's instigation, to cut back on labor costs. Conditions were ripe for a showdown.

The joint council, according to a study of labor relations at Pacific Press done for the 1980 Royal Commission on Newspapers, "evolved from the practice of some unions of sending observers to the negotiations of others."[17] The impetus for starting the council, according to the study, came from Len Guy of the ITU and Bill McLeman of the Newspaper Guild, who became its first co-chairmen. "Since that time, by common understanding, one of the co-chairmen has been a Guild representative and the other a representative of the craft unions."[18] The joint council was an informal, ad hoc body, according to the study.

> The council has no constitution and no bylaws. Any procedural consistency that exists developed through common understanding between the parties. . . . Voting follows the principle of "one union, one vote." Unanimity on all decisions is sought, but when this appears impossible, majority opinion seems to prevail. This voting structure has been a source of conflict.[19]

Negotiations between Pacific Press and the joint council took place on items common to all the unions, such as wages, while issues "peculiar" to individual unions were negotiated separately by the unions involved, often with representatives of other unions sitting in. The arrangement particularly benefited members of the Guild, which although by far the largest union at Pacific Press, was also historically the least militant due to its size and diverse membership. The craft unions, being smaller and more united, were accordingly more powerful, capable of shutting down publication of the Pacific Press papers on short notice with either a legal or illegal "wildcat" strike over any issue that might arise. Pacific Press salaried staff, from journalists to janitors, soon found their wages raised in lockstep with their new-found craft union brothers on the joint council, according to the Royal Commission study. "The Guild, which saw a particular need to participate because key Guild rates were behind journeyman rates, has achieved major wage improvements since formation of the council."[20]

In 1969, talks broke down in September over wage demands. A mediator joined negotiations in October to no avail. Bargaining broke off again once the union contracts expired at the end of the month, and soon the unions unveiled new negotiating tactics. On November 7, printers began a production slowdown.[21] Then on November 12, in protest of the latest wage offer from Pacific Press, the joint council negotiators simply refused to leave the company's conference room where talks had been taking place, staging a "sit-in." The tactic worked, and company negotiators returned to the bargaining table the next day.[22] More contentious than the company's wage offer was its attempt to change the date of contract expiry from just before the lucrative Christmas advertising season until year end, when the unions would not enjoy as much economic leverage with a strike threat. Pacific Press wanted a twenty-six-month contract, which would expire at year's end, and in response the unions took the bargaining stance of asking for a term of twenty-two months.

At the bargaining table on November 14, during a seven-hour session following the joint council sit-in, company negotiator Don Fergusson dropped the company's demand for a longer contract term. He claimed he only lowered it to twenty-five months and promised to take the unions' demand of an 87-cent per hour increase over that period back to the company for consideration. But union negotiators insisted Fergusson not only agreed to a term of twenty-four months but promised to "sell" to the Pacific Press board of directors the deal the joint council claimed to have negotiated when the talks adjourned for the weekend. It was a point that would prove problematic.

Negotiators were so optimistic they had made a deal on that Friday afternoon that they had a company secretary type up a notice to be posted on bulletin boards throughout the Pacific Press Building, announcing to anxious employees heading home for the weekend that the two sides were close to an agreement. A story in Saturday's *Sun* was headlined "Pacific Press Settlement 'Close.'" But by the cold light of Monday morning, things were very different, and negotiations broke down again the next day. The impasse prompted union negotiators to stage a second sit-in at the company boardroom. Newspaper Guild official Bill McLeman, co-chair of the joint council, announced the union team would remain at the bargaining table until company negotiators returned. "All the major economic items appear to be resolved and the major hang-up is the term of agreement," he told a *Sun* reporter.[23] During the second sit-in, according to the joint council leaders, delegations of employees who approached Pacific Press general manager Ed Benson seeking a resumption in bargaining "were told 'go ahead and strike — we have maximum strike insurance.' The suggestion to strike also came from company negotiators at the bargaining table."[24]

Instead of resuming talks, on November 24 the company launched a lawsuit for damages against the craft unions for the production slowdowns that had begun November 7. It claimed the ITU breached its contract by failing to provide printers to work overtime and accused it, along with the pressmen's and mailers' unions, of causing or failing to prevent "concerted production interference by its members."[25] The simmering dispute turned ugly three weeks later, when an anonymous caller to Benson's office made a death threat against the Pacific Press GM. When told by his secretary that Benson was not in his office, the caller left a message: "Tell Mr. Benson unless he changes his mind within two days, he will be shot."[26] When a call five minutes later to Benson's home confirmed the location of his residence, the caller replied: "We just wanted to make sure this was the right place."[27] The joint council issued a statement saying it did not condone the calls, whether genuine or a hoax.[28] Keate doubted the seriousness of the threat and in a memo to Malone derided Benson's subsequent use of a bodyguard, who followed him everywhere. "Such threats, as you know, are common in our business," Keate wrote Malone. "I had one last year. . . . I merely turned the letter over to police and went about my business. The idea of a body-guard is to me theatrical nonsense."[29] Keate complained to Malone about problems with Benson, whom he called "a complete loner and maverick," noting that even meetings he and Auger had with him quickly broke down.

> If we can't communicate with him, how can the unions? I have come around to the view that we will always have trouble as long as he is our chief of labor strategy and that we will never reach a settlement as long as he and Guy are glaring at each other, eyeball to eyeball, in what is essentially a personal vendetta and struggle for power. In short, I believe we are faced with a stalemate between two highly-emotional men involved in a battle of personalities. Benson appears to live in a world haunted by daemons, and to thrive on crises.[30]

The *Sun* publisher had protested a year earlier after a speech Benson made blaming the number of unions at Pacific Press for a lack of labor-management communication. A report in the *Sun* quoted Benson as telling a conference of newspaper production managers in a keynote address that communications companies "are probably the most inept at getting messages across to the public and to our employees."[31] Benson told the Pacific Newspaper Mechanical Conference at the Bayshore Inn that newspaper company planning had to acknowledge the economic facts of life and avoid the "great number of non-economic sentiments, such as pride," that marked the newspaper business.

> Having regard to the sensibilities of the journalist, I agree that it is regrettable that a newspaper has to be a business. But a newspaper in the present economic system just has to be a successful business if it is going to stay alive. . . . It's very often forgotten that, horrible though it may sound to the boys in the newsroom, a newspaper plant is essentially a factory.[32]

According to *Province* editor Paddy Sherman, Benson's erratic behavior was due to a serious drinking problem. "He started drinking a lot and that complicated matters," recalled Sherman in a 2001 interview. "He got very frustrated. When things got very difficult he tended to drink."[33] As for Guy, Keate told Malone that some at the *Sun* who had known him for years "think he is irrational and erratic, to put it mildly."[34] But Guy's power, Keate added, went far beyond his leadership of the ITU, extending to the entire B.C. Federation of Labour, of which he was a vice-president.

Christmas came and went without a settlement, and with the New Year the unions resumed their slowdown tactics in an attempt to force the company's hand. By February the job action began to go beyond mere harassment and caused serious production problems at Pacific Press. On February 5 the slowdowns resulted in the *Sun*'s press run dropping from an average of more than 260,000 to only 72,200 copies printed, and the paper abandoned both its home and final editions. Distribution of the *Province* was delayed by six hours and delivery to suburban Fraser Valley regions was abandoned. Pacific Press applied to the Labour Relations Board that day for an order against the slowdown tactics, and a hearing was set for February 17. On the same day, sixty-one pressmen signed a petition and returned their long-service pins to Benson in protest of what they called his "Machiavellian tactics."[35] Keate explained to Malone that the move came after a secret meeting at the Hotel Vancouver between Benson, Benson's assistant Dave Stinson, and two international union officers, at the initiative of the unions. "Unfortunately, this meeting was 'leaked' — apparently by the unions," Keate revealed in a memo. "The unions have taken the line that this meeting was an attempt to 'divide and conquer.'"[36]

The next day's press run was only slightly better, with 86,600 copies of the *Sun* printed. Management at first tried to have the entire run completed, even if it had to be delivered the next day, but finally abandoned the effort about 9:30 p.m. because the presses were needed for the next day's editions of the *Province*.[37] The subsequent fat Saturday edition of the *Sun* saw only 22,640 copies run off the presses, and the company decided not to wait for the Labour Relations Board hearing ten days hence, applying to B.C. Supreme Court for an injunction against the union slowdowns. Pacific Press also issued a warning to its recalcitrant mechanical staff that it was prepared to suspend publication of both newspapers if production problems continued.

> Because of the actions and tactics you are using we have virtually reached the stage at which there is nothing to be gained by vain attempts to publish the newspapers. When that point is reached, while we do not intend to lock our employees out, we wish to bring to your attention that there will be no work available for

> anybody on staff. And there will be no revenue coming in to pay anybody.[38]

On February 9, Pacific Press lawyer Bill Macdonald told a B.C. Supreme Court hearing the company had already had to refund $150,000 to advertisers because of the undelivered newspapers.[39] The B.C. Federation of Labour waded back into the fray, accusing Pacific Press of "dishonesty" in reporting the dispute. Secretary-treasurer Ray Haynes issued a statement saying he had seen the affidavits signed by union negotiators that swore a bargaining table agreement had been reached on November 14, which the company had reneged on. "It is easy, of course, for them to be dishonest in such matters because they control written news in the Lower Mainland," said Haynes. "It is time this monopoly was broken."[40] According to Sherman, Fergusson had promised the unions nothing that day.

> I was involved in that, and what Don said was, "I do not agree with this and I do not think it will fly, but I'll put it to the management board." He did put it to the management board in those terms and they said, "Drop dead." So he went back and reported that and of course they accused him of reneging. Fergusson was a gentleman of the old school and he would never go back on his word on anything.[41]

The next day only 62,000 copies of the *Sun* were printed, and production of the *Province* was four hours late. The unions conducted strike votes.[42] The court issued an injunction against the union production slowdowns pending a hearing into the company's claim for monetary damages, but February 12 saw less than half the normal press run of the *Sun* completed as results of the union strike votes came back overwhelmingly in favor of a walkout. When production of the next day's *Province* lagged, the company's night foreman suspended the entire shift of thirteen pressmen about 2 a.m., demanding a "competent" crew from the union. He was told none could be provided at that hour, but a meeting produced promises from the pressmen already on shift to "work normally." Production resumed, but jammed machines in the mailing room resulted in a reduced run of the morning paper being distributed.[43] Only 42,000 copies of that day's *Sun* were produced. The resulting company decision was recorded in Keate's typewritten notes.

> At the meeting this morning, attended by Benson, Stinson, Keate, [his assistant Bruce] Rudd, Auger, Sherman, it was decided to take the following immediate action:
>
> 1. Advise ITU contract cancelled.
> 2. Lay off 200 men effective Monday.
> 3. Post notice to staff describing accumulated loss of revenue to date, plus accumulated additional expenses, advising that further staff cuts may be necessary if production does not return to normal. Also, company will consider withdrawing present standing offers.
> 4. If no sign of return to normal production after two or three days of limited-size paper, advise all unions of withdrawal of offers.
> 5. Cancel remaining contracts.
> 6. Shut down if necessary.[44]

The next morning's *Province* announced that the Pacific Press papers would be reduced to between sixteen and twenty-four pages, with no normal advertising content except notices of births, deaths and marriages, and legal notices. "The International Typographical Union has been formally notified that its contract is terminated," it added.[45] Len Guy of the ITU protested the company action. "These are our newspapers which we have helped to build and I don't think any management has the unilateral right to destroy our newspapers," said the joint council co-chair. "We have put our lives into making them and management doesn't have this right. . . . We know what moves we will make to take care of our people."[46] Only 57,000 of the normal Saturday press run of 130,000 copies of the *Province* were produced before its press crew was again suspended about 3:30 a.m. "The press crew suspended early today remained in the work area for several hours," reported George Dobie in that afternoon's *Sun*. "Two of the workers were still there at 8:15 a.m."[47]

Guy told the Canadian Press that his members would report for work as usual despite the staff cutbacks announced by the company, which reduced the number of printers required from 260 to 80. "We work on a slipboard system and it means there will be more subs than usual," he explained. "The number of men working depends on the volume of work."[48] The unions even offered to work for free for a week to help the company make up its financial losses, which Benson dismissed as "meaningless."[49] Not considered without significance was Guy's promise that

ITU members would show up at Pacific Press in force, as Benson told the Canadian Press.

> A spokesman for the unions made it abundantly clear he would not permit production of even a limited service to readers. . . . The threats in union statements over the weekend made it clearer than ever that an illegal strike was in effect. The company decided to suspend publication of both newspapers. One factor in this decision was the need to protect many millions of dollars worth of complex equipment that could take weeks or months to replace or repair.[50]

The company canceled the remaining union contracts and picket lines went up around the Pacific Press Building. The picket signs claimed a company lockout, but the 72-hour lockout notice required under provincial labor law had not been issued. The company action was instead a suspension of publication, said Benson, which would remain in effect "until an element of sanity returns to the conduct of the union leadership."[51] For his part, Guy insisted he was not making threats when he announced that the usual complement of printers would show up on shift. "My statement on Saturday was not that we were devising tactics to restrict publication," said Guy, "but rather that our membership voted to share the work caused by Mr. Benson's decision to lay off 173 of our members."[52] The stunning turn of events at Valentine's Day put 1,100 workers out on the street and left about a million Greater Vancouverites without their daily newspapers. But already the wheels were turning that would shift the balance of power in the struggle of strategies.

Residents of the Lower Mainland went into information withdrawal and turned to the *Toronto Globe and Mail*, the *Seattle Post-Intelligencer*, and the *Victoria Colonist* in an effort to keep up with the news.[53] "That first week, they'd read anything with print on it," said newsstand operator Bud Sowerby. "They bought Seattle papers two or three days old."[54] One downtown newspaper peddler told a reporter his customers were frantic for whatever was available. "They're coming in here crazy for newspapers," said Joe Yacowar, a news vendor for a dozen years. "One guy grabs half a dozen. I'm too old to fight with him. Just like forbidden fruit; there aren't any papers so they want papers real bad."[55] A woman newsstand vendor quipped, "They're buying papers they've never heard of before. They pick up the *P-I* and complain about all the American news but they buy it and run."[56] Even the underground newspaper *Georgia Straight* cashed in on the boom, according to Don MacLachlan of the Canadian Press, who reported passengers "leaping off the bus to pay 25 cents for what they think is *The Sun* and find it is a camouflaged copy of *Georgia Straight,* a hippie weekly."[57] MacLachlan recounted the ruse.

> A bearded youth outside a liquor store is selling papers. The page that shows is peach-colored, like the front of the *Sun*'s final edition. The word *Sun* shows clearly but has two lines through the S, like a dollar sign. It costs 25 cents. The *Sun* regularly costs 10. Buyers don't quibble until they find they've bought a *Georgia Straight.* Some laugh; some are hostile.[58]

According to *Sun* writer Trevor Lautens, who chronicled the travails of daily-deprived Vancouver for *Saturday Night* magazine, some *Straight* staff "urged 'going for the masses,' with additions like television schedules, but the *Straight* kept its principles and lifted circulation from 14,000 to 20,000. . . . Even the *Jewish Western Bulletin* fattened its book from 12-16 to 20 pages."[59] MacLachlan noted that "a current *TV Guide* is becoming worth its weight in gold" and chronicled several other examples of newspaper withdrawal symptoms.

> • A University of B.C. professor buys a *New Westminster Columbian* and puts it on the seat of a bus while he digs out his fare. When he looks up, the paper, and its new owner, have disappeared. . . .
>
> • A cab driver at the airport growls at his passenger: "And you get on the plane and they give you a Calgary paper and you know we got none here and you leave the damn thing on the plane?"
>
> • A man in a hotel lobby apologetically approaches another and asks if he might have his paper when he's through. "Well," comes the reply, "the chap in the sports coat there is next and the fellow sitting next to him is after that and . . ."[60]

By the late 1960s, growth of the newspaper chains in Canada, fueled mostly by the rapid expansion of FP Publications, had begun to alarm many, including Senator Keith Davey. The former federal Liberal Party organizer, who had been dubbed "The Rainmaker" by Scott Young of the *Globe and Mail* for his fund-raising ability, was appointed to the Senate at his own request in 1966 by Prime Minister Lester Pearson. Just 39, he also was hired as commissioner of the Canadian Football League that same year, only to be ousted by unimpressed owners fifty-six days later when he appeared more concerned with the game's fans, going so far as to draft a "bill of rights" for spectators.

Davey came from a newspaper family and as a boy collected newspaper mastheads, he recalled, "the way some kids collect stamps."[61] His father, Charles "Scotty" Davey, rose to the position of production manager of the *Toronto Star*, where he worked for more than fifty years. But despite his interest in newspapers and a stint selling ads for a community paper as a university student, after graduation in 1951 Keith Davey went into the radio business instead as a salesman with the new CKFH in Toronto, which had been started by hockey play-by-play legend Foster Hewitt. "Much as I wanted to be in the newspaper business myself," wrote Davey in his autobiography, "to my way of thinking I could not work at the *Star* because of my father, nor could I work on staff at any other daily newspaper because of him."[62] He stayed at CKFH for ten years before getting into politics full time as the Liberal Party's national director in Ottawa.

First considering a study of the print media only, Davey gave notice in the Senate in November 1968 of his intended motion to establish a committee to study the media, and the country's first national press inquiry began to take form. By the time he formally proposed formation of a Special Senate Committee in a speech on the following March 18, the scope of the study had widened to include broadcasting. Though he initially thought parliament was the appropriate body to consider the question of media power, Davey said he instead decided appointed senators would be better insulated than elected MPs from any political pressure that the press might exert to dissuade enactment of regulatory measures such an inquiry might recommend. Those concerns were confirmed during the committee's hearings, Davey wrote in the preface to its final report, when the elected U.S. Congress passed legislation "which to all intents and purposes legitimizes press concentration. Its easy passage through both Houses of Congress has been popularly attributed, at least in part, to the fact that politicians looking to re-election must depend substantially upon the mass media in the very real world of practical politics."[63]

Davey's committee of fifteen senators set about considering its terms of reference, which included "to consider and report upon the ownership and control of the major means of mass public communication in Canada, and . . . the extent and nature of their impact and influence on the Canadian public." Its first important task, according to Davey, was to decide what constituted "good" media. "The standard we chose, in the words of the report, was pretty straightforward: 'How successful is that newspaper or broadcasting station in preparing its audience for social change?' This was not to endorse anyone's built-in bias. Change remains the central fact of our society."[64] Hearings began on December 9, 1969.

Most of the proceedings went underreported in Vancouver due to the closure of the newspapers. A report to the Senate committee outlined the economic impact of the Pacific Press dispute with a forty-page study. Walter Gray, a Toronto economics and communication consultant and a former journalist, concluded on the basis of telephone interviews with 125 Greater Vancouver residents that the absence of daily newspapers there was creating considerable frustration among the population, along with negative economic and social consequences.

> The daily examination of advertisements for bargains, the crossword puzzle, the horoscope, the weather report, the careful digest of news . . . have been eliminated from the daily ritual. Now, there is the frustration of adjusting the daily routine to radio and television news programming schedules, or unfamiliar out-of-town or weekly papers, of trying to retain news and information that is not written out in black and white.[65]

The sudden disappearance of the Vancouver dailies in early 1970 was felt by advertisers as well as readers. "It's hard to sell your products when you can't advertise," car dealer Alan Eyre told the Canadian Press.[66] The Bay department store published its own sixteen-page flyer.

"Residents, hungry for reading material resembling a newspaper, accepted it with enthusiasm," reported *Marketing* magazine.[67] But the suddenly unfilled demand for printed advertising mostly benefited the area's community newspapers, according to *Marketing*, and "sent a staggering flow of cash into the willing arms of small suburban newspapers."[68] The west-side Vancouver weekly *Kerrisdale Courier* grew fat on advertising that was suddenly without a daily outlet, swelling from eighteen to forty-four pages and boosting its circulation by 50 percent, to 15,000.[69] Publisher Bill Forst, recently of the failed *Vancouver Times*, announced the paper might increase to twice- or even thrice-weekly publication.[70]

In North Vancouver, former *Sun* managing editor Hal Straight operated the Lower Mainland's largest weekly, having bought the *North Shore Press-Review* in 1958 following his return from Edmonton, where he was publisher of Max Bell's *Bulletin* until it folded in 1951. Renaming it the *Citizen*, Straight offered free distribution for a year while a carrier service was developed, and then began charging for delivery. At the end of the year the *Citizen*, by stressing detailed coverage of local happenings, was so popular and accepted in North Vancouver that when a 35-cent monthly charge was introduced, it lost less than 3 percent of its readership, retaining a circulation of 12,000.[71] In the early 1960s, the *Citizen* expanded distribution to adjacent West Vancouver, and its circulation climbed to 20,000, making it the largest community weekly newspaper in Canada.[72]

When the Pacific Press papers closed in 1970, *Citizen* circulation stood at 22,000 copies every Wednesday, and Straight pondered switching to daily publication, even printing a ballot for readers to vote on the move. In an accompanying article, he noted that "past studies have indicated a North Shore daily would not be economically feasible, but if there is sufficient demand we will take this major step as a public service."[73] In the end the question of whether the *Citizen* should go daily was made moot by a lack of adequate press facilities, according to Straight. "There's no equipment in town to put out a daily," he said. "What I have is a hand-stamp compared with Pacific Press."[74] He did increase publication of the *Citizen* to twice a week, boosting circulation to 25,000, and also printed 300,000 department store flyers, increasing his staff by 150 percent. The *Citizen* publisher, according to Lautens,

> also financed and printed the curiously named *Vancouver Classified News* — which had no news, only classified ads. This was

> unblushingly sold at newsstands for fifteen cents, although distributed free in some areas, and claimed an instant circulation of 150,000. "We are making," chortled one of its seven entrepreneurs — erstwhile *Sun* and *Province* ad salesmen aided by two girls — "nothing but money."[75]

The absence of daily newspapers also created a serious information deficit problem for the public. "The B.C. legislature session was more of a mystery than ever," reported Lautens. "Important revisions to the Land Act, Landlord and Tenant Act, Age of Majority Act, Pollution Control Act hardly registered on a community without daily papers."[76] Vancouver council considered postponing a planned March 11 plebiscite on a $29.7-million, five-year plan for upgrading city services due to a lack of publicity on the issues.[77] One stockbroker noted that due to a lack of coverage the Vancouver Stock Exchange had become "an almost entirely professional market . . . with little public participation."[78] The effect of the strike was felt in a wide variety of places. Realtors reported the volume of telephone calls from prospective home buyers fell by half.[79] Libraries were overwhelmed with requests for information. "The arts department gets calls about plays and movies," a librarian reported. "One man wanted every Oscar nomination read to him, and grumbled when we refused."[80] A florist in Surrey found that without daily obituaries, trying to sort out which floral arrangements went to which funeral home became a nightmare. "When the shutdown first started I thought we'd never live through it," said Louise Ruddell. "The morning paper was just like a Bible to us."[81] Allan Fotheringham saw it as "the gradual unbinding of the seams which hold a city together," with the social necessity of newspapers accentuated by their absence.

> There are hundreds of hidden aspects. Attendance at funerals was down 20 per cent. Three employment agencies closed because of the failure of communication. Children's Aid has a backlog of 70 children for adoption. Catholic Children's Aid 25. In both cases, because the papers could not run the usual pictures and appeals.[82]

In an attempt to provide the pressing news of the day, CKNW hotliner Jack Webster gave long, verbatim, on-air accounts of two high-profile libel cases involving Allan Fotheringham. CKWX added an extra newscast on the half hour, sponsored by the Eaton's department store.[83] Television station CHAN, the CTV network's Vancouver affiliate, added a thirty-minute community information program, running free of charge the announcements usually contained on the classified advertising pages of the dailies. "Unless you catch [it] you won't know who died, who had a baby, or who was married," noted MacLachlan.[84] But the city's need for news could not be filled adequately by the electronic media, according to Fotheringham.

> The one clear lesson to the public was how inept are radio and TV. It was a disgrace to their profits how feebly they attempted to fill the gap. . . . Stations larded their newscasts with buckets of foreign news never before contemplated. To give the poor reader a world perspective? Of course not. It was because the stations could no longer scalp the daily papers and pass it off as their own, which is their usual way of faking local news coverage. . . . People are *print* freaks. The superficial radio-TV coverage couldn't satisfy.[85]

Other B.C. dailies seemed reluctant to fill the void left by the suspended Pacific Press dailies, which prompted suspicions of a pact between publishers. Ray Haynes of the B.C. Federation of Labour accused the Victoria papers and the *New Westminster Columbian* of deliberately holding back and announced his group would investigate the matter and look into the "monopolistic practices" of the newspapers.[86] The charge was denied by the general manager of Victoria Press, which published both the *Times* and the *Colonist* in an arrangement similar to Pacific Press, except that the Victoria papers were both owned by the same company, FP Publications. J.C. Melville said circulation of the morning *Colonist* had been boosted considerably on the Mainland, while the evening *Times* was beginning to be circulated. The problem, he said, was distribution. "It's not just a case of getting the papers delivered to Vancouver, but a matter of having them picked up and distributed once they're there."[87] The Lower Mainland's only remaining daily was the *Columbian* in New Westminster, only a dozen miles from Vancouver's city limits. In his written report to the Senate committee on mass media, Walter Gray noted the *Columbian* had increased its edition size and suburban circulation, but according to *Canadian Printer & Publisher*, when questioned by senators "he could not explain why the paper is not sold in downtown Vancouver. Gray said he suspected it was a policy decision on the part of the publisher, or a circulation requirement."[88] According to Lautens, the *Columbian* was slow to fill the daily newspaper void.

> A populist cry rose urging that it penetrate the territory of the paralyzed *Sun* and *Province*. The *Columbian* instantly expanded operations but radio hotliners hinted at a deal between *Sun*/*Province*/Pacific Press and the *Columbian* to keep to their respective sides of the street in times of trouble. *Columbian* management stoutly denied this, saying facilities were being taxed to capacity.[89]

Columbian publisher Rikk Taylor took umbrage specifically with the accusations of collusion made by Ray Haynes on behalf of the B.C. Federation of Labour. "Nothing could be further from the truth," he protested.[90] The Royal City daily's limited press capacity was being used to the maximum, the third-generation family publisher insisted, as press runs had been increased from 30,000 to 40,000 copies of expanded editions. "He termed Mr. Haynes' comments irresponsible and said they showed an unbelievable lack of knowledge of the printing industry," reported the *Colonist*.[91] The *Columbian* had been established in 1861, a full quarter-century before the rail terminus of Vancouver was founded, in the then-provincial capital of New Westminster near the mouth of the Fraser River. It expanded its circulation in the burgeoning suburbs up the Fraser Valley east of Vancouver in the mid-1960s, with different "zoned" editions printed for readers in Burnaby, Coquitlam, and Surrey. "Basically, the four editions are a replate job of the New Westminster edition," reported *Canadian Printer & Publisher* in 1968. "Three pages, including the front page, are remade for each run. Front pages spotlight news from each circulation area. . . . So far, the formula has been successful."[92]

Among the witnesses heard by the Davey committee in Ottawa was *Vancouver Sun* publisher Stuart Keate, who told the senators that labor problems at Pacific Press were due in part to journalists being lumped together with all sorts of other workers in an industrial union. The Newspaper Guild, Keate testified, had expanded its membership far beyond its original concept.

> To take in business-office personnel, telephone clerks and janitors [means] journalists find themselves an outvoted minority, frequently tied in wage negotiations to the aspirations of the non-professional majority. This is patently ludicrous. The logical but unlikely resolution of this situation is for the journalists to break away from the Guild and form their own association.[93]

The Guild's international headquarters responded to Keate's attack in an editorial in its weekly newspaper, the *Guild Reporter*, observing that "sometimes the temptation to pontification is too great for some publishers."[94] The Guild's growth from a craft association to an industrial union, according to the editorial, occurred because "it became evident that an association of editorial workers didn't have the economic strength to deal effectively with publishers, who had their own industrial union — the American Newspaper Publishers Association."[95] Another witness was Bill Hughes, manager of radio station CKNW, who insisted that the electronic media in Vancouver had picked up the information slack left by the closure of the Pacific Press dailies. When he finally regained his public podium, *Sun* columnist Allan Fotheringham could scarcely disguise his dismay at the broadcaster's statement, awarding him "first prize as Funny Man." The city's first experience with prolonged withdrawal symptoms from the newspaper habit had been painful, and apparent to everyone except the radio man. "Sweet, flaming William!" fumed Fotheringham. "What cave has he been hiding in?"[96]

9 The Express

Mike Tytherleigh got out of the newspaper business for several years after the *Vancouver Times* folded in 1965. He went into radio, reading the major newscasts for CKWX and also providing commentary. He tried politics briefly, running unsuccessfully in the provincial election of 1969 as a Liberal candidate in the riding of Vancouver South, but the lure of print was strong. His extensive resume as a journalist soon led to an offer of employment at Pacific Press, and he went back to work as night city editor at the *Sun*. He had started his newspaper career on Fleet Street after serving in the Royal Navy during the Second World War, then traveled the colonies as an itinerant journalist, working on magazines in Australia before arriving in Canada in 1954.

Starting in Ontario at the head of the Great Lakes in Thunder Bay, Tytherleigh worked his way west, first on the *Port Arthur News-Chronicle*, then in Winnipeg at the *Free Press*, where he rose to assistant foreign editor. That led him to his ultimate home in Lotusland and a job at the *Province*, which appointed him city editor but then demoted him to entertainment columnist. His magazine experience led to an offer to edit that section of the upstart *Times*, and he jumped ship to the new offset paper in 1964. When the *Times* foundered a year later, he was at the helm as managing editor of the decimated daily, holding a copy of the final front page as cameras recorded the newspaper's passing for posterity. It was an experiment that would provide him with valuable experience in newspaper production. Walking a picket line with the 1970 shutdown of

Pacific Press, Tytherleigh suddenly saw a way of shifting the balance of power in the long-simmering labor dispute that had boiled over with the precipitous company closure. Together with *Sun* reporters Barry Band and Barry Broadfoot, Tytherleigh cooked up a plan over his kitchen table.[1]

> At the union meeting I suggested — why don't we start our own newspaper? Having worked with offset printing at the ill-fated *Times*, I knew how easy it was to produce a paper. Later in the week, I was called to a meeting of the union bosses, including the poobah from New York, to discuss the feasibility. I said there was no need for a discussion because we were well under way with a planned, 12-page paper to be published on the Saturday.[2]

Meeting with Bill McLeman of the Newspaper Guild, Tytherleigh learned the unions had already incorporated their own publishing company as a contingency after the 1967 strike. Dubbed "Pugstem Publications," the corporate moniker was an acronym for the joint council unions: Pressmen's Union, Guild, Stereotypers, Typographers, Electricians, and Mailers. On Tuesday of the week following suspension of publication by Pacific Press, McLeman told the Canadian Press that the Guild was considering putting out its own paper if the *Sun* and *Province* remained closed. McLeman said in an interview that the Guild "would have to study the situation carefully to determine if advertisers and the general public would accept such a publication."[3] But the unionist wanted most of all to negotiate the contract agreement that had seemed so close months earlier. "We have asked the company to sit down and talk to us for two months at least," McLeman told CP. "Settlement is within our grasp and none of the outstanding contract issues are strike, lockout or suspension issues."[4]

According to the Guild strike newsletter, the *outsider*, after Tytherleigh's union meeting suggestion, the Guild executive had requested a feasibility study on a joint council newspaper. "This study came back in the form of a fait accompli Friday — a newspaper ready to go to press."[5] On Wednesday, Tytherleigh and his journalist colleagues met with their ITU counterparts to work out the details of production. The copy could be set at the ITU's training school on Broadway, they were told, and press time was arranged at nearby Broadway Printers. A price of 15 cents per copy was set, and mailers and circulation staff signed on to arrange distribution. The *outsider* chronicled the clandestine preparations for the strike newspaper's birth.

> The editorial men got on the phone after the meeting and mustered a founding staff of 10. The first step was to mobilize the beats. The next day the writing for 12 pages began. Somehow they had to produce current and interesting local, provincial, national and international news without wire service, with only three telephones (shared by the picket organizers, the ITU hiring officers, and mailers). They had no typewriters, no city directory, none of the simple, convenient tools of a newspaper office. But they had the most skilled talent in the country pooled from two of the nation's leading newspapers.[6]

On Friday, the unions announced the first edition of the *Express* would hit the streets the next day with a press run of 100,000. A statement declared the *Express* would publish three times a week, but would be "strictly an interim, temporary publication" that would go out of existence as soon as the dispute at Pacific Press was settled. It added that the *Express* would be "a true newspaper, completely filled with news, including local news, national and international news, legislature reports, a TV section, sports, entertainment and women's news along with the latest stock market information."[7] The first edition contained no advertising, but the statement said subsequent issues would, and the newspaper would only circulate within the Vancouver city limits. The Canadian Press noted that a Guild spokesman declined to say where the paper would get its national and international news.[8] The CP report quoted a skeptical but unnamed spokesman for Pacific Press. "We are sure the experience will give them a new outlook on the difficulties management faces in producing a newspaper, things they . . . never thought about before," the source said. "We presume they have studied carefully the ramifications of their actions."[9] The *outsider* was more enthusiastic.

> It will probably be the subject of theses and communications studies for years to come. For it is the fastest and most successful newspaper born in a large city. *The Express* is more than just a paper that filled a void of a city starved for the printed word. It is one that changed the mood of 1,100 people, virtually overnight,

> from being stunned and frustrated by sudden joblessness, to optimism and pride in the creation of a product that stands as real proof of the quality and responsibility of the hundreds of men and women of the five unions involved.[10]

At Broadway Printers that Friday night, as the presses rolled to print the first edition of the *Express*, the well-worn machinery gave way under the strain of such a big job. In the middle of the night, before they had printed the first edition of their challenge to Pacific Press, the unionists were faced with disaster in the form of a broken-down press. Luckily, a pressman who owned welding equipment could be roused to make the repair and, according to the *outsider*, "the presses rolled on within 90 minutes of the break."[11] At 4:30 a.m. on February 21, less than a week after the last editions of the Pacific Press papers had been printed, the first issue of the *Express* hit the streets. It printed its own obituary in advance on its front page. "This is both a birth notice and a death notice. We hereby announce the birth of the *Vancouver Express* and the certainty of its death at an uncertain future date. . . . We will cease publication of the *Express* immediately Pacific Press, *The Sun* and *The Province* reach a contract settlement with their employees."[12]

The first edition was a sellout, with more than 100,000 copies snapped up almost as soon as they hit the streets. "There's no question that we'll sell all we can print," Guild president Jim Young told the Canadian Press. "There is more of a demand than we can meet. Unfortunately we don't have the press capacity."[13] Also on the front page was an announcement that advertising would be accepted for subsequent editions at a rate of $5 cash per column inch. "We had no idea the deluge that was coming," recalled Tytherleigh.[14] Soon a flood of requests for ad placement swamped the unionists. "Advertising pleas came in from across the country as soon as word got out that a new paper was aborning," reported the *outsider*. "The second edition was oversold. . . . Deadline for the next (fourth) edition — Saturday — was 4 p.m. today. But by 11 a.m. the small ad space was completely sold out, and by noon all advertising had to be closed off."[15] Copies of the second edition sold out before noon the following Tuesday, according to the strike newsletter, and before the third edition was out stores were "phoning trying to assure stock to cope with rush. Newsies were sold out Tuesday before refill could reach them. Lineups waiting for the paper before it reached the street. . . . First edition bringing offers of $1 as collector's items."[16] With the advertising content, the *Express* quickly doubled its edition size to twenty-four pages, including four full pages of advertising and many partial pages, according to CP. "Woodward's Stores Ltd. bought the entire back page, first of the major department stores to advertise in *The Express*."[17]

The strike paper's makeshift offices lent an air of old-time newspapering. "A small advertiser went through *Express* editorial rooms to basement advertising department and commented: 'Just like an old Humphrey Bogart movie,'" reported the *outsider*.[18] But the editorial content of the *Express* was as professional as were the journalists producing it, which meant bending over backward to cover every news story impartially, including the dispute with Pacific Press that had put them in the publishing business. "It wasn't to be a strike paper, in other words not a labour sheet," recalled Tytherleigh. "In fact, Ray Haynes of the B.C. Fed gave me a sheaf of labour stuff and, when it didn't appear, he called me in to ask why. I told him we were publishing a newspaper and our own labour dispute would be treated as a general news story."[19] Stock tables were reproduced in teletype form as supplied by the exchanges, which led to the look of a school newspaper. Otherwise, idled *Sun* reporter Trevor Lautens judged the product in *Saturday Night* magazine "professional in appearance but stale in national and international news content, scalped from radio newscasts and out-of-town dailies. The absence of bylines and identified columnists contributed to its lack of personality."[20] There was a good reason for the secrecy, at least in the minds of the *Express* staff, one of whom told CP it was "to prevent any possible repercussions after the dispute. No pictures are allowed of the newsroom, nor are there any bylines on *Express* stories."[21]

A Canadian Press report noted the first edition of the *Express* carried out-of-town news, but no wire service copy.[22] The *outsider* identified the problem faced by the *Express* journalists without giving away their secret. "Somehow they had to produce current and interesting local, provincial, national and international news without wire service."[23] But the news stories carried in the *Express* were not just crudely scalped from other media as Lautens surmised, although some other essential newspaper features were. "Canadian Press wouldn't service us, so a wire service employee slipped us a dupe of the day's news," recalled Tytherleigh. "As for the TV programs, we scalped *TV Guide*. A crossword came out of a puzzle book and we had our own horoscoper. Three vital components of a newspaper whatever the ivory tower says."[24]

The horoscope for Pacific Press in its bid to tame the powerful and innovative joint council unions was looking bleak indeed with the birth of the *Express*, which suddenly tipped the balance of power in favor of the enterprising unionists. "It attracted more advertisers than its production and higgledy-piggledy billing facilities could handle," wrote Lautens, "and made bags of money."[25] Meanwhile, Pacific Press was losing money every day it was shut down. "Cost of the strike to date is estimated at nearly $1 million," reported the *Financial Post* after the first three weeks of the dispute.[26] But with advertising revenue that would normally accrue to Pacific Press instead pouring in to the strikers, soon Pugstem Publications was so cash rich it was able to declare a weekly $10 dividend to unionists to supplement their strike pay of $65.[27]

More important than the extra income to the locked-out journalists was the boost in morale the *Express* provided. The *outsider* published the comments of some.

> Never enjoyed newspaper work so much in my life . . . if our publishers had done what our present publishers are doing, pat us on the back and feel the pride in our work that we feel, they might have had greater and more dedicated production . . . nice to escape the feeling of being a pasteurized puppet . . . first time in months we've not had endless headaches from bad lighting and stale air in the Pacific Press mausoleum. Maybe it will be aired out by the time we get back.[28]

Paddy Sherman was the official corporate spokesman for Pacific Press during the 1970 labor dispute, as he had been during the 1967 Guild strike. He was also an early aficionado of the grinding vertical training route up the North Shore's Grouse Mountain. The *Province* editor was a former political reporter and Victoria bureau chief for the morning daily, and his energy and ability were enormous. A wiry English expatriate who joined the *Province* from the *Yorkshire Post* group of newspapers in 1952, Sherman also wrote a biography of B.C. Premier W.A.C. Bennett in 1966 between climbing through clouds in his alternate incarnation of mountaineer.

Sherman had made his name as a reporter in the spring of 1957 with the exclusive story of the fate of a Trans-Canada Airlines plane that had gone missing the previous fall. The vanished North Star aircraft was presumed to have crashed in the mountains east of Vancouver on December 9, 1956, with sixty-two aboard, including five Canadian Football League players returning home after an appearance in the league's annual all-star game at Vancouver's Empire Stadium. The ill-fated flight radioed that it was having engine problems shortly after takeoff and was returning to the Vancouver airport. That was the last heard from the plane, which could not be found despite an extensive search. Sherman liked nothing better than to spend his spare time scaling the craggy peaks of the Coast Mountains that wedge Vancouver into the southwest corner of British Columbia, and he made finding the wreckage his personal mountain-climbing mission. Three mountain climbers, who knew Sherman and his quest for the missing plane well, began scaling 7,910-foot Mount Slesse near Chilliwack in the Fraser Valley on May 12, 1957. They found bits of wreckage and phoned Sherman at the *Province* when they descended two days later. The scoop-hungry *Province* newsroom, led by Sherman, swung into action to get an exclusive at the expense of the rival *Sun*, coincidentally as rumors of the newspaper's impending marriage to its competition began to gather momentum. According to the Southam history by Charles Bruce,

> The three climbers were swept up, rushed to the [*Province*] office, and hidden in the magazine department to tell their story. Bits of wreckage went to TCA. Editor Ross Munro alerted circulation. Managing editor Bill Forst and city editor [Bruce] Larsen headed for Chilliwack for clean-up coverage. By 9:45 TCA confirmed that serial numbers on the scraps tallied with those of the lost North Star. At 10:30 the extra reached the street.[29]

The diminutive but hyperactive Sherman was constantly in search of higher peaks to scale. When Sherman used vacation time to join a trek up a 22,000-foot peak in the Peruvian Andes, *Province* publisher Fred Auger used Sherman's regular column space to explain the editor's absence to readers. "Paddy is one of those peculiar people who derive great satisfaction from mountain climbing," marveled the comparatively sedentary publisher. "When he feels the need for exercise (which is often) he dons a sweatsuit and races the chairlift up Grouse Mountain — would you believe it — jogging a good deal of the way." [30]

While as editor of the *Province* he was the newspaper's top journalist, Sherman made no secret of where his loyalties lay when he took on the role of corporate spokesman. When "summit talks" to end the 1970 labor dispute at Pacific Press were held at the end of February, Sherman announced to the press that Victoria was selected as the site for meetings because it was a "neutral ground away from the hurly-burly of Vancouver."[31] The renewal of negotiations came after FP Publications general manager Dick Malone visited Vancouver on February 24 for a regular Pacific Press board meeting and told reporters the company was prepared to meet with the unions and consider any new offer. Hearing the Brigadier's comments on radio, the union leaders quickly sent Malone a telegram. "We accept your offer unanimously and stand ready and willing to meet at any hour of the day or night," read the message from joint council co-chairmen Bill McLeman and Len Guy. "We await only your communication as to the time and place of such a meeting."[32]

After the negotiations in Victoria broke off after two days without a resolution, Sherman told the press there had nonetheless been "a good thrashing out of all the issues" and said talks were expected to continue later back in Vancouver.[33] But Charles Perlik, the Newspaper Guild's international president, called the Pacific Press spokesman's version of events "totally inaccurate."[34] The *outsider* reported Perlik's perspective. "Contrary to the Sherman report, he said there was NOT a 'good thrashing out of all issues' but rather discussion of one subject, reparations to Pacific Press from the unions."[35] Benson went on radio to outline a company proposal made in Victoria that was rejected by the unions because it called for the damages the company claimed it was owed as a result of union production slowdowns to be paid back by employees foregoing retroactive pay and delaying pay increases.[36] Perlik labeled the proposal a call for "complete capitulation" by the unions. Pay increases in the second year of the offer, he pointed out, would be withheld until the company had recovered all of the money it claimed from the unions. "This could back it right up to the end of the contract," said Perlik.[37] He warned workers they "may have to dig in for a long fight" at Pacific Press.[38]

> He said Benson told the union officers the company has maximum strike insurance, providing top benefits of $30,000 per day for up to 50 publishing days. And he said Benson admitted the company made a profit in November, December and January. He said he came away from the Victoria meeting convinced the company had three R's in mind — "retaliation, retribution and reparation." He said Benson told the unionists he made one mistake, in not closing the plant down earlier than he did.[39]

Perlik also criticized the Pacific Press manager's habit of making personal attacks on union negotiators, noting it was bound to hinder bargaining. "I regret Mr. Benson has resorted to name-calling," he said in a prepared statement. "Perhaps he is aware of disputes settled by such behavior. I am not."[40] But the Guild men had to thank Benson for filling them in on details of the strike insurance policy provided by the American Newspaper Publishers Association. According to a report in the *outsider,* during the Victoria talks Benson revealed more in ninety minutes "than all the spies and investigation by the unions had achieved in 12 years. He gave details: $80,000 in American currency to get $30,000 a day for 50 publishing days, a total of $1.5 million."[41] Guild international officer Chuck Dale told a regular quarterly meeting of the union's strike-bound Vancouver local, which set an attendance record with 431 members turning out on March 22, that because the company had strike insurance, they should not expect serious bargaining until it expired. "You had better resign yourselves to the fact that this is the classic strike insurance dispute," Dale told the packed Guild meeting. "Time and time again we have seen it in the United States. We know when Management runs out of insurance and begins to suffer they bargain — for the first time — in good faith."[42]

When Premier W.A.C. Bennett offered in early March to arbitrate a binding settlement in the dispute, Sherman indicated the company's willingness to agree, announcing that "if . . . both sides agree to accept his decision as final, that would be the answer."[43] But the unions nixed that idea, balking at making binding on their members the decision of a politician beholden to their media employer for his re-election. The ethical dilemma of a journalist like Sherman taking the side of management in a labor dispute with other journalists was outlined by *Sun* columnist Allan Fotheringham. "One wonders what relationship Mr. Sherman, having stepped out of neutral ground, can now have with his returning reporters."[44] But Sherman was more than a mere mouthpiece putting the company position before the public. The memos he wrote to the Pacific Press management team outlined his efforts behind the scenes to use his contacts as a political columnist to the company's best advantage. His keen insights into bargaining strategy revealed an acumen that would propel him to the loftiest peaks of the corporate hierarchy.

Early in March the Newspaper Guild countered the company's lawsuit for damages against the ITU with a grievance claiming $2.1 million in severance pay on behalf of its members laid off by Pacific Press without notice.[45] The company then broadened its lawsuit to include the Newspaper Guild and the Stereotypers' Union as well, claiming a "conspiracy to illegally limit production," and naming 334 union members individually as defendants.[46] The company raised the stakes the next week by filing a notice of motion in court to seize the assets of the unions as collateral or have nineteen of their officers jailed pending the contempt hearing.[47] The unions responded by applying to B.C. Supreme Court for an injunction of their own against the shutdown of Pacific Press, claiming the closure was illegal because it contravened several provincial labor statutes, and seeking monetary damages for lost wages.[48]

On March 19, Sherman phoned Labour Minister Leslie Peterson in Victoria in an attempt to orchestrate a resolution of the dispute. "I asked his advice on how to get the matter of arbitration raised on the floor of the legislature so that we could publicly signify our interest," Sherman reported to his management colleagues in a memo dated March 23. "He said he wouldn't do that unless there was some indication that both sides would be interested, and that most of the preparatory work had already been done beforehand."[49] The major obstacle to convincing the joint council unions to accept binding arbitration, Sherman argued, was the lawsuit brought by the company to recover monetary damages from the production slowdowns and for contempt of court against the union leaders for failing to prevent them despite a court injunction. The latter carried the very real possibility that unionists might be sent to jail, which caused the joint council to balk at bargaining until the lawsuits were dropped, and provincial labor department officials to similarly hesitate to get involved. Sherman saw the possible imprisonment of unionists as putting the company in a no-win situation.

> No matter how it goes, the rules of the game will change markedly when the result comes down. If we should lose, and the unions discover they can hit the company in this way with impunity, then their morale will be stiffened enormously and our prospects of satisfactory bargaining diminish. If we win, and heavy fines are imposed — or even worse, if somebody is jailed — bitterness will reach a new high. In such circumstances, I should be surprised if we could negotiate a settlement before the end of the summer.[50]

While some on the management bargaining team advocated using the lawsuits and any subsequent monetary award for damages as a bargaining tool to extract a settlement favorable to the company, as Southam had done with the ITU in the late 1940s, Sherman disagreed. "This argument suggests that we retain them until the unions are ready to offer us something in bargaining that will make it worthwhile to drop the suits. If we sit waiting for unions to make an approach, then suddenly find ourselves with union people jailed, that lawsuit is no longer a bargaining weapon."[51]

According to Sherman's March 23 memo, Pacific Press lawyer Bill Macdonald shared his view that relying on legal remedies was a mistake by the company. "His feeling is that he does not have a very strong case against individuals named in the contempt charges, and that the damage suit is very distant and hard to assess," Sherman wrote. "He also seems quite concerned that the union counter-actions, which we have been inclined to take lightly, may be better-based than we concede. He refers particularly to the $2.1-million suit against us for 'illegal shutdown.'"[52] The alternative of government mediation also had a downside for the company, according to the *Province* editor, as it "would still leave [Len] Guy clearly in the picture, able to come to the rescue dramatically."[53] The role that Guy, a vice-president of the B.C. Federation of Labour in addition to head of the ITU, would play in any eventual settlement had Pacific Press management of two minds, according to Sherman.

> There are some grounds for thinking . . . that his handling of the whole affair has so damaged him with his people that his future is

> already behind him. . . . The best he can do is contrive a way out of the mess he has got his members into. Some of the negotiators, on the other hand, who know Guy much better than I do, feel strongly that he won't be dead until publicly dismembered and then deep-fried.[54]

With April came an announcement that the unions had agreed to a company proposal of mediation by the provincial labor department. The consent raised some eyebrows, as the B.C. Federation of Labour had boycotted the Mediation Services Commission in the two years since it was created by the Bennett government. The Fed was protesting its power to impose compulsory settlements in matters affecting the public interest. The joint council leaders stipulated in a letter to mediators Alastair Pollock and Pen Baskin that the mediation was informal, that no hearings would be held under the Mediation Commission Act, and "your endeavors on our behalf will not result in any form of compulsion."[55] A condition set by the mediators was that to prevent the spread of rumors and misinformation, only they would release information on the talks to the media.[56] The contempt of court proceedings against the union leaders were adjourned until April 15 while efforts at settlement proceeded.[57] A Court of Appeal hearing on the injunction issued against the production slowdowns went ahead, however, and it was upheld in a ruling issued on April 9.[58]

According to Benson, it was thought to be the first time in B.C., "perhaps even in Canada, that a decision has been rendered that under a closed shop the union is responsible for the actions of its members."[59] The significance of the legal ruling was not lost on Guy, who as head of the ITU's Vancouver local was suddenly in jeopardy of serving jail time if the adjourned contempt hearing found him responsible for the production slowdowns that defied the court injunction issued against them. During a mediation session on April 15, according to a Sherman memo, Guy interrupted proceedings by insisting on a meeting alone with Don Fergusson. The company's chief negotiator refused to meet Guy without a witness, so the mediators attended.

> Guy stressed that it was basic union policy that so long as a jail threat hung over the heads of the union there would be no settlement. He indicated that he was now aware there was a serious chance he would go to jail. Fergusson read his mood as one of genuine and considerable fear of this. Guy said he was now prepared to bargain day in and day out in a genuine way.[60]

Guy asked, according to Sherman's memo dated April 17, that if an agreement could be reached before the next court date, would the company be prepared to do what it could to have the charges against him withdrawn? The hearing scheduled for April 15 had been adjourned to the 27th, so bargaining could proceed without interruption. "He thought that with a little face-saving, an agreement could be reached before the deadline," reported Sherman. "The mediators, of course, were present through all this, and recognized it for the break it was. . . . The mediators began to lean on Guy a little. . . . Guy seemed extremely anxious to get negotiations going."[61] As talks continued, the ITU obstacle seemed to have been overcome, leaving only the Guild issues. "Their alternatives are not encouraging, because there is no doubt McLeman knows that to keep himself out of jail Guy will sell the Guild down the river the moment it suits him — even if it means all four mechanical unions crossing a Guild picket line," Sherman noted. "That would destroy the Guild, I feel sure, and McLeman knows it."[62]

Editions of the *Express* grew fat with advertising, swelling by April to thirty-two pages. Demand for advertising was so great that the papers could have been much bigger, but the limited press capacity at Broadway Printers hindered expansion. Its equipment could only print a twelve-page section with each press run, necessitating three setups to print the larger *Express*. To alleviate the production bottleneck, Pugstem Publications invested some of its profits in a third press, which increased capacity to sixteen pages to keep up with the growing *Express*. According to a report in the *outsider*, plans were afoot for further expansion of press capacity at Broadway Printers.

> In planning for further expansion, the production manager now has a press lined up with a capacity of 32 pages in one run, 64

> total, with a 35,000 run-off in one hour. . . . Saturday's paper will be 40 pages, and even then advertising had to be refused days ago. Every major advertiser, including the most established oil company, has advertised or tried to buy space in *The Express*.[63]

Guild members selling copies of the *Express* on the street pocketed five cents of the 15-cent selling price, supplementing their strike pay to an extent that many were making as much as they had working for Pacific Press.[64] Members of the mechanical unions were paid hourly wages to produce not only the *Express*, but also flyers and community newspapers at overworked job printers. The success of the *Express* started the wheels turning again in Mike Tytherleigh's head, as he wondered if the paper might be able to take on a permanence beyond its strike-void mandate. "As time went on, the paper had a life of its own, becoming part of Vancouver," recalled the *Express* editor. "It was then I wondered about resurrecting the dream that had been that of *The Times* — publishing a third newspaper in Vancouver."[65] He tried to think of who might be willing to finance such a daily. "I flew up to Prince George to see Ben Ginter, the beer baron who had taken on the Liquor Control Board," he recalled, "but he was too busy with his Prince George newspaper. I also approached Don Cromie to see if he wanted to get back in the game. No."[66] When CBC television interviewer Doug Collins, the former *Vancouver Times* columnist, visited Vancouver from Toronto to do a story on the dispute for the public affairs show *Weekend*, the *outsider* ran a review.

> Mike Tytherleigh . . . came through effective, angry and terse over the insult all employees feel in the charges of irresponsibility against the people who worked for them. Executive Secretary Bill McLeman, who gave the Guild story in a half-hour interview, came out on nothing about the Guild in the 30 to 40 seconds he was left on the Eye. And Paddy Sherman was on — as usual.[67]

As the deadline for the contempt of court hearing against the Pacific Press union leaders loomed closer, bargaining under the direction of the mediators bogged down. According to Sherman's memos to management, the April 24 deadline the company had set Guy for reaching an agreement in advance of the court date seemed to add little urgency. "In my view, if a genuine deadline exists, and if Guy has the Joint Council with him on a specific deal, then we won't know whether they are going to fold up until late Friday," wrote Sherman in a memo dated April 22, adding a warning in rock-climbing terms. "This means some rough cliffhanging."[68] Sherman reported that the pressmen's business agent, Dave McIntyre, told Fergusson the joint council was not afraid of the contempt action, insisting the unionists were convinced they would win the case. "There are several ways to read it," Sherman wrote. "McIntyre has been totally in Guy's pocket throughout, which may suggest that at this point he is acting on instructions to confuse us, hoping to stampede us. It may also mean Guy has lost the ability to deliver the Joint Council, even if he himself is still genuinely scared of jail."[69]

Given his previous opinion that the contempt action posed a no-win situation for the company, Sherman suggested that "if Friday passes without a settlement, we shall have no negotiated settlement for a long time."[70] That left the decision of whether Pacific Press would attempt to publish the *Sun* and *Province* using non-union replacement workers from behind a picket line. Sherman reasoned that the ensuing battle might turn into an all-out labor war in the heavily unionized province, which was already suffering almost total shutdowns in the construction industry, the result of a lockout by employers, and in the key forest industry due to a strike by towboat operators.

> Obviously we shall then face the decision on when and how we resume operations. I suspect that this may well be more difficult than we have lately come to believe. I don't normally lean to the conspiracy theory, but there is some reason to believe that the B.C. Federation of Labor is trying to bring about a general strike — which you will recall it wanted to do last year. If this is true, then the absence of the newspapers is clearly something it would want; the resumption is something it would try hard to prevent.[71]

Sherman urged that "if the decision is to resume operations shortly, and not to take the chance that by July B.C. will be an economic disaster area," the company should take the initiative, at least for purposes of public perception, and rather than let matters proceed to court instead seek binding arbitration.[72] "This proposal should be put to the unions Friday afternoon, and arrangements made to milk the proposal for all it is worth via radio and TV. It is faintly possible that the unions would accept it, since it would end the court actions when there seems no alternative."[73] There was another significance to April 27 aside from the scheduled contempt of court hearing for the unionists, noted the union strike newsletter. "The Company's 50-publishing-day strike insurance of $30,000 a day ran out yesterday or will run out tomorrow. That means on Monday Pacific Press is without benefits."[74]

With agreement on most contract issues close, Baskin and Pollock made a move to resolve the drawn-out dispute. First, the urgency of the contempt hearing was reduced with its adjournment, by consent, to June 8.[75] According to a report on labor relations at Pacific Press for the 1980 Royal Commission on Newspapers, the court date was rescheduled "for fear that this might exacerbate an already tense situation."[76] After a two-hour bargaining session on April 29, with the sides unable to agree on some key items, the mediators offered to propose their own package to resolve the dispute. The proposal would not be binding on either side, they explained, and it could be rejected. But if it was accepted, it would have to be accepted in its entirety, without changes. That afternoon at 2 p.m. they put forward their proposed settlement. It called for a three-year agreement retroactive to the expiration of the previous contract, with wage increases of 43 cents an hour in each year, or $10 a week or 9.5 percent, whichever was greater, for salaried Guild positions. To deal with future production slowdowns, a "hotline" system would be set up for a joint union-management committee to immediately deal with the problem. If no solution could be reached within one hour, an independent arbitrator would be empowered to impose one.[77] The *outsider* reported on the joint council meeting.

> The unions listened to the settlement proposal in one room; the Company listened in another. Then both sides caucused to consider it. We don't know what happened in the Company caucus — but the union caucus was neither polite nor quiet: there were more than a few suggestions made by the commissioners that the

> unions found difficult to accept; in fact, there were some suggestions in the package that the unions found intolerable.[78]

The joint council negotiators told Baskin and Pollock the next day that "because of some of the items in, or not in the package, we're reluctant to accept it, [but as] the mediators have taken a very realistic position, we'll do the same in the interests of ending this dispute."[79] The company response came from chief negotiator Don Fergusson on May 1. He told the mediators his committee was "prepared to recommend the package to its principals with the contracts effective from January 1, 1970. Prompt acceptance of this by the union membership would enable our employees to be back at work within a few days."[80] The change in contract date from that proposed by the mediators was something Pacific Press had been trying hard to achieve for months, but in altering the terms of the package, company negotiators had violated the conditions set down for acceptance or rejection in its entirety, with no further negotiation.

The 1980 Royal Commission report concluded that the company tried to alter the effective date of the contract proposed by the mediators "apparently without understanding that, by agreeing, it could not negotiate further any of the items in the package."[81] Union negotiators insisted the conditions of the proposal were made abundantly clear to them by the mediators. "We'd been warned we could not . . . accept part of the package, reject other parts of it and attempt to modify still other areas of the settlement."[82] The joint council negotiators calculated that, in addition to making the contract expire after the lucrative Christmas advertising season, thus putting the unions in a weaker bargaining position in subsequent negotiations, the effect of changing the date to year's end would cost their members more than $500,000 in retroactive pay and delayed wage increases.[83] After a week of recriminations, during which the *Express* reached a record forty-four pages, Pacific Press finally relented and Fergusson accepted the proposal on behalf of the company in a letter of May 8.

> It was not made clear to the company's negotiators . . . that this was a package proposal, not intended to be the subject of further negotiations. Only now has it been made clear to us that the unions were emphatically told that the proposals were not negotiable, and that they accepted them on that basis. In these cir-

> cumstances, while we are not satisfied that the proposals were fair to the company, it would obviously place the union negotiators in an impossible situation if we sought further bargaining.[84]

Union members voted overwhelmingly to ratify the settlement package, and picket lines around Pacific Press came down on May 11 as the *Sun* and *Province* geared up to publish again on May 15 for the first time in three months. To pay the additional labor costs of publication, which the company estimated at $3.5 million in the final year of the contract, both papers hiked their cover price by half to match the 15 cents the *Express* had been charging.[85] The *Province* reported that company negotiators "felt there was very little mediation involved in the end and that the terms suggested by Baskin and Pollock reflected the union positions rather than the company's," and that they had discovered an "'apparent disparity in instructions' that had been given to both sides."[86] The Royal Commission study concluded that management was "bitter at this outcome and the manner in which it had been achieved."[87] Allan Fotheringham left no doubt, in his first *Sun* column after publication resumed at Pacific Press, which side he thought won the power struggle between company and unions.

> No one of course ever "wins" when people are out on a picket line, but if "face" and "pride" are the real issues — as sometimes happens in labor disputes — the five unions clearly bested Pacific Press. They achieved, as the union leaders say, "all we went after" and probably a little more than they expected. (Aided, perhaps, by two volunteer mediation commissioners, eager to win some labor respect.)[88]

Sherman used his first column after publication resumed to defend himself against Fotheringham's allegations of partisanship made the previous day. "For three months I have been, in effect, out of journalism," wrote Sherman in explaining his role as corporate spokesman. "I wasn't involved in bargaining, and I have no intention of re-opening the freshly-healed wounds."[89] The *Province* editor reported that his foray into labor relations had been eye-opening. "One well-known labor leader told me . . . 'The only language the unions understand is a bloody big club.'"[90] As the final edition of the *Express* went to press, Tytherleigh was interviewed by Barbara Frum on CBC radio. "We beat them with a rolled-up newspaper," he told her.[91] Tytherleigh ran into Benson on the street. "He said: 'You're going to take my job,'" recalled Tytherleigh. "I was amazed. But he was right. . . . When I went back into Pacific Press, the Brigadier shook my hand but I counted my fingers afterwards."[92] The B.C. Federation of Labour issued a statement claiming a union victory and praising the workers for their solidarity and dedication, but making no mention of the key role played by publication of the *Express*. According to *Sun* labor reporter George Dobie, the omission was because the union body "believes the temporary newspaper was too conservative [and] maintained a neutral policy on labor issues."[93]

Ed Benson had failed in his bid to tame the tenacious and ingenious Pacific Press unions. In addition to $7.5 million in revenue foregone during the three-month shutdown, the newspapers had lost readers they would never win back.[94] There was only one thing left for Benson to do, and on September 23, 1970 he resigned as the company's general manager, citing "a basic disagreement with the board of directors of Pacific Press."[95]

10 The Perpetrator

Allan Fotheringham's career in journalism almost ended abruptly before it ever began. He had worked his way through school as a student sportswriter for the *Sun* in the early 1950s, but just before his graduation from the University of B.C., the *Ubyssey* student newspaper he edited ran a riotous parody of the daily in its annual year-ending "goon" issue. On campus, the paper published by the Cromie heirs became the *Vancouver Son* published by the "Crummy" brothers. The sports editor, Erwin S. Swangard, appeared as "Squirming S. Vanguard," and the hulking German immigrant was not amused. He let Fotheringham know it, foreshadowing the course of the columnist's career by threatening legal action in the middle of final exams. Fortunately for Fotheringham, Don Cromie had a better sense of humor and wrote a letter to the editor of the student newspaper, which hangs framed on the columnist's wall.

> It has been drawn to my attention that a purported newspaper titled *The Vancouver Son*, imitating the type and head style and satirizing some of *The Sun*'s general styles and manners, has been published, allegedly by *The Ubyssey*. This satirical publication libels, ridicules and generally damages *The Sun* to a grievous degree, with malice aforethought.[1]

But after threatening a lawsuit, Cromie's letter carried a postscript which asked "the identity of author and editor of this work, and ... whether said Perpetrator might be interested in a Salaried Position at *The*

Sun. . . . A person of the skill and ruthlessness of the above mentioned Perpetrator should have no misgivings about advancement once installed."[2] The result was that Fotheringham appeared before Cromie in the old Sun Tower several days later for a job interview, during which the publisher, according to the columnist, "confirmed his reputation as an eccentric genius."[3] Fotheringham recalled that throughout his audience in the publisher's office, Cromie sat "with his feet up on a desk attempting to flip paper clips into the bowl of a ceiling light. We talked and he interviewed, but his attention never wavered from the task that he had obviously spent many hours — and years even — attempting to master."[4]

As punishment, Cromie put Fotheringham to work for Swangard, who refused to even speak to the new recruit for his first six months on the job. "Every Monday morning, at the sports department staff meeting, Swangard would turn to assistant sports editor Merv Peters and instruct: 'Tell Fotheringham to cover the lacrosse game in New Westminster,'" remembered the columnist. "Peters would turn to me and say, 'Fotheringham, cover the lacrosse game in New Westminster.' It was an interesting first six months."[5] Within a few years, however, Fotheringham was a favorite of Swangard, who in 1957 offered him the job of his replacement as sports editor when he moved up to managing editor. Then 24, Fotheringham had been considering a return to school for a law degree if he had not achieved a certain level of success within three years as a journalist. The offer of a senior position confirmed his choice of profession, but he responded with an odd decision. Rather than accept elevation to management, he quit instead to broaden his horizons by traveling and working in Europe.[6]

When Fotheringham returned to Vancouver a few years later, Swangard took him back at the *Sun* and asked him to start a travel page, for which he began writing a Saturday column. In 1964 he won a Southam fellowship to study for a year at the University of Toronto. On his return to the *Sun*, Fotheringham was promoted to editorial writer, writing unsigned columns, but Swangard saw that his flair for the dramatic was wasted with anonymity and convinced Keate to give him his own column in 1968. With it, Fotheringham decided to do something different. Rather than telling the same old tales that appeared in the newspaper every day, he resolved to tell the stories the public did not usually get to read. The best stories, Fotheringham felt, were the ones journalists told each other over drinks at the Press Club after handing in their copy for the next day's paper.[7] The result was unlike anything the city had seen before but, as Fotheringham recalled, he could scarcely take credit for originating the genre.

> Most serious columnists, it seemed to me, came to the office, puffed on their pipes, looked out the window and delivered Olympian overviews of the world's ills. A columnist, someone once said, is simply a good reporter who has strong views. I thought I should get out of the office. It was only sometime later that I learned that, in New York, guys called Gay Talese and Jimmy Breslin and Tom Wolfe were doing the same thing. They called it the New Journalism. In fact, I think it was Old Journalism, applying shoe leather rather than thumb-sucking.[8]

His column ran on the *Sun*'s inside section "front" page five days a week, and within a few years Fotheringham was being hailed by *Time* as "Canada's most consistently controversial newspaper columnist. . . . A tangier critic of complacency has rarely appeared in a Canadian newspaper."[9] By the 1970s, things were changing in journalism, in the newspaper business, and at Pacific Press. The rigid strictures of the inverted-pyramid style of objective reporting were being replaced with a more subjective journalism, in which reporters were given room for interpretation, allowed to "let it all hang out," and expected to "tell it like it is." Controversy was no longer to be avoided, and Fotheringham was the most in-your-face journalist Vancouver had ever seen. While his *Sun* column was nominally on the subject of politics, Fotheringham wrote with such an entertaining style that the result was often more humorous than anything else. He carved up his unsuspecting subjects with what one writer described as a "nasty wit, erudite bitchiness and ratty entertaining savagery."[10]

Within a decade Fotheringham was a national media star, with magazine writer Tom Alderman dubbing him the "King" of Vancouver in 1979. "In close to 11 years as resident hit man for the *Vancouver Sun* . . . Fotheringham has left a delightful trail of mangled, bloodied victims in his wake," wrote Alderman in the *Canadian* magazine supplement included with major weekend newspapers across the country. "That's a lot of clout for a humble columnist and only in Vancouver could it come about. For despite its metropolitan population of more than a million, it's still a self-obsessed little city, steaming with gossip and exaggerated rumor."[11] But as skillful as "Foth" was with his acid pen, what set him apart from other columnists were his network of inside sources and his ability to wheedle information out of the most reluctant of interviews, as Alderman observed.

> As even his detractors admit, the guy's a charmer, a delightful companion. He looks up at you — at his height, with no discernable neck, he looks up at most people — a cuddly teddy bear of a man, soft of build, elegant of dress, a shy smile decorating his . . . country-boy countenance. Overlook the vaguely smarmy tinge to that smile and it's hard not to like him right off. . . . "He's irresistible," says one former victim. "Even after he stuck it to me, two weeks later I find myself letting him pump me for more information."[12]

First turning his attention to city hall, Fotheringham became, according to Sean Rossiter in *Vancouver* magazine, "a far larger figure in civic politics than any candidate. His column became indispensable."[13] Rossiter claimed Fotheringham single-handedly discredited mayor Tom Campbell "in a series of hilarious columns" and "literally elected" alderman Art Phillips as his replacement. "By 1971 he was the central switchboard for information on civic politics," wrote Rossiter. "Information being power, he was conceivably the most important single influence in a complete redirection of priorities at city hall."[14] For Fotheringham, it was like shooting fish in a barrel. The rampant factionalism on Vancouver city council, running from perpetual socialist Harry Rankin on one side to frontmen for land developers looking to carve up the rapidly growing city on the other, the columnist had no shortage of ammunition. "Council at the time had more than its share of pompous fools and buffoons, recurring ingredients in Vancouver politics," recalled Alderman. "All Foth had to do was drop in on their meetings, record their idiocies and add his inappropriate asides. No matter that some said Foth was recording conversations that hadn't even occurred."[15] Fotheringham, noted Alderman, subscribed to the dictum of H.L. Mencken, legendary editor of the *Baltimore Sun*. "The acts of the Administration should be reviewed constantly, and with the deliberate purpose of finding weaknesses in them, and those weaknesses should be denounced in plain terms and without reservations of any kind," wrote Mencken in 1928. "In journalism, it seems to me, it is far better to be wrong than to be timorous."[16]

The decisive moment in Fotheringham's offensive against the Non-Partisan Association that controlled city hall came in November 1972 on the eve of municipal elections. Bill Street had been the party's candidate for mayor in place of the incumbent Campbell, whom Fotheringham had already destroyed. When the columnist pointed out that the lobbyist for land developers had raised campaign funds for NPA candidates far in excess of allowable limits, Street bowed out as the party's candidate and instead ran for mayor as an independent. NPA president Peter Birks called a press conference to denounce the columnist. "One priggish reporter with a history of inaccurate and sloppy reporting has taken it upon himself to bring about the destruction of this association by innuendo, rumor and sly sentence structure," Birks told the assembled media. "He is succeeding in that objective."[17] Fotheringham lurked in the back of the room, wearing a trenchcoat and his trademark smirk as Birks accused him of spreading "half-truths." He did so confidently, according to Rossiter, "knowing he had a column already in print and hitting the streets that would finish Birks as a factor in civic politics."[18] A backroom deal had been made, Fotheringham learned, to allow Birks' Cadillac dealership to remain on a downtown triangle of land on Burrard Street created by the massive Bentall office towers project. The car lot would replace a patch of green space advocated by planners "to let the poor office workers breathe," wrote Fotheringham.[19]

> Mayor Tom Campbell and Peter Birks got together, outside city council's jurisdiction. Early in December, Campbell convened an *in camera* session of council, where so many of the NPA major decisions that affect the future of the city are arranged. He had a surprise announcement — a deal he had arranged to allow Peter Birks and his Cadillacs to remain on the site.[20]

Provincial politicians also became fodder for the columnist's cannon blasts, and W.A.C. Bennett's Social Credit government was full of wayward members who provided Fotheringham with ample ammunition. No target was more inviting than "Flying Phil" Gagliardi, an evangelist minister as well as a cabinet minister who flew around the continent to religious revival meetings and charged his expenses to both his hosts and the provincial government. "When he was highways minister he got to a point where his 'travelling expenses' were almost half as much again as his salary of $17,500 — and that wasn't even including his trips in his Lear jet," pointed out Fotheringham. "The government has paid Gagliardi hotel bills from Anchorage, Alaska; Columbus, Ohio; San Francisco,

Toronto, Winnipeg, Montreal and Portland."[21] Gagliardi's excursions at taxpayer expense were among the worst excesses exposed in the administration of Bennett, who had held power since 1952. "The suspicion remains . . . that the junkets have nothing to do with government business," noted Fotheringham. "They are to do with Gagliardi's private means of earning money — his preaching business."[22]

Fotheringham mustered enough ammunition in that memorable 1972 column to finish "Flying Phil" as a political force after twenty years in cabinet. "Gagliardi, although his departmental offices and his staff are in Victoria and his riding is in Kamloops, lives in the Hotel Vancouver," continued the columnist. "He has maintained — or should I say the taxpayer has maintained — year-round headquarters there for at least four years now."[23] Not only were taxpayers footing the bill to put Gagliardi up in the finest hotel in town, pointed out Fotheringham, but often they were doing it in more than one town at a time. "Gagliardi was caught charging for his Hotel Vancouver room while he was also being paid his sessional indemnity to live in Victoria while the legislature was sitting," noted the columnist, who pointed out the numerous additional road trips. "He never repaid the government after the double-billing was detected."[24] Gagliardi had not only maintained multiple residences at taxpayer expense, pointed out Fotheringham in the same column, but he had managed, despite being forced to sell his private government jet to *Playboy* magazine publisher Hugh Hefner, to fly for free almost three times as often as any other B.C. cabinet minister. "Government planes in one year flew him to Kamloops on 33 weekends. 'On government business,' was his reply when questioned in the legislature. Strange that government business occurs in Kamloops only on weekends, never during the week. It's obvious he uses the private shuttle service not for government business but his own business, his church."[25]

Fotheringham's assault on Gagliardi continued for a week, pointing out that since entering politics from humble beginnings in 1952, the preacher had become a wealthy man. "Over the years he has acquired a ranch outside Kamloops where he bred fine Arabian horses," the columnist noted the next day. "He built a handsome new home in Kamloops overlooking the river. He acquired a summer home in Savona. . . . All this during a life in politics."[26] His sons also had benefited from Gagliardi's position as a government minister, Fotheringham charged. "At one time, their complicated nest of eight companies, dealing in land beside highways, showed land sales to oil companies totalling some $400,000."[27] By the time the columnist was finished, Gagliardi was literally defenseless. "The most interesting aspect of Gagliardi's current troubles is that not a single Social Credit backbencher, nor a single Social Credit cabinet minister, has come forward in his defence," Fotheringham noted. "They feel they can no longer afford, with an election coming up, the luxury of his reputation."[28] According to *Maclean's*, Fotheringham's destruction of Gagliardi was his "proudest accomplishment."[29]

Fotheringham's controversial writing style became both a blessing and a curse for *Sun* publisher Stuart Keate, who watched his newspaper's circulation surge as the columnist became the talk of the town. By the end of March 1969, circulation of the *Sun* stood at almost 261,000, second in Canada behind only the *Star* in megalopolis Toronto and fully 4,000 ahead of the *Globe and Mail*.[30] Household penetration in the Vancouver city zone, Keate reported in a letter to FP president Max Bell at his winter home in Palm Desert, California, had risen from 69 percent to 72.2 percent, and "we are pressing on to Dick Malone's minimum target" of 74 percent.[31]

The downside to Fotheringham's habit of pushing the limits of libel was that it invited lawsuits, including three in one memorable week. Keate noted in the introduction to a 1972 compilation of Fotheringham's *Sun* columns that in person the columnist was "the best of companions — blessed with the gift of laughter, a small-town boy converted to a big-city appreciation of mod clothes, sports cars, fine wines, tennis and the rich, full life," but what appeared in print was something else.[32]

> When he sits down at a typewriter to address himself to the peccadilloes of a wayward Social Credit cabinet minister, a strange transformation takes place. "Foth's" nostrils distend, his glasses fog up, and great gouts of steam emanate from his ears. The earth trembles. Secretaries quake. Lawyers call on his publisher.[33]

A flurry of writs against the controversial columnist arrived on the eve of the 1970 shutdown of Pacific Press. First came a private prosecution on January 2 for defamatory libel by lawyer Arthur Fouks, head of the British Columbia Brewers Institute. A commission of inquiry into the granting of liquor licences had been convened the previous fall, and in his column of

September 10, Fotheringham had described it as involving "high-powered lawyers and public relations men and influence pedlars representing the brewery and beer parlor interests of B.C. The fronts for the very people who have skilfully managed to make drinking a simple glass of beer in this province a vulgar pastime, a distasteful chore in seamy surroundings."[34] The inquiry heard from Prince George brewer Ben Ginter, according to Fotheringham, that "greasing the palm and high-pressure tactics and monopoly agreements constitute the name of the game."[35] Ginter claimed he was unable to get his ale into more than a few beer parlors because he could not match the payola of larger breweries, reported Fotheringham. "I was told to go see Mr. Fouks," the columnist quoted the burly, bearded brewer. "They told me for $10,000 he could fix me up."[36]

Fouks tried to have the column killed before publication, Fotheringham claimed in print on December 3, by calling an unnamed *Sun* executive and quoting the copy verbatim. "This was most interesting, because Fouks' phone call came at 10:40 a.m.," noted Fotheringham. "No one at *The Sun* at 10:40 a.m. had seen a copy of that day's edition. The first papers do not come off the press until 11:00."[37] Fouks complained of "deliberate character assassination by innuendo" when the inquiry resumed, but Fotheringham was not finished with him yet.[38] On December 30 he claimed that Fouks, a business partner of former attorney general Robert Bonner, had been hired as a lobbyist by the Insurance Agents' Association after a bill before the legislature proposed that property damage insurance be eliminated from compulsory automobile coverage, which would have saved the average motorist $24 in mandatory annual premiums. Fotheringham asked in his column: "Is it not true that the fee paid by the Insurance Agents' Association of B.C. to Mr. Arthur Fouks was $10,000? Is it not true that Mr. Arthur Fouks, after some months, was successful in the task for which he was hired?"[39] The summons served three days later on Fotheringham and Keate, on behalf of the *Sun*, alleged injury to Fouks' reputation in a rare private prosecution for criminal libel.

The columnist soon had himself in more hot water with an item on January 27, just as the labor dispute at Pacific Press heated to the boiling point. A *Sun* reporter had given Fotheringham an item for his column after covering a suburban Surrey inquest into the murder of a 7-year-old girl. "Hardened press types who've attended hundreds of inquests are still shaking their heads in disbelief over the callous, unthinking way in which

. . . the inquest was conducted," wrote Fotheringham, noting that in the public gallery the girl's mother broke down in tears on hearing the graphic medical details of her daughter's death. "Not one court official made a move to help the tragic mother. In addition, the coroner, not even bothering to offer his sympathy to the parents, treated the father in a most brusque way in questioning. . . . The press was appalled at the whole performance."[40]

The girl's mother had not been warned to stay out of the courtroom during the grisly medical testimony, Fotheringham claimed, quoting an "experienced reporter" as calling it "one of the worst examples of idiocy by public officials that I've ever seen."[41] The column brought a motion by prosecutors on behalf of coroner Harold Keenleyside for criminal contempt of his court. A hearing was set for February 18, reported the *Sun* in its few editions of February 9 that were printed amid the escalating production slowdowns by the unions. Soon the Pacific Press papers were completely closed in response to the labor tactics, which meant that proceedings against Fotheringham went on in a relative information vacuum, though the case made news across the country.

Fotheringham's source for the alleged insensitivities of coroner Keenleyside turned out to be a memo written by *Sun* reporter Moira Farrow. The columnist testified he had discussed the matter with Farrow, for fear she might have been "emotionally affected" by the proceedings, and also talked to a radio reporter who had attended the inquest. Farrow took the witness stand and admitted that most of Fotheringham's words had been contained in her memo, except for "unthinking," which had been added by the columnist. Prosecutor George Murray called police witnesses who testified that Keenleyside had made several vain attempts to prevent the mother from attending the inquest, and when she insisted, he had instructed the pathologist to minimize the graphic autopsy details to spare her feelings.[42] In the end, while finding that Fotheringham had, according to the Canadian Press, "stretched the limits of criticism beyond the breaking point," B.C. Supreme Court Justice Alan McFarlane said he found no malice in the columnist's remarks and dismissed the Crown's bid to jail him for contempt.[43]

When the case brought by Fouks came to court the next month, Fotheringham narrowly escaped being arrested and fingerprinted after the chief court clerk insisted on the procedure before the columnist could be released on his own recognizance, as ordered by the presiding judge. It was only the intervention of defense lawyer Robert Gardner that convinced Provincial Court Judge David Moffett to quash the customary bench warrant while Fotheringham signed a $100 bond guaranteeing his attendance on the next court date.[44] The case was put over for trial until the fall, when it was thrown out as not meriting criminal prosecution, private or public.[45]

After the two exchanged jousts in their columns following the 1970 shutdown of Pacific Press, one of Fotheringham's favorite targets was Paddy Sherman. When Fred Auger retired in 1972, Southam named Sherman his replacement as *Province* publisher. Sherman in turn recalled his chief political writer from Victoria, elevating Bob McConnell as the morning paper's new editor. "Bob McConnell is one of the new breed of journalists, as much at home with a slide-rule or a computer print-out as with politics, people, or a pungent phrase," wrote Sherman in his Saturday column.[46] Only 29, McConnell held a master's degree from the University of Chicago and had started working for the *Province* as a high-school student. In introducing his new editor to readers, Sherman explained that McConnell had become interested in journalism after a sensational but unfortunately inaccurate *Sun* story in 1960 had spread across its front page tales of a drunken beach orgy, for which classmates at his west-side high school had been blamed. As student president at Magee High School, McConnell protested as part of a delegation to the *Sun* newsroom that items of underwear found at the Spanish Banks scene had been among three tons of clothing collected by teens to assist the needy. When they felt a second story hardly put the facts straight, the students picketed the old Sun Tower with signs reading "Facts not Fiction" and "Journalism not Sensationalism," recalled Sherman.[47] The school board chairman had called it "one of the worst examples of yellow journalism in the city's history," Sherman noted, and had urged publisher Don Cromie to sell his interest in the *Sun*.

> The publisher and other top officials who held the ultimate responsibility at *The Sun* that long ago spring, left years ago. . . . For most people it became nothing more than an almost-forgot-

> ten incident of a journalistic style now mostly outdated. But on a thoughtful 17-year-old it made a marked impression, forming strong views on what journalism should and should not be.[48]

This prompted Fotheringham to respond that, while the appointment of young McConnell was "admirable," and Sherman's account of *Sun* sensationalism a dozen years earlier was basically true, the new *Province* publisher "unctuously rolled on and on, licking his lips rather too much."[49] In retaliation, Fotheringham dredged up the infamous *Province* roorback. "For a new appointee concerned about journalistic integrity, Mr. Sherman seems to have a very leaky memory about the most memorable Canadian journalistic event of that same year," wrote Fotheringham. "*Province* veterans still grow angry with shame when the event is mentioned. It was one of the most despicable newspaper sellouts of the century. The famous *Province* front page of Sept. 10, 1960, is now standard reference in political texts dealing with the roorback technique."[50] Noting that Sherman's 1966 biography of W.A.C. Bennett made no mention of the "real facts behind the affair," the columnist suggested the scenario had been played out repeatedly in provincial elections. "It is Mr. Sherman, presumably, as editor these past few years, who directs the stern anti-Socred editorials between elections — before his *Province* faithfully rolls over and turns Socred each election time."[51] That summer of 1972 saw yet another provincial election campaign, which Bennett habitually called at three-year intervals. This time, however, the premier's luck ran out after twenty years in power, and the socialist New Democratic Party, led by social worker Dave Barrett, topped the polls. According to Rossiter, the columnist went easy on the socialists while they were in power.

> Fotheringham seemed to relax Mencken's dictum somewhat for the NDP government, perhaps to counterbalance some of the overt media bias it was subjected to. He profiled many of Barrett's more astute appointees. Barrett learned, however, that nothing raises the columnist's blood pressure like a failure of character at the decisive moment. Barrett's [1975] election loss occasioned a column of profound, bitter disappointment.[52]

Fotheringham's own politics were undeclared and difficult to determine. The columnist once described his views as "limousine liberal," with a small "l," but others were not so sure.[53] "Al's ideology or political faith was never clear," Stuart Keate told *Vancouver* magazine in 1981. "Some said he was Conservative, a lot said NDP, although I think he was a small-l liberal."[54] A political scientist once invited the columnist to speak to his class on municipal politics but learned little about Fotheringham's own leanings. "I don't know if Foth has a political philosophy," UBC professor Paul Tennant told Alderman in 1979. "I hoped we'd learn something about his point of view. He was very entertaining. But we didn't find out a thing about how he looks at things."[55]

One area in which Fotheringham was no liberal and left no doubt about his leanings was labor relations. The Pacific Press unions were a favorite target of the columnist's pen for their frequent interruptions of his columnizing. The star writer was not required to join the picket line with his co-workers during the three-month strike in 1970, but he revealed in his 1999 book *Last Page First* that he was paid his regular salary by the *Sun* so he wouldn't take his coveted skills to another employer. "My managing editor, the great Bill Galt, met me downtown every two weeks over a martini lunch and handed over the paycheque — under the table, as I recall."[56] In his first column after publication resumed, he publicly calculated the price other journalists had paid by foregoing three months of salary in exchange for the hard-fought contract agreement. "Employees lost one-quarter of their annual salary," noted Fotheringham. "For a good reporter, that would amount to $2,500."[57] After a brief strike in 1972, the columnist again went on record with his analysis of the dispute, claiming the craft unions only settled after "a gutsy group of *Province* reporters" served notice through the Newspaper Guild that they might not necessarily stand behind their ITU brothers this time. "Union solidarity did not force settlement of the Pacific Press troubles," wrote Fotheringham. "It was the threat of some reporters refusing to support printers that spurred on union leaders."[58] That brought a rebuke from Len Guy of the ITU, who called Fotheringham "pathetically inaccurate" and claimed the *Province* reporters' group actually slowed negotiations instead of speeding them as the columnist claimed. "His facts are dead wrong," thundered Guy. "The people in *Province* editorial are just not trade unionists — they are pro-management and historically a very weak group. . . . It gave management hope for a weaker agreement so they put off getting down to serious bargaining."[59]

The issue in joint council negotiations in 1972 was technological change, as Pacific Press was in the process of implementing computerized typesetting, which promised to render redundant the printers who had previously set type in molten lead on large manual "linotype" machines. Already most of the typesetting was being done automatically with punched tape produced by ITU members on computer terminals in the company's data processing department. The tape was then fed into either computerized linotype machines or more modern "cold type" typesetters that composed columns of type photographically for chemical engraving, like photographs that appeared in the newspaper. The next step in the automation process, explained *Sun* labor reporter George Dobie, would be a pioneering joint project between Pacific Press and the Honeywell computer company called "pagination," which would compose entire pages of type on computer.

> The workers in the composing room were skeptical at first that the process could work but now they are worried because they actually see how a machine can make hundreds of decisions involved in making up a page. . . . Fear of the automated future hinges on a machine called the optical scanner which can read typewritten copy. It would bypass punching, make the necessary spacing and hyphenation and put the copy into page form for running on the presses. It could bypass the composing room where the ITU members are employed.[60]

Joint council negotiators wanted an agreement on automation before bargaining began on other issues and refused to discuss wages and working conditions with the company. The unions applied for mediation on September 13 after only two days of what the Newspaper Guild's Bill McLeman called "philosophical debate . . . over the company's responsibility to present and future employees, and the need for guarantees that Pacific Press would not become a totally automated plant 'requiring two or three people to press buttons.'"[61] The new Pacific Press general manager, Dave Stinson, said "to suggest the company is alarmed by this action would understate the case."[62] The B.C. Mediation Commission appointed veteran Clive McKee to intervene in the dispute, while the four mechanical unions conducted strike votes that resulted on October 6 in a 91-percent mandate for a walkout.[63]

Talks broke down on October 26, with Stinson announcing that the company had offered to guarantee the jobs of all present employees, and if, by attrition, staffing levels were reduced by 20 percent as a result of automation, a move to a four-day week would be made to save jobs. "In our view, the proposal shows that fears of massive staff reductions are now groundless," said Stinson.[64] Reducing the workforce through attrition, joint council leaders told union members in a letter, "does not fit our concept of an imaginative — or realistic — solution."[65] When the contract expired on October 31, Stinson proposed extending it by two months to provide time to negotiate further and offered unionists an immediate 5-percent wage increase as a "gesture of good faith."[66] McLeman rejected the offer as "meaningless," pointing out that by law the existing contract remained in effect until a new one was negotiated or a strike was called.[67] The unionists saw the company move as another attempt to move the date of contract expiration to after the lucrative pre-Christmas advertising period, during which the joint council enjoyed considerable bargaining power. "We find it very difficult to believe that Pacific Press management is attempting to embark once again on the same kind of program implemented three years ago that so handicapped genuine bargaining that a long unnecessary lockout resulted," McLeman told Stinson in a letter.[68]

On November 3, twenty-eight delivery truck drivers went out on strike. Pickets appeared only around the loading bay of the Pacific Press Building, allowing other employees to report for work and collect their pay as usual, producing newspapers that the public never read. The strike was widely seen as a pressure tactic in negotiations by the crafty unions. The drivers worked for an independent company, but their small union was affiliated with the pressmen's local. Bruce Moffat, owner of S&P Distributors Ltd., which operated from an office in the Pacific Press Building, said his negotiations with Dave McIntyre, bargaining agent for the pressmen's union, ended after only one meeting. "Then on Halloween night, they served strike notice at 10 p.m. at my home," Moffat told a *Sun* reporter. "Some trick or treat!"[69]

With Pacific Press operations running normally otherwise, the pressmen refused to handle the printing plates prepared by other departments after pickets appeared, claiming the company was "unfair" in its dealings with their brother drivers. The strike notice expired late on a Friday night, which prevented the *Sun* from printing its large and lucrative weekend edition. The frustration felt by some journalists was expressed by *Sun* nightlife reporter Jack Wasserman in an unpublished column contained in internal Pacific Press archives. "For the third time in the past five years I'm sitting in front of a typewriter at 4 o'clock in the morning writing a column for a newspaper that probably won't be published. It's a fearsome, frustrating, dehumanizing experience that underlines the inability of the individual to function in an increasingly collective society he is powerless to alter."[70]

Mediator McKee attempted to resolve the dispute, but soon his efforts appeared ended when the new NDP provincial government passed a bill rescinding the controversial B.C. Mediation Act, under which he had been appointed. "I guess that means I'm out of a job," said McKee, who then agreed to mediate unofficially as a volunteer.[71] Bargaining continued non-stop for thirty-two hours until 8:30 p.m. on November 6, when "exhausted" negotiators called a five-hour recess. "Work proceeded normally in the preparation of the newspaper but no copies left the presses," reported a story prepared for that day's unpublished *Sun*.[72] Spokesmen for the sides, the report noted, refused to disclose if any progress had been made.[73]

Talks resumed at 1:30 a.m. the next day in hopes of getting that day's editions of the *Province* printed, but that plan was abandoned at 4:40 a.m. McKee told the Canadian Press, however, that the technological change issues had been resolved.[74] Finally, at 4:20 p.m., after the longest negotiation session ever at Pacific Press — fifty-four hours of almost continuous bargaining — an agreement was reached. "Moments later copies of Tuesday's *Sun* were rolling off the presses," reported CP. "First papers hit the streets just after 5 p.m., not far behind the normal hour for the *Sun*'s final edition to go on sale."[75] Wage increases of 20 to 24 percent over two years were agreed on, as was a unique formula to deal with technological change.[76] Under the automation agreement, the company retained the right to introduce technological change and reduce its workforce by attrition, but once 5 percent of any union's membership had been eliminated, Pacific Press would pay that union an amount equivalent to the wages due any further displaced workers.[77] "The effect seems to allow management to continue to manage the business, avoid rows over featherbedding, put the brake on automation or slow it down to a degree, and give the remaining workers a share of the proceeds through their unions," wrote Dobie in an analysis.[78]

Some members of the Newspaper Guild were upset they did not get a chance to vote on whether to support the striking drivers and the printers whose jobs were endangered by automation, as members of the craft unions had. The annual B.C. Federation of Labour convention began on November 6, while the Pacific Press papers were prevented from publishing by the picketing of truckers. A Canadian Press report of the first day's proceedings noted "talk — at the grassroots level — of a possible split within the Vancouver Newspaper Guild."[79] The strike had come as a surprise to journalists, reported CP, and no vote was taken at a subsequent meeting of Guild membership. "They say talk of leaving the guild and forming some kind of professional union for journalists has been 'fairly widespread.'"[80]

Fotheringham's distaste for the militant Pacific Press unions seemed to grow over the years. The way the columnist saw it, the labor situation at Pacific Press amounted to "the people who write being jerked around by people who can't form a sentence. . . . People who can write subsidizing people in overalls."[81] According to Fotheringham, it was the printers and pressmen who should have been beholden to journalists, not the other way around. "Such are the arcane politics of union-management relations that reporters have been thrown into a dog's-breakfast alliance with circulation clerks, janitors, ad salesmen and horny-handed pressmen in the principle of solidarity."[82]

The tenuous nature of the alliance between journalists and the tradesmen who produced their words in print was becoming obvious, as was the dysfunctional labor-management relationship at Pacific Press. Bargaining revolved around the formulation of Machiavellian strategies instead of focusing on solving, in a collaborative way, the problems posed by the advances in technology which Pacific Press wished to implement. The adversarial approach prevented the sides from dealing effectively with issues at the bargaining table, as the 1981 Royal Commission on Newspapers report on labor relations at Pacific Press noted. "It is clear that the relationship could not stand the normally protracted negotiations needed to resolve complex industrial relations problems."[83] The 1972 strike showed that because they were unable to engage in productive bargaining due to a lack of trust, the sides were reduced to the repeated use of force in the power relationship.

> It appears that little could occur in the way of serious discussion until the unions undertook job action. The first significant offer from the employer on the subject of technological change was finally made on the day of the strike by S&P employees. The use of power appeared entrenched as the determining factor in resolving disagreements.[84]

The unhealthy power relationship would soon lead to more shutdowns of Pacific Press, with the unions and management alternately engaging in job action and closing down operations in a running battle to establish dominance over the other.

In addition to W.A.C. Bennett leaving politics, another passing of significance to Pacific Press occurred in that summer of 1972. On July 19, Max Bell died at 59 after battling brain cancer for five years. A series of operations at the Montreal Neurological Institute had failed to cure his affliction. A lifelong physical fitness buff who neither smoked nor drank, according to his obituary in the *Sun*, Bell before his illness "was proud of the fact that as he approached his 50th birthday, he could walk across a room on his hands and run a mile in little more than five minutes."[85] FP Publications chain manager Dick Malone was executor of Bell's estate and managed the holdings of his heirs in the company, as he had for Victor Sifton's family. According to Keate, despite holding only about 7.5 percent of FP stock personally, Malone's management of the Sifton and Bell estates gave him effective control over the largest newspaper chain in Canada. "A man whose ultimate fate in life seemed destined to be that of an aide, Malone just happened to be on the spot when his various bosses died."[86]

11 The Power Struggle

Bruce Larsen was from the old school of newspapering, a throwback to the cliches of the 1931 movie *The Front Page*. Midway through the 1970s he still wore his hair in a brush cut, while around him a younger generation of university-educated journalists grew their hair long. A native of Manitoba, he began his newspaper career at 18 in 1945 as a reporter at the *Winnipeg Tribune* before moving to Vancouver for a job at the *News-Herald*. He made his name as city editor of the *Province* in 1956 with an exclusive story that began as just another telephone call to the newsroom. It turned into a sensational front-page "extra" that earned Larsen a National Newspaper Award and may have saved a prison guard's life. "The caller was warden Hugh Christie at Oakalla prison," wrote Charles Bruce in his account of the dramatic events for *News and the Southams*. "Three prisoners held a guard — tied up, a razor to his throat. Their leader wanted Larsen. Could he get out there? Within a minute he was on his way."[1]

The prisoners had just lost an appeal of their twenty-year sentences for attempted murder and were desperate. They had grabbed guard Ernie Loveless and tied him to a cot, threatening to kill him unless their demands were met. Larsen had won a National Newspaper Award for feature writing in 1952 with a series of stories on conditions at Oakalla. Ringleader Robert Tremblay wanted to talk to Larsen, as the Southam history recalled.

> Larsen was the only newspaper name he knew. . . . If Larsen would go down the corridor and listen to Tremblay and print his

> story, Loveless would go free when Tremblay's wife could buy a *Province* that displayed it. Larsen called assistant publisher Ross Munro. . . . Would the *Province* go extra? Munro said yes. In the hostage room Tremblay and Larsen talked for an hour.[2]

The prisoners complained they had not been allowed by their lawyer to testify at their trial, and they wanted their side of the story told. They demanded an investigation by the attorney general and an airing in the *Province* of the facts surrounding their case. "They released Loveless on Larsen's word that the extra would run," wrote Bruce. "It did, under the banner head: THIS STORY FOR A LIFE."[3] The prisoners surrendered and eventually got an extra year added onto their sentences. The story marked the high point of Larsen's reporting career and propelled him as a rising star on a path into management. He jumped to the *Sun* in 1959, where he served as city editor and briefly sports editor. With Erwin Swangard on his way out as managing editor in 1968, Larsen made a bid at age 40 for the top newsroom job. "The continuous time I have spent administering a large metropolitan staff is, I believe, now greater than anyone in your newsroom," he wrote in a memo to publisher Stuart Keate, applying for the managing editor's job. "This in spite of my age." Larsen was also a sportsman, breeding harness-racing horses as a hobby. He had served as president of the British Columbia Standardbred Breeders Society, which gave him valuable financial experience working with budgets he argued in his application to Keate. "If you check the record, I am sure you will find that staff will work for me," Larsen wrote. "If there was a knack that allowed me to survive so long as city editor, I believe it was mainly through operating with staff on a principle of mutual respect." But despite his hands-on experience managing newsroom staff, he was passed over for the managing editor's job in 1968 in favor of Bill Galt, who had been Swangard's assistant.

A bomber pilot during the Second World War and a graduate of the journalism master's program at Columbia University in New York City, Galt had been news editor at the *Victoria Colonist* and Washington, D.C., bureau chief for the *Sun*, when he made his reputation, according to Keate, with "riveting" coverage of race riots in the Southern states in the mid-1960s. While Larsen often rubbed subordinates the wrong way with his gruff old-school manner, Keate found it "impossible not to like Galt," as did most others at the *Sun*. "Quiet-spoken, but with a dry wit and hilarious talent for mimicry, he enjoyed the respect of the newsroom because reporters knew he could do any job they undertook, only better," recalled Keate.[4] Galt was the type of worldly, educated journalist that many saw as the prototype of the future newspaper administrator. "A rumpled, corpulent man with straight black hair combed back over some painful psoriasis on his neck, he was fondly known as 'Injun Joe,'" noted Keate. "His hawk nose and jet-black hair gave him a native countenance, whereas in fact he was a descendent of one of the Fathers of Confederation."[5] Young reporters who joined the *Sun* staff from campuses rife with the generational conflict of the late 1960s represented a new breed of university-educated journalist. They could relate better to Galt than to Larsen, who listed his degree from the School of Hard Knocks. According to Keate, what was demanded by the new breed of reporter was "nothing less than control of their copy, consultation on hirings and formation of a committee which would advise management on day-to-day operations."[6] The rank-and-file bid for newsroom democracy, led by some with openly anarchist leanings, was ably handled by his new managing editor, recalled Keate.

> Galt's solution was to move the renegades (at least two of whom were Maoists) to less sensitive beats, and to stage a few downtown "beer sessions" to which the dissidents were invited, to air their squawks against the paper. There Galt made it abundantly clear that management did not intend to abdicate its control of the newsroom. Eventually the clamour subsided.[7]

Galt's management of the evening newspaper's operations played no small part in the *Sun*'s rise in the ranks of the best-read dailies in Canada. By 1973, *Sun* circulation was back up to 248,000 and climbing steadily toward the pinnacle of 261,000 that the evening daily had hit before the three-month 1970 shutdown of Pacific Press. That interruption had cut circulation by 50,000 and dropped the paper from the second-place status it had enjoyed, behind only the *Toronto Star*.[8] More important to the *Sun*'s corporate owner, soaring advertising revenue more than offset the losses of the lagging morning *Province* and the increased costs of production incurred with the lucrative contract agreements won by the Pacific Press unions. *Sun* advertising linage in 1972 leaped 15 percent to 37.6

million printed lines, including a 35 percent increase in classified advertising.[9] Total ad linage increased another 12 percent during the next year in a booming economy, and the *Sun* boasted the largest classified advertising section in the country, including one Saturday that saw a record forty-nine pages of agate ads.[10]

But Galt, a heavy smoker, contracted cancer and died in 1974, and his death marked a turning point for the *Sun* editorially. By default, Larsen finally occupied the managing editor's chair he had coveted for so long. But his appointment did not sit well with many among a staff that had grown accustomed to having input into operations under the enlightened policies of Galt. Larsen appointed entertainment editor Alex MacGillivray as his assistant and the combination signaled a sudden sea change in the *Sun* newsroom. "Larsen is an unreconstructed siren-chasing reporter of the old, old school," a former staffer told *Vancouver Week*. "Whom else do you know who still has a brush cut?"[11] One senior reporter at the *Sun* told the short-lived weekly newspaper that Larsen's appointment sent newsroom morale into a tailspin. "The mood is one of bitterness, discontent, depression, and a feeling of resignation," the anonymous staff member said. "The fear now is that *The Sun* is going to return to the old cops-and-robbers coverage of the Forties."[12]

Some of Galt's key appointments were soon shunted aside under the new regime. Patrick Nagle, whom Galt had recruited from *Weekend* magazine, abruptly resigned as city editor and was reassigned as a "roving" reporter. Clive Cocking, a former *Sun* reporter, wrote in *Vancouver Week* that with the changes wrought by Larsen, it was likely Nagle was not long for Vancouver. "Noted as a 'reporter's city editor' who was concerned with reporters' development, he is expected to rove right on to a new job in the east."[13] Nagle, who moved to Ottawa as the *Sun*'s correspondent in the nation's capital, saw the subsequent change from proactive investigative reporting back to traditional reactive news coverage as due more to economics than personalities. "Galt and Keate recruited me to change the content of the newspaper," recalled Nagle. "The success of the venture foundered on the 1970 strike-lockout. Then Max Bell died and Keate lost his friend in court. Brig. Malone took over administering the finances of the *Sun* and quality went out the window until the balance sheet was restored (*i.e.* never)."[14]

Promoted in Nagle's place as city editor was Jack Brooks, who had been

Galt's replacement as Washington bureau chief for the *Sun*, only to be recalled by Swangard. "Feeling abused," according to Cocking, "[he] became a sulky rewrite man."[15] Dave Driver stepped down from the key post of news editor and was replaced by Bill Rayner. "He's just to the right of Attila the Hun," commented one *Sun* journalist of Rayner, "and just to the left of Bruce Larsen."[16] The abrupt change in editorial direction, especially after a respite under Galt from the "dark, bitter years of Erwin Swangard's rule," wrote Cocking, signaled a return to newsroom autocracy and qualified as less a disappointment than a disaster.

> Rarely in Canadian journalism has a newspaper with such a large circulation and such huge profits produced such trivial journalism. . . . At a time when elsewhere in North America major dailies have recognized that radio and TV are best for spot news, but papers for investigation and interpretation, *The Sun* continues its peculiar fascination with accident reports, petty crime and the overblown speeches of unimportant people.[17]

Hotliner Jack Webster, another *Sun* alumnus who was doing some of Vancouver's best journalism on his open-line radio program, which he had taken from market-leading CKNW to competitor CJOR, agreed that the promotion of Larsen was a step backward for the newspaper. "With the exception of Jes Odam, there is a total lack of investigative reporting in *The Sun*," said the fiery Scot. "People like me shouldn't be doing their work. It's a pity that they didn't go for a weighty reporter-columnist like Allan Fotheringham, who knows what's going on in the province. Not that Bruce Larsen isn't a good technician, but it's time *The Sun* had a crusading managing editor."[18] Fotheringham had indeed been angling for the managing editor's job, reported Cocking, and, having been passed over by Keate for the more senior Larsen, considered shopping his talents around, with speculation centering on a lucrative standing offer for his column from the *Toronto Star*.[19] At one point in the mid-1970s, according to *Saturday Night* magazine, the *Star* "was so convinced it had landed him that it rented billboard space to announce it. Foth balked at the last moment."[20] *Vancouver Week* carried a full-sized likeness of the columnist on its tabloid cover, headlining Cocking's September 1974 story "Will Allan Fotheringham Quit?"[21] Many *Sun* reporters were hoping the columnist would get the managing editor's job, and the selection of Larsen, according to Cocking, was a major disappointment among the newsroom ranks.

> Fotheringham, who is apparently uncertain how much longer he can take the grind of a daily column, has made clear in private conversations that he believes *The Sun* is doing a rotten job. There is every indication that if he had become managing editor, deadwood would have been cleared out of the newsroom, talented new writers brought in and the reporters sent out to do hard-hitting investigative reporting of what is really going on in our society — rather than re-writing press releases.[22]

Fotheringham put pressure on Keate to reverse the direction in which the publisher had sent the *Sun* with Larsen's appointment, and he did it by threatening to take his column elsewhere. "The paper was being run by the usual cop shop graduates, Bruce Larsen and all these jerks," remembered Fotheringham. "I said to Stu Keate . . . 'unless you start promoting young, educated, well-travelled people like [political correspondent David] Ablett, I don't want to stay around here.'"[23] Keate was in the perilous position as publisher of having to placate Fotheringham's considerable ambitions. The columnist had become well connected with his 1963 marriage to Sallye Delbridge, who was daughter of the *Sun*'s chairman, former *News-Herald* publisher Slim Delbridge. "Thus, if not directly in the money, 'Foth' found himself with rich resources behind him," wrote Keate in his 1980 memoirs. "In an attempt to keep pace with Fotheringham's upward mobility, and to recognize his considerable abilities as a judge of news (and talent) I appointed him as Senior Editor, along with Dave Ablett. It was a title that I had seen working well at Time, Inc. It did not work at the *Sun*."[24]

In a 1981 interview, Keate told Walter Stewart that following the move, "the staff divided like the Red Sea."[25] Older reporters sided with Larsen, while Fotheringham gained the loyalty of younger journalists, who regarded the columnist as "their patron saint."[26] Fotheringham takes credit for convincing Keate to promote him and Ablett above Larsen on the *Sun*'s masthead to meet the newsroom clamor for more modern management, but he also takes the blame for the experiment's disastrous results. His management skills, Fotheringham admits, were described charitably as "clumsy" by a colleague.

> I convinced [Keate] to do this thing and he suddenly announced he was creating two new positions they'd never had before, senior editors, Ablett and myself. We would work beneath him, Ablett in charge of editorial pages. I would keep writing my column. He told us quite honestly he was about three years from retirement. He said "I'll watch you two guys and at the end of three years I'll recommend one of the two of you to the board of directors to succeed me." It lasted eight months.[27]

Sun reporter Karenn Krangle co-authored a 1976 report in *content*, a national magazine devoted to media issues, which revealed that when Fotheringham was appointed to management of the newspaper in June 1975, "staff speculation had it he would remake and enrich Canada's third-largest daily. Fotheringham didn't do much to discourage that theory and that, in the view of some, was his big mistake."[28] Cocking reiterated his tales of *Sun* discontent in the new *Vancouver* magazine in 1975. "As in previous years, there continues to be a crisis in morale in *The Sun* newsroom. If anything, disillusionment among the rank-and-file slaveys has sunk deeper than ever."[29] Fotheringham's appointment above Larsen on the *Sun* masthead was seen by some as a sign the newspaper would focus more on the type of investigative reporting that had recently brought down U.S. president Richard Nixon in the Watergate scandal. The hopeful included *Sun* reporter Moira Farrow, who said the paper "could end up as the *Washington Post* of Canada."[30] With his appointment to management, wrote Cocking, Fotheringham had become the "unseen hand . . . now guiding the journalistic destiny of the *Vancouver Sun*."[31] The columnist's role in the newsroom was left largely undefined, however, as Keate told Cocking that Fotheringham was essentially "an idea man, providing story ideas, backgrounders and advising on the hiring of people."[32] The lack of definition was intentional, Cocking concluded, to avoid the sensitive issue of usurping Larsen's authority as managing editor.

> Obviously the exact nature of Fotheringham's new role has deliberately been kept fuzzy for reasons of internal politics. . . . Keate, one assumes, does not want to publicly convey any impression of a lack of confidence in . . . Larsen, who has held the post for only a year. . . . But it's clear to everyone at *The Sun* that Fotheringham

> has been raised above Larsen in the power structure (the masthead listing is one tipoff), and that Larsen is not regarded as the man to provide the ideas for reshaping *The Sun*.[33]

The appointments of Ablett, who was just 34 but held a master's degree from Columbia; Marjorie Nichols, 31, to replace him as columnist and chief of the *Sun*'s Ottawa bureau; John Sawatsky, 27, to join her there; Frances Russell, 32, to the Victoria bureau; and Don Stanley, a 28-year-old PhD, as television critic, suggested that under Fotheringham's influence, according to Cocking, "youth and talent are to be given greater recognition over strict claims of seniority in the future."[34] The columnist was "deeply concerned about improving newsroom morale," wrote Cocking, but "the question is whether he is determined enough and has strong enough backing from the publisher to carry out a 'purge.'"[35] Fotheringham attempted internal damage control to downplay the insider analyses, telling Keate in a memo "the whole paper has over-reacted to it."[36] Cocking, the columnist pointed out to his publisher, "is not counted among my friends (I believe I have talked to him once in the past two years — about my usual rate of bumping into him) but, as you say, he's obviously an admirer."[37] Fotheringham assured Keate he was not trying to usurp his authority as publisher. "I know who's running the paper," he wrote in a memo on October 5, 1975. "I know where my bread is buttered."[38] That Cocking's analyses in *Vancouver Week* and *Vancouver* magazine displayed his rivals in an unfavorable way was understandable, the columnist argued.

> To be fair to Cocking (if there is such a thing as "fair" to a guy who has done me as much damage as that piece) I didn't read all that bullshit about the unseen hand as meaning Foth ran the paper. I read what he was trying to say was that the future looks as if Foth — and not the managing editor — will have the inside track in influencing SK as to what direction *The Sun* should go.[39]

According to Keate, "serious schisms" developed between Fotheringham and Larsen, who was unimpressed with the younger men who had been promoted ahead of him on the masthead, and his resistance made the new senior editor arrangement unworkable. "The problem was that 'Foth' saw himself as an administrator and was hell-bent to run the shop," wrote Keate in his 1980 memoirs. "Within a few months I realized I had made a mistake."[40] His problems with Larsen began soon after his appointment, Fotheringham reported in the six-page memo to Keate that downplayed the Cocking reports, when his request for a direct telephone connection to the managing editor's office was nixed.

> When Ablett and I enter a gathering in his office, Larsen sneers, "Here come the *seniors*." What he means, of course, is the *juniors*. Larsen obviously makes more money than Ablett and, I presume, more than me and it's quite apparent that he resents the fact that the reporters regard these two upstarts as senior in the pecking order. The resentment is natural (it would be surprising in a way if it weren't there).[41]

Contract negotiations at Pacific Press in 1974 seemed straightforward at first, and in fact an agreement was reached between the joint council and company bargainers in short order. But when a vote was called to ratify the agreement, ITU members turned it down, sending their negotiators back for more. S&P Distributors had been assimilated by Pacific Press since the 1972 strike by delivery truck drivers that had prevented distribution of the newspapers for several days. The drivers then formed their own union within the joint council and became known as "wholesalers." When talks in 1974 broke down, they served strike notice on October 24, and the company responded with lockout notice to prevent the drivers from enjoying the leverage they had two years earlier. "That strike was arranged by the joint council and we were forced to pay everyone while we were struck," said Pacific Press general manager Dave Stinson. "We weren't too happy about that."[42] If and when the drivers prevented printing or distribution of the newspapers, the company made clear its intention to lock out all other employees. "We don't want to be in the position of paying all our employees when we can't put out a newspaper because one of the unions is on strike," said Stinson.[43]

When talks resumed on the morning of November 4, the joint council added some urgency by setting a time limit of twelve hours, threatening to take unspecified "economic action" if an agreement had not been reached by then. The unions had been asking for a $3 hourly increase across all job categories, with the company offering $1.10, but joint council co-chair Jack McKim announced on November 4 that their demands had "come down considerably."[44] Shortly before the union deadline passed, agreement was reached on a raise of $1.27, and over the next few days members of all of the joint council unions voted to ratify the deal, except for the ITU. The printers wanted a bonus for working the midnight "graveyard" shift, over and above the differential already provided under the contract for working nights.[45] After more bargaining, a provision was added allowing graveyard shift printers to rotate onto daytime work for several months a year.[46] The extra consideration was significant, according to the Royal Commission on Newspapers study of labor relations at Pacific Press, because it showed the cracks that were beginning to show in union solidarity. "The attempt by the printers to squeeze a better deal for themselves than for the other unions suggests a lack of solid support by the rank and file for the council."[47]

Fotheringham's bargaining power in his struggle with Larsen for control over the management direction of the *Sun* seemed to increase in the fall of 1975 when the columnist landed a plum post writing a column for *Maclean's* magazine, which had doubled its publication frequency to bi-weekly from monthly and aspired to be a Canadian national news magazine along the lines of *Time* and *Newsweek* in the U.S. The magazine's editor, Peter C. Newman, had written to offer the columnist "a job of your choice," recalled Fotheringham.[48] Newman wanted the columnist as Ottawa bureau chief of *Maclean's*, for which he had been an occasional contributor of feature articles over the previous dozen years, but the Vancouverite balked at moving east. "At one point there was loose talk of $2,000 a weekly column, or $104,000 per annum," reported *Saturday Night*, "but Foth decided once again to stay in Vancouver. His contempt for Ottawa ('Coma City') is in any case well known."[49] Fotheringham flew to Toronto and met with Newman over the proposed national affairs column.

> I told him I couldn't move, for family reasons, to dreaded central Canada but would do a national column for him from Vancouver. He immediately called in his senior editors to sound them out on

> the idea. Managing editor Walter Stewart, an old friend, said, "Foth, we love you. But no frigging way. You can't cover Canada from Lotusland." Newman went around the table . . . listened in silence and then spoke. "You're all wrong," he said. "It may not be a national column, but it will be a Fotheringham column."[50]

Fotheringham's first regular *Maclean's* column appeared in the issue dated October 5, 1975, and he remembered rushing to the newsstand on the magazine's arrival in Vancouver. "A man of no small ego, I instinctively turned to the opening pages, expecting my brilliant tome to be on page 2, if not 3," he recalled. "It wasn't there. I leafed through the mag with a sinking heart. . . . Crushed in the realization that my first effort had been rejected, I finally — completely deflated — turned to the last page."[51] There his column would run for more than a quarter-century in what Fotheringham soon realized was "the most inspired positioning ever in Canadian journalism. There isn't a self-respecting journalist in Canada who wouldn't give his left one for that spot. Newman knew what he was doing."[52] Soon the U.S. news magazines copied the idea, noted Fotheringham. "Today there isn't a magazine in existence without a regular feature on that back page."[53]

The timing of Fotheringham's new national profile coincided perfectly with his power struggle with Larsen. Soon after rushing out to see his first *Maclean's* column in print, the columnist filed with Keate his six-page litany of complaints against the ruling newsroom faction. He attempted to consolidate the power conferred by his elevation over Larsen on the paper's masthead by pointing out that half the *Sun* staff backed him and the other half Larsen, "forcing the troops on the floor into becoming mind-readers and guessers as to who had the real authority."[54] Fotheringham urged Keate to clarify the lines of newsroom power in his favor. "The staff reads the masthead and assumes 'Senior Editor' means senior editor, but is sometimes forced to wonder because of obstructionism mounted by the reporters' immediate superiors."[55] The cold shoulder he and Ablett had received from Larsen and MacGillivray, Fotheringham told Keate, had been "especially tough" for the sensitive young editorial page editor.

> I am a big boy and can take care of myself, but I think some of the treatment handed out to Ablett has been despicable. When he

> started, he came in early every morning to attend the first edition news conference. Alex MacGillivray, who nominally is in charge of that gathering, refused to acknowledge him. Not a welcome, not a hello, not an offer to hear his opinion. Frozen silence. . . . On my few efforts at sitting in on the four-star [home edition] meeting, I received the same treatment.[56]

The six-page memo was written in the "bulleted" format of a *Sun* column, in classic Fotheringham style, without holds barred or prisoners taken, and with typical "Dr. Foth" humor interspersed. "Time out for a commercial," broke up the third page. "You heard that Trudeau is going to star in a movie with Linda Lovelace? It will be called A Frog in Her Throat."[57] The columnist told Keate that others in *Sun* management lacked the "one prerequisite of leadership . . . personality." As that was one quality the columnist had in abundance, he argued it was exactly what the *Sun* newsroom needed. "The problem is that at the moment there are only two chaps with personality in the pecking order: SK and your blushing agent."[58] The result, according to the columnist, had been a flood of reporters and department heads coming to his door for advice. "Practically everyone in the office has been in at one time or another — to offer encouragement or support, to ask advice or guidance or perhaps just chat," wrote Fotheringham. "There have been two exceptions. Bruce Larsen has been in my office once. MacGillivray has never entered it. On all our business, I do the trooping."[59] *Sun* staff was "starved for personality," Fotheringham told Keate. "It is really sad — they want inspiration and praise and criticism. Most of all, some small evidence that there is a real live human being ready to talk to them."[60] The problem, according to Fotheringham, was that they could not find such support in the existing power structure.

> Through perhaps no fault of their own, Larsen, MacGillivray and Brooks have extreme personal problems in relating to reporters on a human level. The failure in one or two of them might not be fatal, but it is extremely unusual to have the entire top echelon in a newsroom suffering from that defect and it makes leading, let alone inspiring, a newstaff [*sic*] almost impossible.[61]

The columnist/senior editor pleaded with Keate to make it clear to *Sun* staff "who has the authority of the publisher behind him and that senior means senior."[62] The management arrangement Keate had created could only work, Fotheringham argued, "if the managing editor learns to get along with the senior editor(s). After all, I am not the one who has trouble communicating with the staff. I don't give the staff $10 to come to my door. They come."[63] He concluded his memo by arguing that "in the *long-term,* I don't think the Ablett-Fotheringham-Larsen relationship will work."[64]

But Fotheringham's rising star as a media darling actually worked against him in his power struggle with Larsen. With 1976 came national attention for the caustic columnist as the rest of the country suddenly discovered the revelation that *Sun* readers had been enjoying for years. "This year the magic buzz-name among Canada's journalistic insiders belongs to Vancouver's peripatetic blower of cobwebs and remover of guff," noted *Sun* columnist Christopher Dafoe in July. "The Fotheringboom, which has been going on for some months now, began to gather speed around the turning of the year."[65] The impetus to stardom came from Newman, according to Dafoe. He not only granted Fotheringham the back page of *Maclean's* in a permanent platform illustrated with riotous drawings by *Sun* cartoonist Roy Peterson, but also expressed his "unstinting devotion" to the columnist in the magazine and in "several telling references" in his book *The Canadian Establishment.*

> The May issue of *Canadian Review* hails him as a paragon, *Take 30* is working on an intimate portrait for afternoon television, outraged citizens of Ottawa have written to *Maclean's* demanding portions of his scalp, Pierre Trudeau insists that he has never heard of him, *Time* Canada is said to have been contemplating a cover story . . . Gordon Pinsent is rumored to be considering an offer to play him in the movie version, and Barbara Frum recently got carried away and referred to him as "Al."[66]

Soon Fotheringham was in demand to appear on television, which he did despite being "awful on camera," according to one broadcaster. "He told me he doesn't want to improve," said an un-named producer. "That he regards TV as beneath him. He's only in it for the money."[67] The columnist appeared regularly on CBC's national weekly investigative television program *the fifth estate*. Producer Ron Haggart, according to *Saturday Night,* had "moved heaven, earth, and a sizeable budget" in an attempt to get Fotheringham to relocate to Toronto as a regular contributor to the program. "It was clear that it didn't matter whether we offered him $3 million or the moon," Haggart told the magazine, which reported that Global television in Toronto had similarly offered Fotheringham "an obscene amount of money" unsuccessfully. "He wasn't going to move."[68] Like Newman and *Maclean's* before him, Haggart had to be content with having Fotheringham contribute to the program from Vancouver.

It was such an appearance on *the fifth estate* in February 1976 that led to Fotheringham's fall from grace in the eyes of Keate, and his besting by Larsen in their struggle for supremacy over the editorial direction of the *Sun*. As the credits rolled at the program's end, the columnist was incorrectly identified as "Editor" of the newspaper. "I'm trying to get rid of these cop shop guys with my usual skill, and they're all laying for me," remembered Fotheringham of the incident. "Bruce Larsen went screaming in to Keate the next day. Keate said, 'That's it.'"[69] According to Denny Boyd, Keate didn't even bother to check out the report. "He ordered the presses stopped in midrun, a costly, emergency-only step. On orders of the publisher, a pressman in oily overalls climbed into the middle of the presses with a hammer and cold chisel and sliced Fotheringham's name off the masthead."[70] But some at the *Sun* saw the issue as political and thought Fotheringham's tumble from management was due to his deviation from the newspaper's traditional support for the federal Liberal Party. A column he wrote on February 7, 1976, was widely seen as contributing to his downfall. In it, Fotheringham complained in venomous terms about being refused an interview with Pierre Trudeau on a visit by the prime minister to Vancouver. "This is a difficult column to explain," began Fotheringham, in words that proved prophetic.

> It has been decided, by the nervous souls who now rule the PM's life, that it would be wise not to submit Mr. Trudeau, probably the finest mind of our time, to a nose-to-nose session with Mr. Fotheringham, whose intellectual inadequacies are well known. . . . It's a result, well-accepted, of the 1974 election that ensconced on high the new gurus of Liberal power — Senator Keith Davey and Jim Coutts, both out of the Toronto advertising milieu.[71]

The column, according to some in the *Sun* newsroom, did not sit well with Keate. *content* magazine reported "major speculation that Fotheringham's anti-Liberal views were a challenge to the *Sun*'s solid liberal backing. . . . That column may have particularly upset Keate."[72] The

Ubyssey student newspaper at the columnist's alma mater reported that Fotheringham's "reclassification" was due as much as anything to the fact he was a "progressive reformist in a nest of Liberal WASPs. His recent attacks on the Liberal god, Pierre Trudeau, his favourable treatment of Dave Barrett, and his sharp jabs at the ruling elite, must have produced some fidgetting and nervousness in the boardrooms of the *Sun*."[73] The student paper saw disfavor with Fotheringham emanating from the top of the newspaper's corporate management. "The *Sun*'s higher-ups, including Keate and R.S. Malone, head of FP Publications, which owns the *Sun*, did not think Fotheringham, as *senior editor* had any right to expect an interview with the prime minister or to complain about the denial of that alleged right."[74] The fact Keate had entertained Trudeau at his home was seen by some as reinforcing the political basis for Fotheringham's removal from *Sun* management. Don Stanley pursued the matter with Keate, after the publisher had left the *Sun*, on behalf of *Vancouver* magazine in 1983.

> To paraphrase his courtly PR locutions: someone on Trudeau's staff gave me a telephone call one night around 10:30 p.m., and said they had heard we had a nice pool and could the PM take a little lunchtime dip tomorrow? We gave him a crab casserole and a glass of white wine and he went away happy. It's a lot of nonsense to think that Mrs. Keate or I harbored any resentment against Allan.[75]

Stanley thought that during Fotheringham's time in *Sun* management he attempted "in general to move the paper to the left, from Liberal to liberal."[76] He reported the misgivings Keate and others in *Sun* management had about the columnist's undeclared political leanings by paraphrasing the retired publisher's reasoning. "I and the other editors — Bruce Hutchison for one — felt that we were never sure what Al stood for and what direction he would take the paper if he were in charge of it."[77] The memo that appeared on the *Sun* bulletin board on February 16, 1976, according to *content*, left the staff stunned. "The title senior editor had been abolished," the magazine reported. "Fotheringham, according to Keate's memo, was considering a *Sun* offer to be an associate editor (editorial writer) and 'other options in the media.'"[78] Even more stunning than Fotheringham's sudden demotion was the way it was carried out. While the first editions of the *Sun* that rolled off the presses that Monday morning listed Fotheringham and Ablett above Larsen on the editorial page masthead, the arrangement suddenly changed in the afternoon, between editions. "When the day's second (four-star) edition rolled off the presses at 2 p.m.," noted *content*, "*Sun* staff discovered Fotheringham and his title gone from the masthead."[79] Ablett was still above Larsen, but with the new title of Editor, Editorial Pages.

Province columnist Lorne Parton, never at a loss for a one-liner, had a field day with the sudden change in the next morning's paper. "A funny thing happened to the *Vancouver Sun* Monday between its first and second editions: someone performed a senioreditorectomy," wrote Parton. "The name of one of the holders of that now-defunct category was not to be seen in the paper at all."[80] Fotheringham was in Toronto covering the Conservative Party leadership convention that would elect Joe Clark as a compromise candidate to head off Brian Mulroney, and Parton reported the rumor mill was going into overdrive in the *Sun* newsroom with speculation about the columnist's future. "It is one of the peculiarities of the so-called 'media' that the inside story of a power-shift in one outlet is usually revealed by another medium," noted Parton. "If my spies are correct, more details on the Fotheringham Affair will be heard this morning at 8:30 — precisely."[81]

Parton was referring to radio hotliner Jack Webster and his signature time-slot phrase, in thick Scottish brogue, and as usual the broadcaster had the inside details for his listeners that morning. After calling Keate, Webster reported that the columnist had embarrassed his boss with suggestions he wielded greater power in management than the publisher. The broadcaster also pointed to Fotheringham's Trudeau column of February 7. "He added Keate owed it to the public to print a story in the *Sun* about Fotheringham's situation," reported *content*. "At least two letters, each over a number of editorial staff signatures, were sent to Keate, seeking clarification and expressing reporters' concerns."[82] Fotheringham complained he had been unceremoniously demoted between editions, while airborne to Toronto, but Keate pointed out to him in a meeting on February 27 that he had been informed of the move three days earlier, which was recorded in the publisher's notes.[83]

> Invited Foth to do a memo outlining what he thought would be workable; suggested consultative role with publisher but not administration (hiring and firing, policy, etc.) of newsroom.

> Reminded Foth that system had broken down because of personality conflicts and subsequent office politicking. Foth said wife distraught about possible move to Toronto; wanted a week's holidays to consider.[84]

In his memoirs, Keate wrote that he "reasoned with 'Foth' as best I could, that he was not cut out to be an administrator; that his great gifts as a writer would be wasted and that he should develop along the lines of a commentator, not only in newspaper but in television and magazines."[85] On March 5, reported *content*, another memo from Keate went up on the *Sun* bulletin board, this one announcing the columnist's decision. "Fotheringham would be a contributing editor, doing three columns a week and special roving assignments. He would, according to the memo, report to the publisher on story ideas and news development suggestions, short- and long-range, and maintain a watching brief on recruitment."[86] But, the magazine pointed out, while Fotheringham would remain a member of the executive committee and editorial board, "he would not be involved in administration."[87] His name would remain above Larsen's on the masthead, but Keate's memo was pointed as to the limits of the columnist's authority.

> Contrary to statements that have appeared recently in other media and which have proven embarrassing to both Fotheringham and myself, Fotheringham is not in charge of hiring and firing, nor is he policy advisor to the publisher. Hiring and firing continue to be the ultimate authority of the publisher. Policy advisors are Bruce Hutchison and David Ablett.[88]

Fotheringham continued his *Sun* column three days a week instead of five in addition to writing the back page of *Maclean's*, which went weekly in 1977. He also dabbled increasingly in television, signing on as an interviewer for CKVU, a third station that went on the air in Vancouver in 1975. The multimedia exposure established the columnist, in Keate's words, as "a communications superstar."[89] Fotheringham would come to see his eight months in *Sun* management as "an insane career diversion."[90] But he would continue to "desperately" seek the *Sun* publisher's chair, according to Alderman.[91] *Saturday Night* reported that amid all the job offers Fotheringham had received, "there are those close to him who argue that the job he most desires is located only a few feet from where he's sitting right now. . . . At the *Sun* there are those who say that Foth still wants to edit the paper. He may do it yet."[92]

Larsen had emerged triumphant from the challenge of the upstart columnist, and the editorial direction he proceeded to take the newspaper in was unlike anything Vancouver had seen before, with Fotheringham fighting the inevitable swing to the political right all the way.

12 The Bulldog

One of the journalists Allan Fotheringham urged publisher Stuart Keate to employ at the *Sun* during his brief tenure as senior editor was Doug Collins, the former *Vancouver Times* columnist and CBC television interviewer. The British expatriate took over as editor of the *Sun*'s Page Six opinion forum in 1975 and immediately began stepping on toes with his reports of bureaucratic and academic excess. Soon he was writing a column again, and the result was explosive. Howls of outrage greeted the right-wing world view that Collins propounded, and pickets descended on the Pacific Press Building in protest of his racist writing. Before long, Collins and Fotheringham were exchanging insults in their respective columns during one of the darkest chapters in the *Sun*'s history.

Sun columnist Lisa Hobbs found Collins full of contradictions. "He is a man who enjoys himself hugely," she told readers in turning over her section-front spot to him in 1978. "He relishes combat. He is a stage lion, roaring across the desert in his own mind. Recently, he took me to lunch. We went to Beaver Lumber and he ordered a pound of nails."[1] Clive Cocking portrayed him in *Maclean's* as an "alternately affable and vitriolic wordsmith, who has the appearance and pugnacious style of a bulldog."[2] The canine comparison to Collins stuck, both for his doggedness and a certain facial similarity. But despite his crude nature and lack of formal education, Collins was an erudite writer, prone to "frequent resort to pejoratives of the 17th century," noted his successor as Page Six editor, Mac Reynolds.

> His favorite terms of endearment are chuff (which he translates as "a rustic boor"), stinkweasel ("self-explanatory"), grubshite ("one who makes foul or dirty"), scapegallows ("one who deserves to hang but somehow has escaped the fate"), caw-handed ("an awkward, bloody useless bugger") and sonsy (dictionary definition: buxom; Collins' definition: big tits).[3]

Fotheringham remembered Collins from his days on the *Sun* in the late 1950s as a "typical working-class, left-wing Brit. He was a natural to take over the labor beat and plunged into B.C.'s vicious union wars with gusto."[4] Collins had moved to Vancouver from Calgary, where he won a National Newspaper Award for the *Herald* in 1953 after exposing the tales of a supposed wartime spy as a fraud. Calgary resident George Dupre had been featured in the Quentin Reynolds book *The Man Who Wouldn't Talk* for his claims of having resisted the most grotesque forms of Gestapo torture following his capture after parachuting into occupied France. Collins saw through the deception, confronted Dupre, and extracted a confession from him. As it turned out, Collins' own wartime experiences gave him good grounds for doubting Dupre's tale. The story rated a full page in *Time* magazine and made the front page of the *New York Times*.[5]

In Vancouver, Collins drew his share of fire as a labor reporter, first for the *Province*. According to Fotheringham, that was an era when "the fights and shenanigans among B.C.'s volatile labor unions were very big news."[6] Collins was assailed by the Vancouver and District Labour Council in 1958 as a "rotten apple," and "the key man responsible for the loss of strikes."[7] Collins took to the airwaves to defend himself on the *Town Meeting of the Air* program on radio station CJOR. "I have never been told, directly or indirectly, to write an anti-labor story," Collins protested. "The day I am told to slant stories will be the day I take to following some other career."[8] Collins soon jumped to the *Sun* and broke a story many unionists considered the most controversial ever on the Vancouver labor scene. His exclusive about the president of the Vancouver Trades and Labour Council making a backroom deal to be hired as a "special assistant" brought the resignation of a member of the council's executive who was accused of leaking the story. "If you get into a little controversy, just get Doug Collins on your back and believe me it will be one of the worst experiences you have ever had," explained the ousted Mel Kemmis. "He will twist and turn and before you know where you are he has got it out of you."[9]

But his first stint at the *Sun* was short-lived, because Collins took increasingly to broadcasting, freelancing as an interviewer for CBC radio and television. Soon the indomitable reporter was butting heads over the issue with the *Sun*'s equally strong-willed managing editor, Erwin Swangard. When Collins ignored repeated warnings about unauthorized outside activities which the managing editor considered to be in competition with the newspaper, he was summarily fired for "gross misconduct."[10] But Swangard failed to follow the required procedure under the Guild contract, and a grievance was launched for wrongful dismissal.[11] An arbitration panel ordered Collins reinstated with back pay.[12] "I recall very clearly the morning when [Collins] reported back for work and was told at 7 a.m. to sit at the rewrite desk answering telephones like some cub reporter," wrote Fotheringham. "He stayed for just two weeks to make his point, then quit on his own to get into a broadcasting career with the CBC on a full-time basis."[13] Collins was just as aggressive on the air as he was in print. A 1963 television interview he did with Highways Minister Phil Gagliardi "precipitated a dramatic situation seldom equaled by anything that gets on Channel 2," according to *Sun* columnist Jack Wasserman.

> In the course of the steamy drama Gagliardi stormed off the set, loudly accusing Collins of "treachery" as the result of the interviewer's pointed questions about Gagliardi's contempt of court episode. The filmed interview was subsequently reshot under Mr. Gagliardi's ground rules, but the film was cancelled out of its scheduled spot on the *7 O'Clock Show*. . . . The CBC brain trust's real concern was that Collins appeared to be hostile to Mr. Gagliardi. That, in turn, is a nice nelly way of saying that he refused to back down on his questions during the hot and heavy interview. Now after all the shouting, and I mean shouting, nobody is talking.[14]

That experience came in handy several years later when Collins interviewed Quebec separatist leader Rene Levesque for the national public affairs television program *Hourglass*. When Levesque got fed up with Collins' confrontational questioning, he similarly excused himself from the hot seat. But the bulldog broadcaster knew exactly what to do this time. He reached out and grabbed Levesque, himself an interviewer for the CBC's French-language network, pulling the Quebec nationalist back for more. "I didn't use much force," remembered Collins. "He came back willingly."[15] Collins was well known as a left-leaning journalist in those days, as *Sun* columnist Trevor Lautens observed after an assault the Bulldog launched on San Francisco hotliner Ira Blue. During an interview for the *7 O'Clock Show* in 1967, according to Lautens, Collins injected his anti-U.S. views on the Vietnam war.

> He began by lumping together as examples of California nuttiness the John Birch Society, Governor Reagan, and the gun-slinging Minutemen. You can bet your ring finger that if he had put, say, Tommy Douglas in the same bag with the Communist party and Mao Tse-tung, he'd have got the hook on the spot. . . . Collins, in short, let fly with a piece of left-wing McCarthyism.[16]

The performance, according to Lautens, "was a disgrace, and the CBC should never let him appear again in this role on its stations."[17] Instead of journalism, Lautens wrote, the Bulldog had engaged in "the ego-serving one-upmanship on which Collins has stamped his brand, and is never so evident as when he interviews a fellow member of the radio, television, or newspaper brotherhood."[18] Soon, amid "some bitterness," according to *Province* columnist James Spears, Collins was dropped from the *7 O'Clock Show* and dispatched by the CBC in 1968 to its headquarters in Ottawa, where he covered parliament for the television programs *Encounter* and *Weekend*, and also worked on the radio show *Capital Report*. "Of all the programs he liked his job on *Capital Report* best," wrote Spears. "It put him in the role of national newspaper critic, and . . . the job of telling editors where to go had its compensations."[19]

But within a few years, *Weekend* expanded to twice weekly, with a midweek edition added on Thursday nights, and Collins was dispatched back to Vancouver in 1971 as its western correspondent. True to form, the Bulldog's shelf life expired after a few years in the position as his relationship with the government broadcaster turned sour. "Once again he had had a blowup with his employer and wondered if I could help 'a broken-down old journalist,'" recalled Fotheringham of their fateful 1975 encounter. "We met for a drink at the Harbourfront Hotel in Toronto and caught up on old lies and gossip. I went back to Vancouver and convinced . . . Stu Keate that I could deliver one of the best scribes in the land."[20] The columnist remembered Collins well from his days on the *Sun* in the 1950s.

> A group of two-bit newsroom debators used to gather at the same cafeteria table each lunch hour and Collins was always in the middle of the fray, berating the callow youth among us for our lack of real political conviction. He had been there about a year, and one day the talk turned to war. Collins casually remarked that he had escaped from 10 German prisoner of war camps. Our chins hit the floor. Why didn't he write a book about it? The toughest man I have ever met allowed that he meant to one day.[21]

Collins' incredible tale of stubborn perseverance was published in 1968 by W.W. Norton as *P.O.W.*, with a foreword by legendary legless fighter ace Douglas Bader. According to Sean Rossiter in *Vancouver* magazine, Fotheringham's review of the book was the most flattering profile column the columnist ever wrote.[22] Suddenly, Fotheringham confessed in his column, he realized what made Collins such an unbending bulldog. "For Collins, it was impossible to approach any issue without being aware of the underlying political motivations," observed the columnist. "Shaking one's head in wonder of this man's experiences, it is easy to see why the political realities mean so much to Collins."[23]

Left behind on the beach at the evacuation of Dunkirk as a teenage sergeant in the Second Gloucester battalion, most of which never returned home, Collins was first imprisoned in a concentration camp at Gleiwitz on the Polish border. He escaped in short order and headed for Russia, but was quickly recaptured. As punishment, he was forced to strip naked and stand for twenty-four hours facing a wall. "It was his 20th birthday and he was in his birthday suit," wrote Fotheringham, "being beaten by enraged German guards."[24] Sent to work in a coal mine, Collins escaped again. This time heading south, he hoped to make it to Yugoslavia and contact the resistance there. "The incredible thing is that Collins began all this in the very early days of the war, before there were organized contacts outside the barbed wire," marveled Fotheringham. "Collins' method was to walk. Walk through the fields and over the mountains at night. Hide in the daytime. Eat raw potatoes. And walk across Europe."[25] He was again recaptured and sent to the more secure Stalag VIII B, from which he escaped twice. Once he cut through barbed wire on an escape attempt only to have the prison searchlights come on. Hurriedly fixing the barbed wire back together, Collins retreated to confinement once more, boasting he was the only prisoner of war to break back into a prison. Once he made it as far as Czechoslovakia, saw Hungary on another jaunt, then escaped to Romania. Fotheringham saw it as a remarkable feat of endurance.

> He was beaten with fist, boot, rifle butt. He was court-martialled by the Hungarian authorities for striking a prison guard who was abusing a mentally-retarded Russian — and was cleared. He was actually before an impromptu firing squad in Romania before being rescued by a Romanian lieutenant. In desperation, the Romanians once set up a special camp in which Collins and Ted Lancaster — a buddy who accompanied him on many of his breakouts — were the only inmates.[26]

When the Bulldog came to him in 1975 in his new position as senior editor, looking for work, the columnist was happy to help out a man he had always held in high esteem, personally and professionally. "Always admiring his gusto," wrote Fotheringham. "I arranged to position him as a columnist." He could have had no idea of the spectacle he was unleashing on *Sun* readers. It soon became apparent to Fotheringham that the man he had known as a strident left-winger had changed his political stripes. The result was as unexpected as it was nasty, and soon the new columnist and the ex-senior editor were feuding in print. "We became bitter enemies on the same paper, my column mocking his spurious new convictions, his column sneering at my limousine liberal views," recalled Fotheringham.[27]

Collins brought his unique style of confrontation to the *Sun*'s Page Six, on which he began his own personal war with investigative articles, first exposing salaries of academics he considered excessive. "It's doubtful whether there's been such a happy jostling and pushing at the public trough since the days of King Farouk and his court."[28] Soon, Prime Minister Pierre Trudeau instituted wage controls to slow runaway inflation, but that did not slow the Bulldog's charge. "In case those wage guidelines don't apply, somebody had better start a movement for local controls," he warned. "Your money is involved — lots of it."[29] Radio hotliner Jack Webster also took up the issue, and together they were vilified in the Vancouver Community College newsletter as "Genghis Collins and Attila Webster." But Collins objected to the hotliner being given equal billing. "I'm a far worse villain than he is," he wrote. "All he's done has been to ask nice polite questions in a nice quiet voice. A regular pussycat."[30] Collins almost relished the fact that he was singled out for special treatment, however, "under the heading 'SCHADENFREUDE,' which, as the author is careful to explain, is a German word with no exact English equivalent. It means 'to take a kind of gleeful pleasure in someone else's misery.' I am seen as a Schadenfreude artist."[31]

Fotheringham recalled that within months of Collins taking over Page Six on his recommendation, *Sun* publisher Stuart Keate expressed astonishment at the Bulldog's increasingly vitriolic reports.

> Where was this mighty left-winger, he demanded, pointing to Collins' latest diatribe. I shook my head sadly, being even more astonished than he was. It seemed the famous CBC bureaucracy in Ottawa had so embittered the left-wing laborite that he had turned into a raving right-winger. He could survive 10 Nazi POW camps but not the CBC; he had snapped and gone over the political wall.[32]

By 1975, the technological changes that began with computerized typesetting in the composing room had spread to other departments at Pacific Press. In the *Sun* and *Province* newsrooms, computers were installed to replace the typewriters on which reporters wrote their stories. Instead of compositors having to rekey their typewritten copy on linotype machines or even as punched tape to be fed into computerized typesetters, stories written on the new "video display terminals" went into the computer's electronic memory. The copy did not have to be retyped before appearing in its final edited version in print, saving a step in the labor process and in theory saving the company some of its high costs of production. The process made whole job classifications redundant, however, and the powerful Pacific Press craft unions fought hard to preserve their livelihoods.

The changes created bitter union jurisdictional disputes and led to renewed production problems beginning that fall in advance of the regular Halloween contract expiry. The wrangle went on more than eight months past that date, while the unions continued to work, and sometimes not work, without a new contract as talks went on. But the issue that prompted a two-week shutdown of publication by the company during the summer of 1976 had less to do with a labor-management dispute than a row with the federal government over its imposition of wage controls. As if the bargaining dynamics at Pacific Press were not delicate enough, the onset of technological change came at the same time that the federal Anti-Inflation Board was introduced. The company found itself not only caught in the middle of its feuding unions, but also at risk of huge fines imposed by Ottawa if it awarded pay increases to its workers beyond the federal guidelines.

When the company announced in March 1975 that it planned to install computer terminals in its newsrooms, the joint council claimed that to do so unilaterally would violate its earlier agreement on automation.[33] The company proceeded with installation, but when the first news story was produced with the computer system on October 15, a printer refused to handle it and was fired, prompting other ITU members to walk off the job.[34] The dismissal, wrote *Province* publisher Paddy Sherman on the paper's front page, was "the only action possible under our contract language."[35] The company complained to the new Labour Relations Board, which had been created by the NDP government to replace the Mediation Services Commission, that the action constituted an illegal strike. LRB vice-chairman Ed Peck worked out a late-night solution, and the fired printer was reinstated. *Province* distribution was not only delayed by seven hours, but what copies did roll off the presses were filled with blank spaces where news stories and columns should have been.[36]

Negotiations could not produce an agreement by the contract expiry date, and a mediator was appointed on November 7, meeting with the sides ten days later. After another week, the Newspaper Guild took a strike vote, which came back 78 percent in favor.[37] The company made several proposals to guarantee the jobs of workers displaced by automation and to retrain them for work elsewhere in the plant, but Pacific Press general manager Dave Stinson complained in a letter to employees that the unions did not even consider the proposals before talks broke off from December 9 until February 5.[38] When they resumed, the focus was on the Anti-Inflation Board guidelines instead of technological change. Stinson reported that spokesmen for the joint council assured him there were no longer any jurisdictional disputes between the unions.[39]

The unions then caucused for almost two months, supposedly on technology issues, but events at the international level were injecting yet another complication into the labor situation at Pacific Press. Pressmen at the *Washington Post* had gone on strike October 1, smashing presses and assaulting a foreman on their way out. Publisher Katharine Graham, who had inherited the newspaper from her father, took a hard line against the pressmen and produced a "scab" newspaper using managers and Guild members who crossed the picket line. In December, the *Post* began hiring non-union pressmen, including some defecting union members, and began settling separately with its other unions.[40]

Back in Vancouver, the Graphic Arts International Union, which represented photoengravers at Pacific Press, suddenly announced in April it was quitting the joint council after a "flareup" in a jurisdictional dispute with the Stereotypers' Union.[41] The stereotypers had previously produced the molded and cast flexible metal printing plates made under the "hot lead" process, but the new computerized "cold type" system used flexible plastic printing plates produced photographically, a process that the photoengravers claimed the right to perform. The company wanted the unions to sort out the dispute, while the unions wanted the company to decide the matter. When Pacific Press washed its hands of the issue, the joint council sided with the stereotypers, who were affiliated with the Pressmen's Union at the international level. The photoengravers, whose union was negotiating a merger with the Guild, quit the group. The company then suggested the LRB or an independent arbitrator rule on jurisdiction, while the joint council asked mediator Charles Stewart to "book out" of the dispute so a strike vote could be conducted in an attempt to "make something happen."[42] All thirty-six members of the Stereotypers' Union voted in favor of a walkout, and strike notice was served on May 6.[43] The joint council submitted the jurisdictional issue to the Canadian Labour Congress, of which all the unions were members. When talks with the company resumed on June 1, joint council spokesman Dave McIntyre said the move was made without the participation of the photoengravers, and the other unions considered the issue settled.[44]

But soon the talks were plagued by production slowdowns, as they had been in 1970. On the night shift of June 3, shop-floor meetings were held by the unions to study the company's offer of a three-year contract and lump-sum payments of up to $5,400 per member in exchange for eliminating restrictive work practices contained in the contracts. As a result, the next morning's press run of the *Province* was two and a half hours late in getting started, mechanical difficulties plagued printing, and rural delivery had to be virtually abandoned. Stinson issued a statement attacking the union leaders for misrepresenting the company's position to their members in shop-floor meetings. "These meetings were calculated exercises in deceit and dishonesty," he said. "The dishonesty with the very employees they claim to represent is reprehensible."[45] McIntyre claimed the company's proposal to retrain and transfer displaced workers to other departments would eliminate the job security of union members. But Stinson said the only employees who would be excluded from the company's offer of lifetime job guarantees would be about twenty printers hired since the previous collective agreement went into effect. McIntyre accused the company of trying to "buy off" union members with the offer of lump-sum payments and guaranteed jobs in exchange for eliminating the restrictive practices, which had been listed by Stinson.

> The pressmen's manning clause, the right of mailers to slow down the presses when counting newspapers, the re-setting of pre-set advertising copy and the premium the company is forced to pay for commercial work. Stinson said the proposal is unique because in similar situations elsewhere when technological change is introduced, companies pay people to go away. Here, people will be paid who stay, he said.[46]

The shop-floor meetings and production slowdowns continued for almost two weeks, and Pacific Press applied to the LRB for a ruling on whether the job action constituted an illegal strike. Under the NDP government's new Labour Relations Act, the new body's jurisdiction over labor matters prevented the company from going to court for injunctions and contempt of court rulings as it had done before. One union "study session" to ponder the latest company offer came on June 10, according to Stinson, when "we were informed they stopped to read the story in *The Sun* about the Pacific Press dispute."[47]

The CLC declined to get involved in the jurisdictional dispute, and it was hard to find anyone who would. Clive McKee, who had mediated a solution to the 1972 strike at Pacific Press and a 1974 dispute at Victoria Press, took a pass, as did LRB chairman Paul Weiler, due to the highly political nature of the negotiations.[48] Finally on June 18 Jim Kinnaird, a unionist who had been an associate deputy labor minister in the NDP government, took on the challenge. One month later an agreement was reached, but the dispute was far from over. He announced a "major breakthrough" in the form of a mechanism to resolve jurisdictional disputes by "mediation-arbitration," under which a mediator would be empowered to impose a solution if one could not be agreed to by the parties.[49]

More problematic was the wage increase Kinnaird helped the parties negotiate, which was well above the Anti-Inflation Board limit of 8.3 percent annually. The two-year deal called for increases of 16 percent in the first year and 8 percent in the second, with the first year's increase retroactive to November 1, almost nine months earlier. The unionists ratified the agreement overwhelmingly and expected a hefty retroactive pay cheque, but the company balked at providing it until the AIB ruled on the deal's legality. Irving Pulp and Paper of New Brunswick had been fined $125,000 during the previous fall for paying out a wage increase well above the guidelines, as it had subsequently been rolled back by the AIB. "There's no way we want to be fined $250,000," said Stinson.[50] The company's change in position was termed "unbelievable" by Guild executive-secretary Jim Young. "If this is so, we'll have to take back our ratification," he said. "Under these conditions, I would have to recommend to our membership that we not ratify it."[51] Stinson was adamant that increases above the AIB guidelines would not be paid without federal approval, while angry unionists insisted he had promised the back pay would be remitted within seven weeks, federal approval or not. A July 26 *Province* story on the dispute made it apparent that Stinson was going back on the deal he had made with the unions. Reporter Kathy Tait pinned the Pacific Press general manager down.

> Asked Sunday if he had signed a statement that proposed increases and retroactive pay would be made in three and seven weeks, respectively, if the contracts were ratified by union members, Stinson said: "Yes, it may be true. In our contract proposal we said something to that effect. We had that in our offer to them. So technically that is quite true. But there is nothing to say there is a contract until the AIB approves it. I'm not agreeing to break the law. I'm not above the law.[52]

The unionists were furious on reading Stinson's comments, and hundreds of them walked off the job that morning, causing the *Sun* to miss its first edition. A group estimated at 250 descended on Stinson's office, where an angry confrontation took place.[53] A similar scene occurred the next morning, when a two-hour walkout took place to protest the turn of events. Stinson told the workers they would get a raise to the AIB limit by mid-August, and the rest of the negotiated increase would go into a trust fund pending a federal ruling on its legality, with interest earned going to whichever side the government body decided should get the money. The problem was in getting an answer from the federal bureaucracy. A report from the *Sun*'s Ottawa bureau fanned the flames further by pointing out there was no mechanism in place to ensure that employers could recover excessive wage increases from workers. "Several officials of the AIB confirmed in interviews that Pacific Press would not be violating regulations by paying the full retroactive amount before the settlement goes to the AIB," reported John Sawatsky.[54]

In an attempt to sort out exactly what promises had been made at the bargaining table, mediator Kinnaird was recalled to the fray. "Obviously there's a misunderstanding by Stinson, in my opinion," he announced on July 29. But that was not the way Stinson interpreted Kinnaird's version of events. "He told me that this was a misunderstanding between the parties," Stinson insisted the next day, "not that I had a misunderstanding." Kinnaird made his recollection crystal clear in a subsequent statement.

> The unions are of the opinion, as I was, that the 16-per-cent increase would be paid no later than the third week after ratification and the retroactive payments within seven weeks. . . . Stinson said consistently he would never place the company in an illegal position. . . . I'm not a lawyer. I don't want to get into a controversy. He has taken his action presumably on the advice of a lawyer.[55]

A local AIB official authorized Pacific Press to pay a wage increase and retroactive pay of 8.3 percent but referred the matter to Ottawa for a ruling on whether any amount above that was allowable. Stinson spent all of July 31 trying to contact the head of the AIB's legal department in Ottawa for a ruling. "Dammit, we've got to get somebody in the AIB," he told a *Province* reporter in frustration. "I want to have somebody tell me to do it or don't do it."[56] To the unionists, it seemed just another broken promise resulting from the fractured corporate control resting in separate Eastern head offices. "All we can say further is that Mr. Stinson's actions certainly confirm our negotiators' belief that his one big happy family concept is nothing but a sham," said joint council co-chair Dave McIntyre.[57] In response, the unions renewed their production slowdowns.

On August 3, Stinson received a telex from Ottawa warning that paying a 16 percent raise without AIB approval could result in Pacific Press being penalized 25 percent of the total payout, or almost $4 million. He urged the union leaders to take up their case for an exemption with the AIB, and "in light of the urgency involved" offered to pay their costs to fly to Ottawa with him.[58] Stinson told the unionists in a letter that he assumed the slowdowns, which caused that day's editions of the *Sun* to be ninety minutes late, constituted "employee misconduct at the individual level," since they had not been authorized by the joint council. "Since we have not had any communication from the authorized representatives in these employee groups, the employees who participate in this activity are placed in a most hazardous position," warned Stinson.[59] The study sessions and job walkouts increased and finally prevented the *Sun* from appearing on August 6. When the next morning's *Province* could not be published, Pacific Press pulled the plug by suspending publication as it had done in 1970 until the dispute could be resolved. Stinson flew to Ottawa in an attempt to get a definitive ruling from the AIB, while the unions went to the LRB, questioning whether there was a valid collective agreement in place at Pacific Press and if the company had bargained in good faith.[60] As in 1970, the unions said the shutdown was illegal and claimed wages from the company for its duration. Pacific Press claimed the right to sue to recover wages paid during the union study sessions.

On August 12, the LRB issued a ruling that backed Pacific Press and sharply criticized the AIB for causing the problem by failing "to issue clear and definitive rulings about the timing of wage increases."[61] Joint council representatives met with LRB vice-chairman Ed Peck the next day, but they could not reach an agreement on the outstanding issue of which side owed which, and how much, as a result of the dispute. Both sides met separately with Peck on August 16, but the impasse continued. Closed-door meetings continued the next day between Peck, Stinson, and McIntyre, but still no resolution was achieved. Finally, on August 18, Peck issued non-binding recommendations in hopes of getting the sides to agree to resume publication.

Peck's formula for resolving the dispute included Pacific Press withholding a day and a half's pay from its workers for its loss of production during the slowdowns. The joint council "reluctantly" agreed to recommend the solution to its members, said McIntyre, who protested that the deal "did not recognize the problems of the unions in dealing with Pacific

Press." Union members ratified the agreement by a reported 75 to 80 percent majority, and Pacific Press resumed publication on August 20 after a thirteen-day shutdown.[62] *Sun* labor reporter George Dobie saw the solution as part of a continuing process toward removing labor disputes from the criminal justice system and instead imposing "labor-oriented" punishment for illegal work stoppages. "This punishment is unprecedented in B.C. labor relations," Dobie wrote several weeks later. "A check of most available authorities confirms that never before has a group of workers willingly given up pay for work they had done."[63]

It took until November 18, four months after the 16 percent wage increase was agreed to, for the AIB to rule it could not be allowed under the federal wage guidelines.[64] The result of the 1976 labor dispute at Pacific Press, according to the 1981 Royal Commission on Newspapers study of labor relations, was increased bitterness.

> Members of some unions believed the closed-door mediation between the mediator, the pressmen's representative, and the employer's general manager produced an unfair settlement. The unions believed the employer showed bad faith in withholding payment, and the employer was bitter over job action against the AIB ruling, over which the company had no control.[65]

The bitterness was soon compounded when the jurisdictional dispute between the photoengravers and stereotypers was finally decided. LRB chairman Paul Weiler served as the mediator-arbitrator under the formula negotiated by Kinnaird and ruled the following spring that the work should go to the photoengravers.[66] The result was the demise of the Stereotypers Union and increased distrust among the joint council unions, a majority of which had sided against the photoengravers. The mechanism to resolve jurisdictional disputes removed a major potential area of conflict between the joint council unions, the Royal Commission report concluded. "It was not sufficient, however, to increase trust among them."[67]

The 1976 Pacific Press shutdown prompted a renewal of the running battle between the *Sun*'s Page Six editor Doug Collins and Jack Webster, with the hotliner wondering loudly when "the great fearless defender of the press" would devote space "to what really happened when dozens of unionists stormed one of the executive offices wanting to know what the doublecross was in the labor agreement."[68] It was Webster's hosting of local Teamster's union boss Ed Lawson that brought the Bulldog's response. Webster told his listeners he was affording Lawson, a prominent Liberal who also held a seat in the Senate, an opportunity to say what the "monopoly press" would not print. Collins replied that allowing Lawson to reply to reports in the *Sun* of the senator's infrequent attendance in the upper chamber amounted to "yet another free-time political broadcast." He also called the hotliner's brand of journalism toothless. "I could also have called it lazily researched, he having allowed Lawson to get away with nonsense piled on nonsense," Collins continued. "Hot-liners, of course, have little time for research. They are too busy 'performing.' As Jack has so often said, he's in showbiz."[69] Webster shot back, calling Collins a "re-cycled corporation lapdog" who was "hiding on Page Six of *The Vancouver Sun*." Collins told readers he played a tape of the hotliner's rebuttal for listeners who "fell down laughing" all day in the *Sun* newsroom. "Hiding? Giving Webster a hiding, that's what. All Jack has these days is a loud voice that's showing distinct evidence of the trembles. He should retire for good to that farm on Saltspring Island, and entertain the sheep and goats."[70]

Soon Collins could hardly be accused of hiding. But the issue that thrust the Bulldog into the national spotlight in the fall of 1976, brought protesters descending on the Pacific Press Building, and defined his career did not begin with an article or column he wrote on Page Six of the *Sun*. Instead it started with a freelance piece he sold to *Weekend* magazine, which was distributed with the Saturday editions of the *Sun* as well as the weekend editions of dozens of other newspapers across the country. In "Fear and Loathing in the Canadian Mosaic," Collins opened a can of worms that exploded in acrimony. He gave public voice to ugly complaints that had been growing for years in beer parlors, behind closed doors, and at the margins of a society whose racial makeup was rapidly changing. "Ottawa's open immigration policies have engendered enormous hatred in this country," wrote Collins. "Tolerance of the wave of colored immigrants is rapidly disappearing, especially in large cities." The establishment of a color-blind immigration policy in 1967 had led to a situation that threatened to explode as it had in Britain, Collins warned, where race riots had killed five in 1976.

> A conservative estimate of the total number of non-whites entering Canada since 1967 would be 500,000. Setty Pendakur, an East Indian and a former Vancouver alderman, has stated that the pace of Asian immigration is simply too great for easy absorption into Canadian society. And Harkirpal Singh Sara, a well-known Sikh, called last year for a five-year moratorium on all immigration so that things could settle down a bit.[71]

The issue had simmered for years amid the unemployment brought by an economic downturn, but Collins brought it out into the open. In Greater Vancouver, entire neighborhoods had been taken over by ethnic groups, making longtime residents feel like outsiders. In South Vancouver and suburban Surrey, immigrants from India congregated in enclaves, and soon neighborhood storefronts were covered in signs in a foreign language. In East Vancouver and suburban Richmond the ethnic mix turned Chinese, and schools there were soon faced with problems posed by English suddenly being the second language of a majority of students. On the affluent west side of Vancouver, wealthy immigrants from Hong Kong were buying up property and driving up house prices permanently beyond the reach of most homegrown Vancouverites.[72]

The city had been discovered, and Vancouver was becoming renowned worldwide for its mountainous, coastal splendor. It was in the process of becoming a multicultural metropolis, but the transformation was not favored by some. With every qualified immigrant allowed into Canada under the Liberals' open-door policy, Collins claimed, came an average of seventeen relatives as well. As Fotheringham had already discovered, Collins always saw underlying political motivations behind any issue. "One wealthy businessman, not normally given to weird thoughts, is convinced that the Liberals are up to some plot," wrote Collins. "What they are doing, he says, is packing as many Asians into western Canada as they can, in order to create a friendly vote and help build the stronger political base they need."[73]

The racial resentment and political conspiracy theories had been festering for years like untended wounds. Collins had exposed the issue to the light of day where it could be the subject of healing discussion, however painful. But the adversarial approach favored by the Bulldog promised that the debate would not be genteel, and it soon became apparent that Collins not only reported the views of those who opposed the influx of non-white immigrants, but also shared them himself. "In short," concluded Collins in his inflammatory *Weekend* article, "the world is to be stuffed down Canada's throat, whether we choke on it or not."[74] Reaction to the article included not just the usual flurry of letters to the editor, but also a mobilization of ethnic groups and anti-racism activists in protest. Soon dozens of pickets appeared outside the Pacific Press Building on Granville Street, carrying signs reading "The *Vancouver Sun* Publishes Racist Lies" and "No Freedom of Speech for Racists."[75]

The tough-as-nails Page Six editor responded to his critics in a two-part retort that covered almost the entire page. Denying he was a racist, Collins pointed to the dictionary definition requiring a belief in racial superiority. "The word has been debased by fools and professional liberals, who are often one and the same," wrote Collins. "And it's been used for a long time now to suppress discussion of [Trudeau's] immigration program."[76] Soon it became clear that Collins had the courage of his convictions, which were becoming equally obvious. He repeated his argument against engendering the kind of race violence that had plagued European cities, and then expanded the scope of his complaints.

> If it is racist to prefer our own traditions and institutions (poor though these may be) to those of others, I am again guilty. If it is racist to think that our own Canadian kids should not become minorities in their own schools, and that they are entitled to learn their own language properly instead of waiting around while newcomers from totally alien cultures attempt to learn it, then I am thrice-damned, because I hold the view that Canadian kids have some rights, too.[77]

The exploding controversy, according to Collins, "has proved once again that there is nothing less liberal than a liberal. ... The liberal demands that his creed be accepted unquestioningly."[78] The issue was debated nationally on CBC radio, and Collins complained of getting short shrift in his replies from host Barbara Black, whom he called "a harmless and knowledgeless little girl." A political science professor from the University of Toronto who provided an opposing viewpoint was "an academic stupid par excellence," according to Collins. "As an exercise in propagandistic do-goodery, it was excellent. As an exercise in examination of an important subject, it was a laugh."[79] As for the pickets who protested outside the *Sun*'s newsroom, Collins labeled them Trotskyists in an accompanying open letter.

> Dear pickets: Thank you for appearing in front of the Pacific Press Building Thursday night with your signs. . . . Your action has given further publicity to a state of affairs that some people would like to ignore, and on which there has been very little reporting. So we are both happy, and we should get together some time and do some kissing.[80]

Collins appeared at a public forum to debate the immigration issue, but when he attempted to speak to the meeting at the Unitarian Church he was drowned out by hecklers from a group calling itself the International Committee Against Racism, which had leafleted the entrance with anti-Collins pamphlets. Police were called to quell the disturbance, and uniformed officers stood by in the lobby of the church while order was restored. Collins complained to the meeting that it was "more desirable to be described as a rapist than a racist."[81] But the Bulldog refused to back down, and soon he was under unfriendly fire from some of his own colleagues at the *Sun*, who objected to his racist diatribes. The result, as one observer put it, would be "blood all over the page."

13 The Reluctant Prince

Harvey Southam did not just carry the surname of his famous great-grandfather, founder of the country's oldest and most respected newspaper chain. He also shouldered the heavy burden of expectations of one of Canada's wealthiest and most powerful families. More importantly for those at Southam's *Province*, Harvey had been born and raised in Vancouver. While he was descended on his father's side from William Southam, founder of Toronto-based Southam Newspapers, his mother was a daughter of H.R. MacMillan, a partner in the largest logging firm on the West Coast, MacMillan Bloedel. Harvey grew up in Vancouver, where he attended private school, and spent summers at the family retreat at Qualicum Beach on Vancouver Island. He began his apprenticeship in the newspaper business in 1972 while still attending the University of Victoria, as a summer reporter at the *Winnipeg Tribune*, and two years later took a posting as a business writer at the *Province*. Allan Fotheringham called him "the only man I've ever seen who was more handsome than Warren Beatty."[1] He was bright, charming, and he carried the magic Southam name. He was also a deeply troubled young man.

Many in the Southam family hoped Harvey would one day prove worthy of leading the chain which bore his name. St. Clair Balfour, the eldest son of company founder William Southam's only daughter and the driving force behind the establishment of Pacific Press, retired in 1975 as president of the newspaper chain. He turned the family firm's reins over to his nephew, Gordon Fisher, whose father Philip had preceded Balfour as Southam president and had led the company through the post-war decades. The family's hopes for Harvey were high, but the brooding young Southam scion was haunted. He was dogged by depression and by the death of his younger brother Gordon in a one-car accident on the night of H.R. MacMillan's funeral in what some said was a covered-up suicide.[2] According to Sean Rossiter in *Vancouver* magazine, Harvey Southam's unhappiness was compounded by the moribund management of the stagnant *Province*, which had for almost twenty years since the Pacific Press amalgamation played second fiddle in the morning to the high-flying afternoon *Sun*. "His friends were aware of his deepening depression over complaints in the newsroom," reported Rossiter. "He was beginning to hate the newspaper business."[3] A telling incident that demonstrated the depths of young Harvey's dissatisfaction with *Province* management, according to Rossiter, came as he contemplated his considerable inheritance on the death of his wealthy grandfather.

> Perhaps he was unhappy at being turned down earlier for an Arctic assignment that would have entailed $3,000 in expenses. Very reliable sources recall his words as: "You know what I'm going to do with that money? I'm going to put it in a special account, and every time that blankety-blank McConnell tells somebody they can't go somewhere, I'm going to give him some of it and tell him, 'Sure, go ahead.'" He apparently said that in full knowledge that Bob McConnell was standing behind him at the time, and the various versions differ substantially whether the editor appreciated the good-natured humor of the moment.[4]

McConnell was soon shuffled east by the Southam chain as general manager of its *Montreal Gazette*, his rapid rise in the company having exposed his weaknesses as a manager, according to Rossiter. "The vaguely intellectual, austere McConnell was so remote from his main responsibility, the newsroom, that it is seriously thought by reporters that he might have been removed barely in time to avert disaster."[5] Pointedly, the *Province* editor's chair languished unfilled. Managing editor Merv Moore, a forty-year veteran of the business, had twice been passed over by Southam for editor in favor of young Victoria correspondents parachuted in above him. This latest refusal to promote him made Moore a three-time loser, obviously on his way out. His seventeen years in the managing editor's chair, according to Rossiter, had served to stamp Moore's conservative approach on the newspaper. "By running a high proportion of wire copy . . . Moore can have most of the day's paper in type by midafternoon," wrote Rossiter. "In consequence, the paper's cityside reporters have comparatively little space to aim for."[6] Lacking any suitable internal candidate to promote as editor, Rossiter's sources speculated the situation had turned into a holding pattern, perhaps awaiting Harvey Southam's maturity. "It seems as if the paper has settled in for a long wait," he reported. "The consensus is that, rather than do anything rash, the paper will wait out the five years until the managing editor retires."[7]

But by 1976, the situation at the money-losing *Province* had came to the attention of the new management in Southam's head office, Rossiter wrote. "During the winter a rumor had started in Toronto that Southam executives had suddenly begun actually reading their Vancouver franchise, and were horrified," he told *Vancouver* readers. "As the story went, *The Province* was given a year to shape up or be folded."[8] The closure threat would not be the last. The inferiority complex from which the *Province* suffered in comparison to its more dynamic afternoon partner translated into defeatism in the paper's management ranks as morale hit rock bottom, according to Rossiter, who interviewed publisher Paddy Sherman.

> Believe it or not, the fact that *The Sun* has far superior columnists is used as an excuse for not even trying to catch up. . . . "How can you compete with Fotheringham?" replies the publisher to an observation about a columnist's shortcomings. It is unfair for the morning paper's sports columnists to be compared with Jim Taylor. So the gap widens. So the depth of such despair defies measurement.[9]

Sherman struggled to rearrange the deck chairs on his foundering vessel while he battled as best he could at the board level to keep the *Province* afloat. *Sun* publisher Stuart Keate recalled the diminutive mountaineer's contortions in the face of FP Publications general manager Dick Malone's continual complaints at the quarterly board meetings of Pacific Press about the morning newspaper's financial underperformance. Sherman countered Malone's demands for cost cutbacks with ingenious arguments, according to Keate. "In boxing parlance, Paddy 'dazzled 'em with footwork,'" he wrote in his 1980 memoirs. "He purported to show, from a maze of statistics, that the *Province* could produce a column of type cheaper than the *Sun*."[10] The Pacific Press agreement, according to Rossiter, provided that the smaller *Province* would contribute only one-third of the company's operating expenses due to its lesser usage of the facilities. Yet under its $3.85-million investment in the 1957 "equalization" payment, Southam was entitled to a half share in the combined profits of both newspapers, which in 1976 amounted to $3.5 million. "Surely no business agreement of recent times in this city is as mysterious," Rossiter noted.[11]

While the arrangement guaranteed the *Province* would make a profit as long as it did not lose more money than the ad-rich *Sun* made, it also ensured the morning paper could never be a serious challenger to the afternoon giant. "The agreement is seen to perpetuate its deficit position, since *The Province* does not actually spend its entire one-third share of costs," reported Rossiter. Some on the *Sun*, he noted, would prefer the *Province* to convert to a tabloid format to at least save on newsprint costs. Keate recalled the boardroom brawls as Sherman made his case for his morning paper at least pulling its weight.

> Wound up, and in full voice, Sherman managed to convey the impression that the *Province* was somehow carrying the *Sun* on its back. At the very least, its cost-conscious operation was subsidizing the *Sun* and making it possible for the evening paper to roll up handsome profits. *Sun* directors often left the meetings chastened and resolved to do better.[12]

The cost-sharing formula in the Pacific Press agreement kept the *Sun*'s production figures artificially low, according to Sherman, which made changes that might have helped the *Province* unacceptable to the afternoon newspaper's owners. "It really went against us and helped the *Sun*," Sherman recalled in 2001. "Dick Malone wasn't going to change anything at the *Sun* because it was his stick to use against the other [FP] papers. It made *Sun* production figures look very good. There was no way he would even listen."[13] The *Province* publisher could protest all he wanted, but under Malone's iron fist the *Sun* representatives on the Pacific Press board of directors, none of whom dared speak out on the issue, exercised their veto over any measures Sherman proposed to improve the morning paper's bottom line. "If I did something that cut the costs, it swung costs over to the *Sun*," explained Sherman. "While in theory that's what I want to do to make the paper profitable, that would increase the costs across the way, and the screams could be heard from Malone without the telephone."[14]

Back at company headquarters in Toronto, Gordon Fisher was consolidating his branch of the family's grip on the Southam corporate chain of command. A mechanical engineer by trade, Fisher had joined the family firm in 1958 as an executive assistant and was promoted to managing director in 1969. The smooth executive, who spent his spare time racing yachts, was set to guide the company for decades to come, it seemed. "A charming, arrogant, confident man, he was immensely popular thanks to the trademark Southam charm and private school finesse," observed Toronto journalist Patricia Best.[15] On his appointment to the chain's top job, Fisher looked ahead to the future in an interview with the *Globe and Mail*. "I think it would be a foolish man who would predict that newspapers as they appear today are going to survive forever," he said.[16]

With the change in leadership of his family's business, and facing the daunting situation at the chain's losing Vancouver enterprise, Harvey Southam, like many *Province* staff members, cast an envious eye past the short counter of the Pacific Press library clippings "morgue," which separated the paper's third-floor newsroom from that of the *Sun*, and jumped. He stunned the already-demoralized *Province* newsroom in the summer of 1976 by bolting across the hall to the *Sun*, taking a post as assistant business editor. The result was a setback for whatever optimism might have existed at the morning newspaper, according to Rossiter.

> How do you measure the impact of a Southam leaving the paper his family owns to join the competition? Reporters who knew him can get quite angry at the episode. Not angry at Harvey Southam; they envy him his freedom. The anger is over the desperation Harvey Southam must have felt to bypass his family's wishes and ignore Paddy Sherman's advice that he hang on as changes were only a month away. Southam's feelings at the time can only be imagined. A senior *Province* man, seething with fury, says, "Here's the guy who's gonna run the paper, gonna be Mr. Big, and he *has* to walk away."[17]

Sherman, however, recalled that Harvey's departure from the *Province* was due more to his lack of aptitude for the family business. "He realized that, as far as I was concerned, he wasn't a very bright young man and wasn't going anywhere in a hurry, so he left shortly afterwards."[18]

By 1976, Stuart Keate also could read the writing on the wall. He would turn 65 in 1978, and retirement was looking attractive. His health was deteriorating, as the onset of Parkinson's disease had set off trembles, which he knew would only get worse. The longtime *Sun* publisher, and even longer-time FP Publications employee, could see that the newspaper chain was imploding under the leadership of Brigadier Malone. The labor situation at Pacific Press, due to union disputes over technological change and company attempts to rewrite archaic manning practices entrenched in its collective agreements, was set to explode. Keate had predicted during the 1976 negotiations that another strike might destroy Vancouver's jointly operating newspapers. "Because of its delicate nature — with problems of jurisdiction, transferability, restrictive practices and so on — it would be a long and destructive shut-down," Keate warned other members of the firm's management committee in a confidential memo. "I suggest it is not inconceivable that it might mark the end of *The Sun* and *The Province*, as we know them. . . . While we may be able technically to produce newspapers, we could not deliver them."[19]

The joint council experiment in 1970 of publishing a strike newspaper, the *Express*, had been replicated during a six-month shutdown in Victoria in 1974, when unionists from the *Times* and *Colonist* had successfully produced their own newspaper, the *Victorian*. The fact the unions had been able to make money with the *Express* by the end of the 1970 strike, Keate argued in his memo to management, had shifted the balance of labor-management power at Pacific Press. To take on the unions would likely result in a protracted shutdown, he said, which would scotch the "handsome" profits the *Sun* was pulling in, amounting to $7 million in the first five months of 1976. "On a per capita basis, this is the most elegant return in Canada and undoubtedly one of the highest in North America."[20] The union jurisdictional problems were promising to be "the unsolvable mediation," Keate warned in urging a settlement. The alternative of shutting down or taking a strike carried the possibility of killing the golden goose and even endangering the dominant position of Pacific Press in the Vancouver media market.

> Under the circumstances, is it not folly to be toying with the idea of strike, or lock-out? I repeat: we have been doing extremely well

> under the status quo — in spite of hefty wage rates, in spite of make-work, shorter hours and longer holidays. Can we, then, afford to risk the crippling — or disappearance altogether — of our two papers? . . . The *Express,* we are told, is all geared up and ready to go. Doubtless it has learned something from its 1970 experience.[21]

With his decision to get out at age 65 in 1978, the question remained of who would replace Keate as publisher of the *Sun.* The Fotheringham experiment had failed in acrimony early in 1976, and Keate's relationship with his other great hope to succeed him also had begun to deteriorate. David Ablett remained as editorial page editor after Fotheringham's departure from management, but soon Keate's chair looked less inviting to him. Financial control of the *Sun* rested with the Pacific Press board of directors and with Malone at FP Publications corporate headquarters, now located in Toronto where the Brigadier had taken over as publisher of the *Globe and Mail.* The newspaper's editorial direction was set by Bruce Hutchison *in absentia* on Vancouver Island. "This seemed to me a recipe for living hell," recalled Ablett. "I don't think he [Keate] understood Pacific Press when he took the job. I don't think most people would have taken the job under those conditions. There wasn't much left for him to do."[22]

Keate professed in his 1980 memoirs to be mystified by his brilliant young protege's disillusionment. "Somewhere along the line, for reasons I could never understand, Ablett turned sour and began to churn out interminable (and, to some extent, incomprehensible) memos," Keate wrote. "By mutual consent we parted company."[23] One of Ablett's issues, according to Keate, was that Pacific Press had "'destroyed the confidentiality of his news sources' by refusing to issue him a company credit-card." Another was a "protracted wrangle over a requested sabbatical, which would have taken Ablett out of the office for seven months."[24] That was not the way Ablett recalled it.

> That's a crock. I sure didn't leave because of a credit card. That [sabbatical] had been agreed on, and he [Keate] changed his mind and withdrew it. He turned out to be a fairly small, vindictive person. The problem was the animosity. It was not a friendly place. It was just a low-grade nastiness. It got worse and worse. It was just far too wearing on me. There were lots of reasons for

> going. I'd done all the good jobs. I was looking for a new adventure, a new learning curve.[25]

Ablett made his mind up to leave and informed Keate of his decision in January 1978. He agreed to stay until September but left instead at the end of June over what he announced as "a misunderstanding with the Publisher regarding my future plans."[26] His departure came, Ablett recalled, after he was taken aside by Bruce Hutchison over cognac after a dinner at the Vancouver Club to commemorate the islander's sixtieth anniversary in the newspaper business. Hutchison, according to Ablett, told him that despite his resignation, both he and Keate were still prepared to recommend him for the publisher's job. But Ablett said he turned down the prospect of serving in what he considered a figurehead position caught between a "warring board of directors" and having to suffer through an "annual strike."[27] After taking time off to spend with his family, Ablett moved to Ottawa and went into the federal civil service with the Privy Council, where he played a key role in repatriating the Canadian constitution from Britain in 1982 and in authoring its accompanying Charter of Rights and Freedoms.

Bruce Larsen had consolidated his grip on the *Sun*'s newsroom operations with his victory over his better-educated, younger challengers, Fotheringham and Ablett, but his unpopularity with many and his lack of a university degree made him unsuitable for the publisher's chair. Paul St. Pierre, who had taken over as editorial page editor and aspired to some day be a publisher, lacked the necessary management skills, according to Keate. "St. Pierre was a poor administrator; a prickly personality who had difficulty in getting along with his staff," Keate wrote in his memoirs. "From time to time, insurrections were threatened. . . . He was tough, unyielding, strongly cynical and disputative. It soon became apparent that he would have to move."[28] Malone, according to Keate, wanted to promote Bruce Rudd, who had been assistant publisher of the *Sun* for five years before moving to FP's head office. But Keate objected that Rudd lacked the necessary news background for publisher. "Trained as a lawyer, he had shown some talent for labor negotiations but had only limited experience on the editorial side and was not in my opinion qualified to direct the affairs of one of Canada's largest metropolitan dailies."[29]

Lacking a suitable internal candidate, at least to Keate's mind, the prospect loomed of an outsider taking over for the first time as publisher of Vancouver's largest daily newspaper. Keate had been the first corporate publisher of the *Sun*, coming in from FP's *Victoria Times*, but at least he was a native Vancouverite who had cut his teeth as a young sportswriter on the *Province* in the 1930s and later worked on the old *News-Herald* with Pierre Berton and Jack Scott. An extensive search was conducted, and a list of ten candidates was drawn up. From the list Keate nominated three men, all outsiders with no experience in the peculiarities of Western Canada's largest outpost or, more importantly, with the delicate balance of competing forces at Pacific Press. Nonetheless, Keate said he was "certain that any one of them would do an elegant job in Vancouver."[30] When Ted Bolwell, an Australian who was editorial director of the FP chain, declined to move from Toronto, the choice came down to former *Winnipeg Free Press* editor Shane MacKay, who was then vice-president of the nickel mining company Inco, or *Globe and Mail* managing editor Clark Davey. The decision, Keate reported in his memoirs, was made by new FP president George Currie, who succeeded Malone in 1978 after the Brigadier had been purged by shareholders dissatisfied with the company's financial performance. "Currie chose Davey on the not unreasonable grounds that he had been intimately involved with the *Globe and Mail* as managing editor for the past fifteen years while MacKay — despite his unquestioned talents — had been out of the business for a decade."[31]

Across the hall at the *Province*, things were finally starting to look up by 1977. Publisher Paddy Sherman had rearranged his staff the previous summer in an attempt to breathe some life into the paper's news operation, despite the defection of Harvey Southam to the *Sun*. City editor Gordon Purver was shuffled sideways to coordinate introduction of computerized operations to the newsroom, and business editor Bob McMurray took his place. It had taken some serious arm-twisting to get McMurray to move city-side from his award-winning business section, according to Sean Rossiter in *Vancouver* magazine. McMurray, who had started at the *Province* as a teenage copy runner almost thirty years earlier, twice turned down entreaties by Sherman before finally agreeing to take on the challenge of revitalizing the newspaper's city desk. His reluctance, reported Rossiter, was symptomatic of the malaise infecting the morning paper.

> Obviously, the paper's management could have saved themselves considerable unrest and a few key defections — not to mention improving the product long ago — by appointing McMurray to the city desk earlier. That it took years to persuade McMurray to leave the safety of the business pages tells the whole story of a newspaper management paralysed with rigor mortis and frozen for decades in the shadow of *The Sun*. McMurray didn't have the confidence to move from his corner of the newsroom to the central position.[32]

As his assistant city editor, McMurray appointed editorial writer Don MacLachlan, a former Canadian Press reporter and *Province* city desker, who had recently returned from a year of studying at the University of Toronto on a prestigious Southam Fellowship. "He is, in the estimation of another former assistant city editor, an amazing 'paper pusher,' in the complimentary sense of being able to deal with story ideas, assignments and copy editing at once," reported Rossiter in his 1977 profile of changes at the morning daily. The return to the city desk of the "tough, bright, no-nonsense" MacLachlan was particularly significant, as he was "respected by reporters for giving fast decisions on story ideas and restoring focus to the city desk." The infusion of new blood immediately revitalized the *Province* staff, according to Rossiter. "It is truly remarkable how two appointments can raise morale at a newspaper. . . . With McLachlan [*sic*] and McMurray running the *Province*, 'It's like night and day,' says a beat reporter. 'There's a whole barrier been broken through.'"[33]

To give the *Province* editorial page some direction, Sherman appointed as its editor Geoffrey Molyneux, the former *Vancouver Times* managing editor who had more recently been director of research for the federal Conservative Party. "The *Province* has lacked a sense of direction ever since W.A.C. Bennett's decline, which has left the paper without much to support," noted Rossiter. "Molyneux has redesigned the editorial page and given it an engaging Tory wit."[34]

The dark clouds of labor unrest that Keate feared would destroy his newspaper continued to gather over Pacific Press in 1977. Extended negotiations were making the bargaining process an annual affair, but with new faces leading the joint council there was hope that relations between Pacific Press and its unions might finally improve. Dave McIntyre had left his post with the pressmen's union to join Len Guy in the leadership of the B.C. Federation of Labour, and his place as joint council co-chair was taken by Harold Dieno of the Mailers. In the Newspaper Guild, *Province* reporter Don Hunter, a street-smart British immigrant, took over as president. Negotiations commenced in early September in advance of the October 31 expiration date, but they did not get off to a good start when the ITU launched a complaint against Pacific Press with the Labour Relations Board.

The union charged that the company had violated the job security and technological change provisions of the collective agreement with a "campaign of non-compliance." The printing staff of 309 was well below the 325 jobs guaranteed in the contract and close to the 5 percent reduction that would trigger company compensation to the union under the contract.[35] Not only did Pacific Press balk at making the required payment to the ITU when another seven jobs were cut, but general manager Dave Stinson warned in a letter of July 11 that due to a decline in business the ranks of printers could be reduced by a further 111 positions for economic reasons, without regard for the technological change provisions of the contract.[36] *Sun* labor reporter George Dobie provided an exhaustive examination of the issues in a full-page feature on September 10.

> The unionists wryly comment that the technological change provisions had originally been hailed as a "model" but the company had removed the "glow" by "trying to expand on what it is entitled to do in the way of reductions." The unionists feel a credibility gap was created when a dispute erupted over the first-year wage terms of the last settlement — was it 16 per cent or eight per cent? — and now the gap is widening.[37]

As point man for the company, the heat was on general manager Dave Stinson, as it had been on Ed Benson before him. Stinson was at least more amiable than the abrasive Benson, but his position between the feuding corporate owners of Pacific Press and its warring unions was an uncomfortable one. "Union negotiators say they don't object to hard bargaining because that is the way they operate," noted Dobie. "But they are critical of Stinson and the company over what happens after negotiations are concluded."[38] The strapping young Stinson, who stood six-foot-four, put on a brave front in the face of union accusations of reneging on the agreements he had made. "If they want to believe the company is dishonest, I can't change their minds," he told Dobie in a long interview just before the 1977 round of negotiations began. "Credibility is extremely important unless you are dealing with somebody you'll never see again. I can't afford to deceive employees. . . . I'm only 40 years old and I'll be here 25 more years."[39]

The Pacific Press gambit of attempting to reduce the ranks of redundant printers by claiming they were not needed due to a drop in business raised the question: What happens when business goes up again? "Machines will do the job but we'll need people in other areas," answered Stinson. "I've tried to explain to the unions that technological change savings are supposed to be passed on to the consumers, otherwise we'll never get a downturn in prices. They don't or won't believe me and that's another part of the credibility gap."[40]

Compounding the company's credibility problem with the unions was another complication that arose shortly after bargaining began in 1977. Negotiations were put on hold September 23 when fifteen of the *Province* advertising department staff called in sick to protest the suspension of a colleague. Hunter told a Guild membership meeting that the union executive had nothing to do with the job action, which was taken by the workers on their own. "We will not be goaded into taking illegal action," Hunter told Guild members. He went on radio to denounce the company's firing of a 61-year-old salesman on a "trumped up and cruel set of charges."[41] An emergency Guild strike vote was scheduled, which came back 88 percent in favor.[42] Hunter laid down the law to Pacific Press, warning on September 29 that the Guild was prepared to strike as soon as it was in a legal position to do so upon expiration of the contract. "In other words," said Hunter, noting that the company had rejected virtually all of the union's proposals at the bargaining table, "no contract, no work."[43] An announcement came the next day that negotiations would resume the following week, but the hope was dimmed by an explosion of journalistic acrimony over a story on the front page of the following morning's *Province*.

Stinson proposed mediation to resolve the dispute in a letter to the joint council, which was rejected by Hunter. "We have no intention of being locked into mediation that would prevent us from going on strike Oct. 31," Hunter was quoted as saying on the front page of the newspaper for which he wrote. The *Province* article also quoted from a bulletin issued by Stinson in response, claiming the joint council had earlier agreed to proceed to mediation "as soon as negotiations became stalled or unproductive."[44] Hunter protested that the *Province* account failed to mention that the Guild had rejected mediation because it felt meaningful negotiations had yet to commence. The *Province* reporters who dominated the Guild executive committee were outraged, charging their newspaper's management with deliberately distorting the issues. Guild vice-president Chuck Poulsen, one of three *Province* reporters on the union's executive, along with Hunter and Alex Young, announced to the *Sun* the imposition of a news "blackout" of their own newspaper because of the ongoing management manipulation of its news coverage of the dispute.

> Poulsen claimed the latest example was on Saturday when "the senior newsroom manager" had some of Hunter's comments removed about the reason the guild did not wish to go to mediation. Poulsen said a headline was changed between editions and both changes "cast the guild in the role of favoring a strike." . . . Poulsen alleged it was being done by the paper's senior management "to suit the purposes of Pacific Press" which prints both newspapers.[45]

The next day the *Province* reproduced both published versions and headlines, which had been changed from "Guild leader has firm vow on mediation" in its first edition to "Guild leader rejects push for mediation" in the final. Managing editor Merv Moore said in an accompanying story that the first-edition headline was changed because it was "sloppy," and he argued the insertion of comments by Stinson, replacing a paragraph that quoted Hunter criticizing company negotiator Jerry Marr's lack of newspaper experience, provided "balance" the first version had lacked. Moore described the original article submitted by Poulsen as a Newspaper Guild press release. "He seems to think that every word in his own press release is sacred, while as a reporter he knows how routinely such releases are condensed."[46]

Stinson observed that the Guild's hard bargaining stance would make negotiations problematic. "If the guild really means 'no contract, no work,' we are going to have a difficult time reaching agreement before the expiry at the rate we are going."[47] When talks resumed, the Pacific Press general manager proposed that as a compromise a private mediator be named rather than a government-appointed one, which would have prevented the unions by law from striking until he "booked out" of the talks. Again on October 7 the Guild balked, insisting that meaningful negotiations still had yet to begin.[48] Finally, five days later, the unions agreed to the suggestion that San Francisco lawyer John Kagel join the talks. The son of University of California law professor Sam Kagel, he had earlier mediated a dispute between Pacific Press and its freelance writers. His father had been the lawyer for the Guild when it was formed, had mediated disputes over technological change on both sides of the border, and had pioneered the technique of "mediation-arbitration."[49]

The same day that Kagel agreed to act as mediator, the technological change jurisdictional issues at Pacific Press became clearer when Labour Relations Board chairman Paul Weiler issued his ruling on the disputed use of video display terminals at the *Sun* and *Province*. Basic jurisdiction over VDTs in the newspapers' newsrooms should rest with the Guild, Weiler ruled as mediator-arbitrator, because their use most closely resembled the typewriters on which journalists had traditionally written their stories. But he awarded to the ITU the job of typing into the computer system copy dictated over the telephone or delivered in written form, such as letters to the editor, TV schedules, and syndicated columns received in the mail.[50]

Hunter's strategy of brinksmanship succeeded in reaching a contract agreement in an all-night bargaining session just before the strike deadline of October 31. The deal allowed printers to save jobs by opting for a four-day week. To do it they would have to forego the 6.2 percent wage increase other unions would receive (the maximum allowed under the tightened Anti-Inflation Board limits), work a longer shift, and give back one statutory holiday. The printers also gave up the right to reset type received by the company in "camera ready" form in exchange for guaranteed jobs for life for all 290 regular printers employed at Pacific Press. In return for extending the lifetime job guarantees to twenty-four substitute printers as well, the ITU agreed to allow the company to accelerate the reduction of printer positions through attrition from 5 percent a year to 5 percent every six months without having to pay the wages of displaced printers to the union. The job guarantees were not just to retirement age, but for life.[51] The unions ratified the agreement by an average vote of 90 percent, but the contract would only be for one year, because AIB controls were expected to be soon lifted. Some Guild issues over reclassification of employees due to technological change remained unresolved, with a joint union-management committee formed to negotiate the changes proposed by Pacific Press.[52]

The apparent ability to resolve contentious issues at the bargaining table for a change, with wages virtually non-negotiable under the AIB guidelines and jurisdictional issues out of the way, appeared to offer fresh hope for labor relations at Pacific Press. But, as the 1981 Royal Commission report noted, the developments "may have given the employer unreasonable expectations about additional gains to be made in the next round."[53] And the next round of bargaining was less than a year away.

On the *Sun*'s increasingly controversial opinion forum, Page Six editor Doug Collins turned his attention in 1977 to the incipient equity wars, and soon he had his own column in which to express his opinions. With it, Collins took on the new movement toward mandated gender and racial equality in hiring. The addition at Vancouver city hall of an equal opportunities officer to enforce new regulations aimed at ensuring employment equity, he argued, would result in "reverse" discrimination. "A better name would be an 'unequal opportunities officer,'" railed Collins. "Once the new bureaucracy is set up, city hall departments will have to say whether they have the right number of East Indians, West Indians, Chinese, Filipinos, Fijians, etc. Merit alone won't count."[54] Achieving gender and racial equity in city hiring by imposing a quota system, Collins noted, might result in the fire department being forced to employ "dwarf blacks or six-months-pregnant women."[55] *Sun* columnist Lisa Hobbs defended the equal opportunity concept against the Bulldog's bite. "There's something about half-baked ideas being passed off as truths that is rather disturbing," she wrote. "What Doug fails to mention is that, in practice, we already have a quota system — something like 90 percent white and male for all the top-paying jobs."[56]

When television station BCTV reported that even a *Sun* advertisement placed by city hall for a male actor to play Captain James Cook in a bicentennial re-enactment of his visit to the West Coast could be prohibited as sexist under the new regulations, Collins had a field day with the issue. "Should Captain Cook have been a woman? *Should he be a woman?* Ms. Cook, perhaps? Anyone daring enough to ask such a silly question in Cookie's day, of course, would have had to walk the plank. Or worse. These days, a guy doesn't even lose his rum ration."[57] Collins soon found a scapegoat in Kathleen Ruff, head of the new B.C. Human Rights Branch or, as he called it, the "Human Wrongs Branch." The Bulldog dubbed Ruff "Big Sister" for her efforts on behalf of equality, but he soon found she would not take such abuse quietly. Ruff called a press conference to defend herself against what she called a campaign of political intimidation. "It's clear that Doug Collins has embarked on a personal vendetta against me," she told reporters.[58] Collins needed make no such media arrangements to fire back at Ruff. "There is nothing more shrewish than a fatcat, well-paid liberal outraged by those who question his — or her — standards," he responded in his next column.[59] Soon the war of words escalated, with Collins winning a more prominent placement, taking over the section-front spot vacated by Hobbs, who moved to Ottawa. There his column would alternate every other day with Fotheringham's.

In May 1978, Collins won top prize in the annual journalism awards sponsored by MacMillan Bloedel for his expose of moonlighting by UBC faculty, and the award seemed to embolden him.[60] When the federal government promoted changes to immigration laws by publishing a booklet whose cover portrayed a smiling Caucasian family group, Collins complained that the racial makeup of the pictured immigrants hardly reflected that of the actual yearly influx. "A good half of the immigrants coming in don't look like that at all," the Bulldog barked. "One or two other races are shown on the inside and back pages but — get this — there are no blacks at all and even the *browns* look white."[61] Ruff issued a statement from the B.C. Human Rights Branch accusing the *Sun* of publishing racist material. "There is no question that at this point in time there are people in B.C. whose minds are warped by feelings of racial superiority," she said. "This material feeds such hatred, paranoia and bigotry."[62]

One news scoop that Collins dug up made the *Sun*'s front page, but with the peculiar spin provided by the columnist it again became a matter of race. A scheme that had defrauded the federal Unemployment Insurance Commission of between $4 million and $5 million was, more importantly to Collins, perpetrated by a particular ethnic group, with the federal government's immigration policies again to blame. "Read all about the racket — the racket run by East Indian farmers and workers in these parts," Collins began his column. "Our shy violets in Ottawa — ever eager not to rock any boats where ethnic groups are concerned — have been reluctant to get tough about it."[63]

Fotheringham could restrain himself no longer and the result, according to *Saturday Night* magazine, shocked *Sun* readers. "Seldom had Canadian journalism seen such a spectacle," reported the national magazine. "There was blood all over the page that strange week last June."[64] Fotheringham fired the first shot with one of his trademark satires, quoting a fictitious Swedish psychiatrist he named Dr. Ebing Spectruum, a supposed expert on patients who make a complete swing through political beliefs, from flaming left-wing radicals to far-right reactionaries in a remarkably short time.

> What makes otherwise intelligent individuals veer suddenly from one violent extreme on the left to an equivalent position on the right? One of the factors, his research has shown, is the understandable matter of age, when disappointment, disillusionment with prospects and ordinary bitterness and past slights bring forth resentment directed at those groups who generally are powerless to strike back.[65]

Collins was never named in the column, but it was obvious to regular *Sun* readers who was the "patient" in question, as his "having been raised in a British working class atmosphere with limited formal education" was a dead giveaway. "Certain British working class immigrants, especially if granted the influence of media, are desperate to boycott others of unfamiliar skin color who might share their largesse," Fotheringham continued.[66] The syndrome under study, the columnist's satirical expert observed, included "a virulence against women in general. This is thought to be a thinly-hidden fear of females as a sex."[67] But the most puzzling aspect of the case in question was the patient's history as a prisoner of war, which typically made others more compassionate instead of less. "It is most unusual, he said, to find a patient who in real life demonstrates the opposite traits: A mean-spirited intolerance that borders on fanaticism toward other than the white race."[68] Collins was unamused, and soon rapt readers read his venomous reply. "The other day, a former friend of mine crept into his office late and wrote a column about me, he not having anything else to write about. These days, that is the way things are with him. I feel sorry for him but that will not prevent me from kicking him in the gonads. (Another lower-class trait.)"[69] The dispute soon descended to name-calling.

> From now on, Fotheringham shall be known as Little Lord Whimsey, his real name. Somehow, I worry Whimsey. I think it must be because I am an up-and-coming young striver while he is an out-of-date hasbeen. . . . In short, I am, as they say in fancy-pants land, his *bete noir*. He used to be Number One, you see. Now there's a new champ and it ain't him. So now he fills Lisa Hobbs' shoes as the *Sun*'s correspondent on Collins, the position being vacant. Whimsey in drag. He yearns to be noticed again and writing about Collins may help.[70]

Fotheringham, Collins continued in his own pseudo-psychoanalysis, suffered from the syndrome of "having married into society and living in a mansion in Kerrisdale — blue rinse land. There, it is easy to be a rich socialist."[71] His rival columnist, he claimed, was "spread too thin, like a tiny pot of shrimp paste on a whole loaf. He's listed on the *Sun*'s masthead as Contributing Editor but he doesn't contribute. He's too busy working for *Maclean's* magazine (which loves lollipop liberals), and for television. When he appears at the *Sun* he has to sign the visitor's book."[72] As for his lack of education, Collins found his real-life experience superior to Fotheringham's "tatty little BA" from UBC, concluding the columnist must have graduated in moonlighting. "What else, UBC being the moonlighting capital of the world?" Collins claimed an honorary degree for his hard knocks. "I want Whimsey and his lollipop clique to know that I, too, am educated. I graduated in international affairs from the University of Dunkirk. *Summa cum laude*, as they say on campus. But that was a long time ago when Whimsey was just a little snob in Gopher Prairie."[73] By the fall of 1978, the movement to oppose Collins began to organize, and the Bulldog dubbed it the "Friends of Kathleen Ruff Society."

> The group is for real, even though it has no name except the one I have given it. Its members show films and play tapes extolling their saint, and probably do a lot of singing, too. Some are pop-eyed Marxists and Trots. Others are former and (they hope) future aldermen. Still others are earnest liberals. But all are in the Kill Collins Movement. You may think I'm joking. Not so. The people I am talking about all hope to bring about the early funeral of the Beast of B.C. (Me).[74]

Collins reported on a gathering of the group at the home of former Vancouver alderman Setty Pendakur, whom the columnist had quoted in his original immigration inflammation. The group had made unsuccessful representations to *Sun* management in an attempt to have him dropped as a columnist, Collins claimed. Their next aim was to organize a mass cancelation of subscriptions to the newspaper, with a goal of lowering *Sun* circulation by 20,000, and also to pressure advertisers to boycott the *Sun*. "Not only that, but they want to kill *The Province*, too, it being published out of the same building as the *Sun* and therefore being equally guilty," wrote Collins, who claimed he had obtained the minutes of some of the group's meetings.[75] He named meeting attendees in successive columns, including several journalists. *Sun* copy editor Bill Barringer was one, and he wrote a response to Collins, explaining that the minutes the Bulldog had obtained told little of the story behind the meeting called to oppose him. "The overwhelming feeling at the meeting was not vengeance or vindictiveness, but sadness, fear and confusion," wrote Barringer in a *Sun* guest column. "These people felt that — by your writing — you create a climate of support for the deranged types in Vancouver who delight in baiting and hating minority groups."[76]

By October 1978, Collins was beginning to attract national media attention for his feuds and diatribes, with *Sun* managing editor Bruce Larsen backing him all the way. *Maclean's* profiled Collins as "the man with the poisoned pen," calling him "the most talked-about, most controversial, most inflammatory columnist on the West Coast."[77] His column, according to Clive Cocking, was "a new phenomenon in Vancouver newspapers where columnists have generally been liberal, moderate and mild-mannered. Not so Collins."[78] The Bulldog's controversial column,

Cocking observed for *Maclean's*, was part of a "conservative backlash that is sweeping the country."[79] Collins told Cocking his columns prompted about fifty letters to the editor weekly, including "about three threats a week. They say things like they'll cut my balls off and 'how would you like to see your wife raped in front of you.' It doesn't bother me."[80] The *Sun*'s managing editor defended Collins staunchly. "We wouldn't knowingly inflame race relations," Larsen told *Maclean's*. "I don't feel that Collins is a bigot. I feel he has very strong opinions. This paper has many columnists with many opinions."[81]

The movement to oust Collins was gaining momentum, but soon the matter became moot as, with little preliminary discussion, the *Sun* and *Province* were closed down immediately after the joint council contracts with Pacific Press expired at the end of October. It was the fifth shutdown in little more than a decade and would prove to be the catastrophic strike now-departed *Sun* publisher Stuart Keate had long feared. Collins took his column elsewhere, and controversy continued to follow him and his increasingly poisonous diatribes for decades. But he was not the only *Sun* writer to bolt the newspaper during the strike, as its new publisher enacted edicts many of the city's best wordsmiths found intolerable even before he had put out his first edition. Included in the losses were the *Sun*'s best columnists, some of whom simply walked across the hall to employment at Southam's morning paper. The exodus would eventually include the long-rumored departure of Fotheringham, as the "King of Vancouver" went into exile in the East he despised so intensely.

14 The Shutdown

Bargaining between Pacific Press and its unions did not get off to a good start in 1978, and talks took a sharp turn for the worse as soon as the contract expired at the end of October. The main issue in that round of negotiations was the number of pressmen required in the pressroom. With advances in automation, the company claimed that the number of pressmen called for under the contract was excessive and amounted to make-work "featherbedding." The pressmen claimed the new "di-litho" printing process the company had introduced as a halfway measure between letterpress and offset printing required more pressmen on shift, not fewer. A secondary company demand was directed at the Newspaper Guild and called for middle management in the newsrooms to be excluded from the union. Journalists feared this would create a non-union skeleton staff the company could use to produce enough editorial content during a strike to continue publishing from behind a picket line.

In a late-night warning at the bargaining table, company negotiator Jerry Marr let his counterparts on the joint council of newspaper unions know just how serious the company was about rewriting the rules at Pacific Press, especially in the pressroom. Marr, who had joined Pacific Press from the auto industry several years earlier, had suffered a bad experience in his initial dealings with the joint council unions during the 1976 fiasco over federal wage controls, Sean Rossiter reported in *Vancouver* magazine, which left what he had to say as the midnight deadline passed reeking of "sweet revenge." What Marr told pressmen's union business agent Gary Dunster across the bargaining table stunned the union side, according to Rossiter.

> "Well, Gary, it's crunch time. This is the year we're going to take you on. We've never been in as good a position in the past, and we don't expect to be in the future. We will take you on for one month, two months, three months" — Marr was counting the months on his fingers — "four months, five months, six months. We've made the calculations and we can recover from a long shutdown." . . . Believe it or not, the pressmen didn't take Marr seriously.[1]

George Dobie, the *Sun*'s veteran labor reporter, reasoned that the company's willingness to shut down immediately revealed the depth of its dedication to achieving its goal of taming the joint council unions. "It was surprising that management would not try to drag on the negotiations to take advantage of the Christmas business," wrote Dobie in *B.C. Business Week*, a 50,000-circulation tabloid published during the Pacific Press strike by the monthly magazine *B.C. Business* to fill the void of financial news. "The fact that they did not do that is ample evidence this dispute is much bigger to them than the short-term Yuletide bonanza."[2] FP Publications was under new management in 1978, with accountant George Currie of the Toronto firm Currie, Coopers & Lybrand named president in April to replace Brigadier Malone. The chain's market-leading *Montreal Star* had been behind picket lines since mid-June in a similar dispute over pressroom manning levels. The issue also had closed the three New York dailies on August 9 after publishers there unilaterally posted revised rules that slashed press crews by 70 percent. The *Washington Post*'s victory over its pressmen in 1975 had been duplicated at newspapers in Kansas City and Dallas, and the latest wave of showdowns seemed a continent-wide push by publishers against the pressmen's union and its entrenched manning clauses.

FP's *Ottawa Journal*, which had historically run neck-and-neck with Southam's *Citizen* in the nation's capital, had been behind ITU picket lines since October 1976, when production slowdowns during bargaining with the joint council of newspaper unions there led to a company lockout. The *Journal* continued publishing with non-union workers, but a labor boycott soon dropped its circulation 50,000 behind the *Citizen*. The Southam paper had weakened the *Journal*'s position by reneging on an agreement to halt publication if its competitor was prevented from publishing by labor problems, signing a deal separately with the unions. The decimated Newspaper Guild finally capitulated early in 1978 and returned to work at the *Journal*, crossing the ITU picket lines to do so, and in June it narrowly survived a decertification vote.[3] A study of newspaper labor relations in Ottawa done for the 1980 Royal Commission of Newspapers placed the blame for the *Journal*'s failure to introduce new technology without labor turmoil squarely on Brigadier Malone, who "apparently thought the new cold-type production process a passing fad."[4]

The opening salvo in the pressroom manning battle at Pacific Press was fired in the summer of 1978, when the *Sun* was prevented from publishing on July 10 by a "wildcat" strike by pressmen. The blowup, as far as Pacific Press was concerned, went to the heart of the problem, which was the $800,000 in annual overtime the company was forced to pay its pressmen. When a paperhandler called in sick that morning, the company assigned a pressmen's union member from another department to fill in. The union insisted that, under the contract, other paperhandlers should cover the work at overtime rates, and when the company disagreed the pressmen walked off the job.[5] The dispute went to the Labour Relations Board and was scheduled for arbitration while work resumed at overtime rates.[6] The company asked the LRB for the permission required under provincial labor law to sue the pressmen's union for revenue lost from missing a day's publication, but it was refused in September.[7]

The pressmen scheduled a strike vote in the first week of October because "negotiations haven't gone too well," Dunster said.[8] The joint council asked for the assistance of a mediator the following week, as the pressmen's strike vote came back 93 percent in favor.[9] As mediator Peter Dowding joined the talks, a Guild membership meeting voted overwhelmingly to hold a strike vote, and a week later it came back 79 percent in favor of a strike.[10] Three days before the contract expired at the end of October, 72-hour strike notice was served by both the Guild and pressmen's union as talks continued non-stop. Guild president Phil Needham said strike notice was served because there had not been "any movement on substantial issues."[11] The company responded with lockout notice, and the joint council asked Dowding to officially "book out" of the talks to clear the way for job action, which he did while remaining in an unofficial capacity to assist negotiations.[12]

When the pressmen turned down a company offer of $5,000 per union member to drop the restrictive manning clauses from the contract, the stage was set for Marr's midnight monologue and the union strike. Needham thought the abrupt breakdown resulted from a tactical error by mediator Dowding, who hoped to force a breakthrough on the main issue of manning. "Had there been any give by either party the strike would probably not have occurred so precipitously, even with the prevailing attitude of 'no contract, no work,'" recalled Needham. "Instead, Marr's statement slammed the door in our faces."[13] The challenge was seen by unionists as part of a larger campaign by publishers to break the pressmen. "If the company defeats the pressmen's union on this issue there will be absolutely no bargaining strength left in the joint council," Dunster told the hastily resumed *Express*. "It's nothing but union busting."[14]

Company spokesman Paddy Sherman downplayed Marr's precipitous bargaining-table outburst. "Sherman said he believes the statement was made at a time when people exhausted by long hours of negotiating were emotionally disturbed," reported the *Express*.[15] But union negotiators saw Marr's challenge as a call to arms. "It's not just a strike — it's war," declared Needham.[16] As he went around the plant informing Guild members of the strike call that morning, however, the *Sun* reporter suffered a sudden sinking feeling. "It was the worst thing I've had to do in my life," Needham told *Sun* colleague Rod Mickleburgh, who reported on the strike for *Maclean's* magazine. "I was damn near crying."[17] For *Sun* reporter Ron Rose, it was his first time on the Newspaper Guild bargaining committee. "It has been a disillusioning experience," he told a union membership meeting. "There was no real bargaining at all — no give at all — until we broke off talks. . . . I'll never forget Halloween night. We sat with the mediator until almost midnight, then the company lowered the boom."[18] Doug Collins noted that the suddenness of developments left some at the *Sun* in shock.

> It was apparent to me, standing in the newsroom the day the strike started, that a lot of guild members were wondering what had hit them. Even many of those who had voted in favor of a walkout didn't expect it to happen that fast. They thought negotiations would continue. Some, of course, had bought the argument that Pacific Press wanted to wipe out the guild. . . . But that is clear poppycock.[19]

Solidarity between journalists and pressmen was tenuous at best. "This is all nonsense," *Sun* reporter Moira Farrow told television cameras that descended on the picket line. "We're being asked to subsidize overtime for the pressmen."[20] It was the fifth shutdown of Pacific Press in eleven years, and many journalists did not know why they were striking. "Most members of The Newspaper Guild, the white-collar union in the joint council and by far its largest component, wondered why they should have to go to the wall for the pressmen, workers they seldom saw or cared about," noted Sean Rossiter in *Vancouver* magazine.[21] A petition was circulated among Guild members calling for a resumption of talks, and a motion instructing its negotiators to attempt to get back to bargaining was passed overwhelmingly at a membership meeting. But the vote was not mentioned in the pages of the *Express*, reported the *Globe and Mail*, which detected "some souring of the spirit of solidarity" between unions.[22] Needham charged that FP Publications management wanted the Guild exclusions to help create a 200-member non-union force that could produce any of its chain of newspapers from behind a picket line. "That's real hashish stuff," countered Paddy Sherman, claiming the exclusions would number two dozen at most.[23]

The joint council had renewed the business licence of Pugstem Publications annually since publishing the *Express* during the three-month shutdown of Pacific Press in 1970, as a contingency in the case of future strike action. As the 1978 showdown with Pacific Press loomed, early preparations to resume thrice-weekly publication of the *Express* enabled the union newspaper to be on the street only two days after the strike began. An office had been rented, phones installed, and department heads appointed. *Province* copy editor Don Brown, the Guild's unit chairman, was named publisher but admitted to being a bit muddle-headed about the paper's publication schedule, as Bruce McLean reported in the *Express*.

> "At our committee meeting on Wednesday, I went along with a 20-pager for Friday because I thought it was still Tuesday," said Brown, left a little punchy by several days at the bargaining table. "Later, I realized it was Wednesday, but I knew it was too late to change anything because the show was on the road." By Thursday the pandemonium settles into a mere confused disarray.[24]

When an unexpected flood of more than 2,000 lines of advertising came pouring in, the *Express* expanded by four pages, which overwhelmed the three print shops pasting up the paper's pages until, according to McLean, "a posse of 45 Pacific Press printers [rode] to the rescue."[25] The biggest problem in the *Express* office in East Vancouver was a shortage of desks, and many reporters wrote their stories on scrounged typewriters balanced on their knees while sitting on the floor. "For some, the incentive is to get even with Pacific Press," observed McLean. "They savor their revenge fish and chip style, hot and wrapped in their own newspaper."[26] On the editorial page, the union position was juxtaposed next to a message from the Pacific Press publishers. An *Express* editorial accused the company of provoking the strike by demanding contract concessions it knew the unions could not accept.

> The operators of Pacific Press are as ruthless as only those who put balance sheets before people can be. . . . Pacific Press . . . clearly sees its duty to the Eastern interests that control it as making the biggest possible profit. . . . We are no longer dealing with newspaper people; we are confronted by cost accountants who wouldn't recognize a good newspaper even if they cared to produce one.[27]

In their quarter-page advertisement, Sherman and new *Sun* publisher Clark Davey pointed out that the pressmen had refused to consider modifying their manning guarantees as their union brothers had in New York, where the three-month newspaper shutdown ended almost as soon as the one in Vancouver began. "The same union has accepted in Toronto a proposal that is not nearly as good for the individual pressmen as the offer we have already put forward," the publishers argued.[28] Due to the impending strike, Davey had rushed out to Vancouver from Toronto ahead of schedule to accept his publisher's post and meet *Sun* staff, and then suddenly he was without a newspaper to put out. Paddy Sherman resumed his role of Pacific Press spokesman, and soon Davey chafed to join the battle himself, something retired *Sun* publisher Stuart Keate had always avoided. As part of middle management at the *Globe and Mail* in 1964, Davey had been one of the strikebreakers trained by the company to do the work of picketing printers, and the tactic succeeded in taming the unions forever after in Toronto.[29] When Davey began arguing the Pacific Press position on local television, he found himself derided as an

Eastern union buster imported to the fray, according to Paul Raugust in *B.C. Business Week*.

> "People said it was stupid of me to say on TV that the pressmen's union was featherbedding," Davey said in an interview. He doesn't believe it was a mistake. ... Davey heard that *Vancouver Province* publisher Paddy Sherman was invited to comment on Jack Webster's morning show on BCTV. Davey called Webster to offer his own views, thereby breaking with *The Sun*'s tradition of "no comment" on its labor disputes, preferring Pacific Press to shoulder that role.[30]

Davey stirred the labor pot again during the second week of the strike, charging that the pressmen had failed to bargain in good faith and that, in his opinion, it would likely take the intervention of a third party to get talks restarted. The company's bad-faith bargaining complaint went to the Labour Relations Board for adjudication while mediator Dowding asked the parties to keep silent on the dispute until it was decided.

Not only did Volume 2 of the *Express* hit the streets even faster than Volume 1, but unlike in 1970 it accepted advertising with its initial issue and was distributed outside the Vancouver city limits, selling in stores from Surrey to West Vancouver. The union newspaper soon encountered organized resistance, however. In an "unusual show of management solidarity," according to *B.C. Business Week*, two business groups urged an advertiser boycott of the *Express* in an effort to assist strikebound Pacific Press. "It is our viewpoint that management should not go out of its way to assist people on strike by prolonging that strike by providing new sources of income," said Bill Hamilton, president of the Employers' Council of B.C.[31] The action was taken, Hamilton told *B.C. Business Week*, because of the unique nature of the newspaper dispute. "Rarely does it happen that striking or locked out union members [are] in a position whereby they can manufacture their previous employer's product."[32]

Don Selman of the Vancouver Board of Trade justified his group's joining the boycott. "We're back to one of these automation issues, and we feel very strongly that if this country is going to get out of its malaise, it's got to become more efficient," he told *B.C. Business Week*. "I think we would not have been so inclined to get involved in this situation if it had been straight wages as the issue."[33] But the boycott had "no significant effect" on demand for advertising, reported the *Express*.[34] That claim was bolstered by the fact the strike paper quickly expanded to thirty-six pages in its second week, including 70 percent advertising.[35] Hamilton also unsuccessfully applied pressure to *New Westminster Columbian* publisher Rikk Taylor, whose Craftsmen Printers division was printing the *Express*. In a telephone call that smacked of "an implied threat," Taylor said Hamilton pointed out the Employer's Council represented major companies. "It sounded like some kind of intimidation," said Taylor. Hamilton claimed he was only gathering information for the council's industrial relations newsletter.[36]

When the advertising boycott failed to slow the *Express*, a sudden shortage of another ingredient even more essential to the publishing process threatened to derail the union paper. In mid-November, MacMillan Bloedel imposed a newsprint quota on its customers as a result of "unforeseen shortfalls," according to Taylor. A strike at thirty pulp and paper mills in the western U.S. earlier that year had created a shortage of newsprint across the continent. The *Columbian* would be allocated only 275 tonnes of newsprint by MacMillan Bloedel, Taylor told his employees in a memo, which was not even enough to meet the suburban newspaper's own needs. As a result, the *Columbian* would have to restrict its editions to a maximum of thirty-six pages, Taylor announced, which meant turning away the revenue from 2,000 to 3,000 inches of advertising a week. Circulation also would have to be kept to 37,000, which meant turning down 400 new subscriptions every day during the Pacific Press shutdown.[37]

The restrictions meant the *Columbian* would not be able to cash in on the strike to make up the financial losses that had been threatening its existence. The Lower Mainland's only other daily newspaper had managed to survive due to income from outside printing contracts. "I am sure you are all aware that a great deal of our newspaper division losses to date could have been eliminated by our continuing gains in circulation and advertising through November and December," Taylor told the *Columbian* staff. "I hope we can keep the advertising and circulation gains we have attained to date."[38] But as serious as the newsprint rationing was for the *Columbian*, it had even more dire consequences for its newest and biggest customer, the *Express*, which suddenly found itself without a supply of vital newsprint, Taylor announced.

> The apparent shortfall of 245 tonnes for *The Columbian* and Craftsmen alone necessitated that we inform the publishers of *The Express* that we would continue to rent our press time only if they could find their own supply of newsprint. . . . Pacific Press newsprint has obviously been withheld or allocated to other FP/Southam sources.[39]

According to general manager Dave Stinson, however, Pacific Press was simply stockpiling its quota of newsprint. "We'd be fools not to stockpile with prices going up," he told *B.C. Business Week*, which itself was threatened by the tightened newsprint supply.[40] On the west side of Vancouver, the *Courier* expanded to twice-weekly publication and began suburban distribution, preparing to go daily if the Pacific Press shutdown continued. The *Courier* claimed it was not affected by newsprint rationing because it was printed at College Printers, which had a guaranteed quota. But like Harvey Southam, *Courier* publisher Robin Lecky was a grandson of H.R. MacMillan, which made it unlikely his expanding tabloid would experience a shortage of paper.

After MacMillan Bloedel's imposition of newsprint quotas, the *Express* was able to continue publishing only by obtaining a ten-week supply of newsprint from the provincial government's B.C. Cellulose newsprint mill at Ocean Falls, but the lifeline was tenuous. Mill spokesman Ted Vesak described the newsprint sold to the strikers as "diverted paper," which had been rejected by the company's regular customers as "not of top quality."[41] B.C. Cellulose president Ray Williston, a former provincial minister of forests, said he had no qualms about supplying newsprint to a strike newspaper. "I was not interfering with a strike situation by selling the paper," he told *B.C. Business Week*. "I would have said I was playing a part in the strike if I had refused to let the *Express* have the paper that no one else wanted."[42] He justified the supply on economic grounds, reported *B.C. Business Week*.

> Williston said it has been very interesting for him to find out that the *Express* is quite capable of using newsprint which other companies have rejected. He said he has started to suspect that many of the rejections, for reasons such as the side of a roll being dam-

> aged, "were pretty fictitious." Normally, he said, this rejected paper has to be reprocessed by Ocean Falls and is a money-losing proposition. "The *Express* took all the crap we had, it was unbelievable," said Williston. . . . "We had stuff sitting there which had been accumulating for months and suddenly the *Express* found that they could use it.[43]

The imposition of newsprint quotas by MacMillan Bloedel as the Pacific Press strike began raised suspicions of a corporate agenda among some observers. "Some unionists are convinced that MB is indirectly seeking to assist the Employers' Council of B.C. in bringing the Pacific Press dispute to a halt," reported *B.C. Business Week*.[44] The family ties between MacMillan Bloedel and Southam were well known, and a study done the previous year for the Royal Commission on Corporate Concentration pointed out the links between their boards of directors. Two directors sat on both the Pacific Press and MacMillan Bloedel boards, while Harvey Southam's father, Gordon, who had married into the MacMillan family, was a director of both Southam and MacMillan Bloedel. The interlocking directorships resulted in MacMillan Bloedel selling newsprint to Pacific Press and other B.C. newspapers at a discount, according to a 1977 study by Simon Fraser University economics professor Richard Schwindt.

> This price difference was explained by a representative of the firm frankly, "Newsprint prices in British Columbia are lower than anywhere else on the U.S. West Coast for political reasons." Whether its links with the media . . . gain the firm a preferential editorial policy from the major British Columbia newspapers is unclear. Nevertheless, the links and the price concessions are facts.[45]

Schwindt admitted he could offer no proof of media influence wielded by MacMillan Bloedel as a result of the price concessions. "All I point out in the paper is there is an uncomfortable connection," Schwindt told the *Sun*. "It just makes me a little nervous." The economist refused to divulge his source for the discount disclosure. "Let's just say it's someone who knows."[46] The connection between the print media and the forestry giant should be investigated further, Schwindt argued, adding he had wanted to conduct a content analysis of B.C. newspaper treatment of the forest firm to examine in detail how news of the company was reported, but he did not have the money to do it.[47] *Sun* publisher Stuart Keate denied any favoritism, pointing to the *Sun*'s "tough, hard-nosed attitude in reporting" on MacMillan Bloedel.[48] Gerry Haslam, vice-president of corporate communication for MacMillan Bloedel, admitted the discount and interlocking directorships existed, but he said the long-standing pricing policy was meant to provide local firms with some benefit of B.C. resources. Haslam, a former Southam journalist at the *Winnipeg Tribune*, said any suggestion that the discount was intended to gain favorable news treatment for MacMillan Bloedel "is simply not the case."[49] *B.C. Business Week* reported that the newsprint brouhaha had the potential to precipitate a major labor-management confrontation, with union action aimed directly at the paper producer.

> Some people in the trade union movement are convinced that the lack of newsprint for the B.C. market is an attempt by Big Business to force the *Express* to stop publishing and thus ensure a speedy end to the strike. As a result, consideration is being given to shutting down some of MB's newsprint operations on Vancouver Island. Informed sources have told *B.C. Business Week* that top management at MB has been made aware of that situation. The betting in industry circles is that . . . the company is prepared to face that risk.[50]

Talks between Pacific Press and joint council negotiators resumed in mid-November, but after several weeks it became apparent to mediator Peter Dowding that nothing was to be gained by bargaining. On December 4 he called for a "cooling-off" period, adjourning talks until "a more appropriate time."[51] In the meantime, he said he hoped "the parties will not further inflame the situation by continuing their dispute in the media."[52] But the Pacific Press publishers rejected the mediator's call to cool their rhetoric, instead raising the temperature by charging the union leaders with misleading their striking members. "Somehow we must get to honest negotiating, with full reporting of what is going on, so that we can end this absolutely unnecessary strike that is doing so much damage to so many," Paddy Sherman said in a letter to employees, in which he termed the mediator's call for a cooling-off period "an abrupt turn for the worse."[53]

The pressroom manning rules, which had been in place since the Pacific Press Building opened in 1966, were known as "unit" manning. Under them, the number of pressmen on each shift was determined by a formula, depending on the number of pages in the newspaper being printed and how many color pages were included. The company wanted a change to "foreman" manning, under which the company's pressroom supervisor would decide how many pressmen would be needed for each day's editions. "Automation isn't the immediate issue but the publishers know if they can get hold of manning and reduce the force by attrition, the Pressmen's Union will be dead," wrote *Sun* reporter Doug Ward in the magazine *Canadian Dimension*. "Its long-term death or even short-term wounding would make it relatively easy for Pacific Press to put out a paper during a strike."[54] The company's claim that the restrictive pressroom practices contained in the contract put it at a competitive disadvantage with suburban printers, such as the *Columbian*, in obtaining lucrative outside printing jobs was not true, according to Ward's research at the Labour Relations Board. "Records show these firms pay their pressmen as much and sometimes more than does Pacific Press. Those records show that Pacific Press has lower shift differentials than most of its printshop competitors."[55]

Not only did the existing rules require them to pay more pressmen than necessary to run the presses, the publishers charged, but the papers were often forced pay them overtime rates. One pressman did not even live in Vancouver, they pointed out, and was able to put in an entire week's worth of shifts in two days by visiting town in his camper from the Cariboo several hundred miles away. "He worked Tuesday morning, worked the next shift on Tuesday afternoon and stayed for a third shift on Wednesday morning," explained the *Globe and Mail*. "Since the two follow-on shifts paid double time, the three shifts put a week's work on his time sheet and he left to resume his briefly interrupted camping."[56] *Sun* columnist Doug Collins backed up the story in a column for *B.C. Business Week*. "That may not happen very often, but it happens, which is why amazed visitors to the pressroom can sometimes spot chaps snoring their heads off on those big rolls of paper."[57] Sherman called a joint council bulletin of December 1, which blamed the overtime problem on the company, "a saddening distortion of the facts," adding that "the prospects now look bleak enough, unadorned, without poisoning the atmosphere with misinformation," reported the Canadian Press.

> He said a union official had said Pacific Press pays overtime to pressmen working into a second shift because it won't hire enough full-time pressmen to do the work. Sherman said the company has complained several times that the union is not providing adequate numbers of pressmen for straight-time pay under the contract. As a result the company is forced . . . into double and triple shifts at premium rates.[58]

Clark Davey wrote a letter to *Sun* staff on December 5, pointing out the joint council had not made any monetary demands in negotiations until the previous week, a month into the strike. "They would only negotiate economic items when the non-economic proposals peculiar to each of the individual unions were resolved," wrote Davey, adding that the monetary proposals finally presented by the unions did not even contain a wage demand.[59] The joint council economic package dealt only with fringe benefits, added Sherman. "But the fringe benefits mentioned alone would have added more than 20 per cent to the wage bill."[60] The publishers also charged in a press release that the Newspaper Guild, which represented 800 of the 1,400 Pacific Press workers, had voted to continue talks. "Nothing could be further from the truth," responded Guild president Phil Needham, adding there had been no Guild vote taken.[61] The cooling-off period had been imposed unilaterally by mediator Dowding, Needham pointed out, which he had the right to do, being in charge of negotiations.[62]

The regular quarterly Guild membership meeting was scheduled for December 12, and a dozen or so unionists prepared a motion calling for the contentious pressroom manning issue to be submitted to binding arbitration. About 450 Guild members attended the meeting, which debated the motion for ninety minutes before voting it down.[63] The meeting also heard details of a settlement in Montreal, where Southam had agreed to pay a 36 percent wage increase over 28½ months in a deal that also included a four-day week. Southam's *Gazette* had continued to publish during bargaining, and its circulation had surged from less than 120,000 to 200,000 while FP's *Star* had been shut down for six months.

The manning issue also had been resolved in the pressmen's favor at the *Gazette*, reported the joint council strike newsletter.

> The situation there is of special interest to us, because in Montreal FP and Southam are competitors, whereas in Vancouver they are allied in the Pacific Press organization. . . . FP and Southam have also gone separate ways in Ottawa and Winnipeg, and in each city the paper that reached agreement with the unions is making gains at the expense of the other. There is a message here, and we hope it is being pondered in the Pacific Press board room as well as on the picket line.[64]

As Christmas approached, the ITU claimed that under the lifetime job guarantees negotiated the previous year, its 300 printers should be receiving full wages and benefits during the Pacific Press shutdown because they had been locked out. "The ITU isn't on strike," union leader Harold Dieno said. "We were asked to leave the building by the company."[65] But Pacific Press general manager Dave Stinson rejected the claim. "A strike by one is a strike by all," he said.[66] By year's end, rumors began to leak out of the picket-ringed Pacific Press Building that Stinson was fed up with the seemingly impossible labor relations at 6th and Granville. A story in the *Express* on December 29 reported that Stinson would soon take a job in the U.S., despite his assurances the previous year that he was in the Pacific Press general manager's chair for the long haul.[67]

As the year ended and the strike moved into its third month, it was becoming obvious the shutdown of Pacific Press would be a long one. Both the company and the pressmen were dug in, their positions entrenched. The resolve of each side was underestimated by the other as neither would blink first or even consider a compromise, and the standoff was prolonged by misinformation. "It was a strike-lockout of people experienced in gathering and transmitting facts, very few of whom were aware of what it was all about," wrote Rossiter in *Vancouver* magazine. "Throughout, they thought of it as a strike that was going to be over in two weeks' time."[68] The "crowning irony" of the strike to Rossiter was the sight of striking reporters keeping secrets from working journalists. "Broadcast reporters trying to cover the strike were subjected to the sight of their print colleagues saying no comment."[69] The silence of the journalists was self-defeating, according to Rossiter, because it allowed Pacific Press to get the upper hand in public opinion. "Aside from the damage to their professional ethics, the result of these hypocrisies was that only the viewpoints of the publishers were aired."[70]

According to Rossiter, the pressmen could be excused for underestimating the company's resolve. "Considering what has happened in the past 10 years at Pacific Press, it was not at all unreasonable for the pressmen to conclude that Jerry Marr's Hallowe'en Night warning was no more than the usual saber rattling," concluded Rossiter.[71] The pressmen thought manning was a side issue, because they had seen the same demand quickly dropped in Winnipeg and Victoria. Even as the company's strike losses mounted beyond what it could ever hope to recoup through pressroom economies, according to Rossiter, the pressmen "simply could not believe" that Pacific Press was not far more interested in economic issues.

> It has been said many times that the most novel, tricky ploy in labor-management negotiations is simply to tell the truth. Had the strikers believed Jerry Marr, they would have saved themselves the frustration of hoping for a settlement in time for Christmas, or in April . . . or by the middle of May. . . . All Marr did was tell the truth. He did the unions a favor.[72]

As the Pacific Press strike dragged on into 1979, the shutdown of Vancouver's two daily newspapers provided a bonanza for the electronic media. "I turned down $7,000 in business on the first day of the strike because we were booked four months ahead," CKWX radio sales representative Barbara Welsh told *B.C. Business Week*. Even radio stations well down in the ratings cashed in on the boom. "In December we really noticed an increase in our business and we've been showing a healthy increase in business," said CHQM sales vice-president Noel Hullah. The radio stations fully expected most of the new business to disappear as soon as the dailies resumed publication, but they counted on keeping some of their new customers. "Every time there's a strike the papers lose some accounts permanently because certain advertisers have discovered that another medium works well for them or costs less," said Bob Speed, general manager of all-news CKO.[73]

The biggest benefactor of the Pacific Press shutdown was television station BCTV, which under the leadership of news director Cameron Bell had emphasized journalism over entertainment. Hotliner Jack Webster had been lured away from radio in 1978 with a lucrative offer to do his morning phone-in show in front of BCTV cameras. As a result, the station's morning viewership soared from 2,300 to an average of 97,300 in just three months.[74] BCTV's biggest gains during the disappearance of the dailies, however, came for its evening *News Hour*, which broke the half-million mark in the first week of February between its CHAN station in Vancouver and its CHEK affiliate in Victoria, reported *B.C. Business Week*.

> It means on weekdays at 6 p.m., 45 per cent of the TV sets turned on in the Greater Vancouver area are tuned to *News Hour*. It means the program on any given weekday during that ratings period was seen by 20 per cent of B.C.'s population. Few shows can boast that penetration. . . . Of course, a natural explanation for any jump in the ratings is the Pacific Press dispute.[75]

Bell predicted that only 15 percent of the extra viewers BCTV had picked up during the newspaper shutdown would go back to the dailies as their main source of news after the strike was over. "TV is a more effective way to tell stories when it's done properly," Bell told *B.C. Business Week*. "I don't accept the premise that TV can't be analytical. TV can ultimately do it better than print journalism."[76] The station's biggest drawing card was anchorman Tony Parsons, a handsome 39-year-old Toronto baritone who had been assigned to Vancouver as a correspondent by the CTV network and liked Lotusland so much he decided to make the West Coast his permanent home. "I had watched BCTV grow and expand and I liked what I saw as they put all their eggs in the news basket," Parsons told reporter Moira Farrow in 1979. "I've turned down two offers from Los Angeles and I've also had chances to go to Denver, Atlanta, Chicago and New York. Five to 10 years ago I would have jumped at the chance but those cities don't appeal to me any more. I love Vancouver and my lifestyle here and I don't like Los Angeles."[77] Parsons had just signed a five-year contract, making him one of the highest-paid broadcasters in Canada, Farrow reported, pointing out that in light of Walter Cronkite's longevity in the U.S., Parsons "probably has a long future in the broadcasting business."[78]

15 The Combination Man

Jim Taylor was as smooth a writer and every bit as witty and entertaining a columnist as *Sun* colleague Allan Fotheringham, but he plied his unique brand of journalism in the sports section instead of on the news pages. In Taylor and Fotheringham, *Sun* publisher Stu Keate boasted the top two writers in Vancouver throughout most of the 1970s, and arguably the top pair of columnists at any newspaper in the country. For years Taylor was Vancouver's best sportswriter "by an embarrassing margin," according to Don Stanley in *Vancouver* magazine, due not just to his writing ability but also to his cynical perspective as a real-life bleacher bum.

> This mythical Regular Guy in his mind acts as a kind of superego over columns that never betray standard market expectations. Thus he never tires of time-tested gags about goon athletes who arrive by vine or walk on their knuckles. As part of the standard newspaper flirtation with impropriety, Taylor's weather is always cold enough to freeze the balls off a billiard table.[1]

The dynamic duo gave the *Sun* good reason to continue trumpeting its long-standing slogan, slightly revised for the 1970s: "*The Sun*: Where The Writers Are." But with Keate's departure from the publisher's chair, that would quickly change. As it had done with Fotheringham before him, the *Toronto Star* took notice of Taylor's popularity, and soon the country's largest-circulation newspaper was courting the sports columnist. The *Star* offered him a healthy raise and a salary of $33,000 in 1977 to move east, but Taylor had an even better reason than Fotheringham not to leave the mild climate of the West Coast. On April 8, 1976, his world had come crashing down when his 14-year-old daughter Teresa was left a spastic quadriplegic from a skiing accident. She had never skied before, so her parents had done the prudent thing and enrolled her in lessons. As she sat in the snow at Manning Park during her first lesson, she was struck by a skier and suffered a brain stem injury. According to *Province* sportswriter Mike Gasher in *Vancouver* magazine, the best column Taylor ever wrote "was not about sports and it did not make anyone laugh. He cried on and off for two days after writing it."[2] The Page Six *Sun* story detailed Taylor's problems obtaining adequate care for his daughter amidst government health care cutbacks.

> When my little girl cries there is no sound, only tears. Her face reddens and her eyes fill. But they fill in silence. She is in there, trying to get out. I know it. "Alert," they call her now, and they say that if she awakens fully she should be able to speak again. But they've put a price tag on her voice, and said it's too high. I think about that a lot.[3]

The 1978 showdown between Pacific Press and its unions posed a financial problem for many *Sun* and *Province* journalists, as the closure promised to be a long one. One by one, they began leaving for more secure jobs in television, public relations or the real world. Don Stanley quit as *Sun* television critic to freelance and write a novel. Neale Adams and Harvey Oberfeld jumped to television, helping BCTV assemble an enviable stable of reporters. Paul St. Pierre took a job on a government commission. Harvey Southam bolted from the newspaper business altogether after jumping from his family's *Province* to FP's *Sun* two years earlier. He took a job as executive producer of CKVU's prime-time *Vancouver* show, which was hosted by his girlfriend and future wife, Pia Shandel. Some Pacific Press writers went to work for the *Courier* rather than walk a picket line, as the west-side community newspaper began publishing twice weekly and geared up to go daily if the Pacific Press strike dragged on. Those who did not take work elsewhere could pitch in at the *Express* in addition to collecting their strike pay.

Taylor had been freelancing with regular radio spots on CKWX for years, and when Pacific Press shut down in 1978 he struck a deal with the local CBC station for television time as well. As *Sun* reporter George

Dobie noted in the *Express*, with Taylor's thick glasses, bald pate, and overbite, "he's not photogenic but he's found a new career in television because he's glib, he's funny and, best of all, he can spot a farcical situation in the super-serious bureaucracy of professional sports faster than anyone west of the Great Lakes."[4] The only problem was that new *Sun* publisher Clark Davey had a firm policy against freelancing by his journalists. That posed a dilemma for many at the *Sun*, especially the paper's lead columnists — Taylor, Collins, and Fotheringham — all of whom had regular outside income from other media. But as Davey had not yet published an edition of the *Sun* because of the strike, his policy had not been challenged. Taylor forced the issue, phoning his new boss as a courtesy to inform him of his career move. "His exact words were, 'You have to remember who your master is,'" recalled Taylor. "I said, 'I'm not phoning to ask if I can. I'm phoning to say I'm going to do this.'"[5] Taylor had lunch with Davey and *Sun* managing editor Bruce Larsen to discuss the issue, but the meeting with the new publisher went no better than the phone call, Taylor recalled.

> He said, "They only want you because you write for the *Sun*. Besides, they'll never hire you." I kept thinking, this time I'm not going to walk around that stupid building. My daughter was still in the hospital. I owed a lot of lawyers a lot of money. That was a bad period of time. I kept working because if I didn't I'd go crazy. I'm a workaholic anyway. The strike really worked out for me, to be brutally honest.[6]

Rumors about Taylor's future were running rampant on radio, and his colleagues at the *Sun* were interested in learning the ramifications of their new publisher's edict against freelancing, especially those with outside income. Taylor's decision was reported by Dobie in the *Express* on May 9. "The columnist says he went home from the luncheon, 'did the math' regarding his income, didn't like what he saw under the freelancing restriction, and wrote his resignation."[7] According to Stanley, Davey's no-freelancing policy, which would have cost Taylor half of his annual income, was based on "the theory that the advertising dollar can only be split so many ways."[8] Multimedia exposure, Stanley reported, made its journalists less valuable to a Clark Davey newspaper, not more. "He rejects Taylor's argument that any high-profile writer without an 'electronic connection' will soon be in serious career trouble. Nevertheless,

Davey resembles a rookie football coach who cuts a star quarterback to get the team's attention."[9]

As Taylor took to television nightly in addition to doing three radio spots a day for CKWX, Dobie saw the erstwhile *Sun* star becoming "the first honest-to-goodness Combination Man in this third largest market area in Canada – a marvel of the Print Media and the Electronic Media all in one."[10] Dobie speculated that once the strike ended, Taylor's column could wind up on the pages of the second-place *Province* instead of the market-leading *Sun*. "If the *Province* really wants to close the gap, a good way would be to pick up a writer of Taylor's talent. And, if Jim is no longer at *The Sun*, why not the man himself?"[11] The radio rumors had Taylor jumping to the *Province* as sports editor, which he quickly denied, noting the morning paper already had a sports editor in Bob Scott. "I would like to think I could be a columnist," Taylor told Dobie.[12]

Negotiations at Pacific Press did not resume under the direction of mediator Peter Dowding until mid-February, after a "cooling-off" period of ten weeks. By the second week in March, with the strike in its fifth month, labor minister Allan Williams announced that talks could "for the first time be classified as productive.... Something is beginning to happen."[13] The company offered a wage increase of 26.2 percent over three years if the sticking point of press manning was referred to binding arbitration, but the pressmen refused to move, so Dowding bowed out of the dispute in mid-March. In his place, the parties sought the services of San Francisco lawyer John Kagel, who had assisted the sides in reaching an agreement on the eve of contract expiry in 1977 and who had been serving as the mediator-arbitrator on technological change issues in Guild jurisdiction. But Kagel's schedule was busy, even with his daily fee of $2,000, and he agreed to assist only if the parties traveled to meet near his home in suburban Palo Alto, which they did on March 22.[14] A recess was called after a week and the sides returned to Vancouver, with Paddy Sherman announcing that Kagel would soon travel to Vancouver to resume attempts to break the deadlock.[15]

On April 17, Kagel finally managed to gain a concession from pressmen's union business agent Gary Dunster on pressroom manning of one pressman per shift, but the proposal was rejected by the company. Dunster then suffered a nervous breakdown, and after a union vote, his replacement as negotiator disavowed the previous manning concession. According to Sherman, management got word that some pressmen who supported referring the manning clause to arbitration were convinced in the crudest manner to change their position. "We were told quietly by one or two of them that they were taken out into the back alley and threatened with two-by-fours by some of the toughest union leaders."[16]

After calling in ten rank-and-file members of the pressmen's union and being told they supported the position of their leaders, Kagel concluded there was "no purpose to be served in continuing negotiations" involving the pressmen, blaming them for the impasse in a scathing indictment.[17] The union's intransigence, he wrote in a report, "is almost a cultural one which has blocked past attempts to have the parties speak the same language."[18] The pressmen's position on manning, concluded Kagel, had to fail in light of their rejection of impartial arbitration.

> What is lacking is the willingness of the Union to move into the same dimension of discussion as the Employer. The moves by the Union have been far too small in light of what it seeks for them – job guarantees and a moratorium on future manning negotiations. . . . The position that manning is not "for sale" is thus an intransigent one which unless the employer folds creates an unbridgable impasse.[19]

Dobie saw the development as signaling a "dangerous point of no return" in the dispute, with the possibility looming of Pacific Press attempting to publish without the strikers. "That could set the stage for bitter encounters on the picket line," he wrote in the *Express*. "Head-bashing is not supposed to be part of B.C. labor relations but it has come down to that in some disputes and could do so in this one."[20] Pacific Press had earlier denied it planned to publish from behind a picket line, but left the option open. Davey declared in February that publishing without union labor would only happen if "the union left us with a whole series of non-negotiable demands."[21] Sherman estimated the company's losses during the strike at between $7 million and $8 million a month.[22] Complaints from members of other unions on the picket line had been growing that the pressmen were earning as much as ever at other employers while the rest of the Pacific Press staff paraded around the plant in the rain to defend their right to guaranteed overtime. "Along with the mailers, it is known they get up to three shifts a week on the outside working in suburban newspaper and commercial shops," reported Dobie. "The way the whole dispute has been manipulated is close to being scandalous.[23] The pressmen attempted to gain the support of the other unions with a mass rally to show solidarity but quit the joint council when Guild leaders were non-committal. Kagel's damning report had been leaked to the press and was excerpted widely in reports of the breakdown in bargaining. *B.C. Business Week* reprinted the memo in its entirety in its edition of May 2.

Kagel continued to oversee often marathon talks between Pacific Press and the remaining joint council unions intermittently between other assignments, but he resigned on May 17 after talks broke off with the parties within what he called "realistic reach of virtually immediate settlement."[24] According to Dobie, the negotiations collapsed after the company changed its offer from a four-step to a three-step increase and the unions complained that change reduced the final compounded wage increase. "The difference over the term of the contract was not sufficient to matter to many workers, by now anxious to get back to their regular jobs," Dobie reported in the *Express*. "But it did make a difference to the bargaining process. Union leaders suggested management had tried to put one over on them while they were groggy at the end of an all-night bargaining session."[25] Newspaper Guild president Phil Needham recalled punching in on his calculator the numbers Kagel relayed from the company, only to obtain a disquieting quotient. "He seemed sort of tentative," recalled Needham of the mediator. "I was doing the math on my calculator when I announced, 'They've taken money off the table.' The response was, 'That's it! We're outta here.' Kagel said, 'I told them not to do it. I told them you'd spot it.'"[26] But in a telephone interview with the *Express*, Kagel refused to blame either side. "I won't get into who's right or wrong," he said from California. "Wrong things were done at the wrong time but I won't say who did them. My function is to make sure people who are consenting adults do things with their eyes open."[27]

In 1974, Robin Lecky and two partners bought the weekly *Kerrisdale Courier*, originally established as the *Point Grey Gazette* in 1908, for $15,000 and expanded it steadily over the next five years. Renaming it simply the *Courier*, they increased the circulation from 12,000 to 20,000 in the first eight months, and then in May 1976 they took over the downtown community newspaper, the *West Ender*, for a combined circulation of 35,000.[28] The *Courier*'s tabloid format proved popular, and so when the *North Shore Times* ceased publication in 1977 after thirty years in West Vancouver, Lecky and his partners decided to expand into that market with a 12,000-circulation free weekly. "We anticipate making money," Lecky told *Sun* business reporter Wyng Chow.[29] The *Courier*'s West Vancouver venture proved disastrous, however. *North Shore News* publisher Peter Speck in adjacent North Vancouver met the challenge to his turf aggressively, according to *Courier* advertising salesman Peter Ballard. "We lasted about six weeks," Ballard told Lisa Smedman for an authorized *Courier* history in 1998. "We left with our tails between our legs."[30] Speck "sent in a sales person after every call we made who would go in and give the [*News*] ad away," added Phillip Hager, another *Courier* account executive.[31]

Now, with no end in sight to the Pacific Press strike, Lecky saw an opportunity to take his west-side community newspaper daily. When his cousin, Harvey Southam, went into the magazine business in 1984 as editor of the new local business publication *Equity*, Southam reported the "inside story" of the *Courier*'s bid to go daily in 1979. Adding a second edition a week during the Pacific Press strike had boosted the *Courier*'s profit to $400,000 monthly, Southam wrote, and Lecky looked for partners to contribute capital to an attempt to publish Vancouver's first daily tabloid since the brief *News-Herald* experiment with the format in the early 1940s.

> He flew back East to talk to Doug Creighton at the *Toronto Sun* about doing a full-blown tabloid newspaper. Contrary to the popular rumor, there was never any deal made with Creighton, although the publisher of Canada's biggest newspaper success story did suggest that Vancouver had great potential as a tab market, and if Lecky could get it up and running, Creighton would consider joining forces later.[32]

The *Toronto Sun* had risen from the ashes of the *Telegram*, which had folded in 1971 during labor negotiations. Creighton and other staff from the *Telegram* set up shop almost immediately with a non-union newspaper. The journalists presented their new *Sun* as a colorful tabloid in competition with the *Star* and *Globe and Mail*, which were both broadsheets. The format proved a marvel of marketing, as a younger audience was attracted to the newspaper, which emphasized sports and entertainment. The disposable income of the younger readership in turn attracted advertisers eager to reach that target market. The employee-owned venture was so successful that it became a newspaper chain in 1978 when it expanded to Edmonton and started a similar *Sun* in competition with Southam's *Journal*, which had enjoyed a wide-open market without competition since Max Bell's *Bulletin* folded in 1951.

Lecky was sure a morning tabloid would fly in Vancouver, even after the Pacific Press papers inevitably resumed publication, but he needed capital to get the venture off the ground. That led him to Gordon Byrn, a Harvard MBA from a wealthy Vancouver family, whose restaurateur wife Jackie wrote a cooking column for the *Courier*. Byrn examined the *Courier*'s books, according to Southam, and declared that the paper could go daily with an injection of $1 million in capital, 60 percent of which he would put up in return for 40 percent equity in the new daily and a post as its Chief Executive Officer. The deal Lecky and Byrn made in early March would become "very misunderstood," according to Southam.[33]

Frenzied preparations were made over the next three months to go daily, as the staff grew to 140 and the Vancouver advertising agency Palmer Jarvis and Associates developed an expensive promotional campaign.[34] A major news conference was held in mid-June to announce the birth of the daily *Courier*, which was scheduled to commence on July 4. "Loaves of bread were sent out to advertisers and the media with the catchline 'Fresh Daily,'" recalled Southam. "Lecky still figures it was one of the greatest ad lines Palmer Jarvis has ever dreamed up."[35] Byrn told the press conference that he was confident a daily *Courier* tabloid could be profitable even after the *Sun* and *Province* hit the streets again. "We're trying to develop a new market and we view television as our competition," Byrn said. "Major advertisers are excited about this, almost as excited as we are."[36] There was a problem with Byrn's bravado, however, according to Moira Farrow in *B.C. Business Week*. "Advertising executives of Eaton's,

Woodward's, the Bay and Canada Safeway Ltd. had not even been contacted by the *Courier* before its announcement of going daily," she reported. "They were non-committal about any future plans for advertising with the *Courier*."[37]

Farrow also recorded Sherman's reaction to the challenge posed for his *Province* by a new morning competitor. "We will go flat out when we go back with a new product of a much higher level than the *Courier* is expecting," said Sherman. "Good luck to them but they are going to need a lot of capital."[38] That raised another problem with Lecky's hastily assembled plan for a new daily newspaper, according to Harvey Southam. "More important to Lecky was the fact that Byrn had still not signed the letter of agreement over the financing in the new *Courier*."[39]

By May settlement of the Pacific Press shutdown, now more than a half-year long, seemed both tantalizingly close and hopelessly remote. While the joint council was down to the nitty-gritty of finalizing wage increases, the absence of the pressmen from the negotiations meant no resolution of the dispute could be achieved as long as their manning issues remained outstanding. If the newspaper shutdown did not end by mid-June, *Sun* business editor George Froehlich observed in an article for *B.C. Business Week*, the papers might close down for the summer due to the inevitable decimation of their carrier networks when the school year ended. "If that were to take place it would certainly be September before the two daily newspapers would resume publication," wrote Froehlich.[40] *Sun* labor reporter George Dobie argued in an accompanying column that part of the problem prolonging the dispute was the fact that both sides were being subsidized. "Pacific Press has had strike insurance while the press unions have bolstered benefits to members by producing ... *The Express*. As a result, the normal amount of pressure associated with a labor shutdown – particularly one of this length of time – is not evident."[41]

Newspaper Guild president Phil Needham recalled being invited to a clandestine meeting with Stinson and joint council co-chair Stan Lepper at the Shaughnessy Golf Club, where the Pacific Press general manager poured drinks in the locker room. Stinson argued the company had no incentive to settle the strike before September and the lucrative back-to-school advertising season, but the Guild leader disagreed.

> I told him the company had a lot to lose if the strike continued into July. At the moment, it still had a nearly intact staff, many of them, such as editorial and sales, still doing what they do. They would be prepared for a quick restart of the papers, a recovery of circulation and no need for a massive hiring and training program. . . . I said I didn't know if that could continue.[42]

Labour Relations Board chairman Don Munroe called the parties together for secret talks and succeeded in convincing the pressmen to accept binding arbitration of the manning clause. The offer was conditional on lifetime job guarantees for all pressmen employed at Pacific Press and delaying any changes to manning levels until the end of the contract. But the company found the conditions unacceptable, Sherman and Davey announced in a joint statement, because they would prevent any significant changes to manning during the life of the contract. "Pacific Press accepted the arbitration concept, but suggested the conditions sought by the union should be left to the discretion of the arbitration board," the statement said.[43] Needham recalled Stinson confiding of the pressmen's turnaround, "It's like a Catholic giving up his rosary beads."[44] Dobie lashed the company in a column in the *Express* for rejecting the "complete turn-around" by the pressmen. "The word is getting around that Pacific Press has a rather bad habit that is prolonging the dispute with the newspaper unions: When someone takes half a step forward to try to meet the company on common ground, the company takes a full step backward."[45]

Jim Kinnaird, the unionist who had negotiated the ill-fated 1976 Pacific Press settlement that was rolled back by the Anti-Inflation Board, then joined the battle. Kinnaird, who had re-entered union politics and been elected president of the B.C. Federation of Labour, accused Pacific Press of getting "greedy" in negotiations. "Everyone involved in industrial relations, whether it be union or management, knows that you just don't increase your demands when a settlement is imminent."[46] He made it clear the pressmen had the support of his powerful labor group, accusing the company of bargaining in bad faith. "It's up to management to get off their butt and bring about a resolution of this thing," Kinnaird told a May 29 press conference. "Pacific Press has chosen to continue the strike-lockout in spite of the fact that the settlement is sitting right in front of them."[47]

Two days later the company and the pressmen's union issued a joint statement, announcing they had agreed on terms of arbitration of the manning clause.[48] The company conceded that changes in manning would not be implemented until the end of the contract if they were unacceptable to the pressmen, but just when it appeared a settlement was imminent, negotiations hit another snag. On rejoining the joint council the pressmen balked at the wage offer on the table, which brought the resignation of joint council co-chairs Needham and Lepper, who had negotiated it.[49] An escalated demand of a 48 percent wage increase over forty months proposed by the pressmen was deemed unrealistic by the joint council negotiators. "According to the best inside sources, they stated flatly they could not be the front men for that kind of approach," reported Dobie. "In effect, they resigned in protest. . . . although, to their credit, they stayed in the council."[50] The crisis in negotiations attracted a summit of heavyweight players to attempt a resolution of the impasse. In addition to Kinnaird, Munroe, labor minister Allan Williams, and his deputy Jim Matkin, according to the *Express*, interested parties boarded flights to Vancouver from all directions.

> George Currie, president of FP Publications, and Gordon Fisher, president of Southam Newspapers, flew out from Toronto for the meeting after being informed objections by their local negotiators to the pressmen's terms could scuttle the settlement. . . . Even Kagel, the high-priced San Francisco mediator who could not settle the whole dispute, flew up at his own expense to help.[51]

Bargaining resumed on June 7, and after forty hours of continuous negotiations, agreement was reached on a wage increase of 35 percent in a forty-month contract from the date of expiry of the previous contract more than seven months earlier. Jerry Marr optimistically announced the *Sun* and *Province* could be back on the streets within seventy-two hours of each union's membership ratifying the contract.[52] But again the hopes for settlement of the longest shutdown of Vancouver's daily newspapers were premature. The deal made at the bargaining table still did not satisfy the pressmen, who rejected the agreement by a vote of 74 percent.[53] "To have it turned down is not particularly encouraging," said Harold Dieno of the ITU, who had helped to negotiate the deal on behalf of the joint council. The pressmen were unhappy with the length of the contract, which would have set the new expiry date at February 28, 1982, as well as a change to the starting date of any pressroom manning changes decided by arbitration. While the company had earlier agreed that any changes in press manning would not be made until the end of the new contract if they were unacceptable to the pressmen, the latest proposal provided for implementation three months before the contract expired.

The mailers and engravers had already voted to accept the agreement, but without the pressmen's concurrence their ratification was meaningless. A Guild meeting, described by the Canadian Press as "sometimes stormy," rejected a motion from the floor to waive the union bylaw requiring a 48-hour period before a ratification vote could be taken. Needham told the meeting that the new agreement was worse than the one he had helped negotiate in April and accused the pressmen of bargaining in bad faith.[54] ITU printers rejected the agreement, 136-119, over provisions which would have allowed Pacific Press to publish a long-rumored Sunday *Province* (at the time there was no Sunday paper), and the wholesalers rejected it by 84 percent, citing contract length.[55] Guild members, who constituted a majority of Pacific Press workers, voted 71 percent in favor of accepting the agreement but were prevented from going back to work by the rejections of the other unions.

Sherman did the math, which showed that more than 60 percent of Pacific Press workers wanted to end the strike, and argued that the ability of one or two small unions to keep hundreds of workers out on strike until they got what they wanted went against fundamental principles of democracy. "At some point, the will of the majority has to prevail," he told the Canadian Press.[56] *Sun* publisher Clark Davey called on labor minister Allan Williams to convert the joint council into a formal bargaining unit under Section 57 of the Labour Code, which would enable a majority vote of all union members to prevail, but Williams responded he could not do so while a dispute was in progress.[57] The labor minister admitted he was at his wit's end as to how to resolve the newspaper deadlock. "Frankly, in this particular dispute, the parties have used up almost every assistance that they can have," he said. "They've already had the services of one of the outstanding mediators on the continent and if he has been unsuccessful, it's difficult to know what other steps might be successful."[58]

On June 19, two weeks before the *Courier*'s planned debut as a daily, a curious new broadsheet called the *Daily News* hit the Vancouver streets with little fanfare. Published by Peter Lasch, a new arrival to Canada from Germany, the twelve-page paper was produced in the Fraser Valley community of Aldergrove, thirty miles from Vancouver. Lasch, 42, told *B.C. Business Week* that the Pacific Press strike had "nothing to do with our new paper. We are so different from them that we do not compete."[59] Containing little advertising, the newspaper depended on street sales for income. Lasch, who had started a harness-racing magazine on his arrival in Canada a year earlier, said the *Daily News* was launched with an initial press run of 50,000 and would sell for 25 cents. It would feature "big headlines, a lot of pictures," and its concept of journalism would be fundamentally different from the Pacific Press papers. "Our reporters will not put their own opinions in stories," said Lasch. "We want our readers to do their thinking for themselves."[60]

Marketing magazine described the effort as "a completely different approach to the newspaper business, somewhat reminiscent of the old-time straight news sheets. It is a strictly no-frills, 12-page newspaper concerned only with the dispensation of international, national, regional and local news. Even advertising is kept to a minimum in the interests of space conservation."[61] Langara College journalism instructor Nick Russell thought the early issues of the *Daily News*, or *DN*, as it called itself, "looked remarkably ghastly and much of the writing and news judgement matched that."[62] He reported in *content*, the national newsletter of the Centre for Investigative Journalism, rumors of the newspaper being backed by a Saudi Arabian contractor. Lasch claimed a paid circulation of 43,000, according to Russell, all from store sales in Vancouver, and planned to increase that to 150,000 by expanding to other B.C. cities.

> Lasch [said] his paper's design is based on *Bildzeitung*, for which he worked in Germany as salesman and reporter for 25 years. Lasch has since diversified and describes himself as an engineer with interests in ship building, oil and a construction company. He says he can break even immediately by keeping costs to an absolute minimum: a total staff of 25, including five in news.[63]

While most dismissed the *Daily News* as an amateur effort, the pending launch of the *Courier* as a daily was shaping up as a more serious challenge to the Pacific Press papers. A half-dozen journalists from the *Sun* and *Province* had already signed on, and the tabloid format was expected to interest advertisers. Reporter Clive Jackson, formerly of the tabloid *Daily Mail* in London, said the *Courier* would be more responsible than the racy Fleet Street scandal sheets, however. "It's not a tit and bum tabloid but we do go for the more off-beat human interest stories that attract the younger reader."[64] A Sunday edition also was planned to take advantage of the seventh-day void, as neither of the Pacific Press papers published on Sunday.

In the suburbs of Vancouver, weekly newspapers sprang up everywhere to fill the demand for print advertising. Some were started by entrepreneurs with little experience in business, such as the *Boundary Road*, a Burnaby weekly founded by several student journalists from Simon Fraser University. Even the weekly *Georgia Straight*, which had started publication as an underground newspaper in 1967, shed its hippie image and re-emerged as the *Vancouver Free Press* in what the *Globe and Mail* described as "the ultimate act in a corporate quest for broader news-stand acceptance with an increasingly conservative readership."[65] During the Pacific Press strike, weekly sales of the *Straight* had doubled to about 22,000. The name and format change, with coverage of news, sports, and entertainment, resulted in the *Free Press* being sold in more than twice as many stores as the *Straight*, which had been held back by the notoriety of its multiple obscenity convictions. "It's been the *Straight* in name only for the last couple of years, anyway," reasoned publisher Dan McLeod.[66]

The only thing that could bring the shutdown of Pacific Press to an end after almost eight months was economic pressure on both sides. As *Sun* labor reporter George Dobie had observed, the bargaining relationship was dysfunctional because each side had outside sources of income: Pacific Press from strike insurance and the unions from printing their own newspaper, the *Express*. The company's bargaining table boast of having six months of strike insurance suggested it was no longer being subsidized, and now Pacific Press faced new daily competition entering the Vancouver market to challenge its government-sanctioned joint monopoly. According to Harvey Southam in *Equity*, "the prospect was scary enough to Pacific Press executives that they started talking turkey with their unions."[67]

On the union side, it was becoming apparent there could be no resolution of the bargaining stalemate as long as the *Express* continued to publish, so the joint council voted to close down the strike newspaper. According to Sean Rossiter in *Vancouver* magazine, "folding *The Express* was the Joint Council's signal to the pressmen that the strike was over."[68] Publisher Don Brown announced on June 17 that the *Express* would cease publication after three more issues due to a shortage of newsprint, adding that "the newspaper was intended to last only as long as the Pacific Press dispute."[69] According to the United Press Canada, however, B.C. Cellulose claimed it had "plenty of newsprint left. Other sources said the decision to fold the *Express* was intended to increase pressure on the three holdout unions."[70] Negotiators for the company and the three unions that had voted against the contract settlement met again with mediator Peter Dowding, and some modifications were made to the agreement. The first union to vote on the revised proposal was the ITU on June 19, reported the *Express*.

> Printers who attended a 90-minute afternoon meeting said Dieno and union vice-president Dick Ainsworth threatened to resign if the proposal was turned down again. . . . Several union members emerged from the typographers' meeting complaining that the contract was being "railroaded" through, and saying it was no different from the pact previously turned down.[71]

The ITU voted 162-80 in favor of the agreement, which left as holdouts only the pressmen and their affiliated wholesalers. Together their two unions represented just 10 percent of workers at Pacific Press. To gain their agreement, B.C. Federation of Labour officials met with the joint council the next day and were given the authority to bargain with the company on behalf of the unions. The talks, reported Peter Comparelli in the final edition of the *Express* on June 22, were "shrouded in secrecy," with both sides maintaining their silence following a three-hour meeting the previous afternoon.[72] As the last copies of the *Express* were being printed in Coquitlam, folder gears on the *Columbian* presses mysteriously failed, causing thousands of dollars in damage and forcing the suburban paper to use commercial printers for several days while repairs were made. "It's never happened before," said *Columbian* publisher Rikk Taylor as the Royal Canadian Mounted Police investigated suspected sabotage.[73]

After a turbulent union meeting the next day, it was announced that another vote would be taken by the pressmen, with Kinnaird admitting they still were "obviously not happy" with the deal. "It's fair to say emotions are running fairly high in the organization in the belief that there is a certain amount of pressure put on them as individuals to ratify the agreement right now," he said.[74] The *Globe and Mail* reported that while there were no changes in the second contract the pressmen voted on, "management did toss them a crumb: It agreed to stall any manning changes for a month, but made it clear they would be implemented during the 39th month of the new contract."[75] The vote results were announced by Dave McIntyre, the former pressman who was secretary-treasurer of the B.C. Federation of Labour. The two unions had agreed to return to work despite being "quite unhappy" with the deal, said McIntyre, who did not release the vote results.[76] Pressmen's union spokesman Keith Jacobsen called the deal "a big fat zero," adding, "It's not going to be a very happy place to work."[77]

Also not happy were a lot of Pacific Press journalists who left to work at the *Courier* or *Columbian*, or switched to television or other livelihoods. Eight had quit the *Sun*, including almost the entire business section, and sixteen had fled the *Province*.[78] Not much happier were those who stayed. Needham declared that bargaining under the joint council arrangement made reaching a settlement without outside assistance impossible. "At the bargaining table, Stinson can speak for the company," Needham told the *Sun*'s Jes Odam. "On the other side the joint council has various interests in many areas and it is more difficult for the council to speak as one."[79] Stinson's imminent departure from Pacific Press was made official after being an "open secret," according to Davey.[80] The recriminations of columnists came thick and furious upon resumption of publication. In the *Sun*, Allan Fotheringham called the pressmen "stubborn and selfish" for causing such protracted grief, and saw their loss of credibility as the ultimate result.

> You can't get around the fact that a small group of men, hiding behind a protective wall of overtime erected over the years,

> weren't about to allow anything that might reduce their earnings to the level of a mere reporter. . . . The ludicrous aspect of 90 per cent of employees wanting to go back to work but held back by a recalcitrant few eventually embarrassed everyone and the city populace in the end viewed us as juveniles – little fit to lecture other people in how to conduct their business.[81]

The next morning, Sherman warned against believing anyone who claimed to tell the "inside story" of the eight-month strike. "There will be many versions of it, but I can tell you one thing with certainty: no one will tell the real story," he wrote in his regular Saturday column. "There will be many 'facts,' but little truth."[82] Truth, he confided, was actually an enemy of labor negotiations in B.C., which he described as "primarily theatre and politics." Ritual statements became perceived as public truths, "even if they reverse reality," Sherman argued, but they destroyed the basis for any informed analysis. "And to tamper with the ritual might be to destroy the perceived reality," wrote the publisher. "In a process that combines the worst features of ideology and the political adversary system that could be disastrous."[83] The process, according to Sherman, meant that "when the minister of labor gets involved in midnight meetings, he must break metaphorical arms in ways that describe common justice because only thus can he make it possible for the other side to move."[84] And union politics required Kinnaird, as president of the B.C. Federation of Labour, to "first make irrational statements to satisfy his constituency" before he could get involved.

> While I can tell the "inside" story better than anybody with perhaps two exceptions, I won't do it. . . . When one party tells the bare, unvarnished truth and the other creates moving fiction, a puzzled public assumes that there are no double standards, and the truth must lie between. . . . To ensure that the charades work in an acceptable way, it is often important for union leaders to tell the voting members little or nothing.[85]

The curious column, according to Sean Rossiter, led him to ask the *Province* publisher to explain what he meant, but Sherman refused to talk, complaining the writer had misquoted him previously. "Not only would he not write the story; he would condemn beforehand anyone else who did," wrote Rossiter in *Vancouver* magazine. "Not only could anyone else not write it accurately, but, as it turned out, he wouldn't even speak to anyone else who tried."[86] Rossiter pointed out that Sherman's claims of a dysfunctional industrial relations system defied the fact that thousands of other labor contracts were negotiated without the chronic shutdowns that plagued Pacific Press. "No, he said, he would not be interviewed on tape," reported Rossiter. "No, he would not be interviewed by anyone else. Paddy Sherman will go to his grave cuddling his precious secrets about the 1978-79 Pacific Press strike."[87]

But twenty-two years after the strike ended — almost to the day — Sherman recalled his thinking behind the cryptic column. The "theatre" he referred to involved the intervention of Labour Minister Allan Williams in an effort to convince the company to accept mediation of the manning dispute. "He said if you will accept the report and go back into operation and then submit to me an application to combine the unions into one, then I will favorably consider it. We did that. The minister [later] denied ever saying anything remotely resembling that."[88]

Rossiter blamed the length of the strike on both sides underestimating the resolve of the powerful pressmen's union to resist in Vancouver the changes that were overtaking its locals at other newspapers across the continent. "It was a strike in which John Kagel was paid $80,000-odd to come to a conclusion that interviews with a few pressmen might have made clear right from the start: they were not going to budge."[89] He saw the result as a wasteful stalemate that did not even resolve the main issue. "Of course, the strike can easily be justified by Pacific Press management on the grounds that they got the thin end of the wedge into the press-room," observed Rossiter. "Any arbitration decision other than the status quo will be their victory."[90] The study of labor relations at Pacific Press for the Royal Commission on Newspapers concluded that the ability to deal with automation issues through arbitration and to conclude an agreement at the bargaining table without a strike in 1977 had obscured the true depth of hostilities. Rivalries were inherent in the confrontational nature of labor relations at Pacific Press between not only the company and the joint council, but between the unions themselves.

> The resolution of jurisdictional disputes should have improved relations between the unions but, under the surface, they were at an all-time low. Secondly, the company's willingness to provide

> compensation and guarantees for change should have provided a basis for settlement, but the trust level between the sides was also at an all-time low.[91]

The resentment between unions as a result of the protracted shutdown would only get worse after the return to work. "There remains much bitterness within the council as a result," the study concluded in 1981, "and there are differing opinions on how to prevent this from affecting solidarity in future negotiations."[92]

16 Black Wednesday

The second Lord Thomson of Fleet was unlike his father in many ways. While Roy Thomson was an ebullient, hard-driving supersalesman, unafraid of any challenge, his son Ken was shy, reserved, and inclined to avoid conflict, especially with the powerful Fleet Street unions. While his father won their hereditary peerage by becoming one of Britain's most powerful media owners and by hobnobbing with the upper crust of English society, Ken Thomson preferred living quietly in Canada. After his father's death in 1976, the country's only billionaire ran the worldwide empire he inherited, with the aid of his most trusted lieutenants, from a twenty-fifth-floor office in the Thomson Building in downtown Toronto. Tall and awkward, the publicity-shy younger Lord Thomson granted few interviews and hated having his picture taken. *Saturday Night* magazine found him remarkably unremarkable.

> There is nothing of the mystery of power about him. His flat, Ontario accent is without the smoothness that Scott Fitzgerald called the ring of money. His sense of humor is unbarbed. His public image, what there is of it, is possessed of the same happy dullness that characterizes a Hallmark Christmas card. But privately, up close, there is a surprising warmth and engaging simplicity.[1]

In London, the absence of the *Times*' new owner from the scene of a bitter labor conflict brewing at the venerable daily infuriated both sides, with one unionist dubbing him "the invisible man."[2] The *Times* had lost money every year since Roy Thomson bought it in 1966, and by 1978 the accumulated losses totaled £16 million. They were more than covered, however, by the huge profits the family fortune was then realizing from North Sea oil exploration, as investments Roy Thomson had made in the early 1970s began to pay off following huge underwater oil strikes. An economic downturn in 1975 accelerated the *Times*' losses however, as advertising revenue declined sharply. In 1968, classified advertising at the *Times* newspapers had seen the first use of cold type in Britain, and in 1974 the newspapers moved into a modern plant, purchasing £3 million in computer typesetting equipment. The only problem was convincing *Times* printers to allow its use.

In Britain, union agreements were not enforceable by law as in North America, and industrial relations at the *Times* newspapers deteriorated in late 1977 as production stoppages increased the number of copies of the newspapers left unprinted. In the first four months of 1978, the production problems increased when twenty-one issues of the *Times* and nine editions of the *Sunday Times* failed to complete their press runs, leaving 7.7 million copies unprinted.[3] In April, *Times* management confronted the printing unions with a list of demands for guaranteed continuity of production, an effective dispute-resolution mechanism, and acceptance of new technology. If the company's demands could not be negotiated by the end of November, *Times* management warned, the newspapers would suspend publication until they were. According to a study by Roderick Martin of attempts to implement technological change at British newspapers in the 1970s, the demands were impossibly ambitious. "In Fleet Street terms, *Times* management was asking for the moon, in seven months," noted Martin, "a programme no print union could accept."[4] The key demand was for direct inputting of copy by journalists on video display terminals instead of by printers. As negotiations with the unions commenced, lost production of the newspapers increased, amounting to 12 million copies worth £1.16 million in revenue between January and November.[5] The printers refused to consider the *Times* demands under the threat of closure.

By the deadline, only journalists at the *Sunday Times* and a small union of engineers had agreed to the demands. The printers reached Thomson in Toronto and implored him to intervene, but he refused. "Suspension of publication is a drastic step," he said in a press release. "One cannot, however, allow the papers to be slowly bled to death. In view of my strong personal commitment, I hope that the suspension will be for the minimum time."[6] An emergency debate in the House of Commons resulted in the labor minister calling for a delay in the closure, and *Times* management agreed to a two-week reprieve. When the holdout unions refused to move, the newspapers began issuing layoff notices. As in the Pacific Press shutdown that had started a month earlier in Vancouver, author Susan Goldenberg observed, the fact that the *Times* was "willing to shut down during the Christmas season, when advertising is traditionally at a peak, was viewed by many as showing their determination."[7]

In Vancouver, the return to life of the Pacific Press dailies at the end of June 1979 could not have been timed worse for Robin Lecky, coming less than a week before the planned launch of his *Courier* as a daily tabloid. *Sun* and *Province* management had been busy redesigning their publications during the eight-month shutdown, and when they hit the streets again they each had a new look. The *Province* included a new tabloid pullout section, similar to that of the failed *Vancouver Times* fourteen years earlier, which alternated between sports, business, and entertainment. As expected, the *Province* sports section now featured Jim Taylor, the erstwhile *Sun* star who quit over new publisher Clark Davey's freelancing ban. *Province* publisher Paddy Sherman admitted his newspaper also prohibited its employees from working for a competitor, but said Taylor got around the restriction by forming his own company and writing for the *Province* on a freelance basis.[8]

At the *Sun*, Davey announced that his long-delayed debut as publisher would bring a new look to Vancouver's leading daily. Section fronts had been redesigned during management's enforced idleness, the business section was given a section front several times a week, and weekly real estate and travel sections were added. New political columnists were appointed in Ottawa and Victoria, but the main change in editorial content was what Davey called a "much greater emphasis on what I call the softer stuff — lifestyles, women's stuff."[9] One regular addition to the *Sun*'s front page that caused consternation among many journalists was a two-column cartoon drawn by Canadian artist Jim Unger, called *Herman*. The journalists felt that running a cartoon on the newspaper's front page suggested its contents had become less serious, but the *Sun*'s new publisher explained that many among management had come to appreciate the humor behind the hulking comic character over the past eight months. "Herman sustained a lot of us during the strike," Davey told the Canadian Press.[10]

The changes signaled a new emphasis on marketing strategy devised during the shutdown of Pacific Press, and Davey was an enthusiastic corporate convert to the idea of giving readers and advertisers what they told market researchers they wanted. "The *Sun* had always been heavily male-oriented, but we've become a great deal more relevant to the female reader who has a great impact on circulation," Davey told *Marketing* magazine.[11] On the business side, the *Sun* began hiring executives from outside the newspaper business, including its new director of marketing. "One of his biggest assets is that he has no previous newspaper experience," said Davey. Advertisers who had taken their business elsewhere during the strike would be wooed back with a new attitude of accommodation at the *Sun*. "We had made so much money for so long that we gained the reputation, partly deserved, partly not, that we were arrogant and hard to deal with," he told *Marketing*. "The watchword now is that we are much more responsive to the advertiser."[12]

On July 4, the *Courier* launched its new daily tabloid to mixed reviews. "The new paper does not have the depth of talent or cheek of the *Toronto Sun*, whose success it is trying to emulate," noted the *Globe and Mail*, "but neither did it have that paper's daunting capital start-up costs."[13] The *Courier*'s star attraction was columnist Doug Collins, who jumped from the *Sun* over Davey's freelancing ban after having been paid by the afternoon paper throughout the long strike. When BCTV reporter Clem Chapple queried Collins as to why he quit his column in one of the largest newspapers in Canada for a start-up daily, the Bulldog gave his answer in print.

> Because new guys who know nothing about Vancouver and its ways are parachuted in from Toronto, and because Collins will be damned if he takes dopey orders from anyone about things like freelancing. . . . It was tempting to leave rude notes behind. Stuff like "Screw Toronto." . . . But we went quietly, pausing only to steal a couple of notebooks, just in case things are in short supply at *The Courier*.[14]

The *Courier*'s debut as a daily provided a type of sensational journalism unseen in Vancouver since the newspaper war between the *Sun* and

Province that ended in the Pacific Press truce of 1957. Through street sales alone, circulation started at 50,000 as Vancouverites who had been starved for newspapers during the past eight months picked up the new publication at newsstands out of curiosity. Home delivery was planned to begin in August, starting first with just the Sunday *Courier*. The target audience for the tabloid was young readers who lived or worked in the city, Lecky told *Marketing*. "There is a big market out there that is presently not reading — or at least not reading to any great degree."[15] Lecky knew that attracting a young readership was essential to win advertising in competition with Pacific Press, so he emphasized that his new morning daily was seeking a new audience not interested in reading the conservative *Province*. "We're going to scrape the mold off certain segments of the establishment," the *Courier* publisher told *Marketing*. "We are going to recognize the emergence of new social patterns as lived by those under 40."[16]

Sherman was unimpressed with his newspaper's new morning competition and its quest for a younger target readership. "Once Lecky's taught them to read a newspaper, they'll be ready for a real one and we'll be happy to supply it," the *Province* publisher told *Maclean's*.[17] To head off the *Courier*'s bid to fill the Sunday newspaper void, Sherman announced the *Province* would begin publishing a Sunday edition on August 12. Provisions in the just-concluded union contract at Pacific Press allowed for the Saturday work required to publish on Sunday, but Sherman denied the steps were taken as a contingency against competition from the *Courier*. He told *Marketing* that a Sunday *Province* had been in the works since 1977 and that market research by the U.S. firm of Belden Associates, which conducted personal interviews with more than 2,000 Vancouver residents, confirmed the demand for a "leisure-oriented" Sunday newspaper. "We don't really regard it as serious competition," said Sherman of the *Courier*.[18]

In early July, the upstart *Daily News*, which had begun publishing in June, closed its doors mysteriously. The odd broadsheet, which had its offices in the Fraser Valley community of Aldergrove and began street distribution in Vancouver on June 20, ceased publication on July 9 after publisher Peter Lasch went into hiding. Lasch claimed to have been kidnapped at gunpoint on July 5 by two men and warned not to run an article about a Canadian oil executive arrested in Saudi Arabia for possession of alcohol, whom Lasch said he had helped to escape the country.[19]

Lasch went underground after the story ran, and the newspaper's printer refused to run the *Daily News* off on its presses without being paid in advance. The unusual publication never reappeared after its payroll and business checks began bouncing.[20]

On the pages of the *Courier*, advertising was sparse, but as circulation leveled off near 40,000 Lecky was confident that his new daily tabloid would soon turn the corner. The financial resources Gordon Byrn had pledged gave the *Courier* the backing it needed to get through the inevitable losses incurred in starting up the newspaper before it could begin to show a profit, Lecky thought. "If we are selling 40,000 copies a day by our target of September 1, I don't think we will ever look back," he told the *Globe and Mail*.[21] But according to Harvey Southam, the "first seeds of the *Courier*'s death" were sown by Sherman three weeks into its effort to go daily.

> He met his former religion editor, David Virtue (now a senior *Courier* staffer), in the *Province* newsroom and spent half an hour telling Virtue that there was no way his current employers were going to be able to survive. A visibly shaken Virtue went back to the *Courier* and related Sherman's comments. Word of the concern got to Lecky who claims Byrn suggested a meeting should be called to reassure staff.[22]

At the *Courier* staff meeting, Byrn pledged his family's considerable wealth to the enterprise. "We are going to give it at least a year," he promised them.[23] But Byrn's promise was hollow, as Lecky had neglected to get his signature on the letter of agreement guaranteeing financial backing for the *Courier*. At the first sign of trouble, Byrn excused himself from the picture, leaving Lecky and his other partners with $600,000 in unpaid bills. By August 14 the *Courier*'s press run was down to 18,500 with little advertising, and Lecky pulled the plug, announcing the short-lived daily would revert to its twice-weekly schedule, including a Sunday edition in competition with the *Province*.[24] "I wonder why it took them so long," Sherman told the *Sun*. "It's rather sad they want to stick with the Sunday market. It's going to be our strongest paper."[25] Byrn insisted he was never more than a financial adviser and said he decided against investing the $2 million he had promised because the terms he had stipulated were not met.[26]

The *Courier*'s death, even quicker than that of the *Vancouver Times* fourteen years earlier, meant that a third daily in competition with the Pacific Press papers would never materialize, predicted Collins. "The disappearance of *The Courier* as a daily means great psychological damage has been done. Potential investors will shy away from any future attempt to launch a daily in Vancouver like peasants running from the plague."[27] That meant there would never be newspaper competition again in Vancouver, he predicted, despite the claims of the Pacific Press publishers that they were engaged in that very thing.

> It isn't competition when two publishers roost in the same building, go out to dinner together, and make any cozy little deals they have a mind to make. . . . Where true competition exists, one publisher is always ready to kick the other publisher in the guts and if necessary gouge his eyes out, too. But that doesn't apply at PP. It's all in the family.[28]

Collins also took a shot at Sherman and his sneering comment about the *Courier*'s demise. "The guy is a four-minute miler in bad taste," concluded Collins. "Let us pray that *The Courier*'s Sunday edition screws up Sherman's Sunday edition. Is that too much to hope for, Lord?"[29] On the *Courier* sports page, columnist Greg Douglas had a more pointed prayer for the *Province* publisher, although it was contained cryptically in his curiously worded piece, which was nominally about Vancouver Canucks goaltender Glen Hanlon. By stringing together the first letter of every paragraph in the carefully crafted column, however, the message Douglas had labored over came clear: F-U-C-K-Y-O-U-P-A-D-D-Y-S-H-E-R-M-A-N.[30] At the end of August, the *Courier* went out of business altogether, an event ironically precipitated by an upbeat assessment in Denny Boyd's *Sun* column on August 30. The brief item declared that a weekly *Courier* "might just make it. . . . with the co-operation of the Bank of B.C."[31] The bank withdrew its support after hearing from many of the *Courier*'s upset creditors who read the item and demanded to be paid.[32]

The revenue losses from the eight-month shutdown of Pacific Press took a toll on both of its corporate owners, but they hit FP Publications hardest. The newspaper chain had suffered an equally long strike in Montreal, where its *Star* had been the leading English-language daily.

When publication resumed in February 1979, a bitter circulation war ensued with Southam's *Gazette*, which under publisher Bob McConnell had taken full advantage of its competitor's absence. By July, with the *Star* hopelessly behind, FP closed it before its losses, amounting to $17.5 million since the strike began, pulled the entire chain under.[33] The 1976 strike at the *Ottawa Journal* and a subsequent labor boycott left the FP paper trailing Southam's *Citizen* by a wide margin and bleeding red ink as a result. Taken together, the losses in three cities left FP Publications in dire financial straits, and its board of directors suspended the regular quarterly dividend as 1979 shaped up as the first year in which the twenty-year-old chain would show a year-end loss.

In December, the sharks began circling the weakened enterprise as financiers saw that conditions were ripe for a corporate takeover. The first bid for the bleeding newspaper giant was made by a group fronted by Conrad Black, the ambitious young chairman of the huge holding company Argus Corp. Black had been in the newspaper business for a decade already, having started a small chain of papers with two school friends, David Radler and Peter White. Sterling Newspapers was headquartered in Vancouver, where the chain's president confirmed it was indeed anxious to expand to the big time. "Our company has always been interested in buying FP if the shares are available," David Radler told *Maclean's*. Radler had turned Sterling's chain of newspapers, most of which were in B.C., into a rich moneymaker through his strategy of cost-cutting. In 1977, Sterling's return on revenue exceeded 20 percent, noted Harvey Southam in the *Sun*, double that of his family's chain.

> Chiselling is what many observers suggest is the Radler way when it comes to operating newspapers.... He once told a friend that if he goes to bed knowing he missed making another $4, he can't get to sleep. It is why Radler is known as a man who squeezed every possible nickel out of Sterling at the expense of editorial and production quality.[34]

Staff at the FP flagship *Globe and Mail* were outraged that the Black group might gain control of their respected newspaper by taking over its corporate parent. Their concern was due mainly to the fact that former *Telegram* publisher John Bassett, whom many blamed for the daily's 1971 death, was among the investors. Howard Webster then entered the bidding, raising Black's offer of $45 a share to $50. Webster, who had bought the *Globe and Mail* in 1955 by outbidding both Roy Thomson and Argus Corp. under its then president E.P. Taylor, already held almost a quarter of FP shares, which he had received in exchange for linking his newspaper to the chain in 1965. His increased offer thus benefited himself as much as anyone. But Black's next offer was even more ingenious. It only raised the bid for the more than 2 million non-voting common shares of FP to $52, but it hiked to $5,000 the offer for each of the firm's 1,448 preferred voting shares. The structure of the offer was directed at one man who held a small block of voting shares dating back to the formation of the company in 1959. Dick Malone, the deposed president of FP, had been given the shares twenty years earlier to enable him to cast the deciding vote when chain founders Max Bell and Victor Sifton could not agree, reported the *Globe and Mail.*

> Although he had no financial stake in the company, he was given votes in its management in case of a deadlock. As FP Publications expanded . . . Malone continued to act as the impartial arbiter on the board, armed with the votes that could break a deadlock in the event of an even split, but with no fiscal interest that could be construed as coloring his judgment.[35]

The original terms under which Malone had been given the voting shares required him to return them to Bell and Sifton when he retired, reported the *Globe and Mail,* but the agreement had expired after the deaths of the founding partners. With Black's second offer, the Brigadier had a definite fiscal interest in the takeover bids for FP Publications, because the new offer for his 112 voting shares suddenly made them worth $560,000. The other four equal holders of the voting stock (the Bell estate, the Sifton estate, Webster, and the McConnell family of the *Montreal Star*) were split on the offer, and Malone thus held the deciding vote. But the next bidder to up the ante for FP Publications put the 70-year-old Malone in an even more awkward position in deciding the fate of the newspaper chain he had helped build.

On Fleet Street, the company closure of the *Times* and *Sunday Times* dragged on into the summer of 1979 without printers budging from their refusal to allow implementation of new "cold type" computer technology Thomson had purchased. In late June, Ken Thomson flew to London and made a fateful decision that allowed resolution of the shut-down of the national newspaper institutions. But by giving in on the key issue of journalists directly inputting copy into the computer system instead of printers, he was seen to have blinked first in the test of wills. By mid-November a series of agreements with the multitude of unions at the *Times* was finally concluded, and the venerable broadsheet reappeared after an absence of almost a year. *Times* management announced it had achieved 70 percent of its initial objectives, but the failure to implement the new computer technology proved pivotal. According to a study of technology and labor relations on Fleet Street, Thomson's weakening of resolve in the showdown with the *Times* unions would prove his downfall.

> The company had made the elementary bargaining error of surrendering their major weapon, the suspension of publication, in exchange for only general commitments, leaving the more important specific details, relating to manning levels and money, to be negotiated subsequently; as the unions recognized, management could not realistically contemplate further suspension and could be "taken to the cleaners" at leisure.[36]

As production problems began again, Thomson contemplated cutting his Fleet Street losses and selling the newspapers, despite promising his late father he would keep them. In the circumstances, the title "Lord Thomson of Fleet" seemed more like a millstone around his neck. The profits from his father's prudent North Sea oil investments continued to flow from the gushers dotting the European seascape, however, and the revenues were more than enough to offset the mounting losses at the *Times*. But the Canadian had lost the respect of many in England, including the *Times* journalists who had remained on the Thomson payroll throughout the dispute, for undermining the hard-line stance management had taken against the crafts.

Unlike his father, Thomson preferred to do business in his own country, which he did in the largest way possible with his growing oil riches early in 1979, winning a high-profile bidding war to purchase Canada's most historic enterprise. The Hudson's Bay Company, which had begun with the fur trade in the seventeenth century, became the country's largest chain of department stores by taking over rival retailers Simpson's and Zeller's earlier in the year, but in doing so it had become overextended financially. That left The Bay vulnerable to takeover itself, and a five-week bidding war ensued, which became known across Canada as "Store Wars." The dizzying battle saw the ante raised five times between Thomson and Weston family interests. With the guidance of his father's most trusted executive, lawyer John Tory, the newspaper baron emerged victorious in the battle for The Bay, paying more than $640 million to become its new owner. According to author Susan Goldenberg, the acquisition was significant because it signaled a new aggressiveness by the oil-rich Thomson organization. "This was a particularly major move because it involved the empire in one of the fiercest takeover contests in Canadian business history, even though the Thomson history is to avoid such fights."[37]

The victory over Weston doubtless whetted Thomson's taste for the takeover arena, and early in 1980 he emerged as the most formidable bidder for FP Publications. Thomson upped the ante in the battle between Black and Webster, raising by more than $10 the bid for non-voting shares of FP in an offer worth $139 million. But Thomson's bid lowered the offering price for the voting shares to $4,000 each, which mattered only to Dick Malone. The other holders of voting shares also owned large tracts of common shares, which more than made up the difference in value to them. But Malone's voting shares were reduced in value under Thomson's offer to $448,000 from the $560,000 they had been worth under the last offer by Black. In addition to his personal holdings, however, Malone also acted as trustee for the Sifton and Bell estates and he was under a legal obligation to vote them in the best interests of their owners. The intrigue escalated when Webster raised his offer for common shares to $69 but dropped his bid for the voting shares to $1,000, for a total of $149 million, reducing the value of Malone's personal holdings even further.

Thomson raised the stakes again on January 10, to $74 for each non-voting share and to $2,000 apiece for voting shares, and Malone voted to sell, giving eight daily newspapers across the country, including the *Vancouver Sun*, a new owner with very deep pockets. The deal made Thomson Newspapers the second-largest newspaper group in Canada behind only Southam, with more than 25 percent of English-language circulation, and the fourth-largest chain in North America with 127 titles across the continent.[38] Included in the purchase, along with the *Vancouver Sun*, came half-ownership of the Pacific Press partnership that had proven so problematic throughout the 1970s. Thomson had paid $159 million for an estimated $125 million in assets, and included in the acquisition were several ailing dailies, so he and his financial experts quickly set about rationalizing the purchase.

The first deal Thomson made to dispose of FP's underperforming assets was selling Max Bell's original daily, the *Calgary Albertan*, to the *Toronto Sun* chain, which had made its nearby *Edmonton Sun* into a lively competitor with Southam's *Journal* in the Alberta capital. FP had converted the *Albertan* to tabloid format in a bid to compete with Southam's *Herald*, but it was a limp effort compared with the colorful *Sun* tabloids. In August 1980, Thomson's attention turned to British Columbia, where both dailies in the provincial capital of Victoria were published in a joint operating arrangement similar to Pacific Press, except that the evening *Times* and morning *Colonist* were both owned by FP Publications and therefore now by Thomson. On August 1, the joint publishing company, Victoria Press, announced it would merge its two broadsheet dailies into a combined *Times Colonist* on September 1. The local Newspaper Guild denounced the merger, which would mean the loss of sixty-one jobs, as "cruel, cold and callous."[39] Journalists at the newspapers withdrew their bylines to protest the arbitrary manner in which the merger and layoffs were announced, but Thomson was just getting started. "The economics in North America are very tough," Thomson told reporters while in Edmonton for a board meeting of the Toronto-Dominion Bank on August 14. "There are very few markets that could support two newspapers."[40] Despite the warning, few were prepared for what would come at month's end.

Allan Fotheringham could read the writing on the wall as well as Stuart Keate, who retired as *Sun* publisher with marvelous timing on the eve of the eight-month Pacific Press strike in 1978. Keate's replacement from Toronto did not sit well with many at the newspaper, not the least of whom was Fotheringham. Instead of its traditional section-front position, under Clark Davey's redesign of the *Sun* Fotheringham's column was moved inside. According to Sean Rossiter in *Vancouver* magazine, the change did not go over well with the columnist. "Naturally, the man who once figured in the outcome of civic elections was not pleased to find his copy replacing the weather report on Page Three."[41] The *Sun*'s other star columnists, Doug Collins, Jim Taylor, and Max Wyman from the entertainment section, had already fled the newspaper because of Davey's ban on freelancing, but Fotheringham continued his weekly back-page column for *Maclean's* and his regular television appearances on CKVU's *Vancouver* show. Soon, however, the town became too small for both Fotheringham and the man who had been given the job he coveted, whom staff derisively dubbed "The Ayatollah" after the Iranian despot then in the headlines.

Fotheringham was becoming a national media star, but it was difficult to cash in on his popularity while remaining in Vancouver, especially under Davey's ban on freelancing, and cash was the columnist's way of keeping score. "I went to university with a lot of lawyers," Fotheringham told *Saturday Night* magazine. "They make a lot of money and they are no brighter than I am. It is a matter of perverse pride with me to be able to do as well. Journalism can afford it. Why shouldn't I get it?"[42] Other Vancouver journalists, such as Jim Taylor and talk-show host Jack Webster, were pulling down six-figure incomes, and Fotheringham knew he could outdo them. "He knows I make more than he does, and it really gripes him," said Webster.[43] But to make the really big bucks, Fotheringham would have to ply his political punditry from the nation's capital.

The scoop on the columnist's departure from Vancouver went to Chuck Davis of the *Province* less than two months into Davey's stewardship of the *Sun*. Rumors from across the hall at Pacific Press had Fotheringham moving east, reported Davis, who admitted he initially treated them with skepticism. "Rumors of his departure have popped up regularly over the years, 25 of them, and perhaps this was just the latest," wrote the gossip columnist on August 22, 1979. "But no. This time it was the real goods. . . . The bulletin board is topped with a headline clipped from the paper: Ayatollah Purge Continues."[44] Davis reported that Fotheringham had signed on with FP News Service as a syndicated columnist for its chain of newspapers, splitting his time between Ottawa and Vancouver. According to Rossiter, when Davey was asked to confirm the rival newspaper's scoop, the newcomer to Vancouver replied, "Who's Chuck Davis?"[45]

Fotheringham's coverage of national politics soon put him in a position of power approaching what he had enjoyed in Vancouver, where he could practically determine the fate of political leaders with his columns. His hilarious accounts of Conservative prime minister Joe Clark's disastrous 1979 world tour, during which he almost impaled himself on a soldier's bayonet while reviewing the honor guard on the Golan Heights, was seen by Walter Stewart as contributing to Clark's image as a bumbling fool and his subsequent election defeat.

> Foth spent most of his effort, throughout the trip, chuckling, guffawing, and sneering; he did it in his column, and he did it in the bars where other journalists — such is the nature of the breed — often form their own attitudes. Everybody got into the act, and soon editors back home were looking for more stories about lost luggage and fouled-up travel arrangements.[46]

Fotheringham was now doing to prime ministers what he had once done to Vancouver mayors and B.C. cabinet ministers. His syndicated column still ran on the pages of the *Sun*, but as Rossiter noted, it was now pushed even further inside "on Page Six, along with features culled from out-of-town rags."[47] The newspaper claimed it had not really lost Fotheringham, whose picture it used in a billboard advertising campaign aimed at regaining the circulation it had lost during the strike, but Rossiter disagreed. "The truth is that we have lost a great deal. We have lost the best writing about this city that any of us has ever seen. Fotheringham is setting out to be the same kind of columnist in Montreal, Ottawa, and Toronto that he was here, and what he will achieve there will be as unique in Canadian journalism as what he did here."[48]

When Thomson took over FP Publications in 1980, Fotheringham again discerned disquieting vertical scribbling. "An instant chill went through the office, their cheapo reputation being well known," he recalled of the reaction at the Ottawa bureau of FP News.[49] Fotheringham had worked for Ken Thomson briefly while on his European tour in the late 1950s after quitting the *Sun* for the first time, toiling as a copy editor at the London-based weekly *Canada News*, which recycled news from home for displaced Canadians. When a meeting in Toronto with Thomson executive St. Clair McCabe confirmed his suspicions that the gold-plated FP News Service would soon fall victim to cost-cutting, Fotheringham accepted an offer in July from the rival wire service Southam News, effective September 1.[50] The change meant that instead of appearing in the *Sun,* his column would now be gracing the pages of the *Province.* To *Sun* worshippers like Rossiter, the changes wrought by Davey were almost too much to bear.

> The *Sun,* which . . . until last year could claim a fine stable of writers who defined Vancouver to itself and anyone else who was interested, was by last fall a shell of the newspaper it had been, published by a man from Toronto. . . . As the Fotheringhams, St. Pierres, Taylors and Wymans filed out the back door, an old question came up again: Was something else unique to Vancouver really second-rate? Or was that Ontario mentality, that sees little good in how things are done elsewhere, breaking up an important local institution?[51]

Southam president Gordon Fisher considered Thomson Newspapers "the one company in Canada with which I found it most difficult being a partner."[52] Dealing with cost-conscious FP Publications in the Pacific Press partnership had been vexing enough, and Thomson was well known for being even more ruthlessly fixated on the bottom line. Now with Thomson's purchase of FP, Southam found itself with an unwanted new partner not only in Vancouver, but also in Montreal. In exchange for the plant and equipment of the folded *Star,* Southam had granted FP an option to purchase one-third ownership of the *Gazette* for $13 million. When Thomson exercised its new option, the urgency increased for Southam to disentangle itself from its new partner and provided the impetus for the greatest upheaval ever seen in the Canadian newspaper industry. The events of August 27, 1980, became immortalized as "Black Wednesday" and resulted in a Royal Commission and a federal criminal case.

Throughout the spring and summer of 1980, Fisher negotiated with

Thomson Newspapers president John Tory in an attempt to dissolve their Montreal and Vancouver arrangements. Fisher agreed to buy back the minority interest in the *Gazette* for $15 million, providing Thomson with a quick $2 million profit. As for Thomson's half-interest in Pacific Press, Fisher let Tory name a price. When the figure came back at $40 million, the deal was done. "After 23 years of frustration with Pacific Press, it was the price we were prepared to pay," said Fisher.[53] But in the course of negotiations over their partnerships in Montreal and Vancouver, Fisher and Tory also discussed their intentions in the two other markets where their companies still competed. In Ottawa, Thomson had been trying to sell the *Journal* it had acquired from FP Publications, because it was hopelessly behind Southam's *Citizen* in circulation following the disastrous strike by printers that had begun in 1976. The *Journal* had lost more than $11 million since then and was facing a further loss of $5 million in 1980. In Winnipeg, Southam's *Tribune* continued to run second to the *Free Press* in their ongoing circulation war, despite an injection of $16 million over the past five years, and it was projected to lose another $3 million by year's end. The chains decided to cut their losses in those two markets, and Thomson agreed to buy the *Tribune*'s plant and equipment for $2.25 million.

When the transactions were announced, the howls of outrage resounded from coast to coast. Executives of the chains insisted they had made their decisions to close the ninety-year-old *Tribune* and ninety-four-year-old *Journal* independently, but the near-simultaneous announcements suggested there had been collusion to lessen competition. The appearance was unavoidable, as Southam and Thomson each gained a local monopoly while 800 staff were thrown out of work. The two chains now controlled 59 percent of daily newspaper circulation in Canada, and English-language daily newspaper competition remained in only four markets: Toronto, Edmonton, Calgary, and far-flung St. John's, Newfoundland. But the deaths of two longtime institutions in Ottawa and Winnipeg overshadowed the transaction in Vancouver, which gave Southam the "newspaper monopoly in the hands of a single owner" of which the 1960 Restrictive Trade Practices Commission report on the Pacific Press amalgamation had warned.[54]

Davey announced the *Sun*'s sale to newsroom staff at an impromptu 7 a.m. meeting and later issued a statement. "Given the hydra-headed nature of Pacific Press's corporate structure and problems it had created, the move to single ownership of the two Vancouver newspaper properties was inevitable."[55] Sherman, who was by then also a vice-president of Southam, denied there were any corporate plans to fold either newspaper. "The status is very much quo," he said. "Our goal here, unlike in Winnipeg or Ottawa, is expansion, not retraction."[56] Fisher issued a statement hinting that instead of losing a newspaper, Vancouver could very well gain one in the near future. "We see the possibility of an additional newspaper directed to a market segment not now reached by the existing products."[57] He justified Southam's acquisition of the *Sun* by pointing to the disastrous series of strikes that had afflicted Pacific Press in the 1970s under its unworkable equal partnership with FP Publications.

> In the last decade Vancouver has suffered from major and costly newspaper strikes that have resulted partly from a shareholders' agreement that had made it impossible to resolve shareholders' differences as to the company's strategy and direction. A priority objective is to improve employee relations. We believe the employees will welcome and benefit from a more clearly defined ownership responsibility. [58]

After personally breaking the bad news in Winnipeg to workers at the *Tribune*, Fisher flew to Vancouver, where *Sun* staff were unhappy that their newspaper was now under Southam ownership. On the newsroom bulletin board, a "ghoul pool" had been posted with predictions of when the Pacific Press newspapers would be combined into one, as Thomson had done in Victoria. "Does this mean we wind up working for *Province* management," asked one reporter. "A lot of people here don't have great respect for the *Province* as a newspaper."[59] Over tea and cigarettes in Paddy Sherman's office, Fisher assured reporters the Pacific Press newspapers would continue to operate independently for the foreseeable future. "There will be no layoffs in this company as a result of Southam's purchase of the other half of the company," he said, adding that more jobs on a third Pacific Press newspaper were a possibility if research showed a market for an urban tabloid such as had been attempted by the *Courier*.[60]

Common ownership of the Pacific Press newspapers infuriated many in Vancouver. The Newspaper Guild asked justice minister Jean Chretien to seek an interim injunction under the Combines Investigation Act blocking the *Sun* sale and closure of the *Journal* and *Tribune*. Bill McLeman, the Guild's Canadian director, called the prospect of a few companies controlling the vast majority of Canada's newspapers "chilling" in light of the fact the companies were no longer simply newspaper chains.

> They are news monopolies run as corporate enterprises, governed by different considerations from those which influenced papers in the past. We face the very real danger, no less real because it has yet to materialize, of a vast newspaper chain controlling the news that reaches the largest portion of the nation's population, manipulating power for self-serving political purposes.[61]

Sherman responded that the union's bid to stop the sale made "no rational sense" and vowed that another owner than Thomson would be found for the *Sun* if its purchase by Southam was blocked. "I don't know how you could block something that has already taken place."[62] B.C. Federation of Labour secretary-treasurer Dave McIntyre, a former pressman, called for a government inquiry into the corporate maneuvering. "Because the corporate manipulation within the newspaper industry is so extensive, it changes the control of the entire structure of news dissemination across the country."[63] At a noon-hour rally outside the Pacific Press Building organized by the Newspaper Guild, hotliner Jack Webster addressed a group of about fifty protesters. "The final disposition of the *Vancouver Sun* is a sad and unhappy thing for Vancouver," he said.[64] Mayor Jack Volrich told a news conference that control over local news by one company was "not only bad for our community, but it's bad for democracy, because the success of democracy relies on an informed public. We would be left with one set of news, one set of reporters, one set of editorial comments with their own particular biases. . . . If there were some bylaw we could pass, believe me we would do it."[65]

In Toronto, Thomson responded to criticism that his inherited conglomerate had just carved up the country's newspaper industry with competitor Southam while killing off two venerable dailies and throwing hundreds out of work. "Each one has to find his own way in the world," the Lord mused.[66] Appearances grew even uglier when it was learned that Thomson Newspapers had been negotiating the $21.5-million purchase of five newspapers in the U.S. even as it was closing the doors of its *Ottawa Journal* and folding the FP News Service. "For most people in the industry as for many outside, Thomson had lost his nice-guy image," observed Doug Fetherling in *Maclean's*.[67] But even more brazen, he noted, was the release by Thomson Newspapers earlier on Black Wednesday of its quarterly financial results.

> With some of the worst timing in the annals of corporate flakery, Thomson Newspapers had earlier that day released its consolidated profit figures for the first six months of 1980. The sum was $34 million, up almost $5 million from the same period in 1979. All across town, as newsmen frowned or wept in their beer, the PR community did little but wince.[68]

17 The Ayatollah

Clark Davey never fit in on the West Coast, and his style of management did not go over well at the *Vancouver Sun*. The first true corporate publisher of the *Sun* was parachuted in from the flagship of FP Publications, the *Globe and Mail* in Toronto, where he had been managing editor for fifteen years, but Davey never really had a chance in Vancouver. In his first fourteen months of actually publishing the *Sun*, Davey reported to a dizzying succession of three corporate owners. He started his new job on the eve of the eight-month strike at Pacific Press in 1978, and during the shutdown all that *Sun* staff heard from their new publisher was anti-union rhetoric and rumors of his edict against freelancing that drove away some of their newspaper's best columnists before he had even published his first edition.

Davey also rankled many with the new political position he brought to the longtime Liberal daily. The new publisher could not resist wielding his influence to support the Conservative Party despite not having a newspaper to do it in. By the time the 1979 federal election campaign rolled around toward the end of the Pacific Press shutdown, noted Sean Rossiter, Davey "had gotten so itchy to pass on some basic guidance, no matter how banal, that [the *Sun*] handed out its endorsement of Joe Clark on press releases and had it printed on billboards. *Bill*boards!"[1] Early on in his tenure at the *Sun*, Rossiter identified the trait that would make Davey's life difficult in Vancouver.

> He has an abrasive personality which challenges men and charms women, several of whom can be seen clustered around

> him at parties. He constitutes a whole new category of chippy new kid on the block. He is your definitive transplanted easterner, a master of that Upper Canadian art form, the insult. His observation that *The Province* would be around as long as his paper makes more than the morning paper loses was typical.[2]

Davey's appointment had been hailed as a triumph at first, recalled Rossiter, as he was renowned as an old-school, hard-news journalist. "Clark Davey was the managing editor of a paper on which the *sportswriters* were scoop artists. There was . . . an immediate anticipation of great things in store for newspaper journalism in Vancouver."[3] According to former colleague Richard Doyle, Davey was "gruff, dogmatic, and sometimes boringly righteous about his political and professional independence, although he would privately confess to being 'somewhat to the right of Attila the Hun.'"[4] Veteran columnist Denny Boyd found him "swashbuckling . . . loud and vain. For some reason, *Sun* staff nicknamed him Waldo."[5]

At the *Globe and Mail,* Davey had not even dealt with budgets, he explained to the *Financial Post* after his appointment in Vancouver. "One of the conditions of employment was that the managing editor didn't even have to worry about money."[6] When he was given the *Sun* publisher's job by new FP president George Currie on the eve of Stuart Keate's retirement, one of the first things Davey had to do was take a crash course in commerce. On October 30 he was hitting the books at the University of Western Ontario, from which he graduated with the school's first journalism class in 1948, when Keate phoned. "He said: 'If you want to be announced as the publisher of the *Vancouver Sun*, you'd better be here at noon tomorrow, not noon Wednesday,'" recalled Davey. "I met Stu walking out with an armful of his memorabilia. He said: 'It's all yours.' And indeed it was."[7]

Davey tried a light-hearted approach on arrival when he addressed the assembled *Sun* newsroom, but the humor was lost on staff who were preoccupied with the pending strike, noted Rossiter. "Davey's joke [was] that he wasn't some alien easterner at all: he was from Western Ontario."[8] The irony of rushing out to Vancouver to accept his long-awaited reward of a publisher's position only to sit idle for eight months without a newspaper to put out was daunting for Davey, and he compensated for his frustration with self-deprecation. "I'm to the publishing business what 7Up is to the soft-drink business," was his standard line during the strike. "I'm the un-publisher."[9] But Davey was hardly idle during his eight months in purgatory. He used the time to become fully imbued in the business ethic he had so studiously ignored during his years as the head journalist at the *Globe and Mail.*

In the newspaper business there was a revolution going on, and it had much less to do with journalism than with marketing. The *Maclean's* magazine on the newsstands as Davey boarded his red-eye flight to Vancouver in 1978 detailed the trend at Canadian dailies toward "disco journalism." The soft features approach emphasizing lifestyles was named after the current dance craze and was aimed at a target readership that *Ottawa Citizen* columnist Charles Gordon described as "people who move their hips when they read."[10] In an effort to boost sagging circulation in competition with television, according to Doug Fetherling in *Maclean's,* newspapers were relying more and more "on the judgment of pollsters hired to tell them what readers want rather than on the judgment of editors."[11] The move, wrote Fetherling, was creating "a change in the very temperature of newspapers . . . a turn away from the controversial, the investigative, the tangible."[12] During the shutdown of Pacific Press, Davey became an enthusiastic proponent of the new approach, according to former *Sun* journalist Ian Gill.

> Denied his daily revelry during the strike, Davey caught the "marketing" bug, and when the strike ended, the *Sun*'s obsession with graphics, color and promotion began in earnest. Davey tinkered every which way, even taking *Vancouver* out of the masthead — "a reflection of our commitment to serve not just Vancouver . . ." It was the beginning of the cosmetic approach to news.[13]

Davey's embracing of the marketing ethic took place at such corporate events as a "brainstorming session" held shortly after the strike ended during a retreat at April Point Lodge, a fishing resort on Quadra Island, 100 miles north of Vancouver.[14] Davey worked with dozens of *Sun* editorial, advertising, and circulation staff to search for ideas to boost circulation back to where it had been before the eight-month shutdown. From more than 240,000 before the strike, *Sun* circulation dipped as low as 215,000 in August 1979. According to *Marketing* magazine, *Sun* managers turned to the time-honored newspaper tradition of enticing readers with cash give-aways, including a ten-week "Win-A-Grand" contest, "complete with garish billboards covered in larger-then-life lips and the caption: 'You could win a thousand smackers.'"[15] Soon the newspaper was wrapped in a page filled with replica dollar bills.

The *Sun* also offered free classified ads after the strike to woo back customers, but it quickly had to pull the plug on the offer when it proved too popular. "They were swamping our facilities so badly that we couldn't take ads from people who wanted to pay us," Davey told *Marketing.*[16] He announced that consumer news would become a staple of the *Sun.* "Business and media have been on a long honeymoon," he told a conference of Junior Achievers. "Now we have a new girlfriend clamoring for attention — the consumer. The rising wave of consumerism is going to demand it."[17] Billboards promoted the remaining *Sun* writers, including new women's columnist Johanne Leach, and promised "boo-boo-free boob tube listings." The campaign spoke volumes about the new *Sun* publisher's approach, according to Rossiter.

> Those ads degraded honest reporters, and, worse, they showed how *The Sun* sees itself in its own house ads. It sees itself as light-weight. Nowhere did the ads mention anything remotely resembling hard news. "The news behind the news," yes, whatever that means . . . but not much about facts. Nothing about what we look to a newspaper for. And with good reason.[18]

Many got the impression that Davey was intent on turning the *Sun* into a dull Western version of the grey *Globe and Mail* and reasoned that was his motive for chasing away such strong columnists as Fotheringham, Collins, and Taylor. "I'm going to bring somebody into this town who's going to make people forget all about Jim Taylor," Davey boasted as the rival *Province* began to load up with discarded *Sun* stars.[19] He hired as his lead sports columnist a world-class literary talent from the *Daily Express* in London, but James Lawton's passionate and lyrical writing style was far removed from the spare, pithy prose of Taylor. "Florid puts it nicely," observed Kevin McGee in the *Georgia Straight.* "Reading a Lawton column gives the mind the same feeling the stomach gets after eating six pounds of chocolates. Verbal overkill, as it were."[20] Lawton was an expert on such sports as soccer, cricket, boxing, and cycling, but he was totally lost when it came to local favorites such as Canadian football. "Lawton is intelligent and industrious, two qualities he requires in abundance to fortify his tenuous grasp of such noted Canadian sports as hockey," observed Don Stanley in a 1980 survey of local sportswriters. "But what his readers lose in information, they gain in lavish Sunday-painter atmosphere."[21] Aside from such perceived blunders, the fact that Davey was an outsider to the peculiar culture of Vancouver did not make it any easier for locals to accept his often eccentric ideas about newspaper journalism.

The revulsion felt by many *Sun* journalists for the abrupt change in direction brought by their new publisher was compounded by his penchant for rubbing people the wrong way. The nickname "The Ayatollah" was pinned on Davey for his management style early in his time at the *Sun*, and it stuck. "Opinionated, blunt, tough and talented is the way some colleagues describe him," reported former *Sun* business writer Paul Raugust in *B.C. Business Week*. "He's a realist to the point of insensitivity to other people's feelings. Those that can't measure up to his standards will undoubtedly call him a tyrant."[22] According to Rossiter:

> The most frequent criticism of him is that he still acts like a managing editor. He communicates his joys and displeasures directly to reporters, instead of having the managing editor, Bruce Larsen, do it. His memos are known as "blue darts," for the paper they are written on. A criticism from the publisher can destroy a reporter's morale for a week, whereas a reminder from the ME is part of the job.[23]

Davey's hands-on management style contrasted with that of retired publisher Stuart Keate, whose *modus operandi* during fourteen years at the *Sun* helm had been to promote the best people he could find and then leave them alone to do their jobs. The micro-management style brought by the new import from Toronto was not well received, and Davey suffered by comparison to the revered Keate. Compounding Davey's maladjustment to his publisher's position at Pacific Press was the maelstrom of local anger surrounding the *Sun*'s purchase by Southam. Many at Vancouver's leading daily were miffed at having to work for rival Southam, while across the hall journalists at the underdog *Province* were suddenly feeling cocky over their chain's control of Pacific Press and their newspaper's acquisition of former *Sun* talent. Those with little seniority at either paper, including dozens of journalists hired to fill the vacancies left after the eight-month strike, feared losing their jobs if Southam merged its two newspapers as Thomson had done in Victoria.

Davey told an advertising conference in September 1980 that under common ownership the Pacific Press newspapers would soon become sharply differentiated products because market research showed readers viewed the *Sun* and *Province* as basically the same. "We now have the freedom, under one owner, to be very markedly different," Davey told a luncheon of the Ad and Sales Association. "Somewhere down the road, you will see two very different products."[24] Southam president Gordon Fisher repeated his earlier hints that Pacific Press might soon publish a third newspaper when he addressed a Board of Trade luncheon on October 1, 1980.

> We have both the physical capacity and personnel resources to produce a third product. Whether we do will ultimately depend on the flexibility and willingness of our employees to expand their service to this market and enhance their job security by doing so — and the willingness of the competition authorities to allow us to use the structure that was created here 23 years ago to the public's great advantage.[25]

Questioned by reporters after his speech, Fisher said a decision on launching a third Pacific Press daily would depend on whether another competitor entered the Vancouver market before the end of the year when, following a detailed analysis, a corporate decision on the project would "almost certainly" be made. He said the new paper might be a tabloid sold only on the street and not available through home subscription, but it would not be the racy Fleet Street type, which featured topless pinups, or even along the lines of the *Toronto Sun* chain of tabloids, which featured clad models, albeit scantily. "As a matter of corporate policy, my board has nothing against beautiful ladies," Fisher told reporters. "But a 'tits and ass' newspaper is another matter." The Southam president squelched any idea of turning the stately morning *Province* into such light reading. "We would almost certainly not convert the *Province* into a tabloid," said Fisher. "That would be illogical."[26]

Many thought Fisher's talk of adding a third newspaper in Vancouver was merely a smokescreen intended to deflect criticism of Southam's now-complete monopoly at Pacific Press. "There's no queue of accountants waiting to endorse that sort of fiscal whimsy," noted *Globe and Mail* columnist Robert Williamson. "And deep down, there isn't a newspaperman in Vancouver who buys it, either. However, upbeat talk of expansion helped soothe nervous Pacific Press employees."[27] Southam's talk of a new tabloid was more likely designed to placate the federal competition bureau, observed the Vancouver correspondent. "It may be that the bureau is a toothless irritant to corporate expediency. But sooner or later Southam . . . will have to seek the Ottawa watchdog's approval of a 'material change' in the Pacific Press setup." Heading off intrusion by the *Toronto Sun* chain into the Vancouver market could be another objective achieved by all the talk of a third Southam daily in Vancouver, predicted Williamson.

> The betting is that after three or four months of study, Southam will propose merging its *Sun* and *Province* into one all-day broadsheet newspaper. . . . A new tabloid would then be launched (forget the twaddle about three papers) aimed at the commuter crowd, for whom staring and snoozing are one-two on transit buses. Southam can't afford to wait the 10 years it will take to get anything resembling trains running in Vancouver.[28]

In the fall of 1980 Southam appointed several of its displaced Winnipeg executives to Pacific Press posts. In November, former *Tribune* publisher Bill Wheatley was named general manager of Pacific Press to replace Dave Stinson, who had taken a job in the U.S. following the eight-month shutdown. The appointment of a strong CEO at Pacific Press, capable of managing the operation without first negotiating with owning partners, was a milestone for the company, noted the *Financial Post*. "It has an executive who can make decisions about the production and financial administration of the two papers without being frustrated by the 'twin vetoes' of the previous ownership structure."[29] George Townsend, another former *Tribune* executive who had been comptroller and acting general manager of Pacific Press, was made director of operations.

In December, Dona Harvey, who had been editor of the *Tribune,* was named the first woman managing editor of the *Province.* Gerry Haslam, who had been head of corporate communications for the forestry firm MacMillan Bloedel in Vancouver before moving back to Winnipeg to help Wheatley boost circulation of the *Tribune,* was hired to research the feasibility of a morning tabloid. "We want to see if we can produce a paper that will meet the needs and interests of the non-readers and casual readers of the other two papers," Haslam said in January, announcing that 500 copies of a printed prototype would be used in marketing research conducted in Toronto.[30] At month's end he was back east poring over the results of the research and of a survey of Vancouver residents conducted by the Goldfarb polling firm, but he admitted reader reaction was a secondary consideration in launching a new tabloid. "No amount of research is going to tell us what's really going to happen to a third newspaper," said Haslam. "Even if the research said there's a great market for a tab, the next step is to find out if you can get advertising. Can you increase the amount of revenue coming into Pacific Press. Our obligation is to our shareholders and employees."[31]

Wheatley's other aim at Pacific Press, aside from maximizing Southam's return from its monopoly on the Vancouver newspaper market, was improving labor relations, which under dual ownership had been so difficult, he told *Sun* business writer Ian Fraser.

> "First of all, we have to get the people here to trust us," said Wheatley. "All of the people. What I have to do is to get everybody here to think that what I'm doing will work for the best interests of us all. I think the best thing that ever happened was [to have] one owner here that would be able to break down those barriers. I don't like the word monopoly. I don't think that in the total community we have one."[32]

Pacific Press officials met with union leaders to try to negotiate a merger of the *Sun* and *Province* circulation and advertising departments now that Southam owned both newspapers. Guild administrative officer Patricia Lane told the United Press Canada the union would resist the attempt if it meant any loss of jobs. "If they try to lay anyone off, we'll fight them," said Lane.[33] A serious setback to the company's hopes of freeing itself from onerous union rules came in the spring of 1981, when the arbitrator named to decide the manning dispute, which had precipitated the eight-month shutdown of Pacific Press, suddenly bowed out. Judge Ted McTaggart, a former labor lawyer, had been appointed the previous summer to solve the dispute over how many pressmen were needed to run the Pacific Press machinery. Failing to achieve an agreement through mediation, McTaggart issued a report in April 1981 outlining his solution. The report sided with the pressmen's claim that the existing manning levels were necessary to print the paper, but the company balked at accepting the decision without first arguing the matter. The pressmen's union claimed that under the agreement which ended the strike the arbitrator's decision was to be considered binding on both sides, but the company pointed to a provision allowing for submissions to be heard before a decision was made.[34] McTaggart was unable to continue with hearings into the dispute because of his busy court schedule, and the company refused to accept his recommendations without a hearing. That led to some press slowdowns, but finally in September Pacific Press declared defeat in its pursuit of the goal for which it had endured such a catastrophic shutdown of its two dailies. Townsend announced the company would accept McTaggart's findings "to try to pave the way to improving the industrial relations atmosphere at Pacific Press. . . . We could have fought the thing forever and we simply would have kept stirring things up."[35]

Following the upheaval of Black Wednesday, calls came to limit the control Thomson and Southam had gained over the newspaper industry across the country. Within a week, Prime Minister Pierre Trudeau, who had regained power after only nine months out of office when a stumbling Joe Clark was forced to call an election following a vote of non-confidence in Parliament, set up a Royal Commission to investigate the effects of increased concentration of newspaper ownership. To head it he named Tom Kent, the former *Winnipeg Free Press* editor, Liberal candidate in Burnaby-Coquitlam, and longtime federal civil servant. Kent had entered politics as an advisor to Prime Minister Lester Pearson in the 1960s, had authored the bill championed by St. Clair Balfour to protect Canadian newspapers from foreign competition, and was widely credited with helping forge the modern Canadian welfare state. He had been appointed to head the Sydney Steel Corp. in Nova Scotia in the 1970s, and in 1980 was newly appointed dean of administrative studies at Dalhousie University in Halifax.[36] Kent vowed to hold hearings across the country and report on the state of the Canadian newspaper industry within a year, selecting former *Toronto Star* editor Borden Spears and former CBC president Laurent Picard as his lieutenants.

In addition to the Kent Commission, as the Royal Commission on Newspapers became known, the federal Justice Department began a criminal investigation of the newspaper transactions. Under the Combines Investigation Act, the newspaper dealings could be ruled illegal if they involved collusion between competitors and resulted in detriment to the public. But the Act had been unsuccessful in preventing increased concentration of newspaper ownership over the decades since hearings into the Pacific Press agreement in 1957, which had failed to result in even its recommended judicial order against changes to the deal without prior court approval. The Act was finally proven toothless by a 1976 Supreme Court of Canada ruling that overturned a 1972 conviction on monopoly charges against New Brunswick industrialist K.C. Irving, who controlled all four English-language daily newspapers in that province through a network of family companies.

On September 9, 1980, federal combines investigators raided the Toronto offices of Southam and Thomson. Fisher proclaimed his company's innocence. "I don't think we've broken the law," he told a reporter. "In fact, we're damn sure we haven't broken the law."[37] St. Clair Balfour, now retired as president but still involved in the company as chairman of the Southam board of directors, protested that the unseemly raid was hardly necessary. The company had offered combines officials the same access to its files as it had for the investigation into the Pacific Press amalgamation more than twenty years earlier, Balfour pointed out. "At that time they apparently trusted us," he said. "This time apparently they don't."[38] The distrust of investigators appeared justified when they retrieved a crudely shredded document from the wastebasket of Southam vice-president William J. Carradine, who was also a member of the Pacific Press board of directors.[39] The memo referred to rival Thomson Newspapers and apparently contained the smoking gun investigators were looking for to prove collusion, detailing the essence of a deal between the chains. It read: "They get out of Ottawa. They get out of Montreal. They get out of Vancouver. They get control in Winnipeg."[40] At the end of the month, investigators raided the offices of Pacific Press, combing through documents for more than a week. "I would say that they took away a stack of stuff about a foot high from everywhere in the building," said company spokesman George Hutchison.[41]

In December, the Kent Commission began its cross-Canada hearings in Winnipeg, where lawyers for Thomson and Southam protested that because of the ongoing criminal investigation their executives could hardly be expected to testify into details of dealings between the chains.[42] In January, the traveling road show visited Vancouver, where *Province* publisher Paddy Sherman testified that no decision on publishing a third newspaper out of the Pacific Press Building was expected before March. "The Pacific Press board meets later this week," said Sherman. "I am looking forward with interest to that meeting." As a result of the federal combines investigation into the 1957 Pacific Press amalgamation, Sherman said, the company was pledged to inform the authorities of any changes to the arrangement. "My understanding is that we do nothing before informing them. After that it becomes a legal problem."[43]

Sun managing editor Bruce Larsen testified the Pacific Press arrangement had been beneficial for both sides, but particularly for the *Province*. "I fully believe the *Province* would not have lasted without Pacific Press," said Larsen. "And if *The Sun* had to bear all the cost of new facilities we might not be as fat as we feel."[44] Perennial Vancouver alderman Harry Rankin predicted that if Southam started a third newspaper as a tabloid, either the *Sun* or *Province* would fold. "I usually offer 10 to one on my bets," said Rankin. "If the proposed new tabloid works, the *Province* will go down the drain."[45] *Columbian* publisher Rikk Taylor explained why his suburban newspaper did not circulate within the Vancouver city limits. "Vancouver Council — which Mr. Rankin did not disclose — has a motion that says that the only newspapers that can be on the property of the City of Vancouver are the two newspapers that are published in Vancouver."[46] Retired journalist Sid Godper testified the *Sun* and *Province* restricted criticism of their joint publishing arrangement and pointed for proof to a letter to the editor he had written which was rejected by both newspapers.

> Back in 1972, Robert McConnell, then publisher [*sic*] of the *Province* personally explained, without a blush, that he could not publish an article I had submitted . . . because there was an agreement that neither paper would print matter critical of the other. My article was highly critical of both papers. If that doesn't constitute an iron curtain, what does? And it appears that the agreement good in 1972 continues good today. So much for the blather about the two papers safeguarding public rights.[47]

In the spring, hearings moved to Ottawa, where Thomson admitted there was a limit to how many Canadian newspapers his worldwide conglomerate should own, but he insisted he would know when a reasonable limit had been reached without a government regulator to tell him. "I have the intent, integrity and judgement to know when to stop," said Thomson.[48] If the public was concerned over so much media power being held in the hands of one man, a "controlling factor" might be necessary, he agreed, but he insisted it should be a non-governmental body. Former FP Publications president George Currie admitted the chain had kept the *Ottawa Journal* alive "so we would have a card to play against Winnipeg."[49] He testified that both FP Publications and Southam had conducted separate market studies in 1979 to find ways to improve the situation at Pacific Press. He told the commission that he and Fisher had discussed many times "what could be done to break the logjam" in Vancouver, but the 1957 Pacific Press agreement made it difficult for competing newspapers to operate as equal partners. He said his preference would have been to turn the *Sun* into an all-day newspaper similar to the *Toronto Star*, with the *Province* playing a secondary role, either as an upscale "mini-*Globe and Mail*" or a down-market morning tabloid such as the *Toronto Sun*. "We would have to find a sharply differentiated role for the *Province* to play," testified Currie. "It was just losing money too heavily."[50]

Fisher admitted that Southam had grown too large already and agreed that an ownership review process for newspaper transactions, similar to what was in place in Britain and which had been proposed for Canada by the Davey Senate Committee a decade earlier, would be appropriate. He testified the *Province* had lost $5.7 million in 1980 and could not survive without being subsidized under the Pacific Press agreement by the profits of the *Vancouver Sun*. He did not deny suggestions by commission lawyer

Don Affleck that keeping the money-losing morning newspaper alive discouraged a new competitor from entering the Vancouver market. "If that is so, it is the result of history, not corporate policy," Fisher said. "I guess the answer is that the existence of *The Province* prevents against intrusion of the *Toronto Globe and Mail.* But I don't think *The Province* would be a very effective blocker against the *Toronto Sun* or any other newspaper that wanted to invade the market." He testified that while a study had been done on the feasibility of publishing a morning tabloid at Pacific Press, he had promised to announce any decision Southam made to its employees first. "I am not at all keen on speculating what we will do in the future," Fisher told Affleck when pressed on what form a morning tabloid might take. "In the tabloid format one can emphasize tits and ass. To date Southam has not published that kind of newspaper. It would be a challenge for us."[51] A decision on a third newspaper also would depend in part on what resulted from the Royal Commission, Fisher testified. "There are arguments that it would be too much for one company to have," he admitted. "I await signals from others."[52]

The Kent Commission concluded its cross-country hearings in mid-April 1981 after hearing almost 800 witnesses and promised to complete its report by July 1. Two weeks later, on May 1, the federal justice department laid charges of conspiracy, monopoly, and merger against the Southam and Thomson chains as a result of their dealings in Ottawa, Winnipeg, Montreal, and Vancouver. Fisher, Thomson, and Currie were named as unindicted co-conspirators but were not charged individually. One executive who was charged with a criminal offence was Carradine, for attempting to "impede or prevent an inquiry being conducted by tearing, mutilating and attempting to destroy and . . . hide documents."[53] A week later, Bill Wheatley announced that Pacific Press had decided against going ahead with a third newspaper in Vancouver. "There is just not that big a market here for that kind of thing. I found out people here are not the kind of readers that the *Toronto Sun* can get." Instead, he said, the company would concentrate on improving its existing newspapers, including distribution of the afternoon *Sun* from the Vancouver printing facilities of Pacific Press, which had become problematic because of traffic problems caused by rush hour starting at 3 p.m. Building a long-needed rapid transit system to alleviate commuter congestion might change the company's mind on introducing a tabloid to Vancouver in the future, Wheatley added.

> But our research does not prove that such a newspaper would appeal on a consistent enough basis to a large enough body of readers to attract the requisite volume of revenue, particularly advertising. A new tab would be a high-risk venture. We feel the risk is too great and have decided not to proceed at this time. However we retain the option of launching a tab at any time in the future.[54]

The Kent commission did not make its self-imposed deadline of July 1, releasing its report on August 18, 1981. An accompanying eight volumes of research reports exhaustively examined the economic and social aspects of the Canadian newspaper industry. The main report concluded to no one's surprise that the Southam and Thomson chains had grown to exert too much control over such an important social institution as the nation's newspapers. It recommended that Parliament enact a Canada Newspaper Act to limit the growth of newspaper chains, and that chains which already controlled an unacceptable number of dailies in any region should be forced to divest themselves of titles. In New Brunswick, the Irving companies should have to sell either their Moncton or Saint John dailies, for example, and in Saskatchewan the Armadale chain, owned by Sifton family interests, should have to choose between its newspapers in Regina and Saskatoon. Most importantly, the Kent Commissioners proposed, Thomson should have to choose between his new *Globe and Mail* and his other Canadian dailies. The *Globe* was growing into Canada's first national newspaper, using satellite technology to print editions in Ottawa and Calgary as well as Toronto, with expansion planned to Vancouver and the far-eastern Maritime provinces. The Kent commissioners were particularly hard on Thomson, whose newspapers they found markedly inferior to those published by Southam. Despite the fact that Southam controlled almost 33 percent of English-language newspaper circulation in Canada, compared with just under 26 percent controlled by Thomson, under Kent's regional perspective no immediate divestitures should be required of the country's largest chain. Even Southam's dominant position in B.C. was exempted from Kent's calls for divestiture of dailies. "Southam's ownership of both Vancouver papers and of one at Prince George puts it in a leading position in British Columbia, but the size of the province and number of smaller dailies qualify the dominance to the extent that we do not recommend a requirement for divestiture now."[55]

The reaction of publishers to the Kent Commission recommendations was as predictable as it was swift and furious. Across the country editorials and columnists deplored the proposed measures as an unacceptable intrusion on freedom of the press to operate as it saw fit. In Ottawa, Trudeau was by then preoccupied with a deepening recession, his government's divisive National Energy Policy, and his planned personal legacy of repatriating the Canadian constitution from Britain. A watered-down version of the Kent proposals was tabled in the House of Commons in June 1982, calling for a 20 percent limit on the share any chain could own of national newspaper circulation. But the proposed Canada Newspaper Act stopped short of requiring the divestiture recommended by Kent, moving merely to freeze the Southam and Thomson chains at their current ownership levels. The Act never got off the order paper, however, as the Trudeau government instead pursued other priorities in its dying days in the face of determined resistance from the powerful publishers' lobby. Thus the warnings of the Kent Commission, like those of the Davey Committee before it, resulted in no government action as the public and political outrage of Black Wednesday eventually died away.

In the Greater Vancouver area, the only other daily newspaper then publishing was the long-independent *Columbian* in suburban Coquitlam. Founded in 1861 in adjacent New Westminster on the Fraser River, then capital of the colony of British Columbia, a full quarter-century before the eventual rail terminus of Vancouver was incorporated, the *Columbian* was by 1982 going through a lingering death. In February the newspaper suffered the first labor dispute in its history when workers occupied the company cafeteria after management attempted to lock them out following rotating union "study sessions" that had prevented publication. The joint council unions were enraged that *Columbian* management had negotiated a secret deal with its pressmen which gave them a higher wage rate than other workers. The other unions demanded parity with the pressmen and shut down the *Columbian* for four days to get it. Publisher Rikk Taylor warned them the family-owned newspaper, one of only four such dailies remaining in Canada, "will not be feasible after any strike or job action."[56] Joint council chairman Terry Glavin admitted unionists were concerned for the *Columbian*'s survival but insisted the principle of parity took precedence. "This parity issue isn't something we created," said Glavin. "The company created it. We told them that no matter how rich or sparse the offer, there has to be parity."[57] The *Columbian* cafeteria took on the look of a dormitory, with mattresses, blankets, and pillows strewn on the floor as the dispute continued. Finally, the company agreed.[58]

But soon the *Columbian*'s financial problems began to become apparent. In March, the newspaper offered Guild members wage parity with the other unions in exchange for foregoing the retroactive pay it owed them. Trading the average $758 owed each Guild member for about $900 apiece paid over the life of the two-year contract saved the company from having to borrow the money to make the lump-sum payments, explained managing editor Neil Graham. "We always have a cash flow problem around April or May and so that's our peak borrowing period. Now we can pay out the parity through general revenue over time."[59] But the *Columbian*'s cash flow problems were more serious than most realized, made worse by the crushing interest rates the newspaper was having to pay on the $2.7 million it had borrowed to computerize its newsroom, which topped 20 percent. In March 1983 it was revealed that the government-owned B.C. Development Corporation had turned the newspaper down for a $1-million loan. Graham explained that the *Columbian* was merely looking at financing the purchase of a new press. "We have a little cash flow problem, but it is nothing too serious. We're going to be around for another 120 years."[60]

Soaring interest rates brought by the policies of U.S. president Ronald Reagan had sent many shaky enterprises into bankruptcy in the resulting recession of the early 1980s, and in May the *Columbian* joined the ranks of companies seeking government protection from their creditors. The newspaper, which was losing more than $2 million a year, filed a proposal under the Bankruptcy Act to restructure its $7.3 million in debts, offering its unsecured creditors fifty cents on the dollar to be paid over the next three years.[61] The offer was accepted, but soon the *Columbian* was short of cash again, despite starting to turn a profit, and by October the newspaper went into receivership. "Basically we have no cash to operate, either from the bank or the creditors," said Taylor. "We're making money. But we're not making what we said we would in our proposal."[62] The historic daily continued to publish into November while attempts were made to find a buyer or secure operating capital. Newspaper Guild officers met with federal officials in an attempt to obtain government support, citing the concern expressed in the Kent Commission report for the survival of independently owned newspapers. "It's time to put their money where their mouth is," said Guild president Roy Tubbs, who added that a group of *Columbian* employees also was looking into taking over the newspaper.[63]

In the end the *Columbian* could not be saved, and many blamed Taylor, whose family had owned the newspaper since his grandfather, Senator J.D. Taylor, became its managing editor in 1900. Inexplicable decisions by the third-generation owner baffled many *Columbian* staff, such as the failure to replace a circulation manager who retired in the early 1980s. "When that happened I think a lot of people gave up," Graham told *Sun* reporter Gerry Bellett, a former *Columbian* staffer. "A newspaper can't really get along without a full-time circulation manager. Someone has to be out there selling what we make."[64] Graham, described by *Sun* columnist Pete McMartin as a "young, personable Scot with extensive journalism experience, and one of the few executives liked by the staff," wrote the newspaper's bitter front-page obituary.[65]

> A phrase by Earle Bradford of [radio station] CKNW comes to mind. "I hope," he said after the Pacific Press strike of 1978–79 when the *Columbian* was selling 50,000 copies a day, "that Rikk Taylor has the courage to stay in the market place now that he has a good product, and not retreat back to New Westminster as he did after the previous strike." Unfortunately, Publisher Taylor did not have that sort of courage.[66]

As circulation dwindled to 21,000, Graham charged that no serious attempt had been made by Taylor to keep the advertising linage or readership the *Columbian* had gained during the eight-month shutdown of the *Vancouver Sun* and *Province*. "The glorious dream of making *The*

Columbian a third force in the Vancouver newspaper market was chopped off at the knees," wrote Graham. "As it became obvious the company had no desire to be more than a weak, suburban daily . . . newsroom talent began to trickle away."[67] Taylor's emphasis on developing the *Columbian*'s chain of five free-distribution suburban weeklies had drained the daily, Graham claimed. "Some bitterness is inevitable. . . . But we all wish the newspaper had been given the dignity of a clean death instead of being allowed to writhe publicly in its death throes. Many of us can never forgive that. The *Columbian* deserved better."[68]

Taylor had saved the moneymaking *Today* publications for himself, scooping them up in an auction of *Columbian* assets held by the company's bankruptcy trustee. The publisher's winning bid was estimated at $300,000, but came in only a few hundred dollars higher than one from a group headed by Graham, which instead started up its own chain of suburban weeklies. As the final edition of the *Columbian* went to press, Graham not only had the last word on its front page, but also added insult to his bitter recrimination. "He instructed composing room staff to cut Taylor's name from the list of employees who wished to thank the public for supporting *The Columbian* through its 123-year history," reported Bellett. "'He's not an employee of *The Columbian*,' he told composing room foreman Don Solomon, 'so take his name out.' Solomon, a 24-year veteran of *The Columbian*, complied."[69]

In the five years Clark Davey spent in Vancouver, a period which included the greatest explosion of fury ever witnessed over the increasing concentration of newspaper ownership in Canada, the city had seen its three daily newspaper owners reduced to just one. In 1983 he returned to Eastern Canada as publisher of the *Montreal Gazette*, where he soon suffered through another strike by pressmen, during which the longtime Liberal newspaper paid for radio airtime to publicize its new political position, supporting the Progressive Conservatives of Brian Mulroney, who swept to victory in the 1984 federal election. Davey did not remember his time in Vancouver fondly, complaining in a 1985 interview with *Media Magazine* that the city had "an undeserved reputation for friendliness."[70] Pacific Press was a "corporate monstrosity," made unworkable by its management structure of three equal leaders, Davey added. "With no control over production facilities and a constant need to compromise, he was frustrated by his lack of power," observed interviewer Mark Abley.[71]

18 Going Tabloid

The *Province* was not Gerry Haslam's first choice of newspapers of which to be named publisher. Even after he took over the ailing daily in 1982, he would have been just as happy to give it a decent burial or convert it into a renamed twice-weekly suburban newspaper. The young Southam executive had spent a month at the morning daily in 1981, producing a prototype tabloid for market research into the feasibility of publishing a third newspaper at Pacific Press. The atmosphere in the *Province* newsroom had made a lasting impression on the former *Winnipeg Tribune* editor, and he did not remember it fondly. "I got the clear impression that the damn place was a war zone," recalled Haslam. "That's why I didn't want to go back."[1]

The red-haired former radio and television talk-show host had been working his way up in the Southam organization, with a brief diversion in the late 1970s into corporate communications for MacMillan Bloedel in Vancouver. In 1973, at just 28, Haslam was named managing editor of the *Tribune*. Three years later he was editor-in-chief of the second-place Winnipeg paper. By 1982, Haslam was 37 and working at Southam's head office in Toronto, heading up the company's initial experiment in electronic publishing, dubbed Videotex. It soon became obvious that delivering news via electronic databases was a concept well ahead of its time, so when the publisher of the nearby *Hamilton Spectator* retired, Haslam looked forward to getting back into the newspaper business at the helm of Southam's oldest daily. Instead of filling the vacancy with their rising young star, however, Southam management decided to shuffle publishers at several of its newspapers, including Paddy Sherman, who moved to the *Ottawa Citizen*. That left the only vacancy in Vancouver.

> Gordon Fisher called me in and said, "We'd like you to go to Vancouver." I said, "Do I have a choice?" He said, "No, Gerry, all the other spots are filled." I accepted the job and prepared to go with great trepidation. Before I left Toronto, I went in to see Fisher and I said, "I'll be back within a year with a plan to spend your money to fix the paper." I had read the research that had been done on the *Province*. It said things like a third of people in Vancouver won't even take it if it was free.[2]

His review of the market research that Southam had already commissioned on its money-losing morning newspaper in Vancouver painted a depressing picture of the challenge Haslam was about to inherit. The polling firm Martin Goldfarb and Associates had concluded from surveys in 1981 that the labor problems which plagued Pacific Press during the 1970s had left Vancouverites with an image of their dailies as "cold, impersonal, aloof, [and] mercenary."[3] A study by newspaper consultant Leonard Kubas found that 63 percent of those who read both the *Sun* and *Province* considered them identical in content. "Neither paper is perceived to stand for something unique from the other," concluded Goldfarb, adding that the only thing the *Province* had going for it was its morning publication time. "There is nothing else unique about it."[4] Haslam concluded the problem was not circulation, which had been growing, but a lack of advertising content that turned off both readers and advertisers. "It was too thin to be taken seriously," he recalled. "The first problem I addressed when I got there was that the paper was too thin. It would jam the stackers in the mailing room."[5]

Haslam's examination of the Pacific Press books showed the brutal financial facts that threatened the newspaper's survival. "This year, on a cost-loaded basis, *The Province* will lose almost $10 million," he concluded in an internal "discussion paper" outlining publishing options for the second newspaper. "Quite apart from political and legal considerations, it is in our own business interest to embark on a program to make our second product a winner. The only alternative is to close the newspaper."[6] Haslam's analysis of the Pacific Press arrangement led him to conclude that the long-standing relationship between the dailies had worked to the detriment of the *Province*. "Pacific Press had been configured, either willingly or by accident to protect the *Sun*'s revenue flow, which was 75 percent of the revenue that came into the building," he argued.[7] The resulting problem for the *Province*, Haslam realized, stemmed from the allocation of production costs between the Pacific Press dailies, as his predecessor Paddy Sherman had so often complained.

> The *Province* was forced because of its losses, these paper losses, to raise its [advertising] rates faster . . . while the *Sun* raised its rates more slowly. The result was that every year got worse because the *Province* base from which you raised the rates was higher. . . . The need was clearly to bring the *Province* economically up to its own ad rates.[8]

The *Province*'s share of Pacific Press retail advertising linage had fallen to 24 percent by 1981, compared with 34 percent in 1971. During that period, *Province* advertising rates had risen by 174 percent, well above the 144 percent increase in inflation, while *Sun* rates had risen by only 122 percent.[9] Lowering adverting rates was not an option, so Haslam decided the *Province* had to be turned into a more attractive media buy. "Instead of lowering the drawbridge, we had to raise the river," he recalled. "We had to bring the circulation and the readership up to where you could justify the rates."[10]

A plummeting economy in 1982 made Haslam's mission of improving the financial fortunes of the *Province* seemingly impossible. A deepening U.S. recession had hit B.C. hard, as stagnant housing starts slowed the entire forestry-based provincial economy. Newspaper advertising linage had been falling sharply nationwide since the New Year, and Southam earnings in the first quarter of the year were half what they were in 1981 as a result of a 6.3 percent dip in advertising at the chain's dailies. Gordon Fisher warned in April that the company's profit margin, 9.8 percent in 1981, would be significantly lower in 1982, due not only to falling revenue but also to its soaring debts, which passed $200 million with financing of a new $70-million plant for the *Calgary Herald*. High interest rates on its borrowing put the company in a "very uncomfortable position," Fisher told reporters at the official opening in Calgary on April 23.[11] By summer, general manager Bill Wheatley admitted that prospects at Pacific Press were bleak, with advertising linage down 12.8 percent at the *Sun* and 14.7 percent at the *Province*. "Our financial condition is very bad," he told *Sun* reporter Phil Needham in July. "Our drop in advertising is bigger than at any of the [other] Southam papers."[12] Haslam took over as *Province* publisher on August 1 and recalled that his initial suggested solution was a drastic one.

> I remember my first [Southam] board meeting. There was a recession going on in '82. Clair Balfour made a speech. I piped up and said, "I know how you can save $10 million." "What was that?" said [Gordon] Fisher. "Close the *Province*." He glared at me down the table. He said, "No, Gerry." He had closed a paper in Winnipeg, and he didn't want to do it again. He sure as hell didn't want to close the *Province*, which had been in the family quite a while.[13]

The appointment reunited Haslam with former Winnipeg colleague Dona Harvey, who had recently been named managing editor of the *Province*. Together with advertising director Bill Peter and circulation manager Al McNair, they undertook a top-secret evaluation of strategies for improving *Province* prospects. They came up with five options and made financial projections for each, based on "hunch" analysis. "For reasons of security, we have not talked to anyone in production," they cautioned in their discussion paper. "So any production dollar figures are sheer guesses."[14] Of the five options, the one Haslam favored would have reduced the *Province* to twice-weekly publication, taken it out of the Vancouver city limits, and changed its name. Two of the options called for the *Province* to "creep" along as it was but to be distributed free to 150,000 additional non-subscribers one or two days a week. Another was to turn the *Province* into a true provincial newspaper as a "B.C. Daily." The least attractive option, according to the revenue projections of the new *Province* brain trust, was to turn the paper into the kind of "Breezy Tab" that had been considered and rejected as an option for a third Pacific Press daily just the year before. The five options considered were:

• *Breezy Tab.* The kind of tabloid newspaper Haslam had market-tested in 1981 would establish the *Province* as a distinctive product, geared to take advantage of the growing commuter market expected with the opening of a light rail transit (LRT) system in 1986 in conjunction with the World's Fair taking place in Vancouver. But unlike the success story of the *Toronto Sun*, the *Province* managers predicted a morning tabloid in Vancouver would follow the pattern of less-successful efforts in Calgary and Winnipeg, hence reduced profit. "The only savings would come from potential editorial staff reductions, which under the contract could be by attrition only."[15] Raising circulation to 180,000 was considered optimistic, but even at that level switching to tabloid format was predicted to drop Pacific Press profits by 41 percent, because the managers foresaw *Province* advertising revenue declining by $6 million.[16]

• *B.C. Daily.* "B.C.'s daily newspaper" would cover the entire province as a single community under the model proposed by Haslam and his managers, with projected population growth in the Fraser Valley increasing circulation to 180,000. More staff on Vancouver Island and in the Interior would enable Southam to invade territory covered by Thomson and Sterling newspapers. "Such an idea would never work in Ontario, which is too disparate, but in B.C. (perhaps because of our separation by the mountains from the rest of Canada), we strongly believe it will," argued *Province* management.[17] Advertising revenue was projected to increase by almost a third, including almost twice the classified linage. Pacific Press profits were predicted to thus increase by 75 percent.[18]

• *"Creep."* Retaining the *Province* in its current format but redesigned with a greater emphasis on news and a "less highbrow" approach would not boost daily circulation, but giving the newspaper away free once or twice a week was projected to have a dramatic effect on advertising revenue. Option A, circulating an extra 150,000 free copies of the *Province* on Wednesdays, was seen as boosting advertising linage by almost 40 percent. Option B, giving it away on Wednesdays and Sundays, was predicted to increase advertising linage by almost 70 percent.[19] The projected results would be 41 and 67 percent increases in Pacific Press profits.[20] But this approach was deemed "risky" by Haslam and his crew: "If my neighbour gets it free twice a week, why should I pay?" The move also might hurt *Sun* linage, they pointed out, which was based on paid circulation.[21]

• *Fraser Valley Times.* The most radical option for Southam under Haslam's projections would have reduced the second-place Pacific Press paper to twice-weekly publication. Distribution would be free, but only in the far eastern suburbs of Greater Vancouver under the most optimistic plan, as the Fraser Valley was projected to see a 64 percent increase in population over the next twenty years.[22] Circulation of such a newspaper was predicted to be 134,000, but advertising linage was projected to grow by almost 40 percent. Circulation and advertising staff would move to offices in Langley or nearby, along with much of the editorial operations. The biggest benefit to Pacific Press under this plan would be a projected 50,000 increase in *Sun* circulation without competition from the *Province* in Vancouver and its closest suburbs. That would boost Pacific Press profits by a projected 233 percent.[23] The downside was that this option effectively eliminated the *Province* and, as Haslam's discussion paper noted, "may cause combines, political and labour problems."[24]

• *Total Market VBR.* Publishing the *Province*, "or whatever we call it," only twice a week, and distributing it free in Vancouver and the close-in suburbs of Burnaby and Richmond, was projected to provide a circulation of 230,500 and an increase of almost 80 percent in advertising linage. The *Sun* would increase its circulation by a "conservative" 55,000 under the predictions of Haslam's team and would have the potential, in the absence of a daily *Province*, to move to all-day publication.[25] But they foresaw the *Sun* losing more than half of its advertising linage to the new paper, reducing it to "the 45–50 page range initially."[26] Giving Pacific Press access to 531,000 households versus the 380,000 it was then reaching would allow it to dominate the primary advertising market in competition with the suburban weeklies that were eating away at its advertising revenue base. The result would be a projected increase in Pacific Press profits of 76 percent, but this raised the same legal, labor and political problems as the *Fraser Valley Times* option. In addition to the legal problems faced by eliminating one daily newspaper in Vancouver, Haslam's team noted this option "effectively moves the *Sun* out of its prime market [and] forces a new strategy on that paper."[27]

The discussion paper compared the projected effect on publishing income of the second Pacific Press paper and, after deducting expenses, on total company profit under each option, compared with keeping the *Province* the way it was.[28]

Option	2nd paper income	Pacific Press profit
Sun/Province now	$1,635,000	$5,536,000
Breezy Tab	-$643,000	$3,258,000
B.C. Daily	$7,799,000	$9,699,000
Creep A	$5,594,000	$7,994,000
Creep B	$7,373,000	$9,273,000
Fraser Valley Times	$3,865,000	$18,411,000
Total Market/VBR	$12,890,000	$9,766,000

The option Haslam favored was the one that generated almost twice as much profit for Pacific Press as any of the others, the twice-weekly suburban *Fraser Valley Times*.[29] The least optimistic option, according to the initial analysis of *Province* managers, was converting the morning newspaper to a tabloid. But Haslam decided to proceed with caution before making any decision on the fate of Vancouver's second newspaper. Under his plan, a final decision would not be made for another nine months. More market research, product testing, and advertising linage projections were needed before then.

On October 1, Southam's head office decided that with the worsening recession it could not wait for Haslam to turn things around at Pacific Press and announced that as part of chain-wide cost cutbacks, seventy-four layoffs would be made in Vancouver. Wheatley claimed in justification that advertising linage had declined in August by 25 percent at the *Sun* and by almost as much at the *Province*. But Southam's annual profit had jumped more than 50 percent in 1981, and earnings for the first quarter of 1982 had only declined to $8 million from $9.9 million during the same period in 1981.[30] The Newspaper Guild filed a grievance to fight the announced layoffs, since under its collective agreement staff cuts could only be made for economic reasons.[31] It also applied to the Labour Relations Board for a ruling that the layoffs amounted to an illegal lockout. In both proceedings, the Guild demanded to see the company's account books, declaring it was not convinced Pacific Press was losing money and instead suspected the company was using the economic climate as an excuse to cut staff.[32] Rumors began circulating that Southam would soon close the *Province* to stem its losses, so Wheatley went on Jack Webster's morning phone-in television show to deny them. "There is no consideration of that at this point in time," he told Webster. "I don't foresee it myself."[33] He admitted that 1981 had been a record profit period for Southam, but added that each of the company's units was expected to show a profit, and that Pacific Press was "slightly in a loss position" in 1982.[34]

As grievance proceedings before arbitrator Bruce McColl began at the Hotel Georgia on November 3, about thirty of the laid-off workers marched on the office of Pacific Press employee relations manager George Townsend, who had issued their termination notices. "Nobody questions the fact that Southam is making a lot less money than they made a year ago," Guild spokesman Rod Mickleburgh told the protesting employees. "But it's also fair to say that Southam isn't in the red. All we're saying is that the company show our accountant, in confidence, why the layoffs are necessary."[35] On November 29, McColl sent shockwaves through the B.C. business community by ruling the Guild was entitled to see virtually every company document relating to the layoffs in its bid to block them, including revenue and expense statements, comparative advertising linage figures, and internal memos.[36] Townsend announced that Pacific Press would comply with the order but added it would appeal the ruling on legal grounds.[37] The documents were not forthcoming, however, after Townsend said the company had received "a lot of pressure from the business community" to reverse its decision.[38] Bill Hamilton, president of the Employers' Council of B.C., denied persuading Pacific Press to fight the landmark ruling. "I'm not in any way denying Mr. Townsend's statement that pressure has been exerted by the business community," Hamilton told a *Sun* reporter. "But there has been no pressure from the council."[39] In January, the Labour Relations Board upheld McColl's ruling and issued its own order for the company to open its books to the Guild in its complaint of illegal layoffs.[40] Still the company refused to comply, announcing it would appeal the LRB rulings to the B.C. Supreme Court. The Guild accused the company in a statement of "stonewalling" the arbitration on the layoffs. "Pacific Press seems determined to play hardball with our membership and return to the 'bad old days' of confrontation and distrust between the parties which existed for many years prior to the 1978 strike."[41]

Finally in June the company opened its books to the union but announced it would fight the legality of the order in court due to its significance as a precedent.[42] Before the arbitration hearing could be concluded, however, a settlement of the dispute over layoffs was negotiated. The point had become almost moot, since by then most of the laid-off workers had been rehired.[43] At the *Province*, the new management from Winnipeg had decided to meet the head-office demands for payroll cuts by laying off their most vulnerable employees, those working part-time and in temporary positions and therefore without job security under the contract. "That was the silliest layoff in the history of man," admitted Haslam.

> The decision was made to have layoffs, so I summoned all the managers. Dona said to me, "We'll have to get rid of all the temps." Naively, not understanding the role of temps in the *Province* newsroom, I said OK. It turns out within weeks we can't function without the goddamned temps. The whole place is built on temps because of all the restrictions that had been put on full-time hiring over the years. You couldn't get rid of them.[44]

The future of the *Province* became clearer in January 1983, when a report by marketing consultant Jim Armitage concluded that a tabloid, despite placing last among the five options in the projections of Haslam and his management team, would be by far the most attractive format for advertisers. "The goal from an advertising standpoint was just to gain credibility," recalled Haslam. "We knew there was enough money in ad budgets in Vancouver to give us the revenue we needed, as long as we could get the circulation up to match the [advertising] rates."[45] Slowly Haslam became persuaded that the market research he had done in 1981 for a tabloid as a third Pacific Press daily was actually the prototype for the repositioned *Province*. "The reason the Tab climbed to the first option in the priorities was we started to believe the third newspaper research, that there really was a market for this thing," he recalled. "Gordon Fisher favored a tab. I remember Gordon saying, 'God damn it, Gerry, why don't we just do it?' I think he knew in his heart it was going to be a tab, and he didn't tell me."[46]

While the 1981 research showed a tabloid would be a hit with Vancouver readers, it concluded there would not be enough advertising revenue for it to survive in the marketplace as a third daily. But as a second newspaper, Armitage argued, it would become more attractive to advertisers because it would appeal to a different readership than the *Sun*. "The demographics sold the paper," said Haslam. "It wasn't unheard of in this country at that time to sell by demographics, but it certainly wasn't done by anybody as aggressively as we did it, because that's all we had. We drove down the [readership] duplication, way down."[47] The distinctiveness of a tabloid audience appealed to advertisers, such as the electronics merchandiser Future Shop, which sought to target younger readers with more disposable income. The advertising content, in turn, attracted new readers who considered that sort of commercial information as important news, explained Haslam.

> I was a first-time publisher. My background was editorial. I was amazed how much I picked up about the marketing side, about the business side. But I still thought we could be a success by tailoring the editorial product to the market. I think I underestimated the importance of both advertising money and advertising content. What the Future Shop ads did was they established the *Province*'s credibility among a group of readers who read stereo ads.[48]

In February it was decided that further test-marketing would be conducted on a second prototype tabloid, and an eighty-page mockup was printed on March 1. When the reaction of 550 members of focus groups proved positive, the decision was made and Haslam prepared his pitch to the Southam board of directors in Toronto on April 22. His decision to convert the *Province* to tabloid format was endorsed unanimously, and on April 25 Haslam was back in Vancouver with the announcement. The newspaper would go tabloid on August 2, he told the *Province* newsroom, adding the switch in format was the result of "the most exhaustive analysis of market position and future options ever undertaken by a Canadian newspaper."[49] But far from a racy tabloid like those in London, or even the version produced by the *Toronto Sun* chain, the *Province* would be a "family tabloid," Haslam cautioned. "In all the pictures of girls we run, unless they are extraordinarily newsworthy, the girls will be clothed."[50] While some staff expressed concern that jobs would be reduced in the smaller format, Haslam said a "modest" overall increase in staffing instead would be needed, although some positions would be eliminated by attrition. Finally, while the prototype tabloid carried the *Province* name, Haslam announced that there was some evidence that a name change would be desirable to better differentiate the new product. "We're going to be looking at the issue, and I'll let you know when it's resolved," Haslam told the newsroom. "Your own views on the matter will be most welcome."[51]

Of all the reaction to the change to tabloid format, the backlash over a possible name change for the *Province* proved most vocal. *Pacific Post* had scored the highest with respondents among eighteen alternatives in the March phase of research and was planned to top the next prototype to gauge public reaction. The prototype third newspaper in 1981 had been called the *Post*, but by itself the name scored poorly. Placing "Pacific" in front of it, however, had narrowly put it first, followed by *The Province, Daily Province*, and *Province Daily News*. Haslam posted a notice on the newsroom bulletin board announcing to *Province* staff the possible title choice of *Pacific Post*: "We will be gauging reactions to it and anticipate making a final decision in late June or early July."[52] Public response to the possibility of a name change for the *Province* had been mixed following Haslam's announcement of the planned switch to tabloid format. But the choice of *Pacific Post* caused such a negative reaction among *Province* journalists that in May Haslam used his weekly publisher's column to scotch the idea even before the final prototype was produced. "As the days went by and the new prototype took shape, reaction came as well from people who work for *The Province*," reported the publisher. "It was soon clear that neither a new name nor the choice of *Pacific Post* excited anyone."[53]

The relaunch of the *Province* as a tabloid was accompanied by a $500,000 advertising campaign, with 1,000 television commercials and 1,600 radio spots hyping arrival of the new format. Extensive market testing had come up with the advertising slogan "All the News! Convenient too!" Even the pages of the *Vancouver Sun* carried promotion for its morning "competition," which was a first for Vancouver.[54] On August 2, curious readers were lined up at the Pacific Press loading dock to get the first copies.[55] The initial edition was ninety-six pages and carried 340 news stories, double the number in a typical broadsheet *Province*.[56] Most were brief items, and even major stories were reduced to summary coverage. The cryptic front-page headline, "Ease Bill 3?" which referred to a story inside on possible revisions to provincial legislation enabling civil service cutbacks, had readers guessing at its meaning. Haslam assured readers that, while delivered in a "crisp, bright and lively style," their morning news would remain responsible. "We're not sacrificing accuracy, but we are giving people news in the way they have said they want it."[57] Sports columnist Jim Taylor as usual saw humor in the situation. "More care will be taken in selecting athletes to be interviewed," he wrote. "People with long names are out of luck — or, as we say in tabspeak, SOL. . . . We're gonna be great. Or possibly grt."[58] Instead of a page-three pinup, the *Province* version of a Sunshine Girl was buried fifty-seven pages inside, with a young, fully clothed female botanist serving as the paper's first "Smile of the Day." The afternoon *Sun,* pointing out that its tabloid cousin was "the first Canadian newspaper to be designed from the start by marketing studies," ran a sneering review.

> Each morning, thousands of pedestrians tilt their heads sideways, not to adjust their clothes or because of nervous tics, but to look at a morning newspaper displayed sideways in a street box. The new *Province* tabloid won't fit upright in more than 1,000 street boxes designed for its former broadsheet format. But despite that marketing problem, The *Province* remains Canada's most carefully market researched and market designed newspaper.[59]

Sales of the first tabloid *Province,* Haslam reported to newsroom staff the next day, were 164,000, for an increase of 27,000 over the previous Tuesday and 37,000 over the same day in 1982.[60] The first week's average circulation of 165,751 was "well beyond" expectations, he told the *Globe and Mail.*[61] More encouraging was an immediate 10 percent increase in advertising linage.[62] By September the novelty had worn off and circulation stabilized at an average of 157,355, almost 20,000 higher than the same month in 1982.[63] Haslam predicted that with projected 8 to 10 percent growth, the *Province* would be in the black within two years.[64] The publisher told the *Financial Post* in the fall that a larger-than-expected increase in advertising linage meant that the *Province* would soon be pulling its weight at Pacific Press. "Haslam says he hopes to make a 'publishing profit' in 1985, which means the paper's revenues will exceed the editorial, advertising, and circulation costs," reported the *Post.* "The next step after that will be to take aim at the *Province*'s share of printing costs at Pacific Press."[65]

In the fall of 1983, the Southam and Thomson chains finally went to trial in Toronto on criminal charges of merger, monopoly, and conspiracy that resulted from the events of Black Wednesday more than three years earlier. Combines branch investigator David Teal testified in the Supreme Court of Ontario that he saw Southam executive William Carradine tear up a document during the September 9, 1980, federal raid on the newspaper chain's head office. The incriminating evidence, seized from Carradine's wastebasket and pieced back together in sixteen parts with Scotch tape, was preserved in cellophane and entered as an exhibit.[66] Dated the month before the closures of the *Ottawa Journal* and *Winnipeg Tribune* and the sale by Thomson of the *Vancouver Sun* to Southam, it estimated increased profits for the chain as a result of the moves. Southam profits were predicted to rise to $15.2 million in 1981 without competition in Ottawa and further losses in Winnipeg, to $18.7 million in 1982, and to $20.3 million by 1983.[67] Crown counsel Claude Thomson argued that another shredded hand-written document seized from Carradine's trash, which had "premature" written beside a reference to an "all-day paper" in Vancouver, was evidence of a contemplated rationalization of its assets at Pacific Press, which the prosecutor called a "cozy arrangement."[68]

Thomson lawyer Lorne Morphy argued that a corporate monopoly was a valid business goal and not necessarily detrimental to the public. "In a free enterprise system, it is legitimate for someone to try to put oneself in a monopoly position."[69] When the Crown's evidence was completed, defense lawyers moved for a dismissal of all eight charges, claiming that a key element of the alleged offences — detriment to the public — had not been proven. On October 28, Justice William Anderson agreed in part, dropping the merger and monopoly charges while allowing three conspiracy charges relating to events in Ottawa, Winnipeg, and Vancouver to stand. On the merger charge relating to Pacific Press, Anderson ruled it had not been proven to have lessened competition there and cited the Supreme Court of Canada precedent in the Irving case that inferences of future lessening of competition were not admissible as evidence.[70]

Southam president Gordon Fisher testified for the defence that there was a good reason to announce the *Journal* and *Tribune* closures and the sale of the *Sun* at the same time. A document outlining the financial dealings was drawn up and held in escrow pending approval of the *Tribune* closure by the Southam board, he testified. He said the chains decided to announce their closures simultaneously because it would "smell like the devil" and attract the attention of federal competition authorities. "If there was going to be a mess, let's have just one mess and deal with it all at one time," Fisher testified. "In that way, there would be no question when the other shoe would drop. . . . It was better to do it once, rather than twice or three times."[71] Thomson Newspapers president John Tory testified the money-losing *Ottawa Journal*, which it had acquired in its takeover of FP Publications, would have been closed even if Southam had not folded its *Tribune* in Winnipeg.[72]

Anderson announced his verdict on December 9. He called Tory and Fisher "witnesses whose credit is unimpeached," and ruled their stories were "a reasonable explanation of the impugned events." He said he was persuaded to acquit the chains on the conspiracy charges because of the "entirely open fashion" in which they conducted business. "There was prompt and full disclosure to anyone who was interested," noted the judge. "It is not the sort of conduct one expects to see exhibited in a criminal conspiracy."[73] As for the Crown's contention that the shredded documents found in Carradine's wastebasket were evidence of guilty intent, he instead saw a "perfectly logical" alternative explanation. "Mr. Carradine may have considered the calculations were sufficiently confidential that he didn't want people to see it, even his own office staff," reasoned the judge. "In the last fortnight, I have destroyed reams of paper. Not because it was incriminating, but because I didn't want anybody to read it."[74]

The verdict of not guilty brought to an end the official fallout from the upheaval of Black Wednesday, which, observed Canadian Press reporter Chisholm MacDonald, had its origins decades earlier in British Columbia. "The sequence of events began many years before — on May 24, 1957, in Vancouver. That was the startup date for Pacific Press. . . . an unsatisfactory arrangement from the start, the publishers said."[75]

Just as prospects for the *Province* appeared to improve with its conversion to tabloid format, the old irritant of labor trouble at Pacific Press arose again in early 1984 to threaten the morning paper's survival. The collective agreement that resulted from the eight-month strike of 1978–79 had expired at the end of February 1982, but neither side was willing to go to war again so soon in the absence of contentious contract clauses. As sole proprietor, Southam was willing to avoid conflict with the most generous wage increases ever granted at Pacific Press, 17 and 13 percent a year in a two-year agreement concluded within a month of expiration.[76] But the deal had been sealed before the full impact of the deepening recession was realized, which led to 400 layoffs at Southam newspapers. Salaries for senior staff at Pacific Press had risen during the 1982 contract from $530 a week to more than $700 while Southam revenue stagnated, dropping profits by more than half in 1983. A recovery in 1983, based in part on a strategy of diversification into non-newspaper ventures, such as the recently acquired Coles bookstore chain, had brought Southam fortunes almost back to their record levels of 1981, but the firm's return on equity of 18.3 percent still lagged behind the 22.7 percent it had seen before the recession.[77]

In 1984, Pacific Press asked its unions to accept a wage freeze in the first year of a three-year contract, but the joint council rejected the notion, pointing to the fact that Southam earnings had doubled from the previous year. A provincial restraint program brought in by the government of Social Credit leader Bill Bennett, son of former premier W.A.C. Bennett, had made wage freezes the norm in B.C. during 1983, as the resource-based economy continued to suffer despite a recovery elsewhere. As a result, the historically powerful union movement in B.C. lost strength to a growing non-union employment sector, particularly in the construction industry. Bill Wheatley, who in addition to his role as Pacific Press general manager had been named *Sun* publisher in 1983 to replace Clark Davey, announced that the $18 million profit of the afternoon newspaper had been offset by $15 million in losses incurred by the *Province* with its costly format switch, leaving Pacific Press with a profit of $3 million, which after taxes amounted to earnings of only $400,000.[78] When the Newspaper Guild executive voted to request mediation, without the knowledge or support of the craft unions, an enraged joint council expelled its largest union on March 20. "The guild just simply violated the code of the council," said co-chair Stan Lepper of the mailers. "The council has been around a long time and we have never had a breach like this before. We are not happy about it."[79]

The craft unions went on strike March 28 after only two hours of bargaining when the company offered a three-year contract with no wage increase in the first year, 3.5 percent in the second, and 5 percent in the third.[80] The joint council demanded 8 percent wage increases in each year of a two-year agreement, but some at Pacific Press suspected the well-paid workers were more interested in taking time off. "They've got more money than they know what to do with so they're going to take a holiday for a couple of weeks," wholesaler Bob Hackney told a *Globe and Mail* reporter while walking the picket line.[81] Craft union members claimed their job action was in support of the larger labor effort against the growing anti-union movement, which had seen the B.C. Federation of Labour form Operation Solidarity the previous fall and also sponsor a weekly newspaper, the short-lived *Solidarity Times*. "This fight has to do with the over-all fight between the unions and Victoria," striking printer Robert Smyth told *Maclean's* magazine. "We are part of the labor force, and it is time we did our share."[82]

The Newspaper Guild went to mediation, but when the company made "final" an offer of 6 percent increases in the final two years of a three-year deal, with a wage freeze in the first year, Guild members voted to strike and on April 11 joined the craft unions on the picket line. "We told the mediator that this ultimatum was unacceptable to the Guild," said union president Jim Young, adding that the Guild understood the offer was less than one the company had made to the crafts.[83] Guild leaders resisted what they considered a company attempt to take advantage of their expulsion from the joint council with a strategy of "divide and conquer." The wage offer of 12 percent over three years was not a legitimate one, they claimed, because it was an ultimatum made without consideration of the Guild's demands for job security in the uncertain economic climate. "Zero percent in the first year is like waving a red flag in front of a bull," said the Guild's Roy Tubbs.[84] Guild members grumbled at a union meeting about their $100 weekly strike pay, which was meager compared with the $250 a week craft unionists were able to withdraw from their well-stocked war chest.[85]

Some journalists went to work for $120 a day at the *Globe and Mail*, which beefed up its Vancouver bureau in order to publish a separate "B.C. News" section during the strike and more than tripled its local circulation to 60,000. "They come around here every morning to sit around and beg for crumbs," *Globe and Mail* bureau chief Ian Mulgrew told *Maclean's* of the idled Pacific Press reporters.[86] The national newspaper, which was transmitted by satellite to College Printers in Vancouver, sold out quickly each morning but could not increase its press run due to the limited capacity of the printer. Plans were made to continue the B.C. section after the strike, but they were shelved after advertising revenue fell far short of the additional costs.[87]

Most of the advertising revenue the *Globe and Mail* sought during the

1984 strike at Pacific Press instead went to community newspapers in the Lower Mainland. The biggest beneficiary of the local advertising bonanza was the *Courier* , which had quietly risen from the ashes of its disastrous foray into daily publication in 1979 with a strategy outlined by Harvey Southam in his capacity as editor of the new *Equity* magazine in 1984.

> They had already made a conscious business decision that they would hold on until the next Pacific Press strike. . . . It was worth the wait. In April the *Courier* pulled in $738,000 with nine editions that grew from a regular 40 pages to 132 pages. Circulation was doubled to 102,000 with the addition of a separate city-wide edition. After the dust settled in early June, the shareholders got their first dividend allocation of $27,500.[88]

Southam Newspapers had attempted to buy up the *Courier* shortly after its 1979 resurrection by a group of investors who each put up $10,000. Publisher Geoff Wellens revealed in early 1980 that a Southam representative "essentially said 'name a price'" for the *Courier* the previous fall, and the offer was confirmed by Gordon Fisher, then Southam president. "We said basically, 'If you're that interested, you name a price,'" said Wellens.[89] The Southam offer was rejected by *Courier* investors when it fell far short of expectations. With the bonanza they reaped in the absence of the Pacific Press dailies in 1984, their decision appeared increasingly astute.

The formula was followed successfully in outlying areas as well. In the North Shore suburbs across Burrard Inlet from Vancouver, Pacific Press penetration was low due to distribution problems caused by snarled bridge traffic. In affluent North and West Vancouver, the market leader was the lively *North Shore News*, which had been founded as a free, all-ad "shopper" in 1969 by advertising salesman Peter Speck, who added editorial content in 1972. He had vanquished dozens of would-be competitors by using an aggressive strategy both editorially and in business. A Sunday paper was added to the weekly Wednesday edition of the *News* in 1977, and by the fall of 1983 circulation stood at 54,000, buoyed by controversial columnist Doug Collins, who had bounced from the *Courier* in 1979 to the *Columbian*, only to have that daily also fold from beneath him. With another strike looming at Pacific Press, Speck announced he would take the *News* daily on February 1, 1984.[90] But after investing $180,000 in computer equipment, he decided to only add a Friday edition for thrice-weekly publication, fearing the fate suffered by the *Courier* and *Vancouver Times* when they challenged Pacific Press with dailies. "I am the King of the North Shore," he told Harvey Southam. "I want to stay being King of the North Shore."[91]

In Toronto, Fisher told the Southam annual meeting on April 18 that the Pacific Press strikers were "playing with fire" by compounding the company's financial problems with yet another publication interruption. "The longer the strike the lower the market penetration," warned Fisher. "Their security of employment in the three years ahead depends mightily on their willingness not to insist that their pay and employment conditions exceed the rest of the company's and Pacific Press's ability to pay by some wide margin."[92] But he denied suggestions that Southam had provoked the latest Pacific Press strike as an excuse to close the money-losing *Province*. "That is sheer nonsense," said Fisher. "The company has publicly committed itself to the publication of two newspapers in Vancouver as long as we can do that with an adequate return on investment."[93]

Four weeks into the strike, B.C. Federation of Labour officials met with joint council negotiators and Guild officers in an attempt to bring them back together in bargaining at Pacific Press, but the effort proved fruitless.[94] In May the joint council agreed on a three-year contract with wage increases of 5, 5, and 7 percent, which members of the craft unions ratified to end their strike after six weeks.[95] Pacific Press refused to bargain further with the Guild, and a membership meeting was called to vote on terms of the company's settlement with the craft unions. The union executive recommended rejection, said Young, after receiving a petition with the signatures of 400 members "telling us not to come to any agreement that doesn't contain provisions for job security."[96] Of the 690 striking Guild members who showed up to vote, 60 percent rejected the company offer at a meeting the *Globe and Mail* described as "stormy."

> Many people in the 950-member Guild say they will no longer be pushed around by the much-smaller craft unions. . . . According to many Guild members, it has been for too long a case of the tail wagging the dog. Now, "We're taking control of our own destiny," one said. They said the Guild has been treated with "utter contempt" by both the company and the craft unions and the vote was as much a vote against the two parties as it was against the proposed contract.[97]

Following Guild rejection of the offer, company negotiator George Townsend said the striking Guild members could be out of work "for a long time," because Pacific Press was unlikely to concede the job security provisions the white-collar workers were demanding. "The choice is theirs," said Townsend.[98] But after the company agreed to recognize seniority rights plant-wide, meaning that senior *Province* employees could "bump" more junior *Sun* workers, and vice versa, in the event the two papers were merged, Guild negotiators agreed to recommend acceptance of the previously rejected wage deal.[99] A second membership vote ratified the deal by 91 percent in what the *Globe and Mail* called an expression of "union pride" as much as anything. "It showed that, if we stand up for our rights, we can win," observed *Sun* reporter Bob Sarti.[100] The new-found Guild solidarity, earned by holding out on strike a week longer than the craft unions, meant that the company would have to deal with a stiffened union resolve three years later, but the question became whether Southam could afford to continue publishing two newspapers in Vancouver. General manager Bill Wheatley informed employees in an October letter that as a result of the strike, a loss of $5 million was forecast for Pacific Press in 1984.[101]

19 The Cheesecake Rebellion

St. Clair Balfour's retirement in the spring of 1985 as chairman of the Southam board of directors at 75 was short-lived. He was forced back into action that summer to prevent a hostile takeover of the newspaper company that had been operated by his family for five generations. His efforts were made urgent by personal tragedy, but their necessity could be traced back to the Pacific Press agreement he had negotiated with Don Cromie almost thirty years earlier. Southam had paid a ransom to Thomson in 1980 to extricate itself from the problematic Pacific Press partnership in hopes of resolving some of the troubles that had plagued the Vancouver newspaper monopoly, but instead the losing proposition began to pull Southam under as it had FP Publications.

Granting rich wage increases at Pacific Press in 1982 could not have come with worse timing; it was on the eve of a recession that cut Southam's earnings in half. High interest rates brought by the fiscal Darwinist policies of Reaganomics meant survival of the fittest in the business world of the early 1980s, and Southam's heavy debt load caused its earnings to suffer as a result. Then the seven-week strike at Pacific Press in 1984 brought more than $5 million in red ink, while a two-week shutdown at the *Montreal Gazette* added another $1.5 million in losses. Company president and newly promoted board chairman Gordon Fisher announced at the 1985 Southam annual meeting in April that the strike in Vancouver the year before had left Pacific Press with a $5.4 million loss for the year and its parent company with an inescapable solution. "The company's only newspaper that is a consistent money loser is the *Vancouver*

Province," warned Fisher. "The inevitable conclusion is that the *Vancouver Province* will not survive another strike at Pacific Press."[1]

Some of the non-newspaper ventures into which Fisher had steered Southam in a bid to diversify into investments less subject to the ups and downs of the economy had proven more of a bust than a boon to the company's bottom line. Coles Books lost more than $6 million in 1982, and the Videotex experiment, now called Infomart, that Southam had pioneered in a partnership with the *Toronto Star* had frittered away another $15 million in profits in the first five years of the decade.[2] When Southam's earnings for the first half of 1985 were released at the end of July, they were down a disappointing 20 percent from a year earlier. Soon the financial sharks began circling the foundering family firm, which became an inviting takeover target in an era of leveraged buyouts by corporate raiders whose strategy typically saw such large acquisitions sold off piecemeal for profit. The purchase of large blocks of widely held Southam shares anonymously through brokerage houses began to fuel speculation of a billion-dollar takeover bid by a mystery investor, pushing the price of Southam stock up more than $10 in two months of heavy trading to a record $65 by August 1. Then, as the crisis mounted, the publishing giant suddenly found itself leaderless: Fisher, only 56, fell ill with liver cancer. Into the breach stepped Balfour, taking over as acting Southam president in the absence of any apparent family successor.

Balfour's first strategy to stave off a hostile takeover of the firm his grandfather had founded in the previous century was to concoct some "shark repellent" to ward off corporate predators. A company bylaw change was proposed that would have required a minimum of 80 percent of shareholders to vote on any transactions involving more than 10 percent of company shares, similar to a provision enacted earlier that year as a defensive measure by the Knight-Ridder newspaper chain in the U.S.[3] As Southam family members still held more than a third of the company's shares, that would have made a takeover impossible without their approval, but the move was opposed by minority shareholders, and a lawyer representing investors threatened to challenge it in court. The motion was adjourned for a week and watered down at a meeting on August 8 to a requirement for a quorum of only 50 percent. After the bylaw change passed, a meeting of the Southam board was informed that Fisher had died.[4]

The diluted shark repellent failed to dissuade the persistent predator, whose identity became a subject of much speculation through August. Many thought the Maclean-Hunter publishing group, which had acquired half-ownership of the *Toronto Sun* chain of tabloids in 1982 to go along with its magazine empire, was the only corporate media player in Canada with the resources to swallow such large prey as Southam. Others speculated the mystery buyer was Conrad Black, who had been outbid by Thomson for FP Publications in 1980 and had recently acquired the troubled *Daily Telegraph* in London to take his Hollinger Inc. international. Some suspected Power Corp., the Quebec-based conglomerate headed by Paul Desmarais, which owned a chain of French-language tabloids. Southam family members secretly feared a non-newspaper company was behind the takeover bid, namely, Toronto real estate magnate George Mann backed by the Bronfman family fortune from Seagram's distillery.[5]

As trading in Southam shares reached a fever pitch in the last week of August, with 800,000 shares or 1.6 percent of outstanding stock changing hands that Friday, Balfour launched a desperate weekend gambit to protect the firm he had helped build. He approached Beland Honderich, the longtime publisher of the *Toronto Star*, whom he had known for decades and with whom he had done some business, although he had never been able to convince Honderich to add the nation's largest-circulation newspaper to Southam's chain. Balfour made an attractive business proposition to the venerable *Star* chairman and CEO, offering to trade a 20 percent stake in Southam for 30 percent ownership of the smaller Torstar Corp. The share swap would make Southam virtually invulnerable to takeover, with Torstar's holdings added to family stock. Honderich at first agreed, and the two giants of Canadian newspapers arranged to convene meetings of their respective boards on Monday morning to finalize the deal in order to head off a takeover bid expected that week. But the Torstar chairman wavered after consulting with aides, so Balfour reserved a room at the Royal York Hotel for an emergency meeting on Sunday to iron out the sticking points. Arriving early, he discovered to his horror that the room had not yet been made up by the hotel's maid service, in a scene described by the U.S. media business magazine *NewsInc.*

> Balfour's worst nightmare was right in front of him. Having just retired as chairman, he faced the prospect of watching his life's work fall into the hands of a complete stranger. . . . As he feverishly set about cleaning the room, he couldn't help but wonder

> what Honderich would think if he walked in to find him folding hospital corners.[6]

The deal was sealed in the tidied suite when Honderich agreed to limit Torstar's further purchases of Southam stock to 5 percent of the total, preventing a takeover of the chain by the daily, and to give Southam first right of refusal if Torstar wanted to sell the shares within the next ten years. After their boards ratified the near-merger the next day, its announcement brought howls of protest from speculators who had bought up Southam stock in expectation of its price being pushed even higher by takeover bidding. As Torstar exercised its option to buy another 5 percent of Southam stock the next day, raising its stake in the chain to 25 percent, Balfour quelled takeover speculation by announcing that the deal he had made with Honderich gave Torstar and Southam family members "absolute control" of the company.[7] But Balfour refused to divulge the exact extent of family holdings, because he still had considerable work to do in bolstering Southam solidarity before the ten-year "standstill" agreement with Torstar expired. "If it jells, we won't have to worry about anything ten years down the road," he predicted. "We'll both know that together nobody can take the company away."[8] The elderly Southam icon then began an attempt to pull together the disparate company holdings of founder William Southam's descendants, by now numbering in the hundreds. The Kent Commission had based its call for ownership restrictions in 1981 in part on the premise that Southam would eventually become vulnerable to takeover by bottom-line financiers unconcerned about editorial quality, the fate of many family newspapers. Fisher had dismissed takeover speculation in 1983 by denying reports that family holdings in Southam had dropped to 30 percent from 40 percent two years earlier. "I don't see how any outsider could figure out what the family interest was because that interest is held in a number of different estates, private companies, the names of which would not be clear to an outsider," he said.[9]

To make the takeover protection he had negotiated with Torstar work, Balfour had to coalesce family shareholders into a united voting block. He set about bringing the extended Southam clan together in an attempt to rekindle the enterprising spirit of his grandfather, commencing a tradition of huge dinners on the eve of annual shareholder meetings. Meanwhile, the search for a successor as company president continued.

Prospects in the family's third generation were bleak, while those in the following generation were mostly too young or uninterested. Desperate to keep the corporate reins in family hands, the Southam board turned to John Fisher, brother of the late company president but totally lacking in a newspaper background. An engineer by trade, he was president of a New Brunswick pulp and paper company with high-level management experience but little interest in, or aptitude for, the family business. "I have difficulty writing a letter," he confessed to a reporter.[10] Fisher first turned down the job, but when the Southam board returned to him in desperation after being unable to find another suitable family candidate, he accepted out of a sense of duty. "I felt it was a company my grandfather, my father and my brother all gave a good part of their life to," he told *Sun* business reporter Don Whiteley, who traveled to New Brunswick for a profile of the new Southam president. "I couldn't say no."[11]

Appointment of the reluctant Fisher was obviously a stopgap measure, and Southam management continued to search for a suitable family leader for the long term. Among the fourth generation of newspapering Southams, there was only one who showed an aptitude for publishing and had demonstrated enough interest in the family business to work his way up in it. According to journalist Patricia Best, family hopefuls "found their candidate in Harvey Southam, [who] was lured from his hometown of Vancouver to Toronto to begin working as an executive at Southam as part of a grooming process."[12] But the free-spirited West Coast native, then 37, was hardly the ideal candidate; in addition to his youth, his sometimes-reckless behavior belied the sober Southam family image. He admitted to *Province* columnist Lorne Parton in 1984 that he had been working at cleaning up his personal life. "A major thing I did 2½ years ago . . . is that I quit drinking," Southam told Parton. "After my first marriage broke up, I spent a lot of time in the press club and drank a lot of whisky. By the time I was 30–31, I got so that every six weeks or so, I would do something really stupid."[13] One of the stupidest was a drunken car crash that had brought an impaired-driving charge. While he was able to beat the rap with the aid of an expensive lawyer, the incident had served as a wake-up call that convinced the Southam scion to go on the wagon, he told Parton.[14]

Balfour returned to his retirement in the hope that his arrangement with Torstar had made Southam safe from hostile takeover for at least the next decade, while the family firm's hopes for the future rested more heavily than ever on the shoulders of troubled Harvey Southam. But the share swap had attracted the attention of regulators, who pointed out that the hastily made deal contravened Toronto Stock Exchange rules for advance disclosure of such arrangements. The TSE notified the Ontario Securities Commission, which began an investigation and set November 15 as the date for a hearing into allegations of impropriety. Within Southam, reported *NewsInc.* in 1993, some felt Balfour had panicked at the prospect of a takeover and instead of preventing financiers from plundering the family empire, he had actually sown the seeds of its inevitable demise.

> "At that time, the family had enough stock that [an acquisition] wouldn't have been a cake walk for anyone," says an executive no longer employed at Southam. "If Gordon [Fisher] were alive, he would have said, '*Try it!*' Clair lost sight of the fact he was doing a business deal and got totally outmaneuvered by people who were far smarter than him in business. I think he knows in his heart that he was the architect of the destruction of Southam."[15]

In Vancouver, the 1985 uncertainty surrounding Southam resulted in a major reorganization of Pacific Press management in March to improve profitability in an attempt to ward off the feared hostile takeover bid. Despite the *Province*'s popularity with readers and advertisers as a tabloid, the B.C. economy continued to slump, preventing any appreciable improvement of the Pacific Press bottom line. In a cost-cutting consolidation, *Sun* publisher Bill Wheatley announced he would move up to chief executive officer while Gerry Haslam became publisher of both newspapers. Norm Weitzel moved from the *Edmonton Journal* to become advertising director of both the *Sun* and *Province*, whose advertising departments were combined to maximize revenue.[16] Wheatley announced that no layoffs were planned, and that Southam had cleared the consolidation with federal authorities. Haslam promoted managing editors Bruce Larsen of the *Sun* and Bob McMurray of the *Province* to new positions as editors-in-chief, which placed them in charge of both news and opinion content of their newspapers. Haslam announced that as "super-publisher" of two newspapers which privately collaborated to divide the market between them but publicly competed for news, he would divorce himself from their editorial affairs. This, he said, meant maintaining confidentiality within editorial departments of the two newspapers, and even providing news tips on an alternating basis. "What is assigned and what is written is the sole preserve of the editors," said Haslam. "I have the right to advise, to warn, to caution, to comment, to express opinion, but I cannot say, under the arrangements that we will have, to McMurray or to Larsen, you will do this or you mustn't do that in terms of what is assigned and what is written."[17]

In April, eleven layoffs were announced as a result of the consolidation of *Sun* and *Province* advertising departments, while another dozen advertising staff who could not be laid off under the job security provisions negotiated by the Newspaper Guild in 1984 were reassigned and given the option of accepting voluntary severance pay.[18] Not only did the Guild not object, but it took the situation seriously and set about formulating its own suggestions for improving the bottom line at Pacific Press in an attempt to save its remaining members' jobs. The Guild submitted a brief to Haslam with proposals for improving business by meeting the challenge of community weeklies for the suburban advertising market, including regaining the advertising flyer distribution business lost during the 1984 strike.[19] The document was leaked to the *Courier*, which published excerpts. With uninterrupted publication in 1985, Pacific Press cuts its losses for the fiscal year to just under $100,000.

In March 1986, new Southam president John Fisher visited Vancouver and warned in a speech to the Canadian Club that while the company was committed to publishing both the *Sun* and *Province* six days a week until the end of the year, negotiations for new union contracts in 1987 would in large part determine the future of the Pacific Press newspapers. "This year if Pacific Press meets its targets, it will achieve a 4.5 per cent pre-tax return on revenue," he said. "The basic cost structures built into our collective labor agreements make the task of turning Pacific Press around particularly difficult. If . . . we cannot foresee a reasonable return for our shareholders from the publication of 12 newspapers [at Pacific Press] each week, we will have to look at publishing less than the 12."[20] Later that year, Fisher told *Media Magazine* that the upcoming contract negotiations at Pacific Press would go a long way to deciding whether Southam could continue its commitment to publish two daily newspapers in Vancouver. "Pacific Press is not a public service," said Fisher. "It is a business that should produce much more revenue than it is doing. . . . We spent close to $50 million buying the other half of Pacific Press and we are getting absolutely no return on that."[21]

In July, a meeting of the Southam board in Vancouver was told that in the absence of an expected economic boom, which had failed to materialize despite the World's Fair that had begun in May, cost cutbacks would have to be made at Pacific Press in order to achieve an "acceptable" profit.[22] A transcript of the remarks was sent to employees by Wheatley, who called "disturbing" a Pacific Press profit of only $1.1 million for the first six months of the year, since it was much lower than projections. "The question of the viability of the company in its present form is still one of doubt by the Southam board, its shareholders, and the financial analysts," he warned.[23] As the collective agreements with the Pacific Press unions expired at the end of February, business analysts taking the pulse of ailing Southam turned their attention to the West Coast to watch bargaining developments in order to ascertain the future financial health of the newspaper chain, observed the *Globe and Mail*.

> Sixteen months after succeeding to the presidency of Southam Inc., John Fisher's date with destiny has finally arrived. . . . Investment analysts have long had March, 1987, circled on their calendars as the true test of Mr. Fisher's mettle. . . . The outcome of negotiations over the next few months could prove crucial both to perceptions of his leadership and the fortunes of the giant Toronto-based communications company.[24]

A pre-tax profit of $6 million at Pacific Press in 1986 represented only a 4 percent return on revenue, far short of the company's target of 15 percent, which had been exceeded that year by Southam's thirteen other dailies. Paddy Sherman, now installed at Southam headquarters in Toronto and in charge of all company newspaper operations, made it his mission to tame the unions that had caused him so much trouble while he was publisher of the *Province*. "Henceforth, the Vancouver papers have to be treated like all the other papers," he told the *Globe and Mail*. "There will be no subsidizing the Vancouver papers. They will have to stand on their own two feet."[25] The story reported unnamed senior Southam executives describing the Pacific Press negotiations of 1987 as the most important in company history. "Southam is determined to tame the most militant newspaper locals in the country and [to] bring costs at its Vancouver papers in line with others in the chain."[26] The strategy formulated in Toronto to solve the Pacific Press problem was extreme and, if implemented, could have caused the same labor chaos Southam had precipitated four decades earlier by publishing the *Province* from behind a picket line. According to the publisher of the *Sun* and *Province* at the time, the plan was to do just that again. To compound the degree of difficulty for Southam in its bid to break the Vancouver newspaper unions in 1987, the level of professional discontent at the *Sun* peaked that fall, when journalists at the afternoon newspaper brewed a rebellion of their own just as contract negotiations reached a climax.

Early in 1986 the *Sun* was redesigned with increased national and international news coverage, backed by a $500,000 advertising campaign that played to the pride of Vancouverites in hosting the World's Fair with the slogan "The whole world in your hands." Haslam announced that "Vancouver" would be returned to the newspaper's title, as market research had found its removal in 1983, in an attempt to appeal to suburban readers, had instead upset many. "We found that Vancouverites are very proud of their city, and more so this year because of Expo 86," said the paper's new publisher.[27] Color was added to every section front, and new headline and body text type faces were introduced, which led to comparisons with *USA Today*, the colorful national newspaper in the U.S. that was founded in 1982 and emphasized colorful graphics over news content.[28] Public reaction to the cosmetic changes was mixed, but the redesign was panned by a cynical *Sun* staff, which did not like sharing a publisher with their newspaper's morning rival. With Haslam's marketing initiatives, *Sun* journalists saw their newspaper being manipulated for marketing purposes as the *Province* had been when it was converted to a tabloid. The *Globe and Mail* noted that since the rejuvenation of its morning cousin, the *Sun* had been left with declining circulation and a sense of ennui.

> The new vigor of *The Province* unmasked the lethargy of the *Sun*. Compared with the flood of new advertising at *The Province*, advertising at the broadsheet was stable — a euphemism for flat — and had been for years. . . . Somehow, the *Sun* had become dis-

> located, alienated, estranged from many of its readers. A history of corporate horsetrading was at the root of its identity crisis. The *Sun* has run through three publishers and three owners . . . in six years.[29]

The *Sun* journalists objected to their newspaper being designed, like the *Province*, to appeal to the wishes of readers as divined by survey takers instead of by editors who had developed the news judgment to decide what the public should know. Haslam convinced Larsen as part of the 1986 typographical redesign to commission market research to better define the *Sun*'s target readership as the *Province* had done, but the old-time journalist proved less amenable to marketing than departed publisher Clark Davey. "I always got the feeling when I was on that side of the building that there was this frostiness toward me," recalled Halsam. "There was resistance, clearly, to the perceived marketing initiatives of a publisher who probably wasn't a journalist. I had been a journalist most of my life, but I wasn't perceived as one at the *Sun*."[30] The attitude of many at the *Sun* was summed up by former assistant city editor Ian Gill, an Australian who quit the afternoon newspaper in disgust for a reporting position at CBC television. "Cowed by the hoofbeats of corporatism, its spirit audited away by bureaucrats masquerading as newsmen, the *Sun* has been lassoed, corralled and broken; all its gallop gone, a snort or a whinny now and then the only vital signs," wrote Gill in a scathing review of the *Sun*'s remake for *Vancouver* magazine. "Six days a week, 'We put the whole world in your hands.' Never has a slogan sounded so hollow."[31] The direction of *Sun* news coverage had increasingly followed the formula employed by the tabloid *Province*, Gill noted, to the chagrin of many in the newsroom.

> Rather than building on a readership that for years had demanded more of it than of the *Province*, rather than fighting the increased acceptance of the *Globe and Mail* by its high-end readership, the *Sun* ducked down the same alley as the *Province* in search of liver-needing tots, savage dogs and terminal diseases — the "human" side of the news.[32]

Since the remake, by late 1987, Gill counted nine *Sun* journalists who had left the newspaper, including star columnist Marjorie Nichols, who moved to the *Ottawa Citizen*. "I was no longer proud to work at the *Van-*

couver Sun," said Nichols. "The *Sun* was a prestigious paper — it is no longer. No one person leaving makes a difference, but we have gone beyond the failsafe."[33] The city affairs column had been given over to consumer columnist Nicole Parton, noted Gill, the wife of *Province* columnist Lorne Parton. "It is almost impossible to find the op-ed pages anyway," groused Gill. "Once on pages four and five (even six, sometimes seven) of the A section — opinions prominently displayed — *Sun* commentary was sent packing to the B section last year. Midway through this year, it was sent even deeper toward oblivion, now holding down the back of the B-section."[34] In a sidebar, former *Sun* investigative reporter Rick Ouston, also then at the CBC, described as "floating" the remade paper's editorial page. "One day on page B6, another on C4 — its significance [is] being destroyed by never having a page to call home."[35] Most seriously in the eyes of many at the *Sun*, the failure to fill a vacancy in the Ottawa bureau due to cost-cutting had left the *Sun* as the only major daily in Canada without a correspondent in the nation's capital. Gill recited a litany of complaints about the afternoon newspaper that surpassed even those chronicled by Clive Cocking and Sean Rossiter in earlier volumes of *Vancouver*.

> Reporters are being worn down by seeing their copy roughly chopped and rewritten, and by seeing original stories killed while having to monitor and "match" the *Province*, the *Globe*, CKNW radio and CBC and BCTV newscasts. . . . Editors do not trust *Sun* reporters to use unnamed sources in all but the rarest of cases, which means the paper has essentially given up breaking political stories. Mildly controversial stories are shipped off to a lawyer, whose legal judgment can obviate a decision being made on a piece's editorial merits.[36]

Soon *Sun* staff began discussing how they could get their newspaper back on the track of editorial excellence they felt it had been derailed from by Haslam's cost-cutting and marketing initiatives. A group of about thirty met surreptitiously across Granville Street from the Pacific Press Building late in the summer of 1987 to plan strategy. "They felt the *Sun* was becoming a newspaper they would not buy if there were any real choice in the city," according to a 1989 internal summary of the uprising.[37] They met not at the boozy, smoky Press Club but at a coffee bar called Cheesecake, etc. down the street to consider their options, which included withdrawing their bylines in protest, going public with their complaints, or taking them to Southam's head office. According to Ouston, the uprising was significant for encompassing journalists of all political persuasions and degrees of loyalty to management.

> It would have been an odd sight to a media-watching fly on the wall. . . . Bob Sarti, perpetual shop steward and left-winger, agreeing with small-T tory Moira Farrow that something was definitely wrong with the newspaper. Gadabout columnist Denny Boyd linking names with sober business editor Judy Lindsay in hopes of improving journalism in our town. The highly regarded Alan Daniels — who writes transportation for the *Sun* and who has never complained publicly about anything — was elected a spokesman for the group.[38]

Sun managing editor Gordon Fisher (not the same man as the late Southam president) caught wind of the meeting and on October 7 wrote a memo to Farrow and Daniels, offering to hold a meeting to air any complaints before they were forwarded to corporate headquarters in Toronto. A letter accepting the offer and outlining their grievances was sent across the street to Fisher on October 11, with copies to Haslam and Larsen. It was signed by fifty-five reporters and editors, a vast majority of *Sun* editorial staff. Describing themselves as "a group of journalists who are concerned at the direction the newspaper has taken in the past two years," the coffeehouse crowd announced that "frustration has built to the point where we can no longer remain silent."[39] Their letter requested an explanation of why the *Sun* had "been changed from an intelligent, occasionally impertinent newspaper to one that so many Vancouver people no longer wanted to read."[40] The lack of an Ottawa bureau, they charged, was a "major embarrassment for Canada's third largest city," while the failure to name a new sports editor for a year had seen the *Sun* "walk away from its responsibilities" to the point where it had stopped sending a reporter on the road with the NHL Canucks.[41] Reaction to the newspaper's lack of suburban council coverage had come from municipal politicians as early as 1984, when the *Sun* suspended its attendance at the meetings.[42] The once-important newspaper, the Cheesecake rebels claimed, was no longer respected as a result of its switch in emphasis from hard news to colorful design.

> We believe it has deteriorated in substance, in style, and its day to day news coverage. The columnists no longer have the depth and range of those who previously adorned this newspaper. Readers apparently agree with our assessment. The Lower Mainland is one of the fastest growing areas in Canada, yet the *Sun*'s circulation continues to drop.[43]

Reprinted in the two-page letter were a half page of comments from Boyd, who admitted that "for the first time in 30 years, I have absolutely no understanding of the philosophy, the direction of the paper." The veteran columnist complained that *Sun* journalists were "working in a vacuum" without being informed of the newspaper's purpose, and their loyalty was being eroded as a result. "If management has a game plan, why doesn't management share it with the players? Surely that is not just courtesy, it is sound management procedure. It is hard to remain loyal to a phantom." Boyd wrote that *Sun* journalists suspected their newspaper was "going the way of *USA Today*, shedding our traditional character for dubious marketing gimmicks."[44] The journalists insisted they sought not confrontation but "some reassurance from management that there is a future for serious journalism in Vancouver. . . . We are proud of our work and want to regain the pride we once held for this newspaper."[45]

Despite Fisher's earlier assurances that his "door was always open," the journalists received no official reply to their complaints. According to Gill, Fisher "offered small group sessions — 'divide and conquer,' as one suspicious reporter put it — instead of the general meeting that had been requested."[46] As a result, they forwarded them, as originally planned, to Paddy Sherman at Southam headquarters in Toronto ten days later. "We all feel Vancouver deserves better," they wrote Sherman. "We want to do better."[47] Only then did they get their meeting with *Sun* management. According to Ouston, seventy journalists attended the weekend confrontation with Haslam, Larsen, and Fisher, who "listened to the complaints and disagreed with most."[48] Three years later, in an update for *Vancouver* magazine, Gill characterized management's reaction as a "shallow and defensive response one might expect from an ossified junta of penny-pinchers who had long since forgotten what battle they were fighting, and appeared to consider everyone an enemy."[49] But according to a 1989 internal summary of the dispute written by *Sun* reporter Douglas Sagi, who had authored the 1987 letters of protest, the "Cheesecakers" felt they had achieved several goals, including the installation of an Ottawa correspondent, the naming of a sports editor, the appointment of several new columnists, and a lessened emphasis on "soft" news.[50] The paper's wandering opinion pages, according to Gill in 1990, "finally bounced back into the A-section, where they belong."[51]

Haslam realized that many of the complaints were valid, but under corporate protocol he could not explain that his hands were tied by the cost-cutting measures instituted by Southam's head office. "It was a legitimate rebellion," he admitted in 1999. "I agreed with them. The problem was I couldn't say the truth, which was I'd been ordered to do it. I hadn't been ordered to move the editorial page around like a ping-pong ball, but I'd been ordered to save X amount of money and that was the only way to do it."[52] The cutbacks were the result of directives from Southam headquarters, he said. "From the moment Sherman took office in 1986, every Friday morning there was a senior management meeting in Toronto. Every Friday afternoon Wheatley would get a fax saying, 'Tell us how you're saving money.' Paddy was funny that way. He said, 'cut, cut, cut,' and when you did and people got mad, he said, 'It's your fault, not mine.'"[53]

Sherman defended the cutbacks he made at Southam head office as necessary to streamline the newspaper chain's operations. "I did work very hard to rationalize a lot of economic factors," said Sherman. "Basically I felt that Southam was being very inefficiently run. There's no doubt about that. . . . I was revising the whole structure."[54]

As usual, contract negotiations at Pacific Press did not get off to a good start in 1987. Bargaining with the Newspaper Guild broke down in January after company negotiators broached issues that the union considered "non-negotiable." Guild president Mel Morris claimed company proposals to cut back on health and welfare benefits and reduce night differential payments, which added 10 percent to the wages of any worker whose shift went past 6 p.m., "strike at the very heart of our contract and . . . would put our members' jobs in jeopardy."[55] In February, mediator Jack Chapelas joined the talks as an observer. Meanwhile, back in Toronto, a corporate plan was formulated to publish at Pacific Press from behind a picket line, which in the testy B.C. labor climate risked turning the square block occupied by the company's Granville Street printing plant into a battle zone. In British Columbia the union movement reached its zenith in 1987 with a one-day province-wide walkout on June 1 to protest changes to provincial labor law planned by new Social Credit premier Bill Vander Zalm. The general strike was called to oppose Bill 19, the Industrial Relations Reform Act, which would have enabled a new Industrial Relations Council to end any strike deemed not in the public interest. An estimated 300,000 unionized workers took the day off and picked up picket signs in protest, shutting down much of the provincial economy, including the Pacific Press newspapers.[56] The enormity of Southam's union-busting scheme became apparent to local Pacific Press managers, who persuaded corporate officials to give up the idea, according to Haslam. "We prepared a plan . . . of how to publish the papers during a strike," revealed Haslam in 1999. "We could have done it. It would have cost us something like $5 million a month. We finally abandoned the idea, thank God."[57]

Paddy Sherman denied Haslam's allegation, which he called outrageous. "I can only remember one occasion when there was very serious thought being given to publishing [behind picket lines]. That was during Dave Stinson's time. We vetoed that." Sherman recalled coming out to Vancouver in 1986 or 1987 to meet with the unions and laying Southam's financial situation on the line to them.

> I remember telling the unions that productivity was appalling and costs were outrageous and that the only thing that differentiated this operation from other Southam operations was that in those other operations management had taken strikes and continued to publish. I said obviously that's something we'll have to consider very seriously here if we can't reach a rational agreement. I phrased it in such a wsay that, as I recall, there was no umbrage taken. I don't recall it ever got to the stage where we actually planned to publish. I certainly never had a plan in place.[58]

Sherman said that whenever a strike loomed, members of management prepared to operate the Pacific Press printing machinery in case Guild members could be persuaded to settle separately and cross craft union picket lines. "But we never said we'd put out the papers without all the unions. When virtually every negotiation came along, and certainly the big ones, we always had a plan if necessary to run the pressroom. . . . I don't think anyone ever seriously thought that would happen. It was all part of the theatre." Sherman recalled that, due to his mountain-climbing agility, during his days in the management suite at 2250 Granville Street his mechanical battle station was in the basement of the Pacific Press Building. "[Press room foreman] Roy Edgell said that all he needed to run a press was four guys who would shut up and do what they're told. He said, 'I want you, because you can clamber around the press much faster than anybody else.'"[59]

It was not until October that bargaining at Pacific Press got serious in 1987. The pressmen's union voted to strike on October 25 but refused to have balloting supervised by the new Industrial Relations Council, which had been placed under boycott by the B.C. Federation of Labour.[60] The pressmen were asking for a four-day week in exchange for allowing the scheduling changes required to publish the *Sun*'s Saturday edition earlier in the morning, but company negotiator Stu Noble called the demand "economically unfeasible."[61] Pacific Press applied to the IRC for an order declaring the pressmen's strike vote invalid, which was granted on October 28.[62] As Newspaper Guild members moved to conduct a strike vote, the union's leaders were warned by the B.C. Fed to respect the IRC boycott and not to break ranks with the craft unions, as they had done in 1984. "If the guild doesn't go along with it, they'll have to answer to the rest of the unions in B.C.," said Federation president Ken Georgetti. "I'm sure the guild will do the right thing."[63] Talks continued without a Guild strike vote being taken, and as bargaining broke off on November 6, the old bugaboo of "production problems" resulted in less than half of the *Province* press run of 210,000 being completed.[64]

Mediator Vince Ready got the sides back together for a marathon bargaining session that weekend, and after twenty-three straight hours of negotiations an agreement was reached on November 8. The forty-five-month contract provided a retroactive wage increase of 2.3 percent for the nine months since the last contract expired, plus wage increases of 3.5, 4, and 4.1 percent over the next three years.[65] The unusually long contract was made more palatable to the unions by including a cost-of-living provision that could raise the final year's increase to 6 percent if inflation exceeded that amount. While the wage increases were meagre by past Pacific Press standards, the unions had done as well as they could have expected in the prevailing climate of financial restraint. More importantly, they had escaped the showdown many had forecast with their rich wages and guaranteed jobs intact. But the settlement was another nail in the coffin for family ownership of Southam, as corporate resolve in dealing with the unions at Pacific Press was seen by financial analysts to have faltered.

In addition to costing Pacific Press millions of dollars over the years in salaries for printers who had long since been made redundant by computer technology, the militancy of the Pacific Press craft unions also cost the company millions in lost revenue. Even as the printers were reduced to typing stories dictated over the telephone by reporters into the computer system or to playing cards in the composing room out of idleness, those who handled advertising copy refused to touch anything from an employer that had been declared "hot" by the B.C. Federation of Labour. In 1984, a lockout of theatre workers by the Famous Players chain cost Pacific Press $750,000 in lost revenue when printers refused to handle its movie ads. A company appeal to the Labour Relations Board failed to get the ad ban declared illegal.[66] In 1985, a strike by workers at Pacific Western Airlines brought a similar "hot" edict, and Pacific Press printers refused to handle the airline ads. PWA went to the B.C. Supreme Court to get the union ban lifted, to no avail.[67] The lost revenue for Pacific Press added up to another $250,000.[68] Then in 1986, when unionized building trades went on strike rather than accept wage cuts, ITU members at Pacific Press refused to handle ads for replacement workers willing to cross picket lines. "They are advertising for scab labor and we are protesting that," said union president Harold Dieno. "We are not going to handle it."[69] Pacific Press decided against forcing the issue, fearing the union response would be a walkout, "which would effectively shut us down," said Stu Noble, the company's vice-president of human resources.[70]

When letter carriers went on strike in 1987, Canada Post placed ads in forty-five newspapers across the country to recruit replacement workers but could not do so in Vancouver because of the ITU's refusal to handle them. Pacific Press applied for an LRB order, confident the "hot" edict would be ruled illegal, because a B.C. Supreme Court judge had earlier that year found the LRB decision in the Famous Players case flawed legally.[71] LRB vice-chairman John Hall threw out the postal application despite the legal precedent, however, ruling that only the provincial legislature could overrule a labor board decision.[72] "Quite frankly, we're all amazed," said Noble.[73] "This is great," said Dieno.[74] In 1988 Pacific Press appealed to the new Industrial Relations Council, which outlawed secondary boycotts such as "hot" edicts. However, in a surprising decision, the IRC ruled that the new provincial legislation did not apply to the postal workers, who were covered by federal labor law.[75]

Switching tack, Pacific Press then went to court for an injunction against the anticipated refusal of printers to handle ads for replacement workers from cabinet maker Citation Industries of Richmond, which had fired 130 striking workers after they defied an IRC order to cease and desist from picketing. That did not work either, as the judge ruled the application speculative.[76] When the Citation ads appeared at Pacific Press, ITU printers handled them "under protest." Then when strike-bound White Spot restaurants placed ads for workers at three of its non-union restaurants, the Pacific Press unions again objected, this time halting the *Sun*'s press run partway through to delete the ads from the remaining 75,000 copies to be printed that day.[77] When Pacific Press again went to the IRC for relief, this time with a dispute firmly in provincial jurisdiction, it hoped to finally put the thorny issue to rest. But instead the IRC ruled the "hot goods" clause in the Pacific Press collective agreement with its unions was not invalid under Bill 19, and such prohibitions could still be imposed.[78]

As Southam earnings lagged with a drop in retail advertising, Paddy Sherman announced from head office that additional cost-cutting measures would be instituted at the chain's newspapers in an attempt to make them "lean and tight."[79] At Pacific Press, where financial returns continued to fall behind the goals set by Southam, Wheatley announced that a hiring freeze would be imposed as a result of the head-office directive.[80] The corporate belt-tightening came after a legal challenge to Southam's 1985 share swap with Torstar again made it vulnerable to takeover. The maneuver had been challenged by minority shareholders who lost money when Southam's stock price fell after the feared takeover bid was foiled, but a 1986 Ontario Securities Commission hearing into irregularities in the deal had resulted in only a six-month trading ban imposed on directors of the two companies.[81] The disgruntled speculators then convinced the federal Department of Consumer and Corporate Affairs to intervene with a lawsuit to force a vote of company shareholders on the share swap and to award financial damages.[82] The lawsuit carried the possibility that Southam and Torstar directors could be held liable for the lost profits of minority shareholders, so on the eve of the trial in September 1988 they negotiated a settlement by agreeing to cut from ten years to five the "standstill" agreement under which Torstar could not increase its Southam holdings.[83]

The result was that Southam would be "in play" as a takeover target again by 1990 instead of 1995, which prompted Fisher to attempt defensive measures in the interim. He resolved to raise the value of Southam over the next twenty-one months to put the company out of reach of corporate raiders. "We have great assets that have been underperforming," Fisher told the *Financial Post*. "Our primary focus is to get the appropriate return from these wonderful assets."[84] As trading in Southam shares again increased, takeover speculation centred on Conrad Black's Hollinger Inc., which had been on a buying spree of U.S. newspapers since turning around the fortunes of its *Daily Telegraph* in London with a move to non-union production away from the militant guilds of Fleet Street.[85] Fisher urged Southam employees to hold onto shares bought under the company's stock purchase plan instituted in 1986 rather than sell them for profit on the open market. "A change in majority ownership, whether friendly or hostile, could reduce or even eliminate the freedom of operation and concern for people which all parts of our company enjoy now," Fisher wrote in a letter to employee shareholders. He added that their 3.5 percent holdings in Southam "will be a critical bloc in any vote for ownership change that might occur."[86]

In an attempt to improve its fortunes in Vancouver, Southam announced in 1988 a plan to upgrade its printing facilities with a new plant in suburban Surrey. The $50-million facility would operate in addition to the Granville Street presses and would use a new water-based printing technology called "Flexography," which printed newspapers whose ink would not rub off on readers' hands.[87] Survey researchers had found black fingers from reading the *Sun* and *Province* to be a major irritant with Vancouverites, along with delivery delays that were caused by increased downtown traffic. It was hoped a new printing plant in the suburbs would alleviate that problem when it opened in 1990. In Toronto, Sherman prepared to move back to Vancouver and take personal control of the situation at Pacific Press.

"I told the [Southam] board there were some things that needed to be done out there," said Sherman. "I would be chairman of Pacific Press while I looked for a new head of the company. There were a lot of problems with [George Townsend's] dealings with the unions at the time, and Wheatley was backing him. The result, in my judgment, was a bit of a mess."[88]

As he posed holding a shovel with Surrey mayor Bob Bose and other Pacific Press management at the sod-turning ceremony for the new Surrey plant on October 25, Sherman had a plan to deal with the problem once and for all.

20 Buying the Competition

In 1989, Paddy Sherman returned to the mountainous coast, whose peaks he loved to climb, after seven years of scaling the Southam corporate hierarchy, first as publisher of the *Ottawa Citizen* and then at the corporate head office in charge of newspaper operations. He came back to Vancouver with a strategy for solving the Pacific Press problem that had plagued him for so long and that was now starting to weigh Southam down and make it vulnerable to corporate takeover due to its faltering financial performance. In September 1988 he had promoted Stu Noble, whose background was in mining, to president of Pacific Press and demoted Haslam to vice-president of marketing, leaving both the *Sun* and *Province* without a publisher.[1] "Publisher in the structure of Pacific Press was a very anomalous character," said Sherman of the decision to go without a top executive at each newspaper.

> Certainly the publisher of the *Province* was only half a publisher in that he couldn't make the decisions that he could be making regarding the profitability of his paper. If everything he wanted to do to improve his paper would run afoul of the structure, then what was the point of having two people sitting there, neither of whom could make the decisions a normal publisher would make?[2]

In July 1989 he reconstituted the Pacific Press board of directors that had been dissolved after Southam bought the *Sun* in 1980, installing on it local heavyweights such as Senator Pat Carney. The former *Province* and *Sun* business columnist had quit Pacific Press during the 1970 strike and gone on to a career in federal politics, holding the Vancouver Centre riding and a series of cabinet portfolios from 1980 until 1988, when she retired.[3] "Paddy wants to have people active in the Vancouver community become involved with the papers there," explained Southam public relations spokesman Brian Butters in suburban Toronto.[4] Now 61, Sherman set himself up as board chairman in charge of Pacific Press operations. Following the corporate housecleaning, he undertook the rebuilding of Pacific Press with a clean slate, as the editors of both papers departed.

Bruce Larsen retired in 1989 after fifteen years as the top editor at the *Vancouver Sun*. Into his spot Southam parachuted Nick Hills, who had headed its news service for seven years. Hills, 50, was a widely respected English newsman whose resume included four years in London as correspondent for Southam News and a five-year posting in Vancouver as its western bureau chief. In 1976, while briefly a *Sun* senior editor, Allan Fotheringham had urged publisher Stuart Keate to hire Hills, whom he described as "a determined little ferret," away from Southam, warning that Sherman might land him for the *Province* if he did not take the editor's job at either the *Montreal Gazette* or *Edmonton Journal*. "Hills' main asset is his sheer enthusiasm for the black art we practice," Fotheringham told Keate in a memo. "He is a born newspaperman in that he is sneaky, a gossip, competitive and deliciously gleeful when he can beat someone to a story."[5] According to former *Sun* editorial writer Richard Littlemore, Hills was "lovingly referred to as 'the Lebanese Truck' for his ability to step into a room and add an unpredictable and not always helpful burst of energy."[6] Ian Gill described Hills in *Vancouver* magazine as a "short and pugnacious" man.

> Hills often self-mockingly portrayed himself as a Napoleonic figure at Southam News, and confessed such a fascination for the emperor's ways that on his departure for Vancouver, Hills' staff at Southam News gave him a richly custom-made Napoleonic hat. He . . . is known for an ego beside which, according to Alan Daniels, the veteran business reporter, "all else pales in comparison."[7]

With the installation of Hills as editor of the *Sun*, the dark years of Larsen's reign were finally over, and many hoped the leadership of a world-class journalist would inject a new vitality into the paper's news coverage. Hills did not disappoint them in that regard, loosening the travel budget to send a team of *Sun* reporters to Alaska to cover the *Exxon Valdez* oil spill in Prince William Sound and assigning Denny Boyd to take a three-week tour of the crumbling Soviet Union. The *Sun*'s new editor insisted the travel budget had not been increased, only used. "In the past, I suspect there was a philosophy that said, let's try and make ourselves look good by not spending a lot of money," he told former *Province* reporter Mike Gasher. "There is a lot of talent here and it's just a question of making the most of it. *The Sun*'s had bad press, as they say. It's just a question of building up the old reputation."[8]

Hills also introduced a new era of introspection at the hitherto secretive daily. "*The Sun* is even covering itself," wrote Gasher in *content*, the magazine of the Centre for Investigative Journalism. "A full-page feature in July scrutinized the newspaper's coverage of Hong Kong immigration. In August, *The Sun* carried a lengthy story on its first business page about the hiring of South African journalist Gerald Proselandis as business editor."[9] Hills' attempt to hire Proselandis, who had applied for the business editor's job while visiting Vancouver on vacation from Johannesburg, noted Gill, was an early indication of both the new *Sun* editor's determination to have his own way and the resistance he would encounter. "In his first real test of will with the Pacific Press unions, Hills found that, Proselandis' qualifications and avowed abhorrence of apartheid aside, no editor was going to hire a South African over a Canadian."[10]

Running a story by *Sun* education reporter Frances Bula on the newsroom revolt sparked by a series on the growing influx of Asian immigrants to Vancouver demonstrated the degree of journalistic openness Hills was determined to achieve, but it also foreshadowed the backlash he would encounter to some of his editorial and managerial initiatives. When a team of *Sun* reporters was assigned to examine the effect of immigration from Hong Kong on Vancouver, several of the journalists balked at covering the story. Reporters rebelled against what they considered an ill-advised inflammation of growing racial tensions, according to Bula, but Hills justified the assignment on the basis of newsworthiness. "There are just too many stories around, says the British-born Hills, about elderly people being forced out of their apartments by Hong Kong buyers, or Chinese people buying million-dollar houses sight unseen, for that not to be a valid story. 'This is not something we've made up.'"[11] According to Ian Gill, Hills' response to criticism from feminists in the *Sun* newsroom about the paper's coverage of the December 1989 massacre of fourteen female university students in Montreal was more pointed. When a petition signed by fifteen journalists complained they were "ashamed" that the *Sun* "had no credible voice that spoke to women's issues," Hills snapped back with a memo of his own that called the criticism "ill-conceived." The political correctness rampant among the ranks of *Sun* reporters was beginning to grate on the paper's new editor, whose memo smacked of petulance. "Journalists ought to write, not whine," he lectured staff.[12]

In part to counter the allegations of racial insensitivity, Hills installed a full-time correspondent in Hong Kong. He also hired longtime local activist Stan Persky, a community college instructor, to write a media column in a new "Saturday Review" section. Persky, who was originator and editor of the B.C. Federation of Labour's short-lived 1983 weekly newspaper, *Solidarity Times*, described himself as a "social critic" when he testified before the Kent Commission in 1981. But others, like Boyd, considered him part of the "renegade flank of the loony left-wing" for which Vancouver had earned itself a reputation as a haven with such measures as the socialist-dominated city council's declaration of Vancouver as a "nuclear-free" zone. "Stan Persky is a Higher Purpose Person," observed Boyd on the occasion of the activist's arrest in 1986 for taking a hammer to bottles of South African wine as television cameras recorded his protest of apartheid.

> Poor Persky, he wants to be famous but he can't pass the means test. He has tried three times to be elected chancellor of the University of B.C. so that he can have a visible platform. He has failed three times. He also failed last month to get the New Democratic Party nomination in Vancouver-Point Grey, but he keeps his name in the news.[13]

Three years later, Boyd and Persky were columnist colleagues as the radical had his own weekly forum in the *Sun* with which to critique the Vancouver media, which meant in large part passing judgment on his own newspaper.

Hills also proved much more amenable to market research than had Larsen, and soon consultants were streaming in and out of his office. Political pollster Angus Reid was hired at a cost of $100,000 to define the afternoon newspaper's "target audience," which Larsen had long resisted doing. Reid divided the *Sun*'s potential audience into groups ranked by their potential to boost the newspaper's sagging circulation as new customers. The segment of the population least attractive to the *Sun* was the 11 percent Reid described as the "insular forlorn," noted Ian Gill in *Vancouver* magazine, and Reid urged editors to "forget this group."[14] Above them were such people as "middle-class joiners," "home bodies," and "post-literate hedonists." According to the consultant, of more interest in building the *Sun*'s target audience should be the 21 percent at the top of the readership spectrum, a group Reid dubbed "literate acquisitors," who "are not reading the *Sun* as often as they should."[15] Literate acquisitors were deemed the *Sun*'s target audience as much as anything for their disposable income, according to Gill.

> Reid's "psychographics" reveal them to be readers and experimenters, neither traditional nor conservative, who are unlikely to see TV as a major source of entertainment, have good self-esteem, do not worry about finances, and possess strong social responsibility. They want a "reliable, in-depth, serious/professional, hard-hitting/investigative, thought-provoking" paper.[16]

Hills set about providing more "literacy" on the pages of the *Sun*, promising that Vancouver "is a very eclectic, sophisticated city and it deserves a sophisticated newspaper and it's going to get it."[17] But the move to target a more upscale readership resulted in resistance from other departments at the newspaper to some measures seen as self-defeating, such as banishing downscale crime stories from the *Sun*'s front page. "Pressure from the circulation department has convinced editors that crime does pay, at least on the front page," noted *B.C. Report*. "Managers are, however, still determined to be up-market on the inside pages. Not surprisingly, some *Sun* staffers feel the paper lacks direction."[18]

Hills next set about diagnosing what was wrong with the management structure he had inherited from Larsen. A consultant commissioned to gauge the state of discontent at Pacific Press concluded from interviewing employees throughout the Granville Street plant in 1990 that management style appeared to be "patterned on the traditional values of news reporting — reactive and crisis-oriented."[19] Employees were "starved for information" as a result, concluded consultant Rodon Communications, as management kept underlings in the dark by failing to hold regular staff meetings. Pacific Press president Stu Noble started a company newsletter, *Newsline*, to keep employees abreast of information, including Rodon's damning indictment of management's poor record of internal communications, which was excerpted.

> Interviewees compared management's attitude to communication to that of a reporter on the trail of a scoop or of a poker player with a royal flush. Information is power and "it is jealously guarded." Employees said communication is top down; that even when information reaches middle management it is rarely passed on; that many managers aren't interested in the opinions of those below them.[20]

The accounting firm of Coopers & Lybrand was commissioned to analyze the *Sun*'s management structure with a "Performance Improvement Program Diagnostic Review." It reported "a high and, we believe, genuine level of unhappiness among departmental employees."[21] The managerial review revealed an operational structure rife with counterproductive practices. "Organizational health (including employee morale and personal job satisfaction) is poor," reported the consultants. "Second-guessing by senior management is too frequent. . . . Many of the basic management practices are not in place or are not working well."[22] Hiring and promotion were seen by the rank and file as a foregone conclusion, the consultants noted, with applications from most staff ignored in favor of candidates preferred by management. As a result, Hills set up an advisory committee to provide journalists with input on management decisions and a seat on hiring panels in an effort to "democratize" the newsroom. "Once remote from decision-making, reporters can now join more committees than a busy MP, although some remain suspicious," noted Gill in 1990. "One reporter says the hiring panel does its work, 'then [the managers] just go into a room and decide what's going to happen.'"[23] A further effort at decentralization under Hills was introduction of a "pod" system, in which reporters worked in teams and reported to a pod leader instead of directly to the city desk, but again the effort proved less than satisfactory, according to *B.C. Report*. "The result, says one editor, is 'the reporters are writing for each other' instead of the paper-buying public."[24]

Increased news coverage, cosmetic changes to the newspaper's design, and managerial rearrangement could not save the *Sun* from the fate suffered by more and more afternoon dailies since the 1970s, as the newspaper's circulation continued to drop ever more steeply. From a six-day average of 248,000 copies sold in 1985, *Sun* sales dropped by several thousand a year until by 1989 circulation was just 230,000 (see Appendix 1). When the semi-annual copy count by the Chicago-based Audit Bureau of Circulations came down in November 1990, alarm bells began going off at Southam's head office. The figures showed that *Sun* sales had fallen more sharply, by 10,000 to 220,000, while *Province* circulation had stabilized at 190,000 despite attempts by Pacific Press to induce tabloid readers to switch newspapers or read both. Monday through Thursday *Sun* circulation had dipped below 200,000, with the six-day average only held up by sales of the Friday edition, which included the *TV Times* magazine, and the fat Saturday paper, which suffered no competition from the *Province*. In desperation, Southam decided to move the *Sun* to "all-day" publication by adding a morning edition, as the *Toronto Star* had done successfully in 1981. A morning edition of the *Sun*, like that of the *Star*, would be sold only on the street and aimed at capturing a segment of the commuter market on which the *Province* had grown. In Canada, only three of the twenty major dailies were still published in the afternoon, but those enjoyed monopoly markets. Southam wanted to save the *Sun* from the fate other afternoon newspapers across the continent had suffered, but moving it to morning publication would place it in direct competition with its *Province*. A second set of presses at the new $50-million Pacific Press satellite plant in Surrey, which opened in September 1990, would enable the morning edition of the *Sun* to be printed at the same time as the *Province*. The biggest problem would be negotiating changes to contract language with the joint council unions to allow the scheduling changes necessary for all-day publication of the *Sun*. Gaining such concessions from the unions meant Pacific Press could forget about taking a hard line in the 1990 round of negotiations, and the unions saw the move as an opportunity to make even more gains in wages and working conditions. But the success of the all-day *Sun* project was essential to reviving the fortunes of Pacific Press, which would, in turn, go a long way toward deciding the fate of faltering Southam. With the June 15 expiry of its "standstill" agreement with Torstar, the publicly traded newspaper chain had again become a takeover target.

***Province* editor Bob McMurray** also resigned in 1989, ending 44 years of employment at the morning daily when an offer of early retirement proved too good to refuse. Southam shuffled 39-year-old Ian Haysom across the hall from the *Sun* into the vacant editor's chair at the *Province*, making the diminutive, bearded Haysom the perfect Pacific Press executive, interchangeable between either of its dailies. Haysom, an enthusiastic English expatriate, had worked his way up in the *Sun* editorial hierarchy since joining the newspaper as a feature writer in 1981 and had served as its city editor and assistant managing editor. "He'd earned the nickname 'the popcorn machine' for his preference for spewing grand ideas over filling pages with solid, original journalism," noted *B.C. Business* magazine. "Many of his ideas were good, but just as many kernels, insiders say, never popped."[25] According to *Sun* columnist Denny Boyd, he won the top *Province* job by promising to concentrate on content over colorfulness. "This paper was designed by a promotions manager," Boyd quoted Haysom as quipping in his pitch for the post. "It's time to let a journalist take a crack at it."[26]

The switch to tabloid format after Sherman's 1982 departure from Vancouver had proven a marketing success, but many considered the newspaper's editorial standards to have been lowered in the process. Foremost among the critics was Boyd, who used a 1986 column to excoriate the *Sun*'s morning competition for "debasing itself and the ethics of the profession by crudely and irresponsibly appealing to the lowest public passions."[27] The tabloid formula of fomenting outrage in an attempt to connect with its target readership was an approach that gave many *Sun* journalists even more reason to scorn their morning bedfellow. "The

Province doesn't report, it agitates," complained Boyd. "It doesn't sell news, it sells anger, resentment and nihilism. It's a cheap appeal to people who would rather throw a brick than think."[28]

> Instead of reporting the story, find one person who is angry about the story. Bury the news in the anger at the news. Readers might not understand or care about the original story, but everyone knows how to get angry. Thus, in the first seven pages of Sunday's *Province*, we had reaction stories about a man who is "lashing out," some neighbors who are "howling," some others who are "fuming," a man who is "raising a stink," a group that is "fired up," a woman who is "irate" and a man who is simply "pissed off."[29]

Haysom used as his template for improving the *Province* the Fleet Street tabloid *Evening Standard*, where he had spent eighteen months as a sub-editor and feature writer. Under McMurray, an old-time broadsheet journalist, the *Province* had suffered from an identity crisis. "One day sensational, the next day trite, the tabloid has lacked direction," noted Mike Gasher in *content*.[30] Haysom's stated intention was to "restore a little bit of integrity" to the morning newspaper. "I think a tabloid can be bright, can be breezy, can be witty, can be sassy, but it can also be intelligent and informative," he told Gasher. "I think what happened in the last three years or so is that *The Province* started to go too far into a sleazy downmarket direction. The front [page], which I think many people form their impressions by, had become far too silly and irrelevant."[31] The colorful cover had featured giant-sized headlines necessarily formed with one-syllable words, which made it difficult to write a headline that accurately reflected the story inside. Under Haysom, the *Province* experimented with smaller front-page headline sizes that told more of the story, while also occasionally running a short article on the cover, keyed to a longer story inside. The changes, according to Gasher, made the morning tabloid less of a journalistic embarrassment.

> Haysom's first steps were to tone down front-page headlines, suppress crime and hero stories, introduce more world, national and provincial news, add a third opinion page and give entertainment its own section. Leads still feature Mohawk Indians "on the warpath" and complex issues are confined to one-paragraph briefs, but the days of such headlines as "Top Red Dead" are gone.[32]

The *Province*'s switch to tabloid format had boosted circulation while carving out a market niche as an advertising vehicle for consumer goods, which the newspaper had not enjoyed as a broadsheet. One year after the 1983 conversion, *Province* circulation rose by more than 10,000 to 156,650, with much of the increase fueled by an 80 percent jump in women readers aged 18 to 34.[33] By 1985 "the Tab" was Canada's fastest-growing newspaper according to the Audit Bureau of Circulations, noted *Province* business reporter David Baines, with an average six-day circulation of 174,000, led by sales of its Sunday edition, which topped 220,000.[34] More importantly, publisher Gerry Haslam told Baines, *Province* retail advertising linage had increased by 11 percent in two years, with classified linage rising 21 percent. The Tab's financial success meant it was able to make a "significant contribution" to overhead costs at Pacific Press, Haslam said, amounting to $2 million more than he had predicted.[35]

During the six-month World's Fair of 1986, *Province* circulation jumped again, topping 190,000, and it kept most of the new readers after the fair ended, aided by the long-awaited introduction of a mass transit system — the automated "Skytrain." In 1987 Haslam was named marketing executive of the year by the Sales and Marketing Executives of Vancouver, but that November the 42-year-old suffered a minor stroke from which he soon recovered, but the aftereffects required him to walk with a cane.[36] By the fall of 1988, with Paddy Sherman preparing to relocate back to Vancouver and take charge of Pacific Press personally, Haslam found himself suddenly out of favor despite the gains to which he had led the *Province*. In September he was demoted to vice-president of marketing for Pacific Press, while former labor relations head Stu Noble was promoted to president.[37] "It wasn't working out," Sherman said of Haslam's ouster. "I was planning a change for him. He had his stroke and I put it off for a long, long time. In my view, he hadn't been up to my standards before the stroke."[38] By 1989, stripped of his power as publisher of both the *Sun* and *Province*, Haslam found it impossible to work under the strong-willed Haysom and Hills to coordinate a marketing strategy for both newspapers.[39]

Province circulation continued to build toward the magic figure of 200,000 as the *Sun*'s dipped perilously close to that psychological barrier, which it had passed in 1957 shortly after gaining the afternoon field to itself when the *Province* moved to mornings following the Pacific Press amalgamation. In the three decades since, afternoon newspapers across the continent had lost circulation as readers turned increasingly to the more passive medium of television to get their nightly news. Morning newspapers had flourished instead, in a role reversal dubbed "Death in the Afternoon" as many long-established afternoon titles in North America either folded for lack of circulation or moved to morning publication to stave off extinction. Executives watched nervously as the morning tabloid cut into the readership and revenue of their afternoon broadsheet moneymaker.

The attempt to infuse life back into the *Sun* journalistically with the appointment of Hills as editor was coupled with a deliberate strategy of holding back the *Province* in many ways, most significantly with a series of cover price increases that slowed its circulation growth, according to Haslam. "It could have been the number one paper in town," he said in 1999. "There's no question in my mind we could have gone to 200,000 in 1988 or early '89 — we had booked the room at the Pan Pacific [Hotel] to have the party in — if we hadn't kept raising the price."[40] In exasperation, Haslam asked for a transfer and in August 1989 he moved to the Interior of B.C. as publisher of Southam's *Kamloops Daily News*.[41]

The *Province* was not the only competition worrying those at the *Sun*. The *Globe and Mail* had established a firm toe-hold in Vancouver during the 1984 Pacific Press strike, and the national newspaper cut into the *Sun*'s high-end readership with the popularity of its respected "Report on Business" section, reaching a morning circulation of 30,000. The national business newspaper *Financial Post* also went daily with Vancouver sales of 15,000. But the biggest losses suffered by Southam in Vancouver were inflicted by community newspapers, which took local advertising revenue away from the *Sun* and *Province* and every few years cashed in big when the Pacific Press dailies were closed by labor problems.

To the east, communities on both sides of the Fraser River had, starting in the 1960s, grown their own weekly newspapers which prospered with advertising revenue from local merchants. Soon an overseas newspaper company began buying up the community papers in a chain that grew to fifteen titles by 1991. Trinity International Holdings of Liverpool, England, began making acquisitions in the early 1960s to diversify its holdings from its original *Liverpool Daily Post* and evening *Echo* when they, like the Pacific Press papers, started to suffer from declining circulation. In addition to the daily *Advocate* in Red Deer, Alberta, Trinity had acquired a chain of weeklies south of Chicago and additional titles in Pittsburgh and Lisbon, Ohio.[42] Beginning with weeklies in the Fraser Valley suburbs of Chilliwack, Abbotsford, and Mission, Trinity had increased its holdings in the Lower Mainland over the next three decades by adding another dozen titles through its subsidiary Hacker Press, including some in the closest Vancouver suburbs, for a total circulation of 500,000.[43] The presence of a well-capitalized competitor at their doorstep was worrisome for Southam and Pacific Press due to the possibility of Hacker pooling the resources of its newspapers to publish a Vancouver daily in competition with the *Sun* and *Province* or, more likely, in their absence.

In 1986, Massachusetts-based Urban and Associates conducted market research in Greater Vancouver for Southam and concluded that the share of local print advertising revenue captured by Pacific Press was an unusually low 27 percent.[44] The problem, concluded consultant Christine Urban, was the result of a "large number of aggressive weeklies in [Greater] Vancouver . . . siphoning revenues" from the *Sun* and *Province*.[45] Area weeklies, argued Urban, were a "competitive force to be reckoned with in determining the future of Pacific Press in the Vancouver market."[46] The speed of the weeklies' growth and "major retailers' faith in their product, is ominous," she warned.[47] In an attempt to compete on the North Shore, the *Sun* began a series of supplements in 1988 that it called *North Shore Extra*. The special broadsheet section, with a full-color front page, local area news, reviews, and advertising, was included with the *Sun* on alternate Wednesdays and also was distributed free to non-subscribing homes.[48]

But at Southam's head office a more aggressive plan was emerging in an attempt to increase the company's size to discourage a hostile takeover, and the strategy emphasized acquisition over competition. A 1988 Southam report, "Agenda for the Future," outlined a bold plan for "bomb proofing" its metropolitan dailies by buying up local community papers.[49] The strategy had proven successful for the *Toronto Star*, which had insulated itself from suburban competition by taking over surrounding weeklies in Southern Ontario throughout the 1980s. On the West

Coast, the *North Shore News* was targeted for acquisition by Southam management, with a 1989 memo describing it as "one of Canada's premier community newspapers," operating in "the single best strategically placed community in the Lower Mainland."[50] The plan, as outlined in the memo, was to hedge the venerable chain's newspaper bets, due to its dependence on dailies, with a diversification into weeklies, starting with the *North Shore News*.

> It's an essential part of any effort to put together a unified community newspaper entity covering the entire Lower Mainland. [Its] acquisition is of significant importance both as a defence against potential competitive thrust by other groups and as part of a new market strategy by Pacific Press and Southam Newspaper Group to develop and expand our revenue base with a much more profitable margin than Pacific Press has presently.[51]

Enriched with the $281 million it had netted from the sale of its cable television holdings in November 1988, Southam made *North Shore News* owner Speck an offer he could not refuse in January 1989, allowing him to retain majority control and remain as publisher while naming his price for a 49 percent interest in the *News*. Minority ownership of a competitor by Canada's largest newspaper chain sparked some local consternation, with Gasher noting in *content* that it "recalled the nationwide newspaper shuffle . . . known as Black Wednesday," since which "Vancouver has been among the least competitive daily newspaper markets in Canada."[52] He interviewed Pacific Press president Stu Noble, who, he reported, "insists Southam has no immediate plans to either invest in or purchase other community papers."[53] *Vancouver Courier* publisher Geoff Wellens, according to Gasher, "said Southam has made no recent offers to buy the *Courier*."[54] But Southam and Pacific Press were just getting started with their new strategy of buying the competition and next began casting covetous glances at the successful *Courier*.

Greater Vancouver had seen a belated economic recovery in the late 1980s turn into one of the boom cycles that the region enjoyed periodically. Local retail advertising expenditures almost doubled from $170 million in 1985 to $326 million in 1990, but the share captured by Pacific Press fell a further 3.7 percentage points to 23 percent.[55] By 1989 the *Sun* and *Province* derived only 34 percent of their advertising revenue from local retail advertising, as opposed to classified and national advertising, which was well below the national average of 51 percent for daily newspapers.[56] The cagy *Courier* had increased its retail advertising revenue by 89 percent between 1986 and 1989 by adding a Sunday edition to its weekly west-side Wednesday paper and distributing it throughout the city for a circulation of 125,000.[57] Retail advertising revenue at the *Province* had climbed by 42 percent during the same period with its popularity as a tabloid, but at the *Sun* retail advertising revenue had stagnated despite the area's economic improvement, growing by only 1 percent.[58] The tabloid *Courier* landed free on every doorstep in Vancouver on Sundays and grew fat with advertising inserts while it bided its time until the next strike at Pacific Press, when it was assured an even greater bonanza.

The three-year collective agreement Pacific Press had reached with its joint council unions in 1987 expired at the end of November 1990, and the presence of the competing *Courier* played a role in Southam's attempts to tame its militant unions in Vancouver. As long as it provided an alternative for advertisers and income for striking journalists to hold out against their regular employers, Southam's bargaining power at Pacific Press was diminished. Taking over the *Courier* would provide a strategic hedge and funnel much of the revenue lost during a strike right back to Southam. On May 8, 1990, Southam acquired 75 percent ownership of the *Courier* for $6 million in a complex deal that also involved the *Now* chain of community newspapers in the eastern suburbs of Burnaby, Coquitlam, and Surrey that had been started by former *Columbian* employees. The purchase also included a chain of fourteen zoned editions of the *Real Estate Weekly* all-advertising tabloids, which had cut sharply into Pacific Press real estate advertising. The acquisition, noted the weekly newsmagazine *B.C. Report*, "was widely decried, except in the pages of the *Sun* and *Province*."[59] While other Vancouver media warned of the possible adverse effects of such concentrated ownership of area newspapers, *B.C. Report* editor Terry O'Neill pointed out, the Pacific Press papers were largely silent on the matter.

> Matter-of-fact reports on the details of the deal prevailed. The sole example of in-depth coverage, provided by the *Sun*, focused on the "newspaper wars" aspect of Southam vs. Hacker. The one major opinion piece was also provided by the *Sun*; business columnist Judy Lindsay heartily defended the deal, and even

went as far as chiding her bosses for being "asleep at the switch" because they did not gobble up the papers sooner.[60]

Southam's acquisition of such a large number of competing publications in the Lower Mainland did not go unnoticed in Ottawa. Ian Waddell, NDP communications critic and a local member of parliament for Port Moody-Coquitlam, called the result "an astonishing ... and dangerous concentration of ownership." Soon politicians were demanding yet another inquiry into the ownership of Vancouver's newspapers. "There's a real danger when so much of the print media is held in so few hands," said Waddell. "The case can be made that these newspapers are protecting their markets against present and future competition."[61] Federal regulators also cast a disapproving eye on the corporate consolidation. Following the acquittal of Southam and Thomson on criminal conspiracy and monopoly charges in 1983, the Restrictive Trade Practices Act had been replaced in 1986 by a Competition Act, which instead provided for civil penalties and proceedings. A new Bureau of Competition Policy was empowered to investigate transactions to determine if they contravened the Competition Act and to order divestiture if it found they unduly lessened competition. Disputes under the new Act were adjudicated by a three-member Competition Tribunal made up of legal and economics experts. On November 29 the bureau's director ordered Southam to divest itself of the *Courier*, the *North Shore News*, and the *Real Estate Weekly* papers because their acquisition would lessen competition substantially for newspaper advertising in their local markets.[62]

In Vancouver, the bureau claimed that acquisition of the *Courier* would increase Southam's share of the market for newspaper retail advertising from 72.4 percent to 86.5 percent and "is likely to enable Southam to unilaterally impose and maintain a material price increase."[63] On the North Shore, the paltry 39.3 percent share of the market held by Pacific Press would immediately be boosted by the 56.9 percent dominance of the *North Shore News*, whose acquisition Southam completed when it purchased the other 51 percent from Speck in February 1991 for a total purchase price of $13.5 million.[64] The increase in Southam's ownership of the *News* even while competition regulators were demanding divestiture resulted in acrimonious negotiations between the bureaucrats and corporate executives over how the disputed publications should be managed pending a ruling from the Competition Tribunal. The bureau sought an order from the Competition Tribunal in March prohibiting Southam involvement in operations of the three newspapers, which the *Globe and Mail* reported "indicates that its relations with Southam have been severely strained by disagreements."[65] Eventually the dispute was resolved when Southam agreed to appoint monitors to ensure the newspapers would be managed independently.[66]

After butting heads in vain with the Pacific Press power structure for two years, Nick Hills' brief but busy tenure was brought to an end in spring 1991 by "a near mutiny in the newsroom," according to *Maclean's*.

> Indeed, the irascible Hills made so many enemies during his two years as editor that he went into hiding to work out a severance package. He emerged with his $110,000 salary intact. In return, he will write a twice-weekly column. But the real triumph, for a man one colleague described as "up and down like a toilet seat," was keeping his *Sun*-paid membership at the posh Vancouver Lawn Tennis Club.[67]

In his memoirs, Denny Boyd suggested instead that Hills was sent packing because he "spent like a caliph."[68] But Paddy Sherman confirmed the contention in *Maclean's* that his departure was more a result of his lack of managerial tact, which caused union problems. "He could never sit down quietly with someone who was opposed to him and work things out," recalled Sherman. "And in a professional sense, he was right more often than he was wrong, but his attitude wasn't very helpful in this sense."[69]

Haysom was recalled from the *Province* in hopes that he could successfully oversee the switch to morning publication that would save the ailing *Sun*. Haysom's plan for the paper's morning relaunch hinged on turning it into the kind of upbeat newspaper product he had helped make the *Province*. He was determined to make the *Sun* more reader-friendly by banishing the bad news that marketing consultants warned editors turned people off reading newspapers. The positive-thinking Haysom, noted *Sun* media columnist Stan Persky, was "the sort of person who would've told a soggy Noah that The Flood was good for the umbrella business."[70] But his "rah rah style," according to Persky, soon wore thin on cynical journalists. As former Haysom colleague Ian Gill observed, the new morning *Sun* would inevitably acquire the personality of its editor.

> Haysom is one of those irrepressibly jocular types, the kind of guy you'd expect to find leading a sing-along at a church camp. Or, to paraphrase Spiro Agnew, a sort of "nattering nabob of positivism." Given his track record at the *Province,* it is little wonder that Haysom's biggest challenge upon taking over the *Vancouver Sun* — to take the paper to mornings — was accomplished . . . with a relentless "happification" of the newspaper.[71]

The problem for Haysom was not only that he lacked the heavyweight columnists which the paper had previously enjoyed, but also that his lead columnists had recently come in for heavy scorn, even on the pages of their own newspaper. Hills had sent featured columnist Pete McMartin to cover the Gulf War in January, but the assignment turned into a disaster when at the first hint of danger the would-be war correspondent beat a hasty retreat home with his journalistic tail between his legs. "Frankly, I was scared," McMartin, a former city hall and sports columnist, told Persky on his return. The media columnist reported, "Naturally, the story of McMartin's misadventures was the choice topic of gossip among B.C.'s journalistic community this week. Among the jokes making the rounds: 'What's the shortest book of the year? Answer: Pete McMartin's War Stories.'"[72]

The McMartin incident, noted the *Globe and Mail,* "would become emblematic of setbacks suffered by the city's largest paper in its efforts to revive its sagging circulation."[73] The *Sun*'s Gulf War coverage had been aided by the headline-writing ability of Pacific Press marketing director Glenn Rogers, a non-journalist who admitted to the *Globe and Mail*'s Deborah Wilson that he had played a "direct role in shaping the *Sun*'s war coverage, including its poster-style front pages and the one-word, five-centimetre headline the day after the first Iraqi missile attack on Israel, which said, puzzlingly, REVENGE. (Israel played no part in the air attack on Iraq.)"[74] The incident, noted Wilson, was another example of the newspaper's stumbling attempts to regain credibility and circulation. "As some *Sun* employees see it, all this has been just another mis-step in the paper's promotional initiatives."[75]

Two months later, the *Sun* suffered one more journalistic black eye when columnist Nicole Parton, who had taken a leave of absence in June

1990 to run for a seat in the provincial legislature, like McMartin beat a hasty retreat from the political wars and returned to the security of the newsroom. After planning to run under the banner of the governing Social Credit Party, Parton declared she could not belong to a party led by Premier Bill Vander Zalm, who had refused to resign despite allegations of influence-peddling. What bothered Persky was the *Sun*'s decision to run the erstwhile candidate's explanation, which he described as an "astonishing piece of local political journalism," on its opinion page.

> The question of publishing Parton must have raised some puzzling ethical questions for the *Sun*'s editors. Was Parton writing as a *Sun* journalist-on-leave, as a public figure offering the paper an exclusive on a current political controversy, or, given the tone of her piece, as a Socred political hack? What made Parton's article questionable was that, rather than merely explaining the reasons for her flip-flop, a good 50 per cent of her piece was devoted to a high-octave rant against NDP leader Mike Harcourt.[76]

As the paper floundered editorially, technological and labor problems also rose up to harass Southam again. The new flexography printing process was proving problematic as unresolved bugs hindered utilization of the new Pacific Press plant and thus delayed the *Sun*'s plans for morning publication.[77] "We made a number of boo-boos along the way," admitted Sherman. "What you have to remember is a lot of these things were done in the context of the very frustrating union situation. They were probably skewed by the need to put in something that might not necessarily be the best system, but the one we could best adapt to the union structure."[78]

Meanwhile, as contract talks dragged on for nine months past the November 30, 1990, contract expiration date, the unions also turned up the heat in the regular ritual of brinksmanship that had come to characterize labor negotiations at Pacific Press. The unions insisted on a four-day week in exchange for allowing morning *Sun* publication, and the old bugaboo of production problems arose again at the end of August. Pacific Press negotiator Mike Pellant warned the unions that the *Sun* would move to mornings with or without them. "There will be a product on September 16 — that's a fact," boasted Pellant.[79] Newspaper Guild leader Mike Bocking responded with a warning that Pacific Press management well understood was backed by the combined power of the entire B.C.

labor movement. "There's no bloody way they could get a paper on the streets in this town," pointed out the *Sun* business reporter.[80] As mediator Vince Ready entered the talks, *Sun* and *Province* press runs were a fraction of normal for three days, causing $1.8 million in lost sales for Pacific Press.[81] Finally on September 1, after a twenty-six hour bargaining session, agreement was reached on a three-year contract that would allow Pacific Press to publish a morning *Sun*.

Harvey Southam had not taken well to Toronto since moving there in 1985 for a posting at the family firm's head office. He was also being groomed as a possible replacement for president John Fisher, who planned to retire in 1992. But Central Canadian corporate life was not to the Vancouver native's liking. He pined for the West Coast, telling his wife Pia Shandel that he longed to escape the corporate rat race by moving to the country and running a bed and breakfast inn. Harvey had been installed in Southam's trade magazine division and had drawn on his experience as editor of *Equity* to found *V*, a glossy monthly supplement to the *Vancouver Sun*, which won Best Magazine of the Year at the 1988 Western Magazine Awards. Not everyone in Vancouver was impressed with the "controlled circulation" magazine, which was distributed only in upscale neighborhoods, targeting affluent readers. "Dividing *Sun* subscribers into haves and have-nots is elitist and discriminatory," wrote *Sun* consumer columnist Nicole Parton, adding that Southam family nepotism was also an issue with some at Pacific Press who were opposed to the project.[82]

Harvey Southam's division was one of the biggest money losers at Southam, and to turn it around the company appointed Bill Ardell in the fall of 1990. Ardell came from Southam's Coles Books subsidiary, which he had returned to profitability after several years of losses. Renowned in the industry as a "hatchet man" who specialized in turning around failing enterprises by slashing jobs, he enlisted Harvey to assist in downsizing the Southam magazine division by firing 120 employees. "He hated his job," recalled Shandel in a 1996 magazine interview. "He didn't know how to get out of it with face."[83] To make things worse Southam had resumed drinking, and early in 1991 he was arrested for impaired driving again, this time losing his license. He couldn't sleep, so his wife convinced him to see a doctor, who prescribed an anti-depressant and observed that

Harvey seemed "a little down about work."[84] The family firm so many Southams hoped he would some day head was rapidly sliding into financial oblivion, and 1990 earnings, announced in the spring of 1991, had fallen by 95 percent despite a boom enjoyed by other media companies.[85] More significantly, the year's fourth quarter had seen a loss of $23.9 million, compared with a profit of $31.2 million during the same period in 1989.[86] The burden and the disappointment had become too much for Harvey Southam, and late on the night of May 30 he took the family dog for a walk and never returned. His body was found the next morning hanging from a bridge over a ravine near his home in the upscale Toronto neighborhood of Rosedale. Only 43, he had committed suicide.

21 The Stolen Newspaper

> I once worked for a Vancouver paper that was owned by Don Cromie, who then sold it to Max Bell and FP Publications, who then sold it to the Thomsons, who then sold it to Southam. After a while you feel like a five-dollar hooker.
>
> ALLAN FOTHERINGHAM, *Maclean's*, FEBRUARY 14, 1994

The story Don Cromie told for public consumption as late as 1986 about how his father gained control of the *Sun* in 1917 was that his dad's boss and benefactor, Colonel Jack Stewart, had to leave Vancouver in a hurry because of a political scandal involving his railroad-building company. A Liberal Party backer, Stewart found owning a newspaper an advantage in gaining the contract to build the Pacific Great Eastern railway to Prince George, which would open the north of the province. But the contract went unfinished when the millions of dollars advanced for the project ran out before the rail line was completed, prompting Stewart and other company principals to flee. Cleaning out the firm's files with company lawyer Fred Anderson after Stewart left town to build railroads on the battlefields of Europe, office boy Bobby Cromie supposedly rescued the worthless *Sun* shares from the wastebasket and was given them by one of Stewart's partners. "[Timothy] Foley apparently had told him he could have *The Sun* if he wanted it, and he wanted it," Don Cromie told Ben Metcalfe for a 1986 *Vancouver* magazine article.[1]

Peter Stursberg, in a 1982 oral history of Vancouver newspapers, also recorded Don Cromie's version, but with a cryptic disclaimer. "How did Robert Cromie do it?" asked Stursberg. "Not even his own son and successor as publisher, Don Cromie, knows the full story."[2] His father "didn't really go into much detail," Cromie told Stursberg. "I guess he was a fairly busy person and looked to the future and the present rather than the past, and he didn't pay much attention to giving the family the history of what he did."[3] Repeating the story of the scandal and Stewart leaving town in a hurry, Cromie got to the part about the wastebasket.

> My father said, "Fred, don't throw those shares into the wastebasket. If they're just going to go into the wastebasket, give them to me and maybe I can borrow the money to make this thing come alive and pay." So my father took those shares, which weren't much good because the paper was losing money."[4]

But there was another version circulating of how the *Sun* became Cromie family property. It did not see print until 1986 but was hinted at for decades, such as in a 1946 *B.C. Historical Quarterly* article, in which longtime *Province* editorial writer Dan McGregor declared the question of Cromie family acquisition of the *Sun* "another of the mysteries of Vancouver newspaperdom."[5] Pierre Berton knew the inside story from his early newspaper days in Vancouver and included it in his 1948 *Maclean's* feature, "Vancouver's Rising Sun," but the incriminating passage was excised by editors after Don Cromie threatened legal action.[6] "What happened next is an unrecorded portion of the Cromie legend," Berton's article declared. "One version has Cromie going through the old stock, which was practically worthless."[7] But after telling the story of how young Bobby Cromie was told he could have the shares, Berton's feature oddly omitted the other version and ended the saga abruptly. "Whatever the truth of the matter," the *Maclean's* article stated, "Cromie got the paper — for no cash."[8]

The inside story gained great currency among journalists, who were bound to let it slip eventually. Berton, by the 1980s one of Canada's foremost popular historians, told the tale to George Bain, who was media columnist for *Maclean's*. Bain corroborated it in 1986 with Allan Fotheringham, who was Washington correspondent for Southam News, and put it in his column. "The story that was told but never proven, Berton says, was that Robert Cromie . . . stole the paper," reported Bain.[9] Fotheringham offered his own version of the "classic story in Canadian newspapering" on the occasion of Don Cromie's death in 1993.

> There were certain legal and conflict matters that had to be sorted out, the proprietors' solution being to put the paper in the name of office boy Cromie until the lawyers and courts got things "cleared" up. When events did ensue and they came back to take legal control in 1917, the shrewd young office boy said no thanks and began a family dynasty.[10]

Newspapers are unique economic commodities in several ways. The fact that the end product is sold to the public at a fraction of its cost of production in labor, capital, newsprint, ink, and other expenses underlines their unusual nature as a "dual market" commodity. The sale of newspapers to readers who are buyers in the market for information is subsidized by the sale of newspaper space to businesses which are in the market for advertising. The subsidy is considerable, as the purchase price of a newspaper usually pays for no more than one quarter of the total cost of its production, often amounting to less that the cost of the newsprint used to print it on. But in addition to the markets for news and advertising, in which newspapers have competed since the commercialization of the industry from the political party press of the nineteenth century, newspapers have recently become subject to the forces of a third market, media critic Ben Bagdikian pointed out in 1978. The incorporation of many newspaper firms as publicly owned enterprises financed by capital raised through the public sale of shares in ownership, according to Bagdikian, means that the stock market has entered the equation of economic forces to which the press is subject.

> The impact of trading newspaper corporate stock on the stock market has meant that news companies must constantly expand in size and rate of profits in order to maintain their position on stock exchanges . . . Instead of the single master so celebrated in the rhetoric of the industry — the reader — there are in fact three masters.[11]

The influence of Bagdikian's third market for newspapers can be clearly seen in the evolution of the daily newspaper market in Vancouver from three competing owners to a tightly controlled single-owner monopoly, as newspapers and then newspaper chains became objects of commodification over the years, bought and sold like properties on a Monopoly board game. The vast resources of the publicly traded Southam chain played no small part in convincing Don Cromie to agree to a truce in the decade-long Vancouver newspaper war in 1956, fearing that his family firm could come in second in a long-term battle of attrition with such a well-financed foe. Widespread public ownership of shares in Sun Publishing Company eventually made it vulnerable to corporate takeover, which convinced Cromie to sell out to the liberal-minded Max Bell and FP Publications in 1963. FP in turn became corporate prey for the worldwide Thomson conglomerate in 1980, which led to increased corporatization of Vancouver's daily newspapers under a single owner after Thomson "flipped" the *Sun*, and thus sole ownership of Pacific Press, to Southam.

But the family newspaper firm, shares of which had been traded publicly since 1945, soon became subject to the same stock market forces that created the Vancouver daily newspaper monopoly and led to its incremental consolidation. Southam's acquisition of much of the Greater Vancouver community press, which was thriving in competition with the *Sun* and *Province*, was in large part a defensive measure to eliminate competition in the Lower Mainland and to grow to such a size as to become an unattractive corporate takeover target. Ultimately the attempt was unsuccessful, and ownership of Vancouver media became even more highly concentrated. Whether ownership of the *Vancouver Sun* and *Province* by one company that also owned the major community newspapers would have been approved in 1960 under the Restrictive Trade Practices Act, weak as it was, is doubtful. But complete control of the city's most important media outlets by one corporation, which was the result forty years later, would almost certainly have been disallowed if government approval of the corporate consolidation had been sought all at once.

The decline in circulation of the Pacific Press dailies under absentee corporate ownership is explained by Bagdikian, a former managing editor of the *Washington Post* and dean of journalism at the University of California, in his landmark 1983 book *The Media Monopoly*. A change in emphasis under corporate ownership from serving the needs of readers to serving the needs of advertisers, who contribute by far the greatest portion of press revenues, led to a fundamental change in management of the medium, according to Bagdikian.

> Increased ownership of local newspapers by distant corporations, often conglomerates with diverse business interests in addition to their media holdings, led to a change in priorities. The ownership of a local newspaper by a distant corporation is not by itself a deterrent to newspaper reading. If papers remained truly unchanged under absentee ownership, changed titles of incorporation would be irrelevant to most readers. But corporate ownership changed the form and content, the strategies of operation, and the economics of newspapers.[12]

Under local ownership, the *Vancouver Sun* exhibited a unique character that provided a strong "connection" with working-class readers who found it essential to understanding their community, while the conservative, corporate *Province* appealed to its own distinct business-oriented readership. But under common corporate ownership the newspapers have increasingly been packaged as products to be marketed like any other rather than presented as a public service. The failure of editors to maximize returns to shareholders over the years resulted in the increasing intrusion into newsroom operations by financial managers unfamiliar with and unbeholden to the principles of journalism in an attempt to boost the bottom line by use of the dual techniques of marketing and cost-cutting. The business-school tactics led to mixed results in the 1980s as daily newspaper circulation continued to decline in spite of the increased influence of professional managers. To many journalists, the marketing and managerial revolutions in newsrooms have had the opposite of their intended effect, with the commodification of news as a product defeating the original purpose of the press.[13] The result has seen newspapers, according to Canadian media critic John Miller, "selling the sizzle of redesign and trying to pander to our elusive tastes instead of investing in what readers really need, which is the substance of quality journalism."[14] Miller diagnosed the fundamental flaw afflicting Canadian dailies in his 1998 book *Yesterday's News: Why Canada's Daily Newspapers are Failing Us.*

> They're putting their money not into training or hiring or figuring out how better to cover the news, but into marketing, which is a business school concept that treats news as a commodity to be manipulated and sold as cheaply as possible. ... Under this model, the audience ultimately determines what news you cover; it's not news coverage that builds the audience.[15]

The phenomenon of corporate ownership and the rise of marketing as the fundamental mission of newspapers is well illustrated in the case of Pacific Press. But in Vancouver, the decline in circulation, which was occurring at daily newspapers everywhere, was exacerbated by a force that counteracted the financial advantages that should have accrued to the government-sanctioned monopoly secured by Pacific Press in 1960. The militant joint council unions largely offset corporate power by using their bargaining leverage to extract guarantees of lifetime employment and entrenched manning practices which, in addition to rich wages and benefits, cut ever deeper into diminishing Pacific Press profits. The attempt by Southam to rationalize labor relations at Pacific Press with its 1980 acquisition of complete control of the impossible partnership could do little to alter the power relationship between labor and management that had become entrenched over years of adversarial dealings. "Concentration of ownership of newspapers in Vancouver has not led to an increased concentration of power," noted the 1981 Royal Commission on Newspapers report on labor relations following Southam's acquisition of the *Sun*. "Concentration of power — in the industrial sense — already existed at Pacific Press."[16]

The regular labor shutdowns of Pacific Press did as much as anything to diminish the franchise for daily newspapers in Vancouver. Again absentee ownership was largely responsible, as bargaining decisions were made at a head office in Eastern Canada instead of by the local managers who dealt with the unions on a daily basis, and a lack of trust developed as a result of the separation of decision-making from the local level. The fundamental victory of the unions in the battle of Machiavellian strategies that ensued was achieved when they were able to publish their own newspaper during the 1970 dispute. The genesis of the demise of Pacific Press, FP Publications, and Southam can thus be traced back to the plan to publish the *Express* that was hatched over Mike Tytherleigh's kitchen table.

The phenomenon of reader withdrawal from the newspaper habit, which was well documented in Vancouver during the three-month shutdown of the *Sun* and *Province* in 1970, had by then been studied for a quarter of a century in one of the earliest avenues of mass communication research known as the "uses and gratifications" school. The research helped establish the concept of an "active audience" that, far from being a passive receptor of media messages as previously thought, goes looking to fulfill its information requirements and other psychological needs. The crucible for this research was New York City, where militant newspaper unions regularly shut down the dailies. During a two-week newspaper strike there in 1945, Bernard Berelson and colleagues from Columbia University conducted interviews with sixty Manhattan residents and found they read the newspaper in "the apparent desire . . . not to be left alone with their thoughts."[17] The gratifications readers receive from newspapers are of two sorts, Berelson concluded, including both "rational" (like the provision of news and information) and non-"rational" (like the provision of social contacts and, indirectly, social prestige).[18] It was as much the daily reading habit as the information for which readers missed newspapers when they suddenly were not available, concluded Berelson. "The newspaper is missed because it serves as a (non-'rational') source of security in a disturbing world and, finally, because the reading of the newspaper has become a ceremonial or ritualistic or near-compulsive act for many people."[19]

Penn Kimball's replication of Berelson's research conducted during a 1958 strike at the seven New York dailies found increased attention to radio news broadcasts was the most notable change in media habits, with the infant medium of television providing a lesser level of news replacement. Neither broadcast medium, however, was able to fill the void left by the absent newspapers, according to respondents, noted Kimball.

> Some need related to news was not being fulfilled by the drenching quantity of alternate media of communication. People seemed to feel drawn to the news as it appears in a newspaper

> without fully understanding what they get out of it, or without knowing how to analyze for themselves what it means to them.... A printed record can be screened when the moment is convenient and stories of interest can be examined at length. Furthermore, it is a process in which the reader participates actively.[20]

A study of the 1962–63 strike at the New York dailies, which lasted sixteen weeks, found that the longer the strike went on, the more frustrated regular readers became. "Nearly one in ten among even the most loyal newspaper readers showed disaffection as the blackout continued," noted Kimball.[21] The result was that "toward the end, newspapers had diminished somewhat in prestige. (Six percent said they would not buy their old papers when they resumed publication.)"[22] The strike had aided the electronic media in displacing newspapers as the primary information source, according to Kimball. "By the time the papers were ready to publish again the prototype New Yorker was one who had settled firmly on television or radio (more often the former) as his primary communication medium — but supplemented by one or more newspapers as a secondary yet highly valued part of his daily experience."[23] By 1967, the number of daily newspapers publishing in New York had been reduced by labor problems from seven to three. A study of the 1990 strike at the *Daily News*, which did not affect the *Times* or *Post*, suggested that publication interruptions serve to steepen the downward trend of readership already under way. "A strike is an accelerant poured on the smouldering fire that has eaten away at national newspaper penetration for decades," concluded John Polich, noting the 36 percent decline in *Daily News* circulation.[24]

The "uses and gratifications" theory, which sees newspapers as a habit from which readers withdraw without access to their daily fix, is clearly seen in the declining circulation of the Pacific Press newspapers. According to figures published by the Audit Bureau of Circulations, sales of the Vancouver dailies dropped almost 15 percent after the labor dispute that closed Pacific Press for three months in 1970 (see Appendix 1). From a steadily building six-day average circulation which topped 250,000, sales of the flagship *Sun* tumbled to 210,000 by the time of the semi-annual fall ABC audit. By 1974 the afternoon daily had rebuilt its circulation to almost 250,000 again, but the labor strife of the late 1970s dropped it back down below 220,000 when publication of the dailies finally resumed in 1979. The extended shutdown of the Pacific Press papers in 1978–79, as

Richard Littlemore noted in *B.C. Business* magazine, had a dual effect. "The absence of the two major dailies from the marketplace for eight months made room for the weekly giveaway papers that have burgeoned in the years since," he pointed out in 1997. "The strike also forced television news reporters to learn how to find stories on their own."[25] *The Sun* never regained its popularity with Vancouverites and suffered sharp declines in the 1980s as an afternoon daily in direct competition with evening television news, especially the high-powered BCTV *News Hour*.

The decline in daily newspaper circulation came during a time of rapid population expansion for Greater Vancouver, which made the downward trend even more pronounced. From just more than a million residents in 1970, the population of the metropolitan Vancouver area grew to more than 1.5 million by 1990 (see Appendix 2). Due to falling family size, the number of households almost doubled during the same period. The result was that with stagnant circulation in the Lower Mainland retail trading zone, market penetration of the *Sun* dropped by half, from 58 percent in 1970 to only 29 percent in 1990. The trend line of the *Province* market penetration during the same time period shows it declining steadily as a broadsheet to less than 20 percent after the eight-month Pacific Press shutdown ended in 1979. The conversion to tabloid format in 1983 boosted *Province* popularity immediately, but by the end of the decade market penetration was again declining.

The success of newspaper market segmentation, as demonstrated by the *Province*'s resurrection from the brink of contemplated closure, has served to contradict the argument made by Southam before the Restrictive Trade Practices Commission for allowing its amalgamation with the *Sun* in 1957. The "economic necessity" argument under the "natural monopoly" theory of newspapers, which won approval of the otherwise illegal merger, has since been demonstrated to be inadequate to explain the dynamics of newspaper markets. Events in Toronto, where the tabloid *Sun* emerged with a sharply differentiated product after the 1970 closure of the broadsheet *Telegram*, provided the example for renewed newspaper competition in Canada. The success of *Sun* tabloids in Ottawa and Winnipeg, where struggling second newspapers were closed by competing corporations because of the adverse effects of the circulation spiral, has shown the natural monopoly theory as it had been applied to newspapers to be simplistic. The spread of the *Sun* chain west to Edmonton and Calgary in Alberta provided all of the impetus needed for Southam to get in on the act with a tabloid of its own in Vancouver in 1983. The move not only revived the fortunes of the *Province* but also doubtless prevented any further daily competition from entering the market with a tabloid.

Stanford economist James Rosse in the 1960s was one of the first theorists to recognize the importance of product differentiation to newspaper competition — publishers find and fill a readership niche which then attracts advertisers.[26] His "umbrella" model of newspaper competition predicted different market levels evolving both above and below the market served by metropolitan dailies. Eventually, a national market for newspapers emerged in North America and a suburban "satellite" newspaper market also began to flourish in metropolitan areas.[27] Both levels can be seen evolving in Greater Vancouver in competition with the Pacific Press papers. At the national level, the *Globe and Mail* emerged as a viable national daily, while in the suburbs the Vancouver dailies suffered revenue and circulation losses to community newspapers at the fringes of their market due to its geographic size and diversity. The inroads made by suburban competitors and other adverse influences on readership of the dailies accelerated during periodic publication interruptions, as hypothesized by Polich, and fragmentation of the Vancouver newspaper market increased.

The intuitive evidence that suggests the Pacific Press monopoly prevented daily newspaper competition from entering the Vancouver market, provided by the demise of the *Vancouver Times* in 1965 and the even faster failure of the daily *Courier* in 1979, is bolstered by research in the U.S. on the effect of newspaper combinations. While setting the amalgamation example on which Pacific Press was formed in 1957, newspaper combinations in the U.S. were found in 1965 to be in violation of federal anti-trust laws against such monopoly practices as price fixing and profit pooling. An ensuing lobbying effort by publishers for an exemption from the law, such as Congress had granted the professional baseball leagues, was rejected by both President Lyndon Johnson and Republican candidate Richard Nixon, according to Bagdikian, "on the grounds that it was harmful social policy."[28] But after the lower court ruling was upheld by the U.S. Supreme Court in 1969, placing forty-four daily newspapers in violation of the law, the publishers pulled out all the stops in their lobbying effort. Bagdikian wrote: "Faced with the terrifying prospect of competing in the open market, they became desperate."[29] He documented how the major U.S. newspaper chains put pressure on Nixon after his 1968 election to reverse his administration's policy on the anti-trust exemption, which he did with the 1969 Newspaper Preservation Act. The Act was designed to save second-place newspapers from extinction under the circulation spiral by exempting the twenty-two existing Joint Operation Agreements from anti-trust laws. It also set up a mechanism to allow new combinations between newspapers that qualified as "failing" operations and their stronger competitors. The political quid pro quo, claimed Bagdikian, was strong editorial support for Nixon's re-election in 1972 despite four years of attacks on the press by the president, including the use of prior restraint against publication of the Pentagon Papers and a growing Watergate scandal, which was largely suppressed by pro-Nixon papers.

> Nixon received the highest percentage of newspaper endorsement of any candidate in modern times. . . . Every Hearst paper, every Cox paper, and every Scripps-Howard paper endorsed Nixon. Scripps-Howard ordered a standard pro-Nixon editorial into all its dailies. Cox ordered its editors to endorse Nixon (causing one editor to resign in protest).[30]

But in the U.S., the arrangements have proven controversial; many scholars and critics claim that they serve to prop up flabby journalistic operations at the expense of readers and advertisers who are forced to pay higher prices to monopoly operators, and that they keep competition out. Research on Joint Operating Agreements has shown that newspapers in the government-approved combinations tend to raise their advertising and subscription rates higher than competing dailies.[31] The result, according to California law professor Stephen Barnett, has been to "make all their owners a good deal richer, at the expense of advertisers and media competitors, and it has helped them smother whatever newspaper competition still exists or might revive in their territories."[32] Jointly operating newspapers are able to keep a market to themselves, noted Barnett, due to their ability not just to set advertising rates jointly, but to "actually choke off newspaper competition, since the monopoly power ... lets them structure their ad rates to soak up revenues that might otherwise go to competitors."[33] The key to dominating the market for daily newspaper advertising, he noted, is the use of "combination" rates such as offered by Pacific Press for inclusion in both newspapers at a discount. "Although today the combination usually is not 'forced' — advertisers remain free to take either paper alone — it effectively compels them to take both papers," observed Barnett in the *Columbia Journalism Review*, "including the weaker one which they might otherwise pass up in favor of a competitor."[34] The demise of the *Vancouver Times* and the daily *Courier* in competition with the Pacific Press papers provides apparent support for Barnett's simply stated hypothesis.

> Since few advertisers have money left in their ad budgets to take both papers and a third one, competition is kept out of the market. The weaker paper, no matter how tired its management or poor its journalism, is shored up as a sentry against potential competition, while the joint rate is set high enough to keep both publishers fat and happy when they split the pooled profits.[35]

The *Vancouver Sun*'s move to morning publication in 1991 could only slow the daily's declining circulation and financial fortunes. After bottoming out at 210,000 in 1991, *Sun* sales blipped up with morning publication to just over 220,000 by 1993, but again began dropping sharply until by 1996 six-day average circulation of the Pacific Press flagship had dipped below 200,000 (see Appendix 1). Worse, the *Sun*'s move to mornings, as expected, affected sales of the *Province* adversely, lowering its circulation from a consistent 190,000 to only 155,000 by 1996. The combined circulation losses of the Vancouver dailies thus amounted to almost 50,000 within five years, or 12 percent of total Pacific Press sales. Ian Haysom's "happification" of the *Sun* failed to excite Vancouverites, who deserted the daily in droves. "The paper is even less readable than before, and less relevant to the times," complained constant critic Ian Gill in late 1991. "As promised in a pre-launch brochure, the tone of the *Vancouver Sun* is now 'more friendly and vibrant' — laudable qualities in, say, a piano tuner, but just plain irritating in a newspaper."[36]

By 1995 Haysom was out as *Sun* editor, replaced by John Cruickshank of the *Globe and Mail* who, according to *B.C. Business* magazine, "won newsroom applause for refusing to bring in a hired gun or initiate another marketing survey to tell him which readers to chase and how to catch them."[37] Five years later Cruickshank was moved on by a new corporate ownership after, according to Richard Littlemore in *Vancouver* magazine, "re-creating the *Sun* in the *Globe*'s image, chasing away everything quirky and light."[38] The regular rotation of editors has resulted in the newspaper continually reinventing itself, concluded Denny Boyd, by then retired from the *Sun*, in a 1999 *B.C. Business* column.

> Every four or five years, a new editor-in-chief/publisher is recruited from the East, arrives here not knowing the territory or readership and re-casts the paper in his own image: new graphics, new headline styles, new columnists, new sections. (I blame the late Stuart Keate. A brilliant publisher, he led the *Sun* to its highest-ever circulation but, tragically, failed to anoint a successor when he retired. But for a petty misunderstanding, that new publisher might have been Allan Fotheringham, who was allowed to get away to the East.)[39]

The failure to turn around the *Sun*'s fortunes with morning publication was due as much as anything to bad timing. The national economy suffered a severe recession in the early 1990s that saw Canadian daily newspaper advertising revenues plunge 27 percent between 1990 and 1995.[40] In 1994, after losing $10 million over the previous three years, Pacific Press was described as a "license to lose money" in the national magazine *Canadian Business*. "Pacific Press's story is one of a rudderless management that let its product deteriorate while failing to respond to changes in the marketplace," observed Daniel Stoffman, a former *Sun* business writer. "It's a case study on the downside of owning a monopoly — everyone gets so complacent that inefficiencies creep into the operation and profitability is destroyed."[41] But as the newspaper business finally turned back up again in 1994 with the rest of the economy, Pacific Press was restored to profitability under new management that had made it a leaner operation. A "downsizing" movement instituted by new Southam CEO Bill Ardell, who replaced John Fisher in 1992 for lack of any suitable Southam family candidate, saw 600 staff pared at Pacific Press through layoffs, early retirement, and "buyout" offers.[42] Under Don Babick, the former *Edmonton Journal* publisher who was appointed president of Pacific Press at the end of 1991, the company finally returned to profitability in 1996. Babick, a former *Sun* advertising department employee, then moved on to head Southam in an attempt to revive its fortunes as well.

But just as Haysom could not save the *Sun*, nothing could save Southam family ownership of their inherited newspaper chain after Torstar sold its holdings in Southam in 1992 to Conrad Black, who was able to incrementally increase his ownership to the point where he assumed complete control of the firm. The international press baron, who by then had added the *Chicago Sun-Times* and *Jerusalem Post* to his worldwide Hollinger stable of dailies, thus became the largest owner of newspapers in his native land, from which he had been shut out for so long. Well known as a hands-on publisher with strong right-wing political views, which he imposes on his newspapers, Black made sport of the vanquished St. Clair Balfour, then 85, at the company's 1996 annual meeting which marked the culmination of his control. Southam, he said, had "long accepted inadequate returns for the shareholders, published generally undistinguishable products for the readers and received exaggerated laudations from the working press for the resulting lack of financial and editorial rigor."[43] Black completed his takeover of Southam in 1998 by taking the company private again after buying up the remaining outstanding shares in an offer financed with the company's own cash reserves, which he distributed in an ingenious extraordinary dividend that enriched Hollinger most of all. Black's Vancouver lieutenant David Radler, who already served as publisher of the *Chicago Sun-Times* and *Jerusalem Post*, was installed as publisher of both Pacific Press newspapers.

But just as Black extended his control over the Canadian newspaper industry with his acquisition of Southam, he overreached his grasp by starting up a new national daily newspaper in competition with the *Globe and Mail*, whose liberal politics he opposed. The *National Post*, built on the former *Financial Post*, which Hollinger acquired from the *Toronto Sun* chain, suffered the same kinds of start-up losses experienced by every other newspaper on entering a market, and Black was forced to sell his Southam dailies in 2000. He passed them on to television network CanWest Global Communications, which already owned the two largest

TV stations in Vancouver, including the giant BCTV it had recently acquired. While required by federal regulators to sell his original Vancouver TV station CKVU, acquisition of the Pacific Press dailies gave CanWest Global owner Israel Asper unprecedented control over the Vancouver media. The "convergence" of print and electronic media has since seen newspaper and television newsrooms working in close collaboration on coverage and in cross-promotion synergies. Before bowing out as owners of Southam, Black and Radler oversaw the installation of libertarian Neil Reynolds as editor of the *Vancouver Sun* to replace Cruickshank, who they moved to their *Sun-Times* in Chicago. The appointment of Reynolds, a far-right devotee of deregulation and government downsizing, has completed the transformation of the *Sun* from its founding as a Liberal Party newspaper, through its evolution under the Cromies and Stuart Keate into a small-"l" liberal daily, through its sudden conversion to a Conservative Party supporter under Clark Davey, to an advocate for more extreme political measures.

The Competition Tribunal hearings into Southam's disputed acquisition of the Lower Mainland community newspapers resulted in a reduced requirement in 1992 that the company sell either the *North Shore News* or the *Real Estate Weekly*, but Southam appealed the ruling to the Supreme Court of Canada and finally succeeded in having it overturned in 1997.[44] The Labour Relations Board granted a 1996 application by Pacific Press to consolidate its multiplicity of unions into one bargaining unit, and a vote by workers chose the Ottawa-based Communications, Energy and Paperworkers Union of Canada to represent them. Jim Taylor jumped from Pacific Press in 1995 to be publisher of the weekly *Sports Only* tabloid started by the *Toronto Sun* chain in an attempt to establish inroads into the Vancouver market, but the challenge was short-lived and the newspaper soon closed. Like Fotheringham before him, Taylor moved his popular long-running column out of Vancouver, to the pages of the *Calgary Sun*. As if to symbolize the complete corporatization of Vancouver newspapers, Pacific Press moved its editorial offices downtown in 1997 to rented space at Granville Square on Burrard Inlet, a building described in a *Sun* survey of local architecture as a "fine monument to '70s Brutalism . . . relying heavily on intimidation of human beings [with] its monolithic, relentlessly undifferentiated tower."[45] Other Pacific Press departments moved to expanded premises in suburban Surrey, while little more than three decades after it opened, the Pacific Press Building went under the wrecker's ball to make way for a condominium development.

The problems of Pacific Press played no small part in prompting the major changes to ownership of Canadian newspapers seen in the 1980s and 1990s and to the media convergence moves seen at the dawn of the twenty-first century. "It was a monopoly that should have enriched Southam," noted *NewsInc.* magazine in 1993. "Instead it sowed the seeds for the chain's paralysis."[46] As a result, Vancouverites have seen not just their daily newspapers, but also most of their community press and now much of their electronic media controlled by a monopoly that was born in an open skiff off Keats Island in Howe Sound on a hot summer day in 1956.

APPENDIX 1

PACIFIC PRESS CIRCULATION, 1957-2001

Year	Sun	Province	Total	+/- (%)
1957	191,031	131,811	322,842	
1958	200,446	112,210	312,656	-3.2
1959	210,505	106,762	317,267	+1.5
1960	215,748	106,333	322,081	+1.5
1961	219,656	98,660	318,310	-1.2
1962	226,102	101,208	327,310	+2.8
1963	231,641	105,477	337,118	+3.0
1964	237,294	98,928	336,222	-0.3
1965	242,619	103,926	346,545	+3.1
1966	240,338	106,501	346,839	+0.1
1967	245,041	104,851	349,892	+0.9
1968	251,266	108,464	359,730	+2.8
1969	254,043	115,536	369,579	+2.7
1970	210,420	104,054	314,474	-14.9
1971	225,146	110,468	335,614	+6.7
1972	235,389	113,898	349,287	+4.1
1973	241,821	121,539	362,360	+3.7
1974	249,278	128,992	378,270	+4.4
1975	236,743	126,553	363,296	-4.0
1976	234,711	129,437	364,148	+0.2
1977	232,505	128,924	361,429	-0.7
1978	240,770	131,623	372,393	+3.0
1979	219,503	127,067	346,570	-6.9
1980	234,983	126,535	361,518	+4.3
1981	240,991	134,991	375,982	+4.0
1982	241,761	136,616	378,377	+1.6
1983	243,419	148,928	392,347	+3.7
1984	245,780	158,428	404,208	+3.0
1985	248,472	175,078	423,550	+4.8

Year	Sun	Province	Total	+/- (%)
1986	245,473	183,268	428,741	+1.2
1987	239,237	183,018	422,255	-1.5
1988	234,528	187,935	422,463	+0.1
1989	230,782	189,028	419,810	-0.6
1990	220,141	190,949	411,090	-2.0
1991	210,917	189,124	400,049	-2.7
1992	214,576	179,461	394,037	-1.5
1993	221,263	175,296	396,559	+0.6
1994	208,639	166,780	375,419	-5.3
1995	206,027	159,815	365,842	-2.5
1996	196,457	155,258	351,715	-3.9
1997	196,890	160,299	357,189	+1.5
1998	205,009	163,149	368,158	+3.1
1999	202,477	163,773	366,250	-0.5
2000	200,420	166,746	367,166	+0.3
2001	201,271	168,065	369,336	+0.6

Source: *Editor & Publisher International Yearbook*, 1958–2001

APPENDIX 2

PACIFIC PRESS GREATER VANCOUVER MARKET PENETRATION, 1970-1991

Year	Population*	Households	Province	%	Sun	%
1970	1.017	310,150	74,196	24	180,210	58
1971	1.017	310,150	72,995	24	176,688	57
1972	1.082	346,215	72,834	22	190,877	55
1973	1.13	361,600	74,834	22	197,983	55
1974	1.146	366,700	85,263	23	202,963	55
1975	1.162	387,500	84,138	22	197,707	51
1976	1.147	376,100	83,754	22	194,510	52
1977	1.201	436,900	86,018	20	191,380	44
1978	1.206	445,000	87,600	20	198,837	45
1979	1.169	439,200	84,588	19	188,406	41
1980	1.209	463,300	84,358	18	189,021	41
1981	1.233	482,500	90,618	19	200,634	42
1982	1.291	447,445	93,852	21	192,153	43
1983	1.295	499,800	98,891	20	196,559	39
1984	1.321	517,000	135,450	26	198,499	38
1985	1.335	524,900	122,772	23	199,641	38
1986	1.433	530,500	135,379	25	198,438	37
1987	1.388	552,000	127,662	24	193,229	35
1988	1.437	557,800	137,260	25	189,593	34
1989	1.491	580,900	138,658	24	185,179	32
1990	1.549	605,600	138,366	23	186,268	31
1991	1.567	619,600	138,554	22	182,526	29

* In millions.

Source: *Audit Bureau of Circulations, Canadian Daily/Weekly Newspaper Circulation Factbook*, 1971/72–1992.

APPENDIX 3

VANCOUVER NEWSPAPER TIMELINE, 1946-1991

1946: ITU strike against Southam; *Province* closed six weeks, June 5–July 22. Victory Square Riot, July 23 — *Province* resumes publication.

1947–57: Newspaper war, *Sun* vs. *Province*.

1957: Pacific Press amalgamation announced, May 15. *Province* moves to morning publication; *Herald* bought from Thomson, closed.

1960: Restrictive Trade Practices Commission Report issued, September 12. Pacific Press approved, judicial order recommended against changes.

1963: FP Publications buys the *Sun* from Cromie family.

1964–65: *Vancouver Times* started as offset evening daily, closes after 11 months.

1970: Pacific Press closed three months by strike. Unions publish *Express*. Senate Committee calls for Press Ownership Review Board.

1978–79: Pacific Press closed eight months by strike. Unions publish *Express*.

1980: Thomson buys FP Publications, including *Vancouver Sun*. Southam closes *Winnipeg Tribune*, Thomson closes *Ottawa Journal*, Aug. 27. Thomson sells *Sun* to Southam for 100 percent ownership of Pacific Press. Royal Commission on Newspapers called.

1981: Kent Commission report calls for restrictions on newspaper ownership. No change to Pacific Press recommended.

1982: Southam, Thomson charged with criminal conspiracy and monopoly.

1983: Chains acquitted on criminal charges. *Province* converts to tabloid. *New Westminster Columbian* closes.
1989: Southam begins buying competing community newspapers.
1990: Southam ordered to sell some competing titles. Company appeals.
1991: *Sun* moves to mornings. Competition Tribunal hearings held.

NOTES

PREFACE

1. Paul Mongerson, *The Power Press: Its Impact on America and What You Can Do About It* (Golden, Colorado: Fulcrum, 1997), 2.

2. Doug Fetherling, *A Little Bit of Thunder: The Strange Inner Life of the* Kingston Whig-Standard (Toronto: Stoddart, 1993), 40–41.

3. *Ibid.*, 47.

4. *Ibid.*, 42.

5. Stanley Tromp, "Editor Speaks Bluntly," *Georgia Straight*, December 7–14, 2000, 9.

6. See "Diversity and Quality in the Monopoly Press: A Content Analysis of Hollinger Newspapers," Campaign for Press and Broadcasting Freedom, April 1997; and Donald Gutstein with Robert Hackett and NewsWatch Canada, "Question the *Sun*!: A content analysis of diversity in the *Vancouver Sun* before and after the Hollinger take-over," School of Communication, Simon Fraser University, 1998.

7. Marc Edge, "Buying Influence: The Growing Newspaper Monolith From the North," Paper presented at the Association for Education in Journalism and Mass Communication Southeast Colloquium, New Orleans, March 1998.

8. See www.guerrillamedia.org/tattler_archive/

9. Marc Edge, "Byline wars at the *Vancouver Province*," *Media*, Spring 2001, 7.

10. *Ibid.*

11. Canada, Special Senate Committee on Mass Media. *The Uncertain Mirror*, Volume I (Ottawa: Information Canada, 1970), 47.

12. *Ibid.*, 63.

13. *Ibid.*, 4.

14. *Ibid.*

15. *Ibid.*, 71.

16. Keith Davey, *The Rainmaker: A Passion for Politics* (Toronto: Stoddart, 1986), 153.

17. Canada, Royal Commission on Newspapers, *Report* (Ottawa: Minister of Supply and Services, 1981), 215–218.

18. Robert Lewis, "The pressure on the press," *Maclean's*, August 31, 1981, 30.

19. *Ibid.*

20. By the 1990s, however, Canada could no longer claim this dubious distinction, despite popular misconception. Acquisitions in Australia by Rupert Murdoch gave his multinational media conglomerate News Corp. control of 67 percent of that country's daily press, with the Fairfax chain controlling most of the rest, with 22 percent. See Paul Chadwick, "The ownership disas-

ter: how journalism failed," in John Henningham, ed., *Issues in Australian Journalism* (Melbourne: Longman, 1990), 225; and Allan Brown, "Newspaper Ownership in Australia," *Journal of Media Economics*, Fall 1993, 59.

21. Peter J.S. Dunnett, *The World Newspaper Industry* (London: Croom Helm, 1988), 199.

22. For details on the voyage of *Markenurh*, visit her web site at www.geocities.com/TheTropics/Paradise/1356/webpage.htm

INTRODUCTION: MOVING TO MORNINGS

1. Tom Arnold, "Sun will 'shine' all day," *content*, January/February 1991, 21.

2. *Ibid.*

3. See Peter C. Newman, *The Canadian Revolution, 1985–1995: From Deference to Defiance* (Toronto: Viking, 1995).

4. Rafe Mair, *Canada: Is Anyone Listening?* (Toronto: Key Porter, 1998), 173.

5. Ellen Saenger, "Southam's unchecked inroads into the B.C. media," *Financial Times of Canada*, September 30, 1991, 12.

6. Ian Gill, "Of Punks, Peach Crumble, and Pitiful Puns," *Georgia Straight*, December 6–13, 1991, 13.

7. Stephen Hume, "Forestry flacks' record: defending the indefensible," *Vancouver Sun*, July 22, A5.

8. Quoted in Ellen Saenger, "'Defending the indefensible,'" *B.C. Report*, September 23, 1991, 31.

9. James Warren, "Escaping afternoon death: Pacific Press moves one of its papers into competition with another," *Chicago Tribune*, May 12, 1991, C2.

10. *Ibid.*

11. Patricia Lush, "*Vancouver Sun* rises earlier," *Globe and Mail*, September 16, 1991, 35.

12. Stuart Keate, *Paper Boy* (Toronto: Clarke, Irwin, 1980), 120.

13. Robert McConnell, "Common ownership and printing in a single plant — the 'illegal' formula for keeping rival dailies alive," *Marketing*, November 10, 1980, 48.

14. David Hogben, "Pacific Press dailies slammed before competition tribunal," *Vancouver Sun*, September 7, 1991, E2.

15. Bruce Constantineau, "Report on advertising in area called worthless," *Vancouver Sun*, September 6, 1991, D3.

16. Hogben, "Pacific Press dailies slammed before competition tribunal."

17. Constantineau, "Report on advertising in area called worthless."

18. In this regard the present work is similar to some notable business profiles of U.S. joint operating agreements, especially those in Detroit (Brian Gruley, *Paper Losses: A Modern Epic of Greed and Betrayal at America's Two Largest Newspaper Companies* [New York: Grove Press, 1993]) and Seattle (Tim Pilgrim, *Nothing Ventured, Nothing Gained: The Seattle JOA and Newspaper Preservation* [Greenwich, CT: Ablex, 1997]).

CHAPTER 1: THE DEAL

1. St. Clair Balfour, telephone interview, Toronto, February 21, 1999.

2. Larry Dampier, interview, Vancouver, March 5, 1999.

3. Kathleen Nairn and James R. Nairn, "The Paper That Likes to Argue," *Saturday Night*, July 26, 1952, 11.

4. *Ibid.*

5. Bruce, *News and the Southams*, 352.

6. David Parry, *A Century of Southam* (Toronto: Southam Press, 1978), 26.

7. Nairn and Nairn, "The Paper That Likes to Argue," 11.

8. Parry, *A Century of Southam*, 27.

9. Bruce, *News and the Southams*, 353.

10. Sun Publishing Company Limited, *Annual Report, 1946* (Vancouver: Sun Publishing Company Limited, 1947), 9.

11. "Sunburst," *Time* (Canadian ed.), October 17, 1949, 29.

12. Robert Cromie's age at his death has been widely misreported as 49, perhaps due to a headline on his newspaper's coverage of the event which read, "He was in his 49th year." Born on July

4, 1887, he died on May 11, 1936, almost two months short of his 49th birthday.

13. Peter Stursberg, *Extra! When the Papers Had the Only News* (Victoria, B.C.: Sound and Moving Image Division, Provincial Archives of British Columbia, 1982), 78.

14. Jack Scott, "Donald Cromie: 'Merger' Is Never Mentioned," *Saturday Night*, July 6, 1957, 35.

15. "Labor Must Be Recognized As Partner, Says Publisher," *Vancouver Province*, May 21, 1946.

16. Pierre Berton, "Vancouver's Rising Sun," *Maclean's*, July 1, 1948, 39.

17. Alan Morley, "It's People's Own Lives That Are the Real News," *Vancouver Sun*, July 14, 1958, 58.

18. St. Clair Balfour, interview, Toronto, February 19, 1999.

19. Pierre Berton, "Papers, Pickets and Profits," *Maclean's*, July 15, 1950, 15.

20. Bruce, *News and the Southams*, 356.

21. *Ibid.*, 355.

22. *Ibid.*, 356.

23. *Ibid.*, 357.

24. *Ibid.*

25. *Ibid.*, 358.

26. "Rioting will be halted, says Cornett," *Vancouver Sun*, July 24, 1946, 1.

27. Bruce, *News and the Southams*, 358.

28. *Ibid.*, 359.

29. "ITU-Southam strike illegal," *Vancouver Sun*, February 19, 1948, 1.

30. Berton, "Papers, Pickets and Profits," 15.

31. Raymond Nixon, "Concentration and Absenteeism in Daily Newspaper Ownership," *Journalism Quarterly*, June 1945, 102.

32. Oscar Garrison Villard, *The Disappearing Daily* (Freeport, N.Y.: Books for Libraries Press, 1944), vi.

33. Stuart Keate, *Paper Boy* (Toronto: Clarke, Irwin, 1980), 104.

34. Canada, Restrictive Trade Practices Commission, *Report Concerning the Production and Supply of Newspapers in the City of Vancouver and Elsewhere in the Province of British Columbia* (Ottawa: Queen's Printer and Controller of Stationery, 1960), 59.

35. Bruce, *News and the Southams*, 366.

36. "Victoria papers join up to cut publishing costs," *Financial Post*, June 2, 1951, 9.

37. R.L. Peacock, *A Study of the Production of the Vancouver Province With Emphasis on Future Expansion* (Vancouver: University of British Columbia, 1956), 16.

38. *Ibid.*, 38.

39. Parry, *A Century of Southam*, 27.

40. Minko Sotiron, *From Politics to Profit: The Commercialization of Canadian Daily Newspapers, 1890–1920* (Montreal: McGill-Queen's University Press, 1997), 94.

41. *Ibid.*

42. Parry, *A Century of Southam*, 21.

43. Bruce, *News and the Southams*, 344.

44. Sotiron, *From Politics to Profit*, 87.

45. Robert Walker, "How the Cost Squeeze Hit Canadian Newspapers," *Saturday Night*, January 18, 1958, 11.

46. W.A. Craik, *A History of Canadian Journalism* (Toronto: Ontario Publishing, 1959), 261.

47. St. Clair Balfour, interview, Toronto, February 19, 1999.

48. Berton, "Vancouver's Rising Sun,"15.

49. St. Clair Balfour, interview, Toronto, February 19, 1999.

CHAPTER 2: THE TOWER

1. Jack Scott, "Jack Scott," *Vancouver Sun*, May 1, 1964, 29.

2. "Sommers Launches Action To Jail 4 for Contempt," *Vancouver Sun*, August 23, 1956, 1.

3. "Sun fined $5,000 in contempt," *Vancouver Province*, November 7, 1958, 1.

4. "Sunburst," *Time* (Canadian ed.), October 17, 1949, 29.

5. Pierre Berton, "Vancouver's Rising Sun," *Maclean's*, July 1, 1948, 7.

6. Jack Scott, "Donald Cromie: 'Merger' is Never Mentioned," *Saturday*

Night, July 6, 1957, 17.
7. *Ibid.*
8. "Sunburst."
9. Berton, "Vancouver's Rising *Sun*," 40.
10. Scott, "Donald Cromie: 'Merger' is Never Mentioned."
11. Michael Kluckner, *Vancouver: The Way it Was* (North Vancouver: Whitecap Books, 1984), 44.
12. Peter Stursberg, *Extra! When the Papers had the Only News* (Victoria, B.C.: Sound and Moving Image Division, Provincial Archives of British Columbia, 1982), 24.
13. *Ibid.*, 21.
14. Bruce Ramsey, *P.G.E.: Railway to the North* (Vancouver: Mitchell Press, 1962), 50.
15. *Ibid.*, 111.
16. *Ibid.*, 114.
17. *Ibid.*, 127.
18. *Ibid.*, 190.
19. D.A. McGregor, "Adventures of Vancouver Newspapers," *British Columbia Historical Quarterly*, vol. X, no. II (1946), 128.
20. *Ibid.*, 129.
21. Howard T. Mitchell, "Cromie of the *Sun*," *Maclean's*, November 1, 1928, 34.
22. *Ibid.*
23. Stuart Keate, *Paper Boy* (Toronto: Clarke, Irwin, 1980), 101, 13.
24. "Coast Co-Operative," *Time*, December 14, 1936, 49.
25. *Ibid.*
26. Mitchell, "Cromie of the *Sun*," 34.
27. "Death of Robert Cromie; Sudden Cardiac Attack," *Vancouver Sun*, May 12, 1936, 1.
28. Stursberg, *Extra!*, 69.
29. *Ibid.*, 36.
30. Scott, "Donald Cromie: 'Merger' is Never Mentioned," 35.
31. Donald Cromie, interview with Peter Stursberg, Vancouver, August 19, 1980, B.C. Archives, Victoria, B.C., Accession No. 3759.
32. Pierre Berton, *My Times: Living with History 1947–1995* (Toronto: Doubleday, 1995), 131.
33. Pierre Berton, *Starting Out: 1920–1947* (Toronto: McClelland and Stewart, 1987), 276.
34. *Ibid.*
35. *Ibid.*
36. Stursberg, *Extra!*, 69.
37. Bruce Hutchison, *The Far Side of the Street* (Toronto: Macmillan of Canada, 1976), 324.
38. Stursberg, *Extra!*, 70.
39. Berton, "Vancouver's Rising *Sun*," 40.
40. Valerie Gregory, "B.C. newspaperman loved a pun, even a bad one," *National Post*, March 3, 2000.
41. Keate, *Paper Boy*, 11.
42. Berton, "Vancouver's Rising *Sun*."
43. *Ibid.*
44. "Sunburst."
45. *Ibid.*
46. Roland Wild, "Columnists in Clover," *Saturday Night*, April 18, 1953, 22.
47. Berton, "Vancouver's Rising *Sun*," 40.
48. Scott, "Donald Cromie: 'Merger' is Never Mentioned," 35.
49. Keate, *Paper Boy*, 106.
50. Canada, Restrictive Trade Practices Commission, *Report Concerning the Production and Supply of Newspapers in the City of Vancouver and Elsewhere in the Province of British Columbia* (Ottawa: Queen's Printer and Controller of Stationery, 1960), 44.
51. Berton, "Vancouver's Rising *Sun*," 40.
52. George Bain, "All the news that's fun to print," *Maclean's*, April 21, 1986, 59.
53. Scott, "Don Cromie: 'Merger' is Never Mentioned," 35.
54. Berton, *Starting Out*, 178.
55. Pierre Berton, as sung to the author during a telephone interview from Kleinburg, Ontario, March 3, 2000.
56. Keate, *Paper Boy*, 103.
57. *Ibid.*
58. Robert Walker, "How the Cost Squeeze Hit Canadian Newspapers," *Saturday Night*, January 18, 1958, 31.
59. "*Edmonton Bulletin* Folds," *Vancouver News-Herald*, January 20, 1951, 1.

60. "Founder's Daughter Sad As Old Bulletin Folds," *Ottawa Citizen*, January 22, 1951, 27.
61. "*Edmonton Bulletin* Closes Up," *Vancouver Province*, January 20, 1951, 1.
62. "*Edmonton Bulletin* Quits Publication," *Vancouver Sun*, January 20, 1951, 1.
63. St. Clair Balfour, interview, Toronto, February 19, 1999.
64. Ben Metcalfe, "Late Editions," *Vancouver*, June 1986, 54.

CHAPTER 3: THE BALANCE WHEEL

1. Allan Fotheringham, "A legend in the news game," *Maclean's*, April 19, 1993, 52.
2. Allan Fotheringham, interview, Toronto, March 6, 2000.
3. "Cromie to be Vancouver's youngest mayor in history," *Vancouver Sun*, November 30, 1948, 11.
4. Pierre Berton, "Vancouver's Rising *Sun*," *Maclean's*, July 1, 1948, 40.
5. "Sam Cromie Had Zest for Life," *Vancouver Sun*, February 18, 1957, 2.
6. Berton, "Vancouver's Rising *Sun*."
7. "Boat Mishap Claims Life of Sam Cromie," *Vancouver Sun*, February 18, 1957, 1.
8. H.F. Inglis, M.D., "Report of Post Mortem Examination on the body of Mr. Sam Cromie," Gibsons, B.C. (Victoria: Provincial Archives of B.C., February 16, 1957), Accession Number 116/57.
9. Canada, Province of British Columbia, "Inquest: Samuel Patrick Cromie," (Victoria: Provincial Archives of B.C., March 20, 1957) Accession Number 116/57, 3.
10. Fotheringham, "A legend in the news game."
11. Charles Bruce, *News and the Southams* (Toronto: Macmillan of Canada, 1968), 366.
12. Larry Dampier, interview, Vancouver, March 5, 1999.
13. "Vancouver Papers To Merge," *Victoria Colonist*, February 26, 1957, 1.
14. "*Sun, Province* To Combine?" *Marketing*, March 15, 1957, 1.
15. Bruce, *News and the Southams*, 367.
16. Canada, Restrictive Trade Practices Commission, *Report Concerning the Production and Supply of Newspapers in the City of Vancouver and Elsewhere in the Province of British Columbia* (Ottawa: Queen's Printer and Controller of Stationery, 1960), 186.
17. *Ibid.*, 185.
18. *Ibid.*, 85.
19. Donald Cromie, "'Home Paper' Stronger — *Sun* Control Stays Same," *Vancouver Sun*, May 30, 1957, 1.
20. *Ibid.*
21. *Ibid.*
22. Scott Young, "Newspaper Merger Unhealthy," *Globe and Mail*, July 11, 1957, 23.
23. *Ibid.*
24. Bruce, *News and the Southams*, 367.
25. *Ibid.*
26. *Ibid.*
27. Canada, Restrictive Trade Practices Commission, *Report Concerning the Production and Supply of Newspapers in the City of Vancouver*, 2.
28. "High-speed presses to print *The Province*," *Vancouver Province*, December 31, 1957, 2.
29. Canada, Restrictive Trade Practices Commission, *Report Concerning the Production and Supply of Newspapers in the City of Vancouver*, 146.
30. Fotheringham, "A legend in the news game."
31. Denny Boyd, *In My Own Words* (Vancouver: Douglas and McIntyre, 1995), 58.
32. Canada, Restrictive Trade Practices Commission, *Report Concerning the Production and Supply of Newspapers in the City of Vancouver*, 133.
33. *Ibid.*, 134.
34. *Ibid.*
35. *Ibid.*, 139.
36. *Ibid.*, 57.
37. *Ibid.*, 104.
38. *Ibid.*, 115.
39. *Ibid.*, 96.
40. *Ibid.*, 56.
41. *Ibid.*, 81.

42. *Ibid.*, 173.
43. *Ibid.*, 63.
44. George Bain, "All the news that's fun to print," *Maclean's*, April 21, 1986, 59.
45. Fotheringham, "A legend in the news game."
46. Allan Fotheringham, *Last Page First* (Toronto: Key Porter, 1999), 11.
47. Allan Fotheringham, *Birds of a Feather: The Press and the Politicians* (Toronto: Key Porter, 1989), 23.
48. Boyd, *In My Own Words*, 55.
49. Pierre Berton, "Introduction," in Peter Murray, ed., *Great Scott! A Collection of the Best Columns by Jack Scott* (Victoria: Sono Nis Press, 1985), 11.
50. Pierre Berton, *Starting Out: 1920–1947* (Toronto, McClelland and Stewart, 1987), 162.
51. Fotheringham, *Birds of a Feather*, 23.
52. Berton, "Introduction," 11.
53. *Ibid.*, 11–12.
54. Boyd, *In My Own Words*, 55.
55. Ben Metcalfe, "Late Editions," *Vancouver*, June 1986, 55.
56. Fotheringham, "A legend in the news game."
57. Boyd, 55.
58. Canada, Restrictive Trade Practices Commission, *Report Concerning the Production and Supply of Newspapers in the City of Vancouver*, 125.
59. Stuart Keate, "Pressures on the Press," in D.L.B. Hamlin, ed., *The Press and the Public: 8th Winter Conference* (Toronto: University of Toronto Press, 1962), 20.
60. "A.W. Moscarella to retire as publisher of *Province*," *Vancouver Province*, November 7, 1958, 2.
61. Young, "Newspaper Merger Unhealthy."
62. Jack Scott, "Donald Cromie: 'Merger' Is Never Mentioned," *Saturday Night*, July 6, 1957, 16.
63. Canada, Restrictive Trade Practices Commission, *Report Concerning the Production and Supply of Newspapers in the City of Vancouver*, 7.
64. *Ibid.*, 159.
65. *Ibid.*, 6.
66. *Ibid.*
67. *Ibid.*, 2.
68. *Ibid.*, 159.
69. *Ibid.*
70. *Ibid.*, 9.
71. *Ibid.*, 11.
72. *Ibid.*, 10.
73. *Ibid.*, 13.
74. *Ibid.*, 12.

CHAPTER 4: THE SELL-OUT

1. Bruce Hutchison, *The Far Side of the Street* (Toronto: Macmillan of Canada, 1978), 215.
2. *Ibid.*
3. Stuart Keate, *Paper Boy* (Toronto: Clarke, Irwin, 1980), 61–62.
4. *Ibid.*, 86.
5. *Ibid.*, 62.
6. *Ibid.*
7. *Ibid.*, 63 fn.
8. Paul Rutherford, *The Making of the Canadian Media* (Toronto: McGraw-Hill Ryerson, 1978), 91.
9. Keate, *Paper Boy*, 105.
10. Charles Bruce, *News and the Southams* (Toronto: Macmillan of Canada, 1968), 369.
11. *Ibid.*
12. *Ibid.*
13. Canada, Restrictive Trade Practices Commission, *Report Concerning the Production and Supply of Newspapers in the City of Vancouver*, 175.
14. *Ibid.*, 176–177.
15. *Ibid.*, 177.
16. *Ibid.*, 178.
17. *Ibid.*
18. *Ibid.*
19. Bruce, *News and the Southams*, 368.
20. St. Clair Balfour, interview, Toronto, February 19, 1999.
21. Bruce Young, "How the Cromie family fought to save the *Sun*," *Canadian Printer & Publisher*, August, 1963, 36.
22. *Ibid.*, 37.
23. Bryce W. Rucker, *The First Freedom* (Carbondale: Southern Illinois University Press, 1968), 22.
24. *Ibid.*, 25.
25. *Ibid.*, 24.
26. Canada, Special Senate Commit-

tee on Mass Media, "Words, Music and Dollars: A Study of the Economics of Publishing and Broadcasting, by Hopkins, Hedlin Limited." (Ottawa: Queen's Printer, 1970), 60.

27. Douglas Fisher, "The case against newspaper chains: Their news is syrup," *Maclean's*, November 17, 1962, 98.

28. Young, "How the Cromie family fought to save the *Sun*," 36.

29. Keate, *Paper Boy*, 105.

30. Hutchison, *The Far Side of the Street*, 325.

31. Keate, *Paper Boy*, 105.

32. *Ibid.*, 106.

33. "Max Bell Buys *Sun* Share Control," *Vancouver Sun*, July 6, 1963, 1.

34. St. Clair Balfour, interview, Toronto, February 19, 1999.

35. Keate, *Paper Boy*, 106.

36. Ben Metcalfe, "Late Editions," *Vancouver*, June, 1986, 54.

37. Keate, *Paper Boy*, 107.

38. *Ibid.*

39. *Ibid.*, 106–107.

40. Denny Boyd, *In My Own Words* (Vancouver: Douglas and McIntyre, 1995), 62.

41. *Ibid.*

42. "Don Cromie To Resign," *Vancouver Sun*, February 6, 1964, 1.

43. "Cromie resigns from *Sun* Board," *Vancouver Sun*, April 28, 1964, 3.

44. Hutchison, *The Far Side of the Street*, 325.

45. *A History of Weekly Newspapers of British Columbia* (Mission, B.C.: British Columbia Weekly Newspapers Association, 1972), 38.

46. *Ibid.*, 108.

47. Bruce, *News and the Southams*, 397.

48. *Ibid.*, 398.

49. *Ibid.*, 399.

50. *Ibid.*, 401.

51. Young, "How the Cromie family fought to save the *Sun*," 36.

52. Canada, Special Senate Committee on Mass Media, "Words, Music and Dollars," 85.

53. "Pacific Press Buys City Block, Plans Call For 7-Story Building," *Journal of Commerce* (Western Canada ed.), April 28, 1962.

54. *Ibid.*

55. "Pacific Press Calls Selected Tenders For $5,000,000 Project," *Journal of Commerce* (Western Canada ed.), October 2, 1963.

56. "Resourcefulness Key to Building," *Journal of Commerce* (Western Canada ed.), December 18, 1965.

57. "Pacific Press probe urged in Commons," *Vancouver Times*, March 30, 1965.

58. *Ibid.*

59. Keate, *Paper Boy*, 107.

60. *Ibid.*, 108.

61. *Ibid.*

62. *Ibid.*, 109.

63. *Ibid.*

64. *Ibid.*, 111.

65. "Points For Publisher of *Vancouver Sun*," March 17, 1964. University of British Columbia Library, Vancouver, Special Collections and University Archives Division, Stuart Keate Papers, Box 10, File 6.

66. *Ibid.*

67. Keate, *Paper Boy*, 112–113.

68. "Dec. 12: (RSM and BH, Hotel Vcr) 1974," University of British Columbia Library, Vancouver, Special Collections and University Archives Division, Stuart Keate Papers, Box 10, File 6.

69. Keate, *Paper Boy*, 113.

70. Young, "How the Cromie family fought to save the *Sun*," 36.

71. Keate, *Paper Boy*, 117.

72. *Ibid.*, 118.

73. *Ibid.*, 119.

74. Stuart Keate, Letter to Bruce Hutchison, July 19, 1966, University of British Columbia Library, Vancouver, Special Collections and University Archives Division, Stuart Keate Papers, Box 10, File 2.

75. *Ibid.*

76. Keate, *Paper Boy*, 118.

77. Hutchison, *The Far Side of the Street*, 327.

78. Keate, *Paper Boy*, 122.

79. *Ibid.*, 123.

80. Douglas Collins, "Press," *Saturday Night*, November 1965, 70.

81. "We can't afford to take a gamble in this election," *Vancouver Province*, September 10, 1960, 1.

82. "$450 million gas, oil plan jeopardized," *Vancouver Province*, September 10, 1960, 1.

83. "Fear Campaign Blamed For Tory, Grit Defeat," *Vancouver Sun*, September 13, 1960, 1.

84. Allan Fotheringham, "Allan Fotheringham," *Vancouver Sun*, July 18, 1972, 29.

85. *Ibid.*

86. Fred Bruning, "'Pandemic' of deceit sweeping country," *Des Moines Register*, September 22, 1996, 1.

87. Fotheringham, "Allan Fotheringham," *Vancouver Sun*, July 18, 1972.

88. Collins, "Press."

CHAPTER 5: THE TIMES

1. Jack Webster, "*The Times*: Bold Vision, Pathetic End," *Vancouver Sun*, August 7, 1965, 15.

2. Alexander Ross, "Hot, hopeful rumors for Vancouverites who are fed up with their newspaper," *Maclean's*, December 14, 1963, 3.

3. Donald Stainsby, "Vancouver's New Newspaper," *Saturday Night*, October 1964, 27.

4. *Ibid.*

5. "How one daily plans to get off the ground," *Marketing*, November 1, 1963, 46.

6. *Ibid.*

7. "A New Dimension in Newspapers," 1963 information package from Vancouver Times Publishing Ltd., in Vancouver City Archives.

8. Stainsby, "Vancouver's New Newspaper."

9. "How one daily plans to get off the ground."

10. Ross, "Hot, hopeful rumors for Vancouverites who are fed up with their newspaper."

11. "Information Package," Vancouver Times Publishing Ltd., Vancouver City Archives, Aubrey F. Roberts papers (Volume 1, File 3), 7.

12. *Ibid.*, 23.

13. *Ibid.*, 26.

14. *Ibid.*, 25–26.

15. "Test runs on press under way as new daily's debut nears," *Canadian Printer & Publisher*, August 1964, 54.

16. "Gremlins, too many subscribers slow first issues of *Times*," *Canadian Printer & Publisher*, October 1964, 56.

17. *Ibid.*

18. *Ibid.*

19. *Ibid.*

20. Stainsby, "Vancouver's New Newspaper."

21. *Ibid.*

22. Webster, "*The Times*: Bold Vision, Pathetic End."

23. *Ibid.*

24. *Ibid.*

25. *Ibid.*

26. *Ibid.*

27. Bruce Young, "*Times* halts publication after 11 stormy months," *Canadian Printer & Publisher*, September 1965, 90.

28. *Ibid.*

29. Webster, "*The Times*: Bold Vision, Pathetic End."

30. "*Times* fights for survival," *Vancouver Times*, March 27, 1965, 1.

31. *Ibid.*

32. *Ibid.*

33. Young, "*Times* halts publication after 11 stormy months."

34. *Ibid.*

35. "*Times* fights for survival."

36. Webster, "*The Times*: Bold Vision, Pathetic End."

37. "*Times* fights for survival."

38. Webster, "*The Times*: Bold Vision, Pathetic End."

39. "*Times* fights for survival."

40. "*Vancouver Times* buys lease on life," *Marketing*, April 16, 1965, 3.

41. "Information Package," Vancouver Times Publishing Ltd., 7.

42. "Plans new daily in Vancouver, Canadian chain of five papers," *Canadian Printer & Publisher*, January 1963, 65.

43. Webster, "*The Times*: Bold Vision, Pathetic End."

44. Young, "*Times* halts publication after 11 stormy months," 90.

45. "*Vancouver Times* buys lease on life."

46. "We have just begun to fight," *Vancouver Times*, March 29, 1965, 1.
47. "This space reserved for Woodward's Stores Ltd.," *Vancouver Times*, March 29, 1965, 18.
48. Webster, "*The Times*: Bold Vision, Pathetic End."
49. "*Vancouver Times* buys lease on life."
50. Canada, *Hansard*, March 30, 1965, 12898.
51. "Pacific Press probe urged in Commons," *Vancouver Times*, March 30, 1965, 1.
52. "MP explains need for Pacific Press probe," *Vancouver Times*, March 31, 1965, 1.
53. *Ibid.*
54. "*Vancouver Times* buys lease on life."
55. "How Pat Burns won fame and fortune by talking on the world's biggest party line," *Maclean's*, November 16, 1964, 79.
56. *Ibid.*
57. Susan Dexter, "The Mouth That Roars," *Maclean's*, October 15, 1966, 24.
58. *Ibid.*
59. Jack Webster, *Webster!* (Vancouver: Douglas and McIntyre, 1990), 101.
60. Jack Wasserman, "Jack Wasserman," *Vancouver Sun*, March 23, 1965, 23.
61. "*Vancouver Times* buys lease on life," *Marketing*, April 16, 1965, 3.
62. "Cooling Off the Hot Line," *Time* (Canadian ed.), April 9, 1965, 17.
63. Dexter, "The Mouth That Roars," 55.
64. "Cooling Off the Hot Line."
65. Dexter, "The Mouth That Roars."
66. "Just about everyone showed up for the show," *Vancouver Times*, March 30, 1965, 1.
67. Jes Odam, "10,000 Rush for 2,800 Seats," *Vancouver Sun*, March 30, 1965, 1.
68. "Cooling Off the Hot Line," 18.
69. "Pat Burns joins *The Times*," *Vancouver Times*, April 1, 1965, 1.
70. *Ibid.*
71. "*Vancouver Times* buys lease on life."
72. *Ibid.*
73. Young, "*Times* halts publication after 11 stormy months."
74. "Independence pledge issued by Warren," *Vancouver Times*, April 30, 1965, 4.
75. *Ibid.*
76. *Ibid.*
77. Webster, "*The Times*: Bold Vision, Pathetic End."
78. "*Times* goes weekly on June 3," *Vancouver Times*, May 26, 1965, 1.
79. "*Vancouver Times* Becomes Weekly," *Vancouver Sun*, May 26, 1965, 2.
80. Young, "*Times* halts publication after 11 stormy months."
81. Webster, "*The Times*: Bold Vision, Pathetic End."
82. William J. Bell, "Warren's 'verve' built *Times*," [letter to the editor] *Vancouver Sun*, July 21, 1979, A5.
83. "Warren Gives Up Control of *Times*," *Vancouver Sun*, May 28, 1965, 7.
84. Webster, "*The Times*: Bold Vision, Pathetic End."
85. *Ibid.*
86. "Day of decision for . . .," *Vancouver Times*, June 2, 1965, 1.
87. "*Times* Faces New Financial Crisis," *Vancouver Sun*, June 3, 1965, 2.
88. *Ibid.*
89. Young, "*Times* halts publication after 11 stormy months," 90.
90. *Ibid.*
91. Victor W. Odlum, "Categorical Message," *Vancouver Times*, June 15, 1965, 1.
92. "Apology," *Vancouver Times*, June 19, 1965, 1.
93. Young, "*Times* halts publication after 11 stormy months," 90.
94. Webster, "*The Times*: Bold Vision, Pathetic End."
95. *Ibid.*
96. *Ibid.*
97. Young, "*Times* halts publication after 11 stormy months," 90.
98. Jake van der Kamp, "*Courier* gets no sympathy from *Times* ex-publisher," *B.C. Business Week*, September 12, 1979, 2.
99. Ben Metcalfe, "Late Editions," *Vancouver*, June 1986, 54.

CHAPTER 6: SIAMESE TWINS

1. Denny Boyd, "A city without a light in the window," *Vancouver Sun*, October 24, 1981, A3.
2. Denny Boyd, "Don't ever give 'em your right name," *Vancouver Sun*, October 21, 1981, A3.
3. *Ibid.*
4. *Ibid.*
5. Douglas Collins, "Press," *Saturday Night*, November 1965, 70.
6. Ormond Turner, "Around Town," *Vancouver Province*, February 19, 1965, 25.
7. *Ibid.*
8. Ormond Turner, "Around Town," *Vancouver Province*, February 22, 1965, 21.
9. *Ibid.*
10. "Columnist accused in House," *Vancouver Province*, February 24, 1965, 15.
11. Canada, *Hansard* (Ottawa: Queen's Printer, 1965), 11669.
12. Charles Lynch, "Liberals muff the ball again," *Vancouver Province*, February 25, 1965, 5.
13. Canada, *Hansard*, 11670.
14. *Ibid.*
15. Lynch, "Liberals muff the ball again."
16. "Vote fraud probe ordered as government loses out," *Vancouver Province*, February 25, 1965, 1.
17. Canada, *Hansard*, 11671.
18. *Ibid.*
19. *Ibid.*
20. *Ibid.*
21. Lynch, "Liberals muff the ball again."
22. Collins, "Press," 71.
23. "Election talk is in the air again," *Vancouver Province*, February 26, 1965, 1.
24. "Lawyer Charges Hearsay In Irregular-Voting Stories," *Vancouver Sun*, March 27, 1965, 29.
25. Michael Cobb, "No Vote Evidence, Says B.C. Druggist," *Vancouver Sun*, April 2, 1965, 15.
26. "Mystery two speak in vote lists inquiry," *Vancouver Province*, April 23, 1965, 14.
27. Nathan T. Nemetz, *Report into certain charges of election irregularities in the federal election of 1963* (Victoria: Queen's Printer, 1965), 12 .
28. "Columnist Claims Called 'Fantasy,'" *Vancouver Sun*, May 10, 1965, 2.
29. "Many election errors ignored, claims lawyer," *Vancouver Province*, May 11, 1965, 32.
30. Collins, "Press," 73.
31. Nemetz, *Report into certain charges*. . ., 33.
32. *Ibid.*, 9–10.
33. Ormond Turner, "Around Town," *Vancouver Province*, August 19, 1965, 21.
34. Collins, "Press," 69.
35. "'Invaders' Flayed By Saucer Addict," *Vancouver Sun*, May 2, 1968, 26.
36. Canada, Restrictive Trade Practices Commission, *Report Concerning the Production and Supply of Newspapers in the City of Vancouver and Elsewhere in the Province of British Columbia* (Ottawa: Queen's Printer and Controller of Stationery, 1960), 75.
37. *Ibid.*, 142.
38. "Building Valuable Addition To Vancouver," *Journal of Commerce* (Western Canada ed.), December 18, 1965.
39. "Resourcefulness Key To Building," *Journal of Commerce* (Western Canada ed.), December 18, 1965.
40. *Ibid.*
41. "Building Valuable Addition To Vancouver."
42. *Ibid.*
43. *Ibid.*
44. *Ibid.*
45. "Pacific Press complex is new fully automated giant of Canadian west," *Canadian Printer & Publisher*, April 1966, 54.
46. "Unique Features in Pacific Building," *Journal of Commerce* (Western Canada ed.), December 18, 1965.
47. Tom Hazlitt, "Rolling again — on schedule," *Vancouver Province*, December 28, 1965, 1.
48. *Ibid.*
49. *Ibid.*

50. "Statue recalls an era," *Vancouver Province*, September 27, 1967, 1.
51. "Building Valuable Addition To Vancouver."
52. Nat Cole, "Newspaper Milestone Acclaimed by Pearkes," *Vancouver Sun*, March 15, 1966, 20.
53. *Ibid.*
54. George A. Norris, "It's Sort of a Fantasy," *Vancouver Sun*, March 14, 1966, 2.
55. Stuart Keate, *Paper Boy* (Toronto: Clarke, Irwin, 1980), 141.
56. *Ibid.*
57. *Ibid.*
58. Kathy Tait, "Red all over," *Vancouver Province*, August 29, 1966, 1.
59. Keate, *Paper Boy*, 142.
60. "Parish repels bishop's attack," *Vancouver Province*, December 21, 1966, 1.
61. *Ibid.*
62. Stuart Keate, Memo to Fred Auger, December 21, 1966, University of British Columbia Library, Special Collections and University Archives Division, Stuart Keate Papers, Box 1, File 7.
63. *Ibid.*
64. Stuart Keate, Letter to Dick Malone, December 23, 1966, University of British Columbia Library, Special Collections and University Archives Division, Stuart Keate Papers, Box 1, File 7.
65. *Ibid.*
66. Fred Auger, Memo to Stuart Keate, F.A. (no adjective) [signed] Fred, "Stu, since you won't answer the phone I'm writing to say —" undated, University of British Columbia Library, Special Collections and University Archives Division, Stuart Keate Papers, Box 1, File 7.
67. Stuart Keate, Memo to Fred Auger, December 23, 1966, University of British Columbia Library, Special Collections and University Archives Division, Stuart Keate Papers, Box 1, File 7.
68. *Ibid.*
69. *Ibid.*
70. *Ibid.*

CHAPTER 7: THE LEGEND

1. Vaughn Palmer, "Bruce Hutchison," *Vancouver Sun*, September 15, 1992, A12.
2. Denny Boyd, "He was the best of his time, even in the worst of our times," *Vancouver Sun*, September 19, 1992, B1.
3. Peter C. Newman, "The voice of Canada," *Maclean's*, September 28, 1992, 56.
4. Pierre Berton, *Starting Out: 1920–1947* (Toronto: McClelland and Stewart, 1987), 125.
5. *Ibid.*
6. Bruce Hutchison, *The Far Side of the Street* (Toronto: Macmillan of Canada, 1976), 147.
7. Palmer, "Bruce Hutchison."
8. Hutchison, *The Far Side of the Street*, 174.
9. *Ibid.*, 213.
10. *Ibid.*, 216.
11. *Ibid.*, 214.
12. Stuart Keate, *Paper Boy* (Toronto: Clarke, Irwin, 1980), 65.
13. *Ibid.*, 67.
14. Hutchison, *The Far Side of the Street*, 216.
15. Vaughn Palmer, "Foreword" in Bruce Hutchison, *To Canada With Love and Some Misgivings* (Vancouver: Douglas and McIntyre, 1991), 10–11.
16. Hutchison, *The Far Side of the Street*, 215.
17. *Ibid.*, 326.
18. Allan Fotheringham, "Cry, my beloved country," *Maclean's*, October 5, 1992, 68.
19. Keate, *Paper Boy*, 101.
20. "Canadian Papers Struck 14 Times," *Victoria Times*, December 9, 1967, 3.
21. "Toronto ITU Strike Echoes in City," *Vancouver Sun*, August 15, 1964, 3.
22. "Papers' Tactics Scored," *Vancouver Sun*, November 4, 1964, 55.
23. *Ibid.*
24. Pat Carney, "Business on business: Pacific Press' Benson," *Vancouver Province*, December 6, 1963, 20.
25. *Ibid.*
26. *Ibid.*
27. "Planners OK Pacific Press Heli-

port Try," *Vancouver Sun*, October 21, 1967, 11.

28. "Vote Okays Strike," *Vancouver Sun*, October 4, 1967, 2.

29. Pat Carney, "Pat Carney," *Vancouver Sun*, October 4, 1967, 30.

30. *Ibid.*

31. "No strike agreement claimed by publishers," *Vancouver Province*, October 21, 1967, 8.

32. "Company Loses Anti-Strike Bid," *Vancouver Sun*, October 27, 1967, 12.

33. "Manager Refuses to Shut School," *Vancouver Sun*, November 9, 1967, 31.

34. "Company Accepts Mediation Offer," *Vancouver Sun*, November 10, 1967, 16.

35. *Ibid.*

36. "Guild Rejects Offer From Pacific Press," *Vancouver Sun*, November 10, 1967, 16.

37. "Four Press Unions File Strike Notice," *Vancouver Sun*, November 13, 1967, 1.

38. *Ibid.*, 2.

39. "Mediation Moves Made in Pacific Press Disputes," *Vancouver Sun*, November 14, 1967, 2.

40. "Newspaper Guild Suspends Talks," *Vancouver Sun*, November 16, 1967, 2.

41. *Ibid.*

42. "Pacific Press working conditions, wages and fringe benefits are among the best in Canada," *Vancouver Sun*, November 16, 1967, 32.

43. *Ibid.*

44. *Ibid.*

45. "Pacific Press Talks Resume," *Vancouver Sun*, November 17, 1967, 2.

46. *Ibid.*

47. "Bennett Makes Suggestion: 6-Month Pacific Press Pact," *Vancouver Sun*, November 17, 1967, 1.

48. *Ibid.*

49. "Press talks," *Vancouver Province*, November 17, 1967, 2.

50. "Pacific Press Talks Resume."

51. *Ibid.*

52. *Ibid.*

53. "Press Discussions Continue Monday," *Vancouver Sun*, November 18, 1967, 2.

54. *Ibid.*

55. *Ibid.*

56. Norman R. Severud, "Newspaper Strike Could be Long, Bitter," *Victoria Colonist*, November 18, 1967, 1.

57. "City Union Protests News Lack," *Victoria Times*, November 18, 1967, 2.

58. Maurice Rush, "Who is Pacific Press?" *Pacific Tribune*, November 24, 1967, 1.

59. "Blank Spaces Dot *Vancouver Province*," *Victoria Times*, November 30, 1967, 2.

60. "An Apology," *Vancouver Province*, November 30, 1967, 1.

61. *Ibid.*

62. "Press strike set for 8 a.m.," *Vancouver Province*, December 8, 1967, 1.

63. "Pacific Press talks collapse," *New Westminster Columbian*, December 8, 1967, 1.

64. "Newspaper Strike On, Off, On Again," *Victoria Times*, December 8, 1967, 1.

65. "Mayor's Bid Fails To Stop Strike," *Victoria Colonist*, December 9, 1967, 1.

66. *Ibid.*

67. "No Break Near In Press Strike," *Victoria Times*, December 9, 1967, 1.

68. Sean Rossiter, "Pacific Pressed," *Vancouver*, February 1980, 64.

69. "Press strike settled by 3 a.m. agreement," *Vancouver Province*, December 11, 1967, 1.

70. "P. Press contract ratified," *Vancouver Province*, December 12, 1967, 1.

71. "17-Hour Parley Brings End To Strike at Pacific Press," *Vancouver Sun*, December 11, 1967, 1.

72. *Ibid.*, 2.

73. Rossiter, "Pacific Pressed," 64.

CHAPTER 8: THE SHOWDOWN

1. Stuart Keate, *Paper Boy* (Toronto: Clarke, Irwin, 1980), 121.

2. *Ibid.*, 120.

3. *Ibid.*

4. *Ibid.*

5. Robert Fulford, "The hands of these 4 men steer Canada's biggest newspaper chain," *Toronto Star*, January 29,

1966, 8.

6. *Ibid.*

7. *Ibid.*

8. Keate, *Paper Boy*, 187.

9. *Ibid.*, 198, fn.

10. *Ibid.*, 192.

11. *Ibid.*, 220.

12. *Ibid.*, 195.

13. *Ibid.*, 200.

14. St. Clair Balfour, interview, Toronto, February 19, 1999.

15. Keate, *Paper Boy*, 120.

16. Canada, Restrictive Trade Practices Commission, *Report Concerning the Production and Supply of Newspapers in the City of Vancouver and Elsewhere in the Province of British Columbia* (Ottawa: Queen's Printer and Controller of Stationery, 1960), 72.

17. C.R.P. Fraser and Sharon Angel, "Vancouver: a history of conflict," in Gerard Hebert, *et al.*, eds., *Labor Relations in the Newspaper Industry* (Ottawa: Minister of Supply and Services, 1981), 28.

18. *Ibid.*

19. *Ibid.*, 28–29.

20. *Ibid.*, 28.

21. *Ibid.*, 33.

22. "Talks Resume At Pacific Press," *Vancouver Sun*, November 14, 1969, 19.

23. "'Impasse' Reached At Pacific Press," *Vancouver Sun*, November 20, 1969, 2.

24. Len Guy and William McLeman, "An Open Letter From The Joint Council of Newspaper Unions," December 2, 1969, University of British Columbia Library, Vancouver, Special Collections and University Archives Division, Stuart Keate Papers, Box 10, File 4.

25. "Press vote 68 per cent for strike," *Vancouver Province*, November 25, 1969, 1.

26. "Threatening call made," *Vancouver Sun*, December 17, 1969, 2.

27. "Security net mounted after threat on life," *Vancouver Province*, December 18, 1969, 13.

28. *Ibid.*

29. Stuart Keate, memo to R.S. Malone, February 7, 1970, University of British Columbia Library, Vancouver, Special Collections and University Archives Division, Stuart Keate Papers, Box 10, File 4.

30. *Ibid.*

31. "Unions' Multiplicity Rapped By Pacific Press Manager," *Vancouver Sun*, August 23, 1968, 3.

32. *Ibid.*

33. Paddy Sherman, interview, West Vancouver, June 28, 2001.

34. Stuart Keate, memo to R.S. Malone, February 7, 1970, University of British Columbia Library, Vancouver, Special Collections and University Archives Division, Stuart Keate Papers, Box 10, File 4.

35. "Press production lags again," *Vancouver Province*, February 7, 1970, 2.

36. Keate, memo to Malone, February 7, 1970.

37. "Press production lags again," *Vancouver Province*, February 7, 1970, 2.

38. "Press unions get warning of shutdown," *Vancouver Sun*, February 9, 1970, 1.

39. *Ibid.*

40. "Press Negotiators Draw Haynes Fire," *Vancouver Sun*, February 10, 1970, 7.

41. Paddy Sherman, interview, West Vancouver, June 28, 2001.

42. "3 Press Unions Call Strike Vote," *Vancouver Sun*, February 11, 1970, 1.

43. "Three More Press Unions Vote for Strike Action," *Vancouver Sun*, February 13, 1970, 1.

44. "At the meeting this morning . . ." typewritten note, February 13, 1970, University of British Columbia Library, Vancouver, Special Collections and University Archives Division, Stuart Keate Papers, Box 10, File 4.

45. "Papers cut out ads as trouble continues," *Vancouver Province*, February 14, 1970, 1.

46. *Ibid.*

47. George Dobie, "Pressmen Suspended for Second Time," *Vancouver Sun*, February 14, 1970, 1.

48. "Staff Lopped, Papers Shrink," *Victoria Colonist*, February 14, 1970, 1.

49. "*Province* and *Sun* Cease Publication," *Victoria Times*, February 16, 1970, 1.
50. *Ibid.*
51. *Ibid.*
52. *Ibid.*
53. "Unions Trying to Renew Pact Talks," *Victoria Colonist*, February 18, 1970, 6.
54. Trevor Lautens, "When the Newspapers Had to Stop," *Saturday Night*, May 1970, 33.
55. Don MacLachlan, "Camouflaged '*Sun*' Leaves Some Burning," *Victoria Times*, February 26, 1970, 15.
56. *Ibid.*
57. MacLachlan, "Camouflaged '*Sun*' Leaves Some Burning."
58. *Ibid.*
59. Lautens, "When the Newspapers Had to Stop."
60. MacLachlan, "Camouflaged '*Sun*' Leaves Some Burning."
61. Keith Davey, *The Rainmaker: A Passion for Politics* (Toronto: Stoddart, 1986), 8.
62. *Ibid.*
63. Keith Davey, "Preface," *The Uncertain Mirror: Report of the Special Senate Committee on Mass Media*, Vol. I (Ottawa: Information Canada, 1970), vii.
64. Davey, *The Rainmaker*, 153.
65. Walter Gray, "Vancouver Without Papers," *Vancouver Province*, May 15, 1970, 5.
66. "Dispute Hurting Business," *Victoria Times*, March 5, 1970, 9.
67. "Windfall for Vancouver suburban newspapers," *Marketing*, March 2, 1970, 2.
68. *Ibid.*
69. *Ibid.*
70. "Weeklies Take Up Slack on Mainland," *Victoria Times*, February 18, 1970, 3.
71. "The Citizen," *A History of Weekly Newspapers of British Columbia* (Mission: British Columbia Weekly Newspapers Association, 1972), 37.
72. *Ibid.*
73. "New Paper Weighed By Union," *Victoria Colonist*, February 19, 1970, 49.
74. Lautens, "When the Newspapers Had to Stop," 34.
75. *Ibid.*
76. *Ibid.*
77. "5-Year Plan Plebiscite Delay Opposed by Two Aldermen," *Vancouver Express*, February 24, 1970, 2.
78. *Ibid.*
79. "Dispute Hurting Business," *Victoria Times*, Mar. 5, 1970, 9.
80. *Ibid.*
81. *Ibid.*
82. Allan Fotheringham, "Allan Fotheringham," *Vancouver Sun*, May 15, 1970.
83. "Windfall for Vancouver suburban newspapers."
84. MacLachlan, "Camouflaged '*Sun*' Leaves Some Burning."
85. Fotheringham, "Allan Fotheringham," May 15, 1970.
86. "Mainland Circulation Boosted by *Colonist*," *Victoria Colonist*, February 19, 1970, 49.
87. *Ibid.*
88. "Vancouver shutdown is affecting BC economy," *Canadian Printer & Publisher*, April, 1970, 33.
89. Lautens, "When the Newspapers Had to Stop," 34.
90. "Mainland Circulation Boosted by *Colonist*."
91. *Ibid.*
92. "Columbian company is big in suburbs with four dailies keyed to local scene," *Canadian Printer & Publisher*, February 1968, 40.
93. Stuart Keate, "A brief to the Special Senate Committee on Mass Media," in Canada, *Proceedings of the Special Senate Committee on Mass Media* (Ottawa: Queen's Printer), January 22, 1970, 8–9.
94. "Thanks, But No Thanks," *The Guild Reporter*, March 13, 1970, 8.
95. *Ibid.*
96. Fotheringham, "Allan Fotheringham," May 15, 1970.

CHAPTER 9: THE EXPRESS

1. Mike Tytherleigh, e-mail to author, September 26, 2000.
2. *Ibid.*

3. “New Paper Weighed by Union,” *Victoria Colonist*, February 19, 1970, 49.
4. *Ibid.*
5. “The Birth of a Newspaper,” *The outsider*, February 26, 1970.
6. *Ibid.*
7. “*Express* Hits Streets Today,” *Victoria Colonist*, February 21, 1970, 8.
8. *Ibid.*
9. *Ibid.*
10. “The Birth of a Newspaper.”
11. *Ibid.*
12. “This is both a birth and a death notice,” *Vancouver Express*, February 21, 1970, 1.
13. “*Express* Races Into News Gap,” *Victoria Colonist*, February 22, 1970, 1.
14. Mike Tytherleigh, e-mail to author, September 26, 2000.
15. “The Birth of a Newspaper.”
16. “Full *Express* run was sold out by noon Tuesday,” *The outsider*, February 25, 1970.
17. “*Express* Doubles at Third Edition,” *Victoria Colonist*, February 27, 1970, 15.
18. “Full *Express* run . . .”
19. Mike Tytherleigh, e-mail to author, September 26, 2000.
20. Trevor Lautens, “When the Newspapers Had to Stop,” *Saturday Night*, May 1970, 34.
21. “*Express* a Sellout, Another Out Today,” *Victoria Colonist*, February 24, 1970, 3.
22. “*Express* Races Into News Gap.”
23. “The Birth of a Newspaper.”
24. Mike Tytherleigh, e-mail to author, September 26, 2000.
25. Lautens, “When the Newspapers Had to Stop,” 34.
26. “Long siege in view for Vancouver,” *Financial Post*, March 7, 1970, 34.
27. “Pugstem Payoff,” *The outsider*, March 3, 1970.
28. “The Birth of a Newspaper.”
29. Charles Bruce, *News and the Southams* (Toronto: Macmillan of Canada, 1968), 364.
30. Fred Auger, “If it’s there Paddy will find it — and climb it,” *Vancouver Province*, June 7, 1969, 4.
31. “Press Talks Shift To ‘Neutral’ Island,” *Victoria Colonist*, February 26, 1970, 1.
32. “Press Unions Okay Talks,” *Vancouver Express*, February 24, 1970, 2.
33. “Further talks set in press dispute,” *Vancouver Express*, February 28, 1970, 1.
34. “Newspaper guild initiates action,” *Vancouver Express*, March 3, 1970, 5.
35. “‘Benson Proposal Means Complete Capitulation,’ — Perlik,” *The outsider*, March 4, 1970.
36. *Ibid.*
37. *Ibid.*
38. “Long Fight Seen In Press Dispute,” *Victoria Times*, March 3, 1970, 2.
39. “Newspaper guild initiates action,” *Vancouver Express*, March 3, 1970, 5.
40. “‘Benson Proposal Means Complete Capitulation,’ — Perlik.”
41. “Benson Does Unions a Favor,” *The outsider*, March 23, 1970.
42. “The Anniversary Meeting,” *The outsider*, March 23, 1970.
43. “Bennett Arbitration Rejected by Unions,” *Victoria Times*, March 11, 1970, 14.
44. Allan Fotheringham, “Allan Fotheringham,” *Vancouver Sun*, May 15, 1970, 29.
45. “Newspaper guild initiates action,” *Vancouver Express*, March 3, 1970, 5.
46. “Pacific Press Files Suit,” *Victoria Times*, March 7, 1970, 2.
47. “Pacific Press seeks seizure of chattels,” *Vancouver Express*, March 12, 1970, 1.
48. “Union accuses Pacific Press,” *Vancouver Express*, March 19, 1970, 5.
49 Paddy Sherman, “Memo from P. Sherman,” March 23, 1970, University of British Columbia Library, Vancouver, Special Collections and University Archives Division, Stuart Keate Papers, Box 10, File 4.
50. *Ibid.*
51. *Ibid.*
52. *Ibid.*
53. *Ibid.*
54. *Ibid.*

55. "Mediation launched in newspaper dispute," *Vancouver Express*, April 2, 1970, 2.
56. "Special Notice on Mediation," *The outsider*, May 1, 1970.
57. *Ibid.*
58. "Vancouver Injunction Upheld on Appeal," *Victoria Times*, April 10, 1970, 9.
59. E. Benson, letter to The Directors, Pacific Press Limited, April 13, 1970, University of British Columbia Library, Vancouver, Special Collections and University Archives Division, Stuart Keate Papers, Box 10, File 4.
60. Paddy Sherman, "Mem [*sic*] from P. Sherman," April 17, 1970, University of British Columbia Library, Vancouver, Special Collections and University Archives Division, Stuart Keate Papers, Box 10, File 4.
61. *Ibid.*
62. *Ibid.*
63. "The *Express* Expanding," *The outsider*, April 17, 1970.
64. C.R.P. Fraser and Sharon Angel, "Vancouver: a history of conflict," in Gerard Hebert, *et al.*, eds., *Labor Relations in the Newspaper Industry* (Ottawa: Minister of Supply and Services, 1981), 34.
65. Mike Tytherleigh, e-mail to the author, September 26, 2000.
66. *Ibid.*
67. "National Publicity," *The outsider*, March 23, 1970.
68. Paddy Sherman, "Memo from P. Sherman," April 22, 1970, University of British Columbia Library, Vancouver, Special Collections and University Archives Division, Stuart Keate Papers, Box 10, File 4.
69. *Ibid.*
70. *Ibid.*
71. *Ibid.*
72. *Ibid.*
73. *Ibid.*
74. "Rumour Machine Pours Out a Flood — Again," *The outsider*, April 24, 1970.
75. "Pacific Press court date set," *Vancouver Express*, April 28, 1970, 6.
76. Fraser and Angel, "Vancouver: a history of conflict," 34.
77. "Papers get ready after 3 months" *Vancouver Express*, May 12, 1970, 1.
78. "What's Going On?" *The outsider*, May 6, 1970.
79. *Ibid.*
80. D.E. Fergusson, letter to Pen Baskin and Alastair Pollock, May 1, 1970, quoted in "Special Notice on Mediation," *The outsider*, May 1, 1970.
81. Fraser and Angel, "Vancouver: a history of conflict," 34.
82. "What's Going On?"
83. "A Simple Matter of $500,000," *Vancouver Express*, May 7, 1970, 1.
84. D.E. Fergusson, letter to Pen Baskin and Alastair Pollock, May 8, 1970, quoted in "Papers get ready after 3 months," *Vancouver Express*, May 12, 1970, 1.
85. "Vancouver's Papers Back on Streets Friday," *Victoria Times*, May 12, 1970, 10.
86. "Wages, pensions, 'hot-line' plan end press tieup," *Vancouver Province*, May 15, 1970, 30.
87. Fraser and Angel, "Vancouver: a history of conflict," 34.
88. Fotheringham, "Allan Fotheringham," May 15, 1970.
89. Paddy Sherman, "Is B.C. headed toward a general strike?" *Vancouver Province*, May 16, 1970, 4.
90. *Ibid.*
91. Mike Tytherleigh, e-mail to the author, September 26, 2000.
92. *Ibid.*
93. George Dobie, "Can newspapering survive if labor strife continues?" *Vancouver Sun*, May 15, 1970, 51.
94. Fraser and Angel, "Vancouver: a history of conflict," 35.
95. "Benson quits Pacific Press," *Vancouver Sun*, September 23, 1970, 2.

CHAPTER 10: THE PERPETRATOR

1. Don Cromie, letter to Allan Fotheringham, quoted in Allan Fotheringham, *Last Page First* (Toronto: Key Porter, 1999), 16.
2. *Ibid.*
3. Fotheringham, *Last Page First*, 16.
4. Allan Fotheringham, "A legend in

the news game," *Maclean's*, April 19, 1993, 52.

5. Fotheringham, *Last Page First*, 16.

6. Allan Fotheringham, interview, Toronto, March 6, 2000.

7. *Ibid.*

8. Fotheringham, *Last Page First*, 18.

9. "Fotheringham's Harpoon," *Time*, May 1, 1972, 10.

10. Tom Alderman, "Foth: That's Allan Fotheringham, the king of Vancouver," *Canadian*, May 5, 1979, 3.

11. *Ibid.*

12. *Ibid.*

13. Sean Rossiter, "The Mayor and the Columnist," *Vancouver*, November, 1976, 26.

14. *Ibid.*

15. Alderman, "Foth: That's Allan Fotheringham, the king of Vancouver," 4.

16. H.L. Mencken, quoted in *ibid.*

17. Hall Leiren, "Birks rejects NPA accounting," *Vancouver Sun*, November 21, 1972, 1.

18. Rossiter, "The Mayor and the Columnist," 27.

19. Allan Fotheringham, "Allan Fotheringham," *Vancouver Sun*, November 21, 1972, 33.

20. *Ibid.*

21. Allan Fotheringham, "Allan Fotheringham," *Vancouver Sun*, April 7, 1972, 19.

22. *Ibid.*

23. *Ibid.*

24. *Ibid.*

25. *Ibid.*

26. Allan Fotheringham, "Allan Fotheringham," *Vancouver Sun*, April 8, 1972, 33.

27. *Ibid.*

28. Allan Fotheringham, "Allan Fotheringham," *Vancouver Sun*, April 14, 1972, 33.

29. "Inside *Maclean's*," *Maclean's*, December 1, 1975, 1.

30. Stuart Keate, letter to G.M. Bell, April 11, 1969, University of British Columbia Library, Special Collections and University Archives Division, Stuart Keate Papers, Box 9, File 15.

31. *Ibid.*

32. Stuart Keate, "Introduction," in Allan Fotheringham, *Collected and Bound* (Vancouver: November House, 1972), x.

33. *Ibid.*

34. Allan Fotheringham, "Allan Fotheringham," *Vancouver Sun*, September 10, 1969, 27.

35. *Ibid.*

36. *Ibid.*

37. Allan Fotheringham, "Allan Fotheringham," *Vancouver Sun*, December 3, 1969, 21.

38. David Ablett, "Fouks Attacks the *Sun*," *Vancouver Sun*, December 4, 1969, 44.

39. Allan Fotheringham, "Allan Fotheringham," *Vancouver Sun*, December 30, 1969, 17.

40. Allan Fotheringham, "Allan Fotheringham," *Vancouver Sun*, January 27, 1970, 13.

41. *Ibid.*

42. "Columnist decision reserved," *Vancouver Express*, March 5, 1970, 9.

43. "Columnist Cleared In Contempt Case," *Victoria Colonist*, March 7, 1970, 5.

44. "Bid to arrest Fotheringham quashed in court by judge," *Vancouver Express*, April 18, 1970, 2.

45. "Criminal libel case rejected," *Vancouver Sun*, October 27, 1970, 1.

46. Paddy Sherman, "Memo *about* the editor," *Vancouver Province*, July 15, 1972, 4.

47. *Ibid.*

48. *Ibid.*

49. Allan Fotheringham, "Allan Fotheringham," *Vancouver Sun*, July 18, 1972, 29.

50. *Ibid.*

51. *Ibid.*

52. Rossiter, "The Mayor and the Columnist," 28.

53. Allan Fotheringham, "I've created a journalistic monster," *Financial Post*, May 13, 1997, 19.

54. Don Stanley, "All About Allan," *Vancouver*, November 1983, 66.

55. Alderman, "Foth: That's Allan Fotheringham, the king of Vancouver," 4.

56. Fotheringham, *Last Page First*, 22.
57. Allan Fotheringham, "Allan Fotheringham," *Vancouver Sun*, May 15, 1970, 25.
58. Allan Fotheringham, "Allan Fotheringham," *Vancouver Sun*, November 10, 1972, 43.
59. "Pacific Press union heads rap Fotheringham column," *Vancouver Sun*, November 13, 1972, 37.
60. George Dobie, "Newspaper talks get 'specific,'" *Vancouver Sun*, October 17, 1972, 2.
61. "Technological changes at issue," *Vancouver Sun*, September 14, 1972, 12.
62. *Ibid.*
63. "4 Press Unions Vote For Strike Action," *Vancouver Sun*, October 7, 1972, 83.
64. "Newspaper negotiations recessed," *Vancouver Province*, October 27, 1972, 21.
65. *Ibid.*
66. "Guild rejects Pacific Press proposal," *Vancouver Sun*, November 2, 1972, 21.
67. *Ibid.*
68. "Newspaper unions' joint council rejects bid to extend contracts," *Vancouver Sun*, November 3, 1972, 8.
69. "Newspaper truck drivers serve strike notice on distributor," *Vancouver Sun*, November 2, 1972, 21.
70. Jack Wasserman, "Jack Wasserman," *Vancouver Sun*, November 4, 1972 [unpublished].
71. "Presses Roll in Vancouver," *Victoria Colonist*, November 8, 1972, 1.
72. "Pacific Press talks going on," *Vancouver Sun*, November 6, 1972 [unpublished].
73. *Ibid.*
74. "Technology Issue Solved But Still No Press Pact," *Victoria Times*, November 7, 1972, 1.
75. "Presses Roll in Vancouver," *Victoria Colonist*, November 8, 1972, 1.
76. "Pact ends news famine," *Vancouver Sun*, November 8, 1972, 1.
77. "Pacific Press operators vote to accept pay boost," *Vancouver Sun*, November 9, 1972, 22.
78. George Dobie, "A pioneer formula is born," *Vancouver Sun*, November 10, 1972, 34.
79. "Press Talks Recess," *Victoria Colonist*, November 7, 1972, 2.
80. *Ibid.*
81. Allan Fotheringham, "The talented subsidize those who can barely grunt," *Toronto Sun*, November 5, 1994, 12.
82. *Ibid.*
83. C.R.P. Fraser and Sharon Angel, "Vancouver: a history of conflict," in Gerard Hebert, *et al.*, eds., *Labor Relations in the Newspaper Industry* (Ottawa: Minister of Supply and Services, 1981), 35.
84. *Ibid.*, 36.
85. "Max Bell dies in Montreal," *Vancouver Sun*, July 20, 1972, 1.
86. Stuart Keate, *Paper Boy* (Toronto: Clarke, Irwin, 1980), 189.

CHAPTER 11: THE POWER STRUGGLE

1. Charles Bruce, *News and the Southams* (Toronto: Macmillan of Canada, 1968), 363.
2. *Ibid.*
3. *Ibid.*
4. Stuart Keate, *Paper Boy* (Toronto: Clarke, Irwin, 1980), 119.
5. *Ibid.*
6. *Ibid.*
7. *Ibid.*
8. Doug Jansen, "The paper that carried 49 pages of classified," *Marketing*, October 29, 1973, 25.
9. *Ibid.*
10. *Ibid.*
11. Clive Cocking, "Promotion of 'undynamic duo' seen as editorially disastrous," *Vancouver Week*, September 26, 1974, 5.
12. *Ibid.*
13. *Ibid.*
14. Patrick Nagle, e-mail to the author, October 23, 2000.
15. Cocking, "Promotion of 'undynamic duo' seen as editorially disastrous."
16. *Ibid.*
17. *Ibid.*, 5, 28.
18. *Ibid.*, 28.

19. "The media drama: Waiting for Fotho," *Saturday Night*, January/February 1979, 4.
20. *Ibid.*
21. Cocking, "Promotion of 'undynamic duo' seen as editorially disastrous."
22. *Ibid.*
23. Allan Fotheringham, interview, Toronto, March 6, 2000.
24. Stuart Keate, *Paper Boy* (Toronto: Clarke, Irwin, 1980), 124.
25. Walter Stewart, "Fathoming Fotheringham," *Saturday Night*, May 1981, 43.
26. *Ibid.*
27. Allan Fotheringham, interview, Toronto, March 6, 2000.
28. Karenn Krangle and Lin Moody, "Fotheringham affair shows unhealthy situation at Canada's third-largest daily," *content*, April 1976, 8.
29. Clive Cocking, "Will Allan Fotheringham Make the *Sun* Shine?" *Vancouver*, September 1975, 21.
30. *Ibid.*
31. *Ibid.*
32. *Ibid.*
33. *Ibid.*, 22.
34. *Ibid.*
35. *Ibid.*, 26.
36. Allan Fotheringham, "Being, The Fotheringham Papers, Mk.III or The Moving and Scraping of Musical Chairs," [Memo to Stuart Keate], October 5, 1975, University of British Columbia Library, Vancouver, Special Collections and University Archives Division, Stuart Keate Papers, Box 9, File 15.
37. *Ibid.*
38. *Ibid.*
39. *Ibid.*
40. Keate, *Paper Boy*, 124.
41. Fotheringham, "Being, The Fotheringham Papers, Mk.III . . ."
42. "Notices served in press talks," *Vancouver Sun*, October 29, 1974, 12.
43. "Press negotiations resume today," *Vancouver Province*, October 30, 1974, 28.
44. "Press talks resumed," *Vancouver Sun*, November 4, 1974, 2.
45. "ITU members want more," *Vancouver Province*, November 18, 1974, 10.
46. "Newspapers' printers okay altered pact," *Vancouver Province*, November 29, 1974, 39.
47. C.R.P. Fraser and Sharon Angel, "Vancouver: a history of conflict," in Gerard Hebert, *et al.*, eds., *Labor Relations in the Newspaper Industry* (Ottawa: Minister of Supply and Services, 1981), 36.
48. Allan Fotheringham, *Last Page First* (Toronto: Key Porter, 1999), 11.
49. "The media drama: Waiting for Fotho."
50. Fotheringham, *Last Page First*, 11.
51. *Ibid.*
52. *Ibid.*
53. *Ibid.*
54. Fotheringham, "Being, The Fotheringham Papers, Mk.III . . ."
55. *Ibid.*
56. *Ibid.*
57. *Ibid.*
58. *Ibid.*
59. *Ibid.*
60. *Ibid.*
61. *Ibid.*
62. *Ibid.*
63. *Ibid.*
64. *Ibid.*
65. Christopher Dafoe, "Christopher Dafoe," *Vancouver Sun*, July 6, 1976, 18.
66. *Ibid.*
67. Tom Alderman, "Foth: That's Allan Fotheringham, the king of Vancouver," *Canadian*, May 5, 1979, 3.
68. "The media drama: Waiting for Fotho."
69. Allan Fotheringham, interview, Toronto, March 6, 2000.
70. Denny Boyd, *In My Own Words* (Vancouver: Douglas and McIntyre, 1995), 99.
71. Allan Fotheringham, "Allan Fotheringham," *Vancouver Sun*, February 7, 1976, 39.
72. Krangle and Moody, "Fotheringham affair shows unhealthy situation at Canada's third-largest daily."
73. John Ince, "Frothy's lifespan shortening fast," *The Ubyssey*, February

27, 1976, 3.

74. "What to do with Foth?" *The Ubyssey*, February 27, 1976, 4.

75. Don Stanley, "All About Allan," *Vancouver*, November 1983, 66.

76. *Ibid.*

77. *Ibid.*

78. Krangle and Moody, "Fotheringham affair shows unhealthy situation at Canada's third-largest daily."

79. *Ibid.*

80. Lorne Parton, "Lorne Parton," *Vancouver Province*, February 17, 1976, 11.

81. *Ibid.*

82. Krangle and Moody, "Fotheringham affair shows unhealthy situation at Canada's third-largest daily."

83. "Al Foth came to see SK 10.30–11.30 a.m. today," [typewritten note] February 27, 1976, University of British Columbia Library, Special Collections and University Archives Division, Stuart Keate Papers, Box 9, File 15.

84. *Ibid.*

85. Keate, *Paper Boy*, 125.

86. Krangle and Moody, "Fotheringham affair shows unhealthy situation at Canada's third-largest daily."

87. *Ibid.*

88. Quoted in Krangle and Moody, "Fotheringham affair shows unhealthy situation at Canada's third-largest daily."

89. Keate, *Paper Boy*, 125.

90. Allan Fotheringham, "I've created a journalistic monster," *Financial Post*, May 13, 1997, 19.

91. Alderman, "Foth: That's Allan Fotheringham, the king of Vancouver."

92. "The media drama: Waiting for Fotho."

CHAPTER 12: THE BULLDOG

1. Lisa Hobbs, "Lisa Hobbs," *Vancouver Sun*, January 27, 1978, B1.

2. Clive Cocking, "The man with the poisoned pen," *Maclean's*, October 2, 1978, 56.

3. Mac Reynolds, "Git along little Dougie," *Vancouver Sun*, January 28, 1978, A6.

4. Allan Fotheringham, "I've created a journalistic monster," *Financial Post*, May 13, 1997, 19.

5. See Douglas Dales, "'Hero' of War Book Admits Exploits As Cloak-Dagger Spy Were a Hoax," *New York Times*, November 15, 1953, 1; and "The Man Who Talked," *Time*, November 23, 1953, 55.

6. Allan Fotheringham, "Allan Fotheringham," *Vancouver Sun*, April 7, 1977, 25.

7. "Labor raps reporter as 'rotten apple,'" *Vancouver Province*, May 21, 1958, 1.

8. "Press Upheld And Attacked," *Vancouver Province*, May 26, 1958, 17.

9. "Whalen Faction Attacks Reporter," *Vancouver Sun*, June 17, 1959, 2.

10. "Reporter Dismissed," *Vancouver Sun*, February 29, 1960, 38.

11. "Board Probes Case Of Fired Reporter," *Vancouver Sun*, June 11, 1960, 12.

12. "Reporter Ordered Reinstated," *Vancouver Sun*, July 4, 1960, 33.

13. Fotheringham, "Allan Fotheringham," April 7, 1977.

14. Jack Wasserman, "Jack Wasserman," *Vancouver Sun*, March 2, 1963, 21.

15. James Spears, "Look out, Phil! Collins is back in town," *Vancouver Province*, August 19, 1971, 27.

16. Trevor Lautens, "Trevor Lautens," *Vancouver Sun*, May 12, 1967, 41.

17. *Ibid.*

18. *Ibid.*

19. Spears, "Look out, Phil! Collins is back in town," 27.

20. Fotheringham, "I've created a journalistic monster," 19.

21. *Ibid.*

22. Sean Rossiter, "The Mayor and the Columnist," *Vancouver*, November 1976, 28.

23. Allan Fotheringham, "Allan Fotheringham," *Vancouver Sun*, January 2, 1969, 37.

24. Allan Fotheringham, "A lifelong fight for freedom," *Maclean's*, May 24, 1999, 56.

25. Fotheringham, "Allan Fothering-

ham," January 2, 1969.

26. *Ibid.*

27. Fotheringham, "I've created a journalistic monster."

28. Doug Collins, "BCIT brass harvests money tree," *Vancouver Sun*, September 27, 1975, 6.

29. Collins, "Wanted: open salaries openly arrived at," *Vancouver Sun*, October 21, 1975, 6.

30. Doug Collins, "Regarding Genghis Collins and Attila Webster," *Vancouver Sun*, October 27, 1975, 6.

31. *Ibid.*

32. Fotheringham, "I've created a journalistic monster."

33. "*Vancouver Sun* plans 'electronic newsroom,'" *Vancouver Sun*, March 11, 1975, 33.

34. Paddy Sherman, "Production problems," *Vancouver Province*, October 16, 1975, 1.

35. *Ibid.*

36. "Labor Dispute Delays Paper," *Vancouver Sun*, October 16, 1975, 1.

37. "Pacific Press guild workers favor strike by 78 per cent," *Vancouver Sun*, November 24, 1975, 28.

38. D.J.H. Stinson, "Pacific Press Limited," [letter to all employees] April 30, 1976.

39. "Complicated newspaper talks centre on wage guidelines," *Vancouver Sun*, February 6, 1976.

40. Andrew Zimbalist, "Technology and the Labor Process in the Printing Industry," in Zimbalist, ed., *Case Studies on the Labor Process* (New York: Monthly Review Press, 1979) 120.

41. "Union Quits Joint Council," *Vancouver Sun*, April 10, 1976, 37.

42. "Mediator asked to withdraw," *Vancouver Sun*, April 29, 1976, 10.

43. "Union serves strike notice," *Vancouver Sun*, May 6, 1976, 2.

44. "New talks try to avert strike as press case goes to umpire," *Vancouver Sun*, June 1, 1976, 20.

45. "Contract discussions delay press production," *Vancouver Sun*, June 4, 1976, 2.

46. *Ibid.*

47. "LRB to review press dispute," *Vancouver Sun*, June 10, 1976, 2.

48. "Weiler appointment in doubt in Pacific Press labor dispute," *Vancouver Sun*, June 17, 1976, 2.

49. "Pacific Press settlement '24 per cent in two years,'" *Vancouver Sun*, July 20, 1976, 8.

50. "Dispute arises on payment of Pacific Press pay boost," *Vancouver Sun*, July 24, 1976, 2.

51. *Ibid.*

52. Kathy Tait, "Uncertainties feared in Pacific Press pact," *Vancouver Province*, July 26, 1976, 29.

53. "250 walk off job in Pacific Press row," *Vancouver Province*, July 27, 1976, 19.

54. John Sawatsky, "Curbs board to enforce pay recovery," *Vancouver Sun*, July 28, 1976, 16.

55. "Pacific Press pay raise okayed — up to 8 per cent," *Vancouver Sun*, July 30, 1976, 2.

56. "Pacific Press seeks quick AIB ruling," *Vancouver Province*, July 31, 1976, 8.

57. *Ibid.*

58. "Pacific Press told 16 pct. would be illegal," *Vancouver Sun*, August 4, 1976, 7.

59. *Ibid.*

60. "Pacific Press Row to Labor Board," *Victoria Times*, August 11, 1976, 6.

61. "Labor Board's precedent backs papers in pay fuss," *Victoria Colonist*, August 13, 1976, 1.

62. George Dobie, "LRB plan ends press dispute," *Vancouver Sun*, August 20, 1976, 1.

63. Dobie, "Punishment should fit crime in sphere of labor relations," *Vancouver Sun*, September 15, 1976, 25.

64. "Board vetoes above-guidelines press settlement," *Vancouver Sun*, November 18, 1976, 1.

65. C.R.P. Fraser and Sharon Angel, "Vancouver: a history of conflict," in Gerard Hebert, *et al.*, eds., *Labor Relations in the Newspaper Industry* (Ottawa: Minister of Supply and Services, 1981), 38.

66. "Weiler Rules Against Stereotypers

in Pacific Press Jurisdiction Row" *Vancouver Sun*, May 27, 1977, 23.

67. Fraser and Angel, "Vancouver: a history of conflict," 38.

68. Collins, "Around (again) with Collins and Webster," *Vancouver Sun*, August 20, 1976, 6.

69. *Ibid.*

70. *Ibid.*

71. Doug Collins, "Fear and Loathing in the Canadian Mosaic," *Weekend Magazine*, September 11, 1976, 8.

72. See Donald Gutstein, *The New Landlords: Asian Investment in Canadian Real Estate* (Victoria, B.C.: Press Porcepic, 1990); and Freda Hawkins, *Canada and Immigration: Public Policy and Public Concern* (Kingston, Ont.: McGill-Queen's University Press, 1988).

73. Collins, "Fear and Loathing in the Canadian Mosaic," 8.

74. *Ibid.*, 10.

75. "'Racist' writing protested," *Vancouver Sun*, September 24, 1976, 18.

76. Doug Collins, "Racism: Collins answers critics," *Vancouver Sun*, September 28, 1976, 6.

77. *Ibid.*

78. *Ibid.*

79. *Ibid.*

80. Doug Collins, "Thank you, pickets, for boosting the issue," *Vancouver Sun*, September 28, 1976, 6.

81. Dave Stockand, "Police calm hecklers at immigration debate," *Vancouver Sun*, November 26, 1976, 16.

CHAPTER 13: THE RELUCTANT PRINCE

1. Katharine Govier, "Surviving Harvey," *Toronto Life*, December 1996, 90.

2. *Ibid.*

3. Sean Rossiter, "Number Two in a Two-Paper Town," *Vancouver*, January 1977, 24.

4. *Ibid.*, 24–25.

5. *Ibid.*, 25.

6. *Ibid.*, 22.

7. *Ibid.*, 26.

8. *Ibid.*, 24

9. *Ibid.*, 26.

10. Stuart Keate, *Paper Boy* (Toronto: Clarke, Irwin, 1980), 121.

11. Rossiter, "Number Two in a Two-Paper Town," 22.

12. Keate, *Paper Boy*, 121.

13. Paddy Sherman, interview, West Vancouver, June 28, 2001.

14. *Ibid.*

15. Patricia Best, "How an empire was lost," *Toronto Star*, June 9, 1996, D1.

16. Nicholas Cotter, "Technological changes seen reinforcing dailies' status," *Globe and Mail*, April 23, 1975, B1.

17. Rossiter, "Number Two in a Two-Paper Town," 23.

18. Paddy Sherman, interview, West Vancouver, June 28, 2001.

19. Stuart Keate, "Labor Negotiations," Memo to Members of Management Committee, July 1, 1976, University of British Columbia Library, Special Collections and University Archives Division, Stuart Keate Papers, Box 10, File 11.

20. *Ibid.*

21. *Ibid.*

22. David Ablett, telephone interview, Toronto, January 9, 2001.

23. Keate, *Paper Boy*, 123–124.

24. *Ibid.*, 124.

25. David Ablett, telephone interview, Toronto, January 9, 2001.

26. "Ablett resigns position at *Sun*," *Vancouver Sun*, July 4, 1978, A2.

27. David Ablett, telephone interview, Toronto, January 9, 2001.

28. Keate, *Paper Boy*, 199.

29. *Ibid.*, 205.

30. *Ibid.*, 212.

31. *Ibid.*, 212–213.

32. Sean Rossiter, "Number Two in a Two-Paper Town," 26.

33. *Ibid.*, 25.

34. *Ibid.*, 26.

35. "Printers claim pact violated," *Vancouver Sun*, September 5, 1977, 35.

36. George Dobie, "Technological changes leave the industrial elite behind," *Vancouver Sun*, September 10, 1977, 20.

37. *Ibid.*

38. *Ibid.*

39. *Ibid.*

40. *Ibid.*

41. "Press pact talks 'suspended' as

workers book off sick," *Vancouver Sun*, September 23, 1977, A2.

42. "Guild members vote 88 pct. for strike action," *Vancouver Sun*, September 29, 1977, A10.

43. *Ibid.*

44. "Guild leader rejects push for mediation," *Vancouver Province*, October 1, 1977, 1.

45. "Another problem arises in Pacific Press talks," *Vancouver Sun*, October 3, 1977, A19.

46. "'Balance' Required," *Vancouver Province*, October 4, 1977, 19.

47. *Ibid.*

48. "Press unions again reject mediator," *Vancouver Sun*, October 8, 1977, A8.

49. George Dobie, "Looking for hopeful signs in chronology of mediation," *Vancouver Sun*, October 20, 1977, C10.

50. "Newspaper jobs switched from guild by mediator," *Vancouver Sun*, October 14, 1977, A14.

51. "Printers offered four-day week," *Vancouver Sun*, November 1, 1977, A1.

52. "Seven Pacific Press unions accept one-year contract," *Vancouver Sun*, November 7, 1977, B1.

53. C.R.P. Fraser and Sharon Angel, "Vancouver: a history of conflict," in Gerard Hebert, *et al.*, eds., *Labor Relations in the Newspaper Industry* (Ottawa: Minister of Supply and Services, 1981), 40

54. Doug Collins, "Equal opportunity? How mealy-mouthed!" *Vancouver Sun*, September 24, 1977, A6.

55. *Ibid.*

56. Lisa Hobbs, "Lisa Hobbs," *Vancouver Sun*, September 28, 1977, C1.

57. Doug Collins, "Aye, aye, ma'am: Ruff strikes again," *Vancouver Sun*, October 13, 1977, A6.

58. "*Sun* columnist accused of conducting 'vendetta,'" *Vancouver Sun*, October 18, 1977, D3.

59. Doug Collins, "Come on and kiss me, Kate," *Vancouver Sun*, October 20, 1977, A6.

60. "Collins takes top MB prize," *Vancouver Sun*, May 31, 1978, B9.

61. Doug Collins, "Doug Collins," *Vancouver Sun*, July 7, 1978, B1.

62. "Ruff says Collins is a racist," *Vancouver Sun*, July 8, 1978, B1.

63. Doug Collins, "Doug Collins," *Vancouver Sun*, May 29, 1978, C1.

64. "Meet Doug Collins, self-proclaimed New Champ," *Saturday Night*, January/February 1979, 6.

65. Allan Fotheringham, "Allan Fotheringham," *Vancouver Sun*, June 6, 1978, C1.

66. *Ibid.*

67. *Ibid.*

68. *Ibid.*

69. Doug Collins, "Doug Collins," *Vancouver Sun*, June 9, 1978, C1

70. *Ibid.*

71. *Ibid.*

72. *Ibid.*

73. *Ibid.*

74. Doug Collins, "Doug Collins," *Vancouver Sun*, September 18, 1978, C1.

75. *Ibid.*

76. Bill Barringer, "People fear the hatred you inspire, Doug," *Vancouver Sun*, September 20, 1978, A23.

77. Clive Cocking, "The man with the poisoned pen," *Maclean's*, October 2, 1978, 56.

78. *Ibid.*

79. *Ibid.*

80. *Ibid.*

81. *Ibid.*

CHAPTER 14: THE SHUTDOWN

1. Sean Rossiter, "Pacific Pressed," *Vancouver*, February 1980, 66.

2. George Dobie, "Press foes ignore way out of their woes," *B.C. Business Week*, December 5, 1978, 7.

3. Donald Schwartz and Eugene Swimmer, "Ottawa: a failure of management," in Gerard Hebert, *et al.*, eds., *Labor Relations in the Newspaper Industry* (Ottawa: Minister of Supply and Services, 1981), 124.

4. *Ibid.*, 107.

5. "Manning dispute behind *Sun*'s non-appearance," *Vancouver Province*, July 11, 1978, 1.

6. "*Sun* Presses Rolling Again As Row

Goes To Arbitration," *Vancouver Sun*, July 11, 1978, A1.

7. "LRB Denies Consent To Sue Press Union," *Vancouver Sun*, September 27, 1978, A17.

8. "Strike vote scheduled," *Vancouver Sun*, October 7, 1978, A19.

9. "Pacific Press Pressmen Vote For Strike Action In Dispute," *Vancouver Sun*, October 14, 1978, A17.

10. "Guild votes 79 per cent for strike," *Vancouver Province*, October 24, 1978, 9.

11. "Pacific Press served strike notice," *Vancouver Sun*, October 28, 1978, A2.

12. "Mediator asked to report out of press talks," *Vancouver Sun*, October 30, 1978, A2.

13. Phil Needham, e-mail to the author, May 2, 2001.

14. "It's war, say press unions," *Vancouver Express*, November 3, 1978, 2.

15. *Ibid.*

16. *Ibid.*, 1.

17. Rod Mickleburgh, "Manning strikes again," *Maclean's*, November 20, 1978, 50.

18. Ron Rose, "I know you're all concerned . . .," *On The Line Bulletin* [joint council strike newsletter], December 1, 1978.

19. Doug Collins, "Doug Collins," *B.C. Business Week*, November 14, 1978, 3.

20. Stuart Keate, *Paper Boy* (Toronto: Clarke, Irwin, 1980), 214.

21. Sean Rossiter, "Pacific Pressed," 64.

22. Robert Williamson, "Vancouver dailies hold the line," *Globe and Mail*, November 18, 1978, 11.

23. *Ibid.*

24. Bruce McLean, "Pitch-in spirit of pioneer days gets presses rolling," *Vancouver Express*, November 6, 1978, 5.

25. *Ibid.*

26. *Ibid.*

27. "Press ganged," *Vancouver Express*, November 3, 1978, 3.

28. Clark W. Davey and Paddy Sherman, "The Newspaper Strike," *Vancouver Express*, November 3, 1978, 3.

29. Robert L. Perry, "The rise and rise of Clark Davey — and the *Vancouver Sun*," *Financial Post*, September 22, 1979, S4.

30. Paul Raugust, "*Sun* Publisher: Captain Without a Ship," *B.C. Business Week*, November 21, 1978, 2.

31. "Bosses fight *Express*," *Victoria Colonist*, November 8, 1978, 9.

32. "Pacific Press fight for future," *B.C. Business Week*, November 14, 1978, 2.

33. *Ibid.*

34. Jan O'Brien, "LRB to enter Pacific Press dispute," *Vancouver Express*, November 10, 1978, 2.

35. "Gut feeling of hope grows in Pacific Press dispute," *Vancouver Express*, November 8, 1978, 2.

36. "Strike paper's printer feels pressure," *Victoria Colonist*, November 4, 1978, 2.

37. R.D. Taylor, "Notice To: All Employees of the Columbian Company Ltd.," November 14, 1978, University of British Columbia Library, Vancouver, Special Collections and University Archives Division, Stuart Keate Papers, Box 30, File 6.

38. *Ibid.*

29. *Ibid.*

40. George Froehlich and Eleanor Boyle, "Confrontation Possible Over Newsprint Quota," *B.C. Business Week*, November 21, 1978, 1.

41. "*Express* runs low on paper, morale dips," *B.C. Business Week*, June 20, 1979, 20.

42. *Ibid.*

43. *Ibid.*

44. *Ibid.*

45. R. Schwindt, "Study Number 15, The Existence and Exercise of Corporate Power: A Case Study of MacMillan Bloedel Ltd.," *Royal Commission on Corporate Concentration* (Ottawa: Minister of Supply and Services, 1977), 234.

46. "Report's newsprint 'connection' challenged," *Vancouver Sun*, May 16, 1978, A10.

47. *Ibid.*

48. *Ibid.*

49. *Ibid.*

50. Froehlich and Boyle, "Confrontation Possible Over Newsprint Quota."

51. "Paper row heats after 'cool off,'" *Vancouver Express*, December 6, 1978, 9.
52. *Ibid.*
53. *Ibid.*
54. Doug Ward, "Stop the presses," *Canadian Dimension*, July/August 1979, 11.
55. *Ibid.*, 12.
56. Williamson, "Vancouver dailies hold the line."
57. Collins, "Doug Collins," *B.C. Business Week*, November 14, 1978.
58. "Unions United, Newspaper Guild Says," *Victoria Colonist*, December 8, 1978, 7.
59. Clark Davey, letter to *Sun* staff, December 5, 1978, University of British Columbia Library, Vancouver, Special Collections and University Archives Division, Stuart Keate Papers, Box 30, File 6.
60. "Unions United, Newspaper Guild Says."
61. "Paper row heats after 'cool off.'"
62. "Unions United, Newspaper Guild Says."
63. "No Press Arbitration Bid," *Victoria Colonist*, December 13, 1978, 11.
64. "On The Line . . ." *On The Line Bulletin*, December 18, 1978, ITU fonds, City Archives, Vancouver.
65. "Printers claim pay guarantee," *Vancouver Express*, December 18, 1978, 8.
66. *Ibid.*
67. "Pacific Press boss quitting?" *Vancouver Express*, December 29, 1978, 2.
68. Rossiter, "Pacific Pressed," 67.
69. *Ibid.*, 69.
70. *Ibid.*
71. *Ibid.*, 68.
72. *Ibid.*, 66.
73. Moira Farrow, "Newspaper gloom brings radio joy," *B.C. Business Week*, March 28, 1979, 18.
74. George Froelich, "Success follows the roar that sells," *B.C. Business Week*, January 16, 1979, 1.
75. Jake van der Kamp, "BCTV's *News Hour* tops in B.C.," *B.C. Business Week*, March 7, 1979, 1.
76. *Ibid.*, 2.
77. Moira Farrow, "Anchorparson won't lift anchor," *B.C. Business Week*, May 23, 1979, 7.
78. *Ibid.*

CHAPTER 15: THE COMBINATION MAN

1. Don Stanley, "How They Play The Game," *Vancouver*, October 1980, 113.
2. Mike Gasher, "Ironic Columnist," *Vancouver*, September 1984, 26.
3. Taylor, "'You tell Teresa, Mr. McClelland — I can't,'" *Vancouver Sun*, October 16, 1976, 6.
4. George Dobie, "Something . . . different," *Vancouver Express*, May 9, 1979.
5. Jim Taylor, telephone interview, West Vancouver, January 30, 2001.
6. *Ibid.*
7. Dobie, "Something . . . different."
8. Stanley, "How They Play The Game," 112.
9. *Ibid.*
10. Dobie, "Something . . . different."
11. *Ibid.*
12. *Ibid.*
13. "Press talks 'productive,'" *Vancouver Express*, March 9, 1979, A5.
14. Peter Comparelli, "Press talks moving to U.S.," *Vancouver Express*, March 19, 1979, A1.
15. "Press dispute talks recessed," *Vancouver Express*, March 30, 1979, A3.
16. Paddy Sherman, interview, West Vancouver, June 28, 2001
17. "Kagel's memo: Union willingness lacking," *B.C. Business Week*, May 2, 1979, 4.
18. *Ibid.*
19. *Ibid.*
20. George Dobie, "Press dispute at the crisis stage," *Vancouver Express*, April 25, 1979, A4.
21. "Management won't publish," *Victoria Times*, February 16, 1979, 11.
22. "Mediator says they must ease stand, pressmen leave bargaining council," *Globe and Mail*, April 26, 1979, 10.
23. George Dobie, "Press dispute at the crisis stage."
24. "Strike-Lockout Talks Off At Two Vancouver Dailies," *Victoria Times*,

May 17, 1979, 35.

25. Dobie, "Kagel goodbye could get foes to say hello," *B.C. Business Week*, May 30, 1979, 13.

26. Phil Needham, e-mail to the author, May 2, 2001.

27. "Mediator out in press dispute," *Vancouver Express*, May 18, 1979, 2.

28. Harvey S. Southam, "The Inside Story," *Equity*, July/August 1984, 42.

29. Wyng Chow, "Weekly papers fighting for survival, but they're not admitting it," *Vancouver Sun*, June 13, 1977, 7.

30. Lisa Smedman, "*The Courier*," in George Affleck, *Paper Trails: A History of British Columbia and Yukon Community Newspapers* (Vancouver: B.C. and Yukon Community Newspaper Association, 1999), 129.

31. *Ibid.*

32. Harvey S. Southam, "The Inside Story," 42.

33. *Ibid.*

34. *Ibid.*, 43.

35. *Ibid.*

36. Moira Farrow, "New *Courier* didn't tell advertisers," *B.C. Business Week*, June 20, 1979, 2.

37. *Ibid.*, 1.

38. *Ibid.*, 2.

39. Southam, "The Inside Story," 43.

40. George Froelich, "'Paperboy' deadline looms for press foes," *B.C. Business Week*, May 16, 1979, 16.

41. George Dobie, "Press dispute: call it abnormal, weird," *B.C. Business Week*, May 16, 1979, 16.

42. Phil Needham, e-mail to the author, May 2, 2001.

43. "Long press strike going even longer," *Victoria Times*, May 29, 1979, 7.

44. Phil Needham, e-mail to the author, May 2, 2001.

45. George Dobie, "Pacific Press accused of playing dirty pool," *Vancouver Express*, May 30, 1979, A7.

46. "Fresh talks expected in newspaper dispute," *Vancouver Express*, June 6, 1979, A11.

47. Jan O'Brien, "Get off your butt now, Fed tells Pacific Press," *Vancouver Express*, May 30, 1979, A1.

48. "Press talks breakthrough?" *Victoria Times*, June 2, 1979, 13.

49. "Press Union Duo Out," *Vancouver Express*, June 4, 1979, A1.

50. George Dobie, "Press Unions Spitting Against The Wind," *Vancouver Express*, June 6, 1979, A4.

51. "Press Union Duo Out," A2.

52. "Tentative pact ends long press shutdown," *Victoria Times*, June 9, 1979, 1.

53. Peter Comparelli, "Pressmen's union rejects new offer," *Vancouver Express*, June 11, 1979, A1.

54. "No quick press vote," *Victoria Times*, June 12, 1979, 21.

55. "Second union torpedoes Pacific Press settlement," *Victoria Times*, June 14, 1979, 27.

56. "Largest Pacific Press union says yes to proposed contract," *Victoria Times*, June 15, 1979, 15.

57. "Close vote forecast on press pact," *Vancouver Express*, June 13, 1979, A2.

58. "New try at Pacific Press," *Victoria Times*, June 16, 1979, 25.

59. Lindsay Corbett, "The papers start scrapping," *B.C. Business Week*, July 4, 1979, 2.

60. *Ibid.*

61. Ray Norman, "Battle of the dailies begins out west," *Marketing*, July 16, 1979, 35.

62. Nick Russell, "Strike Ends, New Dailies In For Fight," *content*, August 1979, 4.

63. *Ibid.*

64. Corbett, "The papers start scrapping."

65. Robert Williamson, "The *Georgia Straight* goes straight," *Globe and Mail*, May 31, 1979, 8.

66. *Ibid.*

67. Southam, "The Inside Story,"43.

68. Rossiter, "Pacific Pressed," 72.

69. "ITU votes yes on Pacific Press pact," *Victoria Times*, June 20, 1979, 25.

70. "Strike paper dies, unions twist arm," *Victoria Colonist*, June 19, 1979, 23.

71. Peter Comparelli, "Papers a step closer," *Vancouver Express*, June 20, 1979, A2.

72. Peter Comparelli, "Silence veils press talks," *Vancouver Express*, June 22, 1979, A1.

73. "Strike newspaper's press sabotage suspected," *Victoria Times*, June 23, 1979, 39.

74. "Further vote at press," *Victoria Times*, June 25, 1979, 24.

75. Robert Williamson, "Vancouver papers return to life on Friday," *Globe and Mail*, June 27, 1979, 9.

76. "Eight-month Pacific Press strike over, papers Friday," *Victoria Times*, June 26, 1979, 1.

77. "Vancouver papers scrambling," *Victoria Times*, June 27, 1979, 6.

78. "Eight months to get out a newspaper," *Vancouver Province*, June 29, 1979, 7.

79. Jes Odam, "First the handshake, then a sense of commitment," *Vancouver Sun*, June 29, 1979, D2.

80. *Ibid.*

81. Allan Fotheringham, "Union credibility biggest loss in strike," *Vancouver Sun*, June 29, 1979, A3.

82. Paddy Sherman, "Labored truths," *Vancouver Province*, June 30, 1979, 21.

83. *Ibid.*

84. *Ibid.*

85. *Ibid.*

86. Rossiter, "Pacific Pressed," 70.

87. *Ibid.*, 71.

88. Paddy Sherman, interview, West Vancouver, June 28, 2001.

89. Rossiter, "Pacific Pressed," 67.

90. *Ibid.*, 68.

91. C.R.P. Fraser and Sharon Angel, "Vancouver: a history of conflict," in Gerard Hebert, *et al.*, eds., *Labor Relations in the Newspaper Industry* (Ottawa: Minister of Supply and Services, 1981), 47.

92. *Ibid.*, 48.

CHAPTER 16: BLACK WEDNESDAY

1. David MacFarlane, "The Accidental Tycoon," *Saturday Night*, October 1980, 30.

2. Susan Goldenberg, *The Thomson Empire* (Toronto: Methuen, 1984), 158.

3. Linda Melvern, *The End of the Street* (London: Methuen, 1986), 75.

4. Roderick Martin, *New Technology and Industrial Relations in Fleet Street* (Oxford: Clarendon Press, 1981), 279–280.

5. Goldenberg, *The Thomson Empire*, 153.

6. Arthur Johnson, "*Times* of London presses stop today, Thomson says," *Globe and Mail*, November 30, 1978, 2.

7. Goldenberg, *The Thomson Empire*, 155.

8. Mike Hughes, "Dailies launch 'new look,'" *Victoria Times*, June 29, 1979, 2.

9. "Papers ease back after eight months," *Victoria Colonist*, June 27, 1979, 28.

10. *Ibid.*

11. Tom Douglas, "Pacific Press: Brainstorming to bump up circulation to pre-strike levels," *Marketing*, November 5, 1979, 63.

12. *Ibid.*

13. "Old-time newspaper wars make lively reading in three Canadian cities," *Globe and Mail*, July 31, 1979, 3.

14. Doug Collins, "Doug Collins," *Vancouver Courier*, July 4, 1979, 5.

15. Rob Wilson, "Vancouver's *Courier* goes daily," *Marketing*, July 2, 1979, 6.

16. Ray Norman, "Battle of the dailies begins out west," *Marketing*, July 16, 1979, 35.

17. Mark Budgen, "'*The Courier*' also rises," *Maclean's*, June 25, 1979, 17.

18. "*Vancouver Province* prepares its Sunday," *Marketing*, July 23, 1979, 13.

19. "Police probe publisher's kidnap claim," *Vancouver Sun*, July 7, 1979, A3.

20. "*Daily News* out for the duration," *Victoria Times*, July 13, 1979, 10.

21. "Old-time newspaper wars make lively reading in three Canadian cities."

22. Harvey S. Southam, "The Inside Story," *Equity*, July/August 1984, 43–44.

23. *Ibid.*, 44.

24. "*Courier* calls it quits in the daily market," *Marketing*, September 3, 1979, 14.

25. "Short of cash *Courier* halts daily publication," *Vancouver Sun*, August 15, 1979, A10.

26. "Byrn admits pulling the rug out

on *Courier*," *Vancouver Sun*, August 16, 1979, A3.

27. *Ibid.*

28. *Ibid.*

29. *Ibid.*

30. Greg Douglas, "Greg Douglas," *Vancouver Courier*, August 16, 1979, 28.

31. Denny Boyd, "Guy's got moxie," *Vancouver Sun*, August 30, 1979, B4.

32. "*Courier* show comes quietly to close as 'economic wounds' prove fatal," *Vancouver Sun*, September 1, 1979, A3.

33. David Yates, "FP learns the hard way," *content*, November 1979, 11.

34. Harvey Southam, "Bottom-line newspapers: The Sterling stable," *Vancouver Sun*, October 14, 1978, C6.

35. Edward Clifford, "Thomson makes bid for FP Publications," *Globe and Mail*, January 3, 1980, B1.

36. Martin, *New Technology and Industrial Relations in Fleet Street*, 290.

37. Goldenberg, *The Thomson Empire*, 201.

38. Jack Willoughby, "Thomson firm will control total of 127 newspapers," *Globe and Mail*, January 12, 1980, B1.

39. "Unions reaction swift and angry," *Victoria Colonist*, August 2, 1980, 1.

40. "Thomson gloomy on two-paper city," *Winnipeg Free Press*, August 15, 1980, 23.

41. Sean Rossiter, "Pacific Pressed," *Vancouver*, February 1980, 74.

42. Walter Stewart, "Fathoming Fotheringham," *Saturday Night*, May 1981, 42.

43. *Ibid.*

44. Chuck Davis, "Fotheringham exits *Sun*," *Vancouver Province*, August 22, 1979, B8.

45. Rossiter, "Pacific Pressed," 74.

46. Stewart, "Fathoming Fotheringham," 40.

47. Rossiter, "Pacific Pressed," 74.

48. *Ibid.*

49. Allan Fotheringham, *Birds of a Feather* (Toronto: Key Porter, 1989), 113–114.

50. *Ibid.*, 114.

51. Rossiter, "Pacific Pressed," 43.

52. "No collusion with Thomson chain on closings, Southam's Fisher says," *Globe and Mail*, September 16, 1980, 11.

53. Douglas Sagi, "Southam's president says changeover won't kill *Province* or *Sun*," *Vancouver Sun*, August 28, 1980, A16.

54. Canada, Restrictive Trade Practices Commission, *Report Concerning the Production and Supply of Newspapers in the City of Vancouver and Elsewhere in the Province of British Columbia* (Ottawa: Queen's Printer and Controller of Stationery, 1960), 177.

55. "*Sun* bought by Southam group," *Vancouver Sun*, August 27, 1980, A1.

56. *Ibid.*

57. *Ibid.*, A2.

58. *Ibid.*

59. "Staffers worry for jobs," *Vancouver Sun*, August 27, 1980, B1.

60. Sagi, "Southam's president says changeover won't kill *Province* or *Sun*."

61. "Guild moves to block *Sun* sale," *Vancouver Sun*, August 28, 1980, A1.

62. "Attempt to block sale of *Sun* called senseless," *Vancouver Sun*, August 29, 1980, A11.

63. *Ibid.*

64. "New work schedules ignored," *Vancouver Province*, September 3, 1980, A4.

65. "Newspaper motion planned," *Vancouver Sun*, September 3, 1980, A2.

66. Michael Valpy, "Finding one's own way in the world," *Vancouver Sun*, August 28, 1980, A4.

67. Doug Fetherling, "Two deaths in the family," *Maclean's*, September 8, 1980, 42.

68. Doug Fetherling, "The day the news caught fire," *Maclean's*, September 8, 1980, 24.

CHAPTER 17: THE AYATOLLAH

1. Sean Rossiter, "Pacific Pressed," *Vancouver*, February 1980, 67.

2. *Ibid.*, 73.

3. *Ibid.*, 44.

4. Richard Doyle, *Hurly-Burly: A Time at the Globe* (Toronto: Macmillan of Canada, 1990), 187.

5. Denny Boyd, *In My Own Words* (Vancouver: Douglas and McIntyre, 1995), 101.
6. Robert L. Perry, "The rise and rise of Clark Davey — and the *Vancouver Sun*," *Financial Post*, September 22, 1979, S4.
7. *Ibid.*
8. Rossiter, "Pacific Pressed," 45.
9. *Ibid.*, 67.
10. Doug Fetherling, "All the news that's soft enough to print," *Maclean's*, October 30, 1978, 80.
11. *Ibid.*
12. *Ibid.*
13. Ian Gill, "Clouded *Sun* Today," *Vancouver*, December 1987, 66.
14. Tom Douglas, "Pacific Press: Brainstorming to bump up circulation to pre-strike levels," *Marketing*, November 5, 1979, 62.
15. *Ibid.*, 63.
16. *Ibid.*
17. "Newspapers 'must woo the consumer' in future," *Vancouver Sun*, August 22, 1980, A10.
18. Rossiter, "Pacific Pressed," 75.
19. Mike Gasher, "Ironic Columnist," *Vancouver*, September 1984, 26.
20. Kevin McGee, "Local Sportscaster Fractures Language, Ties Own Tongue," *Georgia Straight*, September 26-October 3, 1986, 23.
21. Don Stanley, "How They Play the Game," *Vancouver*, October 1980, 113.
22. Paul Raugust, "*Sun* Publisher: Captain Without a Ship," *B.C. Business Week*, November 21, 1979, 2.
23. Rossiter, "Pacific Pressed," 75.
24. "*Sun, Province* 'now have freedom to be different,'" *Vancouver Sun*, September 24, 1980, A15.
25. "Fisher says capacity there for third Vancouver paper," *Vancouver Sun*, October 1, 1980, B12.
26. Larry Still, "Third paper decision likely by year's end, Fisher says," *Vancouver Sun*, October 2, 1980, A7.
27. Robert Williamson, "Epitaph on hold for another daily?" *Globe and Mail*, September 3, 1980, 8.
28. *Ibid.*
29. Deborah Dowling, "West a ripe market for daily newspapers," *Financial Post*, February 21, 1981, 9.
30. "Prototype newspaper set," *Vancouver Sun*, January 21, 1981, A2.
31. Ian Fraser, "Southam launches 2-way fight," *Vancouver Sun*, January 31, 1981, C1.
32. *Ibid.*
33. "Department merger at Pacific Press?" *Victoria Times-Colonist*, November 5, 1980, 8.
34. "Manning report splits union and employer," *Vancouver Sun*, April 16, 1981, G5.
35. "Company accepts terms to end pressroom dispute," *Vancouver Sun*, September 29, 1981, E3.
36. Terrance Wills, "Press investigator Tom Kent was once Dief's 'Paper Tiger,'" *Montreal Gazette*, October 4, 1980, 26.
37. Margaret Mironowicz, "Combines investigators raid Thomson, Southam," *Globe and Mail*, September 10, 1980, 2.
38. "Southam and Thomson offices raided," *Vancouver Sun*, September 10, 1980, B5.
39. Robert Lewis, "The Press Barons," *Maclean's*, May 11, 1981, 25.
40. Ian Austen, "The case against the media giants," *Maclean's*, October 3, 1983, 40.
41. "Pacific Press Papers Probed," *Vancouver Sun*, October 11, 1980, A15.
42. Patrick Nagle, "Probe won't bow to Thomson," *Vancouver Sun*, December 9, 1980, A7.
43. Patrick Nagle, "Sherman, probers skirmish over *Province*'s future," *Vancouver Sun*, January 20, 1981, A8.
44. "Increased newspaper competition predicted," *Vancouver Sun*, January 20, 1981, A3.
45. *Ibid.*
46. Canada, Royal Commission on Newspapers, *Proceedings* (Ottawa: Minister of Supply and Services, 1981), Vol. VII, 1696.
47. *Ibid.*, Vol. VI, 1479–1480.
48. Robert Lewis, "Nobody here but us chickens," *Maclean's*, April 27, 1981, 32–33.
49. *Ibid.*

50. Patrick Nagle, "Newspaper partners sought ways to break Vancouver 'logjam,'" *Vancouver Sun*, March 24, 1981, F8.
51. "'Loser' *Province* isn't kept alive to block a rival paper: Southam," *Vancouver Sun*, April 13, 1981, A9.
52. Patrick Nagle, "3rd daily newspaper for city 'hinges on commission findings,'" *Vancouver Sun*, April 8, 1981, H7.
53. "News chains facing conspiracy charges," *Vancouver Sun*, May 2, 1981, A1.
54. "Pacific Press shelves plans for 3rd newspaper here," *Vancouver Sun*, May 8, 1981, A10.
55. Canada, Royal Commission on Newspapers, *Proceedings* (Ottawa: Minister of Supply and Services, 1981), 241–242.
56. Doug Ward, "*Columbian* employees stage sit-in," *Vancouver Sun*, February 10, 1982, B2.
57. *Ibid.*
58. "4 Unions Ratify *Columbian* Newspaper Pact," *Vancouver Sun*, February 12, 1982, B5.
59. "Guild gains parity," *Vancouver Sun*, March 11, 1982, C9.
60. "BCDC turns down *Columbian*," *Vancouver Sun*, March 14, 1983, B9.
61. Der Hoi-Yin, "*Columbian* offers its creditors a deal," *Vancouver Sun*, May 21, 1983, A3.
62. Doug Ward and Der Hoi-Yin, "Creditors place *Columbian* in receivership," *Vancouver Sun*, October 11, 1983, A1.
63. "*Columbian* wins three-week reprieve," *Vancouver Sun*, October 15, 1983, A13.
64. Gerry Bellett, "*Columbian* staff resigned to fate," *Vancouver Sun*, October 11, 1983, B4.
65. Pete McMartin, "Putting things in perspective," *Vancouver Sun*, November 16, 1983, A5.
66. Neil Graham, "It's all over for *The Columbian*," *New Westminster Columbian*, November 15, 1983, 1.
67. *Ibid.*
68. *Ibid.*
69. Gerry Bellett, "Recrimination, bitterness rule at last rites for *The Columbian*," *Vancouver Sun*, November 16, 1983, A1.
70. Mark Abley, "Davey of the *Gazette*," *Media Magazine*, March 1985, 14.
71. *Ibid.*

CHAPTER 18: GOING TABLOID

1. Gerry Haslam, interview, Richmond, B.C., March 11, 1999.
2. *Ibid.*
3. Gerald Haslam, "Summary of Vancouver Newspaper Research," July 1982, provided to the author by Gerry Haslam.
4. *Ibid.*
5. Gerry Haslam, interview, Richmond, B.C., March 11, 1999.
6. "Discussion Paper: Publishing Options for the Second Newspaper in Vancouver," August 1982, provided to the author by Gerry Haslam.
7. Gerry Haslam, interview, Richmond, B.C., March 11, 1999.
8. *Ibid.*
9. "Discussion Paper," 8.
10. Gerry Haslam, interview, Richmond, B.C., March 11, 1999.
11. "Southam president warns of staff cuts as ads drop," *Vancouver Sun*, April 23, 1982, B7.
12. Phil Needham, "That thump at the door tells the story: Recession cuts local media revenues," *Vancouver Sun*, July 10, 1982, C1.
13. Gerry Haslam, interview, Richmond, B.C., March 11, 1999.
14. "Discussion Paper," 10.
15. *Ibid.*, 18.
16. *Ibid.*, 15.
17. *Ibid.*, 19.
18. *Ibid.*, 22.
19. *Ibid.*, 25.
20. *Ibid.*, 28.
21. *Ibid.*, 29.
22. *Ibid.*, 30.
23. *Ibid.*, 33.
24. *Ibid.*, 34.
25. *Ibid.*, 37.
26. *Ibid.*

27. *Ibid.*
28. *Ibid.*, 40.
29. Gerry Haslam, interview, Richmond, B.C., March 11, 1999.
30. *Ibid.*
31. Marc Edge, "Guild fighting layoffs," *Vancouver Province*, October 3, 1982, A4.
32. "Guild asks to see company books," *Vancouver Sun*, October 6, 1982, C9.
33. "*Province* 'lives' says Wheatley," *Vancouver Sun*, October 6, 1982, C9.
34. *Ibid.*
35. "Press arbitration set," *Vancouver Sun*, November 2, 1982, C5.
36. "Pacific Press arbitration ruling causes stir in labor circles," *Vancouver Sun*, December 1, 1982, B11.
37. *Ibid.*
38. "Council 'did not push appeal,'" *Vancouver Sun*, December 3, 1982, A9.
39. *Ibid.*
40. Jes Odam and Doug Ward, "2 LRB rulings back newspaper union," *Vancouver Sun*, January 8, 1983, A8.
41. "Pacific Press accused of 'stonewalling' guild layoff appeal," *Vancouver Sun*, January 14, 1983, B5.
42. "Union Has Books But Pacific Press To Fight Order," *Vancouver Sun*, June 2, 1983, B4.
43. "Pacific Press, Guild, Near Settlement on 65 layoffs," *Vancouver Sun*, June 24, 1983, D7.
44. Gerry Haslam, interview, Richmond, B.C., March 11, 1999.
45. *Ibid.*
46. *Ibid.*
47. *Ibid.*
48. *Ibid.*
49. Don Hunter, "*The Province* to change format, perhaps even name," *Vancouver Province*, April 26, 1982, A1.
50. *Ibid.*
51. "*The Province* to become a 'family tabloid,'" *Vancouver Province*, April 26, 1982, B4.
52. Gerry Haslam, "To: All Employees of *The Province*," [Memo] May 10, 1983, provided to the author by Gerry Haslam.
53. Gerald Haslam, "*The Province* will remain *The Province*," *Vancouver Province*, May 22, 1983, B2.
54. David Wishart, "Keeping tabs on *The Province*," *Marketing*, November 7, 1983, 16.
55. "Readers line up for tab," *Vancouver Sun*, August 2, 1983, A2.
56. Dan Smith, "Vancouver paper goes tabloid — but 'tame,'" *Toronto Star*, August 3, 1983, D10.
57. "*Province* turns page to new era," *Vancouver Province*, August 2, 1983, 3.
58. Jim Taylor, "Will somebody pick up the tab?" *Vancouver Province*, August 2, 1983, 61.
59. Catherine Marshall, "Small paper lands new readers," *Vancouver Sun*, September 10, 1983, D1.
60. Gerry Haslam, "To All Staff," [memo] August 3, 1983, provided to the author by Gerry Haslam.
61. Albert Sigurdson, "*Province* calls switch to tabloid successful," *Globe and Mail*, August 17, 1983, B4.
62. Wishart, "Keeping tabs on *The Province*."
63. Jim Lyon, "Vancouver's media are making lots of news," *Financial Post*, November 12, 1983, 34.
64. Marshall, "Small paper lands new readers."
65. Lyon, "Vancouver's media are making lots of news."
66. Rick Haliechuk, "Southam officer tore up document, court told," *Toronto Star*, September 28, 1983, E10.
67. *Ibid.*
68. Lorne Slotnick, "Closing of *Winnipeg Tribune* was key to deals, court told," *Globe and Mail*, October 20, 1983, 10.
69. Lorne Slotnick, "Monopoly legitimate, Thomson lawyer says," *Globe and Mail*, October 15, 1983, 5.
70. "Judge drops some charges in chains' case," *Vancouver Sun*, October 29, 1983, A12.
71. Chisholm MacDonald, "Same-day closures done for a reason, Southam boss says," *Vancouver Sun*, November 8, 1983, A13.
72. Lorne Slotnick, "Thomson official maintains closing not linked to deals,"

Globe and Mail, November 3, 1983, 11.

73. Lorne Slotnick, "Newspaper chains cleared of Combines Act charges," *Globe and Mail*, December 10, 1983, 1.

74. *Ibid.*, 5.

75. Chisholm MacDonald, "Newspaper trial had origin in the '50s," *Vancouver Sun*, December 10, 1983, A18.

76. "Tentative pact reached by Pacific Press, unions," *Vancouver Sun*, March 31, 1982, A2.

77. Dan Westell, "Southam denies strike excuse to close *Vancouver Province*," *Globe and Mail*, April 19, 1984, B1.

78. "Unions reject a wage freeze in Pacific Press negotiations," *Globe and Mail*, April 3, 1984, BC1.

79. "Guild, five press unions split," *Vancouver Sun*, March 21, 1984, A2.

80. "Vancouver dailies shut down," *Victoria Times-Colonist*, March 29, 1984, 1.

81. "Press unions ready for long strike," *Globe and Mail*, March 31, 1984, 5.

82. Ross Laver, "The *Globe* muscles in on Vancouver," *Maclean's*, April 16, 1984, 52.

83. "Guild strikes Pacific Press," *Globe and Mail*, April 12, 1984, BC3.

84. Patricia Lush, "Strikers, papers fail to communicate," *Globe and Mail*, April 25, 1984, BC3.

85. Robert Sheppard, "Press unions at odds over strike pay, attitudes," *Globe and Mail*, April 7, 1984, 4.

86. Laver, "The *Globe* muscles in on Vancouver."

87. David Wishart, "*Globe* to cancel its B.C. section," *Marketing*, May 21, 1984, 2.

88. Harvey Southam, "The Inside Story," *Equity*, July/August 1984, 41.

89. "*Courier* newspaper rejects 'inadequate' Southam bid," *Vancouver Sun*, January 11, 1980, C2.

90. Shelley Fralic, "Small papers press onward," *Vancouver Sun*, October 25, 1983, 1.

91. Southam, "The Inside Story," 44.

92. "Lengthy strike will kill paper, Southam hints," *Winnipeg Free Press*, April 19, 1984, 33.

93. *Ibid.*

94. Patricia Lush, "Talks aimed at bringing paper unions together," *Globe and Mail*, April 27, 1984, BC3.

95. "Craft unions favor PacPress contract," *Victoria Times-Colonist*, May 11, 1984, C6.

96. *Ibid.*

97. Patricia Lush, "Vancouver news guild votes to continue strike," *Globe and Mail*, May 14, 1984, 16.

98. "B.C. newspaper strike could last 'for a long time,'" *Montreal Gazette*, May 15, 1984, B8.

99. "PacPress gets pact with guild," *Victoria Times-Colonist*, May 17, 1984, 1.

100. "Vancouver's dailies to resume Thursday," *Globe and Mail*, May 21, 1984, 5.

101. Doug Ward, "$5 million loss forecast for Pacific Press," *Vancouver Sun*, October 17, 1984, A2.

CHAPTER 19: THE CHEESECAKE REBELLION

1. "Strike would kill paper: Fisher," *Vancouver Sun*, April 26, 1985, F7.

2. Murray Campbell, "Southam seeks new chief who respects its traditions," *Globe and Mail*, August 29, 1985, 17.

3. Harvey Enchin, "Southam taking evasive action against takeover," *Globe and Mail*, July 6, 1985, B1.

4. Bud Jorgensen, "Southam rule set to protect shareholders," *Globe and Mail*, August 9, 1985, B1.

5. Patricia Best, "How an empire was lost," *Toronto Star*, June 9, 1996, D1.

6. Shaun Assael, "Northern Exposure," *NewsInc.*, January 1993, 29.

7. Harvey Enchin, "Torstar raises Southam stake to 25 per cent," *Globe and Mail*, August 28, 1985, B1.

8. *Ibid.*

9. Kevin Dougherty, "Southam boss doubts newspaper chain is in danger of takeover," *Toronto Star*, August 8, 1983, B7.

10. Frances Phillips, "Southam bets on keeping it all in the family," *Finan-*

cial Post, November 2, 1985, 4.

11. Don Whiteley, "Challenge is making money: Southam boss," *Vancouver Sun*, November 5, 1985, D1.

12. Best, "How an empire was lost."

13. Lorne Parton, "The Southam maverick," *Vancouver Province*, June 22, 1984, 40.

14. *Ibid.*

15. Assael, "Northern Exposure," 30.

16. "Papers announce major reorganization," *Vancouver Sun*, March 8, 1985, A1.

17. "Union lauds papers' shake-up," *Vancouver Sun*, March 9, 1985, A16.

18. "11 Pacific Press employees receive termination notices," *Vancouver Sun*, April 23, 1985.

19. David Wishart, "Balancing the books," *Marketing*, November 11, 1985, 37.

20. "Southam gives Pacific Press mixed reviews," *Vancouver Province*, March 30, 1986, 38.

21. Sheri Craig, "Reorganization at Southam: An Interview with John Fisher," *Media Magazine*, July/August 1986, 8.

22. "Press workers told of need to cut costs," *Vancouver Sun*, August 14, 1986, F1.

23. *Ibid.*

24. Edward Greenspon, "Vancouver the real test for latest Southam boss," *Globe and Mail*, March 6, 1987, B1.

25. *Ibid.*

26. *Ibid.*

27. David Wishart, "A new-look *Sun* rises in Vancouver," *Marketing*, March 17, 1986, 37.

28. *Ibid.*

29. Harvey Enchin, "Southam sticks to policy of 2 Vancouver papers," *Globe and Mail*, June 23, 1986, B2.

30. Gerry Haslam, interview, Richmond, B.C., March 11, 1999.

31. Ian Gill, "Clouded *Sun* Today," *Vancouver*, December 1987, 63.

32. *Ibid.*, 66.

33. *Ibid.*

34. *Ibid.*

35. Rick Ouston, "Patrick Nagle: 'Nobody Ever Published A Newspaper In A Beer Parlor,'" *Vancouver*, December 1987, 135.

36. Gill, "Clouded *Sun* Today," 67.

37. "Cheesecake Background," [memo to Nicholas Hills] September 21, 1989, provided to the author by Douglas Sagi.

38. Ouston, "Patrick Nagle."

39. "Cheesecake, Etc.," [letter to Gordon Fisher] October 11, 1987, provided to the author by Douglas Sagi.

40. *Ibid.*

41. *Ibid.*

42. Larry Pynn, "News coverage cuts anger council," *Vancouver Sun*, March 20, 1984, A11.

43. "Cheesecake, Etc."

44. *Ibid.*

45. *Ibid.*

46. Gill, "Clouded *Sun* Today," 134.

47. Concerned Journalists at *The Vancouver Sun*, letter to Paddy Sherman, October 21, 1987, provided to the author by Douglas Sagi.

48. Ouston, "Patrick Nagle."

49. Ian Gill, "Just in the Time of Nick," *Vancouver*, July 1990, 28.

50. "Cheesecake Background."

51. Gill, "Just in the Time of Nick."

52. Gerry Haslam, interview, Richmond, B.C., March 11, 1999.

53. *Ibid.*

54. Paddy Sherman, interview, West Vancouver, June 28, 2001.

55. Valerie Casselton, "Union halts Pacific Press talks," *Vancouver Sun*, January 29, 1987, A14.

56. Marc Edge, "Labor Talks Tough," *Vancouver Province*, April 3, 1987, 3; Jeff Lee, "Journalists faced work-or-walk dilemma of ethics," *Vancouver Sun*, June 2, 1987, B3.

57. Gerry Haslam, interview, Richmond, B.C., March 11, 1999.

58. Paddy Sherman, interview, West Vancouver, June 28, 2001.

59. *Ibid.*

60. "Pressmen at Pacific Press back strike action in disputed vote," *Vancouver Sun*, October 26, 1987, A3.

61. "Validity of strike notice queried," *Vancouver Sun*, October 27, 1987, A12.

62. "Pressmen leave strike option

open," *Vancouver Sun*, October 29, 1987, A13.

63. *Ibid.*

64. "Pacific Press unions break off contract talks," *Vancouver Sun*, November 7, 1987, A3.

65. "Pacific Press and unions reach tentative agreement on contract," *Vancouver Sun*, November 9, 1987, A3.

66. "Movie ads ban not illegal strike: LRB," *Vancouver Sun*, November 3, 1984, A2.

67. Phil Needham, "PWA loses court action on newspaper ads," *Vancouver Sun*, December 11, 1985, A27.

68. "Appeal denied over 'hot' ads," *Vancouver Sun*, July 25, 1986, A2.

69. "Pacific Press won't try to force handling of ad," *Vancouver Sun*, May 31, 1986, A2.

70. *Ibid.*

71. Miro Cernetig, "Pacific Press fails to get unions to handle post office ads," *Vancouver Sun*, June 17, 1987, A3.

72. Miro Cernetig, "Unions' ad ban up to legislature, LRB says," June 18, 1987, A18.

73. Cernetig, "Pacific Press fails to get unions to handle post office ads."

74. *Ibid.*

75. Valerie Casselton, "IRC supports newspaper unions," *Vancouver Sun*, January 15, 1988, B7.

76. "Court rejects Pacific Press bid to make union handle ad," *Vancouver Sun*, August 4, 1988, A10.

77. Valerie Casselton, "Press unions defend balking over 'hot' ads," *Vancouver Sun*, September 9, 1988, B7.

78. Valerie Casselton, "IRC backs unions in 'hot' advertising fight," *Vancouver Sun*, September 3, 1988, A8.

79. Harvey Enchin and John Partridge, "Belt-tightening urged at Southam's dailies," *Globe and Mail*, August 24, 1988, B1.

80. "Pacific Press puts on a hiring freeze," *Vancouver Province*, August 25, 1988, 40.

81. Harvey Enchin, "OSC bars Torstar, Southam directors," *Globe and Mail*, June 4, 1986, B1.

82. Renate Leach, "Ottawa readying case against Southam-Torstar share swap," *Financial Post*, April 18, 1988, 43.

83. John Partridge, "Southam, Torstar avert trial with agreement," *Globe and Mail*, September 20, 1988, B1.

84. Renate Leach, "Fisher faces Southam defence task," *Financial Post*, September 26, 1988, 21.

85. John Partridge, "Hollinger not bidding for Southam, but interested if price right," *Globe and Mail*, December 21, 1988, B6.

86. Jaimie Hubbard, "Southam urges employees to hang onto their stock," *Financial Post*, November 30, 1988, 21.

87. "New plant in works," *Vancouver Province*, May 6, 1988, 43.

88. Paddy Sherman, interview, West Vancouver, June 28, 2001.

CHAPTER 20: BUYING THE COMPETITION

1. "Pacific Press executive shuffle leaves papers without publisher," *Toronto Star*, September 15, 1988, D7.

2. Paddy Sherman, interview, West Vancouver, June 28, 2001.

3. "Carney among new directors of Pacific Press," *Vancouver Sun*, July 6, 1989, C1.

4. Jaimie Hubbard, "'Fine-tuning' beginning at Southam newspapers," *Financial Post*, June 14, 1989, 4.

5. Allan Fotheringham, "Looking ahead to 1976," [memo to Stuart Keate] January 12, 1976, University of British Columbia Library, Vancouver, Special Collections and University Archives Division, Stuart Keate Papers, Box 9, File 15.

6. Richard Littlemore, "Bigger. Better. Smarter.: How to Use Consultants to Help Your Company Outstrip the Competition," *B.C. Business*, April 1999, 69.

7. Ian Gill, "Just in the Time of Nick," *Vancouver*, July 1990, 30.

8. Mike Gasher, "A tale of two editors," *content*, September/October 1989, 24.

9. *Ibid.*

10. Gill, "Just in the Time of Nick," 33.

11. Frances Bula, "Hong Kong: The Story Behind The *Sun* Story," *Vancouver*

Sun, July 8, 1989, B5.

12. Gill, "Just in the Time of Nick," 73.

13. Denny Boyd, "100 years old, but this city's not yet grown up," *Vancouver Sun*, September 15, 1986, B2.

14. Gill, "Just in the Time of Nick," 32.

15. *Ibid.*

16. *Ibid.*

17. *Ibid.*

18. Ellen Saenger, "Fat and floundering," *B.C. Report*, November 19, 1990, 27.

19. "Report an eye-opener," *Newsline* [Pacific Press newsletter] December 1990, personal collection of the author.

20. *Ibid.*

21. Gill, "Just in the Time of Nick," 31.

22. *Ibid.*

23. *Ibid.*, 32.

24. Saenger, "Fat and floundering."

25. Robin Ajello, "The Cruickshank redemption: can the new editor-in-chief of the *Vancouver Sun* save the paper from hopeless mediocrity?" *B.C. Business*, December 1995, 28.

26. Denny Boyd, *In My Own Words* (Vancouver: Douglas and McIntyre, 1995), 138.

27. Boyd, "100 years old, but this city's not yet grown up."

28. *Ibid.*

29. *Ibid.*

30. Gasher, "A tale of two editors," 25.

31. *Ibid.*

32. *Ibid.*

33. Gerald Haslam, "Publisher's Notebook," *Vancouver Province*, August 2, 1984, 17.

34. David Baines, "Your tab's a grabber," *Vancouver Province*, September 8, 1985, 33.

35. *Ibid.*

36. Mia Stainsby, "Haslam named marketer of year," *Vancouver Sun*, May 22, 1987, C10.

37. "3 Senior Executives Appointed," *Vancouver Province*, September 14, 1988, 5.

38. Paddy Sherman, interview, West Vancouver, June 28, 2001.

39. Gerry Haslam, interview, Richmond, B.C., March 11, 1999.

40. *Ibid.*

41. "Haslam to head Kamloops paper," *Vancouver Sun*, August 25, 1989, B2.

42. William Boei, "Trinity anchored by Liverpool papers," *Vancouver Sun*, May 12, 1990, A10.

43. Bob Mackin, Jr., "Southam Takes Hold In The West," *Marketing*, May 13, 1991, 16.

44. Patricia Lush, "Vancouver dailies 'bomb proofed,'" *Globe and Mail*, September 5, 1991, B2.

45. Ellen Saenger, "Southam's stranglehold," *B.C. Report*, September 23, 1991, 31.

46. *Ibid.*

47. *Ibid.*

48. Tony Whitney, "Supplements a success for *Sun*," *Marketing*, November 18, 1988, 44.

49. Lush, "Vancouver dailies 'bomb proofed.'"

50. Ken MacQueen, "Papers called protective wing," *Vancouver Sun*, September 5, 1991, D1.

51. *Ibid.*

52. Mike Gasher, "Southam consolidates Vancouver monopoly," *content*, May/June 1989, 23.

53. *Ibid.*

54. *Ibid.*

55. Bob Mackin Jr., "Will *Sun*'s Move Help Southam?" *Marketing*, November 18, 1991, 30.

56. *Ibid.*

57. Lisa Smedman, "*The Courier*," in George Affleck, *Paper Trails: A History of British Columbia and Yukon Community Newspapers* (Vancouver: Arch Communications, 1999), 132.

58. *Ibid.*

59. Saenger, "Southam's stranglehold," 30.

60. Terry O'Neill, "Smothered by Southam," *B.C. Report*, June 4, 1990, 36.

61. *Ibid.*

62. Drew Fagan, "Southam purchase challenged," *Globe and Mail*, November 30, 1990, B1.

63. *Ibid.*

64. Bob Mackin Jr., "Tribunal decision on *News* purchase expected in spring," *North Shore News*, January 29, 1992, 3.

65. Drew Fagan, "Watchdog wants limits on Southam," *Globe and Mail*, March 6, 1991, B1.

66. Drew Fagan, "Competition bureau allows Southam plan," *Globe and Mail*, March 18, 1991, B13.

67. "Mutiny on the flagship," *Maclean's*, March 11, 1991, 9.

68. Boyd, *In My Own Words*, 138.

69. Paddy Sherman, interview, West Vancouver, June 28, 2001.

70. Stan Persky, "Teenagers stand up to trashy stereotypes," *Vancouver Sun*, September 28, 1991, C2.

71. Gill, "Of Punks, Peach Crumble, and Pitiful Puns," *Georgia Straight*, December 6–13, 1991, 13.

72. Stan Persky, "Being a war reporter can be hell, too," *Vancouver Sun*, January 26, 1991, D2.

73. Deborah Wilson, "*Sun*'s quest for readers plagued by setbacks," *Globe and Mail*, January 28, 1991, A5.

74. *Ibid.*

75. *Ibid.*

76. Stan Persky, "Parton should have spared us the farewell rant," *Vancouver Sun*, March 9, 1991, D2.

77. "Southam president calls Pacific Press worst performer in newspaper group," *Vancouver Sun*, March 2, 1991, C2.

78. Paddy Sherman, interview, West Vancouver, June 28, 2001.

79. "Vancouver papers face walkout," *Globe and Mail*, August 29, 1991, B2.

80. "Southam plans to publish during strike," *Vancouver Sun*, July 25, 1991, A2.

81. "Dispute Costs B.C. Dailies $1.8 million," *Marketing*, September 9, 1991, 2.

82. Nicole Parton, "Why the magazine is a good deal for all," *Vancouver Sun*, April 13, 1987, F1.

83. Katharine Govier, "Surviving Harvey," *Toronto Life*, December 1996, 90.

84. *Ibid.*

85. John Partridge, "Newspaper chief on tight deadline," *Globe and Mail*, May 2, 1991, B1.

86. "Southam president calls Pacific Press worst performer in newspaper group."

CHAPTER 21: THE STOLEN NEWSPAPER

1. Ben Metcalfe, "Late Editions," *Vancouver*, June 1986, 53.

2. Peter Stursberg, *Extra! When the Papers Had the Only News* (Victoria, B.C.: Sound and Moving Image Division, Provincial Archives of British Columbia, 1982), 17.

3. *Ibid.*

4. *Ibid.*, 18.

5. D.A. McGregor, "Adventures of Vancouver Newspapers," *British Columbia Historical Quarterly*, Vol. X, No. II (1946), 128.

6. Pierre Berton, telephone interview, Kleinburg, Ontario, March 3, 2000.

7. Pierre Berton, "Vancouver's Rising *Sun*," *Maclean's*, July 1, 1948, 39.

8. *Ibid.*

9. George Bain, "All the news that's fun to print," *Maclean's*, April 21, 1986, 59.

10. Allan Fotheringham, "A legend in the news game," *Maclean's*, April 19, 1993, 52.

11. Ben Bagdikian, "Conglomeration, Concentration and the Media," *Journal of Communication*, Spring 1980, 64.

12. Ben Bagdikian, *The Media Monopoly* (Boston: Beacon Hill, 1983), 199.

13. See Doug Underwood, *When MBAs Rule the Newsroom* (New York: Columbia University Press, 1993).

14. John Miller, *Yesterday's News: Why Canada's Daily Newspapers are Failing Us* (Halifax: Fernwood, 1998), 9.

15. *Ibid.*, 9–10.

16. C.R.P. Fraser and Sharon Angel, "Vancouver: a history of conflict," in Gerard Hebert, *et al.*, eds., *Labor Relations in the Newspaper Industry* (Ottawa: Minister of Supply and Services, 1981), 48.

17. Bernard Berelson, "What 'Missing the Newspaper' Means," in Paul F. Lazarsfeld and Frank N. Stanton, eds., *Communications Research: 1948–1949* (New York: Harper, 1949, 129.

18. *Ibid.*

19. *Ibid.*

20. Penn Kimball, "People without Papers," *Public Opinion Quarterly*, 23,

(1959), 394.

21. Penn Kimball, "New York Readers in a newspaper shutdown," *Columbia Journalism Review*, Fall 1963, 50.

22. *Ibid.*, 48.

23. *Ibid.*, 52.

24. John Polich, "*Daily News*, its unions, newspaper market lose in 1990 strike," *Newspaper Research Journal*, Winter 1995, 80.

25. Richard Littlemore, "The biggest moments of the last 25 years: our take on the events that have made Lotusland what it is," *B.C. Business*, April 1997, 50.

26. James Rosse, "The Decline of Direct Newspaper Competition," *Journal of Communication*, Spring 1980, 67.

27. See Stephen Lacy, "Competing in the Suburbs: A Research Review of Intercity Newspaper Competition," *Newspaper Research Journal*, Winter 1988, 69.

28. Bagdikian, *The Media Monopoly*, 96.

29. *Ibid.*

30. *Ibid.*, 100.

31. See Robert Picard, "Pricing Behavior of Newspapers," in Picard, *et al.*, eds., *Press Concentration and Monopoly: New Perspectives on Newspaper Ownership and Operation* (Norwood, N.J.: Ablex, 1988), 55.

32. Stephen R. Barnett, "Monopoly games — where failures win big," *Columbia Journalism Review*, May/June 1980, 40.

33. *Ibid.*, 41.

34. Stephen R. Barnett, "Combination ad rates: the monopoly stinger," *Columbia Journalism Review*, May/June 1980, 44.

35. *Ibid.*

36. Ian Gill, "Of Punks, Peach Crumble, and Pitiful Puns," *Georgia Straight*, December 6–13, 1991, 13.

37. Robin Ajello, "The Cruickshank redemption: can the new editor-in-chief of the *Vancouver Sun* save the paper from hopeless mediocrity?" *B.C. Business*, December 1995, 28.

38. Richard Littlemore, "The Daily Double," *Vancouver*, Summer 2000, 29.

39. Denny Boyd, "Who said print journalism was dead?" *B.C. Business*, January 1999, 15.

40. Miller, *Yesterday's News*, 11.

41. Daniel Stoffman, "A Licence To Lose Money," *Canadian Business*, March 1994, 45.

42. One of which the author accepted.

43. Quoted in Miller, *Yesterday's News*, 62.

44. Brenda Dalglish, "Top court sides with Southam on B.C. newspapers ownership," *Financial Post*, March 21, 1997, 18.

45. Lance Berelowitz, "Granville Square," *Vancouver Sun*, March 25, 2000, E2.

46. Shaun Assael, "Northern Exposure," *NewsInc.*, January 1993, 29.

BIBLIOGRAPHY

UNPUBLISHED DOCUMENTS

Archival collections containing material relating to the history of Pacific Press are not extensive, but anyone interested in reading more of the "inside story" of the Vancouver dailies, especially the *Vancouver Sun*, could spend many informative and entertaining hours in the Special Collections and University Archives Division at the University of British Columbia Library in Vancouver. There are housed the dozens of boxes comprising the personal papers of Stuart Keate, a UBC alumnus who was publisher of the *Vancouver Sun* from 1964 until his retirement in 1978. The Vancouver City Archives contains the records of the defunct International Typographical Workers Union local, as well as the papers of Aubrey F. Roberts, a former managing editor of the *Province* and assistant publisher of the short-lived *Vancouver Times*.

BOOKS

Affleck, George. *Paper Trails: A History of British Columbia and Yukon Community Newspapers*. Vancouver: Arch Communications, 1999.

Altschull, J. Herbert. *Agents of Power*. New York: Longman, 1984.

Bagdikian, Ben. *The Media Monopoly*. Boston: Beacon Hill, 1983.

Berton, Pierre. *My Times: Living with History 1947-1995*. Toronto: Doubleday, 1995.

——. *Starting Out: 1920-1947*. Toronto: McClelland and Stewart, 1987.

Boyd, Denny. *In My Own Words*. Vancouver: Douglas & McIntyre, 1995.

Bruce, Charles. *News and the Southams*. Toronto: Macmillan of Canada, 1968.

Busterna, John and Picard, Robert. *Joint Operating Agreements: The Newspaper Act and its Application*. Norwood, N.J.: Ablex, 1993.

Canada. Royal Commission on Newspapers. *Proceedings*. Ottawa: Minister of Supply and Services, 1981.

Canada. Royal Commission on Newspapers. *Report*. Ottawa: Minister of Supply and Services, 1981.

Canada. Special Senate Committee on Mass Media. *Proceedings*. Ottawa: Queen's Printer, 1970.

Canada. Special Senate Committee on Mass Media. *The Uncertain Mirror*. Ottawa: Queen's Printer, 1970.

Canada. Special Senate Committee on Mass Media. *Words, Music and Dollars*. Ottawa:

Queen's Printer, 1970.
Commission on Freedom of the Press. *A Free and Responsible Press*. Chicago: University of Chicago Press, 1947.
Craik, W.A.. *A History of Canadian Journalism*. Toronto: The Ontario Publishing Company, 1959.
Davey, Keith. *The Rainmaker: A Passion for Politics*. Toronto: Stoddart, 1986.
Desbarats, Peter. *A Guide to Canadian News Media*, 2nd ed. Toronto: Harcourt Brace, 1996.
Doyle, Richard. *Hurly-Burly: A Time at the Globe*. Toronto: Macmillan of Canada, 1990.
Dunnett, Peter J.S. *The World Newspaper Industry*. London: Croom Helm, 1988.
Fotheringham, Allan. *Birds of a Feather: The Press and the Politicians*. Toronto: Key Porter, 1989.
——. *Collected & Bound*. Vancouver: November House, 1972.
——. *Last Page First*. Toronto: Key Porter, 1999.
Goldenberg, Susan. *The Thomson Empire*. Toronto: Methuen, 1984.
Gruley, Brian. *Paper Losses: A Modern Epic of Greed and Betrayal at America's Two Largest Newspaper Companies*. New York: Grove Press, 1993.
Gutstein, Donald. *The New Landlords: Asian Investment in Canadian Real Estate*. Victoria, B.C.: Press Porcepic, 1990.
Hawkins, Freda. *Canada and Immigration: Public Policy and Public Concern*. Kingston, Ont.: McGill-Queen's University Press, 1988.
Hebert, Gerard, *et al.*, eds. *Labor Relations in the Newspaper Industry*. Ottawa: Minister of Supply and Services, 1981.
Holmes, Helen and Taras, David, eds. *Seeing Ouselves: Media Power and Policy in Canada*, 2nd ed. Toronto: Harcourt Brace, 1996.
Hutchison, Bruce. *The Far Side of the Street*. Toronto: Macmillan of Canada, 1978.
——. *To Canada With Love and Some Misgivings*. Vancouver: Douglas & McIntyre, 1991.
Keate, Stuart. *Paper Boy*. Toronto: Clarke, Irwin, 1980.
Kluckner, Michael. *Vancouver: The Way It Was*. North Vancouver: Whitecap Books, 1984.
Lacy, Stephen and Simon, Todd. *The Economics and Regulation of United States Newspapers*. Norwood, N.J.: Ablex, 1993.
Lazarsfeld, Paul F. and Stanton, Frank N., eds. *Communications Research: 1948-1949*. New York: Harper, 1949.
Martin, Robert. *Media Law*. Toronto: Irwin Law, 1997.
Martin, Roderick. *New Technology and Industrial Relations in Fleet Street*. Oxford: Clarendon Press, 1981.
Melvern, Linda. *The End of the Street*. London: Methuen, 1986.
Miller, John. *Yesterday's News: Why Canada's Daily Newspapers are Failing Us*. Halifax: Fernwood, 1998.
Murray, Peter, ed. *Great Scott! A Collection of the Best Columns by Jack Scott*. Victoria: Sono Nis Press, 1985.
Newman, Peter C. *The Canadian Revolution: From Deference to Defiance, 1985-1995*. Toronto: Viking, 1995.
Osler, Andrew M. *News: The Evolution of Journalism in Canada*. Toronto: Copp Clark Pitman, 1993.
Overbeck, Wayne. *Major Principles of Media Law*. Fort Worth: Harcourt Brace, 1997.
Owen, Bruce. *Economics and Freedom of Expression: Media Structures and the First Amendment*. Cambridge: Ballinger, 1975.
Parry, David. *A Century of Southam*. Toronto: Southam Press, 1978.
Phillips, Paul. *No Power Greater: A Century of Labour in British Columbia*. Vancouver: B.C. Federation of Labour, 1967.

Picard, Robert G. *Media Economics: Concepts and Issues.* Newbury Park: Sage, 1989.
Picard, Robert, *et al.*, eds. *Press Concentration and Monopoly: New Perspectives on Newspaper Ownership and Operation.* Norwood, N.J.: Ablex, 1988.
Pilgrim, Tim. *Nothing Ventured, Nothing Gained: The Seattle JOA and Newspaper Preservation.* Greenwich, Ct.: Ablex, 1997.
Ramsey, Bruce. *PGE: Railway to the North.* Vancouver: Mitchell Press, 1962.
Romanow, Walter I. and Soderlund, Walter C. *Media Canada: An Introductory Analysis.* Toronto: Copp Clark Pitman, 1992.
Rucker, Bryce W. *The First Freedom.* Carbondale: Southern Illinois University Press, 1968.
Rutherford, Paul. *The Making of the Canadian Media.* Toronto: McGraw-Hill Ryerson, 1978.
Severin, Werner J. and Tankard, James W. Jr. *Communication Theories: Origins, Methods, and Uses in the Mass Media,* 4th ed. New York: Longman, 1997.
Sherman, Paddy. *Bennett.* Toronto: McClelland and Stewart, 1966.
Shoemaker, Pamela J. and Reese, Stephen D. *Mediating the Message: Theories of Influences on Mass Media Content,* 2nd ed. New York: Longman, 1996.
Siegel, Arthur. *Politics and the Media in Canada,* 2nd ed. Toronto: McGraw-Hill Ryerson, 1996.
Siklos, Richard. *Shades of Black: Conrad Black and the World's Fastest Growing Press Empire.* Toronto: Minerva, 1996.
Smith, Anthony. *Goodbye Gutenberg.* Oxford: Oxford University Press, 1980.
Sotiron, Minko. *From Politics to Profit: The Commercialization of Canadian Daily Newspapers, 1890-1920.* Montreal: McGill-Queen's University Press, 1997.
Stursberg, Peter. *Extra! When the Papers had the Only News.* Victoria, B.C.: Sound and Moving Image Division, Provincial Archives of British Columbia, 1982.
Udell, Jon. *The Economics of the American Newspaper.* New York: Hastings House, 1978.
Underwood, Doug. *When MBAs Rule the Newsroom.* New York: Columbia University Press, 1993.
Villard, Oscar Garrison. *The Disappearing Daily.* Freeport, N.Y.: Books for Libraries Press, 1944.
Webster, Jack. *Webster!* Vancouver: Douglas & McIntyre, 1990.
Winter, James. *Democracy's Oxygen: How Corporations Control the News.* Montreal: Black Rose, 1997.
Zimbalist, Andrew, ed. *Case Studies on the Labor Process.* New York: Monthly Review Press, 1979.

REPORTS

Canada. Restrictive Trade Practices Commission. *Report Concerning the Production and Supply of Newspapers in the City of Vancouver and Elsewhere in the Province of British Columbia.* Ottawa: Queen's Printer, 1960.
Canada. Restrictive Trade Practices Commission. *Report on the Production, Distribution and Supply of Newspapers in the Sudbury-Copper Cliff Area.* Ottawa: Queen's Printer, 1964.
Canada. Restrictive Trade Practices Commission. *Report Relating to the Acquisition in 1962 of the Times-Journal Newspaper Published in Fort William, Ontario.* Ottawa: Queen's Printer, 1965.
Nemetz, Nathan T. *Report Into Certain Charges of Election Irregularities in the Federal Election of 1963.* Vancouver: Queen's Printer, 1965.

THESES AND DISSERTATIONS

Peacock, R.L. *A Study of the Production of the Vancouver Province With Emphasis on Future Expansion*. Vancouver: University of British Columbia, 1956.

MAGAZINES AND JOURNALS

Abley, Mark. "Davey of the *Gazette*," *Media Magazine*, March 1985.

Ajello, Robin. "The Cruickshank redemption: can the new editor-in-chief of the *Vancouver Sun* save the paper from hopeless mediocrity?" *B.C. Business*, December 1995.

Alderman, Tom. "Foth: That's Allan Fotheringham, the king of Vancouver," *Canadian*, May 5, 1979.

Arnold, Tom. "*Sun* will 'shine' all day," *content*, January/February 1991.

Assael, Shaun. "Northern Exposure," *NewsInc.*, January 1993.

Austen, Ian. "The case against the media giants," *Maclean's*, October 3, 1983.

"ANPA goal: publish when unions strike," *Editor & Publisher*, April 25, 1970.

Bagdikian, Ben. "Conglomeration, Concentration and the Media," *Journal of Communication*, Spring 1980.

Bain, George. "All the news that's fun to print," *Maclean's*, April 21, 1986.

Barnett, Stephen R. "Combination ad rates: the monopoly stinger," *Columbia Journalism Review*, May/June 1980.

——. "Monopoly games — where failures win big," *Columbia Journalism Review*, May/June 1980.

Berton, Pierre. "Papers, Pickets and Profits," *Maclean's*, July 15, 1950.

——. "Vancouver's Rising *Sun*," *Maclean's*, July 1, 1948.

Boyd, Denny. "Who said print journalism was dead?" *B.C. Business*, January 1999.

Brown, Robert U. "The illegal sitdown," *Editor & Publisher*, April 18, 1970.

Budgen, Mark. "'*The Courier*' also rises," *Maclean's*, June 25, 1979.

Cocking, Clive. "The man with the poisoned pen," *Maclean's*, October 2, 1978.

——. "Will Allan Fotheringham Make the *Sun* Shine?" *Vancouver*, September 1975.

Collins, Doug. "Fear and Loathing in the Canadian Mosaic," *Weekend Magazine*, September 11, 1976.

——. "Press," *Saturday Night*, November 1965.

"Columbian company is big in suburbs with four dailies keyed to local scene," *Canadian Printer & Publisher*, February 1968.

"Cooling Off the Hot Line," *Time* (Canadian ed.), April 9, 1965.

"*Courier* calls it quits in the daily market," *Marketing*, September 3, 1979.

Craig, Sheri. "Reorganization at Southam: An Interview with John Fisher," *Media Magazine*, July/August 1986.

Dexter, Susan. "The Mouth That Roars," *Maclean's*, October 15, 1966.

"Dispute Costs B.C. Dailies $1.8 million," *Marketing*, September 9, 1991.

Douglas, Tom. "Pacific Press: Brainstorming to bump up circulation to pre-strike levels," *Marketing*, November 5, 1979.

Fetherling, Doug. "All the news that's soft enough to print," *Maclean's*, October 30, 1978.

——. "The day the news caught fire," *Maclean's*, September 8, 1980.

——. "Two deaths in the family," *Maclean's*, September 8, 1980.

Fisher, Douglas. "The case against newspaper chains: Their news is syrup," *Maclean's*, November 17, 1962.

Fotheringham, Allan. "A legend in the news game," *Maclean's*, April 19, 1993.

——."A lifelong fight for freedom," *Maclean's*, May 24, 1999.

——. "The revenge of Mila Mulroney," *Maclean's*, February 14, 1994.

"Fotheringham's Harpoon," *Time*, May 1, 1972.

Gasher, Mike. "A tale of two editors," *content*, September/October 1989.
——. "Ironic Columnist," *Vancouver*, September 1984.
——. "Southam consolidates Vancouver monopoly," *content*, May/June 1989.
Gill, Ian. "Just in the Time of Nick," *Vancouver*, July 1990.
——. "Clouded *Sun* Today," *Vancouver*, December 1987.
Govier, Katharine. "Surviving Harvey," *Toronto Life*, December 1996.
"Gremlins, too many subscribers slow first issues of *Times*," *Canadian Printer & Publisher*, October 1964.
"How one daily plans to get off the ground," *Marketing*, November 1, 1963.
"How Pat Burns won fame and fortune by talking on the world's biggest party line," *Maclean's*, November 16, 1964.
"Inside *Maclean's*," *Maclean's*, December 1, 1975.
Jansen, Doug. "The paper that carried 49 pages of classified," *Marketing*, October 29, 1973.
Kimball, Penn. "New York Readers in a newspaper shutdown," *Columbia Journalism Review*, Fall 1963.
——. "People without Papers," *Public Opinion Quarterly* 23 (1959).
Krangle, Karenn and Moody, Lin. "Fotheringham affair shows unhealthy situation at Canada's third-largest daily," *content*, April 1976.
Lacy, Stephen. "Competing in the Suburbs: A Research Review of Intercity Newspaper Competition," *Newspaper Research Journal*, Winter 1988.
Lautens, Trevor. "When the Newspapers Had to Stop," *Saturday Night*, May 1970.
Laver, Ross. "The *Globe* muscles in on Vancouver," *Maclean's*, April 16, 1984.
Lewis, Robert. "Nobody here but us chickens," *Maclean's*, April 27, 1981.
——. "The Press Barons," *Maclean's*, May 11, 1981.
——. "The pressure on the press," *Maclean's*, August 31, 1981.
Littlemore, Richard. "Bigger. Better. Smarter.: How to Use Consultants to Help Your Company Outstrip the Competition," *B.C. Business*, April 1999.
——. "The biggest moments of the last 25 years: our take on the events that have made Lotusland what it is," *B.C. Business*, April 1997.
——. "The Daily Double," *Vancouver*, Summer 2000.
MacFarlane, David. "The Accidental Tycoon," *Saturday Night*, October 1980.
Mackin, Bob Jr., "Southam Takes Hold In The West," *Marketing*, May 13, 1991.
——. "Will *Sun*'s Move Help Southam?" *Marketing*, November 18, 1991.
McConnell, Robert. "Common ownership and printing in a single plant — the 'illegal' formula for keeping rival dailies alive," *Marketing*, November 10, 1980.
McGregor, D.A. "Adventures of Vancouver Newspapers," *British Columbia Historical Quarterly*, Vol. X, No. II (1946).
Metcalfe, Ben. "Late Editions," *Vancouver*, June 1986.
"Mutiny on the flagship," *Maclean's*, March 11, 1991.
Nairn, Kathleen and Nairn, James R., "The Paper That Likes to Argue," *Saturday Night*, July 26, 1952.
Newman, Peter C. "The voice of Canada," *Maclean's*, September 28, 1992.
Nixon, Raymond, "Concentration and Absenteeism in Daily Newspaper Ownership," *Journalism Quarterly*, June 1945.
Norman, Ray. "Battle of the dailies begins out west," *Marketing*, July 16, 1979.
O'Neill, Terry. "Smothered by Southam," *B.C. Report*, June 4, 1990.
Ouston, Rick. "Patrick Nagle: 'Nobody Ever Published A Newspaper In A Beer Parlor,'" *Vancouver*, December 1987.
"Pacific Press complex is new fully automated giant of Canadian west," *Canadian Printer & Publisher*, April 1966.
"Plans new daily in Vancouver, Canadian chain of five papers," *Canadian Printer & Publisher*, January 1963.

Polich, John. "*Daily News*, its unions, newspaper market lose in 1990 strike," *Newspaper Research Journal*, Winter 1995.
Ross, Alexander. "Hot, hopeful rumors for Vancouverites who are fed up with their newspaper," *Maclean's*, December 14, 1963.
Rosse, James. "The Decline of Direct Newspaper Competition," *Journal of Communication*, Spring 1980.
Rossiter, Sean. "Pacific Pressed," *Vancouver*, February 1980.
——. "The Mayor and the Columnist," *Vancouver*, November 1976.
Russell, Nick. "Strike Ends, New Dailies In For Fight," *content*, August 1979.
Saenger, Ellen. "'Defending the indefensible,'" *B.C. Report*, September 23, 1991.
——. "Fat and floundering," *B.C. Report*, November 19, 1990.
——. "Southam's stranglehold," *B.C. Report*, September 23, 1991.
Scott, Jack. "Donald Cromie: 'Merger' Is Never Mentioned," *Saturday Night*, July 6, 1957.
Southam, Harvey S. "The Inside Story," *Equity*, July/August 1984.
Stainsby, Donald. "Vancouver's New Newspaper," *Saturday Night*, October 1964.
Stanley, Don. "All About Allan," *Vancouver*, November 1983.
——. "How They Play The Game," *Vancouver*, October 1980.
Stewart, Walter. "Fathoming Fotheringham," *Saturday Night*, May 1991.
Stoffman, Daniel. "A Licence To Lose Money," *Canadian Business*, March 1994.
"Sunburst," *Time* (Canadian ed.), October 17, 1949.
"Test runs on press under way as new daily's debut nears," *Canadian Printer & Publisher*, August 1964.
"The media drama: Waiting for Fotho," *Saturday Night*, January/February 1979.
"*Vancouver Province* prepares its Sunday," *Marketing*, July 23, 1979.
"Vancouver shutdown is affecting BC economy," *Canadian Printer & Publisher*, April, 1970.
"*Vancouver Times* buys lease on life," *Marketing*, April 16, 1965.
Walker, Robert. "How the Cost Squeeze Hit Canadian Newspapers," *Saturday Night*, January 18, 1958.
Whitney, Tony. "Supplements a success for *Sun*," *Marketing*, November 18, 1988.
Wild, Roland. "Columnists in Clover," *Saturday Night*, April 18, 1953.
Wilson, Rob. "Vancouver's *Courier* goes daily," *Marketing*, July 2, 1979.
"Windfall for Vancouver suburban newspapers," *Marketing*, March 2, 1970.
Wishart, David. "A new-look *Sun* rises in Vancouver," *Marketing*, March 17, 1986.
——. "Balancing the books," *Marketing*, November 11, 1985.
——. "*Globe* to cancel its B.C. section," *Marketing*, May 21, 1984.
——. "Keeping tabs on the *Province*," *Marketing*, November 7, 1983.
Yates, David. "FP learns the hard way," *content*, November 1979.
Young, Bruce. "How the Cromie family fought to save the *Sun*," *Canadian Printer & Publisher*, August, 1963.
——. "*Times* halts publication after 11 stormy months," *Canadian Printer & Publisher*, September, 1965.

INTERVIEWS

St. Clair Balfour, Toronto, February 19, 1999.
Larry Dampier, Vancouver, March 5, 1999.
Allan Fotheringham, Toronto, March 6, 2000.
Gerry Haslam, Richmond, B.C., March 11, 1999.
Paddy Sherman, West Vancouver, June 28, 2001.

TELEPHONE INTERVIEWS

David Ablett, Toronto, January 9, 2001.
St. Clair Balfour, Toronto, February 21, 1999.
Pierre Berton, Kleinburg, Ontario, March 3, 2000.
Jim Taylor, West Vancouver, January 30, 2001.

E-MAIL CORRESPONDENCE

Patrick Nagle, October 23, 2000.
Phil Needham, May 2, 2001.
Mike Tytherleigh, September 26, 2000.

INDEX